If you're looking for a trustworthy guide through the financial maze, consider what these respected leaders have said about Austin Pryor and *Sound Mind Investing*.

"I have known Austin Pryor for over twenty years now, and I regard him as a good friend. I have found his counsel to be both biblical and practical. I know of no other individual with whom I would consult with more confidence on the subject of mutual fund investing than Austin. If you will spend the time to read carefully the counsel Austin provides in this book, you will find it both time and money well spent."

Larry Burkett
Founder and President / Christian Financial Concepts

"I have had the privilege of knowing Austin Pryor since the beginning of my Christian life. There are few that I have as much respect for and confidence in than Austin. His counsel in the investment area has proven to be extraordinarily wise and discerning over a long time period. I can recommend this book without hesitation as a 'must read' for anyone interested in investing in very uncertain economic times. I consider it a privilege to be able to make this recommendation."

Ron Blue
Founding Partner / Ronald Blue & Co.

"Austin Pryor's book, *Sound Mind Investing*, is a masterpiece on the subject of Christian economics. It is clearly a comprehensive hand-book for any person seeking professional guidance in investments. As a minister, of course, I am especially appreciative of the godly orientation manifest throughout this important work, and of the powerful testimony presented in Section Six, 'Investing That Glorifies God.'"

D. James Kennedy, Ph.D.
Senior Minister / Coral Ridge Presbyterian Church

(Turn the page for more comments from Christian leaders and teachers.)

"I have known Austin personally since 1973, and find him to be a man of integrity who is committed to serving our blessed Lord and Savior. His book is an outstanding compendium of helpful investment information. It is thorough, easy-to-understand and has a uniquely appealing style and readability. But most important, it incorporates Scriptural principles to help the reader be a better steward of God's resources."

Bill Bright
Founder and President / Campus Crusade for Christ

"I have never outgrown the enjoyment of a book with lots of pictures. This book clearly explains what before was difficult to understand. A true expert knows his field well enough to explain it in simple terms yet with profound insights. Austin Pryor deciphers the bewildering jargon of the investment world for the first-time investor, yet also provides profound insight for the seasoned money manager. As a book that applies biblical principles to an area of great need, I highly recommend *Sound Mind Investing*."

Howard Hendricks
Chairman, Center for Christian Leadership
Distinguished Professor, Dallas Theological Seminary

"*Sound Mind Investing* gives important steps to help you prepare before you invest. You'll learn how to set priorities, avoid risk, and develop reasonable long-term financial goals. It will tell you everything you need to know to make wise financial choices for your family. And Austin does it without getting bogged down in complex financial terms that might make things confusing for lay people like you and me. This is a vital tool that you'll want to refer to again and again as you make your financial decisions."

Beverly LaHaye
Founder / Concerned Women of America

"In my book *Saving Money Any Way You Can*, I noted that Austin Pryor is a rising star in the financial advice arena. *Sound Mind Investing* covers the waterfront—everything from stocks, bonds, mutual funds, and annuities. What makes the book extremely readable are the eye-popping graphics, sidebars, post-it notes, and graphs. If you are going to self-manage your retirement (and this is something I recommend), then this book is for you."

Mike Yorkey
Focus on the Family Magazine editor

"If you're looking for an attractive easy-to-follow investment guide written in plain English, look no further. Austin Pryor writes without vested interests in any specific plan or fund. This means greater candor and objectivity. I'm frankly skeptical of a lot of stuff coming out of the financial realm with its short-term 'for this life only' perspective. Austin is a man with a larger and better perspective. May every reader seek to make wise investments of money and time in God's kingdom, investments that will pay off not only in this life, but in the eternal life to come!"

Randy Alcorn
Director of Eternal Perspective Ministries / Author of <u>Money, Possessions & Eternity</u>

"One of the main reasons I wrote *Wake Up, Women!* was to encourage the endless number of Christian women who seem to know little or nothing about finances. I included Austin's excellent book in my bibliography because it's an inviting, easy-to-understand, step-by-step primer for anyone who finds the subject difficult (if not terrifying). If you're in the process of 'waking up' in this area, I heartily recommend you pick up a copy of *Sound Mind Investing*."

Florence Littauer
Author and Speaker

"Austin Pryor's *Sound Mind Investing* does more than offer its readers easy-to-understand access to the intricacies of investing in today's world. The author is a Christian who obviously has a sincere desire to help other Christians gain the basic knowledge they need to protect themselves and help secure their future financial security."

Dr. Ron Nash
Professor of Theology / Reformed Theological Seminary of Orlando
Author of <u>Poverty and Wealth</u> and <u>The Closing of the American Heart</u>

"I have known Austin Pryor personally for over two decades, and have found him to be not only a knowledgeable investment consultant, but a man with a deep relationship with the Lord Jesus Christ. In this world, where distrust seems to prevail, it is very encouraging to know that in the Christian community there is a man with integrity that is backed up by years of professional experience. I 100% endorse *Sound Mind Investing*."

Bob George
President of People to People / Author of <u>Classic Christianity</u>

It's reassuring that so many respected leaders gave *Sound Mind Investing* high marks. Equally gratifying were the comments from "everyday ordinary folks" like these who read the first edition and found it a reliable road map as they made important financial decisions.

Your book is one of the best that I've read on financial matters. Your writing was clear and easy to understand. I especially liked the Godly principles that the book was based on. I believe you have helped many people (including me), and have brought honor and glory to God through this book.

Alan Fyfe
Coal Valley, Illinois

SMI is written in an easy-to-read, easy-to-understand, and easy-to-apply manner. I was elated to find the book to fill my needs in a Christian bookstore written by a God-fearing man. God fills our every need, and He has filled a need of mine through Mr. Pryor.

Daniel Rawn
San Diego, California

I want to thank you for writing such a clear, complete guide to investing which incorporates Biblical wisdom. *Sound Mind Investing* has been a tremendous help in sorting out my investment planning for my family.

John Wieloszynski
Buffalo, New York

I have been reading and studying your book *Sound Mind Investing*. What a great help! Before my wife gave me this book, I was in total ignorance about finances. Now I am so grateful that I have this tremendous resource to help me invest wisely and make financial decisions to honor the Lord with all that He has given my family.

Kevin Golde
Cranston, Rhode Island

Awesome, powerful, a masterpiece! I am so grateful that the Lord would lead me to read such a beautiful book as He prepares me to be a steward of His blessings in my life.

George Avila
Miami, Florida

I have never seen so much useful information compiled in one source. Until we found SMI, we had very little information with which to guide ourselves. With the help of your book, we were able to analyze our investments, find several weak areas, and structure an investment plan that I know will help us achieve Godly financial goals.

Becky Kiefer
Rolling Meadows, Illinois

I want to commend you on this book as it is well written, helpfully illustrated, and easily understood. I have read many books and articles about money, investing, etc., and I find that your book tops them all. I want to thank you for giving us a volume written in simple, clear language that is educational, enjoyable, and very practical for those who have any interest in the world of finances.

Richard Kidd
Romulus, New York

I've been reading the SMI book—wow! Praise God that He saw fit to bless you with wisdom that you share so effectively! I was just about to head into the field of investing "blind," but now I understand where I'm going. Thanks!

Pamela Miller
Concord, California

I found SMI to be a wonderful resource manual that I will always be able to refer to. It is so nice to be able to have access to information as important as finances that is backed with a Biblical understanding. I would like to commend you on such a fantastic job.

Paul Fesler
Charleston, South Carolina

Your book has been helpful in enabling me to set up a plan. All of this investing "stuff" was new to me and after talking to three brokers and one CPA it was overwhelming. Your book helped tie it together and give me some confidence and knowledge so I can structure and chart my own plan. Thank you.

Cheryl Guilzon
Westerlo, New York

I have felt so ill-informed in an area that has always appeared to be so intimidating, that of investing. Your book has put the whole notion of investing into a context which I have been able to understand and act upon. I found your book so interesting that I couldn't put it down. I was so delighted to see that you have linked investing with a Christian perspective.

Barbara Apostol
Sutherlin, Oregon

I was planning to start an investment portfolio when I saw your book on the shelf of my local Christian bookstore. It was an answer to my prayers. There were many books dealing with personal and family finances, but only yours on investing. The book was easy and educational reading. Especially interesting were the four investing "risk personalities." They helped my wife and me come to a suitable compromise in our investing strategy. I frequently refer back to SMI as I make purchasing decisions.

Ronald Lee
Miami, Florida

Your book has been very informative. I am the CEO of a Federal Credit Union. I am telling you this to let you know that your book is not only for beginners, but for all levels of investors.

Harry Ovitt
Fredericksburg, Virginia

I just received a copy of your book and wanted you to know how much I'm enjoying it. It's a home run! You have covered the areas that we novices all want to know more about, and you've done it in such a creative way. The charts, graphs, and visual enhancements have made the concepts so easy to understand. Congratulations on a great job!

Lee Ellis
Gainesville, Georgia

Thank you for having developed such a superior educational book as SMI. The book is rich in information from the basics to the subtle elements of investing. The layout of the book has enhanced my understanding and made the subject matter less daunting. For the first time ever, I feel that I have begun to truly understand the operation of investing, instead of parroting the "rules" of investing. Your work has been—for lack of a better word—a blessing to me at this time in my life.

Robert P. Regitano
Albany, New York

First of all, thank you for writing *Sound Mind Investing*! I had stayed away from investing because I believed that the "small investor" did not have a chance these days. I was happy to learn that I was dead wrong. In particular, I appreciate the confidence which you have given me in making my own decisions—a real sense of empowerment! I have purchased multiple copies of your book which I have given to my children, relatives, and friends.

David Goldman
Springfield, Virginia

A road map that includes what you

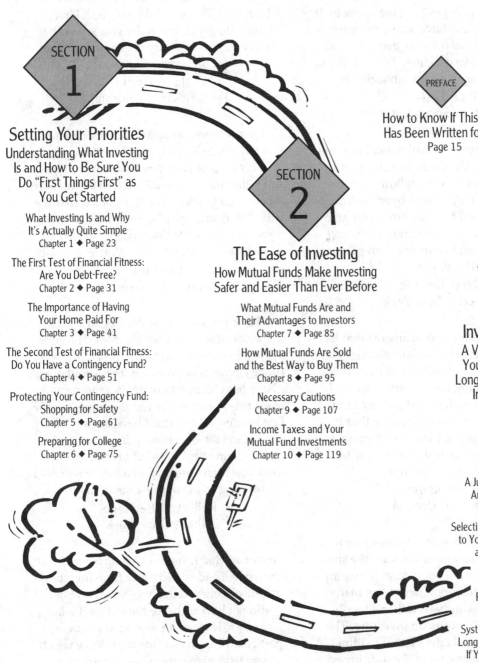

need to know and where to find it.

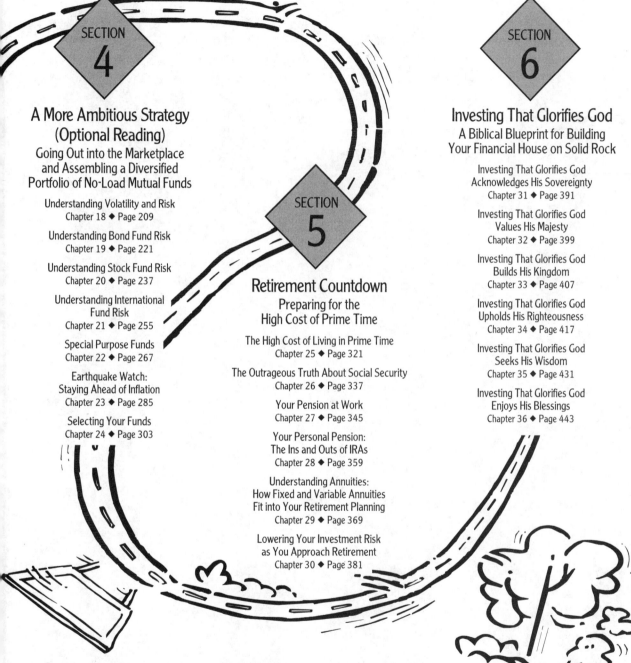

SOUND MIND INVESTING

A Step-by-Step Guide to
Financial Stability & Growth As
We Move Toward the Year 2000

BY
AUSTIN PRYOR

MOODY PRESS
CHICAGO

BY LARRY BURKETT

I have known Austin Pryor for almost twenty years now, and I regard him as a good friend. As I have observed him over the years, I have found his counsel to be both biblical and practical. I know of no other individual with whom I would consult with more confidence on the subject of mutual fund investing than Austin.

I believe the true character of an investment adviser is not only the degree of success he has achieved, but the integrity that is maintained in the process. Austin has achieved success in the business world, but, more important, he has done so with truth and honesty.

When Austin began his monthly investment journal, he asked for my help in getting the word out to Christians. Since I regard the reputation of the ministry I represent as more important than any friendship, I imposed some conditions for helping. First, Austin had to agree to forego building his investment advisory business (which was his primary source of income). I felt that to sell an investment newsletter while accepting investors' money would be a potential conflict of interest. Because he felt it was more important to teach Christians investment strategies, Austin readily agreed to cease accepting new clients.

My second condition was perhaps even more restricting since it required him to submit his newsletter to our editorial staff for review and critique every month. Without hesitation, Austin also agreed to this condition. We have since found this review to be unnecessary and have discontinued it.

I say this only to emphasize that I endorse the integrity and honesty of Austin Pryor. Obviously you, the reader, must evaluate his advice yourself. No one individual has the right advice for everyone, and anyone can, and will, be wrong in the changing economy we live in. But if you will spend the time to read carefully the counsel Austin provides in this book, you will find it both time and money well spent.

I encouraged my good friends at Moody Press to contact Austin about writing this book since I felt he had information that would benefit God's people. We are in no way competitors. None of us, individually, are indispensable to God's plan; we are all merely *a part* of God's plan. Austin and I are collaborators in God's plan to help His people become better stewards of His resources.

SPECIAL THANKS!

FROM THE AUTHOR

To Larry Burkett . . .
. . . the idea of offering investment help especially for Christians was yours to start with, and without your gracious support, the monthly journal would never have gotten off the ground. Thanks for believing in me, and for helping me launch a new career in writing that has proven so very gratifying.

To Doug and Gena Cobb . . .
. . . for your help in teaching me the ropes of desktop publishing. Your consistent interest and personal prayer support was, and continues to be, immensely appreciated.

To Catharine Smith . . .
. . . a lot of people have good secretaries, but you're definitely off the top of the scale when it comes to getting things done. Your loyalty, hard work, and unselfish spirit have blessed me and our family. Thank you!

To Vicki Mosher and Lynn Mosher . . .
. . . you've come alongside to help grow our ministry. Your willingness to be servants, and the genuine interest you have shown in the welfare of our readers, are evidence that you have been heaven-sent. You are appreciated!

To Mimi and Sim Fulcher . . .
. . . our extended family in Christ. Susie joins me in praising our Father for your faithful, creative, and generous love and prayers.

To my three terrific sons . . .
. . . Andrew, thank you for seeking God's leading and joining our team just in time to help with the layout and graphics of this second edition. I couldn't have made it without you! Tre, your proven faithfulness to our Lord and to your young family blesses me deeply as your father. And Matthew, as I see your life lived to bring many to a personal relationship with our Savior, I praise our heavenly Father for sending you into our lives. Guys, thanks for making me so proud of you!

And to all my journal readers . . .
. . . who have shown their support and prayed so faithfully that the Lord would give His blessing to our work. To get anything of value accomplished, there's no substitute for people who are willing to pray!

How to Know
If This Book Has
Been Written for You

"C'mon, Herb. We've got to go.
Are you going to buy the book or not?"

**The foundation of every successful investment program
begins with a clear understanding of one's motivation:
"What's my purpose in investing?"**

For the Christian, the answer is two fold: (1) to provide financially for the needs of your household, and (2) to increase your assets in order to serve God more fully. This book was written to help you do both.

If you're like most Americans these days, you look with bewilderment at the flood of investment opportunities passing before you. You're being encouraged to invest in stocks, zero-coupon bonds, mutual funds, commodities, options, certificates of deposits, Ginnie Maes, and other complicated securities. You're even told to invest by borrowing against the equity in your home.

During the 1980s, the variety of financial opportunities available to the average investor multiplied greatly. For most people, it's too much of a good thing—this "option glut" often serves to paralyze them. Many of the alternatives seem very complicated. Strategies that used to occupy only the wealthy now appear to be urged on everyone. Even everyday economic decisions that should be routine seem to require as much research and planning as a takeover of one major corporation by another!

Finding your way is not made any easier by the investment industry.

To a large degree, any intimidation felt by the average investor is the result of the way the industry conducts itself. For one thing, investment "experts" make your task of learning more difficult because everything they say sounds so complicated. They create the impression that investing is very hard, and that it might be best if it were not entrusted to amateurs (like you).

And then there's the matter of the industry's preoccupation with making forecasts. It's one thing to help investors make more informed decisions by giving out economic data, corporate profiles, historical trends, and the like. But then to use that information as the basis for market predictions is quite another. The fact is that nobody knows for sure what's coming next year, next month, next week, or even tomorrow. Forecasts from the brokerage community and investment media, at best, are conflicting and confusing. At their worst, they're totally misleading and eventually will prove extremely expensive to any investor who takes them seriously.

**Most people have only vague notions as to what their
long-term investment goals are. As a result, they move
through life as responders . . .**

. . . deciding on a case-by-case basis whether to say yes to the various investment opportunities that randomly come to their attention. Their thinking is short-term. Depending on their mood that day, or the advice of a friend who's in on a "good thing," or even how persuasive a salesperson is, they make a decision whether to invest. Often, they give little thought as to exactly where that particular investment fits in fulfilling their long-term goals.

Responders feel a need to "do something" when a major news story hits. Because they're not quite sure where *they're* going, they tend to watch the crowd to see where *it's* going. They begin listening for the hot tips, taking the gurus seriously, and putting too many eggs in the same basket. They might realize they're going somewhat out of bounds, but they're looking for that extra edge. The problem is they're drinking from "broken cisterns." The crowd and the experts don't know what's coming next any more than they do.

In order to find peace of mind in your investment decisions, you need to become *an initiator* rather than *a responder*.

Initiators have a concrete game plan in mind. They have made the effort to develop a strategy that specifically takes into account both their long-term financial goals as well as their own personal investment temperament. It is shaped around what they hope to accomplish in the future, and it fits who they are "inside."

Make it your goal to become an initiator! Be like a shopper at the food market who buys only those ingredients needed to prepare a specific recipe. Before she goes to the supermarket, Lynn knows what she is looking for. When she is confronted with special promotions for products that aren't on her shopping list, she readily passes them by. Lynn won't need to spend any time at all considering whether to buy them *because her shopping is purposeful.* Similarly, before you begin to invest, put together a strategy that takes into account the risk of loss you can comfortably carry both financially *and* emotionally.

If you're ready to spend a little time learning a few basics, you can be of good cheer! This book is written especially with your needs in mind . . .

. . . to equip you to have the confidence to take charge of your financial life—to become an initiator. I plan to help you do this in four primary ways.

❶ **I'm going to teach you only what you *need to know*, not all that there *is to know*.** (That should be pretty good news, right there!) I don't

> The plans of the diligent lead to profit as surely as haste leads to poverty.
> Proverbs 21:5
>
> Suppose one of you wants to build a tower. Will he not first sit down and estimate the cost to see if he has enough money to complete it? For if he lays the foundation and is not able to finish it, everyone who sees it will ridicule him, saying, "This fellow began to build and was not able to finish."
> Luke 14:28–30

THE "COMPLETE GUIDE" APPROACH TO TEACHING

THE "ONLY WHAT YOU *NEED* TO KNOW" APPROACH TO TEACHING USED IN THIS BOOK

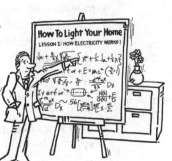

take the "complete guide" approach. Instead I assume that you just want the bare essentials for now. And put that way, there really isn't all that much for you to learn. Just as you can throw a wall switch and enjoy the benefits of electricity without understanding how it all works, so it is with mutual funds. I will cover just enough information here to teach you to "throw the switch" that will enable you to establish a practical (and relatively easy to supervise) long-term investment strategy.

❷ **I'm going to give you a framework for setting priorities on how to spend (or invest) your monthly surplus.** It's based on working your way through Four Levels toward financial security. If you have consumer debt outstanding (Level One) or lack a sufficient contingency fund (Level Two), I believe it's best to apply your surplus in those areas. However, that doesn't mean you are free from making important investment decisions in connection with stock, bond, and money market securities.

If you have an IRA, you've got the responsibility for managing it. Or perhaps you have a pension plan at work, like a Keogh, SEP-IRA, or 401(k), where you are allowed to make decisions as to how your share is invested. Perhaps you've purchased a variable annuity, which offers you similar choices. These retirement investments represent money that was set aside in the past, and although you may not be adding to them at present, you still must decide how best to invest the money that's already there. To one degree or another, you will do a better job of making these decisions if you have a basic understanding of the investment markets. Even if you're still at the first two levels, you can use this time productively to build your understanding of investing principles. Then, when you have larger amounts to manage in the future, you won't need a crash course—your knowledge and confidence levels will be up to the task!

❸ **I'm going to introduce you to four basic investment temperaments—four approaches to risk-taking.** Each is represented by a cartoon image that will reappear throughout the book to reinforce the lessons. I'll lead you through a process of discovering which of the four is most appropriate for your basic emotional makeup and financial situation. Once you learn this, you'll have a yardstick for measuring risk that will be helpful to you for years to come.

❹ **I'm going to teach you in an extremely user-friendly way.** The lessons are worded in everyday "plain-English" language, and come in small, easy-to-digest portions. Also,

The Daredevil
"There's a lot of money to be made by people who aren't afraid to go for it! I may be overly optimistic (and a tad impulsive), but I don't usually worry about my investment decisions once they're made."

The Explorer
"To be successful in investing, you've got to keep in step with the latest trends. I'm open to new investment opportunities with potentially large returns even if they are a little more risky."

The Researcher
"I don't believe in investing in something just because everyone else is doing it. Once I make a decision, I have a lot of confidence in it, even if other investors around me are changing their minds."

The Preserver
"You can't be too careful when it comes to investing your money. I am much more interested in minimizing my chances for losses than I am in taking greater risks to earn possibly higher returns."

I've put lots of extra time into making the layout and design of these pages as clear, interesting, and easy-to-follow as possible (as I hope you're beginning to notice by now).

❺ I'm going to base all of the above on the time-tested principles taught in Holy Scripture. There's nothing new under the sun, so you should not be surprised to learn that the underlying values and priorities that shape the very practical strategies taught in this book are merely the outworkings of concepts taught in God's Word for centuries. Investing at the dawn of the twenty-first century, we may be tempted to feel we have grown too sophisticated for biblical lessons. In truth, the current census and economic statistics reveal that our need for biblical truth is more serious than perhaps we realize. Individually, and as a nation, we have built our financial houses on the sand and are reaping the consequences. We dare not ignore God's wisdom any longer.

I have devised this book to serve as a tool to help you follow through and build on the biblical principles that Larry Burkett, Ron Blue, and others have written about so well.

Where they usually stay with general principles, I want to take you the next step—showing you how to apply those principles in specific ways out in the financial marketplace. I've often used the analogy of learning how to "dress for success." Books that teach fashion concepts (including information about fabrics, color coordination, fit, and style) help build an understanding of the basics. But you still need to get in your car, travel to the local mall, and purchase your wardrobe. I think of myself as the person who goes with you, helps you pick the clothes out, watches you try them on, and offers you opinions on whether the style, color, and fit is a good one for *you*. I also know a few things about the reputations of various stores and clothing manufacturers, and steer you away from the bad ones.

LET ME TELL YOU HOW THIS SECOND EDITION OF <u>SOUND MIND INVESTING</u> DIFFERS FROM THE FIRST ONE.

First, there's a wealth of totally new material. About 40% of the content in this book was not in the first edition. The new material includes:

♦ Preparing for college
(chapter 6)

♦ Necessary cautions about new risks in the mutual fund industry and how to deal with them
(chapters 9 and 13)

♦ A "controlling your risk" table that helps you select the right portfolio balance given your current age, goals, and emotional tolerance for risk
(chapter 14)

♦ Understanding volatility and risk
(chapter 18)

♦ Investing internationally
(chapter 21)

♦ Earthquake watch and staying ahead of inflation
(chapter 23)

♦ Factors to consider when selecting funds for your personal portfolio
(chapter 24)

♦ An extensive retirement planning worksheet
(chapter 25)

♦ Lowering your risk as you approach retirement
(chapter 30)

♦ An appendix that includes two dozen short lessons to help guide your financial planning and shopping
(see bottom of pages 6-7 for the topics included)

Additionally, the material has been reorganized so that more advanced topics are gathered in one section. If you just want the basics for now, save Section 4 for a future day—you'll still have all you need to knowledgeably take control of your financial future. Finally, and importantly, all the economic, investment, and mutual fund data have been updated through 1995.

If you read the first edition of this book, you may be wondering if there is a sufficient difference in this new edition to make its purchase worthwhile. Naturally, as the author, I've no doubt there is! If you'll give a quick scan through the book of the improvements cited above, I believe you'll agree.

In order to avoid information overload, you need to develop a sense of proportion. Everything doesn't have to be learned or done yesterday. There's no such thing as "wealth without risk," so accept that you'll make a few mistakes along the way. But that's OK. You'll do fine over the long haul if you follow the basics, exercise self-discipline, and stay the course.

Greater self-confidence — the kind needed to be an initiator rather than a responder — comes with knowledge and experience.

In this book, I'm working on adding to the first, *but you're the only one who can add to the second.*

Let me encourage you to keep at it. It's worth the effort because nobody will take as much of a genuine interest in your finances as you will. And, when you think about it, you know yourself better than anyone else does. You know how much money you have to work with and whether you're really willing to risk losing any of it. You know how much you'd reasonably like to make, how much time you have before you need it, and how much patience you bring to the task. I believe that most people know, perhaps even subconsciously, what's best for them.

I've seen this demonstrated time and again in the counseling sessions I have with my readers. After listening to them explain the various alternatives they have, I usually ask, "What would you *like* to do?" or sometimes, "What are you hoping I'll tell you to do?" The responses are almost always reasonable and carefully thought out. They knew the answers; they just wanted me to confirm them. In the same way that most of us know which foods we *should* be eating and how much exercise we *should* be getting, we also generally know how much risk we should be taking. You'll find that all of this isn't as complicated as it might sound, because there are really only two basic ways to invest your money — as we will see in chapter 1. ◆

Setting Your Priorities

Understanding What Investing Is and How to Be Sure You Do "First Things First" As You Get Started

"That's it? But can't you tell me more than just 'buy low and sell high'?"

1

CHAPTER PREVIEW

What Investing Is and Why It's Actually Quite Simple

I. **Investing occurs when you put your money to work in a commercial undertaking subject to modest levels of risk. You expect a reasonable return over time.**

  A. It is not the same as speculation, which also puts your money to work in a commercial undertaking but involves a very high level of risk. With speculation, there's a possibility of a very large return in a relatively brief period of time. Options and futures are speculations.

  B. It is not the same as gambling, which subjects your money to a very high level of risk in an attempt to profit from the outcome of a contest or game of chance. With gambling, there's a possibility of an unusually large return in an exceptionally brief period of time.

II. **Investing is simple because you have only two basic choices.**

  A. There are investments where you become a lender.

   1. These are generally the lower-risk kind. The primary risk to watch out for is that you might get locked in to a poor rate of return for many years, so the financial strength of the borrower is of great importance.

   2. The most common borrowers include (1) banks and savings and loans, (2) local, state, and federal governments, (3) large corporations, and (4) insurance companies.

  B. There are investments where you become an owner.

   1. These are generally the higher-risk kind. The primary risk here is that the value of what you own could fall, so the economic outlook and its effect on your holdings are of great importance.

   2. The most common investments where you become an owner include common stocks, real estate, precious metals, and collectibles.

  C. How you divide your money between these two basic choices has a greater impact on your eventual investment results than any other single factor.

III. **The one fundamental rule of investing you should never, ever, *ever* forget is:**

  A. The greater the return being offered, the greater the risk you're taking.

  B. This is always the case—whether those making the offer tell you or not, whether it's obvious or not, and whether you know it or not.

**I've been an investment adviser for almost fourteen years.
During that time, I've had the courage of my convictions
(some might say audacity!) to go to people and say . . .**

. . . "You can trust me with your hard-earned money. I'll protect it while
I make it grow." There have been good years, accompanied by rankings in
the top 5% of money managers nationwide. It seemed as if everyone was my
friend, and I loved coming to work in the morning. I thought, *What a great
business to be in!*

There have also been years when I was too conservative. My clients' profits
were not as high as they might have been. I made money, but not as much as
some of my competitors made that year. Asking, "What have you done for
me lately?" many of my clients left in search of greener pastures. After several months of this, I dreaded coming to work in the morning. I thought, *What
a terrible business to be in!*

Most people seem to have the impression there's something special about
being an investment adviser. I've been at social gatherings where people who
throughout the evening had hardly noticed me suddenly came alive when
they learned that I manage investments for a living. Judging by their new
interest in me, I have been instantly transformed from my usual normal self
into someone of great charisma and charm. What accounts for this?

**I've come to believe it's because people secretly think
of investing as being like magic.**

It's the kind of "wow" reaction a magician receives when, after placing a
little kitten into a cage and covering it, he removes the cover to reveal a growl-
ing, full-grown tiger. "Amazing—did you see *that?* How'd he do that?!"
Where did the kitten go? Where did the tiger come from? What happens under that cover, anyway? It's amazing and mysterious! *We* could never do that
. . . *unless the magician would teach us his secrets.*

Isn't this similar to the kind of reactions we have when we read of the
futures trader who made millions in a single week? Or the real-estate tycoon
who always seems to know where to buy next? Or the college student who
started out buying penny stocks in meager amounts and a few years later is
worth more than $20 million? It all seems so impossible. How do they ever
do it?

Our imaginations and curiosities are kindled. *We* could never do that—
unless the magical investor would teach us his secrets. Unlike the kitten, which
doesn't actually turn into a tiger (I hope I haven't spoiled it for you), the modest sums of these gifted investors do turn into fortunes. But—and here's where
the misconception comes in—it's a mistake to call what they do "investing."
It's "speculating."

Investing occurs when you put your money to work in a commercial undertaking, subject to modest levels of risk, and expect a reasonable return over a long period of time. What's reasonable? About 3%–5% more than the rate of inflation.

Speculating, while it also involves putting your money to work in a commercial undertaking, involves a level of risk so great that it's theoretically possible to lose most or all of your capital (the actual amount you invested). In return for this high risk, the speculator has the possibility of making an unusually large return (perhaps doubling or even tripling his/her money) in a relatively brief period of time—usually a couple years at most. This is also frequently accompanied by borrowing additional sums for the undertaking and accepting personal responsibility for repaying those sums regardless of the outcome of the venture. Financial options, commodity futures trading, and leveraged real estate projects are common forms of speculation.

Note that this is not the same as gambling, which subjects your money to an exceedingly high level of risk in an attempt to profit from the outcome of a contest or game of chance. There is the possibility of an unusually large return in an exceptionally brief period of time—perhaps measured in minutes or hours. A sure sign that an activity falls under the "gambling" heading is when *the activity exists solely for the sake of creating wagering opportunities*. For example, apart from wagering, there would be no reason for casinos, horse racing, or lotteries to exist.

Gambling should be avoided by all. Speculating should be avoided by all except those with a professional interest and degree of expertise. But investing is an activity that all of us, as stewards of God's resources, are unavoidably called to. Once you understand that investing involves only taking prudent risks and seeking reasonable returns, it takes a lot of the magic and mystery out of it.

Like it or not, as a steward of God-given time, talents, and resources, you're an investor.

Investing is simply giving up something now in order to have more of something later. When you put your money into a savings account, you are making an investment decision (less spendable money now in order to have more spendable money later). When you volunteer your professional services or personal talents now in order to serve in a ministry, you're making an investment decision (less free time or current income now in order to have a greater sense of fulfillment and eternal gains later). When you take a day off without pay in order to spend time with your family, you're making an investment decision (less income now in order to have stronger family ties and happy memories later).

> Do not wear yourself out to get rich; have the wisdom to show restraint. Cast but a glance at riches, and they are gone, for they will surely sprout wings and fly off to the sky like an eagle.
> Proverbs 23:4–5
>
> People who want to get rich fall into temptation and a trap and into many foolish and harmful desires that plunge men into ruin and destruction. For the love of money is a root of all kinds of evil. Some people, eager for money, have wandered from the faith and pierced themselves with many griefs.
> 1 Timothy 6:9–10

Your goals seem reasonable: Make as much as you can but don't lose any of your savings. You're eager for good advice but wonder whom you can trust. You would like to feel confident but usually feel a little confused. You are caught in the constant tension between risk and reward. If you feel this way, I've got good news!

Investing is actually quite simple . . .

. . . because you really only have two basic choices: investments where you become *a lender to someone* and investments where you become *an owner of something*.

Investments where you *lend* your money are generally the lower-risk kind. Assuming you do a good job of checking out the financial strength of the borrower, the primary risk is that you might get locked in to a poor rate of return for many years. We'll cover investing-by-lending in detail in chapter 11.

Investments where you *own* something are generally the higher-risk kind. The primary risk here is that the value of what you own could fall, so the economic outlook and its effect on your holdings is of great importance. We'll look at the various forms of investing-by-owning in detail in chapter 23.

INVESTING BY LENDING

| Banks, S&Ls, and Credit Unions (which you loan to when you open savings accounts and buy their certificates of deposit) | Large Corporations (which you loan to when you give your money in return for corporate IOUs— commercial paper and bonds) | The National Government (which you loan to when you give your money in return for Treasury IOUs—bills, notes, and bonds) | Local and State Governments (which you loan to when you give your money in return for their IOUs—that is, bonds—which pay tax-free interest) | Insurance Companies (which you loan to when you give your money in return for insurance company IOUs—cash value life insurance and fixed annuities) |

What I'm about to tell you is very important, so please pay close attention: The way in which you divide your investment capital between these two basic choices of "loaning" or "owning" *has a greater impact on your eventual investment returns than any other single factor.*

Think of your investments as being like a garden. Some people like to grow flowers and others prefer to grow vegetables. Some enjoy doing both. The one decision that has the greatest influence over what your garden looks like and the kind of harvest you'll ultimately have is this: How much of your garden should you devote to flowers and how much to vegetables? Once you decide that, you know a lot about what to expect in terms of the risks involved and the potential results *even if you haven't yet decided which kinds* of flowers or vegetables you're going to plant. Once you decided how you were going to allocate your space, the kind of harvest you were going to have was, to a great extent, already predetermined.

Now, let me shift your thinking to the investment arena. Studies have shown that 80%–90% of your investment return is determined by how much of your portfolio is invested in stocks (flowers) versus bonds (vegetables), and

INVESTING BY OWNING

Stocks	Real Estate	Oil & Gas Syndications	Precious Metals	Farmland
(where you become part owner of a business—"preferred" stock shares give you first claim on dividends)	(where you become an owner of land and/or buildings purchased primarily for their income-generating potential)	(where you pool your money with other investors and head for the great outdoors in search of undiscovered sources of energy)	(where you become an owner of actual gold, silver, or platinum—some investors prefer to hold gold/silver in the form of coins)	(where you become an owner of land used for growing crops—typically held for future price appreciation rather than income)

THE RISKS AND RETURNS OF OWNING VS. LOANING OVER VARIOUS 5-YEAR HOLDING PERIODS

5 Year Period	"Own" (Stocks)	"Loan" (Bonds)	50% Each
1940–1944	7.7%	3.3%	5.8%
1941–1945	17.0%	3.4%	10.5%
1942–1946	17.9%	3.2%	10.7%
1943–1947	14.9%	2.2%	8.7%
1944–1948	10.9%	2.4%	6.9%
1945–1949	10.7%	2.2%	6.6%
1946–1950	9.9%	1.8%	6.0%
1947–1951	16.7%	0.9%	8.9%
1948–1952	19.4%	2.0%	10.8%
1949–1953	17.9%	1.9%	10.0%
1950–1954	23.9%	2.3%	13.4%
1951–1955	23.9%	2.0%	13.2%
1952–1956	20.2%	1.1%	10.9%
1953–1957	13.6%	2.1%	8.4%
1954–1958	22.3%	1.0%	12.3%
1955–1959	15.0%	−0.3%	7.8%
1956–1960	8.9%	1.4%	5.7%
1957–1961	12.8%	3.8%	8.8%
1958–1962	13.3%	3.6%	9.0%
1959–1963	9.9%	4.5%	7.5%
1960–1964	10.7%	5.7%	8.5%
1961–1965	13.2%	3.8%	8.8%
1962–1966	5.7%	2.9%	4.6%
1963–1967	12.4%	0.3%	6.6%
1964–1968	10.2%	0.4%	5.5%
1965–1969	5.0%	−2.2%	1.6%
1966–1970	3.3%	1.2%	2.5%
1967–1971	8.4%	3.3%	6.1%
1968–1972	7.5%	5.8%	6.8%
1969–1973	2.0%	5.6%	3.9%
1970–1974	−2.4%	6.7%	2.4%
1971–1975	3.2%	6.0%	5.0%
1972–1976	4.9%	7.4%	6.5%
1973–1977	−0.2%	6.3%	3.4%
1974–1978	4.3%	6.0%	5.5%
1975–1979	14.8%	5.8%	10.4%
1976–1980	13.9%	2.4%	8.4%
1977–1981	8.1%	−1.3%	3.7%
1978–1982	14.0%	5.6%	10.2%
1979–1983	17.3%	6.9%	12.5%
1980–1984	14.8%	11.2%	13.4%
1981–1985	14.7%	17.9%	16.4%
1982–1986	19.9%	22.5%	21.4%
1983–1987	16.5%	14.1%	15.4%
1984–1988	15.4%	15.0%	15.2%
1985–1989	20.4%	14.9%	17.7%
1986–1990	13.1%	10.4%	11.9%
1987–1991	15.4%	10.4%	13.0%
1988–1992	15.9%	12.5%	14.3%
1989–1993	14.5%	13.0%	13.8%
1990–1994	8.7%	8.4%	8.6%
1991–1995	16.6%	12.2%	14.4%

only 10%–20% is determined by how good a job you did at making the individual selections. This surprises most people, because the investment industry gives far more attention to telling you about hot stocks and mutual fund performance rankings than to explaining the critical importance of asset allocation (that is, how much space you make in your investment garden for stocks versus how much room you allocate to bonds). We'll look at this in great detail in chapter 13 where I'll teach you a very simple strategy which puts your focus on "how much you put where" rather than "which ones."

For now, I just want you to recognize that the economic forces that influence the two basic choices are different. It's possible for you to lend your money to a corporation in return for one of its bonds and have that corporation be financially strong enough to meet all of its interest and principal obligations, even in the midst of a deep recession. On the other hand, it's also probable that if you had invested your money in the stock of the same corporation and become one of its part owners, the same recession would have caused serious harm (hopefully temporary) to the company's earnings and dividend payments. As a part owner of the business, rather than one of its creditors, you would have likely watched the value of your investment in the company lose value.

Of course, that's just looking at the risk part of the equation. The other side of that coin is that the owners of a company can enjoy great prosperity during those times in the business cycle that the economy is healthy and growing. The creditors merely continue receiving the interest payments to which they are due.

The reference table of annualized returns (at left) illustrates this risk/reward relationship. Consider the five-year period from 1987 to 1991 near the bottom. The table indicates that investors who allocated 100% of their capital to being owners (by investing in the shares of stocks in those blue-chip companies that are part of the Standard & Poor's 500 Stock Index) would have received a total return of 15.4% *per year* during that time. This is despite the fact that the crash of 1987 occurred early in the period. By comparing the "own" column with the "loan" column, you can also readily see that with rare exceptions since World War II, stockholders who held for at least a five-year period did far better than bondholders during the same period.

Investors who decided to allocate 100% of their money to becoming lenders would have earned 10.4% per year during the 1987–1991 period. (This assumes their returns were similar to the bonds included in the Salomon Brothers Long-Term High-Grade Corporate Bond Index, which is an average of more than 1,000 publicly issued corporate debt securities.) They would have made less money and taken less risk. The final column on the right shows the experience of investors who don't want to cast their lot entirely with either camp, but choose to split their capital equally between the two basic choices—50% in stocks and 50% in bonds. (The reason the 50/50 column is not simply the average of the other two columns is due to the effects of *reallocating the portfolio back to one-half of each kind of investment at the beginning of each new year*. This annual process is often referred to as "rebalancing.") You'll note that this middle-of-the-road course has consistently been profitable.

The point I want to make is this: All investing eventually finds its way into the American economy. It provides the essential money needed for businesses to be formed and grow—for engineering, manufacturing, construction, and a million and one other services to be offered and jobs to be created. You can either be a part owner in all this, tying yourself to the fortunes of American business and sharing in the certain risks and possible rewards that being an owner involves. Or, you can play the role of lender, giving your money to others in order to let *them* take the risks and knowing you are settling for a lesser, but more secure, return on your money. How to divide your funds between these two kinds of endeavors is your first and most important investing decision. Everything else is fine-tuning.

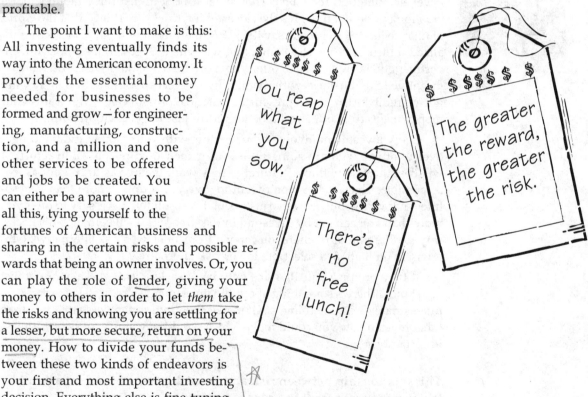

THE POTENTIAL FOR HIGHER RETURNS ALWAYS CARRIES A PRICE TAG

You reap what you sow.

There's no free lunch!

The greater the reward, the greater the risk.

Of course, no discussion of investing is complete without including the potential risks involved in making an investment. There is one fundamental rule that you should never, ever, *ever*, forget . . .

. . . the greater the potential reward being offered, the greater the risk involved in making that investment. Let me say that again. The greater the potential reward being offered, the greater the risk involved in making that investment. Or, in everyday plain English, *There's no free lunch*.

Countless people have learned this simple lesson only after losing thousands (and often hundreds of thousands) of dollars in an investment that was "just as safe" as a money market account but offered a higher return. The truth is that the link between risk and reward is as certain as the link between sowing and reaping. It's inescapable. Anyone who tells you differently is either self-deceived or is trying to deceive you.

Think about it for a second. The world's safest and most liquid investment is a 90-day U.S. Treasury bill. Investors in T-bills are loaning money to the U.S. government (which represents the world's largest economy and has never defaulted on its debts). They'll get it back in just three months, not a very long period of time. It's the closest thing to a "sure thing" that the world of finance has to offer. Let's say the U.S. government will pay you a 5% annualized return. Anyone else competing with the U.S. government for your investment dollar will have to offer you more than 5%; otherwise, you have no incentive to do business with them. Why not? Because by definition they are not as creditworthy and represent a greater risk. Anyone else who wants your money *will have to* offer you a better return just to get your attention.

Every investment involves your parting with your money and handing it over to others who are going to use it for their own purposes. In return, it will cost them something. Naturally, they want their costs to be kept as low as possible. That is, they don't want to give you a dollar more than is absolutely necessary. But, as we've just seen, it *is* absolutely necessary to offer you more than you can get by investing in risk-free U.S. T-bills. In fact, it's necessary to offer you more than you can get from *any* lower-risk alternative. Otherwise, you'll always select the lower-risk alternative.

If they promise you 10%, it's only because *they have to*. They're not just being nice. There's something about the investment—credit risk, market risk, interest rate risk, something—that makes their investment less attractive than other investments you could make which would pay you, say, 9½% with less uncertainty.

This relationship between risk and reward is one of the fundamental truths you must accept in order to succeed in investing.

Throughout the book, I'll be giving you some basic rules of thumb concerning this and various other investing truisms. My goal will not be just to help you understand them—I want you to "own" them. I want you to develop convictions concerning them. It will be the strength of these convictions that, in future years, will continue to provide you with a reliable compass for navigating the often turbulent waters of economic life. ◆

2

CHAPTER PREVIEW

The First Test of Financial Fitness: Are You Debt-Free?

I. **Before you begin investing your surplus funds, you should pay off any outstanding consumer-type debts.**

   A. Debt is defined as that which one is bound to pay or perform. It is a financial obligation that must be met.

   B. For purposes of this chapter, consumer debt includes credit card debt, local charge accounts, auto loans, and home equity loans. First mortgage loans on one's home will be covered separately in the next chapter.

II. **If you presently have the means to pay part or all of a debt but are investing with those funds instead, you are playing a very dangerous game. There are only three possible outcomes:**

   A. You could lose part or all of your investment money, in which case you are worse off than ever.

   B. You could make a profit, but the profit could be less than the interest you are paying on your debt. You are still worse off.

   C. You could *consistently* make profits, after taxes, that exceed the interest payments you are making on your debt. For an amateur investor, this is *extremely* unlikely.

III. **A thoughtful and workable plan for getting debt-free is a sign of maturity.**

   A. Getting debt-free is all the more important in light of the economic outlook for the coming years.

   B. Goal setting is important. Your goals should be consistent with God's Word and reflect His guidance. They should also be set with your spouse (if married) and in writing.

   C. Many helpful resources—newsletters and books—exist to help you in your efforts to get debt-free. Several are suggested for your consideration.

   D. Getting debt-free requires self-control but is attainable by everyone.

   E. For the Christian, getting debt-free is a matter of obedience, integrity, and preserving your allegiance to Christ alone.

Before you begin your stock and bond market investing, you need to achieve a certain level of financial fitness. It's like those exhortations . . .

. . . to see your doctor for a physical exam before launching out on a new exercise program. Think of it as practicing financial aerobics. Now, I know working out isn't any fun. Personally, I haven't gone to work out at the fitness center in several months. Not once. *Nada*. Zero. Zip. I'm too lazy.

My workout schedule usually goes something like this. I work out faithfully for three months, starting in early March, to get ready to go out in public in my beachwear. Then, it's off to the beach where I have a great time with family and friends. Upon my return, I carefully avoid the fitness center until the following March. During the recurring nine-month periods of well-deserved rest from exercising, I've made a discovery. It's tedious, hard work to get in shape, but getting out of shape is remarkably simple. All you have to do is. . .nothing. Just relax. Stop investing time in it. It's amazing how easy it is to get out of shape. I wish it weren't like that, but it is. Being in shape, it turns out, has a very short shelf life.

We all would like great health and physical fitness, but only the people with self-discipline achieve such goals. Other areas of life are the same way. Invest time, commitment, and sacrifice in your marriage or dating relationship, and it grows stronger by the month. Replace that with neglect and making decisions just to please yourself, and the relationship weakens. The same is true of your career and a host of life's other activities—including your financial affairs. They also need time, commitment, and sacrifice in order to be healthy and grow. Are you in shape financially?

If you're not, I'm writing this book with the assumption that you're serious about making progress. After all, you handed over more than twenty bucks to get this information. At the very least, you've got good intentions. I'm hoping that this book will help those good intentions lead to determined action.

Now, let's get started with your financial fitness tests to see what kind of shape you're in. The first fitness test you need to pass is the "debt" test . . .

. . . with special emphasis on credit card and other consumer-type debt. Webster's says that debt is that which one is bound to pay or perform; an obligation; the state of owing something. Using that definition, very few Americans are free of debt.

So, why place an emphasis on getting debt-free as the first step toward a sound investing strategy? Because debts are obligations, and they must be honorably met no matter the circumstances.

"Ten Motivating Reasons to Get Debt-Free" by Wilson J. Humber. Excerpted from The Financially Challenged. See Briefing 1, page 456.

The wicked borrow and do not repay, but the righteous give generously.
Psalm 37:21

Give everyone what you owe him: If you owe taxes, pay taxes; if revenue, then revenue; if respect, then respect; if honor, then honor. Let no debt remain outstanding, except the continuing debt to love one another, for he who loves his fellowman has fulfilled the law.
Romans 13:7–8

If you have the means to pay your debts off now but are investing with that money instead, you're playing a very dangerous game. There are only three possible outcomes . . .

. . . from a money management point of view. First, you might lose part— or even all—of your investment money. It does happen, you know. Then, how will you meet your obligations? The anxiety, pressure, and embarrassment this could cause you would be nightmarish. In fact, the leading reported cause of divorce is financial pressures. Yes, it could even destroy your family.

Second, you might make a profit, but the profit could be less than the interest you are paying on your debt. The prevailing interest rate charged by banks for major credit cards is 14%–18% per year. It's quite difficult to consistently make more than that on your investments. Yet making less would mean you were continuing to lose ground financially.

Third, you might make a consistent after-tax profit exceeding 20% per year. If this happens, you should consider leaving your present employment and moving to Wall Street! There are top professionals there, being paid hundreds of thousands of dollars per year, who aren't as good at investing as you appear to be. As of December 31, 1995, *less than 1% of all stock funds* had returns as high as 20% per year for the previous ten-year period (a time, if you'll recall, when the stock market was booming).

The dilemma facing those who would try to invest their way out of debt reminds me of Darrell Royal, who coached several University of Texas Longhorns football teams to national titles. When asked why his teams ran with the football so much, he replied: "Because when you pass, three things can happen and two of them are bad!" Keep this truth in mind: No investment is as secure as a repaid debt.

Putting your desire to invest ahead of repaying your debt obligations is usually a sign of immaturity . . .

. . . not financial sophistication. It requires thoughtful self-discipline not to overuse your access to credit. Even if you've made past mistakes, it's never too late to correct poor spending habits!

The time to start is now—if you're to escape the "squeeze" of the coming decade.

The 1980s were a decade of economic confidence and robust consumer spending. The 1990s will be different. . . . The era of the squeezed consumer is upon us. In this era, middle-class Americans will use their resources to fend off powerful economic assaults. Consumption will be driven less by whim and more by necessity. . . . The 1980s were enormously positive years for consumption. The 1990s may prove far less friendly. The new "squeezed" consumer will pay higher taxes, save more, and devote

Do not withhold good from those who deserve it, when it is in your power to act. Do not say to your neighbor, "Come back later; I'll give it tomorrow"—when you now have it with you.
Proverbs 3:27–28

Now listen, you who say, "Today or tomorrow we will go to this or that city, spend a year there, carry on business and make money." Why, you do not even know what will happen tomorrow. What is your life? You are a mist that appears for a little while and then vanishes. Instead, you ought to say, "If it is the Lord's will, we will live and do this or that." As it is, you boast and brag. All such boasting is evil. Anyone, then, who knows the good he ought to do and doesn't do it, sins.
James 4:13–17

The rich rule over the poor, and the borrower is servant to the lender.
Proverbs 22:7

more income to paying off their debts.

So speaks James Hughes, a professor of urban planning and policy development at Rutgers University. He foresees "years of debt without end." Here's his basic scenario:

The 1980s were great growth years primarily because the baby boomers were big spenders. Helped along by the Reagan tax cuts, they were in their prime family-forming, home-building years. Their spending was generally unrestrained by personal budget limitations and the traditional debt-averse ethic; they readily borrowed to support their spending desires. The result is that, as we entered the 1990s, it would take 90% of the average household's annual income to pay off all its debts. This is up from 70% ten years earlier.

We're now entering a period where slower growth in our annual incomes appears likely. The economic recovery is uneven and uncertain, housing values have flattened out (and in many areas declined), and the income tax reductions of the 1980s are being replaced with income tax hikes in the 1990s at the federal, state, and local levels. What's going to happen when our reduced income growth meets head-on with our record debt levels and interest burdens?

Larry Burkett, in his best-selling book *The Coming Economic Earthquake*, outlines a plausible scenario for our financial futures, both as individuals and as a country. For those who take his concerns seriously and wish to take steps to protect themselves, his primary recommendation is to get debt-free.

The problem with carrying out this sound bit of advice and getting completely debt-free is that we are our own worst enemies.

It's not hard to spend money. With a little practice, most of us get really good at it. Advertisers show us things that (they say) will make our lives more fun, exciting, and fulfilling. And if our eyes are bigger than our wallets, lenders shower us with credit cards

12 WARNING SIGNS OF EXCESSIVE DEBT

How about a financial health checkup? If any of these twelve warning signs describe your current state of affairs, you are "past due" to get on the road to recovery. Be honest.

❑ You are unable to pay each month's bills on time.

❑ You routinely receive overdue notices because of late or missing payments.

❑ You pay the minimum amounts required on your credit card bills.

❑ You've reached your credit limits on your credit card bills.

❑ You've applied for more credit cards to keep up your spending.

❑ You have used a cash advance from one credit card to make payments on others.

❑ You regularly take cash advances on your credit cards to pay routine living expenses such as food, rent, or utilities.

❑ You owe more on your car than it is worth as a trade-in.

❑ You postdate checks and cover them on payday or with new borrowings.

❑ You don't know the total amount of installment debt you owe.

❑ You no longer contribute to a savings account.

❑ You have no savings at all!

and encourage us to pamper ourselves. It may be expensive, but after all "we're worth it." For the most part, we're all prone to being tempted by the neat stuff we see around us. That's why we need a plan to keep us on course. To remind us where we're going. To match our outgo with our income. To help us actually live out our priorities.

A friend once heard a sermon by a noted pastor in which the pastor read a poem called "The Land of Beginning Again." The speaker then presented the claims of Christ, explaining that He is King in the Land of Beginning Again. The message made quite an impact on our friend, and as we listened to the tape he sent us, we knew why. The pastor explained that each of us has experienced his share of errors, failures, and missed opportunities. We all have things that we would do differently if given a second chance. What wonderful news to know that, in Christ, the slate is wiped clean and we do have the opportunity of beginning again.

Have you ever wished you could "begin again" financially?

Many who have become weighed down by debt wish they could get free. They have learned that the satisfaction that comes with spending is brief indeed compared to the pressure of making monthly payments, which often go on for years. For some, it seems hopeless. You may sometimes feel this way yourself.

If so, take heart! You can make great strides this year. It will require planning, discipline, sacrifice, and singleness of purpose. A friend of mine likes to say that the most powerful force in the universe (humanly speaking, of course) is singleness of purpose. Individuals or groups, no matter how determined, disciplined, or talented, will never realize their potential for growth and accomplishment without singleness of purpose. Their time, money, and energies must be focused on common goals. One thing that successful people seem to have in common is an emphasis—perhaps that's putting it too lightly, make that *an obsession*—concerning setting goals.

Without singleness of purpose and specific goals, we can become like the person described in Scripture as double-minded. "That man should not think he will receive anything from the Lord; he is a double-minded man, unstable in all he does" (James 1:7-8). So let me encourage you to engage in a meaningful goal-setting exercise as you work to get debt-free. Here are some suggestions for effective goal-setting in any area of life; adapt them to your financial situation.

◆ **Set goals that are consistent with God's Word.** Many successful people have accomplished much, yet remain unhappy. Having singleness of purpose toward the wrong goals only leads to wrong results. Examine your motivations, as well as your actions, in the light of God's wisdom. With respect to financial

"Enjoying the Benefits of a Spending Plan" by Stephen and Amanda Sorenson. Excerpted from Living Smart, Spending Less. See Briefing 2, page 457.

"Financial Deceptions" by Ron Blue. Excerpted from Taming the Money Monster. See Briefing 3, page 458.

You must teach what is in accord with sound doctrine. Teach the older men to be temperate, worthy of respect, self-controlled. . . . Likewise, teach the older women. . . . Then they can train the younger women to love their husbands and children, to be self-controlled. . . . Similarly, encourage the young men to be self-controlled. . . . For the grace of God that brings salvation has appeared to all men. It teaches us to say "No" to ungodliness and worldly passions, and to live self-controlled, upright and godly lives in this present age.
Titus 2:1–6, 11–12

Recommended Resource
The Financial
Planning Organizer
by Larry Burkett

Just the tool you need to get
your budget into shape. You
will receive a ten-inch three-
ring binder, the newly revised
Financial Planning Workbook,
20 pages of special addenda
to the workbook, and a set of
20 divider tabs. To order call
1-800-722-1976.

goal-setting, one implication of this is that your plan provides for your tithe to the Lord. To help you through the process, I recommend *The Financial Planning Organizer* from Christian Financial Concepts (see sidebar). It combines biblical principles with financial planning forms and how-tos.

◆ **Ask God for His guidance.** This is not the same as having scripturally sound goals. This has more to do with having the wisdom needed to set the right personal priorities. God promises to guide us if we're willing to submit to Him. It's not: "Show me Your will, Lord, so I can decide if I'm willing." Rather, it's: "Before You even reveal Your will to me, Lord, the answer is yes."

◆ **If married, set your goals together.** If two have become "one flesh," how critical that they have a singleness of purpose in their commitment toward common goals. Few areas will so quickly affect a couple's relationship as a financial plan that limits their spending freedom because it brings mutually conflicting goals into the open. If you can't reach a meeting of the minds on what your priorities should be, perhaps the marriage relationship itself needs some work. Russ Crosson's *Money & Your Marriage* is an excellent book that deals with this area (see page 37).

◆ **Put your goals in writing, signing your name and date.** This act helps cement in your thinking that you really have made a firm commitment of your will to achieving your goals. It is also helpful to have your goals posted where you will see them daily as additional motivation to stay the course when the inevitable temptations to compromise arise.

Before you compete in the stock market and other investing arenas, you must get in shape.

"Practical Guidelines
to Control Spending"
by Randy Alcorn.
Excerpted from
Money, Possessions,
and Eternity.
See Briefing 4,
page 460.

"How to Make Money
the Easy Way"
by Scott Houser.
Excerpted from the
Sound Mind Investing
newsletter.
See Briefing 5,
page 461.

Part of being in shape is getting good at spending. Enjoying spending is not the same as getting "good" at it. Getting good at it is when you have it under control. Fortunately, frugality is "in." This means you can live more simply, progress toward financial freedom, and be fashionable all at the same time!

The trendiness of frugal living has given rise to several helpful newsletters on how to live well on less money. Here are several that are worth checking out. The following brief reviews were taken from articles written by Vicki Mosher, a member of my staff, which appeared in my monthly newsletter during 1995. I'd suggest sending for samples of each to see which ones best fit your needs and lifestyle.

◆ *The Pocket Change Investor.* Cleverly written by Marc Eisenson and Nancy Castleman, this quarterly newsletter offers you a smorgasbord of money saving strategies. You'll discover how to save thousands of dollars (like I did!) through prepayments on your home mortgage and credit cards and the importance of retiring these and other debts. I especially like the wide variety of interesting topics featured in every issue. In recent issues, subscribers enjoyed: "25 Tips to a Penny Pinching Home Closing," "Home Insurance Can Cost Less," and "What To Do When the Lease Bug Bites." (For an example of the Eisenson/Castleman style, see Briefing 6, "Cutting Credit Card Costs," on page 463.) *The Pocket Change Investor,* Box 78, Elizaville, NY 12523 is $12.95 for four quarterly, eight-page issues. Send $1.00 for a sample issue.

◆ *No-Debt Living.* This newsletter is committed to helping God's people reach their goals of becoming and remaining debt-free. Leading financial professionals contribute to the newsletter, sharing their wisdom with you in bite-sized nuggets. You will find a broad range of topics covered in each issue, filled with timely tips that will enable you to save in all areas of your finances. In the past two years, it has addressed such topics as: reducing college costs, minimizing taxes, refinancing your mortgage, creating a workable budget, choosing smart loans, eliminating credit card debt, reducing insurance costs, and investing in no-debt stocks. *No-Debt Living,* Post Office Box 282, Veradale, WA 99037 or call (509) 927-1322. It costs $25.95 for eleven, eight-page monthly issues. Send $1.00 for a sample issue.

◆ *The Cheapskate Monthly.* With wit and humor, editor Mary Hunt makes saving money a pleasant experience. She defines cheapskates as those who "save consistently, give generously and never spend more money than they have." Mary has gained national recognition by appearing on such programs as "Good Morning America" and "Focus on the Family." The design is great, and the content is even better. The testimonials of success and struggle found in Turning Point, along with the Money Makeovers, give you confidence that you can be a better steward of your financial resources. You will discover answers to your personal budgeting questions to help make living within your means easier. There's a wealth of money-saving information and encouragement in this publication. *The Cheapskate Monthly,* P.O. Box 2135, Paramount, CA 90723-8135 or call (310) 630-8845. The cost is $15.95 for a twelve-page newsletter that is published monthly. A free sample issue will be sent upon your request.

Plus, there are some excellent books on the market as well. Three of my favorites are:

◆ *Money & Your Marriage* by Russ Crosson. When married couples come to me for financial counseling, a book I often recommend first is this one by Russ Crosson. As a certified financial planner, Russ has seen how money is a source of friction, frustration, and anxiety for many couples. But he believes that the conflict over money in most marriages is more likely the result of incorrect thinking on the part of a husband and wife about money. This is complicated by a lack of communication as well as a lack of financial strategy. Published by Thomas Nelson. Softcover. $9.99.

If you're still working to get debt-free, should you tithe?

"I have heard Christians say, 'I don't think it honors God to tithe while I still owe a past due debt.'

I could accept that argument if they would do one thing for me. Write the Internal Revenue Service, and say, 'I'm sorry but I don't think I should pay taxes while I'm in debt. I'll wait until I get out of debt, and then I'll pay my taxes again.'

Why do they pay their taxes? Because they fear the government. Proverbs 1:7 says that the fear of the Lord is the beginning of knowledge.

I have also had creditors call and say, 'I don't see why I should take a reduced payment while they're giving to their church.'

I simply share with the creditors the principle of the tithe—that it's a commitment to God, not to a church. I also share an observation that those who tithe are almost always better money handlers, and as a result of their commitment to God, they will honor their commitment to their creditors. Rarely does a creditor object after that. In fact, almost everyone respects the commitment, even though most aren't Christians themselves.

God's Word says that, if we tithe, God will give us His wisdom (Deut. 14:23). If there were ever anyone in the world who needs God's wisdom in finances, it is those who are in debt."

Excerpted from Answers to Your Family's Financial Questions by Larry Burkett

Copyright 1987 by Focus on the Family

◆ *Debt-Free Living* by Larry Burkett. For the couple facing financial crisis, this book offers a scriptural way back. In addition, *Debt-Free Living* provides a layman's guide to consumer rights. With the financially troubled in mind it summarizes federal codes and acts covering credit agencies, credit reports, debt collection agencies, and bankruptcy. Published by Moody Press. Hardback. $16.99.

◆ *Taming the Money Monster* by Ron Blue. This Focus on the Family release offers the expert advice of a leading financial counselor on how to get out of debt, stay out of debt, and experience true financial freedom. It shows why we tend to slip into debt, how we're manipulated into making unwise borrowing decisions, and how to evaluate the opportunities when borrowing seems the right thing to do. Softcover. $9.99.

Here are others I liked well enough to add to my library. Several have contributed excerpts to my monthly newsletter over the past few years. The book descriptions (within quote marks) are taken from their respective covers:

◆ *Finding Dollars for Family Fun: Creating Happy Memories on a Budget* by Gwen Weising. "Fun activities are essential for a family's sense of unity and well-being. Yet funds for these activities are usually the first to be cut from overextended budgets. Believing that fun doesn't always have to cost a lot of money, or any money at all, Gwen Weising offers hundreds of ideas for creating happy and affordable family memories." Gwen Weising is the managing editor of Focus on the Family Books. Published by Revell. Softcover. $8.99.

◆ *Living Smart, Spending Less: Creative Ways to Stretch Your Income and Have Fun Doing It* by Stephen and Amanda Sorenson. "Many books can tell you how to multiply your income . . . and run yourself ragged in the process! But few offer proven, simple tips on how to stretch the dollars you have and enjoy life more. This one does. It's your survival manual for the frugal '90s. Just because income is tighter doesn't mean you have to watch your bank account shrink or enjoy your family less. Why? Because it's not what you make that counts, it's how much you spend. Organized so that you can pick and choose which tips apply to your situation, this eye-opening book lets you in on a 'living smart' adventure, including: •Sixteen spending categories where every family can win key battles •How to untangle needs from wants •How to make wise shopping decisions (and avoid costly blunders) •Simple financial secrets to rescue both your savings and sanity." Stephen Sorenson has worked for Compassion International and NavPress, and Amanda is a former editor of *Bookstore Journal*. Published by Moody Press. Softcover. $9.99.

◆ *Downsize Your Debt: How to Take Control of Your Personal Finances* by Andrew Feinberg. "Being in debt is a fact of life for tens of millions of Americans. But the average consumer could save hundreds, perhaps thousands, of dollars a year simply by knowing more about the ins and outs of borrowing. This extremely helpful book will show you how to: •Manage credit—from cards to car loans •Save money every time you borrow •Establish a solid credit rating and keep it from going sour •Fix a damaged credit rating and reestablish credit •Negotiate with creditors •Break bad borrowing habits •Deal with the IRS." Andrew Feinberg is a regular contributor to *Money* and *Worth* financial magazines. Published by Penguin Books. Softcover. $10.95.

◆ *Saving Money Any Way You Can: How to Become a Frugal Family* by Mike Yorkey. "They say that money doesn't grow on trees, but tell that to the super shoppers in this book. Full of advice and engaging stories from consumers just like you, it takes the mystery out of s-t-r-e-t-c-h-i-n-g your dollars. In 1989, Mike Yorkey and his wife Nicole wanted to buy their first home. When they sat down to figure their budget, they discovered they had regularly been borrowing from their savings in order to make ends meet. Shocked and disheartened, they were forced to tighten their belts and make better buying decisions. Now they—and the numerous families interviewed for this book—say they spend less but enjoy it more. They include tried-and-true tips on: •How you can save dollars by using (not abusing) credit cards rather than cash •Ways to deflate the pressure on your kids to wear designer clothing •Maximizing your grocery dollars so that you don't have to scrimp on food •Creative and effective ways to put aside money for your child's college education •Getting the best price for your family car. Written by a consumer for consumers, this book is fun, easy-to-read, and practical—and it works!" Mike Yorkey is the editor of *Focus on the Family* magazine. Published by Vine Books. Softcover. $8.99.

◆ *The 15 Minute Money Manager* by Bob and Emilie Barnes. "A money management book for busy people! Watch your finances come into focus as you apply the authors' proven 15-minute principle: Invest a small amount of time and make a big difference. Sixty-two short, quick-reading chapters have hundreds of ready-to-use ideas that will help you: •Streamline and simplify your budget •Develop a strong financial plan •Cut costs without crimping your style •Plan for the future." The Barneses are the founders of More Hours in My Day Time Management Seminars. Published by Harvest House. Softcover. $9.99.

◆ *1,001 Bright Ideas to Stretch Your Dollars* by Cynthia Yates. "With energy and sparkling wit this dynamic 'Queen of Thrift' will inspire you to learn to live within your means. Cynthia Yates and her imaginary sidekick 'Grim' interview grocers, merchants, financial consultants and others to show you how to make your dollars S-T-R-E-T-C-H! This handy, hilarious guide for today's thrifty woman incorporates 'Ten Commandments of Thrifty Living' into every aspect of daily life: food preparation and storage, hospitality, gift-giving, car and home purchase and maintenance, home decorating, and much, much more.

to the Holy Spirit's promptings to give generously to meet others' needs. Here I am talking not just about the tithe but the freewill giving, that which is above and beyond the minimum. If my indebtedness leaves me unable to respond to God in this way, I have robbed myself and others of incalculable blessings.

◆ Debt is especially dangerous when it restricts our freedom to respond to the Holy Spirit's call to make a move or change. If God called you today to go to the mission field, how long would it take you to free yourself from your financial responsibilities in order to follow him? Is it impossible for you to pull up stakes in response to God's leading because the stakes have been driven so deep by your debt on your tent?

◆ Debt is especially dangerous when it tempts us to violate our convictions. A Christian couple assumed a large home mortgage based on both their incomes. But when the wife became pregnant, they realized that in order to keep the house they would have to violate their convictions against leaving their child in a day-care center while the mother worked. Once they realize their dilemma, it would be better to confess their error, ask God's forgiveness, and take whatever losses they might need to take in order to get out of their house and into one appropriate for a single income."

Adapted from
Money, Possessions,
& Eternity
by Randy Alcorn
Copyright 1989
by Randy C. Alcorn

"Cutting Credit
Card Costs"
by Marc Eisenson.
Excerpted from The
Pocket Change Investor
newsletter.
See Briefing 6,
page 463.

"How to Save on Credit
Card Interest and Fees"
by Gerri Detweiler.
Excerpted from
The Ultimate
Credit Handbook.
See Briefing 7,
page 466.

"Bankcard Holders
of America"
by Vicki Mosher.
Excerpted from the
Sound Mind Investing
newsletter.
See Briefing 8,
page 468.

As you follow her advice, your family will be amazed—and God will be glorified—by the results!" Cynthia Yates is a humor columnist and public speaker. Published by Vine Books. Softcover. $8.99.

◆ *The Ultimate Credit Handbook: How to Double Your Credit, Cut Your Debt, and Have a Lifetime of Great Credit* by Gerri Detweiler. "You will find out how the credit bureaus rate you, how to improve your credit rating, and how to correct credit bureau errors that can wreck your financial life. You will master the secrets of good credit and find out how to turn a credit rejection into an acceptance. You will learn how to get through credit catastrophes and how to fix your credit if it has already been damaged. You will be armed with information to help you battle credit-card fraud, bank foul-ups, and merchandising rip-offs. You will learn your credit rights and how to enforce them. And, best of all, you will discover painless ways to cut your spending and get out of debt—forever. Credit can be a blessing, or a curse. The choice is yours—this book is a tool that can make a difference." Gerri Detweiler is the former director of Bankcard Holders of America, a national nonprofit consumer credit organization. Published by Plume Books. Softcover. $11.95.

Aside from the practical advantages of getting debt-free—less financial stress and huge savings on interest expense—there are biblical ones as well. Here are three that seem compelling to me:

❶ **To be obedient.** "Give everyone what you owe him: If you owe taxes, pay taxes; if revenue, then revenue; if respect, then respect; if honor, then honor. Let no debt remain outstanding, except the continuing debt to love one another, for he who loves his fellowman has fulfilled the law" (Romans 13:7-8).

❷ **To maintain your integrity.** "The wicked borrow and do not repay, but the righteous give generously" (Psalm 37:21).

❸ **To preserve your allegiance to Christ alone.** "The rich rule over the poor, and the borrower is servant to the lender" (Proverbs 22:7).

Most debt problems result from an excess of spending, not a lack of income. The solution is deceptively simple: You must develop a plan to assure that you spend less than you earn. Then you'll have a monthly surplus that can be applied to gradually eliminating your debts.

In chapter 3, we look at another source of indebtedness that affects a majority of working Americans—the house mortgage. What priority should paying it off have in your financial plan? ◆

3

CHAPTER PREVIEW

The Importance of Having Your Home Paid For

I. **As a general rule, surplus funds are better used for paying off the mortgage on your home than they are for investing because:**

    A. You could lose your home if the investments don't work out as planned, possibly leaving you more in debt than ever.

    B. You could lose your home if your present level of income falls due to being disabled or laid off, general economic recession, or childbearing.

II. **The parable of two families: the LiveHighs and the ThinkSmarts.**

    A. In identical financial situations, the LiveHighs choose to finance their higher standard of living by taking a thirty-year mortgage when buying their home; the ThinkSmarts elect a fifteen-year mortgage on a less expensive (but functionally similar) home.

    B. After fifteen years, the ThinkSmarts paid their mortgage in full and began redirecting their monthly mortgage payments into their retirement investment account. You'll likely be greatly surprised at how much more the ThinkSmarts have in their retirement account after thirty years than the LiveHighs have.

III. **My recommendation is that you *not* consider other investments (as opposed to paying off your mortgage) unless the three listed conditions are met.**

IV. **Home equity loans are quite dangerous because you can lose your house for nonpayment. They should have the top priority for repayment, even ahead of other consumer debt.**

V. **If you can't afford to make extra principal payments on your home mortgage and at the same time put money into a retirement plan, which should have the priority?**

    A. As we see by following the experiences of Rob and Dan, contributing to the retirement plan is more profitable from an economic viewpoint. Ultimately, it's a decision based on your personal convictions with respect to debt.

    B. It's generally not advisable to cash in one's retirement plan in order to retire the mortgage.

As a general rule, surplus funds are better used to pay off the mortgage on your home than they are for investing.

First, as we've already discussed, investments don't always pan out as hoped. You might be left with more debt than ever—and possibly even lose your house! Second, you probably are assuming that your income will continue at its present level or higher. But what if you are disabled, or laid off, or unexpected developments harm your business? Be careful about presuming on the future. And third, your patience will eventually be rewarded. The guaranteed interest savings from a faster pay-down will free up other funds that can be used for future investing.

Consider the saga of the LiveHighs and the ThinkSmarts . . .

Two partners named LiveHigh and ThinkSmart had a lot in common. They each owned half their business, paid themselves equal salaries, were both married, and had two kids each. They had both saved $20,000 and were ready when the big moment that they'd worked so hard for finally arrived: the day they went looking for that first new house for their families.

They each were planning to start investing $200 per month into their new retirement accounts, and both had also decided they could afford monthly payments of around $925 on their house mortgages. LiveHigh knew just the house he wanted—it had an extra large corner lot and a spacious deck for cookouts. He figured that with interest rates down now, he could pick up a thirty-year, 7.75% mortgage that, along with his down payment, would enable him to afford the $150,000 price tag.

"Housing Decisions: Should You Buy or Rent?" by Marc Eisenson. Excerpted from <u>The Pocket Change Investor</u>. See Briefing 9, page 469.

ThinkSmart liked the house next door. It was just like LiveHigh's except it was on a much smaller lot and lacked the backyard deck. The $120,000 price was appealing because it meant his $925 monthly payment would fit just right with a fifteen-year, 7.5% mortgage. He put down his $20,000 and signed on the dotted line.

As time passed, the business grew slowly but steadily. We pick up our story fifteen years later as ThinkSmart is writing the check for his final mortgage payment. What a great feeling! He and his wife decide to go out for the evening to celebrate. They talk about how much fun it would be to "trade up" to a nicer home but agree they don't want to get back into mortgage debt again. Instead, they decide to increase the amount they put into their retirement account. Every month they deposit the $925 that formerly went to the mortgage company.

We can fast-forward fifteen more years to the end of our story. Mr. and Mrs. LiveHigh are happy. After thirty years, they have written their final mortgage check. As they think of the future, they agree: "With this taken care of at last, it's time to begin putting more money into our retirement account."

Next door, ThinkSmart and his wife are also thinking of the future. Their quarterly statement came today, and the current balance in their investment account is quite impressive! As they look through some travel brochures, they agree: "With this much in savings, it's time to begin enjoying some of the fruits of our labor."

Assuming that both families earned 8% on their retirement investments over the years, how much more do the ThinkSmarts have than the LiveHighs?

First, let me point out the *reason* the ThinkSmarts have more: they were willing to accept a lifestyle with more modest amenities. Although the houses themselves were quite similar, the ThinkSmarts were willing to do without the backyard deck and more spacious lot size. For most couples who have debt problems, their difficulties began when they obligated themselves to a larger mortgage payment than was reasonable given their income.

This is especially true if they relied on two incomes when computing their ability to comfortably make long-term monthly mortgage payments. In that event, if either income is interrupted for any reason—the economy, corporate strategic planning, technical obsolescence, disability, or childbearing—they automatically have a financial problem on their hands.

Now, here are the numbers reflecting the surprisingly high costs of the LiveHighs' lifestyle. After thirty years of paying on their mortgage and contributing to retirement, the LiveHighs have $300,059 in their retirement account. Meanwhile the ThinkSmarts, after paying off a smaller mortage in only fifteen years, have $622,278 in their retirement account. Thus, they have $322,219 more. The extra amenities ended up costing the LiveHighs far more than they could have ever imagined!

I would recommend that you *not* consider other investments (as opposed to paying down your house mortgage) unless all three of these conditions are met:

❶ Both spouses are in *complete* agreement that the investment should have the top priority;

❷ The remaining unpaid balance on your mortgage is *less than 50% of the current value* of your house (for example, your house would sell for around $120,000 and you owe less than $60,000 on your mortgage); and

❸ The investment will provide a return that is *guaranteed* to be greater than the interest rate on your mortgage.

If these three criteria are met, using your surplus income for investing rather than paying extra on your mortgage could be considered a reasonable and prudent decision. (This assumes you already have an adequate contingency fund in place—see next chapter.) I want to make clear, however, that what we are talking about here applies only to first mortgages.

I denied myself nothing my eyes desired; I refused my heart no pleasure. My heart took delight in all my work, and this was the reward for all my labor. Yet when I surveyed all that my hands had done and what I had toiled to achieve, everything was meaningless, a chasing after the wind; nothing was gained under the sun.
Ecclesiastes 2:10–11

But godliness with contentment is great gain. For we brought nothing into the world, and we can take nothing out of it.
1 Timothy 6:6–7

"Home equity loans" are another story altogether. Americans used to take out second mortgages as a last resort. Now . . .

. . . many consider them a sign of savvy tax planning. Why the change in our thinking?

Aside from the obvious fact that our entire society has become increasingly addicted to debt, we should understand the major roles played by the federal government and our friendly bankers. First, Congress got the ball rolling when it passed tax legislation that eliminated the income tax deduction for consumer interest payments unless they were made on a home mortgage. Then, lenders made it easy for us by offering low teaser rates and often waiving closing costs and other fees. Toss in the fact that, with interest rates so low, the cost of borrowing is less than it has been for quite a while. Now homeowners are using these loans to pay for everything from vacations to college tuition to new cars. Everybody seems happy, so what's the problem?

I don't like these loans for the same reasons that banks love them. First, these loans greatly increase the amount of money banks can safely lend you (and therefore the amount of interest they receive). One thing most Americans don't need is more credit and more debt. Second, if anything goes wrong with your loan, the bank is protected and can always foreclose on the house. It's one thing when getting laid off or having unexpected medical expenses shoots a hole in your monthly budget and your new car is repossessed. It's quite another when they come for your house!

There are other concerns as well. Some lenders are letting homeowners borrow up to 100% of their equity—where would you ever get the money to pay off such a large loan? Years of building equity through your monthly payments can be completely erased by one problem loan. Especially beware of loans that allow you to pay interest-only during the term of your loan and then call for immediate payment of the full principal. Finally, if the loan has a variable rate, check how high your rate could conceivably get during the life of the loan. Interest rate "caps" vary widely, from as low as 15% to as high as 25%! All in all, they're a threat to your financial safety, and their payment in full should be a priority.

Refinancing your mortgage, in order to take advantage of lower interest rates and/or shorten your payment schedule to a fifteen-year maturity, can result in significant savings on interest expense.

Refinancing your mortgage involves paying your existing mortgage off early by taking out a new one at a lower rate. The key statistic in deciding whether to refinance is learning how far down the road you "break even." Here's what you do. First, shop for the best deal and learn what your new monthly payment will be. Next, subtract the amount of your new payment from your old one. This tells you how much you'll save each month. Finally, divide this monthly savings into the total spent for points and other refinancing costs. This tells you how many months before the refinancing pays for itself (tax considerations aside). That's your break-even point; after that, you're saving every month.

Here's an example: If your new monthly payment would be $120 less than your current one, and if your total closing costs (including points) were $2,400, then it would take twenty months' worth of savings to pay your expenses (2,400 divided by 120). After that, you'd be ahead an extra $120 each month.

It can get confusing trying to compare different proposals, so here's a handy way to convert points into a percentage rate: treat each point as if it added ¼ of 1% to your loan rate. Example: a 9% rate with two points is roughly the same as a 9½% rate with no points.

Once you know the break-even point for each loan you've been quoted, the main consideration is how long you expect to be in your present home. If you don't think you'll be there long enough to reach the break-even point, forget it. If you think you'll be there past break-even and decide to go ahead, you still have to decide whether to take a loan that features a lower rate but more points, or a higher rate with fewer points. The general rule is that the shorter the time past break-even that you expect to live there, the more you should lean toward the lower transaction costs. That means a shorter stay equals fewer points with a higher rate; a longer stay equals more points but a lower rate.

> ## MORTGAGE "POINTS"
>
> A typical mortgage loan, in addition to the interest rate you pay, carries two or three "points." Each point is equal to 1% of the loan amount and is charged by the lender to cover the up-front costs of originating the loan, appraisals, title search, legal fees, and so on. These points are subtracted from your proceeds at the time of your loan closing.
>
> For example: If your new mortgage is for $80,000 and you are charged three points, then you really only receive cash of $77,600 at the loan closing ($80,000 times 3% equals $2,400 in points paid).

To keep things simple, many lenders offer a "no points" option where they let you skip the points and closing costs entirely . . .

. . . in exchange for a higher interest rate. Then it becomes simply a matter of comparing the interest rate they quote you with the rate you're paying now. For example, if you're currently paying 7.75% but can get a "no points" rate of 7.40%, you're guaranteed to save. In fact, there's no reason you wouldn't want to refinance many times over the years when the advantages are this clear cut. Sure, there's some paperwork involved, but there's probably nothing else you can do that will pay you (in saved interest) such a high hourly rate for your time! I'd check every ninety days, and consider refinancing whenever you can save at least one-quarter of a percent. Depending on the overall level of rates, you'll save $6,000–$7,000 in interest over thirty years on a $100,000 mortgage for *every* one-quarter of percent reduction in your rate.

Here are some other shopping tips that can help you save money. First, look into getting a fifteen-year mortgage rather than a thirty-year one. The monthly payment will be higher, but the interest rate is lower. The savings in interest is dramatic! Second, if you refinance and end up with a lower monthly payment than you're now making, the temptation will be to take the savings and spend it elsewhere. Don't do it! Instead, send in the same amount using two checks. One check will be for the new monthly payment; the other can be applied to pre-paying principal and hastening the day when you own your home free and clear. Other points to keep in mind:

◆ You can refinance with the original lender or go to a new one. However, often you will save on closing costs by staying with your current lender.

◆ Find out when the rate on your loan will be "locked in" (permanently set). Is it when you apply? When the loan is closed? Many borrowers have been hurt when interest rates rose after the original proposal was made but before the lender locked in the rate.

◆ Get a commitment in writing of the exact terms of the mortgage being offered and how long the offer is good for. It should include the circumstances under which the lender would be allowed to back out (for example, in case of a dispute over the appraised value of your home).

◆ Keep in touch with your loan officer as your application is being processed. Find out when the appraisal and credit agency reports are supposed to be back, and call on the expected dates to see if everything checks out.

"Big Savings Through Mortgage Prepayments" by Marc Eisenson. Excerpted from The Pocket Change Investor. See Briefing 10, page 470.

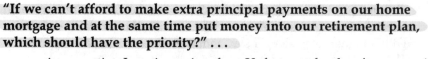

"If we can't afford to make extra principal payments on our home mortgage and at the same time put money into our retirement plan, which should have the priority?" . . .

. . . is a question I receive quite often. Unfortunately, there's no one-size-fits-all answer—your age, your tax bracket, what you would do with the tax savings from your mortgage interest, how long you expect to live in your home, and your general attitude toward being debt-free all play significant roles.

Let's say that two readers of this book who have different goals are each wrestling with this question. Rob is leery of Social Security and wants to begin building his retirement funds immediately. Dan thinks being in debt is more of a concern and plans on using any monthly surplus to make additional principal payments on his mortgage.

For comparison purposes, let's make their two situations identical: They both have new $50,000, fifteen-year fixed rate mortgages; both can set aside $600 out of each month's paycheck (their monthly mortgage payment is $507, leaving them each an extra $93 for payment of the principal or investment in a retirement account); both are in the 34% tax bracket (federal plus state), and both have the opportunity to contribute to a retirement plan at work that will earn 9%, the same rate as their mortgages.

When they make their first month's mortgage payment, $375 of it is tax deductible as interest expense. This will lower each of their taxes by $128 a month (34% of $375). What they do with that $128 savings can make a big difference.

Let's assume that both Rob and Dan would like to get their hands on that savings sooner rather than later. They would get it back when they filed their income tax returns anyway, so why wait? So, they both change the withholding instructions they give their employers so that about $128 less is withheld for income taxes each month. By adding that amount to the extra $93 left from their monthly surplus, they each now have an extra $221 to work with. Rob contributes his into his company's 401(k) plan while Dan takes the cash and makes an extra principal payment on his mortgage.

Now here's where it can really get confusing. To construct an accurate picture, we have to recognize that Rob gets a second tax deduction—this time for putting money into the retirement plan. Rob's $221 contribution is worth another $75 tax savings, which he could then also put into his 401(k). But then that $75 contribution would save him an additional $25 in taxes, which he could also put into his 401(k). But then that $25 . . . well, you get the idea. If Rob took maximum advantage of this, he could ultimately put $334 into his company retirement plan that first month (the $93 extra plus his tax savings of $128 for mortgage interest plus another $113 in tax savings for contributing to the company 401(k)).

ROB EMPHASIZES SAVING FOR RETIREMENT

At End of Year	Balance Due on Mortgage	Value of 401(k) Account	Tax Savings Mortgage Interest	Tax Savings 401(k) Contributions
1	$48,347	$4,172	$1,507	$1,350
2	46,540	8,651	1,454	1,323
3	44,562	13,458	1,397	1,294
4	42,400	18,617	1,334	1,261
5	40,034	24,149	1,265	1,226
6	37,447	30,081	1,189	1,187
7	34,617	36,438	1,107	1,144
8	31,521	43,247	1,017	1,098
9	28,135	50,539	918	1,047
10	24,431	58,342	810	991
11	20,380	66,690	692	930
12	15,949	75,616	562	864
13	11,102	85,154	421	791
14	5,800	95,341	267	711
15	0	106,215	97	624
Summary	$0	$106,215	$14,037	$15,841

Assume that both men are able to take the maximum advantage of the available tax savings as the years pass. Dan pays down as much extra on his mortgage each month as he can and pays it off completely in nine years. At that point, he shifts all the money he formerly put toward his mortgage each month into his retirement plan. He also adjusts his withholdings to take maximum advantage of the tax savings his contributions create.

At the end of fifteen years, their experiences can be summarized this way. Both men had the same out-of-pocket expenditures—$600 per month over fifteen years, totaling $108,000. In return, they both accomplished paying their $50,000 mortgage loans in full and were able to invest for retirement. It's interesting to note that, although they proceeded according to different time tables, Rob and Dan ultimately saved an equal amount ($29,878) on their taxes. This was due to each of them always taking full advantage of the tax-deductibility of mortgage interest and 401(k) contributions with their surplus dollars.

The important difference in their financial situations after fifteen years is found in the value of their retirement accounts. Rob's 401(k) grew to $106,215 and Dan's to $87,454. Although they had both saved the same amount in taxes which could then be invested for retirement, Rob's savings were "front-loaded." That meant he could put them to work in his 401(k) earlier than Dan could. In this way, Rob was able to take greater advantage of the tax-deferred compounding of profits. The difference in his 401(k) would have been even greater if Rob's employer contributed matching funds. Dan's retirement account later came on strong, but Rob's head start was too great.

Should you follow Rob's example? Not necessarily. To make it work, you've got to be able to aggressively use all of the tax savings, and more important, you need fifteen years of relative stability in your job, the economy, and the tax code. That seems to be asking a lot from the next decade.

The advantage of following Dan's approach is: It quickly provides the security of debt-free home ownership, which will better enable you to weather any economic storms; in case of an emergency, the wealth in your home is more accessible than assets tied up in a retirement plan; and while Rob's return in the 401(k) could fall below 9%, Dan's interest savings on his mortgage will not.

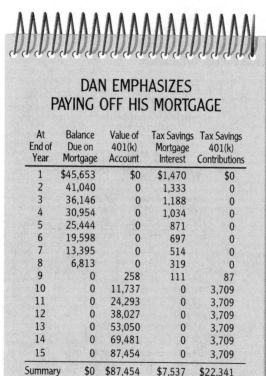

DAN EMPHASIZES PAYING OFF HIS MORTGAGE

At End of Year	Balance Due on Mortgage	Value of 401(k) Account	Tax Savings Mortgage Interest	Tax Savings 401(k) Contributions
1	$45,653	$0	$1,470	$0
2	41,040	0	1,333	0
3	36,146	0	1,188	0
4	30,954	0	1,034	0
5	25,444	0	871	0
6	19,598	0	697	0
7	13,395	0	514	0
8	6,813	0	319	0
9	0	258	111	87
10	0	11,737	0	3,709
11	0	24,293	0	3,709
12	0	38,027	0	3,709
13	0	53,050	0	3,709
14	0	69,481	0	3,709
15	0	87,454	0	3,709
Summary	$0	$87,454	$7,537	$22,341

It's one thing to temporarily lower or eliminate putting money into a retirement plan in order to work on a debt-reduction plan; it's another altogether to close out your retirement plan.

Questions such as, "Should I cash in my pension plan in order to pay off my mortgage?" or, "Should I close my IRA and take the proceeds to pay off my consumer/car loans?" involve much more serious decisions than the example we just discussed.

The steps, once taken, are irreversible. You can't change your mind later. So it's important to understand and weigh all the factors. Be sure you understand the tax consequences of prematurely withdrawing money from a tax-deferred plan. Let's say you cash in $10,000 before age 59½ (or 55 in some plans). First, the IRS hits you with a 10% penalty. That leaves $9,000. Next there are the ordinary federal income taxes. Assuming you're in the 28% marginal bracket, there goes another $2,800 (the penalty isn't deductible). So you only have $6,200 of your original $10,000 left to apply against your debts. Then there is the opportunity cost of not having the $10,000 compounding tax deferred for years into the future. So, it's a pretty costly decision from a tax standpoint.

To look at it from a strict financial planning point of view, I have asked my friend Jim Shoemaker — who is a certified financial planner (CFP) and the president of his own financial planning firm, J.H. Shoemaker & Co. in Memphis, Tennessee — what advice he would give in such a situation:

> *To a large degree, it depends on the person's age and whether they are currently managing their debt successfully. By "managing" I mean they are making consistent progress month by month and can see the day coming when they will be debt-free, even if it's a few years off. The 40-45 year age range is roughly the dividing point — getting one's debt under control before the end of this five year period is critically important.*
>
> *If a person is 40 or younger and is currently managing their debt, I would advise they leave their retirement funds alone. However, if they are heavily debt-ridden (for example, $25,000-$35,000 in debt with an income of $35,000-$50,000 and no realistic options of getting the debts paid), I would say to go ahead and get the debt under control even though there is a heavy penalty and tax bite. Now, I'm not talking about home mortgages here, just consumer-type debts and home equity loans.*
>
> *If a person is over 45 and has still not overcome their debt, it becomes very difficult to effectively deal with debt as well as retirement. It's a difficult decision, but I would be hesitant to eliminate one's retirement fund because, at that late date, time is no longer on their side.*

Don't be too quick to give up on the idea of making short-term lifestyle adjustments that would result in a greater monthly surplus. Examine all of your budget items closely — are there ways to lower them further? Or, are there assets you could sell (a second car, bicycles, boats, guns, stereos, etc.) and apply toward your debt retirement?

Naturally, the intensity of one's beliefs about the importance of being free of debt should play a major role . . .

. . . in balancing the various pros and cons. Steve Humphrey, who is the director of counseling at Christian Financial Concepts and also a CFP, has this to say:

Recommended Resource
<u>The Banker's Secret</u>
by Marc Eisenson

If you have a mortgage, this could be one of the most important books you'll ever buy! Eisenson has a simple premise: Prepayments on your loan prove that there is no reason to keep your family enslaved in debt for thirty years while you pay the bank back three to four times the mortgage money you borrowed. "In fact, the only difficult thing about pre-paying is understanding how such a good idea could have been kept a 'banker's secret' for so long." Highly recommended!

<u>By wisdom a house is built</u>, and through understanding it is established; through knowledge its rooms are filled with rare and beautiful treasures.
Proverbs 24:3–4

. . . For some who are carrying large sums of consumer debt (not mortgage debt) and have convictions about the importance of being debt-free, it might be the best thing for them to cash in a retirement plan. Eliminating the debt burden gives them a fresh start. From that point, they can begin to address other goals, such as retirement planning and mortgage reduction. The most important thing is that people need to have clearly stated goals that are based on their Christian convictions rather than on income tax considerations.

Retiring debts that are carrying interest charges of 12%–24% is obviously more economically advantageous than adding to a 5% savings account. On the other hand, if you don't have any savings at all, then any unexpected setback (for example, a car problem or medical bills) will just put you even deeper in debt. In the next chapter, we take a look at the role savings for such contingencies plays in your financial fitness program. ◆

CHAPTER PREVIEW

The Second Test of Financial Fitness: Do You Have a Contingency Fund?

I. **The Sound Mind Investing "Four Levels" sequence is designed to protect you as well as help you set your financial priorities.**

    A. Level One (getting debt-free) and Level Two (saving for future needs) are prudent objectives that should be met before moving into the stock and bond arenas. The dollars you apply here are *guaranteed* to help you progress financially.

    B. Level Three (investing your surplus) and Level Four (diversifying for safety) involve risks that should not be undertaken without the solid foundation provided by achieving the first two levels.

II. **Before risking your money in the stock and bond markets, you should have an adequate contingency fund set aside in a separate savings account for short-term uses.**

    A. It serves as a cushion to help you deal with emergency expenses or it can be used to pay for large-ticket items like cars and home improvements.

    B. Financial planners frequently recommend six months' living expenses as an adequate size. I would recommend that, if you are married, your fund be no smaller than $10,000.

III. **An automated savings program is an effective way of imposing self-discipline and helping you build your contingency fund.**

    A. Offered by most savings institutions and money market mutual funds; the amount you wish to save is automatically deducted from your paycheck and put into your savings.

    B. The amount you save should be based on your age and gross income. Financial planners commonly suggest saving 5%–10% of your income while in your twenties, eventually moving up to 15%–20% prior to retirement.

IV. **Money makes money (simple interest), and the money that money makes, makes more money (compound interest).**

    A. "Compound" interest refers to an arrangement where you earn interest on both the initial principal *and* the interest previously earned on that principal.

    B. Our tale of two savers—Jack and Jill—has a surprising winner. The moral is to invest early and often. Small amounts can make a big difference.

Even if you have not completely reached your Level One goal of becoming debt-free, it's still a good idea to begin setting aside some money for emergencies or large purchases.

The Scriptures encourage us to plan for the unexpected, equating planning with being wise: "Go to the ant, you sluggard; consider its way and *be wise!* It has no commander, no overseer or ruler, yet it stores its provisions in summer and gathers its food at harvest" (Proverbs 6:6-8); "In the house of the *wise* are stores of choice food and oil, but a foolish man devours all he has" (Proverbs 21:20).

When I created what I call the "Four Levels" sequence in my *Sound Mind Investing* newsletter, the idea was to help my readers set reasonable and prudent priorities. As discussed in chapters 2 and 3, I believe you are best served if you make getting debt-free your first priority. In my newsletter, I refer to this as working at Level One. Now we come to the subject of this chapter—the importance of building a contingency fund for future needs. This is Level Two.

Only after these two primary objectives are reached do we move into the arena of stock and bond market investing at Level Three. The reason for this is straightforward: up to that point, every dollar of surplus was used in a manner that *guaranteed* the reader would advance financially. When you invest in stocks or bonds, an element of financial risk is being introduced for the first time. Such a move should only be undertaken if a person can bear to lose part (sometimes a significant part!) of his capital. Finally, as you can see from our investment "runners" below, at Level Four we move beyond using a few securities in order to diversify into several types of stock funds as well as into various kinds of bond funds. I'll give you the "how-tos" on diversification in Section 3.

It is appropriate to work on Level One and Level Two at the same time. Although it is economically sensible to first pay off debts that are carrying high interest charges, I don't feel you should use every spare penny for that purpose. Everyone needs a contingency fund, which serves two purposes.

LEVEL
1
Getting Debt-Free

LEVEL
2
Saving for Future Needs

First, it is an emergency fund for dealing with the unexpected. Perhaps you will have unanticipated medical or auto repair expenses. Or, it might be a case of a temporary layoff at work or a disabling injury. If you don't have a "cushion" to fall back on, you'll eventually wind up back in debt because of the unhappy financial surprises that come everyone's way occasionally. By having this money set aside and readily available, you can "borrow" from yourself rather than from family members or your bank.

Second, the fund can be used to finance major expenditures that are not in your monthly operating budget—such as replacing your old car, buying some new furniture as the family grows, or funding that home remodeling project you've been looking forward to.

How large should your contingency fund be? Many financial planners recommend having from three to six months' living expenses set aside. In my monthly newsletter, I suggest a fund of $10,000. The amount is up to you, but I would think living expenses for at least three months would be a minimum. Where should you invest it once you've saved it? We'll look at several options in the next chapter.

Pay yourself first.

When one of my sons came to me for help in getting his finances organized, the first thing I did was get him set up on a pay-as-you-go basis using the so-called "envelope" system. That's where you cash your paycheck(s) and immediately divide your income into several envelopes, one for each of your major spending areas. When the money in a particular envelope is gone, that means no more spending in that area until the next payday.

LEVEL 3

Investing Your Surplus

LEVEL 4

Diversifying for Safety

Modern technology has enabled us to improve on this approach—now we use the "Ziploc™ bag system" so all the loose change doesn't fall out!—but there's one thing technology can't do, and that's to restrain us from overspending. That part still requires self-discipline, sacrifice, and a long-term perspective. Arriving at financial independence is very satisfying, but the journey can be tough along the way.

"God's Plan for Systematic Giving" by Bill Bright. Excerpted from <u>As You Sow</u>. See Briefing 24, page 488.

Here's the process my son used as he worked on building his Level Two contingency fund. *After* setting aside his tithe and taxes, what was left was his spendable income. This was the "pie" that he proceeded to "cut" several ways. The first piece of 10% went into his Level Two contingency fund account. Then, the remainder of his spendable income went into bags for his current bills, debt repayment, and monthly living expenses.

His contingency fund came in handy twice during his first few months using the system—to pay for emergency brake and transmission repairs. The money in the savings account was used up, and he had to begin building it anew. But having it on hand prevented him from going back into debt to pay for those items. That's why it makes sense to set aside some savings in a contingency fund.

Automation beats procrastination.

When it comes to saving, despite your best intentions, it's easy to rationalize putting it off until the next paycheck. So it often helps to have some of your money put aside automatically before you have the opportunity to spend it. Here are three paths to automated savings:

◆ Sign up to have part of your paycheck (you decide how much) automatically deposited into your savings account at your credit union or local bank. It's easy, convenient, and offers some useful discipline. Plus, your savings are insured and available for withdrawal without penalty whenever you wish.

◆ For a higher rate of return, set up automatic transfers from your bank account to a money market mutual fund (which we'll look at in detail in the next chapter). Such funds typically accept transfers of $50 and up on either a weekly, every other week, or monthly basis. Most money market mutual funds offer this service; call them and ask for the forms to get started.

◆ Although part of your retirement planning (rather than building your contingency fund), an employer-sponsored savings plan known as a 401(k) plan is also a good bet. Under this plan, your employer takes some of your pay before it's taxed and puts it into a savings account. Many employers have provisions in these pension plans that call for the employer to match every $2 of yours with $1 of theirs. It is designed primarily as a retirement program, and you cannot freely withdraw money from this kind of program except for emergencies (and then there is a 10% early withdrawal penalty). But the tax savings and employer matching dollars make this an attractive program in spite of its relative inflexibility.

Consider a strategy of saving 5%–10% of your gross income when you're in your twenties. Initially, this will go toward building your contingency fund. Once that's in place, your savings can be used for a down payment on a house and other large purchases. (Eventually, the primary use of your savings will be to invest for retirement.) Then, move up to 10%–15% in your thirties and forties. In your fifties, as home buying and child-rearing costs are tapering off, you might be able to boost your savings rate to the 15%–20% area in final preparation for your approaching retirement years.

Sometimes, Level Two folks feel they can't do anything very exciting from an investing point of view.

The folks at Levels Three and Four seem to have all the fun. Meanwhile, you're still trying to save $10,000 for those "contingencies." It can seem like an impossible task. If you feel that way, you're short-changing the impact you can make. The power of compounding works to help you as you save.

YEARS NEEDED TO ACCUMULATE $10,000					
If you start with	Assuming you add this much each week:				
	$10	$20	$30	$40	$50
$0	12.8	7.6	5.4	4.2	3.5
$1,000	11.0	6.7	4.8	3.8	3.1
$2,000	9.4	5.8	4.2	3.3	2.7
$3,000	7.9	5.0	3.6	2.8	2.3
$4,000	6.5	4.2	3.1	2.4	2.0
$5,000	5.3	3.4	2.5	2.0	1.7
$6,000	4.1	2.7	2.0	1.6	1.3

This table assumes your money will earn interest at 6% per year. Although rates are lower than that at present, the average money market return over the past decade has been greater than 6%. There has been no adjustment for taxes because they may or may not apply to a given situation.

For example, let's assume you're starting today with nothing in the bank. If you can save $10 each week and put it in a savings account, it will grow to $10,000 in 12.8 years. Admittedly, that seems pretty far away. How about working harder on your budget and increasing your savings from $10 a week up to $30? That gets you to your $10,000 goal in just 5.4 years. That's much better. And if you start out with $5,000 in the bank rather than from scratch, the time required drops to only 2.5 years.

You can alter the variables to fit your particular situation (see table at right). Just keep in mind that every dollar in additional savings and interest earned contributes to the compounding process and gets you to your destination that much faster. You can achieve your Level Two goal sooner than you think through commitment and careful planning.

Many years ago, I came across a book with a rather unforgettable title: *Money Makes Money, and the Money Money Makes Makes More Money.*

As you might expect, it was about the power of compound interest. The word "compound" refers to something composed of two or more parts. Familiar examples include a chemical compound (a substance composed of two or more elements) and a hospital/medical compound (a building where two or more functions, like surgery, doctors' offices, nursing care and laboratory, are combined into one large facility).

In financial terminology, "simple" interest refers to interest being paid on the principal only. Assume you deposited $1,000 in a one-year bank CD that paid simple 7% per year interest. After the first month, you would have "earned" a small amount of interest, around $5.83. But the bank isn't going to pay it to you until the year is up; it is going to hold onto it. And even though it's yours, it is not going to pay you any interest for having it around to use over the coming year. The bank is obligated to pay you interest only on one part of your account—your principal. After the year, you'd have earned $70.00 in simple interest (see table on the next page).

CONSUMER QUIZ

Which of the following one-year certificates of deposit will pay the greatest interest?

- ❑ A: 7% CD with semi-annual compounding?
- ❑ B: 7% CD with quarterly compounding?
- ❑ C: 6% CD with weekly compounding?
- ❑ D: 6% CD with continuous compounding?

Now, let's change the terms of the CD to one of "compound" interest, where interest will be paid on *both the principal and the monthly interest earned* as the year goes along. The first month, the bank pays you only on your principal, just as before, because you haven't earned any interest yet. But after the first month, it credits your account with that $5.83. Now, for the coming month, you're going to earn interest on $1,005.83 instead of your original $1,000.00 of principal.

The second month you earn $5.87 in interest, only 4¢ more. By the end of the year, you've earned total interest of $72.29. That's $2.29 more than simple interest would have paid, and it came your way just by changing one word in the CD agreement and without increasing your risk. Suppose we change the CD to pay weekly compounding. Instead of giving you credit for your earned interest just once a month, the bank will do it once a week. It turns out that at year's end you've earned $72.46 in interest.

Daily (or "continuous") compounding has become the most common offer. If we used daily compounding in our CD example, the total interest earned would have been $72.50. That's the same as a simple interest rate of 7.25%. So, by changing from simple interest to daily compounding, you would have effectively improved your return by ¼% per year.

Does it seem too small an amount to really matter? For just $1,000 and for only one year, perhaps so. But when you consider how much you will have on deposit in a savings account over your lifetime, the difference of ¼% per year in return can amount to tens of thousands of dollars.

Investments that offer more frequent compounding are *not always* the best choices. A more important consideration is . . .

. . . the interest rate used in the compounding formula. The Consumer Federation of America sponsored a nationwide test to see how well consumers understood products that strongly affect their financial or physical health. Only 25% of those taking the test answered the question on compound interest correctly (see quiz at far left). Which do you think is the correct answer?

You may be surprised, but the correct answer is B. Look again at our "compound interest" table below, which shows the results from various savings offers on a $1,000 investment over a one-year period. Notice how the benefit from increasing the frequency of compounding gradually decreases. Take the 6% line, for example. The $60.00 in interest earned from no compounding (simple interest) improves to $61.36 by compounding four times a year. But if you move from quarterly compounding to daily (or "continuous"), you pick up only another 44¢. It's more, of course, but not as much as you might have expected. In general, while increasing the frequency of compounding is desirable, the benefits are not enough to compensate for a lower rate of interest to begin with. If in doubt, refer to the compound interest table when you are shopping for a new savings account.

The unrelenting power of compound interest is one of your greatest investing weapons.

Consider this updated version of the saga of Jack and Jill. Jack started a paper route when he was eight years old and managed to save $600 per year. He deposited it in an IRA investment account that earned 10% interest. Jack

COMPOUND INTEREST TABLE

How much interest will you earn in one year on $1,000 invested in a savings account or CD with various approaches to compounding?

	Simple	Semi-Annual	Quarterly	Monthly	Weekly	Daily
At 5%:	$50.00	$50.63	$50.95	$51.16	$51.25	$51.27
At 5½%:	$55.00	$55.76	$56.14	$56.41	$56.51	$56.54
At 6%:	$60.00	$60.90	$61.36	$61.68	$61.80	$61.83
At 6½%:	$65.00	$66.06	$66.60	$66.97	$67.12	$67.15
At 7%:	$70.00	$71.23	$71.86	$72.29	$72.46	$72.50
At 7½%:	$75.00	$76.41	$77.14	$77.63	$77.83	$77.88
At 8%:	$80.00	$81.60	$82.43	$83.00	$83.22	$83.28

continued this pattern through high school and "retired" from the paper-delivery business at the ripe old age of 18. All told, he saved $6,600 during that time. He left his savings to compound until he reached 65 and never added another dollar during the entire intervening 47 years.

Jill didn't have a paper route, but waited until her post-college days to start her savings. At age 26, she was sufficiently settled to put $2,000 into her IRA retirement fund. This she continued to do each year for 40 years. She also earned a 10% compounded return on her savings. Now, the question is which fund was larger at age 65—Jack's IRA into which he put $6,600 or Jill's into which she put $80,000?

Surprisingly, Jack is the winner. His IRA has grown to more than $1,078,700, an amount equal to *more than 162 times* what he put in as a child. Jill also did quite well with hers, which grew to $973,700. But Jack's earlier start, even with smaller amounts and deposits for far fewer years, was too much to overcome thanks to the tremendous power of compounding. That's because when Jack was 26, the age at which Jill began her IRA savings, the interest earned in his account was more than the $2,000 Jill was putting in. The moral is: invest early and often—even small amounts can make a big difference!

"Every time we almost reach our contingency fund goal of having $10,000 set aside for future needs, a reason to spend some of it comes along (car dies, hospital bill). Do we have to postpone moving into the stock market until we replenish what was spent . . .

. . . or can we apply our monthly surplus to Level Two and Level Three at the same time?" This question from one of my readers gave voice to the frustration that many investors feel. After building their contingency fund (often from scratch over a period of a few years), they're tired but exhilarated. *At last*, they think, *debt-free, a large contingency fund to serve as a financial safety net, and we're finally ready to begin working on our long-term retirement portfolio.* Then, boom! An unexpected expense comes along and knocks down the balance in their contingency fund. Now they have to return to the drudgery of building it back up again. It seems they'll never get beyond this stage. Is all this caution about having a contingency fund really necessary?

Many of my monthly newsletter readers, having a conscientious desire to do the "right" thing in terms of setting priorities and following the counsel I offer, have tended to look at the Four Levels process as a set of laws rather than guidelines. I often receive questions with the words "do we *have* to?" and "*can* we?" in them. Such questions make me a little nervous because they imply that there are right and wrong answers that are absolute. There aren't. That's why I constantly alert my readers to beware of the self-proclaimed "experts" who have all the answers.

Financial management involves making highly personal decisions, and every counselor should avoid appearing dogmatic unless obedience to a biblical command is at stake. My primary goal is to encourage you to take reasonable and informed steps, which I believe will provide you with emotional comfort in the present and financial security in the future. The point is simple: although I can make recommendations, *you have to live with the consequences.* Therefore, it is my expectation that, ultimately, you will do what you believe is best and take responsibility for the results.

If you want to begin investing in stocks and bonds while still building (or replenishing) your contingency fund, that's a decision you're free to make. It's not as safe a strategy because you're entering a high-risk undertaking without the solid foundation that is desirable. For example, what if the investments don't pan out, and more unexpected events arise to further deplete your contingency fund? On the other hand, everything could go well and you might even be better off financially a few years down the road.

There is no way of knowing ahead of time which would end up being the more profitable course. But it is obvious which approach is the more prudent—rebuilding the contingency reserve first. The general rule, then, is when you withdraw funds from your contingency account, you should make every effort to rebuild it as quickly as possible.

Making the sacrifices necessary to complete Level One (getting debt-free) and Level Two (saving for future needs) is not a lot of fun. But laying this foundation is vitally important and, if you'll commit yourself, it can be done. So, be diligent and be prayerful.

The passage in John 6 is a familiar one. The people had followed Jesus into the countryside where He was resting with His disciples. When Jesus posed the question of where they might get food to feed the great crowd, the disciples responded in terms of what man could do. "Eight months' wages would not buy enough bread for each one to have a bite!"

Jesus, however, always saw such situations in terms of what God could do. When He took action, He routinely made things happen that not only were humanly impossible, but up until the very moment He did them, were completely unimaginable!

To the disciples, the situation seemed hopeless ("Here is a boy with five small barley loaves and two small fish, but how far will they go among so many?"). So I wonder what their reaction was when Jesus, in the face of the impossibility of the situation, said, "Have the people sit down." As they moved to carry out His instructions, did they understand the implications?

I'd like to think that at least a few of them got an immediate thrill. Sort of like, "Wow! Did you hear that? The Teacher is up to something. There's no food,

---

Do you have a $23,892 habit?

I am going to point out something about your spending that you may never have thought of (and may not be able to get out of your mind once I put it there). Have you ever stopped to consider what the "future value" of the money you spent today could have amounted to? That is, if you'd saved it rather than spent it, what would it be worth as you neared retirement, say in twenty years?

For example, let's say you spend $4 each workday for lunch on the job. What if you decided to fast once a week and save that $4 rather than spend it? You continue to do this once a week for twenty years. Invest it at 7% and it would grow to . . . (drum roll) . . . $9,067!

Surprised? I thought so.

Now, start applying that same logic to other adjustments you can make in your lifestyle. Would you rather have a soft drink once a day, or $7,964 in extra liquidity in twenty years? Or what if you could save $60 a month in gas and parking if you were to carpool or take the bus? You might be more inclined to endure the extra hassle when you realized you were going to have an extra $31,256 waiting for you down the road. And if you buy cigarettes at a pack-a-day rate, that's $23,892 up in smoke. Well, you get the idea. Think about it.

nowhere to get any food, and no money to pay for the food even if we knew where to get it! And He just says, 'Have the people sit down.' Man! I don't know what He's got in mind, but I bet it's going to be spectacular!" And it was.

This account reinforces several truths about God's faithfulness that are taught elsewhere in Scripture. God's provisions include our physical needs as well as our spiritual ones. God's provisions are unmerited; we've done nothing to deserve them. God's provisions often come after we wait in expectant obedience. God's provisions are generous and overflowing. And over all of this is Christ's complete sufficiency regardless of the circumstances. Ron Dunn once illustrated the truth of Christ's sufficiency this way:

> He said to John on the island of Patmos: "I'm the beginning and the end. I'm the Alpha and the Omega." He was saying: "I'm the A and the Z." He's the whole alphabet. Isn't that amazing? I just bought a set of the Encyclopedia Britannica, and you know, I made a discovery the other day. I think I'm going to read through the whole encyclopedia and see if this is really true, but I believe they wrote that entire encyclopedia with only twenty-six letters. Boy, that's something, isn't it? Now my little nine year old girl has a book "See Dick Run," and I can imagine that they wrote that with twenty-six letters, but to come to the Encyclopedia Britannica or to any book you want to write, and to say I wrote this with just twenty-six letters, I tell you that's amazing to me. You don't need to go outside the alphabet to write anything! And I'll tell you something else — you never need to go outside of Jesus for anything that you need. He's the Alpha and the Omega. He's all that you need.

I know that sometimes the effort to be a responsible steward can be tiring. Whether it's giving faithfully, getting debt-free, saving for the future, making prudent investing decisions, or planning for retirement, it usually includes a sacrifice of time and material comforts. Let me encourage you to continue trusting Him to provide all that you need to be obedient and victorious in these areas.

While our circumstances differ, we all have areas in our lives and work that desperately need His sufficiency. What we hope to accomplish will never happen apart from His provision. From my own experience, I can say that my monthly newsletter is one of them. Even before the first issue was published, my wife Susie and I began setting aside a regular time to pray for God's blessing in our efforts to minister through it. We've kept a prayer journal throughout, and it's very faith-enriching and humbling to see His answers over the years.

God encourages us in His Word to pray expectantly. "This is the confidence we have in approaching God: that if we ask anything according to his will, he hears us. And if we know that he hears us—whatever we ask—we know that we have what we asked of him" (1 John 5:14-15).

We're to do all we can do, and then "sit down" and expect Him to do what only He can do. Are you sitting down?   ◆

5

CHAPTER PREVIEW

Protecting Your Contingency Fund: Shopping for Safety

I. **Your emergency fund is not a part of your long-term investment portfolio and should be handled quite differently.**

A. You should look for a "parking place" for your money that is absolutely safe. The value of your investment should not fluctuate with the markets.

B. Your investment should be easily convertible to cash without penalties. The rate of return is a lesser consideration than immediate availability.

II. **Local savings institutions (banks, savings and loans, and credit unions) provide convenient and safe havens for your money.**

A. Bank certificates of deposit offer safety and reasonable returns but lack some flexibility due to the early withdrawal penalties. You should be willing to shop nationwide if you want the best rates.

B. Building a "savings ladder" is one way to diversify the interest-rate risk while maintaining a degree of flexibility.

III. **Money market mutual funds also offer a safe haven. They are virtually as safe as FDIC-insured bank accounts but pay 1%–2% more in annual interest.**

A. There are three basic varieties of money market funds: those that invest in IOUs from big businesses, those that invest in IOUs from the federal government and its agencies, and those that invest in IOUs from local and state governments. The interest from the latter is largely tax-exempt.

B. Shopping for the best deals and opening your money fund account is a relatively simple process. This chapter offers pointers.

IV. **A third safe haven is found in U.S. Treasury bills. They offer the greatest degree of safety and liquidity.**

A. T-bills pay the current short-term interest rate and can be purchased in three, six, nine, and twelve month maturities. They can be sold before maturity (if necessary) without a penalty.

B. The easiest way to invest in T-bills is either through a money market mutual fund or by buying them at your local bank. The most profitable way, because it avoids operating expenses and bank fees, is to buy them directly from the U.S. Treasury.

Your contingency fund is not a part of your long-term retirement portfolio and should be handled quite differently than your other investments.

You should look for a "parking place" for your money that is absolutely safe and can be easily converted to cash without early withdrawal penalties. The interest rate earned is a lesser consideration than assured immediate availability. In this chapter, we'll look at three safe havens that are suitable for this purpose, starting with your local bank.

There are many different ways you can save at your local bank. They may be convenient, but usually they're not your best choice.

In my financial newsletter, I have consistently recommended money market mutual funds as my preferred way to save. They're safe, convenient, offer check writing, and pay higher interest than bank money market accounts. (We'll get into this shortly.) But for those of you who like keeping some of your savings with your friendly neighborhood banker, here's a guide to the often-confusing variety of accounts being offered.

◆ **Passbook Savings.** This name is a holdover from the days when most people kept track of their savings through the transactions recorded in their little bank savings book. Banks typically offer the lowest rate but have low minimum requirements. They may pay interest either from the day of deposit or, in some cases, the first of the following month. The only reason to have a passbook account is if you can't meet the minimums required for the better-paying types of accounts.

◆ **NOW Accounts.** This is an interest-bearing checking account rather than a savings account. It is convenient for earning interest while still having your money available for check writing at the same time. When shopping around, look for the one with the lowest "minimum monthly balance" required. To earn your interest, you cannot let your balance fall below this amount. If you do, not only might you lose interest, you may incur additional charges. The minimum is usually around $1,500.

◆ **SuperNOW Accounts.** These are glorified NOW accounts that require you to maintain a higher minimum balance and in return pay you slightly higher interest. The minimums are usually set at $2,500. If you have that much cash, you want it in a genuine savings account rather than a low-paying checking account.

◆ **Bank Money Market Accounts.** Notice I said *accounts*. These should not be confused with money market *funds* offered by the mutual fund industry. Bank MMAs pay you lower returns than the open market rates paid by money market mutual funds. Each bank is free to set its own rates. They change daily or weekly and can vary widely between banks. Some banks charge penalties if the

Things You Should Know About FDIC Insurance

The $100,000 insurance limit applies per person and not per account. This means that all checking accounts, savings accounts, certificates of deposit, and business accounts (if run as sole proprietorships) combined at any one bank or S&L are limited to $100,000 of protection.

The $100,000 limit includes any interest you might have coming. For example, if you had $98,000 in CDs which earned $4,000 in interest before the failure, your total recovery would be limited to $100,000 and you would lose $2,000 of the interest.

Not All Banks and S&Ls Carry FDIC Insurance Protection

Many rely on state-sponsored programs instead. Unfortunately, state deposit insurance has proven unreliable in many instances. Here are two precautions you can take. One, immediately move any deposits you have in an institution that carries only state deposit insurance to one protected by FDIC insurance. And two, never exceed the $100,000 limit at any one institution.

balance falls below a certain minimum. The primary advantage of bank MMAs is that they are guaranteed by the FDIC up to $100,000.

◆ **Certificates of Deposit (CDs).** As with other bank offerings, you are loaning money to your bank for a fixed rate of interest. Unlike the others, however, you agree not to withdraw your money for a set period of time. If you take it out early, you forfeit a large part of the interest you would have earned.

Only certificates of deposit force you to face the interest-rate risk, which is . . .

. . . the chance you take that after you lock in your deal—which might seem pretty good at the time—interest rates will rise and make your yields look bad in comparison. This is the dilemma faced when you invest in a CD, which can be purchased for periods as brief as one week or as long as five years. The longer you commit to leaving your money, the higher interest rate the bank will usually pay you.

What you should do depends on your personal goals and needs. If your needs can be met by locking in the higher return, then that's probably the thing to do. You trade off the possible opportunity of making a little more in return for the knowledge that the present deal will *assure* that you reach your goal (which is, after all, the primary objective).

Another way to decide is to ask yourself: Which scenario would frustrate me the most—missing the opportunity to lock in a satisfactory rate, or missing the opportunity to make a little more?

GOOD DEALS IN SAVINGS ACCOUNTS

Tables similar to those shown below can be found in each issue of Money magazine, Kiplinger's Personal Finance magazine, and Barron's weekly financial newspaper.

Money Market Accounts

Institution	Location	Telephone Number	Minimum Deposit	Recent Rate	Effective Yield
Stearns Cnty Natl	St. Cloud, MN	(800) 320-7262	$75,000	5.37%	5.50%
Bluebonnet Svgs	Dallas, TX	(800) 343-5874	25,000	5.30%	5.43%
1st Deposit Natl	Tilton, NH	(800) 821-9049	5,000	5.07%	5.20%
Key Bank USA	Albany, NY	(800) 872-5553	5,000	5.05%	5.17%
Aetna Bank	Chicago, IL	(800) 989-5101	10,000	5.02%	5.14%

Six-Month CDs

Institution	Location	Telephone Number	Minimum Deposit	Recent Rate	Effective Yield
Sterling Bk & Trust	Newport Beach	(800) 676-2630	$500	5.57%	5.65%
Safra Natl Bank	New York City	(800) 223-2311	10,000	5.47%	5.62%
1st Deposit Natl	Tilton, NH	(800) 821-9049	10,000	5.46%	5.61%
Key Bank USA	Albany, NY	(800) 872-5553	5,000	5.45%	5.60%
Sthrn Pac T&L	Los Angeles, CA	(800) 428-5056	5,000	5.45%	5.60%

In mid-1996, these rates were the highest yields on these types of accounts offered by federally insured banks and savings associations nationwide. Yields are based on the stated rate and compounding method in effect at week's end and are subject to change. You should call to verify the current rates before investing or sending money. Source: Barron's.

If the above suggestions don't help you reach a decision, I would suggest taking the short-term CD. This will give you another chance to make the decision in a few months when either (1) your own circumstances are more clear, or (2) the trend in interest rates seems more settled.

**One popular strategy for dealing with the interest-rate risk
is to build a "savings ladder."**

Assuming you find current interest rates satisfactory, you might desire to lock
them in for the next few years. That's where a strategy of building a "ladder" of
staggered maturities can help you obtain the higher long-term rates on a portion
of your savings while not altogether sacrificing your liquidity.

Say you have $10,000 to invest. Tell your bank that you want to divide it
evenly among CDs with the following maturities (yields shown were available
in mid-1996): six months (5.6%), twelve months (5.9%), eighteen-months (6.1%),
twenty-four months (6.2%), and thirty months (6.3%). Each time a $2,000 CD
matures, reinvest the proceeds in a new thirty-month CD. Eventually, all your
savings will have been invested at the higher-paying thirty-month CD rate, yet
one-fifth of your savings will reach maturity (and be available to you without
penalty) every six months. You'll still have some flexibility.

SHOPPING FOR CDS LONG DISTANCE

As you phone around for the best deals in bank
CDs, here are some questions to ask.

❑ Are my deposits here insured by the FDIC?

❑ What is the stated rate of interest (the rate before
compounding)?

❑ What is the "annual effective yield" (the return after
compounding)?

❑ If I don't keep a certain minimum amount on deposit,
or if I close my account within a certain period of time,
will I be charged a fee?

❑ Will I earn interest from the day of deposit without a
hold being placed on my check?

❑ What penalty do you charge for early withdrawal on
CDs?

❑ When my CD matures, how much time do I have
before you automatically roll it over into a new CD?

❑ Will you notify me first?

*get pre assigned acct #
(for dep. only + put on ck
when open)*

**Barron's is an inexpensive source of data
for savers. If you've spent much time . . .**

. . . looking through financial magazines,
names like *Money*, *Kiplinger's*, *Forbes*, *Smart
Money*, and *Worth* are probably familiar to you.
What you may not know, however, is that a lot
of up-to-the-minute data and other helpful information is available in *Barron's*, the Dow Jones
company's weekly newspaper. Published every
Saturday, it contains investing data and articles
on various markets. It is current up through the
previous day. At $3, it's a bargain.

Each issue of *Barron's* is divided into two sections. The first section contains articles that deal
with the economy, mutual funds, stock and bond
markets, and real estate. There are also interviews
with money managers who discuss their investing
styles and their opinions on the markets. There is often some very interesting reading here, but this is not
the main reason I'm suggesting you familiarize yourself with *Barron's*. It's the second section, called "Market Week," where you'll find the data of most interest
to savers. On its cover, you'll find a table of contents
divided into three sections—Markets, Indicators, and
Indexes. Let's look at one of the regular features you'll
find listed there—savings deposit yields.

If you're interested in certificates of deposit and are willing to go outside your local area to get the best deal, *Barron's* will point you in the right direction. The rates shown are the highest yields reported for various savings-type investments offered by federally insured banks and savings associations across the country. The categories include money market accounts and CDs of three, six, twelve, thirty, and sixty months duration. The minimum amount required for each and 800 numbers to call are also included.

When shopping for CDs long distance, be sure to verify that you will earn interest from the day of deposit without a "hold" being placed on your check. Obtain a pre-assigned account number, and write it on your check along with the inscription "For Deposit Only." Send a cover letter with instructions as well as your daytime phone number.

Credit unions are to banks what generic drugs are to name brand prescriptions . . .

. . . excellent substitutes that typically give you good value for your money and are just as safe. These nonprofit consumer organizations were started with the idea of providing higher savings rates and lower loan rates than profit-making institutions like banks and S&Ls. Approximately one in every five Americans has an account at one of these nonprofit cooperatives. Here's a brief rundown of their strengths and weaknesses to help you assess whether they're a good place for you to stash your contingency fund savings.

👍 **Service.** Much as with banks, the range of services offered by a credit union largely depends on its size. Areas where they might cut corners include the frequency with which statements are issued, the availability of automated teller machines and electronic transfers, and the number of branches. On the plus side, many credit unions offer discounts on automobile and life insurance. A survey reported by *Consumer Reports* indicated that members of credit unions were, on average, twice as likely to voice satisfaction with the service they received as were customers of commercial banks.

👍 **Safety.** Approximately 90% of credit unions are protected by a federal agency that insures their deposits just like the FDIC does for banks. (Don't settle for state-sponsored or private deposit insurance—many have had problems in the past.) However, the rules governing which kinds of accounts are insured and for how much can be confusing. To be absolutely sure you're fully covered, request the booklet *Your Insured Funds* from your credit union (or you can write for a copy to the National Credit Union Administration, Washington, D.C. 20456). Have an officer go through it with you and explain which sections apply to your account.

👍 👎 **Rates.** The good news is that surveys have routinely indicated that credit unions pay better savings rates than banks. The bad news is that there

Wire Transfers are a very quick way to move your money between banks. Your funds travel through the Federal Reserve bank wire system (it generally takes a few hours) and, if done early enough in the day, the receiving bank will give you credit for your money the same day you send it. Check with your bank to find out how early in the day they need to receive your instructions and what they charge for this service.

are two possibly offsetting drawbacks: (1) The surveys reflect national averages, but the credit union you are eligible to join may be "below average." Make sure yours measures up. (2) Many credit unions do not pay interest based on your *average* monthly balance but on your *lowest* monthly balance. Such a policy discourages you from drawing on your savings; if that's your intention, a money market fund might be preferable.

☞ **Eligibility.** Most credit unions are sponsored by employers or trade and community associations, and they limit membership to employees or those with geographical proximity. However, there are some that cater to the investing public at large, so it's worth calling the Credit Union National Association (800-358-5710) to see if there is one in your area that you could join.

Now, let's turn to a second safe haven for your savings — money market mutual funds. What is a money market fund, anyway?

When you open a savings account or buy a CD at your bank (that is, loan them your money), your bank turns around and lends your money to others at a higher rate than it's paying to you. Obviously, the less it pays you on your savings, the more profit it makes. The problem with this arrangement is that you and your bank are financial adversaries.

Fortunately, there are other borrowers, the "big time" players, who would like you to loan to them *and will pay you more interest than your bank will*. These organizations include the federal government, big corporations, and even other banks. However, to do business with them readily, you need a go-between. That's where a special type of mutual fund comes in, one that specializes strictly in the short-term lending of money in the financial markets. Hence, its name: money market fund.

Your money market fund is on *your* side; it will try to get you the best rates it can, while still not taking undue risks. You give the fund your money; the fund gives you one of its shares for every $1 you put in. It takes your money and loans it out to the big time players, almost always getting a rate of interest 1% to 1½% higher than your bank will pay you over the same time period. The value of your money market fund shares doesn't fluctuate; they're

CHARACTERISTICS OF MONEY MARKET FUNDS

1. Safety. Although not insured by the government, money market mutual funds operate under Securities and Exchange Commission guidelines that make them very safe.

2. Liquidity. You can have your money back whenever you want with no withdrawal penalties. This is important to you because you might need your contingency funds on short notice.

3. Higher returns than bank money market accounts. Money market mutual funds have historically paid 1.0%–1.5% more than bank-sponsored money market accounts.

4. More responsive to interest rate trends. When interest rates finally begin moving higher, money market funds will be leading the way due to their ultra short maturities.

kept at a constant $1—the same amount you paid for them. As the fund earns interest from its investments, it "pays" you your portion by crediting you with more shares. You earn interest, that is, receive more shares, every single day. The longer you leave your money in, the more shares you'll have. In this way, you are assured of getting all of your money back, *whenever* you want it, plus all the interest you've earned in the meantime. And, thanks to Securities and Exchange Commission regulations, money market mutual funds are essentially as safe as insured bank accounts. Opening a money market fund account is like opening a checking account—a few forms to sign and you're on your way (see page 70).

With these advantages, you wonder why anyone would still use the traditional bank savings-type accounts. Yet the data show . . .

. . . that hundreds of billions of savers' dollars continue to reside in savings accounts. It seems to me that many savers simply don't understand the difference between bank money market *accounts* and money market *funds* sponsored by mutual fund organizations. They think it's all the same kind of thing. But there's a big difference! Investors in a money market mutual fund receive all of the fund's investment income after very small operational expenses are paid. Depositors in a bank money market account, on the other hand, are merely creditors of the bank and are paid as little as the market will bear. Because it comes out of their pockets, banks naturally want to pay as little as they can get away with. That explains why banks and S&Ls will always offer interest rates lower than money market mutual funds (unless they're desperate for cash, in which case you don't want to loan them your money, anyway).

There are three different kinds of money market funds.

❶ The most common are the ones that loan money to businesses and banks. I'll refer to these as corporate money market funds because they invest primarily in bank certificates of deposit and commercial paper. This kind pays the highest yield to investors and is the most popular.

❷ For people who want added safety, there are money market funds that loan money only to the federal government and its agencies. Given the excellent track record of the corporate kind, it's debatable whether the added caution of sticking strictly with Uncle Sam's securities is worth the slight reduction in yield. For the past fifteen years, the value has been more in the peace of mind investors receive rather than in actually providing additional safety.

❸ For people who are in high tax brackets, there are money market funds that invest only in tax-free municipal bonds that are very close to maturity. The income is free from federal income taxes, and if you invest in a single-state tax-free fund for your state of residence, your income is exempt from state income taxes as well.

Money Market Funds are specialized funds that take your money and make very short-term loans to big businesses, the U.S. Treasury, and state/local governments. They are a way of pooling your money with other small investors and getting a better deal on interest rates. Think of it as a savings account disguised as a mutual fund.

Advantages of Money Market Funds Great for savings or for using as a temporary holding place for money that might be needed in the near future. Virtually as safe as FDIC-insured bank accounts but typically pay 1%–1.5% more.

Disadvantages of Money Market Funds There's no set level of interest that you can count on earning. You receive whatever the short-term rate is, and it changes constantly.

Commercial Paper is the term for very short-term corporate IOUs of large, creditworthy corporations. Credit-rating agencies, such as Moody's and Standard & Poor's, monitor the commercial paper market. They continually study the financial strength of the corporations that issue the IOUs, and assign ratings of 1, 2, or 3. Under SEC rules, money funds may not own any 3-rated paper because of its higher risk, and they are severely limited in the amount of 2-rated paper they can hold.

corporate
MMF
pays Best + most popular

BIG BUSINESS/
Banks

FEDERAL
GOVERNMENT +
their agencies

STATE/LOCAL
GOVERNMENTS
exempt from taxes

There is a fiercely waged competition for money market fund deposits (like yours). And one of the principal weapons is a sales tactic called an "expense waiver."

Money market funds, by definition, invest in short-term money market instruments. This means all of them are pretty much investing in the same securities — bank CDs, commercial paper, and U.S. Treasuries. This being the case, you wouldn't expect a great deal of difference in the yields they earn for their shareholders. But you'd be wrong. The operating expenses they charge for running the fund, which come out of their investors' profits, can vary dramatically. Some funds charge up to four times as much as others that run a tighter ship. Many, in an attempt to attract new business, go so far as to absorb all (or a portion) of the operating expenses themselves. This practice is called "undertaking." *"pay*
interest)

Since these "undertakers" don't pass on their full costs to the shareholders, they can pay them higher returns. The industry average for money fund operating expenses is sixty "basis" points. (A basis point is 1/100 of one percent, so sixty basis points equals .6% per year.) If your money fund earned 4.8% on its investments and charged the industry average for operating the fund, your yield for the year would be just 4.2%. But if the fund manager absorbed all the operating expenses, you'd get the full 4.8%.

In effect, they're discounting their services, and will often continue this practice for a year or more in order to more quickly build their assets under management. Testimony to the intense competition for your savings dollar among money funds is the fact that about half of all money funds have engaged in undertaking to some degree.

Dreyfus used this tactic in launching its Worldwide Dollar Fund a few years ago. Initially, the fund engaged in an aggressive undertaking strategy and, as a result, its yield regularly placed number one in the money fund rankings. This enabled the fund to grow very quickly. After it became one of the largest money market funds in the country, Dreyfus decided to start charging the full fare, and then some. Recently, the yield on Worldwide Dollar was a full 1.25% below the yield offered by the leading money funds. Thousands of investors still have their Worldwide Dollar accounts at Dreyfus, either because they have not kept informed and do not understand that their formerly top-ranked fund is now performing poorly or they simply are not willing to expend the effort to change. Such a casual approach will cost them a lot of money over a lifetime of investing.

Is there anything "bad" about investing with funds that engage in under-taking? No, as long as you understand that they can decide to stop being so gen-erous at any time. If you ask them, they will generally tell you how long they plan to continue their undertaking strategy. Once their growth targets are met, they will understandably want to charge the going rate for their services and be-gin to profit from their success. Naturally, they're hoping you'll remain a share-holder. But why should you? Don't be like the indifferent or uninformed share-holders of Dreyfus Worldwide Dollar. You shop the sales at your local mall, don't you? You should shop money funds the same way.

The leading money market mutual fund in 1994 was Benham Prime, a fund that was waiving its expenses. In 1995, the leader was Strong Money Market, which also pursued an undertaking strategy. The leaders in the years to come are likely to come from the ranks of those following the same course. That's why your attitude toward money market funds should be, "What have you done for me lately?" Call your fund each month and ask for the most recent seven day compounded yield. You should be willing to change money funds once or twice a year if need be, always moving to the fund that is "hav-ing a sale," that is, virtually giving away its fund management services and passing the savings on to its shareholders.

To intelligently shop for a good money market fund, you need to understand the way yields are listed in the paper.

The "Market Week" section of *Barron's* also contains money market fund listings. They are updated weekly, and provide current yield and average ma-turity information on many hundreds of money market funds, of both the tax-able and tax-free variety. Many are designed for large institutions and require exceedingly large minimums (you can tell because the word "institution" or "institutional" is usually part of their names), but the majority are available to the average investor. Plus, they indicate which funds are temporarily ab-sorbing part or all of their operating expenses and passing the savings on to shareholders. In a table at the top, industry-wide data is shown so you can see what the average money fund is paying. Then you'll know whether your fund is above or below average in its performance.

Since most of the major money market mutual funds offer similar ser-vices and portfolio risk, the decision as to which to buy usually rests on where the best returns are to be found. In researching this information in the news-paper, it is common to find two different yields listed for each fund.

The first percentage listed is usually called the "Seven Day Average (or Current) Yield." This reflects the annualized equivalent of what the fund earned for its shareholders over the past week. The limitation of this measure is that it ignores the long-term benefits of daily compounding. So, to more

SEC Safety Regulations
The average maturity of a money fund portfolio cannot exceed ninety days, so there's not much time for something to go wrong with the IOUs that wasn't known up front. The short time period also reduces the risk of rising interest rates hurting the fund's net asset value. Other restrictions include no more than 5% of a fund's assets can be invested with a single corporate borrower, and no more than 5% of the portfolio can be invested in commercial paper that carries less than the best rating.

accurately reflect the actual results from investing in a money fund over time, another yield is shown. This percentage is listed second and is called the "Seven Day Compounded (or Effective) Yield." This is what an investor would actually earn over a one-year period at last week's rate.

The rate of interest you earn changes a little bit every day because the funds have such short average portfolio maturities. This simply means that their "loans" are ultra short-term—almost every day, at least one of these loans is repaid to the fund. The fund must then take this money and loan it out all over again at a new rate. This constant process of re-loaning the money in the pool causes money market fund yields to change rather quickly; last week's rate is somewhat obsolete by the time the numbers are published. Still, it's helpful for comparison purposes.

The general rule is that you want a long average maturity when rates are falling (so the fund can enjoy the old, higher rates for as long as possible), and you want a short average maturity when rates are rising (so the fund can get its money back quickly and reinvest it in the newer, higher-paying securities). And the stars of the show will be those that know how to keep their expenses down—or waive them altogether—and thereby pass the greatest returns through to their shareholders.

MONEY MARKET MUTUAL FUNDS

A listing of hundreds of taxable and tax-free money market funds appears in most newspapers at least once a week. You can also find one in Barron's and the Thursday edition of The Wall Street Journal.

The Average Maturity indicates the number of days before the average CD or corporate commercial paper is due to be repaid to the fund. The money will then be re-loaned at the current rate. The lower the average maturity, the more quickly the fund will reflect changes in interest rates.

The Seven Day Compounded Yield is the number you're interested in. Remember though, when interest rates start moving, these yields will change quickly to reflect the new realities.

Most mutual fund organizations offer at least two kinds of money funds, and some offer three or four.

Most money funds invest primarily in bank CDs and corporate IOUs. They are identified by names like MM, Cash, or Prime.

The money funds that limit their investments to the U.S. government use names like Treasury, Federal, or simply Govt.

This fund's portfolio is $448 million in size. Economies of scale can benefit investors once a fund surpasses about $5 billion. Note the Vanguard Prime fund has over $19 billion.

Fund	Avg Mat	7Day Yield	7Day Comp	Assets
USAA Money Market Fund k	72	4.98	5.10	1753
USAA Treasury MM Trust k	60	4.88	5.00	76
United Serv Govt Secs k	76	5.01	5.14	585
United Serv Treas Secs	44	3.96	4.04	147
Value Line Cash Fund	33	4.71	4.82	350
VanKampen Amer Capital	39	4.36	4.45	502
Vang Admiral US Treas MMP	58	5.04	5.17	2151
Vang MMR / Federal Port	49	4.99	5.11	2800
Vang MMR / Prime Port	48	5.04	5.17	19665
Vang MMR / US Treas Port	57	4.87	4.99	2760
Victory Prime Oblig Fund	42	4.58	4.68	448
Victory US Govt Oblig Fund	36	4.73	4.84	1196

Moving your savings to a money fund really isn't a difficult process. These pointers should help make the transition an easy one.

First, call the funds in which you're interested and ask a few questions. After learning which offer the most attractive combination of yield and features, ask them to send their information package. Don't worry, this doesn't obligate you to do business with them.

The material you receive will include an application form and prospectus. The application form may look intimidating, but is actually quite simple and will take only a few minutes to complete. If you have any questions, you can call the fund's toll-free number and get all the help you need. Some of the questions request that you make choices (which can be changed at any time) among different convenience options. Most fund companies offer an option where you can automatically have your savings invested with them. Check the appropriate box if this is what you desire. To take advantage of check-writing privileges (which I recommend — see below), simply check this option and provide the appropriate authorized signature(s). One disadvantage is that some funds do not return your canceled checks; however, they will send a copy of any check you may need if you request it.

Finally, fill in the amount that you will be depositing into your new money market mutual fund account and attach your check. Getting started in saving with money funds is as easy as 1-2-3 — and now you're on your way!

Money market mutual funds offer check-writing privileges that make them a much better deal than a similar account at your local bank.

One of the most popular accounts offered by banks and S&Ls is the NOW account, which is basically an interest-bearing checking account. Such accounts typically require minimum balances of $1,500 and pay interest of only about 1% less than the leading money funds. Many savers are not aware that a money market mutual fund set up with check-writing privileges is a better alternative. While most money funds request that checks not be written for small amounts (say less than $250), they place no limit on the number of checks written, nor do they charge for the service.

This presents individual savers with the opportunity to safely and quickly improve their rate of return by a full 1% and more. And for businesses, which by law are not permitted to earn interest on their checking account balances, money market mutual funds represent the difference between earning interest or not earning interest. That doesn't seem too difficult a choice.

Here's how to use your money fund as a checking account. First, order a full supply of checks. Usually you'll get no more than a handful unless you make a specific request. Also, you'll want to give written authorization to your fund to make *wire transfers* to your bank (and possibly your

SOME LEADING MONEY MARKET FUNDS FOR YOUR CONSIDERATION

Fund Name	Minimum	Telephone
Benham Price Money Market	$ 1,000	(800) 472-3389
Dreyfus BASIC Series: Money Mkt	25,000	(800) 645-6561
Evergreen Money Market Fund	2,000	(800) 235-0064
Fidelity Cash Reserves	2,500	(800) 544-8888
Nicholas Money Market Fund	2,000	(800) 227-5987
Schwab Value Advantage Money	25,000	(800) 526-8600
Strong Money Market Fund	1,000	(800) 368-3863
USAA Money Market	1,000	(800) 531-8181
Vanguard Admiral: U.S. Treasury	50,000	(800) 662-7447
Vanguard Prime Portfolio	3,000	(800) 662-7447

Building a savings ladder with Treasuries

The "ladder" strategy explained on page 64 can also be done with Treasuries, but it requires a larger amount of money due to the higher minimums. The initial implementation will need to be modified slightly because the Treasury doesn't issue four-year notes. Here's how you could go about investing $25,000:

This year, purchase $10,000 of fifty-two week bills, $5,000 of two-year notes, $5,000 of three-year notes, and $5,000 of five-year notes. Next year, when your $10,000 in bills matures, purchase $5,000 of new three-year notes and $5,000 of new five-year notes. Thereafter, as each note matures, roll it over into a new five-year note. In this way, you'll have $5,000 in savings coming to maturity each year. You can use it for cash flow needs or continue to roll it over into new five-year notes.

The advantage is that if interest rates fall, you can sell your notes at a profit if you wish. If rates rise, your notes will decrease in market value, but that won't affect you *as long as you hold them until they reach maturity*. If circumstances compel you to cash some in early, you can sell the ones nearest to maturity to minimize any capital loss.

The *easiest* way to implement your Treasury ladder is at your local bank. For a fee, it will make the purchases you want and take care of all the paperwork. This cost, which can amount to as much as 1% of the amount you invest, may be stated as a service fee, commission, or may simply be reflected in the yield you are quoted, and obviously reduces the net return you'll receive on your investment.

The *most cost effective approach* is to avoid the fees altogether by dealing directly with the government yourself.

brokerage firm) in response to your telephone request.

Second, use your local bank checking account for all salary and investment income deposits. Once a week, transfer the bulk of your account balance to your money fund. In order to get it to your money market fund even faster, you can ask your bank to "wire it" through the Federal Reserve. Banks charge extra for this service, so you would only want to transfer money this way if the interest you would earn by getting it there a few days faster would exceed the bank wire charge.

Third, pay all bills of $250 and up with a money fund check. This can include your rent or mortgage payments, credit card and auto loan payments, major repairs, insurance, and schooling, among others. And last, be sure to let your fund know that you want your canceled checks back. Some funds hold them in their files unless you request them, and this complicates reconciling your monthly statement.

With this arrangement, not only do you earn a market rate of interest on your idle checking balances, but interest is earned until the checks you write clear your money fund (which can take a week or more). Interest earned on routine checking account balances can be significant for an individual and dramatic for a business.

Before departing this subject of safe "parking places" for your contingency fund, let's take a brief look at the merits of using U.S. Treasury securities.

When the government issues bonds that have very short-term maturities, they are called Treasury "bills" (or "T-bills" for short). T-bills are initially sold to investors in three-month, six-month, nine-month, and one-year maturities. The minimum denomination is $10,000. You can buy them when they are newly issued, either directly from the Federal Reserve or through your bank or broker. You can also buy them after they've been issued (in what's called the "secondary" market to distinguish it from newly issued securities that are being purchased directly from the issuer). When you buy your T-bills in the secondary market, you are buying them from another investor who wishes to sell. Your broker serves as the intermediary. Regardless of how you buy them, you can always sell them before maturity through your bank or broker without an interest-rate penalty.

The greatest advantage of T-bills is their safety and liquidity. The disadvantage is that you can't lock in long-term yields due to their short-term nature. In a period of rising rates, however, they make a good choice because they mature quickly and allow you to reinvest at the new, higher rates.

There is one aspect to T-bills that often confuses the new investor: they are sold in "discount" form. That simply means you buy them at less than their face value, and when they mature you get the full face value. The difference between what you pay and what you get back at maturity is your "interest." For example, assume you bought a one-year $10,000 T-bill at a 6.00% discount. That means you paid $9,400 ($10,000 face value less the 6% discount of $600). You hold it for one year, during which time you receive no interest. After the year is up, you receive the full $10,000 face value. This means you earned interest of $600. Now, here's the tricky part. Even though your discount was only 6.00%, your actual rate of return was 6.38% (the $600 return you received divided by the $9,400 you actually invested).

Get better returns: Buy T-bills directly from the U.S. Treasury.

The easiest way to buy T-bills (as well as avoid the $10,000 minimum) is through a money market mutual fund that specializes in investing only in very short-term securities of the U.S. government. T-bills can also be purchased at your broker or local bank for a fee (usually one-half to one percent). However, this convenience comes at a cost—the fund operating expenses and bank fees reduce your net return.

If you can meet the minimum purchase requirements, you can avoid fees and realize better returns by skipping the middleman and dealing directly with the government. This can be done by opening your own "Treasury Direct" account. Here are the steps involved in buying a thirteen-week T-bill.

1. Obtaining the forms. Call the Federal Reserve branch nearest you

U.S. Treasury Bills are issued in three-, six-, nine-month, and one-year maturities.

U.S. Treasury Notes are issued for periods ranging from two to ten years.

U.S. Treasury Bonds are issued for periods of longer than ten years.

All of the above are highly liquid and combine maximum safety with a relatively low rate of return. The interest earned on Treasuries is exempt from state and local—but not federal—income taxes. Treasuries are not issued in certificate form, but are created and monitored as bookkeeping entries in the records of the U.S. Treasury. New issues are sold through the regular Federal Reserve auctions, and there is an active secondary market which makes it easy to buy or sell them through a broker.

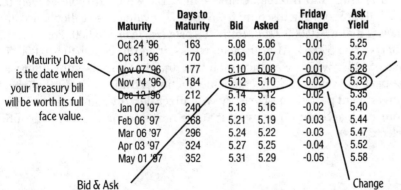

U.S. TREASURY BILLS

Maturity	Days to Maturity	Bid	Asked	Friday Change	Ask Yield
Oct 24 '96	163	5.08	5.06	-0.01	5.25
Oct 31 '96	170	5.09	5.07	-0.02	5.27
Nov 07 '96	177	5.10	5.08	-0.01	5.28
Nov 14 '96	184	5.12	5.10	-0.02	5.32
Dec 12 '96	212	5.14	5.12	-0.02	5.35
Jan 09 '97	240	5.18	5.16	-0.02	5.40
Feb 06 '97	268	5.21	5.19	-0.03	5.44
Mar 06 '97	296	5.24	5.22	-0.03	5.47
Apr 03 '97	324	5.27	5.25	-0.04	5.52
May 01 '97	352	5.31	5.29	-0.05	5.58

Maturity Date is the date when your Treasury bill will be worth its full face value.

Asking Yield is the return you would earn by buying this Treasury bill at the dealer's asking price and holding it until it matures.

Bid & Ask are the prices at which dealers are willing to buy and sell Treasury bills expressed in terms of the bill's yield. Ignore these numbers and focus on the column on the far right.

Change shows how much the yield to investors changed during the previous day of buying and selling. A negative change means that your cost of buying Treasury bills actually rose, leaving you with a lower yield. A positive change means that your cost of buying Treasury bills fell, thereby offering you a better yield.

and request the useful book, *Buying Treasury Securities.* You'll also need the "Tender For 13-Week Treasury Bill," which is your order form. If the book is unavailable in your area, try contacting the Fed branch in Louisville (502-568-9238) or Richmond (804-697-8372). As you'll learn, T-bills are sold most Mondays through an "auction" process. The minimum order is $10,000 and in multiples of $1,000 above the minimum. They are issued in "book entry form" similar to a savings account; in other words, transactions are documented by recording them in your personal Treasury account rather than by issuing certificates.

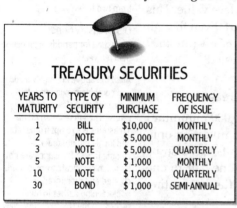

TREASURY SECURITIES

YEARS TO MATURITY	TYPE OF SECURITY	MINIMUM PURCHASE	FREQUENCY OF ISSUE
1	BILL	$10,000	MONTHLY
2	NOTE	$ 5,000	MONTHLY
3	NOTE	$ 5,000	QUARTERLY
5	NOTE	$ 1,000	MONTHLY
10	NOTE	$ 1,000	QUARTERLY
30	BOND	$ 1,000	SEMI-ANNUAL

2. Opening your Treasury account. After reviewing pages 6-16 of *Buying Treasury Securities,* turn to page 72 (Exhibit H) where the New Account Request is found. Complete the form in its entirety. You'll find detailed instructions on pages 73-75.

3. Ordering your T-bill. Complete the "Tender For 13-Week Treasury Bill" form. To be sure your order is filled, mark it as "noncompetitive." This means you are willing to accept, sight unseen, the yield that results from the auction process. If you are unclear on any of the information required, call for clarification. If you want the proceeds from your investment automatically reinvested after thirteen weeks, you can indicate that on the form. Accepted forms of payment are certified personal checks or cashier's checks made out to the Federal Reserve Bank (or branch) nearest you. When mailing, the notation "Tender for Treasury Bill" should be printed at the bottom of the envelope. If your tender is not received in time, it will be held for the next auction.

4. Collecting your interest. Unlike bank CDs, which are sold at their face value, T-bills are sold at a discount from their face value (also called par value). This means that a $10,000 T-bill initially costs *less than* $10,000. For example, it might cost you $9,863. After thirteen weeks, it would be worth $10,000. The increase of $137, which was the amount of the discount, is your interest. It will be paid to you a few days after the auction. At the end of the thirteen-week investment period, the Treasury will direct-deposit your original $10,000 into your bank account (or reinvest it at the next auction if that is the option you selected). ◆

6

Preparing for College

I. **Investing for college is no different than investing for any other long-term financial goal.**

   A. You should have a plan that provides for systematically setting aside money on a regular basis.

   B. It's important to get an early start in order to maximize the benefits of compound interest, as well as to provide a long time horizon that permits reasonable risk-taking.

II. **Series EE savings bonds are popular investments because of their special college-related tax advantages, but I can't recommend them because you would be trying to fund an expense that has been rising faster than inflation with an investment that historically has lagged behind inflation.**

   A. Among their advantages: safety, income tax advantages, and the convenience and discipline of a payroll deduction program.

   B. Among their disadvantages: relatively low return, limitations on the income tax exclusion, and limitations on how the interest proceeds can be spent in order to receive the college-related tax benefit.

III. **Mutual fund companies offer college investing programs that are easy to establish and monitor.**

   A. Such programs allow you to begin with small amounts and add to your account on a regular monthly basis.

   B. Six no-load fund organizations that offer special college-related investment services are discussed.

IV. **Financial aid possibilities should be thoroughly explored. A brief overview of the subject of college grants and scholarships is provided.**

V. **Giving careful thought to the income tax consequences of your college investing strategy is also important. The pros and cons of using family trusts and custodian accounts are briefly discussed.**

The Gallup organization has reported that 86% of Americans believe that a college education will be beyond the reach of most families in the future.

Investing for college is no different than investing for any other long-term financial goal. It is attainable if a sound plan is put into place early enough. One popular strategy is to dollar-cost-average (DCA) monthly investments in no-load growth mutual funds. DCA involves investing an unchanging dollar amount every month, regardless of market conditions. This strategy passes three important tests.

COLLEGE SAVINGS CALCULATOR

Years Until College	Monthly Investment Per $1,000	Expected 4 Yr Share of Costs	Monthly Investment Needed
1	$80.23	$29,414	$2,360
2	38.71	30,885	1,196
3	24.90	32,429	807
4	18.01	34,051	613
5	13.89	35,753	497
6	11.15	37,541	419
7	9.21	39,418	363
8	7.76	41,389	321
9	6.64	43,458	289
10	5.74	45,631	262
11	5.02	47,913	241
12	4.43	50,309	223
13	3.93	52,824	208
14	3.50	55,465	194
15	3.14	58,238	183
16	2.82	61,150	172
17	2.55	64,208	164
18	2.31	67,418	156

Footnotes: The second column shows the amount of monthly investment needed to accumulate $1,000 over the period of time shown assuming an annual return of 7% net after taxes. Example: $13.89 per month will grow to $1,000 over five years. The source for college costs (tuition, books, fees, room and board) is The College Board's estimate that the cost for public schools for 1995–96 is $9,285. The numbers shown assume costs will increase at the rate of 5% per year and that financial aid will cover 30% of the cost. Private colleges cost about twice as much as public ones. The final column shows the amount needed to fund the expected four-year cost not covered by financial aid. Example: For a child who will be entering college in ten years, a regular monthly investment of $262 would grow to approximately $45,631 during that time.

First, you are funding an expense that will rise with inflation via an investment that historically has outpaced inflation. On the other hand, fixed-income investments, like savings accounts and U.S. Treasury Series EE bonds, fail this test. (Series EE bonds, discussed next, do have some college-related tax advantages.)

Second, dollar-cost-averaging mechanically guides your investing so you acquire more shares when they are more attractively priced. You don't have to worry about timing. (I'll discuss DCA in detail in chapter 16.) And third, it allows you to begin with small amounts. This helps you to begin sooner rather than later so you can take greater advantage of the principle of compound interest.

The table at left dramatically illustrates the importance of getting an early start. As with any set of projections, there are several general assumptions built in to the data that will ultimately miss the mark. But they are useful for their shock value and getting your attention. Here are a few pointers to keep in mind.

(1) It is no longer assumed that parents pay the full costs of their children's college education. According to the American Council on Education, parents and students now combine to pay a little under 60% of college costs; student aid, either from the school itself or from the taxpayers, pays the remaining 40%. The table assumes a more conservative 30% level of assistance. It's imperative that parents and students understand the ins and outs of financial aid.

(2) Your college portfolio is not part of your own retirement portfolio, so keep it separate in your thinking.

(3) The earlier you begin, the more risk you can take. This means selecting an aggressive portfolio that is 100% stocks and adding short-term bonds or money markets only when you get within a year or two of when you'll need the money.

(4) **Separate accounts for each child make record-keeping simpler,** but you may want to initially combine each child's savings into one account (be able to document what percentage of the account each child owns) in order to meet the account minimums or to make it easier to diversify into several funds.

A word of caution: As costs escalate, many parents are turning for help to a variety of heavily advertised services and products specifically promoted as ideal for funding college expenses. Be careful when considering many of the most common "college investment" strategies such as variable and universal life insurance policies, zero-coupon bonds, and prepaid tuition plans. Often, the high commissions, the investment risk, or a lack of flexibility in selecting the school of your choice more than offset the tax benefits. You must look past the hype and focus on the investment merits.

"Paying for College" by Scott Houser. Excerpted from the Sound Mind Investing newsletter. See Briefing 11, page 471.

One safe and popular strategy for saving for college involves the purchase of Series EE savings bonds.

Series EE bonds are sold through most banks and come in many denominations. The purchase price is one-half of the face amount, so a $50 bond can be purchased for $25 and, if held long enough, will grow to be worth its face value of $50. This doubling in value is, in effect, your interest. The length of time it will take to double depends on the "guaranteed minimum rate" of interest prevailing at the time you purchase the bond. Series EE bonds purchased after March 1993 carry a guaranteed minimum rate of 4%. This means it will take about eighteen years for them to double in value. Some of their advantages include:

☙ **Safety.** They are backed by the full faith and credit of the U.S. government.

☙ **Tax advantages.** The interest is exempt from state and local taxes, and the federal taxes aren't payable until you cash them in.

☙ **Saving for college.** If you buy them and later cash them in to pay for college tuition, you may owe no taxes on the interest you earned. They carry a federal tax exclusion which, for families meeting an income test, makes the interest tax-free.

☙ **Discipline.** They are most commonly purchased through payroll deduction savings plans, so you can impose discipline on yourself by automating your savings. Also, since you don't receive the interest until you redeem your bonds, it is automatically reinvested for you. It has been said that there are better ways to invest, but few better ways to save than through a payroll savings plan.

On the other hand, Series EE bonds have these drawbacks:

☙ **Relatively low return.** Savings bonds carry two rates, depending on how long you hold them. If held for less than five years, you receive the guaranteed minimum of 4% as described above. If you hold them longer than five years, however, you are eligible to receive a "market-based" rate that might be higher than 4%. The market-based rate is equal to 85% of the five-year Treasury note rate, and is adjusted every May and November. For example, if five-year Treasuries are yielding 7.00% at the

Smart credit strategies for college students

Sixty percent of college students end up with credit cards before commencement. At least a third got their first credit card before they entered college. But most teens have never been taught how to manage credit cards, and the bills they run up in college can haunt them long after graduation.

To help them use credit to their advantage while avoiding its pitfalls, Gerri Detweiler (former director of Bankcard Holders of America, a national nonprofit consumer organization) has developed a new audiotape called "Smart Credit Strategies for College Students." On the tape, she explains how to avoid the hype that has already put millions of Americans in debt far beyond their ability to repay in the short term. She warns students that by getting caught in the minimum payment trap, they'll be obligating themselves to years of expensive payments, long after they've graduated.

"It's difficult enough," Detweiler says, "for a college grad to make ends meet, without having to pay for pizzas they polished off years ago."

(continued on next page)

time of one of the semi-annual adjustments, the Series EE market-based rate would be set at 5.95% (85% of 7.00%).

☞ **Limitations on tax exclusion.** The tax exclusion starts to phase out when the family's adjusted gross income, modified to include Social Security and other retirement income, exceeds $63,450 (or $42,300 for single filers). The income test is applied *when you cash them in, not when you buy them.* So, if your income outpaces inflation over years of industrious saving and investing, you could end up going over the income limit and facing an unexpected tax bill.

☞ **Limitations on college expenditures.** To be tax-free, the interest proceeds can only be used for tuition and related expenses (e.g., books and lab fees). This excludes using them for room and board, two of the major cost components. Also, should your child decide to skip college, the bonds' interest is fully subject to federal taxes.

If you purchased your bonds prior to March 1993, it's important to consider your timing when you cash them in. For the first thirty months, their increase in value is reflected monthly. After that, however, the government adjusts their value for earned interest only twice a year. If you happen to cash them in the week before that semi-annual increase in value is official, you're going to get the old value. In other words, you lose five months and three weeks worth of interest. So if you're considering cashing any in, first be sure to check with your bank to see when your bonds will next go up in value. That trap has been eliminated on Series EE bonds issued since March 1993—their interest is accrued monthly. If you're thinking of using Series EE savings bonds for college, be sure to pick up the buyer's guide available at most banks. It will explain in detail the strict rules that apply.

Even with Series EE bonds' possible tax advantages, I feel that in order to build a college fund whose buying power will outpace inflation, a consistent long-term plan of investing in a good stock fund is still your best bet.

Many mutual fund companies offer college investing programs that are easy to establish and monitor.

As of mid-1996, all of the organizations listed below: (1) provide step-by-step worksheets that will help you estimate educational expenses and establish a strategy for meeting those needs, (2) waive their usual minimums if an automatic monthly investment of $50-$100 is chosen (electing this option is a great way to exercise self-discipline), and (3) are no-load. As a result, 100% of your money goes to work for you.

◆ **The Dreyfus Guide to Investing for College** takes you systematically through a plan for establishing four different growth-oriented portfolios from a wide range of Dreyfus funds. The portfolios gradually adjust from 100% stocks for the early years of investing to a more conservative mix of stocks, bonds, and money markets as the time for college approaches. You can call their toll-free number anytime for individual advice on which funds would be most appropriate. Call (800) 782-6620 for more information.

◆ **T. Rowe Price's College Planning Kit** features a step-by-step personalized strategy for allocating educational funds. There are three different recommended college portfolios. If you have more than four years until college, you might follow the "aggressive" portfolio and when you get within four years, switch to the "average risk" portfolio. Call (800) 638-5660.

◆ **20th Century's College Investment Program** primarily relies on the Select Investors fund, a growth fund that invests in common stocks. As college draws near, the program gradually and automatically reallocates your investment into the Cash Reserve money market fund, thereby preserving your capital. This rebalancing feature is one where you specify the time period for completion, and 20th Century accepts the responsibility for monitoring your account. Be aware, however, that every time the account is "rebalanced" by selling Select shares and moving into the money market, you have a taxable event. If you don't mind this added complication, the program does offer great convenience. On the chosen completion date, the accumulated balance is waiting in your Cash Reserve account. You can even write checks for your child's tuition from it. Call (800) 345-2021.

◆ **The Fidelity College Savings Plan** offers five Fidelity mutual funds that have been especially selected to help meet your college investment needs. They range from stock mutual funds to hybrid and cash reserves. Along with a Fidelity representative, you decide which funds to choose. You can use them individually or in any combination, making the necessary adjustments as college draws closer. Call (800) 544-8888.

◆ **Stein Roe's Young Investor Fund** is a stock fund that invests in large, growth-oriented companies. It has had excellent returns in its relatively brief history. The fund is designed to meet future educational needs by investing in the securities of companies that provide goods and services to children and teenagers (toy and entertainment companies, restaurants, computer product manufacturers, etc.) Participation in the fund is intended to be a fun learning experience. To help motivate and educate the child in the area of investing, a welcome kit is sent including material on basic economic and investment principles, along with a fun wall poster, activity book, and certificate of enrollment. Call (800) 338-2550.

◆ **Neuberger & Berman** has a helpful resource entitled *9 Tips for College Savers* that is full of helpful information on investing strategies, financial aid, and possible tax breaks for college savers. There are fourteen Neuberger & Berman equity, income, or money market funds available for your college savings program. Invest in one or any combination of funds depending upon your desired aggressiveness. It's up to you to decide which funds to invest in, but a representative is always available if guidance is needed. Call (800) 877-9700.

Don't overlook the possibility of financial aid.

As college tuitions and associated expenses continue to skyrocket, it's not surprising that a U.S. Department of Education survey found that only one family in

She suggests these guidelines for students to use in deciding when to borrow and when to say no.

Pay cash, she advises, if:

◆ It will be gone by the time you get the bill (a burger).

◆ You wouldn't borrow money to make the purchase (a pair of jeans).

◆ You don't know how or when you can pay the bill in full.

Detweiler believes teens should consider getting a card in college—for emergencies and also because it will be harder to get one once they graduate if they don't have a credit history.

"Smart college students will get a credit card in college and use it carefully," says Detweiler. "That way, they'll graduate with a good credit rating—but without a lot of credit card bills."

The tape contains some good pointers along with a few sobering warnings. In a concise way, it offers money saving advice on choosing and using credit cards in language teens will understand. It makes an excellent graduation gift. To order, send $15.95 to: Good Advice Press, Box 780, Elizaville, NY 12523.

ten has plans for the parents to pay the full cost of their children's education. Students are expected to contribute from their own savings. Working one's way through, receiving financial aid, and obtaining student loans are also in the mix. For more and more families, a realistic goal is that parents contribute half and the student arranges for the other half.

In *No-Debt Living* newsletter, publisher Robert Frank included this introduction on the subject of the ins and outs of obtaining college grants and scholarships:

> *About 74% of all financial aid available in the United States comes from federal or state grants and loans. The vast majority of that money is awarded based on "financial need" and is doled out on a first-come first-served basis. Financial aid applications or forms for college enrollment are accepted beginning on January 2nd for the following fall quarter. If you're serious about getting financial aid, you need to get that form in as close to New Year's Day as possible.*

> *Even if you don't expect to qualify for a government grant, you should submit a Financial Aid Form (FAF) as early in the year as possible. Most colleges have an arsenal of scholarships and grants available, but they want to stretch that money as far as they can. Consequently, many colleges won't consider you for scholarships until they know you have already tried to land a government grant and how much you will receive. College scholarship recipients are usually selected early in the year. So in order to have a clean shot at that money, you must submit your FAF as soon as possible.*

> *Before you fill out your FAF, however, you need to understand how the game is played. The basic primer is a free, 54-page government pamphlet called* The Student Guide, *which you can obtain through most college financial aid offices or by calling the Federal Student Aid Information Center at 800-4FED AID. A highly rated book providing strategies for obtaining funding is* Don't Miss Out: The Ambitious Student's Guide to Financial Aid, *by Robert and Anna Leider, which you can find at most libraries.*

> *Here's the bottom line. Government grants are based primarily on financial need, as opposed to merit. Don't confuse the term "need" with "needy." The amount of money a person can receive is determined by the income and assets of the student (and his or her family if the student is a dependent). Other items taken into account include the number of family members, how many dependents are attending college, and how much tuition and fees are.*

> *Generally speaking, the lower your assets and income, the more financial aid you may receive. When it comes to Pell Grants, for example, a family of four with an income of $50,000 is approaching the eligibility cutoff line. Families with less income should qualify for some funding.*

> *If you make more than $50,000, don't give up. That line is not as distinct as it seems. It is arrived at through a formula. In fact, people with higher incomes and assets can qualify for government financial aid depending upon where they have their money invested and saved.*

> *The FAF form considers income and assets in the form of cash, dividends, savings, checking, certificates of deposit (CDs), stocks, real estate investments (excluding your house) and other forms of taxable and nontaxable income. The form does not consider life insurance cash values, or money already invested in Keogh, IRA, 401k and 403b plans.*

Recommended Resource
<u>No-Debt Living</u> is a monthly newsletter dealing with financial, home management, and investing news with a Christian perspective. Subscription cost is $25.95 for 11 monthly issues. Sample issues are $2.00. Call (800) 560-3328 for more information.

So, advance planning can make a big difference in the amount of assets you must claim and how much funding you can receive. In fact, it is best to begin this planning at least one or two years early. Even if you surpass the income/assets eligibility line, you need to send in an FAF, because there are many "no-need" funds available through colleges and private sources. Millions of dollars in scholarships go unused every year because nobody applies for them. The FAF form is the key that opens the first door to those funds.

As you consider financial strategies, the question of ethics often arises . . . and rightfully so. Government rules are relatively clear and there are many things you can do "legally." The more important question is what would the Lord have you do? (Proverbs 3:5-6 and 16:2). It is more important to maintain your integrity and provide a godly witness than to save a few dollars.

Financial aid is not the only way to lower the cost of college. A wide variety of options are available. Here are a few tips:

◆ *Depending upon the student's major area of study, consider starting at a two-year college and transferring. The cost of tuition can drop from as much as $18,000 or more per year to as low as $1,000 per year. And, if you like, you can complete your degree at a prestigious university.*

◆ *Many companies and community service organizations offer substantial scholarships for children of employees and members, respectively. Even extended family members can nominate your children. Don't forget to ask. Even if the amount is small, every little bit helps.*

◆ *Consider taking advanced placement courses in high school or take an advanced placement examination. This can save a great deal of time and money.*

◆ *If a student has his/her heart set on an out-of-state university, but can't afford the tuition, consider working six to twelve months in that state to qualify for in-state tuition rates. The savings is substantial.*

◆ *Live on or near campus, so you can go without a car. You save the cost of an automobile, insurance and fuel.*

Giving careful thought to the income tax consequences of your college investing strategy is also important.

Most of the questions I receive from parents in regard to saving for college are directed toward *where* to invest the money being set aside. But because the top rates for federal and state taxes combined can easily exceed 40%, you should also understand the various trade-offs involved when deciding *who owns* the investments—the parents or the child.

The natural inclination of most parents is to retain ownership of the savings being set aside. Not only are many parents reluctant to simply turn property over to an immature or spendthrift child, there's also the desire to have the flexibility to use it for something else if an unexpected need arises. A drawback, however, is that the college funds are vulnerable to creditors. If the investments are owned in your name and you are successfully sued for any reason, the courts can reach the assets to satisfy any claims against you. This is of more practical importance to professionals such as doctors and accountants.

Unless your annual taxable income (for those married, filing jointly) exceeds $40,100, there's no tax reason to give up ownership—you're paying the lowest rate of 15% on investment income already. However, between $40,100 and $96,900 your marginal rate rises to 28%. When you're in this bracket it can pay to look for ways to move the tax rate on the kids' investments back down to the 15% level.

One popular alternative to parental ownership is forming a family trust. This is an arrangement where, by signing a trust agreement, you create a new legal entity that the law treats as a separate taxpayer. Before 1993, the trust could earn investment income up to $3,750 before paying the 28% rate; now, that rate kicks in at $1,600 and moves even higher to 31% for income earned above $3,800 and to 36% for income earned above $5,800. Under the new tax law, some families could end up paying more by using a trust than without one! Fortunately, smaller trusts are unlikely to be much affected. For example, assume a trust has assets of $15,000 and earns 10% a year. All $1,500 of the earnings would be taxed at the low 15% rate. There are, however, initial legal costs of forming the trust that can run $300-$1,000, as well as ongoing maintenance chores such as filing annual tax returns. (All income amounts shown above reflect the rules governing tax year 1996. They are indexed for inflation, which means they are adjusted upward annually.)

The other favored ownership alternative is to give the money to the child outright but keep it under the control of a parent or other relative as custodian. Most state laws provide a way to do this under the heading of either the Uniform Gifts to Minors Act (UGMA) or Uniform Transfers to Minors Act (UTMA). All that needs to be done for paperwork purposes is to have the investment registered as: "Mr. John Doe as custodian under the Uniform Gifts to Minors Act." (If you have a number of children to whom you wish to give money, you will need to have a separate account for each child.) It's so commonplace that virtually all banks and mutual funds should be able to help you set one up. Like the family trust, once money is put into this account, the parent has *permanently* given up ownership.

There are potential tax savings; however, the savings differ depending on the child's age. *For children fourteen and older*, the gains on the investments are taxed to the child and not the parents. Since children usually have limited taxable income, this means the investment earnings would be taxed at the 15% tax rate. *For children under fourteen*, the so-called "kiddie-tax" comes into play if the gains in any one year exceed $1,200. In that event, all income of more than $1,200 is taxed at the parents' marginal tax rate (which is likely higher) rather than the child's. How significant a deterrent is this tax? Again using our example of a college fund with $15,000 that earns 10% while the child is still under fourteen, the return would be enough to trigger the kiddie-tax. But it's only the $300 earned in excess of $1,200 that is taxed at your marginal tax rate.

From a tax perspective, the younger the child, the greater the case for a family trust. That's because (1) the trust offers more tax protection than a UGMA account for children under age fourteen, and (2) the cost of establishing the trust could be spread over a greater number of years. For children over fourteen, the primary benefit of a trust is that you can specify the ages at which the assets are given to the child rather than the child automatically receiving them upon reaching legal age. ◆

The Ease of Investing

How Mutual Funds Make
Investing Easier Than Ever Before

"Hey, isn't that the new guy the boss hired
to manage our Aggressive Growth stock fund?"

7

What Mutual Funds Are and Their Advantages to Investors

I. **For most investors, mutual funds represent the best way to assemble a well-balanced, diversified portfolio of securities.**

    A. A mutual fund is simply a big pool of money formed when thousands of small investors team up in order to gain advantages that are normally available only to wealthy investors.

    B. The money in the pool is managed by a hired professional who is paid based upon the size of the pool and, in some cases, on his/her performance results.

    C. The money in the pool can only be invested according to the "ground rules" that were drawn up when the pool was first formed. Most mutual funds limit their investments to a particular kind of stock or bond that is the specialty of the professional managing the pool.

II. **Mutual funds can make your investing easier and safer. Twenty advantages of mutual fund ownership are listed and explained. Among them are:**

    A. They reduce risk by providing extensive diversification. This means their price movements are less volatile and more predictable than individual stocks.

    B. They keep commission costs low while managing the pool.

    C. They provide experienced, full-time professional management that gives your holdings individual attention on a daily basis.

    D. Their past performance is a matter of public record.

    E. They allow you to efficiently reinvest your dividends.

    F. They offer many convenient services, such as automatic investing and withdrawal plans, check-writing privileges, handling all the paperwork, creating reports for tax purposes, and providing safekeeping of your money.

    G. They can be used for your IRA and other retirement plans.

    H. They allow you to sell your shares and leave the pool at any time.

Abraham Lincoln received an invitation to deliver a college commencement address. The exact date had not yet been set . . .

. . . and he was asked how much advance notice he would need. He said that depended on how long they wished him to speak: "If you want me to speak for just fifteen minutes, I'll need three weeks' notice. If it's for an hour, I'll only need three days' notice. And if you'll let me speak all day, I can start right now!"

The point behind his humorous answer is that it takes a great deal of preparation time to be economical in one's presentation while still covering all the essentials. I thought of Lincoln as I was reviewing all the books in my investment library that were written solely on the subject of mutual funds. I've collected fourteen different ones over the years; they average more than 264 pages each! Can I hope to teach you more about mutual funds than is already covered in those fourteen books? Probably not, especially when you consider that they run collectively to over 3,700 pages!

I'm going to do something that may be even more valuable to you—teach you a lot *less*. I'm going to mercifully leave out . . .

. . . a lot of material that is best reserved for a more in-depth study, and focus on only those things you need to know about mutual funds in order to benefit from them. And put that way, there really isn't all that much for you to learn. This section of the book will serve as a primer, and a primer teaches only the basics.

One last word before we begin. The fund industry has experienced explosive growth over the past decade. The sheer number (more than 6,000 at last count!) and types of different funds is overwhelming. As a result, I find that many people feel a little confused, if not intimidated, by the whole topic. Of course, it can be scary tackling a brand new subject, especially one that can so dramatically affect one's financial future. If you feel the same way, take heart! I've written this book especially for you. Ready? Let's get started!

The easiest way to understand a mutual fund is to think of it as a big pool of money.

The *Barron's Dictionary of Finance and Investment Terms* defines a mutual fund as a "fund operated by an investment company that raises money from shareholders and invests it in a variety of securities." My plain-English definition is that it's (1) a big pool of money (2) collected from lots of individual investors (3) that is managed by a full-time professional investment manager (4) who invests it according to specific guidelines. When you put money in a mutual fund, you are pooling your money with other investors in order to gain advantages that are normally available only to the wealthiest investors. You are transformed from a small investor into part owner of a multimillion dollar portfolio!

Investment Company is the technical name for a mutual fund.

Mutual Fund is a company that combines the funds of many investors into one larger pool of money, and invests the pool in stocks, bonds, and other securities consistent with its area of specialization. For this service, the company typically charges an annualized management fee that approximates 1% of the value of the investment.

Portfolio is a collection of securities held for investment.

Net Asset Value is the market value of a single mutual fund share. It appears in the newspaper listings under the "bid" heading, which means the fund was willing to bid that amount to repurchase any shares that investors wanted to sell.

Security is a financial instrument that is bought and sold by the investing public. The majority are stocks, bonds, mutual funds, options, and ownership participations in limited partnerships. All publicly traded securities are subject to the regulation of the Securities and Exchange Commission.

What do you get in return for your investment dollars? You receive shares that represent your ownership in part of the pool. The value of the shares is calculated anew at the end of every day the financial markets are open. Here's how it's done. First, you take the day's closing market value of all the investments in the fund's pool. To that number, you add the amount of cash on hand that isn't invested for the time being (most funds keep 3%–5% of their holdings in cash for day-to-day transactions). That gives you the up-to-the-minute value of all the pool's holdings. Next, you need to subtract any amounts the pool owes (such as management fees that are due to the portfolio manager but haven't yet been paid). This gives the net value of the assets in the pool. Finally, you divide the net value by the total shares in the pool to determine what each individual share is worth. This is called the net asset value per share and is the price at which all shares in the fund will be bought or sold for that day. It is also the number that is reported in the financial section of the newspaper the next morning.

What kinds of securities do mutual funds invest in? That depends on the ground rules . . .

. . . set up when the pool was first formed. Every mutual fund is free to make its own ground rules. The rules are explained in a booklet called the prospectus that every mutual fund must provide to investors — that is where you learn what types of securities the fund is allowed to invest in.

As we learn about mutual funds, I'll be using examples that might give you the mistaken impression that they invest only in stocks. This is most assuredly not the case. Mutual funds invest in just about every type of security around, including corporate, government, and tax-free bonds, federally backed mortgages, and the ever-popular money market instruments like bank CDs, commercial paper, and U.S. Treasury bills. For the average person, mutual funds are the very best way to assemble a well-balanced, diversified portfolio containing many different kinds of securities. But in order to simplify things, I'll primarily use mutual funds that are stock-oriented when I'm explaining how funds work.

HOW THE XYZ MUTUAL FUND CALCULATES ITS DAILY CLOSING PRICE

List of Investments	Closing Price	Shares Owned	Market Value
Alcoa	$ 65.500	6,400	$ 419,200
Allied-Signal	58.000	8,900	516,200
American Express	46.750	9,700	453,475
A T & T	62.375	7,500	467,813
Bethlehem Steel	13.125	12,000	157,500
Boeing	82.375	3,000	247,125
Caterpillar	68.750	7,200	495,000
Chevron	58.500	4,400	257,400
Coca-Cola	45.500	3,800	172,900
Disney	60.750	2,200	133,650
DuPont	80.000	3,500	280,000
Eastman Kodak	76.500	9,100	696,150
Exxon	83.875	6,000	503,250
General Electric	79.875	4,600	367,425
General Motors	55.500	6,600	366,000
Goodyear	52.250	8,400	438,900
IBM	108.625	3,300	358,463
International Paper	41.250	2,900	119,625
McDonald's	47.750	9,500	453,625
Merck	62.125	4,000	248,500
Minnesota Mining	67.375	3,500	235,813
J. P. Morgan	86.375	7,700	665,088
Philip Morris	91.500	2,300	210,450
Proctor & Gamble	87.75	3,100	272,025
Sears	50.25	5,000	251,250
Texaco	82.125	8,600	706,275
Union Carbide	43.375	9,200	399,050
United Technology	109.875	6,800	747,150
Westinghouse	18.250	7,000	127,750
Woolworth	20.500	9,500	194,750

Market Value of Investments	$ 10,962,100
Plus: Cash on Hand	+ 265,321
Less: Expenses Payable	– 6,744
= Net Value of Pool Assets	$ 11,220,677
Divide By: Number of Shares	524,388
= Net Asset Value Per Share	$ 21.40

(The thirty stocks shown for our hypothetical XYZ Fund are the same companies that make up the Dow Jones Industrial Average.)

Prospectus
is a formal written offer to sell a security. Mutual funds provide them free to investors. They explain the fund's investment objectives, its performance history, the fees they will charge, the special services they offer, and a financial statement.

Basically, a prospectus explains the ground rules under which a mutual fund operates.

A mutual fund will usually limit its investments to a particular kind of security. For example, assume you want to invest only in quality blue-chip stocks that pay good dividends. As it turns out, there are a large number of mutual funds whose rules permit them to invest only in such stocks. No small company stocks, stock options, long- or short-term bonds, precious metals, or anything else. By limiting their permissible investments, mutual funds allow you to pool your money together with that of thousands of other investors who wish to invest in similar securities.

Mutual funds are almost certain to play an important role in your financial future because they offer many benefits which will make your investing program easier and safer. Here are twenty of their major advantages.

Advantage #1: Mutual funds can reduce the anxiety of investing.

Most investors constantly live with a certain amount of anxiety and fear about their investments. This is usually because they feel they lack one or more of the following essentials: (1) market knowledge, (2) investing experience, (3) self-discipline, (4) a proven game plan, or (5) time. As a result, they often invest on impulse or emotion. The advantages offered by mutual funds can go a long way toward relieving the burdens associated with investing.

Advantage #2: Mutual fund shares can be purchased in such small amounts that it makes it easy to get started.

Dreyfus

The Dreyfus
Third Century
Fund, Inc.

Prospectus

If you have been putting off starting your investing program because you don't know which stocks to invest in and you can't afford your own personal investment consultant to tell you, mutual funds will get you on your way. It doesn't require large sums of money to invest in mutual funds. Most fund organizations have minimum amounts needed in order to initially open your account, which run from $500 to $3,000. And if even $500 is too much, the 20th Century Investors fund group has no minimum account requirement *if* you'll agree to make regular monthly deposits to build your account.

Advantage #3: Mutual fund accounts can also be added to whenever you want—often or seldom—in small amounts.

After meeting the initial minimum (if any) to open your account, you can add just about any amount you want. To make your purchase work out evenly, they'll sell you fractional shares. For example, if you invest $100 in a fund selling at $7.42 a share, the fund organization will credit your account with 13.477 shares ($100.00 divided by $7.42 = 13.477).

Advantage #4: Mutual funds reduce risk through diversification.

Most stock funds hold as many as 200 stocks in their portfolios. They do this so that any loss caused by the unexpected collapse of any one stock will have only a minimal effect on the pool as a whole. Without the availability of mutual funds, the investor with just $2,000 to invest would likely put it all in just one or two stocks (a very risky way to go). But by using a mutual fund, that same $2,000 can make the investor a part owner in a very large, profession-ally researched and managed portfolio of stocks.

Advantage #5: Mutual funds' price movements are more predictable than those of individual stocks.

Their extensive diversification, coupled with outstanding stock selection, makes it highly unlikely that the overall market will move up without carrying almost all stock mutual funds up with it. For example, on May 20, 1996, when the Dow jumped 61 points, more than 98% of stock mutual funds were up for the day. Yet, of the more than 3,000 stocks that traded on the New York Stock Exchange, only 42% ended the day with a gain. The rest ended the day unchanged (25%) or actually fell in price (33%).

> **"DIVERSIFICATION"**
>
> The spreading of investment risk by putting one's assets into many different kinds of investments.
>
> Mutual funds are usually regarded as relatively low in risk because they are so widely diversified. While some of their holdings are moving up in value, others are standing still or moving down. So, the price changes somewhat cancel each other out. The effect of this is to increase the price stability of the overall portfolio. Thus, while an investor is unlikely to score a huge gain in any one year holding mutual funds, he is also unlikely to incur a huge loss. For the average investor, this relative price stability is one of the primary advantages of investing through mutual funds.

Advantage #6: Mutual funds' past performance is a matter of public record.

Advisory services, financial planners, and stockbrokers have records of past performance, but how public are they? And how were they computed? Did they include every recommendation made for every account? Mutual funds have fully disclosed performance histories, which are computed according to set stan-dards. With a little research, you can learn exactly how the various mutual funds fared in relation to inflation or other investment alternatives.

Advantage #7: Mutual funds provide full-time professional management.

Highly trained investment specialists are hired to make the decisions as to which stocks to buy. The person with the ultimate decision-making authority is called the portfolio manager. He possesses expertise in many areas, including

Risk is usually defined in terms of the potential an investment has for wild swings up and down in its market value. The term "volatility" refers to the extent of these price swings. An investment with high volatility (meaning very wide, often abrupt, swings in its market value) is defined as high risk. An investment with low volatility (meaning narrow, usually gradual swings in its market value) is thought of as having low risk.

Blue-chip Stocks
are shares of large, well-
known companies that have
long records of profit growth,
dividend payments, and
reputations for quality
products or services.

Dividends
are payments to shareholders
as their share of the profits.
They are usually made
quarterly and are taxable in
the year they are received.

Bull Market
is a market with rising prices
of sufficient duration to
indicate an upward trend.

Bear Market
is a market with falling prices
of sufficient duration to
indicate a downward trend.

accounting, economics, and finance. He is experienced, hopefully having learned to avoid the common mistakes of the amateur investor. And most important, he is expected to have the self-discipline necessary to doggedly stick with the mutual fund's strategy even when events move against him for a time.

Advantage #8: Mutual funds allow you to efficiently reinvest your dividends.

If you were to spread $5,000 among five different stocks, your quarterly dividend checks might amount to $10 from each one. It's not possible to use such a small amount to buy more shares without paying very high relative commissions. Your mutual fund, however, will gladly reinvest any size dividends for you *automatically*. This can add significantly to your profits over several years.

Advantage #9: Mutual funds offer you automatic withdrawal plans.

Most funds let you set up the selling of your shares in an amount and frequency of your choosing automatically. This pre-planned selling enables the fund to mail you a check for a specified amount monthly or quarterly. This allows investors in stock funds that pay little or no dividends to receive periodic cash flow.

Advantage #10: Mutual funds provide you with individual attention.

It has been estimated that the average broker needs 400 accounts to make a living. How does he spread his time among those accounts? The common-sense way would be to start with the largest accounts and work his way down. Where would that leave your $1,000 account? But in a mutual fund, the smallest member of the pool gets exactly the same attention as the largest because everybody is in it together.

Advantage #11: Mutual funds can be used for your IRA and other retirement plans.

Mutual funds offer accounts that can be used for IRAs, Keoghs, and 401(k) plans. They're especially useful for rollovers (which is when you take a lump sum payment from an employer's pension plan because of your retirement or termination of employment and must deposit it into an IRA investment plan account within sixty days). The new IRA rollover account can be opened at a bank, S&L, mutual fund or brokerage house and the money then invested in stocks, bonds, or money market securities. These rollover accounts make it possible for you to transfer your pension benefits to an account under your control while protecting their tax-deferred status. They are also useful for combining several small IRAs into one large one.

Advantage #12: Mutual funds allow you to sell part or all of your shares at any time and get your money quickly.

By regulation, all open-end mutual funds must redeem (buy back) their shares at their net asset value whenever you wish. It's usually as simple as a toll-free phone call. Of course, the amount you get back will be more or less than you initially put in, depending on how well the stocks in the portfolio have done during the time you were a part owner of the pool.

Advantage #13: Mutual funds enable you to instantly reduce the risk in your portfolio with just a phone call.

Most large fund organizations (usually referred to as "families") allow investors to switch from one of their funds to another via a phone call and at no cost. One extremely popular use of this feature is to switch back and forth between a growth-oriented stock fund (during bull markets) and a more conservative income or money market fund (when the stock market weakens and a bear market threatens). This exchange feature enables you to act quickly on the basis of your stock market expectations.

Advantage #14: Mutual funds pay minimum commissions when buying and selling for the pool.

They buy stocks in such large quantities that they always qualify for the lowest brokerage commissions available. An average purchase of $3,000 of stock will cost the small investor $150 to buy and sell. That's a 5% commission charge. On the other hand, the cost is a mere fraction of 1% on a large purchase like $100,000. Many investors would show gains rather than losses if they could save almost 5% on every trade! The mutual-fund pool enjoys the savings from these massive volume dis-

A GLIMPSE INTO A MUTUAL FUND PORTFOLIO

Most mutual funds report to their shareholders each quarter, providing market commentary, performance data, and a list of the fund's current holdings.

Note that this growth fund is reporting that only 85% of its portfolio is invested in stocks. Most funds, even those dedicated to investing in stocks, will keep a small percentage of their holdings in CDs and Treasury bills to use for future purchases as well as to pay shareholders who wish to sell their fund shares on any given day.

COMMON STOCKS (85.3%)

	Number of shares	Current market value (in millions of dollars)
Retail and Distribution (15.9%)		
Dayton-Hudson Corp.	205,000	$ 11,634
Gap, Inc.	48,000	2,568
Liz Claiborne, Inc.	58,000	1,552
Toys "R" Us, Inc.	568,000	14,413
Wal Mart Stores, Inc.	548,000	15,618
Walgreen Co.	180,000	8,212
Group Total		$ 53,997
Consumer (13.2%)		
American Brands, Inc.	51,000	$ 3,417
Walt Disney Co.	16,000	1,638
McDonald's Corp.	132,000	3,679
PepsiCo. Inc.	197,000	14,775
Philip Morris Co., Inc.	358,000	16,155
Rubbermaid, Inc.	135,000	4,995
Group Total		$ 44,659
Technology (6.4%)		
Automatic Data Processing, Inc.	247,000	$ 12,443
Computer Sciences Corp.	20,000	782
MCI Communications Corp.	251,000	8,503

Percent of the total portfolio that's invested in a particular industry or sector of the economy.

counts, enhancing the profitability of the pool. Eventually, then, part of that savings is yours. These commission savings, however, should not be confused with the annual operating expenses which every shareholder pays (see pages 97-98).

Advantage #15: Mutual funds provide a safe place for your investment money.

Capital Gains
are the profits you make when you sell your investment for more than you paid for it.

All mutual funds are required to hire an independent bank or trust company to hold and account for all the cash and securities in the pool. This custodian has a legally binding responsibility to protect the interests of every shareholder. No mutual fund shareholder has ever lost money due to a mutual fund bankruptcy.

Advantage #16: Mutual funds handle your paperwork for you.

Closing Price
is the price at which a security last traded before the close of business on a given day.

Capital gains and losses from the sale of stocks, as well as dividend and interest income earnings, are summarized into a report for each shareholder at the end of the year for tax purposes. Funds also manage the day-to-day chores such as dealing with transfer agents, handling stock certificates, reviewing brokerage confirmations, and more.

Advantage #17: Mutual funds can be borrowed against in case of an emergency.

Volatility
refers to the tendency of securities to rise or fall sharply in price within a relatively short period of time.

Although you hope it will never be necessary, you can use the value of your mutual fund holdings as collateral for a loan. If the need is short-term and you would rather not sell your funds because of tax or investment reasons, you can borrow against them rather than sell them.

Advantage #18: Mutual funds involve no personal liability beyond the investment risk in the portfolio.

Open-End versus Closed-End Funds
Open-end funds sell as many shares as necessary to satisfy investor interest. They are the most common kind.

Closed-end funds have only a limited number of shares available. To invest, you purchase shares through a stockbroker from other investors who wish to sell theirs.

Many investments, primarily partnerships and futures, require investors to sign papers wherein they agree to accept personal responsibility for certain liabilities generated by the undertaking. Thus, it is possible for investors to actually lose more money than they invest. This arrangement is generally indicative of speculative endeavors; I encourage you to avoid such arrangements. In contrast, mutual funds incur no personal risk.

Advantage #19: Mutual fund advisory services are available that can greatly ease the research burden.

Due to the tremendous growth in the popularity of mutual fund investing, there has been a big jump in the number of investment newsletters that specialize in researching and writing about mutual funds. In the current edition of *The Hulbert Guide to Financial Newsletters*, fifty-four were listed, and that just includes the ones that have been in existence since the beginning of 1991. Even within this group, there are different approaches. Some promote timing strategies that tell you when to buy and sell, others focus on just the funds at one of the giant organizations such as Fidelity and Vanguard, and others recommend balanced, diversified portfolios of mutual funds geared to your risk tolerance and stage of life. They usually publish once a month, and average $152 per year (although the majority range from $89 to $149) in cost.

Advantage #20: Mutual funds are heavily regulated by the SEC and have operated largely scandal-free for decades.

The fund industry is regulated by the Securities and Exchange Commission and is subject to the provisions of the Investment Company Act of 1940. The act requires that all mutual funds register with the SEC and that investors be given a prospectus, which must contain full information concerning the fund's history, operating policies, cost structure, and so on. Additionally, all funds use a bank that serves as the custodian of all the pool assets. This safeguard means the securities in the fund are protected from theft, fraud, and even the bankruptcy of the fund management organization itself. Of course, money can still be lost if poor investment decisions cause the value of the pool's investments to fall in value.

Securities and Exchange Commission (SEC) is an agency in Washington that regulates the securities industry. SEC rules govern the way investments are sold, the brokerage firms that sell them, what can be charged for selling them, what information must be disclosed to investors before they invest, and much more. The SEC is charged with looking after the general welfare of the investing public. All mutual funds come under SEC supervision.

Think of mutual funds as offering the convenience of something you're pretty familiar with: eating out! Someone else has done all the work of . . .

. . . developing the recipes, shopping for quality at the best prices, and cooking and assembling the dinners so that foods that go well together are served in the right proportions. For mutual funds, that's the job of the professional portfolio manager — he develops his strategy, shops for the right securities at the best prices, and then assembles the portfolio with an appropriate amount of diversification. And the analogy doesn't stop there. Just as there are many different dinner entrees to choose from at most nice restaurants (such as steak, seafood, chicken, pasta, and so on), there are also many kinds of mutual funds to choose from at most fund organizations. Each kind has its own "flavor."

IN A NUTSHELL

With mutual funds . . .

1. The fund portfolio manager decides what stocks to buy and sell and when's the best time.

2. You get the added safety that comes from diversifying among lots of different stocks.

3. You can invest any amount you want (above the minimum) and receive fractional shares.

4. You can easily and efficiently reinvest all of your dividends.

5. You can transfer your money between funds the same day.

6. You pay no sales charges when buying or selling no-load funds.

With individual stocks . . .

1. You decide what stocks to buy and sell and when's the best time.

2. You get the high-risk, high-reward potential that comes from concentrating on just a handful of stocks.

3. Stock prices affect how much you can invest because you have to buy whole shares.

4. It's difficult to reinvest all your dividends because the amounts are usually so small.

5. It usually takes five business days to get your money when you sell.

6. Even discount brokers' commissions can cost 1% each time you trade.

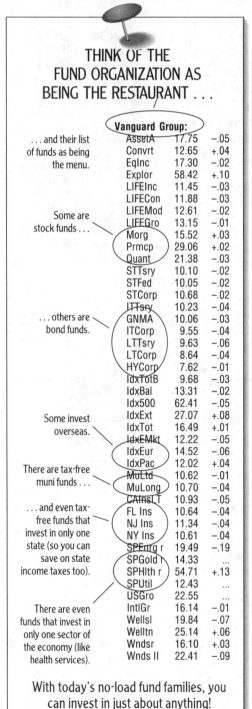

THINK OF THE FUND ORGANIZATION AS BEING THE RESTAURANT . . .

. . . and their list of funds as being the menu.

Some are stock funds . . .

. . . others are bond funds.

Some invest overseas.

There are tax-free muni funds . . .

. . . and even tax-free funds that invest in only one state (so you can save on state income taxes too).

There are even funds that invest in only one sector of the economy (like health services).

Vanguard Group:

AssetA	17.75	−.05
Convrt	12.65	+.04
EqInc	17.30	−.02
Explor	58.42	+.10
LIFEInc	11.45	−.03
LIFECon	11.88	−.03
LIFEMod	12.61	−.02
LIFEGro	13.15	−.01
Morg	15.52	+.03
Prmcp	29.06	+.02
Quant	21.38	−.03
STTsry	10.10	−.02
STFed	10.05	−.02
STCorp	10.68	−.02
ITTsry	10.23	−.04
GNMA	10.06	−.03
ITCorp	9.55	−.04
LTTsry	9.63	−.06
LTCorp	8.64	−.04
HYCorp	7.62	−.01
IdxTotB	9.68	−.03
IdxBal	13.31	−.02
Idx500	62.41	−.05
IdxExt	27.07	+.08
IdxTot	16.49	+.01
IdxEMkt	12.22	−.05
IdxEur	14.52	−.06
IdxPac	12.02	+.04
MuLtd	10.62	−.01
MuLong	10.70	−.04
CAInsLT	10.93	−.05
FL Ins	10.64	−.04
NJ Ins	11.34	−.04
NY Ins	10.61	−.04
SPEnrg r	19.49	−.19
SPGold r	14.33	...
SPHlth r	54.71	+.13
SPUtil	12.43	...
USGro	22.55	...
IntlGr	16.14	−.01
WellsI	19.84	−.07
Welltn	25.14	+.06
Wndsr	16.10	+.03
Wnds II	22.41	−.09

With today's no-load fund families, you can invest in just about anything!

The graphic at left is a partial listing of the daily mutual fund section that appears in the newspaper. Vanguard is one of the giants in the no-load fund industry, and it offers quite a "menu" for its investors. The point here is to show you *how many different funds you can find at a single fund organization.* Want a conservative blue-chip stock fund? Try Windsor. Perhaps something a little more aggressive? Check out Explorer or U.S. Growth. Prefer bonds instead? Vanguard has funds that specialize in corporates, governments, and tax-frees. Want short-term bonds instead of long-term? No problem—it offers funds that have different portfolio maturities for all three bond categories. The trend among fund organizations is to offer investors a choice in just about every investing specialty and risk group imaginable.

There are three primary ways you can profit from investing in mutual funds.

When you make your mutual fund investment, you will receive shares to show how much (that is, what portion) of the pool you own. The value of those shares fluctuates daily according to how well the investments in the pool are doing. If the overall value of the stocks held in the pool goes up today, the value of the fund's shares will go up today, and vice versa. The greater the volatility, the greater the risk. The price you pay for your shares is based on the worth of the securities in the pool on the day you buy in. Typically, the closing price is used for establishing their market value. For this reason, mutual funds are usually bought or sold only at the day's closing prices. This means that it doesn't matter what time of day the fund receives your order—early or late—you'll still get that day's closing price.

You can profit from your shares in three primary ways. First, the dividends paid by the stocks in the portfolio will be paid out to you periodically, usually quarterly. Second, if the portfolio manager sells a stock for more than he paid for it originally, a capital gain results. These gains will also be paid out periodically, usually annually. And third, when you're ready to sell your shares in the pool, you might receive back more than you paid for them. ◆

8

CHAPTER PREVIEW

How Mutual Funds Are Sold and the Best Way to Buy Them

I. **There are two primary ways to go about investing in mutual funds.**

   A. "Load" fund organizations sell their shares to investors through a sales network of brokers, insurance professionals, and financial planners. A percentage of every dollar you invest (which can run as high as 8½%) goes to the salesperson with whom you do business.

   B. "No-load" fund organizations sell their shares to investors directly. They don't have a sales force to represent them, and so there need not be a "load" charged to the investor; 100% of every dollar invested goes to work on the investor's behalf.

II. **There are ongoing costs associated with owning mutual fund shares.**

   A. All mutual funds charge for the portfolio manager's fee and other operating expenses. This is the way they make their money. The average charge is around 1% of the value of your investment per year.

   B. There are other potential costs that *some* funds charge. These include marketing expenses, back-end loads, and exit fees. These are avoidable through selective shopping.

III. **Fund organizations vary in the excellence and variety of their funds as well as in the account minimums they require. You should select a fund organization based on the amount of money you have to start with and the kinds of investments you wish to focus on.**

   A. If you have $2,000 or less to begin with, you must initially look for fund organizations with low account minimums.

   B. As your portfolio grows in value, you may eventually want to open accounts with more than one fund organization in order to have a greater selection of funds to choose from.

   C. For maximum convenience, flexibility, and selection, investigate the mutual fund brokerage services offered by Charles Schwab and Fidelity Brokerage. There are costs associated with such services, however, that makes them inefficient for smaller accounts.

What does it cost to buy mutual funds? That depends on how you buy them . . .

. . . whether you go to them or they come to you. Mutual funds earn their profits by the management fees they charge, which are based on the amount of money they are responsible for investing. The more investors' money they manage, the more they make. Naturally, they want to attract as many customers as possible.

Load Fund
is a mutual fund that is sold to investors through a sales network, typically by stock brokers, financial planners, and insurance agents, and for which the investor pays a markup or sales charge.

So-called "load" funds get new customers by having a sales force of stock-brokers, financial planners, and insurance professionals sell their funds for them. These funds charge a sales fee, which is added on top of the fund's net asset value. This markup cost can run as high as 8½% on every dollar you invest. The load applies to all purchases you make in the fund, not just the first time; some load funds even charge to reinvest your dividends for you (which I think is going a bit far). In return, the salesperson comes up with recommendations as to which funds might be best suited for your goals and completes all the paperwork to get your account opened. The load is the way the salesperson is rewarded for opening and servicing new accounts. If you would never get around to doing the research needed to select funds that are right for you, the salesperson provides an important service by doing this work for you and motivating you to action.

No-Load Fund
is a mutual fund that is sold without a sales markup. This is usually done by the mutual fund organization not using a sales network and selling directly to the investor. However, be careful. There are some funds that still charge a sales load although they are selling directly to the public.

"No-load" funds, on the other hand, have chosen to deal directly with investors. They don't have a sales force to represent them — they believe plenty of investors are willing to do their own research and paperwork in order to save on the sales load. *They don't come to you; you go to them.* Of course, they make it as easy as possible through their advertising, 800 numbers, and customer service departments. Since they don't have salespeople to pay, they don't charge the load (thus the name "no-load"). By showing some initiative, you can save the 5%–8½% load that is commonly charged. That means *all the money* you put into your fund account goes to work for *you*. I recommend you limit your investment shopping to no-load funds. You'll learn all you need to know in this book to select the funds that are right for you, and you'll save thousands of dollars in loads over the years.

But (I can hear many of you asking) what about investment performance? Is it true that load funds get better results than no-load funds?

Sometimes they do, and sometimes they don't. Let me explain it to you this way. One of the major college basketball rivalries is the one between the University of Louisville and the University of Kentucky. People around here are fiercely devoted to their favorite teams. The question of who's best is settled once a year — but only briefly. Bragging rights only last until the next time they play. Since the team lineups are constantly changing, the question of superiority is fought anew each season. If you look at the two programs over time, they're pretty evenly matched.

That's also the way it is in the great "load fund" versus "no-load fund" debate. Which kind has the better performance? The truth is they're pretty evenly matched. Neither group is inherently better than the other, just as none of the top college programs is inherently superior to the others. One year college A is best, the next year college B, and so on (although a John Wooden or a Dean Smith can come along and dominate every now and then, but that's to their credit, not the institution's).

In the same way, one year several of the no-load categories will outperform their load counterparts. The next year it could well be the other way around. Each group will have their share of winning results, and the "margin of victory" is usually quite small. They're so close that it's anyone's guess who will lead in performance in the coming year. Both load and no-load fund organizations hire top professionals in an attempt to bolster their performance results, which are, after all, what they are selling. So why should you expect either type to be inherently superior to the other? You shouldn't.

COSTS OF INVESTING IN MUTUAL FUNDS		
Type of Fee:	Applies To:	You Pay:
Sales Loads	Load funds only	When you buy
Operating Expenses	All mutual funds	A little each day
12b-1 Fees	About 1/2 of all funds	A little each day
Deferred Sales Charges	Load funds only	If you sell within 4–6 years
Exit Fees	A few no-load funds	If you sell within 30–180 days

However, that doesn't mean they're equally attractive. The load that investors pay comes out up-front, which means they're "in the hole" the day their account is opened. Load funds *must* be consistently superior over time in order to be a better investment than a comparable no-load fund. This places the burden of proof on the load funds.

What costs are involved in owning mutual funds?

Most investors understand the one-time costs of investing in load funds. What's not always so clear, however, are the ongoing operating expenses that are charged by *all* mutual funds, whether load or no-load. These are the costs of owning mutual funds over the long haul. They include:

◆ **Operating expenses.** The lion's share of operating expenses goes toward making the investing decisions. This means paying for an experienced portfolio manager as well as a staff of financial analysts to help with all the research. Next, there's a lot of administrative overhead involved in having a large office, staff, and equipment. Then there's the cost of having a bank maintain the shareholder accounts and safeguard all the money and securities that are constantly coming and going. Finally, there are the costs of presenting regular reports to shareholders, as well as for legal and auditing services. Operating expenses for the average stock mutual fund cost shareholders around 1% per year; that is, $10 for every $1,000 of account value.

◆ **Marketing expenses.** On top of operating expenses, almost 60% of stock funds also charge some of their marketing expenses to shareholders. These expenses are referred to as "12b-1" fees because of the SEC ruling that permits them, and the money from them can only be used to advertise and sell the fund to prospective investors. Such fees are predominantly favored by load funds (eight out of ten funds charging 12b-1 fees are sold through a sales network). Most funds do not yet levy these charges, but it is a growing (and controversial) practice. Marketing fees can reduce shareholders' returns by another $3 to $10 per $1,000 of account value annually.

◆ **Back-end loads, also sometimes called deferred sales charges.** These are most commonly assessed by funds affiliated with major brokerage firms. This approach allows the firms that use them to sell shares through their commissioned brokers without charging front-loads. The firm is able to pay the brokers from these back-end loads and from the hidden 12b-1 charges. Typically, if you sell during the first year, you are charged a back-end commission ranging from 4% to 6% of the amount originally invested. The percentage drops each year, gradually declining to zero after four or five years. They are deducted from your proceeds check when you pull your money out.

◆ **Exit fees.** Charged by a relatively few funds, these fees are intended to discourage you from making frequent trades. Such fees can range from a flat $5.00 per withdrawal to as much as $1.00 for every $100 withdrawn. Like back-end loads, they are deducted from the check sent you at the time you sell your shares.

The first two categories, operating and marketing expenses, are deducted from the pool's value daily. Therefore, a fund's performance rating, which is based on the change in a pool's value over a period of time, already takes the effects of these costs into account. The mutual funds that I recommend in *Sound Mind Investing* have reasonable operating and marketing expenses; however, I generally do not recommend funds that charge front-end or back-end loads.

Investors are frequently told that they can enhance their returns by purchasing stock funds with below average expenses.

While this idea passes the commonsense test — "If the fund takes less for

"Load Funds and
Classes of Shares"
by Austin Pryor.
Excerpted from the
<u>Sound Mind Investing</u>
newsletter.
See Briefing 13,
page 474.

overhead and marketing, that leaves more for me" — the surprising fact is that there doesn't seem to be a reliable correlation between the level of expenses a stock fund charges and the returns it earns for its shareholders. One study, by investment adviser Burton Berry, examined more than 400 stock funds and found that less than 2% of the variability of returns was due to differences in the expenses they charged. (This is in dramatic contrast to fixed income funds, where expenses are a more significant factor. For example, 86% of the variation in money funds returns was found to be a function of expense ratios.)

The table below shows the results of a study where I divided several kinds of stock funds into five groups based on their expense ratios (which include both operating fees and, where applicable, 12b-1 marketing fees). Although I observed a greater correlation than Berry found — average returns did tend to go down as average expenses went up — it wasn't consistent. For example, in group one, funds in the "least expensive" quintile had an average expense ratio of 0.66% and returned the best performance in that category. However, in group four, funds in the least expensive quintile had the second *worst* performance.

The bottom line is that buying a fund with low annual expenses won't necessarily get you top performance. On the other hand, buying a fund with high annual expenses does make it more likely you'll get below-average performance. Perhaps the best use of expense ratios might be as the "deciding factor" when trying to choose between two similar funds.

Are load funds worth the extra costs?

They're worth it for *some* people. My thoughts on this are summarized in an exchange of letters I once had with a financial planner who sold load funds.

More on Load vs. No-Load Performance
"As far back as 1962, a special study was performed by the Wharton School of Finance for the Securities and Exchange Commission. It found 'no evidence that higher sales charges go hand-in-hand with better investment performance. Instead, the study showed that fund shareholders who paid higher sales charges had a less favorable investment experience than those paying less.'. . .One of the best studies was an exhausting comparison of loads versus no-loads covering income, growth, and stability. Conducted in 1971 by Fundscope, it concluded: 'Because so many no-load and so many load funds perform both above-average as well as below-average, you must reach the conclusion there is just no relationship, no correlation, between load and results.'. . ."

From <u>The Handbook for No-Load Fund Investors</u>

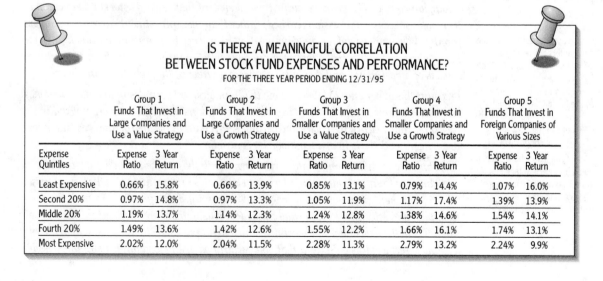

IS THERE A MEANINGFUL CORRELATION BETWEEN STOCK FUND EXPENSES AND PERFORMANCE?
FOR THE THREE YEAR PERIOD ENDING 12/31/95

Expense Quintiles	Group 1 Funds That Invest in Large Companies and Use a Value Strategy		Group 2 Funds That Invest in Large Companies and Use a Growth Strategy		Group 3 Funds That Invest in Smaller Companies and Use a Value Strategy		Group 4 Funds That Invest in Smaller Companies and Use a Growth Strategy		Group 5 Funds That Invest in Foreign Companies of Various Sizes	
	Expense Ratio	3 Year Return	Expense Ratio	3 Year Return	Expense Ratio	3 Year Return	Expense Ratio	3 Year Return	Expense Ratio	3 Year Return
Least Expensive	0.66%	15.8%	0.66%	13.9%	0.85%	13.1%	0.79%	14.4%	1.07%	16.0%
Second 20%	0.97%	14.8%	0.97%	13.3%	1.05%	11.9%	1.17%	17.4%	1.39%	13.9%
Middle 20%	1.19%	13.7%	1.14%	12.3%	1.24%	12.8%	1.38%	14.6%	1.54%	14.1%
Fourth 20%	1.49%	13.6%	1.42%	12.6%	1.55%	12.2%	1.66%	16.1%	1.74%	13.1%
Most Expensive	2.02%	12.0%	2.04%	11.5%	2.28%	11.3%	2.79%	13.2%	2.24%	9.9%

Banks Faulted for Mutual Fund Sales Tactics

Imagine you've been hired by First Union Bank to sell mutual funds to its customers. Let's listen in to a training session where you're being given guidelines on how to explain the risk of loss.

(This dialogue was reported in a <u>Wall Street Journal</u> article about a legal action that resulted in First Union being assessed $500,000 in punitive damages for coaching its brokers on how to sidestep questions about mutual fund risk.)

"Why don't I want you to say, 'Yes, you could lose money,'" First Union's Mark Gibson asks a class of brokers.

"You don't want to be negative," a woman in the audience replies.

"Exactly right," says Mr. Gibson.

Rather than giving a yes-or-no answer, Mr. Gibson suggests that brokers describe what could happen to an investment. They might explain that a fund's value "can fluctuate," or that an investor "might get more or less, depending on market conditions."

He also suggests to his students that they put potential investors at ease by emphasizing that the customers are purchasing the mutual fund at a bank. "You haven't bought mutual funds before and what's important is you're buying them through the bank, and look at the return, 12%. That's better than what you were doing before."

A few years ago, banks began bringing brokers into their lobbies and selling mutual funds in a big way. Since that time, <u>Money</u> magazine has been highly critical

(continued on page 102)

Dear Austin:

I have been in the financial services business for five years. God has blessed my business, and I am very proud of the fact that my clients place a lot of confidence in me in giving them sound, unbiased and godly financial advice. I serve most of my clients as a financial planner in the type of work I do, but I have never charged fees for this. . . . Obviously, I've seen how you recommend that people should primarily consider no-load funds. Why pay a sales charge when you could use a no-load fund, and I have to agree with that.

The problem I have is that no-load funds don't put bread on my family's table. I do think there are many good funds to choose from that are loaded. I tend to sell funds that are 1½%–4% and not ones that are more expensive. I sell mostly larger, reputable funds with long successful track records. Yet, in all this I certainly don't feel I've done my clients a disservice, since they have not had to pay me a fee for the financial planning. I guess what I would like you to do is simply comment on how you feel about this kind of service and how I might better communicate to my clients the reasons I use load funds.

Sincerely, Alan

Dear Alan:

When I first decided to try making a go of it in the investment advisory business, I was fortunate to have one of my closest friends as a business partner. After ten years as a stockbroker, he was ready to make a change. There were many reasons, both personal and professional, for this, but the one that most stands out in my mind after all these years is that he wanted to get away from the potential conflicts of interest he routinely faced.

He wanted to give his customers the very best service and investment counsel. He wanted to honor his commitment to Christ. And yes, he wanted to provide for his young and growing family. Often, he was thrust into situations where he felt these goals might be on a collision course. The primary culprit was a system that rewards stockbrokers based on their sales success (commissions earned) rather than their investment success (customers' profits). When my friend resigned his position in order to team up with me and launch our new company, Wall Street's loss was my gain. He taught me much about the technical aspects of investments, and displayed a sincere interest in the welfare of our clients.

I recount this experience to let you know that I understand your desire to render an honest service for a fair wage. Furthermore, there are millions of people who are not willing to invest the time to learn the basics and become self-reliant in the area of finances and investing — they need the help of a trustworthy counselor.

A pastor once completed one of my survey forms with the comment: "I do not have the time or inclination to study financial matters, yet I know it is important." He is the kind of person who could benefit from your knowledge and objectivity. In helping him formulate a long-term plan and selecting good mutual funds (obviously, there are excellent funds to choose from in both the load and no-load camps) suited to his personal situation, you are rendering a valuable service. It is only right that you be fairly paid, and load funds make this possible.

READING THE DAILY MUTUAL FUND LISTINGS

These initials stand for net asset value. Each day after the markets close, all of the investment securities owned by the pool are valued at that day's closing price. The total is then divided by the total number of shares in the pool in order to find out how much an individual share is worth. The value of an individual share is called its Net Asset Value and is the price at which shareholders were permitted to redeem (sell back) their shares on that day. The NAV continually fluctuates, depending on how the securities owned by the fund performed during the day. It also is affected by: (1) the costs of running the fund (2) 12b-1 marketing expenses, and (3) periodic distributions when the fund passes along capital gains, dividends, and interest to the shareholders.

This column shows the per share change in the value of the fund from the previous day. Small rises and dips are normal and should not cause undue concern. In weekly mutual fund listings, such as those found in Barron's and many Sunday papers, this column will reflect the change for the entire week. A string of declines over several weeks during which similar funds are climbing is an early warning sign that a change may be needed.

The maximum initial sales charge represents the cost of buying the fund shares. This cost is shown in percentage terms. For example, the number "4.75" in this column means that 4.75% comes out of your purchase to pay the sales markup, and 95.25% is left to purchase your shares at the net asset value shown. No-load funds (which do not charge a sales markup) are indicated by "0.00" in this column. Although there is no front-end load, there may be back-end loads or exit fees.

The headings indicate a fund organization that has several funds that it operates. Such groups of mutual funds are called fund "families." It is quite easy to move your investments from one fund to another within the same family, usually with just a phone call. This makes the larger no-load fund families, such as Vanguard and Price, more attractive because they have such a large variety of funds from which to choose.

The name of each fund is listed in normal type. Often you can tell what the fund's special emphasis is by its name. The abbreviations can be puzzling at first. Here's how to decipher some of those appearing in the AARP listing: CaGr stands for capital growth, GthInc indicates a growth and income fund, HQ Bd is their high quality bond fund, and TxFBd is their tax-free bond fund. In the Babson Group, Intl is their international stock fund, and TaxFrS is a tax-free bond fund, but with a short-term portfolio. In the AIM family, note there are two versions of many of their funds. HiYld is a high yield (junk) bond fund which offers both "A" shares (front load) and "B" shares (higher operating expenses and deferred load).

	NAV	Net Chg	Max Init Charge		NAV	Net Chg	Max Init Charge
AAL Mutual:				**Babson Group:**			
Bond p	9.61	−.04	4.75	Bond L	1.52	.....	0.00
CaGr p	19.10	.....	4.75	Bond S	9.62	−.02	0.00
Intl p	11.06	+.01	4.75	Enterp2	22.02	+.03	0.00
MuBd p	10.91	−.04	4.75	Enterp	17.95	+.02	0.00
SmCoStk p	18.04	+.23	4.75	Gwth	15.73	+.01	0.00
Util p	11.03	−.04	4.75	Intl	18.23	+.05	0.00
AARP Invest:				Shadw	11.93	+.01	0.00
BalS&B	17.30	−.04	0.00	TaxFrL	8.72	−.03	0.00
CaGr	42.23	−.16	0.00	TaxFrS	10.68	−.02	0.00
GiniM	14.90	−.03	0.00	Value	34.78	−.05	0.00
Glbl	15.55	−.04	.....	**Bailard Biehl&Kaiser:**			
GthInc	42.75	−.11	0.00	Diversa	13.29	−.04	0.00
HQ Bd	15.76	−.03	0.00	IntlEq	5.96	.....	0.00
TxFBd	17.74	−.05	0.00	IntlBd	8.09	.....	0.00
AHA Funds:				**Baird Funds Group:**			
Balan	13.47	−.01	0.00	AdjInc	8.68	.....	3.25
DivrEq	17.63	−.02	0.00	BlChip p	25.93	+.02	5.75
Full	9.64	−.03	0.00	CapDev p	25.75	+.01	5.75
Lim	10.12	−.01	0.00	BaronA	26.73	+.02	0.00
AIM Funds:				BaronGrl	18.08	−.01	0.00
Agrsv p	50.51	+0.25	5.50	**Bartlett Funds:**			
BalA p	20.73	+.01	4.75	BasVl	18.64	−.04	0.00
BalB t	20.71	+.01	0.00	FixedI	9.79	−.02	0.00
Const p	26.22	+.08	5.50	ShtTmBd	9.70	−.01	0.00
HiYld A p	9.46	.....	4.75	Vl Intl	13.04	−.03	0.00
HiYld B t	9.46	.....	0.00	Bascom	23.35	−.06	0.00

Many of the funds have single letters following their names. These are footnote codes to convey something extra you should know about that fund. The most commonly used code letters are:

"f"   yesterday's price was not available by press time, so the price from the day before is still being used;
"p"   12b-1 marketing costs are paid from the pool's assets;
"r"   redemption costs (exit fees) are charged under certain circumstances;
"t"   12b-1 marketing costs as well as redemption costs are charged (footnotes p and r apply); and
"x"   today's net asset value was reduced by the amount of a dividend soon to be paid out to shareholders.

of many banks' handling of their fiduciary responsibilities. By sending testers into the field who posed as customers, Money found salespeople who failed to ask basic questions (concerning the customer's objectives, risk tolerance, income level, or tax bracket) or who imparted misleading or factually incorrect information. More recently, the General Accounting Office of the federal government conducted its own investigation. Its staffers posed as customers and visited eighty-nine banks across the country. In a report released late last year, the GAO faulted banks for:

◆ Not disclosing fund-related costs. The sales brochures given to customers failed to adequately explain the fees which they would pay.

◆ Inappropriate sales locations. The GAO report indicated that 34% of the banks visited did not clearly separate their mutual fund sales areas from their deposit-taking activities.

◆ Allowing customers to assume that mutual funds offer the safety of savings accounts. Only about one-third of the banks surveyed included all four of these risk disclosures in their sales presentations: funds aren't federally insured, funds aren't guaranteed by the bank, funds are not the same as savings deposits, and funds go up and down in value.

◆ Inadequate disclosure of interest rate risk. Investors accustomed to traditional savings accounts usually regard rising interest rates as a good thing—they'll get a better return on their investments. However, when interest rates go up, bond values go down. In 30% of the banks surveyed, this risk was not mentioned to customers who, seeking to improve on low yields, moved their savings into bond funds.

It's obvious, but bears repeating: Make sure you understand the potential risks, transaction fees, and tax consequences associated with an investment before making a final decision.

Unfortunately, there have been so many well-publicized episodes of blatantly deceptive and self-serving brokers and planners taking advantage of trusting investors that the public is becoming cynical and wary. It does take a good bit of time to persuade potential clients that you are a person of integrity.

To assure that the welfare of your clients remains uppermost in your mind as you serve them, I would suggest these guidelines: [1] go the extra mile to make sure the portfolio you are recommending is truly fitted to your clients' needs; [2] make sure they understand the risks and the possible worst case scenarios if they were to withdraw their money earlier than expected; [3] put them in fund families with a wide variety of offerings to accommodate possible future changes; and [4] always remember that we live our lives moment by moment in the sight of God. "To do what is right and just is more acceptable to the Lord than sacrifice" (Proverbs 21:3).

Sincerely, Austin

If you fit the description given above as someone who has neither the time nor inclination to select your own mutual fund investments, then your task is to locate someone like Alan who is informed, experienced, and objective.

On the other hand, if you're interested in doing your own fund "shopping" and saving the costs associated with load funds, which fund organization is best?

Well, best for what purpose? How long do you expect to hold your fund investments? What kinds of funds are you interested in? Are you willing to monitor your funds' progress, or do you want to just buy a few and forget them for the next few years? There is no "best" in an absolute sense; the selection must take place within the context of your personal goals and risk tolerance. A greater number of choices, it seems, creates greater anxiety about making the right decision. Here are some things to keep in mind as you contemplate selecting a no-load fund organization.

1. Each fund organization has its own areas of excellence. For example, if you're primarily going to be investing in bond and money market funds, Vanguard is hard to beat. If you're interested in having access to stock funds across the entire risk spectrum, T. Rowe Price has a good selection. Or if a large selection isn't important, 20th Century's stock funds are super during periods of rising stock prices (but beware of them in a bear market!).

2. Consider opening more than one account. If you don't mind the paperwork and can manage the initial minimums, open accounts at two (or more) of the no-load organizations. Having an account at Vanguard so you can invest in their fixed income funds, and one at Price to have access to their stock funds, would be a good combination. Or, if you're

A TYPICAL AD FOR A NO-LOAD FUND ORGANIZATION

No-load fund organizations attract investors through direct advertising in financial publications (like <u>The Wall Street Journal</u>, <u>Barron's</u>, <u>Forbes</u>, and <u>Money</u>) rather than via a sales network of brokers, insurance agents, and financial planners. They typically call attention to their performance histories or variety of fund offerings in an attempt to motivate you to call for more information. Other features of these ads include the words "no-load" prominently featured and a toll-free 800 number for you to call. There is no charge for the material they send you, and they usually do not bother you with personal follow-up calls.

An account application form is included with the information package you receive. By contacting their toll-free number, you'll get all the help you need in completing the form.

No sales commissions are charged because they are selling directly to the investing public—they have no sales force to pay. To be sure it's a no-load fund, always look for these words to appear in the ad.

The sponsoring fund organization is usually referred to as a "family" if it offers a wide assortment of funds to choose from.

No-load funds are excellent places to maintain your IRA. They will even do the work for you of transferring it from its present location.

The free prospectus explains the fees and expenses charged, the investment guidelines and strategy used, and the benefits and services offered by the fund.

Toll-free number makes it easy to call for information.

This is a listing of the variety of funds offered.

A Strong Portfolio Is Built On A Solid Foundation.

And **Founders no-load Blue Chip Fund** is built primarily on the financial strength of well-established, mature "Blue Chip" companies with long records of profitability. Founders Blue Chip Fund pays quarterly dividends and is designed for those looking for long-term growth of capital and income.

Founders offers a family of nine no-load mutual funds with objectives to meet both the conservative and aggressive investor. Call us today to receive a free prospectus.

Please read the prospectus carefully before you invest or send money. It contains more complete information including management fees and expenses.

1-800-934-GOLD (4653)

≡Founders
Based In Denver Since 1938.

AGGRESSIVE		MODERATE			CONSERVATIVE			
Founders Discovery Fund	**Founders Frontier Fund**	**Founders Special Fund**	**Founders Worldwide Growth Fund**	**Founders Growth Fund**	**Founders Blue Chip Fund**	**Founders Equity Income Fund**	**Founders Government Securities Fund**	
Small Capitalization	Aggressive Growth	Capital Appreciation	Global Growth	Long-Term Growth	Growth & Income	Income & Capital Appreciation	Fixed Income	

moving two IRAs, put them at different organizations and enjoy a greater selection. The additional annual charges are insignificant.

3. *Performance leadership is always changing.* Organization A could be doing great now, but its funds could all become un-load candidates a year from now. No problem. With no-load funds, you can move your money easily and at no cost. The SMI philosophy involves diversifying across several risk categories. While it's important that you discipline yourself to have a long-term commitment *to the diversification strategy,* you need only make short-term commitments to individual funds and organizations.

When you are ready to begin building your mutual fund portfolio, your "starting place" will primarily depend on how much you initially have available.

If you're just getting started, I suggest you consider either the 20th Century or Invesco organizations due to their willingness to take very small accounts. 20th Century has the very unusual policy of requiring no initial account minimum; Invesco requires just $500. Fortunately, both are well run and have funds to choose from with outstanding performance records.

A SAMPLING OF THE GREAT VARIETY OF NO-LOAD FUNDS OFFERED BY SEVEN LEADING FUND ORGANIZATIONS

No-Load Fund Family	Number of U.S. Stock Funds	Number of U.S. Fixed Income Funds	Number of International Funds
Dreyfus	43	20	6
Fidelity	74	27	25
Invesco	18	7	7
T. Rowe Price	22	17	13
Scudder	8	9	10
20th Century	15	22	3
Vanguard	37	24	7

If you have at least $3,000 available for stock market investing . . .

. . . you will find your needs well met by choosing among the many no-load investment companies listed in the graphic on the left. They are all reputable organizations that offer a variety of funds from which you can choose. They also allow you to move your money from one of their funds into another simply by making a toll-free phone call. As with all true no-load funds, there are no commissions charged to you, either when you invest or when you take your money out. These organizations provide you with a very cost-effective way to proceed with your program. We will really get into the specifics of how to do this in Section 4.

As your portfolio grows, you will want to diversify further. Although each of the above-mentioned organizations offers a variety of stock funds, you could run into either of two "problems." One, they might not offer a fund in the exact risk category or area of specialty you are seeking. Or, even if they do offer one, you might find that it is a relatively poor performer. At this point, it might be time to open a second mutual fund account at a different organization with strengths that complement those of your first organization and match up well with your current needs.

However, along with having such a variety of choice comes housekeeping chores that can be inconvenient and occasionally confusing. You've got multiple sets of 800 numbers, application forms, investment account numbers, organizational policies, and monthly statements to contend with. When you want to sell shares at one organization and buy them at another, you've got to wait for a check from the first fund before sending your check off to the next one. And then there's all the tax information to keep track of.

An alternative to multiple fund accounts is to open a single investment account at either the Charles Schwab Company or Fidelity Brokerage Services.

In addition to stocks and bonds, they each offer a very convenient way to invest in mutual funds. These services allow you to quickly and easily buy/sell no-load mutual fund shares for your account without having to open separate accounts at all the various fund organizations. They perform this service *commission-free on some funds* or for a small charge for others.

Why pay for this when you can go to a no-load organization and buy its fund shares for free? Greater convenience and greater selection. Because Schwab and Fidelity offer hundreds of different funds to choose from, many of them will be superior performers to those of the one or two no-load organizations where you might have accounts (especially in the stock fund categories). In view of the far greater convenience and variety of funds, these services constitute the "new look" of fund investing for the nineties.

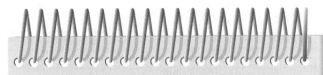

STEPS NEEDED TO MOVE YOUR MONEY FROM ONE MUTUAL FUND ORGANIZATION TO ANOTHER

Why go through a brokerage firm like Schwab or Fidelity and pay them to do what you can do for yourself? The answer is simple: convenience when moving your investment dollars from one mutual fund organization to a new one where you don't already have an account.

For example, let's pretend that you want to sell your shares at Organization A and invest the money in one of the funds at Organization B. If you weren't using Schwab's mutual fund service, here's what you'd need to do:

❑ Mail written instructions to Organization A (with your signature guaranteed by your local bank or broker) to sell your shares.

❑ Wait seven to ten days for your proceeds check to arrive from Organization A.

❑ While you're waiting, contact Organization B and ask them to send you the new account application forms.

❑ When they arrive, complete the forms.

❑ Mail them to Organization B with your check to pay for the new fund shares you want to purchase.

❑ Finally, wait two to three days before you know your order has been processed. (What's been happening in the stock market while you're doing all this waiting is anyone's guess!)

Charles Schwab pioneered its Mutual Fund Marketplace a few years back. For a small service fee, Schwab offered access to hundreds of no-load funds through one investment account. It wasn't long before Fidelity, the giant mutual fund organization, came along to one-up Schwab by offering the same service with even more funds to choose from.

Schwab struck back with its OneSource service which *eliminated the service fees completely for certain fund families.* In 1993, Fidelity responded by introducing a similar no-transaction-fee service of its own. Both of these companies are now battling it out to see which one can sign up the most funds and thereby offer the widest selection. Free competition in the marketplace has once again resulted in better and less costly service for investors!

Now you can choose from hundreds of "no transaction fee" (NTF) no-load funds at either organization. New funds are being added all the time. With one toll-free call to phone lines that are answered twenty-four hours a day, you can make changes in your portfolio. You'll get one monthly statement that includes your transaction history, dividends, and the current market values for all your holdings. Plus, both Schwab and Fidelity offer their clients free performance reports that include helpful data on all the funds they offer and are completely updated every three months.

The commissions these firms charge are well worth it unless your account is a small one, say under $25,000. In that case, the fees are too high in proportion to the amounts invested. For more on Schwab OneSource, call (800) 435-4000, and for Fidelity's FundsNetwork, call (800) 544-9697. ◆

THE CONVENIENCE OF ONE-STOP SHOPPING
(CURRENT AS OF MID-1996)

Mutual Funds Offered with No Transaction Fees	Fidelity Funds Network	Schwab One Source
Berger	3	3
Dreyfus	35	35
Fidelity	135	0
Founders	10	10
IAI Funds	13	13
Invesco	0	31
Janus	15	15
Lexington	12	13
NeubergerBerman	9	11
Schwab	0	17
SteinRoe	15	15
Strong	21	25
20th Century/Benham	0	35
Other	163	296
Total	431	519

9

CHAPTER PREVIEW

Necessary
Cautions

I. **The rapid growth of the mutual fund industry in recent years has created an exceptionally crowded and competitive playing field.**

   A. This has led many funds to take added investment risks as they seek to gain a performance edge over their rivals.

   B. The fund industry's system for classifying risk is subjective and open to misinterpretation and abuse.

II. **As a result of the exceptional growth and the ways in which many funds have responded to it, red flags have been raised that are a legitimate cause for concern to mutual fund investors.**

   A. Red Flag #1: You can't necessarily accept a fund's "investment objective" at face value.

   B. Red Flag #2: You can't necessarily accept a fund's diversification claims at face value.

   C. Red Flag #3: You can't necessarily accept a fund's implied performance excellence at face value.

   D. Red Flag #4: You can't necessarily accept a fund's rankings at face value.

III. **Mutual fund investors must accept the responsibility for learning how to shop intelligently.**

   A. One source of information often bypassed by investors is the fund prospectus. Pointers are offered on how to read it for the essentials.

   B. Other sources of information include your local library.

IV. **To help you neutralize the difficulties described above, I'll show you two ways to help assure that the funds you purchase are suited to your personal needs.**

   A. The use of index funds, as explained in chapters 13 through 15, enables you to avoid the "red flag" traps described above. I'll show you how to assemble them into a portfolio that reflects your current age, goals, and tolerance for risk.

   B. Additionally, in chapters 18 through 21, I'll teach you a new way to evaluate stock and bond fund risk that doesn't rely on the standard industry groupings, which are prone to abuse.

When I began my career as an investment adviser in the late 1970s . . .

. . . I chose to specialize in the study of mutual funds. They offered my clients quick and easy diversification within specified boundaries, as well as seasoned professional management. Plus, since there were only about 800 to choose from at the time (compared to thousands of common stocks), the selection process was greatly simplified.

How times have changed! The number of funds has multiplied at a phenomenal 30% annual rate over the past few years. And the number of fund *categories* increased 50% from 1986 to 1994 according to a report from Goldman, Sachs. Morningstar, one of the country's three leading mutual fund reporting services, now carries data on more than 7,000 mutual funds in its database. These days the selection process is no longer a simple one. The sheer number and variety of funds has caused investors to be confused about what is available, let alone what is appropriate.

This stunning growth, which many have characterized as mutual fund mania, has raised some eyebrows among fund industry observers.

In 1994, one researcher found such an abundance of material on the subject that he wrote a 250-page book that detailed what he sees as dangerous changes afoot (*Surviving the Coming Mutual Fund Crisis* by Donald Christensen). The popular magazines have also weighed in:

"Today, the risks of investing in mutual funds may actually outweigh their benefits. The dangers include too many derivatives and foreign currency bets, too little disclosure and portfolio diversity." (Fortune, 3/6/95)

"Investors now have more than 7,500 mutual funds to choose from. Is the fund industry picking up speed or running off the rails?" (Worth, 6/95)

"The industry has spliced and diced too much to come up with new funds. We'd be better off if some were left on the shelf." (Money, 8/95)

The fund industry's explosive growth has increased the complexity of monitoring mutual fund performance and being sure you understand the risks. Arriving at a decision is more difficult than it used to be, not merely because you have more choices now, but, regrettably, because it can no longer be safely assumed that fund managers are investing your money prudently.

In recent years, too many fund executives have made poor decisions as they attempted to gain an edge in the face of the enormous competitive pressures that now characterize the fund industry. To better understand the dynamics at work, let's use an analogy based on a business we're all familiar with—the neighborhood supermarket.

Assume that in the "old days" you had three grocery stores in your small town. There was friendly competition, but there was enough business to go

---

Risk Category is a way of classifying mutual funds that groups together those with similar investment strategies and similar possibilities of profit and loss. The idea is that they be useful in helping investors compare "apples with apples" when measuring mutual fund performance.

Unfortunately, there is no "official" list of categories used consistently throughout the industry. The mutual fund trade associations, Morningstar, Lipper, and Value Line, are the most influential authorities on mutual funds, and they each have their own different (albeit similar) ways to classify funds. Because of the great diversity of funds, their systems have grown to include as many as thirty different risk categories.

In this book, I have created a simplified system that involves just four basic categories for stock funds and four for bond funds. These will be explained in detail in Section 4.

around. Then, in a period of fifteen years, the size of your town tripled. With a larger population to feed, the local grocers responded by opening additional stores. The town's growth did not go unnoticed by the grocery chains that had not previously operated in your community, and they came in with new stores as well. Now there are two dozen supermarkets—it seems like there's one on every corner.

The population tripled, but the number of grocery stores grew eightfold. The grocers know that the town can't support all of them and that a shakeout is inevitable. They also know that low prices are the key to attracting shoppers because they see their sales go up and down in direct proportion to how their prices compare to their competitors' prices. So, there is a great deal of pressure on each grocer to have his prices appear as attractive as possible. Each is determined to do what he must in order to be among the survivors, even if it means cutting a few corners here and there.

In the same way, the number of new mutual funds has far surpassed the number of new investors. Mutual fund organizations have hundreds of millions of dollars in fees riding on their ability to attract and keep customers, and the key for them isn't low prices—it's investment performance. In the *Fortune* article mentioned above, the situation was summed up this way:

> In a recent Smith Barney survey of investors, when asked the single most important reason for selecting a fund, 51% looked to past performance over one to five years, not the composition of the fund portfolio or the fund's management philosophy. . . . That emphasis has sent a message to fund companies: short-term performance is paramount. . . . The trouble with this seemingly harmless focus is that fund managers can be pressured to throw caution to the wind as they try to jockey into the winner's circle for one-year performance. The swelling number of mutual fund rankings in almost every business publication has reinforced the short-term bias, moving one-year performance into an elite class. . . . Such measurements have become the standard for investors and the fund managers who serve them.

In this chapter, we're going to look at some of the "red flags" that are a legitimate cause for concern to mutual fund investors. They all stem, ultimately, from the way the fund industry has taken advantage of the difficulty inherent in categorizing funds by risk. This is important because it allows investors to "compare apples to apples." Let's begin by laying some important groundwork.

In order to analyze their performance, mutual funds are placed into groupings called risk categories.

Morningstar and the other firms place every mutual fund into one of three major camps: equity (stock) funds, fixed-income (bond) funds, and hybrid (a mix of both stock and bonds) funds. This is the easy part.

Within each of the three camps, however, there are sub-categories of risk

Morningstar
Lipper Analytical
Value Line
are large companies that are in the business of collecting, analyzing, and distributing information about mutual funds. They sell their data to financial institutions, publishers, and investors. When you read about mutual fund performance in The Wall Street Journal, Barron's, Business Week, Money, Forbes, or other leading financial publications, the data shown came from one of these three organizations. Because their dominance of the industry is so total, the way they categorize funds for risk and performance is extraordinarily influential in the decision-making of millions of mutual fund investors.

Equity Funds
are mutual funds that primarily invest in stocks.

Fixed Income Funds
are mutual funds that primarily invest in bonds.

Hybrid Funds
are mutual funds that have characteristics of both equity and fixed-income funds.

based on a fund's "investment objective." A problem arises at this point because there are no official categories that all analysts and rating services can apply uniformly when assigning funds to a given category. For example, the graphic below shows four major risk categories for stocks. For each one, you'll find the definitions used by the Investment Company Institute—the mutual fund trade organization—and Morningstar. Notice that they are different.

These definitions are little more than the most commonly stated portfolio objectives as found in fund prospectuses, which describe a fund's theoretical goals and strategies. A fund's actual portfolio has tremendous room for variance while still staying within the broad, subjective guidelines given in the prospectus.

The very fact that there are no official categories that everyone can agree to proves how subjective the risk-assessment process is. After reading a fund's prospectus, the Morningstar (or Lipper or Value Line) analyst assigns the fund to the risk category that seems right to him. In other words, it's merely *each analyst's opinion* based on what the fund says it *intends* to do. Risk, like beauty, is in the eye of the beholder.

What you're looking for in a fund's stated investment objective is an indication of the road the fund is traveling in terms of risk and possible reward. If you

THE FOUR MAJOR INVESTMENT OBJECTIVES OF STOCK FUNDS

	Annualized Return 1991-1995	Standard Deviation 1991-1995	Definitions Used by the Investment Company Institute	Definitions Used by Morningstar Mutual Funds
Aggressive Growth	20.1%	15.6	Seek maximum capital appreciation (a rise in share price); current income is not a significant factor. Some may invest in out-of-the-mainstream stocks . . . and may also use specialized investing techniques such as option writing or short-term trading.	Seek rapid growth of capital and use investment techniques involving greater-than-average risk, such as short-selling, leveraging, and frequent trading.
Growth	16.2%	11.8	Invest in the common stock of companies that offer potentially rising share prices. These funds primarily aim to provide capital appreciation (a rise in share price) rather than steady income.	Seek capital appreciation by investing primarily in equity securities of companies with earnings that are expected to grow at an above-average rate. Current income, if considered at all, is a secondary objective.
Growth & Income	14.8%	9.9	Invest mainly in the common stock of companies that offer potentially increasing value as well as consistent dividend payments. Such funds attempt to provide investors with long-term capital growth and a steady stream of income.	Seek growth of capital and current income as near-equal objectives, primarily through equity securities.
Equity Income	14.7%	8.2	Seek a high level of income by investing primarily in stocks of companies with a consistent history of dividend payments.	Seek current income by investing at least 50% of their assets in equity securities with above-average yields.

Standard deviation is a measurement of risk that we'll learn more about in chapter 17. The highest risk funds are at the top and the lowest risk funds at the bottom. Because there is a direct correlation between risk and reward, it's not surprising that they both decline as you move down the list.

saw your neighbor loading up the car for a trip and asked him where he was going, you wouldn't learn very much if all he said was "somewhere warm." That would eliminate a lot of places he *wouldn't* be going, but it really wouldn't pinpoint where he *was* going. That's also true of the way many mutual funds state their objectives. They tell you in very general terms what they are allowed to do, but beyond that the door is left open for a lot of "creativity" on the part of the manager. It's the irresponsible use of this creative freedom on the part of some fund managers that is now a growing cause for concern, as we shall now see.

Red Flag #1: You can't necessarily accept a fund's "investment objective" at face value.

The investing boundaries that guide a portfolio manager ("it's OK for our fund to invest in this area but not in that area, to take these risks but not those") have become even more blurred as funds have changed their by-laws in order to broaden their investing horizons. Funds are being more aggressive in seeking a performance advantage. I have read of instances where:

◆ six U.S. stock funds had invested 40% or more of their portfolios in foreign stock holdings.

◆ a growth-and-income stock fund held large positions in high-yield bonds and dropped 20% in value in six months when the junk bond market fell.

◆ two-thirds of equity income funds, which purportedly specialize in high-dividend-paying stocks, yielded less than 3% during 1995 because they went for growth instead.

◆ a leading bond fund in the "high quality corporate" category owes its superior record compared to its peers to the fact that it routinely invests about one-third of its portfolio in lesser quality bonds rated BBB or lower.

◆ a supposedly stable short-term government bond fund dropped 22% in one year because the manager had made a big bet on the direction of interest rates by investing heavily in "derivatives" (complicated securities—which I don't begin to understand—whose value is derived from some other underlying asset or index).

Consider the table above. As before, the highest risk category is at the top, lowest risk group at the bottom. Look first at the high/low range of performance for the funds in each category over the twelve-month period. I can understand a very wide range of results in the aggressive growth group because those funds are taking large risks and can make or lose money more quickly. The best fund in the group gained 82.3% while the worst

THE INADEQUACY OF USING A FUND'S STATED INVESTMENT OBJECTIVE AS A GUIDE TO RISK
FOR THE PERIOD ENDING 8/31/95

Investment Objective	12 Month: High	Low	Yield: High	Low	HighTech As High As	Foreign As High As
Aggressive Growth	82.3%	−29.9%	3.4%	0.0%	71%	37%
Growth	70.7%	−13.8%	4.3%	0.0%	78%	25%
Growth & Income	26.8%	−29.5%	3.7%	0.0%	30%	24%
Equity Income	18.4%	5.9%	7.8%	1.2%	19%	15%

performer lost 29.9%. Investors who buy these funds understand the high risk/
reward potential, so the numbers don't surprise me. But look at the growth-and-
income group, where the worst performing fund lost 29.5%. During the same
period, the Standard & Poor's 500 stock index (a mix of growth and income stocks)
gained more than 20%. If the categories were useful guides to risk, how could any
fund in that category lose money, let alone such a huge amount?

Next, look at the yield columns, which are a measure of the dividends paid to
shareholders. The table shows the best and worst yielding funds in each category.
You would normally expect *no* dividends from funds in the aggressive growth
group and *significant* dividends from those in the equity-income group. Yet there
was a fund in the aggressive growth category that yielded 3.4%, and more surprisingly, nine funds in the growth-and-income category that yielded 0.0% (paid
no dividends at all). If they're not going to generate current income, why are they
in this group? Furthermore, although not shown in the table, 72% of the growth-
and-income funds yielded less than 2%.

Another area where category labels can be misleading has to do with the
degree to which U.S. stock funds hold shares in companies overseas. You might
think that if you wanted to invest internationally you would need to choose a
"global" fund (which can invest anywhere) or a "foreign" fund (which can invest anywhere except in the U.S.). Not so. As the table shows, there are funds in
three of the four categories that have as much as one-fourth of their entire portfolios invested outside the U.S.

Not only does this kind of behavior mean investors are taking risks of which
they are unaware, but it also makes it more difficult to evaluate the quality of the
job being done by the portfolio manager. For example, if Fund A moves significantly ahead of Fund B in its performance, is it because the manager has done a
better job of selecting securities, or because he took a big risk, loaded up on options,
and made a speculative killing? In their attempts to achieve top-performing results,
many funds have resorted to high-risk strategies that are not readily apparent on
the surface. Raw performance rankings, which previously implied excellence, may
now merely represent temporary speculative success.

Red Flag #2: You can't necessarily accept a fund's diversification claims at face value.

One of the big selling points of mutual funds is that they offer lower risk
due to the diversification in the portfolio. Many funds, however, in the pursuit
of higher performance numbers, are turning that concept on its head by concentrating their investments in just a few sectors of the economy.

In a meeting with my staff in late 1995, I illustrated this by pointing to
Robertson Stephens Value + Growth, one of the leading funds in the performance
rankings at that time. Whereas most funds in its peer group showed gains over

the previous twelve months of 16%–28%, the Robertson Stephens fund was up a stunning 70%! It was a case where the fund's performance was *too* good. I indicated there was no way the fund could have achieved such returns without making a huge speculative bet on the high-tech sector, 1995's hottest area.

I hadn't looked this up; it was self-evident. It was apparent the shareholders of that fund were being exposed to a high degree of risk. When I checked the Morningstar data, I was able to confirm that the fund entered 1995 with an 80% stake in high-tech. I wondered if the shareholders knew this. After all, the fund was categorized as a medium-risk growth fund (not a sector fund or even an aggressive growth fund). It also contains the word "value" in its name, which implies a lesser degree of risk.

Nor was this fund alone. At the end of 1995, more than thirty equity funds had committed 50% or more of their portfolios to technology stocks. Now, there's nothing wrong with investing in technology. It's an exciting area. I'm merely saying that funds that have such heavy concentration in a single area of the economy should be clearly labeled as such lest investors assume they are as diversified as their name would imply.

Another way that funds shoot for higher performance is to concentrate their holdings in a smaller number of stocks. The Fidelity Magellan fund, managed by the renowned Peter Lynch during its rise to prominence, was $10 billion in size and invested in approximately 1,000 different stocks at the time Lynch stepped down in 1990. Five years later, its size had grown to over $50 billion, but it held only about 450 stocks under its current manager. Five times as much money was invested in one-half as many stocks. That is a significant reduction in diversification with a corresponding increase in risk. This could present an especially difficult situation if the manager is forced to sell some of his holdings quickly due to shareholder redemptions.

Red Flag #3: You can't necessarily accept a fund's implied performance excellence at face value.

Mutual funds are promoted on the basis of how much money they've made for their shareholders. That's why their ads are usually filled with claims of "great" performance. The job of any fund's marketing department is to take that fund's performance history and make it look as good as possible. Fortunately for them, rare is the fund that hasn't hit a hot streak somewhere along the way. Using the hypothetical results of the three funds shown on the next page, let's look at some of the ways that mutual funds will present their performance histories in the manner most likely to attract investors.

◆ **Picking the best time period.** The Standard & Poor's 500 stock index serves as the benchmark to beat for most stock market professionals. If they have significantly outperformed the S&P 500 over the long haul, they will

Sector funds specialize in just one industry (or sector) of our economy, such as banking and financial services, health care, high-tech, or precious metals. They often attract attention because they can turn in excellent performance if their sector of the economy is growing rapidly. The trade-off, however, is a much higher degree of risk due to their lack of industry diversification.

On Fund Names Under the rules set by the Securities and Exchange Commission, a fund can name itself after a particular kind of security as long as it invests at least 65% of its portfolio in that type of security. For example, in an effort to gain a performance edge, a bond fund could invest up to 35% of its portfolio in higher-yielding, lower-quality corporate bonds and still represent itself as a super-safe "government securities" fund.

certainly trumpet that in their ads. If not, one trick is to find a shorter time period in which they had relatively good performance. Take the Allen Fund, for example. It didn't compare too well over the past decade—the S&P grew at an average compounded rate of return of 11.0% versus just 10.1% for Allen. Shortening the time period to five years doesn't help, either, because Allen still trailed the S&P. But the final three-year period looks pretty good, thanks to a strong 1991. In their ads, the managers of the Allen Fund play up the market conditions of recent years and proudly show off their superior performance.

◆ **Using average returns rather than compounded returns.** Unfortunately for the Brown Fund, it's difficult to select *any* time frame that makes it look like a particularly promising performer, so the managers adopt a different strategy in their advertising. Rather than deal in *compounded* returns as is customary, they present their gains in *average* terms. A $1,000 initial investment in Brown over the past ten years would have grown to $2,600, a total gain of 160%. Divide that by ten years and you get an average return of 16.0% per year.

However, achieving 160% over ten years requires a *compounded* return of just 10.0% (which was inferior to the 11.0% compounded growth turned in by the S&P). But to the casual reader of the ad, an average return of 16.0% per year sounds pretty impressive.

◆ **Emphasizing dollars earned rather than percentage returns.** The Cole Fund has a ten-year record that is slightly better than the S&P, but not enough to boast about. Besides, most of that was due to an exceptionally good year way back in 1985. More recently, the fund has done relatively poorly, although it has managed to eke out some gains each year. So the managers of Cole decide to advertise their performance in dollar terms rather than in percentage terms. A shareholder who held through the entire ten-year period would have seen his initial investment triple in value, and the graph in the ad (far left) illustrates the steady growth. To make the fund's

WHEN IT COMES TO MUTUAL FUND PERFORMANCE, SEEING IS BELIEVING . . . OR IS IT?

THE AD YOU SEE VERSUS THE DATA YOU DON'T

The Cole Fund Does It Again!
$1,000 invested in 1984 would have more than tripled!
Cole: The inflation killer!

	S&P 500	Allen Fund	Brown Fund	Cole Fund
1984	1.4%	−8.3%	−2.7%	6.2%
1985	26.3%	30.2%	25.5%	41.8%
1986	14.6%	15.3%	12.3%	14.0%
1987	2.0%	−2.5%	3.7%	1.3%
1988	12.4%	16.6%	10.6%	10.3%
1989	27.3%	18.4%	23.3%	15.2%
1990	−6.6%	−8.2%	−5.3%	2.5%
1991	26.3%	31.6%	24.7%	18.2%
1992	4.5%	9.3%	8.8%	7.1%
1993	7.1%	6.6%	4.4%	5.2%
10 Yrs	11.0%	10.1%	10.0%	11.7%
5 Yrs	10.9%	10.8%	10.6%	9.5%
3 Yrs	12.2%	15.3%	12.3%	10.0%

performance appear even more powerful, the results are shown in contrast to inflation rather than the S&P 500 benchmark, which it barely surpassed. An investor coming across the Cole Fund ad would likely have reacted favorably to its performance claims. So, be alert. There's often much more than meets the eye in mutual fund performance claims.

Red Flag #4: You can't necessarily accept a fund's rankings at face value.

This problem flows logically from Red Flag #1. If you can't count on the risk categories to be consistent in comparing apples to apples, then the performance rankings based on them are potentially misleading. Assume that the ABC Fund is classified as an aggressive growth fund by Morningstar while the Lipper analyst, due to using slightly different criteria, puts it in the growth category.

In that event, which is the "correct" classification to use when evaluating the excellence of the ABC Fund's performance? For example, if the fund averaged 19.5% per year over the past five years, was that good? For an aggressive growth fund, it was slightly below average (see table on page 110). Consequently, as far as Morningstar was concerned, the fund didn't perform all that well, and Morningstar's rankings would reflect that.

Meanwhile, Lipper would rank its performance against that of its peers in the growth fund group. On that basis, it was good enough to rank in the top 20% of growth funds. When you're being "graded on the curve," it's good to be in a class of underachievers. This is a mighty important matter to the folks at the ABC Fund. It determines whether they can advertise their fund as an excellent performer or an also-ran. Which measurement service's rankings do you believe ABC will refer to in its full-page ads? Lipper's, of course.

In this example, the fund has done nothing wrong. It is merely taking advantage of a difference of opinion between Morningstar and Lipper. There have been instances, however, where funds have been suspected of "gaming" the fund rankings, that is, attempting to have their fund placed in a risk category where its performance would earn it a high ranking relative to the other funds in that group. *Worth* magazine, in its March 1995 issue, explained it this way:

> *Fund managers can accomplish this sleight of hand in part because fund categories are so loosely defined, and because funds are commonly listed under the heading suggested by the vaguely worded investment objectives found in their prospectuses. This allows managers, in effect, to choose the heading under which their funds will be ranked, a cozy arrangement from the not-too-distant time when the whole industry was small and stodgy rather than the cutthroat world of 7,500 or more funds it has become.*

> *Wall Street professionals have suspected for years that gaming was widespread. Until recently, they haven't had much evidence to back them up, but two independent studies now appear to confirm that gaming not only exists, but may be more widespread*

than anyone imagined. Both research efforts concluded that more than half of all mutual funds are misclassified in performance rankings. And more than one out of ten is listed inaccurately enough that investors could be misled about their true nature, according to one study. . . . Many funds that are drastically out of place are spotted by the data gatherers. Morningstar, Lipper, and others work diligently to find badly misclassified funds. Morningstar, for example, changed 205 listings in 1994, Lipper 154.

In spite of these concerns, I'm not ready to throw the baby out with the bath water.

As we saw in chapter 7, mutual funds offer many advantages to the average investor. The answer is not to avoid mutual funds entirely, but rather to learn how to shop for them intelligently. This means you must accept responsibility for getting the information you need and reading it sufficiently well that you understand the risks as well as the rewards. The place to start, even though it has its limitations, is with the fund's prospectus.

Mutual fund prospectuses are usually boring, filled with unfamiliar terms, and set in small print. Although investors are continually admonished to "read the fund prospectus carefully before you invest or send money," I doubt that many do so. If you're among the legions who routinely toss fund prospectuses onto your read-it-when-I-find-the-time stack, you're missing out on some important information the government wants you to have.

Basically, putting your money in a mutual fund is like taking an investment journey, and the prospectus outlines the details of the trip—where it wishes to go in terms of its goal, what strategy it will use to get there, how much risk it will take on the way, and what it will charge you to ride along. Here are some things you should know about prospectuses.

❶ A prospectus is a legal document. That's why it reads so poorly. The fund's attorneys have made sure that it contains only those promises that the fund is fully confident it can keep. As a result, it contains no performance guarantees.

❷ A prospectus has a limited shelf life, usually a little over a year. Aside from the historical data that needs to be updated, there are other items that can change as well: the amount of sales loads (if any); the level of management fees and operating expenses; policies that govern buying (e.g., the minimum required to open an account) and selling your shares (e.g., how frequently you can exchange them for shares in other funds within the same organization and if there's a charge).

❸ A prospectus is for marking in. Don't hesitate to make notes in the margins or mark in some way the items that you don't understand. Then use that as a checklist when taking your questions back to the fund or your broker. Don't leave a concern unaddressed or a doubt unresolved.

❹ Of all the sections in a prospectus, five are of greatest interest. Get your yellow highlighter out—here's how you can find the essentials in ten minutes flat.

◆ **Investment objectives.** This is the section we've been talking about in this chapter. It is supposed to tell you what the fund hopes to accomplish (regardless of what the name of the fund implies). The objective is usually stated in terms of stability (protecting you from loss), growth (buying securities that go up in value), and income (making regular dividend or interest payments to you). Most funds will mention two of these objectives as being primary; because of the risk trade-offs involved, no fund can do a good job on all three at the same time.

◆ **Investment policies.** Here you'll find the strategy the fund will use as it attempts to achieve its objectives. Does it have a value or growth orientation, or prefer small companies over large ones? You'll learn if the fund is *committed* to buying certain kinds of securities ("80% of the fund's assets will be invested in investment grade bonds rated AA or higher"), or merely *permitted* to buy them ("manager may engage in trading exchange-traded covered options").

◆ **Performance and per share data.** This includes a listing of the fund's annual total returns to shareholders over several years, usually in comparison to a benchmark like the S&P 500 index. Look to see if there is a great deal of year-to-year variability (big gains, small gains, and some losses all seemingly mixed together) versus consistent performance. Does the fund have a strong record because of just one or two good years? Also, how consistently has the fund outperformed the benchmark it is being compared with? The table showing up to ten years of financial history is another place to look for consistency, especially in the areas where the fund is supposed to be strong (stability, growth, or income). Caution: even a good long-term record can be misleading if the manager who achieved it is no longer running the fund. Don't assume there's any correlation between the fund's past and your future.

◆ **Summary of fund expenses.** Here's where you'll find a breakdown of the maximum sales loads (if any). Are the sales loads up front, or contingent on how long you own your shares? Do they apply to reinvested dividends as well as your initial deposit? Are there redemption fees to pay? There is also data on the annual operating expenses of the fund. These are the invisible fees charged by every mutual fund that you never see on your monthly statement. They include management fees, 12b-1 fees, and other expenses, and are deducted before the fund's yield or net asset value is quoted. Performance numbers, such as those published in financial magazines, already take operating expenses (but not sales loads) into account.

"How to Exchange Fund Shares Quickly by Mail" by Vicki Mosher. Excerpted from the Sound Mind Investing newsletter. See Briefing 12, page 473.

◆ **How to buy/redeem shares.** This lays out how you buy/sell shares in the fund as well as services offered like reinvestment options, wire transfers, check-writing privileges, etc. The important thing here is to be clear on what you have to do to sell your shares. Can you do it over the phone? How long before you'll get your money? Make sure you understand this thoroughly and have any necessary forms on file with the fund.

The most important paragraph in any prospectus is found on page one. It says,

"These securities have not been approved or disapproved by the Securities and Exchange Commission nor has the commission passed upon the accuracy or adequacy of this prospectus." The SEC doesn't endorse the fund nor the information in the prospectus. It's up to you to ask the right questions.

In addition to the prospectus, you might be able to get additional information from your local library.

Many libraries subscribe to the Morningstar or Value Line fund services. If yours doesn't, you can get reports on individual funds by calling *Morningstar OnDemand* at (800) 876-5005. Reports are available on more than 1,500 funds. The cost is $5 per report, and they will either fax it to you or send it via first class mail.

If this chapter has been discouraging, take heart! Later in this book, I'm going to show you two additional ways to help assure that the funds you buy are suited to your personal needs.

First, in chapter 13 I'm going to introduce you to a special breed of mutual funds called "index" funds that, by their very nature, avoid the red flag traps we've just discussed. In chapter 14, I'll then show you how to assemble them into a portfolio that reflects your current age, goals, and tolerance for risk. And in chapter 15, we'll go out into the marketplace and look at some funds that are suitable for those who are just getting started. You need go no further than this to have a winning long-term strategy.

Second, if you're not convinced that indexing is the way to go, I'll teach you a new way to evaluate stock and bond fund risk that doesn't rely on the standard industry groupings. It's based on what is actually owned in a mutual fund's portfolio, not on what the fund says its objectives are. This is the approach to categorizing risk that I use in my monthly newsletter, and it's all explained in chapters 18 through 22. ◆

CHAPTER PREVIEW

Income Taxes and Your Mutual Fund Investments

I. **Mutual funds are simply conduits through which you invest. The capital gains and losses and dividend and interest income they receive are treated as if they were yours personally.**

   A. Investment companies periodically pay to their shareholders the interest and dividends the funds receive on their investments.

   B. Investment companies periodically pay to their shareholders the capital gains the funds make when selling their investments.

   C. The date that these distributions are set aside from the fund's assets for payment to shareholders is called the "ex-dividend" date. This is the significant date as far as income taxes are concerned, not the later date on which you receive the distribution check in the mail.

II. **The tax accounting for mutual funds can be confusing, even to veteran investors.**

   A. Buying just prior to a fund distribution does not result in an actual gain, but merely results in incurring an immediate tax liability.

   B. Distributions are taxable in the year they are declared, not in the year they are received by the investor.

   C. There are two kinds of capital gains to keep in mind — those the funds can earn by buying and selling within the fund portfolios, and those investors can earn by selling their fund shares for more than they paid for them.

   D. The IRS recognizes three different methods for computing capital gains on fund shares. If you sell part (rather than all) of your shares in a fund, you can select the one that results in the lowest tax liability.

III. **Timing your selling so as to minimize or postpone your tax liability is a natural inclination; however, it should not supersede the normal common sense disciplines built into your long-term strategy.**

If you're tempted to skip this chapter until next year at tax time, don't do it! The sooner you understand what will be needed to complete next year's 1040 form . . .

. . . the sooner you can begin organizing your thinking and record keeping to make things much easier on yourself. Also, you can avoid making a costly year-end investment that will unnecessarily raise your taxes (see common misconceptions one and two on pages 121-122). I promise to do my best at making this as clear as possible — but nobody can keep it from being boring! So go for a cup of coffee if need be, and get ready to make some good notes in the margins.

Mutual funds are among the most flexible of all investments from a tax standpoint. That's the good news. Calculating your taxable income, however, is made more complicated by a maze of rules and exceptions to the rules at both the federal and state levels. That's the bad news. Because tax laws vary so widely from state to state, I can't proceed very far into planning tax strategies; there are just too many possible scenarios. What I will do is give you a basic foundation so that you can read and plan intelligently in relation to your particular tax bracket and state of residence.

The first major point I want to emphasize is that mutual funds are simply conduits through which individuals invest in securities.

In the process of investing, mutual funds incur capital gains and losses and receive dividend and interest income on their investments. From a tax point of view, all of this is done in behalf of their shareholders. *It's as if you owned all the investments outright, and the gains and losses that result are all your personal gains and losses.* There are three ways mutual funds can generate profits in your behalf:

❶ They invest in stocks that pay dividends. Mutual funds collect the dividends and pay them out to you periodically.

❷ They invest in bonds or short-term debt securities that pay interest. They collect the interest and pay it out to you periodically.

❸ They sell one of their investments for more than they paid for it, thereby making a capital gain. They keep track of these gains (and offset them against any capital losses) and pay them out to you periodically, usually annually. If they end up with more capital losses than gains, they carry the losses over to the next year; you would receive no payment for the year just ending.

All of these payments to you, regardless of the source — whether dividends, interest, or capital gains — are called "distributions." The fund decides whether to make these periodic distribution payments monthly, quarterly, semi-annually, or annually.

A fund goes through a two-step process in making distributions. First, it "declares" the amount of the distribution . . .

. . . it intends to make, and sets aside the appropriate amount of cash that will be needed to write you a check. Let's say your fund declares a 25¢ per share distribution, and that there are one million shares owned by investors. This means the fund will be paying out a total of $250,000 to its shareholders at this time. Once the money is earmarked for distribution in this way, the fund no longer counts the $250,000 when it does its daily bookkeeping (see page 87). This has the effect of suddenly lowering the net asset value of the fund—one day the money was being counted as part of the fund, and the next day, the day of the declaration, it wasn't. To indicate to investors that the net asset value is lower than it otherwise would be because of the distribution, an "x" appears next to the name of the fund in the daily newspaper listings (see page 101). The date this happens is called the "ex-dividend" date, *and it is the significant date as far as your taxes are concerned.*

The second step of the distribution process is when the fund actually mails your check to you. It can be anywhere from a few days to a month later. This is called the "payment date" and is important only to you (and the other shareholders) because that's when you finally receive the cash that has been promised. The payment date has no significance when computing your taxable income.

Let's look at some of the common misconceptions that investors have about fund taxation.

Misconception #1: "It's a good idea to invest in a mutual fund just before one of its periodic distributions."

Actually, it's a bad idea because it will create an immediate tax liability for you. There is no actual profit in owning a fund on the day it goes ex-dividend because the amount the shareholders are to receive is deducted from the value of the fund that same day (see note at right). If an investor buys a fund today and the fund declares a distribution tomorrow, *the investor owes tax on the amount of the distribution.* This may seem unfair, as the profits were earned by the fund long before the new investor made his purchase. Still, someone has to pay the tax on those profits, and it falls to the "shareholders of record" *at the time of the distribution* to do so.

When a fund makes a distribution, the price of its shares falls by the exact amount of the distribution. This has the effect of reducing the investor's capital gains tax liability in

HOW DISTRIBUTIONS ARE REPORTED IN THE NEWSPAPER

Monday's closing price for the XYZ Fund was $6.00 per share, up 4¢ from Friday's closing price. On Tuesday, the net asset value fell 10¢ a share due to a slight drop in the stock market that day. The fund also declared a 60¢ per share distribution on Tuesday. The listing for XYZ in the newspaper for those two days would look like this:

Monday	XYZ Fund	6.00	+ .04
Tuesday	XYZ Fund	x5.30	– .70

the future. Most funds make distributions at roughly the same time each year, and most funds announce distributions in advance. This presents an opportunity for savings. Just before purchasing shares of any mutual fund, call the fund and ask if a distribution will be made soon. If a distribution is scheduled within a few days, you might want to wait and purchase your shares the day after the distribution to avoid its tax impact.

Misconception #2: "If I don't receive my distribution check until after the end of the year, I don't have to pay taxes on it this year."

From a tax standpoint, distributions fall into two classifications: (1) "capital gain" as described above, and (2) "income," a mutual fund's dividend and interest earnings, less its management fees and other operating expenses. Short- and long-term capital gains, interest, and dividend income distributions are all currently being taxed at identical rates.

Your tax liability is based on the ex-dividend date, not the payment date. If the ex-dividend date falls in the current year, your tax liability will also. The fund is required to prepare IRS Form 1099-DIV (similar to the one you receive from your employer) for everyone who was a shareholder on any day a distribution was declared. You will receive a copy (and so will the government), which lists the various distributions you will be taxed on, and where to report them on your form 1040 return.

Misconception #3: "As long as I don't sell any of my mutual fund shares, I can't have any capital gains."

This seems logical. Assume you buy fund shares at $10 and still own them at the end of the year. Since it is too soon to know whether you will receive more or less than $10 per share when you sell them, it would seem to follow that it is also too soon to know whether you'll have a capital gain to pay taxes on. What this overlooks is that the mutual fund *itself*, within its portfolio, is continually buying and selling securities. Each time it sells one, it has another capital gain or loss. Since the tax law considers all of this as being done in your behalf, you participate in your fair share of that gain or loss *whenever a fund declares a capital gain distribution.*

When you eventually do redeem (sell) your fund shares, any capital gain or loss from the original purchase must be reported on Schedule D of your form 1040 tax return just like any other investment. One easy way to put off paying this kind of capital gains tax is simply to avoid selling mutual funds for gain just before the end of the year. If you sell in December, then taxes will have to be paid by April 15, just three and a half months later. Instead, you might wait to sell out of a profitable position until the first week of January. The tax on such gains would then not be owed until April of the following year. This postpones paying your tax liability more than fifteen months. By the same token, a good time to sell a fund if you have a loss is in December, as the loss will be deductible on the tax return filed only a few months later.

Misconception #4: "To calculate my capital gain from selling my fund shares, I subtract the amount I paid for them from the proceeds I received when selling them."

This is only true in the simplest instance—where you bought all your shares at the same time, received no distributions while you owned them, and sold them all at the same time. In that case, it's pretty straightforward as described. However, if you either receive distributions, acquire your shares over time (for example, through dollar-cost-averaging or reinvesting your dividends), or sell only part of your holdings, there is more work to be done. Let's look at the most common situations.

◆ **When you receive a distribution.** Keep in mind: *you aren't really gaining anything when you receive a distribution because the amount of the distribution is deducted from the value of your shares.* For example, assume you buy 100 fund shares at $8.00 each. Your total cost is $800. The value grows to $12.00 per share, and your investment becomes worth $1,200 (100 shares multiplied by $12.00 each). If a $1.00 per share dividend distribution is declared, you will receive a check for $100 (100 shares multiplied by $1.00). However, on the ex-dividend date, the value of your shares immediately drops to $11.00 each because $1.00 per share has been taken out of the fund's asset pool to be mailed to shareholders. You haven't gained; you still have $1,200 in value—$1,100 in fund shares (100 shares multiplied by $11.00) and $100 cash. The fund has merely "robbed Peter to pay Paul."

The tax consequences work like this. If you had sold your shares *before* the ex-dividend date, you would have a $400 capital gain ($1,200 proceeds minus $800 cost). If you sell your shares *after* the ex-dividend date, you would have a $300 capital gain ($1,100 proceeds minus $800 cost) *plus* $100 in dividend income; thus, you still have total taxable income of $400. The ex-dividend date didn't change the amount of your profit; it only changed the tax nature of your profit.

◆ **When you reinvest your dividends.** If you routinely have your fund distributions reinvested in more shares, you must be careful to avoid double taxation. When calculating your tax liability, you must add the cost of the additional shares purchased with your dividends to the amount originally invested in the fund. This will raise your tax "basis" in the fund shares you've acquired. In this way, you'll avoid being taxed twice—initially on the dividends and again later as a capital gain when the fund shares are sold.

For example, let's take our previous example and make a change: Instead of receiving the $100 distribution in cash, you instruct your fund to reinvest it in more shares. On the ex-dividend date, the value of the fund dropped to $11.00 per share. At that price, the $100 would purchase an additional 9.09 shares, bringing your total shares to 109.09. The $100 distribution must be reported on that year's federal 1040, and taxes must be paid. Later, you sell all of your shares for $11.00 each, which brings in proceeds of $1,200 (109.09 shares multiplied by $11.00 per share). Will you be taxed on your $400 gain? No. The total cost of the shares (for capital gains purposes) is the initial $800 *plus the $100 on which tax has already been paid,* making a total of $900. Thus, the taxable capital gain from the $1,200 proceeds received the following year is only $300 rather than $400.

◆ **When you dollar-cost-average.** If you routinely add to your fund holdings through frequent new purchases, you should be especially careful to keep careful records of the dates, amounts invested, and number of shares purchased. That's because you will later need detailed and accurate information concerning your many different purchases in order to compute any capital gains that might result when your shares are eventually sold. This is all the more true if you later sell part (rather than all) of your shares. See the chart at left for an explanation of the choices you have under the tax laws. Once you select one of these methods for a particular fund, you must use it every time you sell shares from that fund.

HOW TO COMPUTE YOUR TAXABLE GAINS AND LOSSES

	Using the First-In, First-Out Method	Using the Average Cost Method	Using the Specific Cost Method
How to Do It	Unless you say otherwise, the IRS assumes that you sell your shares in the same order as you bought them.	You calculate the average price paid for all the shares in the fund that you own. Divide the total dollars invested (including any distributions reinvested) by the number of shares you own.	Send the fund written instructions saying that you are selling the shares purchased on such-and-such a day at such-and-such a price.
Advantages and Disadvantages	If your early purchases were at higher levels, this method will give you tax losses; if your early purchases were at lower levels, this method will create taxable gains.	Could either raise or lower your taxes depending on how the other alternatives work out.	A little more trouble, but gives you the most flexibility for managing your tax liability from year to year.

Under the general heading of "other assorted things you should know" are the following items.

◆ The IRS is available year-round to answer your tax questions—call (800) 829-1040. It also offers free materials on various topics—call (800) 829-3676 to request IRS forms and publications. You can begin with publication 910, which is an explanation of all the *other* publications that are available.

◆ The best tax advantage available for mutual fund investing is to carry out as much of your long-term program as possible within an IRA or other tax-deferred type of account.

◆ Whenever you "switch" between funds at the same mutual fund organization, it's the same as selling your shares in the fund you are leaving. Calling it a switch doesn't change the fact that you are selling one fund and buying another. Unless you are moving out of a money market fund, every switch has tax consequences.

◆ Using the special checks your bond fund might supply also has tax consequences. That's because the fund sells some of your shares in order to honor your check. As a result, you'll have a taxable gain or loss on the shares sold. This is not the case with money market funds because they always maintain a level $1.00 per share value.

◆ Investors in tax-free funds don't completely avoid dealing with tax considerations. For example, capital gains distributions from the funds and capital gains you might make on the sale of your shares are taxable just like with any other security. Tax-free income is generally free from federal tax, but not all the dividends you receive will necessarily be exempt from state tax; check with your fund if in need of clarification. Also, special rules apply under a variety of situations (for example, investors who receive tax-exempt income from shares in a municipal bond fund that was held for six months or less and sold for a loss). Request IRS Publication 564 for more information on the taxation of mutual funds.

◆ If you invest in international stock and bond funds, mutual funds are to notify you if you are entitled to claim a tax deduction for taxes that the fund paid to a foreign country. For more information, request IRS Publication 514.

◆ The tax documentation you will receive from your mutual fund each year includes: confirmation statements telling you the date, price, and number of shares transacted when buying and selling fund shares; form 1099-B reports the proceeds from selling shares during the year (it can be used to help you compute your capital gains or losses); and form 1099-DIV reports the details of dividend and capital gain distributions for which you owe taxes.

I felt it was important to equip you with some basic tax-planning knowledge. My recommendation, however, is that you not buy or sell primarily for tax reasons.

Although I acknowledge that it is legitimate to minimize one's tax liability by using any of the applicable strategies mentioned here, a preoccupation with taxes can be counterproductive. Sometimes a few days in the market can make a big difference as to the price you pay or receive for your shares. Don't let tax considerations sidetrack you from following the disciplines you will be building into your long-term strategy. ♦

Investing on Your Own

A Very Simple Strategy That You Can Tailor to Your Own Long-Term Goals and Personal Investing Temperament

"I'm sorry, but Mr. Hutton left very strict orders he couldn't take any drop-in appointments today."

11

CHAPTER PREVIEW

The Basics of Bonds

I. **Bonds are merely long-term IOUs.**

   A. They are a promise to repay the amount borrowed at a specific time in the future.

   B. They pay a fixed rate of interest that doesn't vary over the life of the bond.

   C. They carry higher risks than money market funds due to their longer average maturities.

II. **There are two major risks associated with investing in bonds, both of which can be neutralized.**

   A. The first risk is that you might lend to someone who is not creditworthy. This risk is neutralized by loaning only to the federal government and financially strong corporations. Investing in a bond mutual fund adds safety through diversification.

   B. The second risk is that you could get locked into a below-market rate of return. This risk can be neutralized by loaning only for the short term.

      1. The advantage of longer maturities is that you receive a higher yield.

      2. The disadvantages of longer maturities are that the value of your bonds can go down due to either their quality rating being lowered or rising interest rates.

      3. The direction of interest rates is important in making bond investing decisions, but even the experts have proven inept in predicting their future direction.

III. **It's important to understand the difference between "yield" and "total return."**

   A. The yield is the amount you receive back on your investment over the course of a year, but expressed in percentage terms rather than dollar terms. This is what we commonly think of as "interest."

   B. The total return includes the yield, but also takes into account how much the value of your investment went up or down while you owned it. With investments that fluctuate in value, you won't know your total return *for sure* until you convert your investment back into dollars.

   C. You should pay careful attention to the total return, not just the yield.

IV. **The primary advantage of lending your money is the relative safety it offers.**

Bonds
are IOUs in the form of
investment certificates.

Issuer
is the business or government
that is borrowing the money.

Maturity Date
is the time at which the borrower
is due to pay the bond in full.

Coupon Rate
is the percent of interest stated
on the bond that the borrower
agrees to pay to investors. It
stays fixed throughout the life of
the bond.

Par
is the face value on the bond,
usually $1,000. This is what
investors are to receive when the
bond matures.

Deep Discount Bonds
are those that can be purchased
far below their par value. This
means investors receive, in
addition to the regular interest
payments, the added benefit of
getting back much more at
maturity than they paid for the
bond originally. This extra
enticement is needed either
because the coupon rate being
paid is below the current
levels available to investors or
because the issuer's credit rating
has slipped and full payment at
maturity is in doubt.

Average Maturity
is the average number of years it
will take for all the bonds in the
portfolio to mature. The longer
the average maturity date, the
greater the risk in the portfolio.

America's largest banks and corporations (not to mention our local, state, and federal governments) need your help . . .

. . . they'd like to borrow some money from you. For a few months or, if you're willing, for several decades. To make sure you get the message, their ads are everywhere. The government promotes safety of principal and has created certain kinds of bonds with special tax advantages. Banks and S&Ls want your deposits and want you to know your money is safe with them because it's "insured." Bond funds tantalize you with suggestions of still higher yields, although in their small print they remind you that "the value of your shares will fluctuate." And of course, insurance companies promote the tax-deferred advantages of their annuities. You're in the driver's seat. To all these institutions, you're a Very Important Person.

Have you ever thought of renting out your money for a while? Chances are, you do it all the time. You probably think of it as buying a certificate of deposit (or Treasury bill, bond, or fixed annuity), but actually, you're making a loan. The "rent" you're being paid is called interest. In the financial markets, investors with extra money (lenders) rent it out to others who are in need of money (borrowers). The borrowers give their IOUs to the lenders.

Bonds are basically IOUs.

They are a promise to repay the amount borrowed at a specified time in the future. The date on which the bonds will be paid off is called the maturity date and may be set at a few years out or as many as (believe it or not) one hundred years away. At that time, the holder of the bond gets back its full face value (called par value). In order to make bonds affordable to a larger investing public, they are usually issued in $1,000 denominations.

Bonds promise to pay a fixed rate of interest (called the coupon rate) until they mature (are paid off). *This rate doesn't vary over the life of the bond.* Remember that. Once the rate is set, it's permanent. That's why bonds are referred to as "fixed income" investments. As we'll soon see, it's the unchanging nature of the interest rate that causes bonds to go up and down in value.

Why buy bonds?

If you want to protect your principal and set up a steady stream of income, then bonds, rather than stocks, are the answer. Current income is traditionally the most important reason people invest in bonds, which usually generate greater current returns than CDs, money market funds, or stocks.

They also can offer greater security than most common stocks since an issuer of a bond will do everything possible to meet its bond obligations. (Even Donald Trump accepted a humbling at the hands of his banks in order to gain the money necessary to meet his bonds' interest payments.)

The interest owed on a corporate bond must be paid to bondholders before any dividends can be paid to the stockholders of the company. And it's payable before federal, state, and city taxes. Being first in line helps make the investment safer.

Bond funds carry higher risks than money market funds. The primary difference has to do with . . .

. . . the *average maturity* of the portfolio. Bond funds diversify among a great many individual bond issues, each of which has its own maturity date. By adding up the length of time until each issue matures and then dividing by the total number of bonds owned, you learn the average amount of time needed for the entire portfolio to be paid off.

While time is passing, many things can happen to interest rates or to the bond issuer (whoever borrowed the money from investors in the first place) to affect the value of the bonds. The more distant the maturity date, the more time for things to potentially go wrong. That's why bond funds with longer maturities carry more risk than ones with shorter maturities.

THE DIFFERENCE BETWEEN MONEY MARKET FUNDS AND BOND FUNDS

Money Market Funds	Bond Funds
Yields are relatively low	Yields are higher
Interest is paid by giving you more shares	Interest is paid in cash
Shares are set at a constant $1 per share	Shares fluctuate in value daily
Maturities are measured in days	Maturities are measured in years
Guaranteed to always show a gain	Possible to lose money

Any drop in the market value of the bonds is offset against the fund's interest income. If these losses are greater than the interest received by the fund, the price of the bond fund drops that day. *That's why it's possible for investors in a bond fund to get back less than they put in!*

Let's learn how bond values fluctuate by working through an example. Assume XYZ Inc. wants to borrow $200 million for advanced research . . .

. . . and doesn't want to have to pay the loan back for thirty years. Rather than ask its banks, which generally don't like to loan their money out for such long periods of time, the company decides to issue some bonds.

Let's say that XYZ agrees to pay a coupon rate of 9% annual interest. Bond traders would call these bonds the "XYZ nines of 2026." (XYZ will pay 9% interest and repay the loan in 2026.) No matter what happens to interest rates

Current Yield
is the rate of return that the investor receives per year as a percent of the amount invested.

WHAT BOND RATINGS MEAN

Standard & Poor's and Moody's are the two leading credit rating agencies. They use slightly different rating terminology. S&P is shown on the left (AAA) and Moody's on the right (Aaa). Credit ratings attempt to alert bondholders to the risks of not being paid the interest when due or the principal upon maturity. The lower the rating, the higher the risk *and* the higher the interest rate the borrower will have to pay to attract investors.

AAA / Aaa
Highest rating; extremely strong capacity to pay interest and repay principal; smallest degree of investment risk.

AA / Aa
High quality; very strong capacity to pay interest and repay principal; safety margins are strong, but not quite as exemplary as the AAA level.

A / A
Upper-medium grade; strong capacity to pay interest and repay principal; good debt-service coverage, although vulnerable to cyclical trends.

BBB / Baa
Medium grade; adequate capacity to pay interest and repay principal; however, no room for error. Any further deterioration and these will no longer be considered investment grade bonds.

BB / Ba
Speculative grade; only moderately secure.

B / B
Low grade; lacking characteristics of a desirable investment.

CCC / Caa
Very speculative, with significant risk. May be in danger of default.

CC / Ca
Highly speculative, often in default or otherwise flawed; major risk.

C / C
No interest is being paid, or in default with poor prospects of improvement.

over the next thirty years, XYZ is obligated to pay investors 9% per year on these bonds. No more. No less.

Let's say that you decide to purchase one of these new XYZ bonds. This means that you will receive $90 per year from XYZ on your $1,000 investment (9% times $1,000). Since bond interest is usually paid twice a year, you would receive two checks for $45 spread six months apart.

The simplest transaction would work this way. Assume that when XYZ first sells its bonds (through selected stock brokerage firms), you buy one of these brand-new bonds at par value. In effect, you loan XYZ $1,000. You collect $90 interest every year for thirty years. It doesn't matter how high or how low interest rates might move during this period, you're still going to get $90 a year because that was "the deal" that you and XYZ agreed to. Finally, in 2026, XYZ pays you back your $1,000. You made no gain on the value of the bond itself; your profit came solely from the steady stream of fixed income you received over the thirty years.

There are two major risks to watch out for in the world of lending. The first is that you might not get all your money back.

The pros call it the "credit risk" because you're depending on the creditworthiness of the borrower. You're taking the risk that the issuer of the bond might go into default. This means the borrower is not able to keep up its interest payments or even pay off the bonds when they mature. This is the worst-case scenario that faces all bond investors.

To help evaluate this risk, ratings are available that help determine how safe the bonds are as an investment. Standard & Poor's and Moody's are the two companies best known for this. There are nine possible ratings a bond can receive (see margin notes). Most bond investors limit their selections to bonds given one of the top four ratings. As you might expect, the lower the quality, the higher rate of interest investors demand to reward them for accepting the increased risk of default.

By definition, all other borrowers are less creditworthy than the U.S. government (which is still the world's most creditworthy borrower despite the damage done by the reckless and irresponsible deficit spending of Congress in recent years). Therefore, borrowers who are in competition with the federal government for your money *must* pay you more in order to give you an incentive to lend to them instead of Uncle Sam. That's why U.S. Treasury bills establish the floor for interest rates. Other rates are higher than the T-bill rate depending on how creditworthy the borrower is.

If XYZ gets into trouble due to poor management and earnings, its ability to pay off its bond debts . . .

. . . may come into question. Assume its quality rating is lowered from AAA to A, and that shortly thereafter you need to sell your XYZ bond to meet an unexpected expense. A buyer of your bond will now want a greater potential profit to reward him for the possibly greater risk of default. As a practical matter, it may seem to be a very minor increase in risk, but the buyer will want compensation nevertheless.

But remember, the interest that XYZ pays on these bonds is fixed at $90 per year and can't be changed. The only way anyone buying your bond can improve his profit potential is *if you will lower the price of your bond*. Then, in addition to the interest received from XYZ, the buyer will also reap a profit when he ultimately collects $1,000 (if all goes well) for a bond he bought from you for only, say, $800.

Thus, as the quality rating of a bond falls, sellers must lower their asking prices in order to make the bond attractive to buyers. Always remember that a bond can become completely worthless if the issuer gets into financial difficulty and defaults.

How can you minimize the credit risk? One way to eliminate it altogether is to stick solely with U.S. Treasuries. The drawback, however, is that because U.S. government bonds are widely regarded as the world's most creditworthy investments, the interest rates they pay investors are lower than those of corporate bonds. The most common way to minimize the credit risk is to add safety through diversification. Spread your holdings out among many different bond issues. That's where bond funds (which we'll discuss in detail in chapter 19) can play a helpful role.

The second major risk facing bondholders, and the one that is the greater of the two, is that you could get locked into a below-market rate of return.

The pros call this the "interest-rate risk." It's the same dilemma you face when trying to decide how long you should tie up your money in a bank CD, but it has even greater significance when investing in bonds. If you invest in a two-year CD when it turns out that a six-month one would have been better, you're only missing out on better rates for eighteen months. Try making that eighteen *years,* and you get an idea of how painful it can be when holding long-term bonds during a period of rising interest rates.

A fear of inflation leads to rising long-term interest rates. Just for the moment, assume that you're back in 1980 and inflation is running at 12% per year. Now ask yourself this question: Would you be willing to pay full price for a thirty-year, $1,000 bond with an 9% coupon rate? Not likely. The bond would only be paying you $90 in interest per year at a time when you need $120 just to keep up with inflation. You'd be agreeing to a deal that would guarantee you a loss of purchasing power of $30 each year. Eventually, you'd get your $1,000 back, but it wouldn't buy nearly as much then as it does now.

But what if the seller would lower the price of the bond so you could buy that bond at a big discount? If you only had to pay $750 for a $1,000 bond, it might make economic sense. The $90 interest per year—remember, the coupon rate stays fixed throughout the life of the bond—would represent a 12% return ($90 received in interest divided by the $750 invested). Now, at least you're even with inflation. Plus, when the bond matures thirty years down the road, you get a full $1,000 back for your $750. That's 33% more than you paid for it.

So you can see that high inflation (or even the fear of high inflation) causes bond buyers to demand a higher return on their money in order to protect their purchasing power. And in order to create that higher return, bond sellers must lower their asking prices. That's why the bond market usually goes down when any news comes out that could reasonably be interpreted as leading to higher consumer prices.

Here's how this affects your XYZ bond. Although you originally intended . . .

. . . to hold onto your XYZ bond for the full thirty years, real life is rarely quite that simple. Very few investors hold onto their bonds for so long a period of time. Let's say that you decide to sell your XYZ bond and use the money for a really worthwhile purpose—like buying tickets to the Final Four basketball championship. You want your money back *now*, not in 2026.

Where do you sell it? In the bond market where older bonds (as opposed to new ones just being issued) are traded. Your stockbroker can handle it for you. Assuming that XYZ is still in tip-top financial condition with a AAA credit rating, you might expect to get all of your $1,000 back. Well, maybe you will, and maybe you won't. The big question is: *what is the rate of interest being paid by companies that are now issuing new bonds?*

If the rate of interest being paid on new bonds is higher than what your bond pays, you've got a problem. Assume that interest rates have gone up since you bought your XYZ bond, and that new bonds of comparable quality are now paying 11%. Why would any investor want to buy your old XYZ bond that will pay him just $90 per year in interest when he can buy a new one that will pay $110? Obviously, if both bonds cost him the same price, he wouldn't. So, to sell your bond you will have to reduce your asking price below $1,000 to be competitive and attract buyers.

On the other hand, if interest rates have *fallen*, to let's say 8%, then the shoe is on the other foot. Your old bond that pays $90 per year looks pretty attractive compared to new ones that pay only $80. This means you can sell it for a premium, meaning more than the $1,000 par value you paid.

"How the Federal Reserve Affects Interest Rates and Bond Prices" by Austin Pryor. Excerpted from the Sound Mind Investing newsletter. See Briefing 14, page 475.

Here's the lesson: anytime you sell a bond before its maturity date, it will either be worth less than you paid for it (because interest rates have gone up since you bought it) or worth more than you paid for it (because interest rates have gone down since you bought it).

That's why it's possible to lose money even with investments like U.S. Treasury bonds (see page 140). They're safe from default, but nobody can protect you against rising interest rates.

Of course, if you hold onto your XYZ bond until it matures in 2026, it will be worth $1,000. At that time, XYZ will repay the par value to whoever owns its bonds. The closer

NEW YORK EXCHANGE BONDS

Surprise! Did you know you can buy bonds on the New York and American Stock Exchanges? These are bonds that were issued in the past and are now being bought and sold in what's called the "secondary" market (the primary market is when new bonds are sold to investors when they are first issued). The secondary market is where you go to sell a bond you bought when it first came out, but then changed your mind and decided you didn't want to hold onto for twenty years after all. Your broker, who is a member of the Exchange, can sell it for you there just like stocks.

Name
is the company that borrowed the money initially and is (1) responsible for paying the interest regularly and (2) paying the amount owed on the bond when it matures.

Maturity Date
is the year when the bond matures. Only the last two digits are shown. This Borden bond issue would be known as the "eight and three-eighths of sixteen" and would mature in 2016.

Coupon Rate
is the interest the borrower pays to the bondholder. It stays constant throughout the life of the bond. Since bonds usually come in $1,000 denominations, this DuPont bond pays $84.50 per year interest (8.45% x $1,000).

Bonds		Cur Yld	Vol	Close	Net Chg
AldSig 9 7/8	97	9.2	21	107 3/4	– 3/8
ATT 5 5/8	95	5.7	145	99 1/2	+ 1/8
Amoco 7 7/8	96	7.6	15	103 1/8	– 3/4
Banka 8 7/8	05	8.7	55	102 1/4	+ 1/4
BellPa 7 1/8	12	7.7	43	92 1/2	+ 1/8
BethSt 8.45s	05	9.3	73	90 3/8	+ 3/8
Bordn 8 3/8	16	8.4	33	100	– 1 1/2
Chiquta 11 7/8	03	11.3	98	105 3/8	– 1/2
ChryF 9.30s	94	9.2	175	100 5/8	+ 1/8
Chrysir 8s	98	8.4	9	94 7/8	+ 3/4
Citicp 8.45s	07	8.6	29	98 1/4	+ 1/4
CmwE 7 5/8	03F	7.8	4	98	+ 7/8
DetEd 9.15s	00	9.0	6	101 1/2	– 1 1/2
duPnt 8.45s	04	8.3	29	102	+ 1/8
Exxon 6s	97	6.2	20	97 1/2	+ 3/8
GMA 7.85s	98	7.8	40	101 0/0	– 3/4

Net Change
is almost always the result of movements in interest rates. As we'll soon see, bond prices and interest rates move in opposite directions. Since most of these changes indicate that bond prices rose, it's reasonable to assume that interest rates fell the previous day.

Volume
is the dollar value (expressed in thousands) of all the bonds of this issue traded yesterday. $145,000 of this AT&T bond traded. The bigger the better, because it means you have lots of trading activity—which is what you want because it will help the market be more efficient and you'll get a better price when buying or selling.

Current Yield
is the number you're interested in as a buyer. It tells what your return would be if you bought the bond at yesterday's closing price of $1,020 for a $1,000 bond. It's computed by dividing your annual interest by the amount you invest ($84.50 divided by $1,020 = 8.28%).

you get to a bond's maturity date, the more the bond's price reflects its full face value. That's why interest rates eventually lose their power to affect the market value of a bond.

The longer you have to wait until maturity, the longer you are vulnerable. How can you shorten the wait (and therefore reduce the risk)? Buy old bonds that were issued many years back and are now only a few years from their maturity. The shorter the maturity, the less volatile a bond's price will be.

Short-term bonds, then, represent a middle ground between the money market and the long-term bond market. They have much less interest-rate risk than long-term bonds and still pay higher yields than money market funds.

Where are interest rates headed? No sense in asking!

Since the direction of interest rates is so critical to bond investors, *The Wall Street Journal* routinely surveys leading economists to get their take on economic matters in general and the direction of interest rates in particular. For investors seeking insights on this important matter, their track record is not a hopeful one.

Since 1981, the *Journal* has been taking a poll of more than three dozen leading economists. They do this twice a year, asking the economists to make predictions as to the direction of the economy, inflation, and interest rates for the coming six to twelve months. An analysis of the economists' track record shows that their projections concerning inflation have been fairly good, their record on the economy is mixed, and their predictions concerning in-

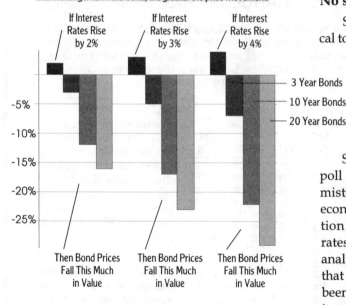

BOND PRICES FALL WHEN INTEREST RATES RISE

This graph shows the various effects on short-term, medium-term, and long-term bond portfolios when interest rates go up. The point is not only that interest rates and bond prices move *opposite* to each other, but also that the longer term the bond, the greater the price movement.

If Interest Rates Rise by 2%

If Interest Rates Rise by 3%

If Interest Rates Rise by 4%

- 3 Year Bonds
- 10 Year Bonds
- 20 Year Bonds

Then Bond Prices Fall This Much in Value

Then Bond Prices Fall This Much in Value

Then Bond Prices Fall This Much in Value

terest rates rather amazing. Amazingly bad. Consider the record:

♦ The consensus opinion as to whether rates would be higher or lower a mere six months later have been wrong 75% of the time.

♦ Out of the thirty-four economists who participated in the surveys most often, only five of them managed to be right *even half the time* concerning the direction of long-term bond yields.

♦ A passive strategy of just holding a basket of medium-term T-bonds would have done a better job for you than following the survey advice, giving you an average annual return of 12.5% versus just 8.8% from following the consensus. Only two of the thirty-four most-frequent participants produced forecasts that would have done better.

In fact, their track record has been so bad on long-term rates that you could actually have done quite well *by doing the opposite of what the experts said* would happen! Let's say that, starting in 1981, if the economists thought interest rates were *going up* over the next six months, you would assume they were wrong and that rates were, in fact, *going down*. So you would invest in long-term bonds (which go up the most as interest rates fall). The first time the consensus said that interest rates were *going down*, you would interpret that to mean that rates would probably be *going up* over the coming six months. The obvious move would be to swap your long-term T-bond fund shares for a money market fund that invested in T-bills. After eleven years, you would have enjoyed impressive average returns of 13.7% per year!

The inability to forecast rates accurately and consistently is well known among investment professionals. A Senior V.P. at Fidelity acknowledges, "Some people can be right for short periods of time, but the track record of most institutional investors has not been very good." The former chairman of the nation's largest bank admits, "We lost our teeth trying to guess rates at the bank. . . . You have to treat these forecasts with a large saltshaker." And John Kenneth Galbraith, renowned Harvard economist and author, has said, "There are only two kinds of interest rate forecasters: those who don't know where rates are going, and those who don't know that they don't know."

WHEN IT COMES TO INTEREST RATES, EVEN THE EXPERTS DON'T KNOW WHAT'S COMING NEXT

(Graph Shows Yields of Ninety-Day T-bills)

Wall Street Journal reports that the winner of its semi-annual interest rate forecasting survey, which included forty economists, was Raul Gonzalez, a thirty-one-year-old doorman at a Manhattan apartment building.

In early 1991, Hulbert Digest announces that the bond newsletters that have the best track records at predicting rates are mostly in agreement — the decline in interest rates is now over. The "experts" were two years early.

The Hulbert Financial Digest reports that none of the bond investment newsletters it monitors was able to outperform the bond market during the previous five years. A VP of Prudential observes: "Timing the bond market is a game many people play but few win."

So don't ascribe unwarranted powers of foreknowledge to economists or market professionals (this writer included). Just because people study money all the time doesn't mean they have special insight into what's coming next.

What kinds of bonds should you buy, since you don't know where interest rates are headed?

First, remember Galbraith's observation and be thankful that at least you know you don't know! Second, make your mistakes on the side of caution. To minimize risk, don't go further out than about ten years — the reward just isn't worth the risk. According to the respected Ibbotson Associates research firm, since the late 1920s, ten-year Treasuries have averaged 5.1% per year (with just six losing years) versus 4.8% for the higher risk thirty-year bonds (which had eighteen losing years). Another study indicated that nine out of ten years, the yield on a ten-year Treasury is equal to 85%-95% that of a thirty-year bond but with just 60% of the risk.

In chapter 13, I'll show you a middle-of-the-road approach you can use which doesn't require that you do the impossible—consistently guess the coming direction of interest rates.

It's important that you understand what "yield" means and how it's different from "gain" and "total return."

Interest
is the return you get from lending-type investments, such as CDs and bonds.

These terms may sound like they're saying the same thing, but they're not. When evaluating whether an investment has been successful, there are two questions to be addressed. First, how much income from your investment did you receive while you were waiting to get it back? And second, did you get back more than you put in, less than you put in, or the same as you put in?

Dividends
are the returns you get from your ownership in a business, such as from stock shares.

The income you received while your money was tied up is called the *yield* and is always expressed in annualized terms. If you invest $1,000 in an XYZ bond and it pays $90 every year in interest, it is yielding you 9% per year ($90/$1,000). Now, when you eventually sell your investment, if you receive back more than you paid for it, you have a *capital gain*. Let's say your $1,000 investment is sold after three years for $1,300, giving you a $300 gain.

Yield
is the interest or dividends you receive each year as a percentage of an amount you invested.

Both the yield and the gain represent partial returns; only when you combine them do you get the total picture, hence the name *total return*. The total return is usually expressed in annual compounded terms. In our example, you invested $1,000 and received back a total of $1,570 over three years ($270 in dividends plus the $300 gain).

Gain/Loss
is the difference between what you paid for a security and what you got back when it was sold or reached maturity.

To learn what your total return was in annual percentage terms, you ask, "What rate of growth is needed to turn $1,000 into $1,570 in three years?" By using a financial calculator that can perform time-value-of-money computations, you learn that it takes about a 16.3% per year rate of growth to do that. In other words, if you could invest $1,000 at 16.3% for three years, you'd have approximately $1,570 at the end of that time. In the example, you know that part of the growth came from that 9% annual yield. But how did you get from 9% to that 16.3% total return? By selling for a gain and picking up that extra $300. The 9% *yield* that you received as you went along, *plus* the $300 *gain* at the end, made it possible for you to achieve a very nice 16.3% annualized *total return*.

Total Return
is the annualized return taking both the yield and the gain/loss into account.

But what if you had sold at a loss? Say the bond went *down* $300 instead of up $300. That makes the result look quite different. Now you have invested $1,000, and after three years have just $970 ($270 in dividends minus a $300 loss) to show for your efforts. *Your total return is now negative;* while you were collecting your 9% yield with the thought that you were making money, you were actually losing, on average, about 1% per year!

As you can see, the yield tells you only part of the story. Your total return is what you're really interested in . . .

. . . and you can't know that for certain unless you know exactly how much you'll be getting back and exactly when you'll be getting it. Now here's why all this should be understood by savers. Some fixed income investments—such as insured savings accounts, CDs, and money market funds—do not fluctuate in value. You'll *always* be repaid what you put in, plus any interest you earned; there is never a loss of your original capital to worry about. *That means your total return is always a positive number.*

However, there are other fixed income investments that do fluctuate in value day to day. When you eventually sell, you might get back more than you put in or you might get back less. If you get less back, it could even be that you lose more on the sale than you received in interest during the time you owned it. And that means a negative total return!

Look at what happened in the late 1980s. As interest rates fell, the interest paid by CDs and money market funds dropped below what savers had grown accustomed to. In search of higher returns, they saw that some highly publicized bond funds were "yielding" 12% and more. They thought, *Hey, that looks pretty good!* So off they went. When the junk bond market (see chapter 19) crashed, investors found they could be receiving a great yield and still lose money! The average high-yield bond fund fell about 10% in value in 1990. A few dropped more than 20%. Focusing on yield alone carries high risk because the highest yielding funds are the ones with the lower quality ratings or the longest average maturities.

WHO DECIDES WHETHER INTEREST RATES ARE SET HIGH OR LOW?

When I describe rates as "moving up" or being "low," I'm referring to a whole set of interest rates that change every day. Interest rates are charges for the use of money, and they're determined the same way that the prices of meat and vegetables and just about everything else is—by supply and demand.

Changing rates behave similarly . . .	. . . to changing oil prices.
Interest rates can go up either because (1) the Federal Reserve reduces the supply and there's not enough to meet the normal loan demand, or (2) the supply stays the same, but because we have an economic expansion, loan demand from businesses and consumers who want homes, cars, etc., rises. Either (or both) of these will cause rates to rise.	Oil prices can go up either because (1) oil producers (typically OPEC) reduce the supply and there's not enough to meet the demand, or (2) the supply stays the same, but because we have a severe winter, our demand for heating oil rises. Either (or both) of these will cause oil prices to rise.
Interest rates can go down either because (1) the Federal Reserve increases the supply and there's more than enough to meet the demand, or (2) the supply stays the same, but because of a recession, we don't need or want to borrow as much and our demand for money decreases. Either (or both) of these will cause rates to fall.	Oil prices can go down either because (1) OPEC increases the supply and there's more than enough to meet the demand, or (2) the supply stays the same, but because of our energy conservation efforts, we don't use as much and our demand for oil decreases. Either (or both) of these will cause oil prices to fall.
It's the combined interaction of hundreds of millions of people making billions of personal decisions that affects interest rates. Nobody "sets" them—for long—independently of these market forces.	It's the combined interaction of hundreds of millions of people making billions of personal decisions that affects oil prices. Nobody "sets" them—for long—independently of these market forces.

Most investors are surprised to learn that it's possible to lose money in U.S. Treasury securities.

If you buy a Treasury security and hold it until it matures, you can ignore market fluctuations. When the maturity date arrives, the government will pay you the $1,000 face value regardless of how much the bond may have moved up or down in market value in the meanwhile. But as we've seen, anytime you sell a bond before its maturity date, it could be worth less than you paid for it if interest rates have gone up since you bought it. And, the further away from maturity, the greater the loss in value that takes place when rates rise (see page 136). The table below shows what happened to Treasury values during a period of rising interest rates in 1993–1994. The thirty-year bonds, which enjoyed the greatest gains while rates were falling, likewise suffered the greatest losses once the interest rate pendulum began to swing in the other direction. They lost over 14% in value in just five months.

U.S. TREASURY NOTES & BONDS

Years to Maturity	Coupon Rate	Maturity Date	Value 10/15/93	Yield 10/15/93	Value 3/10/94	Yield 3/10/94	Loss in Value
1	4.25%	Oct 1994	$1,008.44	3.35%	$1,001.56	4.00%	−0.7%
3	6.87%	Oct 1996	$1,078.13	4.09%	$1,040.00	5.23%	−3.5%
5	7.12%	Oct 1998	$1,112.19	4.57%	$1,051.25	5.84%	−5.5%
10	5.75%	Aug 2003	$1,044.06	5.16%	$947.19	6.51%	−9.3%
30	6.25%	Aug 2023	$1,065.94	5.78%	$914.38	6.94%	−14.2%

If you invest in Treasuries through a mutual fund rather than buying individual bonds, you have a different risk. The portfolio manager is constantly buying and selling bonds with many different maturities. The fund has an "average" maturity, but not a single date when all the bonds will mature together. When some of the bonds in the portfolio do mature, the money is reinvested in more bonds. As a result, a bond fund never reaches maturity. That means there's no future date when you're guaranteed to receive a certain amount. You can't necessarily count on recouping any losses in value just by holding your shares long enough. The reason you invest in bond funds (as opposed to staying in money market funds) is they can offer higher yields, but the trade-off is that you incur some additional risk.

The primary advantage of *lending* your money (versus equity-type investments) is the relative safety it offers. You *need* never risk losing even a penny of your capital.

Of course, it is possible to lose money when lending it out, but that usually happens because investors are reaching for the higher yields being offered by the higher risk borrowers. You need to gauge the risks when lending, and guard against only two things — loaning money to poor credit risks who don't pay you back, and loaning your money out for too long a period of time (and therefore losing important flexibility to take advantage of new opportunities that might come along). ◆

Stock Market Basics

I. **Stock shares represent part ownership in a business.**

   A. As an owner, you have the right to participate in the future growth of the company.

   B. You will receive dividends if the company decides to distribute money to shareholders rather than retain it for future growth needs.

   C. The other way you can profit is if the company grows and prospers; your ownership stake will grow in value as well.

II. **The stock market is where the buying and selling of part ownerships in businesses takes place.**

   A. Stock market prices rise and fall for the same reasons other prices do: from supply and demand forces that reflect economic conditions.

   B. Stock market "indexes" chart the price movements in the stock market, and are useful for describing what is happening in the market as well as for helping investors measure the relative performance of the investments in their portfolios.

III. **There are two major risks to your capital when you invest in stock shares and become a part owner in a company.**

   A. The first is the risk that the company might fail and your investment be totally lost. This risk can be controlled through prudent selection and diversification.

   B. The second is that the entire market for stocks can be adversely affected by economic conditions that might have nothing to do with your company. This risk can't be avoided but is minimized by holding your shares through a complete economic cycle.

IV. **Major stock market uptrends are called "bull markets" and downtrends are called "bear markets." To avoid losses during bear markets, many investors practice a strategy known as market timing.**

   A. Market timing represents an attempt to move out of stocks near market highs and buy back in near market lows.

   B. Market timing is difficult to execute successfully over the long term and is not recommended for the average investor.

What we call "stocks" are actually pieces of paper that represent ownership in a company.

When corporations desire to raise money from investors for long-term working capital, they have two choices. One, they can borrow it by selling bonds. This approach means that the company will have to make regular interest payments to the bondholders, as well as pay all the money back some day. The investors play the role of lenders. Or two, the company can sell part ownerships in the company by offering *stock*. In that case, the investors play the role of owners. They are usually entitled to voting rights (which allow them to participate in electing the board of directors who oversee the running of the company, to vote on whether to merge with or sell to another company and under what terms, etc.), and they share in any dividends the board of directors may decide to pay out. However, they will not receive any interest payments on their investments (because they are owners, not lenders) and cannot necessarily count on ever getting their investment money back. Their fortunes are tied in with the future success or failure of the company.

When you decide to invest in shares of stock you've actually made a decision to "go into business." Just as with any business owner . . .

. . . you're last in line when it comes to dividing up the money that's (hopefully) pouring in from happy customers. Your company has to pay the suppliers that provide a variety of needed goods and supporting services. It has to buy equipment and then keep it well maintained. It has employees' salaries, related payroll taxes, health insurance, and retirement benefits to support. It needs to carry property, liability, and workman's compensation insurance. It regularly needs financial and legal services and must continually deal with government reporting requirements and other red tape.

Depending on the business, it might also need to invest large sums in product research and development, or massive sums for sales and marketing. And if it has borrowed any money for expansion or seasonal cash flow needs, it must pay the interest in full. Finally, if your company manages to pay all these bills and still has any money left over at year's end, governments at the local, state, and federal level all show up demanding a share of the profits.

All of this happens before you, the owner, receive a penny. Nobody said it would be easy.

Investors buy stock with the hope of profiting by either receiving dividends while they own the stock, or by eventually selling their shares . . .

. . . for more than they paid. Whatever money is remaining at the very end, if any, is called the net profit. What you are hoping for is that (1) there will be

---

Common Stock
is the term used to describe the units of ownership in a corporation.

Initial Public Offering (IPO)
is when a corporation offers to sell its stock to investors for the first time. The proceeds, less what the company owes for the broker's services, go to the company.

Secondary Offering
is when a corporation offers to sell previously issued stock which is held by founders and other insiders. The proceeds, less what is owed for the broker's services, go to the individuals who are selling, not to the company.

Limited Liability
is one of the attractions of stock ownership. It means that shareholders have no financial obligation to assist the company should it be unable to pay its liabilities.

Preferred Stock
is a special class of stock that pays dividends at a promised rate. Holders of preferred stock must receive their dividends before any may be paid to common shareholders. They also take preference over common shareholders in receiving back the par value of the stock in the event the company is liquidated. Preferred stock typically does not carry voting rights.

Par Value
is the face value printed on a security. In the event of a corporate liquidation, preferred shareholders receive preference over common shareholders to the extent of receiving back the par value of their preferred shares.

some net profits every year, and (2) the net profits this year will be greater than the net profits last year. If these two things happen consistently—and despite the odds, they occasionally do—then you have a good chance of prospering along with the company.

For example, you might receive cash payments from the company as it distributes some of its accumulated profits to the owners—that's called dividend income. Or the board of directors might decide it's better to pay little or no dividends for the time being, preferring instead to keep the money to use for the additional expansion of the company. As the company's sales and profits grow over time, the price of its shares will hopefully gain in value as well—that's called capital growth. Dividend income and capital growth are the two primary rewards investors hope to receive in return for the risks they assume when they become shareholders in companies.

Newcomers to stock investing are often confused as to what it is that makes the price of shares go up or down each day. Perhaps you've seen scenes of the stock trading activity at the New York Stock Exchange (NYSE) on the news and wondered what's going on down there. Well, "what's going on" is that thousands of investors worldwide have sent buy and sell orders through their brokers for stocks listed on the NYSE, and they all collide on the floor in a kind of controlled chaos.

Come along, and I'll take you through a typical trade. Let's start by assuming that you own 100 shares of stock in Ford. As a shareholder . . .

. . . you are one of the owners of Ford Motor Company. Perhaps not a major owner, but an owner nevertheless. As a part owner, you share in Ford's profits, if any. When Ford pays its shareholders a dividend, all the owners receive some money in proportion to how much of Ford they own.

As it so happens, there are new people every day who decide they, too, want to own stock in Ford. Perhaps they are portfolio managers who have extra money from investors to put to work and believe that Ford is the best value in the auto industry. Or, perhaps they are people who like the fact that Ford pays an annual dividend of $1.60 per share. If they buy shares for $40 each, that $1.60 represents a yield of 4.0% on their money. For whatever reason, they want to buy shares in Ford.

It is also apparent each day that some of the current part owners of Ford decide they don't want to be part owners anymore. Let's say you're one of them. Perhaps you've decided that foreign imports are going to devastate American car makers, and you don't want to be in the automobile manufacturing business anymore. Or maybe you still like Ford's competitive position in the industry but fear the economy is heading into a recession that will hurt Ford's profits and possibly cause Ford to reduce its $1.60 dividend. Or maybe

Leverage
means owning a larger amount of securities than you can pay for in cash by borrowing the rest. It can greatly magnify gains and losses, and is considered a high-risk strategy.

Short-Selling
is the practice of borrowing shares (from a broker) in a company and selling them at the current price. This is done in the hope the price will fall, allowing you to repay the borrowed shares at a later date with ones repurchased at a lower price.

Portfolio Turnover Rate
indicates the speed at which one's portfolio is replaced with new holdings. A 100% turnover means that trading volume equal to the value of the entire portfolio takes place every year. In short, a high rate means a lot of buying and selling is going on rather than buying and holding the securities for the longer term.

it has nothing to do with Ford or the economy; you just need the money for a down payment on a house, or for college tuition, or something else.

The point is you want to sell your shares in Ford. Now, where do you find all those new buyers I said were out there? For the most part . . .

Stock Exchange
is an organized marketplace where the shares of companies that meet certain criteria with respect to size and shares outstanding are traded among its members. Such shares are said to be "listed" on the exchange.

. . . on the trading floor of the NYSE where people stand around all day buying and selling part ownerships in companies. That's where your stockbroker comes in. All the major brokerage firms are members of the NYSE, and they have employees there whose job it is to carry out your orders.

So, you call your broker and tell him to sell your 100 shares immediately at the best price he can get. The order is sent to a floor worker, and when the market opens at 9:30 EST, he goes to the place on the floor where Ford stock is traded. When he arrives, he encounters workers from other firms who are also carrying customer instructions to sell or buy Ford shares. On this particular morning, let's assume there are many more shares of Ford ready to be sold than there are to be purchased. In other words, the current supply of Ford stock for sale is greater than the demand for Ford stock at the current price. Although Ford last traded the day before at $40, it seems the most any buyer will offer this morning is $39. Since that's the best price available, your representative sells your shares at that price. Soon, "F 39" flashes across stock quotation machines all over the country, recording the fact that 100 shares of Ford (so well-known it is noted by the single-letter symbol F) just changed hands at $39 a share.

Over-the-Counter
is a market where securities are traded between brokers over the phone or through a computer network rather than on the floor of an organized exchange.

Secondary Market
involves the trading of securities on stock exchanges and over-the-counter which takes place after the securities are originally issued. The proceeds from such transactions go to the investors who are selling, not to the companies that originally issued the securities. For example, when Ford stock is traded daily on the New York Stock Exchange, the money paid by buyers goes to the investors who are selling, not to Ford, which received its money when the shares were initially sold in the "primary" market.

Who decided the price of Ford should drop that morning? The free market did — that is, the collective decisions of buyers and sellers (like you) from all over the world acting in their own self-interest made it happen. At the old price of $40, there were more shares of Ford to be sold than there were buyers for them; to attract more buyers, a lower price was necessary.

Throughout the day, every time Ford shares change hands, the number of shares and price will appear on the ticker tape. The price of the very last transaction of the day will appear in the next morning's paper as the "closing price." If that closing price is less than the previous day's closing price, then Ford will be said to have gone down that day.

What does it mean when we say that "the market was up" today?

Ford Motor is just one of more than 5,000 stocks for which daily price quotes are available. In order for the stock market to "go up," do all of them have to go up, or just a majority, or just a few of the important ones?

In a sense, there's no such thing as "the stock market." The term is so broad that it's misleading. It sounds so singular, as if all stocks were moving as one. In fact, they rarely do. Some stocks go soaring to the heights while others are disappearing into bankruptcy. Some represent companies that are larger and more powerful than many countries, whereas others are little more than wishful thinking disguised as businesses.

Asking what the stock market did yesterday is akin to asking what the weather was like yesterday. In some places it was unseasonably warm and others below zero; some places it was wet and others dry. To make sense of the question—and get a meaningful answer—you have to be much more precise: "What was the weather like *in Atlanta* yesterday?"

To help investors speak about the stock market with greater precision, market "averages" (or "indexes") were invented.

Stock indexes attempt to measure changes in value, over time, *of a specific group* of stocks. Some are very broad-based (Wilshire 5000), which means they communicate information in only the most general of terms. Others are more narrow in their focus (Dow Jones Utilities), which makes them more useful for understanding how stocks with specific characteristics are performing. Indexes serve as benchmarks against which you can evaluate the investment performance of the stocks or mutual funds you own, but it's important to use one that is similar in content to your portfolio (to be sure you're comparing "apples to apples").

There are dozens of them listed in *The Wall Street Journal* each day, but let's just look at three you should become familiar with.

◆ **Dow Jones Industrial Average (DJIA).** This is the oldest and most widely quoted of all market indicators. The DJIA is an average of the stock prices of thirty of the nation's strongest blue-chip companies. The value of these companies represents 15%–20% of the total value of all the stocks traded

DIFFERENT INDEXES FOLLOW DIFFERENT GROUPS OF STOCKS

Index	Characteristics	1988	1989	1990	1991	1992	1993	1994	1995
Wilshire 5000	Very broad-based; includes almost entire stock market	13.3%	24.9%	−9.3%	30.3%	6.2%	8.6%	−2.5%	33.4%
Russell 3000	Very broad-based; includes almost entire stock market	13.8%	25.0%	−8.3%	29.6%	6.6%	8.1%	−2.4%	33.6%
Russell 1000	Reflects the price movements of 1,000 large companies	13.1%	25.9%	−7.5%	28.9%	5.9%	7.3%	−2.4%	34.4%
Standard & Poor's 500	Reflects the price movements of 500 large companies	16.5%	31.6%	−3.1%	30.2%	7.6%	7.1%	−1.5%	34.1%
Dow Jones Industrials	Reflects the price movements of 30 large companies	15.8%	31.5%	−0.5%	24.1%	7.3%	13.7%	2.1%	33.5%
Nasdaq Composite	Almost all of the smallest companies	15.4%	19.3%	−17.7%	56.8%	15.5%	14.8%	−3.2%	39.9%
Russell 2000	Most of the smallest companies	22.4%	14.2%	−21.5%	43.7%	16.4%	17.0%	−3.2%	26.2%

This table illustrates how indexes can be useful in understanding where the strength is in the market. In years when the market is strong overall, such as 1988, there is not a really large difference between the various indexes. Most years, however, meaningful differences are observable. Consider 1989 and 1990 when the large companies in the Dow and S&P 500 turned in far better performance numbers than the small companies in the Russell 2000. In 1991, that trend was reversed. And in 1994-1995, their performance was similar once again.

on the New York Stock Exchange. Unfortunately, the DJIA was originally conceived as a "price-weighted" index. This means higher priced stocks have more influence than lower priced ones. For this reason—and the fact that only thirty stocks are included—some analysts consider the Dow the worst of the major indexes. Although the best known, it is actually the least representative of daily market action. This is ironic in light of the stature it enjoys.

◆ **The Standard & Poor's 500 Index (S&P 500).** This market-weighted index is published by Standard & Poor's, another giant financial news and information company. It represents about 80% of the market value of all NYSE-traded stocks. Composed of 500 large companies from all the major sectors of the economy, it is more representative than the DJIA as to what the overall market did on a certain day. As such, it has long been used by investing professionals as the benchmark against which they measure the excellence of their own investment performance results. Further testimony to its perceived accuracy, the U.S. Commerce Department selected this index to represent the stock market in its Index of Leading Economic Indicators.

MARKET-WEIGHTED INDEXES

A stock's total market value—also referred to as its market capitalization—is what it would cost you to buy all the shares outstanding at yesterday's closing price. In an unweighted index, each stock has an equal weight. However, in a market-value weighted index, which most of the leading indexes are, each stock influences the index in proportion to its total market value. In the example below, AT&T accounts for 75% of the movement in the index.

Company	Unweighted Index	Share Price	Total Shares Outstanding	Total Market Value	Market Value Weighted Index
American Telephone	33.3%	$55	1,336 million	$73.5 billion	75.1%
Compaq Computer	33.3%	$88	78 million	$6.9 billion	7.1%
Texaco	33.3%	$67	259 million	$17.4 billion	17.8%
	100.0%			$97.8 billion	100.0%

◆ **Wilshire 5000.** This is the broadest of all the market indexes. If you had to pick one index that most closely represents the behavior of the *entire* U.S. market, this would be the one. It represents the value, in billions of dollars, of all the New York Stock Exchange (NYSE), American Stock Exchange (AMEX), and over-the-counter (Nasdaq) stocks for which quotes are available. The name is outdated because the index, which covered about 5,000 issues when it was first published in 1981, now includes 6,000+ stocks. It represents approximately 99% of the total investable U.S. market. The Wilshire 5000, like most stock indexes, is "market-value weighted."

In our imaginary sale of Ford stock, we saw both of the major risks of owning a business come into play.

First, there's the risk that *the company you own* will fall on hard times. This is called the "business risk." In the example, this was manifested by concerns of sellers about the effects that foreign manufacturers are having on Ford's sales and profits. It could be due to poor management, technological obsolescence, overwhelming competition, a shift in cultural behavior patterns, changing government policies, or any number of things. Considering all the things that can go wrong, it's a wonder that there are a large number of successful businesses. Separating the future winners from future losers requires knowledge, experience, wisdom, and a fair amount of good fortune. It is very difficult to do well on a consistent basis. If it were not, we'd all be making easy money in the stock market.

The second major risk of owning stocks is called the "market risk." This refers to those times when the stock market *as a whole* is being adversely affected by economic events. This takes place during the periodic recessions that the American economy goes through. In our example, it could be that Ford as a company is doing great, but lots of people still want to sell their Ford shares because they (1) fear a recession is coming and don't want to own any stocks, (2) have already been hurt by a recession and need to sell some of their stock to raise cash for living expenses, (3) have seen the recession drive down home prices and interest rates and are going to sell their stock in Ford to come up with the down payment money for a new house, and so on and so on.

As you can see, people often sell stock shares for reasons that have nothing directly to do with the prospects of the company. Many times, the sale of stock reflects the unfolding realities in the American and world economies and the level of interest rates. At other times selling takes place for purely emotional reasons. It has been said that "fear"

MAJOR PRICE TRENDS IN THE STOCK MARKET

(The graph below omits the smaller up and down cycles, and shows only those price moves of 20% or more as measured by the Standard & Poor's 500 Stock Index from 1961–1995)

Over the past sixty years, through recessions, wars, inflationary spirals, rocketing interest rates, investment scandals, and economic crises too numerous to mention, American stocks have nevertheless generated an average annual return of 10% a year to investors.

Still, that doesn't mean the occasional setbacks aren't nerve-wracking—especially if one comes along just before you need to sell your shares for college, retirement, or emergency needs.

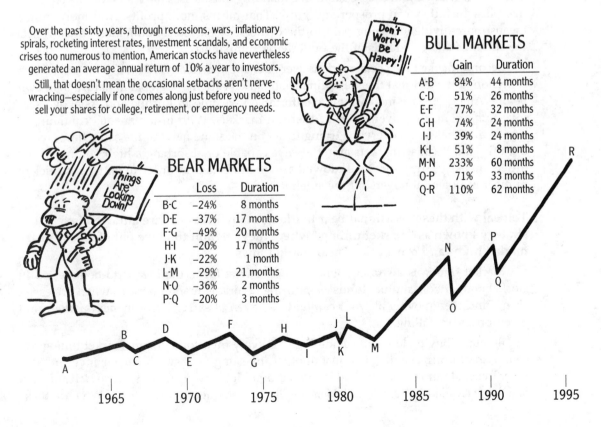

BULL MARKETS

	Gain	Duration
A-B	84%	44 months
C-D	51%	26 months
E-F	77%	32 months
G-H	74%	24 months
I-J	39%	24 months
K-L	51%	8 months
M-N	233%	60 months
O-P	71%	33 months
Q-R	110%	62 months

BEAR MARKETS

	Loss	Duration
B-C	–24%	8 months
D-E	–37%	17 months
F-G	–49%	20 months
H-I	–20%	17 months
J-K	–22%	1 month
L-M	–29%	21 months
N-O	–36%	2 months
P-Q	–20%	3 months

1965   1970   1975   1980   1985   1990   1995

and "greed" are the two primary forces that continually drive market activity. It's important to understand that ultimately your shares are worth what the market says they're worth, regardless of how seemingly well or poorly the company itself may be doing.

If you're beginning to think that the risks of owning stocks are considerable, that's good. You must . . .

. . . have a realistic view of this! The past twelve years provided such a positive economic environment for stocks that many people have lost sight of the fact that stocks can lose value as well as gain it. Let's take a look at the historical record to put things into perspective. "Major Price Trends" (previous page) shows stock price movements over the past thirty-five years. I have simplified the picture by drawing in only the major price moves of 20% or more. The accompanying tables explain the letter codes on the graph, showing the amount of each move and how long it lasted. For example, the bull market indicated by the letters *A-B* gained 84% over a forty-four-month period.

Notice two key elements in the graph. First, the overall trend is up. Even the long sideways movement of the 1960s and 1970s had an upward bias. This upward trend reflects the underlying strength of American free-enterprise capitalism. As long as the economy is healthy and the population expanding, businesses have a favorable environment in which they can prosper and grow. That means more profits. And more profits means more dividends being paid to the owners. Stock prices, ultimately, must reflect the earnings and dividends of the underlying companies.

Second, the last two bear markets were abrupt and relatively brief. This might be a reflection of the fact that the major financial markets are more global in nature than ever before. Americans are increasingly comfortable investing in Europe and Asia; overseas investors are major players in the American markets. With instantaneous communication of financial news, everyone trying to act on the same news at the same time creates a traffic jam. Because markets aren't always capable of absorbing a high volume of sell orders quickly, large price markdowns are often needed in order to entice a sufficient number of potential buyers off the sidelines.

To deal with these occasional bear markets, many investors are attracted to a strategy known as "market timing" where they attempt to move out of stocks near market highs and buy back in near market lows.

Market timing is a strategy where, in its purest form, the idea is to be invested in stock, bond, or gold mutual funds *only* during favorable market periods when prices are rising, and then moving all your capital to a haven of safety like a money market fund when prices are falling.

Because "buying low and selling high" is every investor's dream, market timing can sound an alluring call. But is it just another investing fantasy? Superstar investors like Peter Lynch, John Templeton, and Warren Buffett don't even attempt it. The *Harvard Business Review* called it "folly," and *Money* magazine frequently ridicules it. Why are these knowledgeable observers lined up against it? They say it's too difficult to be done *on a consistently* profitable basis, and that newsletter writers have grossly exaggerated its value in order to sell more newsletters. While it sounds good in theory, they submit it doesn't deliver as advertised.

Enter Mark Hulbert, respected publisher of *The Hulbert Financial Digest*. For more than fifteen years, Hulbert's work has served as a kind of *Consumer Reports* of the investment newsletter field. Over time, his research, performance statistics, and writing has gained wide acceptance in the industry. In addition to his own newsletter, he writes a regular column for *Forbes* that covers the investment newsletter scene. What has Mark Hulbert's fifteen years of tracking newsletter recommendations taught him about market timing? In his words:

> *It is an undeniable fact that some newsletters have beaten a buy-and-hold approach with their timing. . . . The proportion of timing newsletters which have beaten the market is significant and can't be explained away as just luck. . . . One goal is to beat the market – to do better than simply buying and holding. But the other goal, which is far less widely recognized, is to reduce risk. Whatever else one might say about the market timing newsletters, this is a goal on which they can, and have, delivered. . . . More than half of the market timing newsletters beat the market on a risk-adjusted basis in each of the three time periods measured. This is a very impressive achievement.*

Hulbert's findings are in line with my own experience – that market timing can indeed reduce risk while improving returns; however, it's not as easy as some would have you believe and it's often mentally and emotionally exhausting. I gained this insight the old-fashioned way – I earned it.

In 1978, a close friend and I decided to launch an investment advisory service based solely on market timing. We were one of the early entries in what eventually became a crowded field. During periods of market weakness, we performed exceedingly well for our clients due to our ability to sell out and move quickly into money market funds. When the eventual rallies occurred, we were nimble enough to get back in and enjoy most (but not all) of the ride up. Our strategy generated returns which saw our average managed account more than triple in value during our first five years of operations.

Our "glory days" faded during the bull market of the mid-1980s. Market timing doesn't work well in bull markets (as even its supporters will admit) because the occasional moves out of the market eventually prove unnecessary, and you often find yourself buying back in at higher prices. Investors become impatient with these miscues; during bull markets they forget the need to be ready with a defensive game plan. The summer of 1987 still stands out in my memory as one of the worst periods of my professional life. I'll share the grim details with you in chapter 36.

For now, just accept my word for it that successful market timing demands enormous self-control, more than most people are conditioned to give. I'm not a proponent of average investors attempting a market timing strategy on their own. It's just too challenging emotionally. First, there's our natural greed. Peering blind-eyed into an impenetrable future, we hope for the best and talk ourselves into expecting the best. So if our trade turns into a loss and our timing system says to sell, we think, *Surely the market won't go straight down from here. There's bound to be at least a little bounce and I can get out without a loss.* How many times have you decided to sell an investment "just as soon as the price gets back up to what I paid for it?"

Second, there's simple fear. Your system says "buy," but you're convinced by what you've been reading and hearing to expect further weakness instead. This causes you to lack confidence in your system's signal. You decide that if the market can prove itself by rising to Point X, *then* you'll buy. When Point X is reached, you feel better about the market's prospects, but don't want to pay the higher price. Your plan becomes, "I'll buy on a pullback to Point Y." Assume you are given this second chance and Point Y is reached. Perversely, the very weakness that you were hoping for now causes you to doubt the authenticity of the rally. You again hesitate. While you're racked with indecision, the market roars off without looking back. When last seen, you were still trying to muster the courage to get invested.

Unfortunately, many of us exhibit a market timing mind-set even while engaged in seemingly "normal" investing activities.

We need not consider ourselves market timers or even follow a formal market timing strategy in order to fall into the trap of focusing on short-term satisfactions rather than on long-term objectives. A good example of this was on display in *The Wall Street Journal* in 1994. The markets were going through some dramatic market swings, and the *Journal* reported on how investors were making market-related decisions.

It included the story of a grocery store executive who had a lifelong habit of investing only in the safety of bank CDs. I was struck by his impatient, childlike reactions. Here are some quotes from the article, along with what appear to be his driving motivations enclosed in brackets: "I got fed up *[anger]* with making 3% while everyone else I knew *[peer pressure]* was making 8%-9% *[envy]* in bond mutual funds. I felt like I wasn't a smart *[feelings of inferiority]* investor." So he invested in bonds. When his bond funds dropped in value, he sold half his holdings and is debating whether to sell the rest. "How can bonds lose money in a month's time *[short-term thinking]*? Why should I sit there *[impatience]* while I'm losing money in these funds every day?" Did he understand the risks of his new investments or have any long-term commitment to them? Apparently not.

The article also related the tale of a young attorney who retreated back to his CDs after venturing into overseas stock funds. He gave up on his new holdings after just a four-month period. "I couldn't sleep *[anxiety]* at night. It proves, I guess, that I'm just not that kind of investor." Then why did he leave his CDs in the first place? "Everybody in my office *[peer pressure]* was talking about emerging markets mutual funds, and how they were the hot *[following fads]* thing." After he initially made about 15% on his investment, he says he "thought this fund was going to keep going up *[unrealistic expectations]*. But it's been dropping like a stone. All I could think of *[fear of failure]* was getting out before I lose any more."

I mention these two accounts not to ridicule these people but to illustrate how intelligent, educated adults can be surprisingly childlike in decision-making. Against all reasonable expectations, we seem to somehow expect to astutely select the cream of the investment crop, ride our holdings to the crest of a glorious bull market, and then wisely take our profits. We'll move to the sidelines and let other (presumably less savvy) investors suffer the frustrations of the inevitable correction that follows. We're living, like children, in a fantasy world, and when our fantasies don't come true, we often react with bitter disappointment, anger, or fear.

Many would object at this point and say, "I know that's unrealistic. I don't try to do that." But what then is the motivation, conscious or subconscious, behind the most common questions investors ask, such as: *When* will the rise in interest rates stop? Where is the market headed *next*? Are stocks a buy *yet*? Should I buy gold *now*? These are the questions the financial media constantly raise, appealing to our natural desire to make profitable decisions.

Yet, they are largely irrelevant to the investor with his eyes fixed on the distant horizon. The long-term investor is asking a different set of questions: Is it even appropriate for me to take on the risks of investing in securities that fluctuate in value? If so, how should I divide my capital between the different kinds of investments (stocks, bonds, gold, real estate, etc.)? What are the growth prospects for the next five years, both in America and various overseas economies? Am I getting good value for my money?

We need to say, along with the apostle Paul, "When I was a child, I talked like a child, I thought like a child, I reasoned like a child. When I became a man, I put childish ways behind me" (1 Corinthians 13:11). To be profitable, we need to put away childish things—such as demanding immediate gratification—and invest by using our reason rather than our emotions.

Every successful investing strategy requires a degree of self-discipline.

Self-discipline is the ability to do the right thing at the right time every time. By the "right" thing, I don't mean always making the most profitable decision. That's impossible. Rather, I mean the right thing is to ignore the distractions of news events and well-intentioned advice and stay with your plan. This is more difficult than it sounds because the markets don't always offer positive reinforcement. In the short run, you can lose money following your plan or you can make money deviating from it. When that happens, "good" behavior is penalized and "bad" behavior is rewarded. It weakens your commitment to following your strategy. If this continues, it isn't long before you're back where you started—making every decision on a what-seems-best-at-the-moment basis. Unless you have a rare and natural gift for investing, that's the last place you want to be.

In the next chapter, I'm going to offer you a "Just-the-Basics" strategy that has been designed to minimize the wear and tear on your emotions by making it easier for you to exercise self-discipline and do "the right thing." It's been my experience that:

◆ **Doing the right thing is easier when the strategy is simple.** Our Just-the-Basics portfolios use relatively few ingredients, and I use plain-English explanations to tell you what to do and why we're doing it. The simplicity lets you see how everything fits together, so you can feel more comfortable making decisions.

◆ **Doing the right thing is easier when the rules are clear-cut.** Just-the-Basics offers specific guidelines that determine your mix of stocks and bonds and fund selections. You can have more confidence when you know you're making buy/sell decisions that fit into a coherent plan.

◆ **Doing the right thing is easier when it's not time consuming.** You don't need to read *The Wall Street Journal*, monitor the mutual fund rankings, keep daily charts, calculate moving averages, or anything else. The Just-the-Basics requires only an hour or so once a year, usually in January, to perform a little routine maintenance.

◆ **Doing the right thing is easier when you know that your losses won't kill you.** No strategy is perfect, so you know ahead of time you will have some losses. But when you're well diversified, they won't be devastating. The Just-the-Basics track record in this regard is reassuring.

◆ **Doing the right thing is easier when you know you're in for the long haul.** You needn't be overly concerned about the quarterly performance in your Just-the-Basics portfolio. There will be occasional setbacks. But we're realistic and understand that's going to happen from time to time. Investing often involves taking two steps forward and one step back. But that needn't alarm us because we've got time on our side.

This book, as well as my monthly newsletter, gets its name from 2 Timothy 1:7. In the King James Version, it reads: "For God hath not given us the spirit of fear; but of power, and of love, and of a sound mind." It's interesting that the New International Version translates "sound mind" as "self-discipline." We can look forward to maturing in our faith beyond childish things because *"His divine power has given us everything we need for life and godliness through our knowledge of him who called us by his own glory and goodness. . . . For this very reason, make every effort to add to your faith . . . self-control"* (2 Peter 1:3, 5-6). ◆

13

CHAPTER PREVIEW

A Just-the-Basics Strategy
Built Around Six Model Portfolios

I. **Historical data show that, over time, 80% of professional money managers and newsletter writers fail to "beat the market."**

    A. A "loser's game" is that kind of competition where the winner is determined primarily by the mistakes of the loser rather than the skill of the winner. Investing has become a loser's game.

    B. The path to success when playing a loser's game is to play a passive, patient game where the emphasis is on minimizing one's mistakes.

II. **The mutual fund world offers a product that is perfectly suited to playing a loser's game. It's called an "index" fund.**

    A. An index fund doesn't try to beat the market. Its goal is to equal the market by replicating the performance of a major market index like the S&P 500.

    B. The growth in index funds has been explosive in recent years as pension funds, insurance companies, and other large institutional investors, recognizing how extremely difficult it is to regularly outperform the market, have placed huge sums in them.

III. **Our Just-the-Basics strategy uses no-load stock and bond index funds in various combinations to create six portfolios with varying degrees of risk.**

    A. Your most important investing decision is how you divide your money between stocks, bonds, and cash reserves. One industry leader cites a study which concludes that 94% of the differences in returns achieved by investors is due to how this decision is made.

    B. A primary advantage of Just-the-Basics is that its primary focus is on this all-important asset allocation decision rather than on which mutual funds to purchase.

    C. Other advantages of this strategy include guarding against sub-par investment returns, lower expenses, fewer taxable distributions, and easy accessibility.

    D. Just-the-Basics allows you to tailor-make the risk and reward aspects of investing to your personal temperament.

Traditional money management is founded on the questionable assumption that . . .

. . . professional managers can consistently beat the market through research, intelligent risk-taking, and exploiting the mistakes of others. But what if this assumption is largely false?

In this chapter, we'll look at historical data that show that the vast majority of mutual funds and investment newsletters underperformed the market over the past decade. It turns out that the secret to winning the money game may be to not try winning at all.

We'll begin our study with an analogy from the world of tennis. I have spent many a Thursday afternoon risking bodily injury and public humiliation on the tennis courts. As a beginner, I concentrated my efforts on trying to learn how to hit the ball correctly. My pregame strategy had little to do with specific plans for hitting the ball to my opponent's forehand or backhand or placing it shallow or deep. My primary concern was pretty simple: Try to keep the ball in bounds! I lost many more points due to the mistakes *I* made than as a result of the actions of my opponents.

In his book on tennis strategy, *Extraordinary Tennis for the Ordinary Player*, Dr. Simon Ramo describes the kind of amateur tennis I play as a "loser's game." By that he means it is the kind of competition *where the winner is determined by the behavior of the loser*. The amateur doesn't win by defeating his opponent; he wins by letting his opponent defeat himself.

Ramo contrasted this with the "winner's game" played at the professional tennis level. In those matches, we are accustomed to seeing consistently precise serves, stunning recoveries, and long, dramatic rallies. Eventually, one player takes a calculated risk and attempts to put away his opponent with an exceptionally powerful or well-placed shot. At the expert level, it is the winning of points that drives the action and determines the outcome.

In short, Ramo observed, amateurs *lose* points and professionals *win* points. To test his hypothesis, he compiled an extensive database of points scored in actual tournaments at both levels. He found a surprisingly consistent and symmetrical tendency. In professional tennis, about 80% of the points are won due to superb offensive execution—a winner's game. On the other hand, in amateur tennis about 80% of the points are lost due to unforced errors—a loser's game.

OK, so what does this have to do with selecting a mutual fund portfolio? In his highly acclaimed book *Investment Policy*, money manager Charles D. Ellis applied Ramo's work to the investing arena. When Ellis studied the investment markets, he saw that it was not uncommon for 80% of the managers of stock and bond mutual funds to underperform their respective markets (see graphs on next page). In their efforts to "score" for their shareholders, they were hitting the ball into the net or out of bounds far too often. It appeared that investing had become a loser's game. It hadn't always been this way:

> *Winner's games can and do sometimes become loser's games. That is what has happened to the "money game" we call investment management. A basic change has occurred in the investment environment; the market came to be dominated in the 1970s by the very institutions that were striving to win by outperforming the market. And that shift made all the difference. No longer was the active investment manager competing with cautious custodians or amateurs who were out of touch with the market. Now he was competing with other experts. . . . So many professional investment managers are so good, they make it nearly impossible for any one to outperform the market they now dominate.*

> *The key question under the new rules of the game is this: How much better must the active manager be to at least recover the costs of active management? Recovering these costs is surprisingly difficult. Such superior performance can be done and is done every year by some, but it has not been done consistently over a long period of time by many. . . .*

Believing that investment management had evolved into a loser's game, Ellis drew this conclusion: Just as the path to victory in amateur tennis is to play a passive, patient game while letting your opponent take the risks, so the logical strategy for the amateur investor should be the same.

Survivorship Bias is the term given to describe the distortion that creeps into mutual fund performance data due to funds passing out of existence each year. For example, in the graphic below, there would have been many more than 294 stock funds which underperformed the index, but they have been liquidated or merged into other funds. Thus, they're no longer in the database to drive the average performance down. As a result of survivorship bias, the number of funds which outperformed the index was actually lower than the 25% shown.

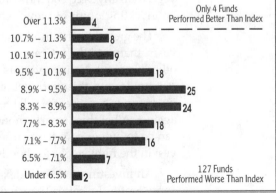

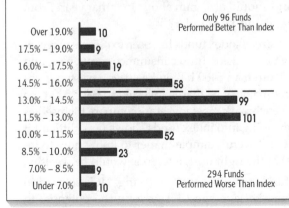

IT'S TOUGH TO BEAT THE MARKET!
For ten-year period ending 12/31/95. Source: *Morningstar Ondisc.*

STOCKS

This is a picture of the annualized returns for the ten-year period ending December 1995 for the 390 diversified stock funds that have track records going back to 1986. It shows that ten funds had returns of less than 7% per year, nine returned more than 7.0% but less than 8.5%, and so on. During this period, the S&P 500 returned just a little over 14.5% per year (dotted line). Only about 25% of the funds (top four bars) did better during this particular ten-year period.

Only 96 Funds
Performed Better Than Index

Range	Funds
Over 19.0%	10
17.5% – 19.0%	9
16.0% – 17.5%	19
14.5% – 16.0%	58
13.0% – 14.5%	99
11.5% – 13.0%	101
10.0% – 11.5%	52
8.5% – 10.0%	23
7.0% – 8.5%	9
Under 7.0%	10

294 Funds
Performed Worse Than Index

BONDS

Similarly, this graph depicts the annualized returns for the same ten-year period for 131 general purpose bond funds (excluding mortgage, zero coupon, and limited maturity funds) that have track records going back to 1986. During this period, the Salomon Brothers Long-Term High Grade Corporate Bond Index (dotted line) returned 11.3% per year. Only 3% of the funds (top bar) did better. Expenses are a bigger factor for bond funds.

Only 4 Funds
Performed Better Than Index

Range	Funds
Over 11.3%	4
10.7% – 11.3%	8
10.1% – 10.7%	9
9.5% – 10.1%	18
8.9% – 9.5%	25
8.3% – 8.9%	24
7.7% – 8.3%	18
7.1% – 7.7%	16
6.5% – 7.1%	7
Under 6.5%	2

127 Funds
Performed Worse Than Index

There are advantages to playing a loser's game.

Most investors, consciously or subconsciously, are caught up in playing a winner's game. They're trying to "beat the market." They buy financial magazines and investment newsletters that offer a dizzying array of stock recommendations and mutual fund rankings, and they feel they must respond to fast-breaking news events and trade with a short-term perspective. Theirs is an active strategy where they work harder and take extra risks in what is usually a futile attempt to "win." One investor/writer expressed his frustration over the investing rat race this way:

> *I could keep my money in stocks, either in many companies or in just a few good ones; I could invest abroad or bring my money home; I could buy and hold or entrust portfolio choices to hot mutual funds; I could shift to bonds; I could prepay my mortgage; or, last — and in the view of Wall Street wisdom, unutterably stupid — I could simply sit on my cash. Like other investors, I balance my fears against my greed, my distrust in easy money against my belief in the eternal upward movement of the market. Like others, I tramp from sage to wizard to priest, gathering portents and signs, each more bewildering than the last, always believing that ahead lies a successful end. In other words, I am a fool.[1]*

[1]Ted C. Fishman, "The Bull Market in Fear," Harper's magazine, October 1995, 58.

In a loser's game, the strategy is more passive (and relaxing!). The path to victory lies in minimizing one's mistakes and being patient. This describes our Just-the-Basics portfolios where we refuse to play the performance game. Instead, we simply invest in selected "index" funds, which, by definition, are going to give us returns similar to the market as a whole.

An index fund is a special kind of mutual fund that has only one objective: to mirror the performance of a market index . . .

. . . such as Standard & Poor's 500 stock index. The portfolio manager invests in the same securities that are used in calculating the index. The fund will make or lose money to the same extent the index after which it is patterned shows gains or losses. For example, if the S&P 500 gains 15% in a given year, then any S&P 500 index fund should also gain about 15% that year. From an investing point of view, what could be simpler?

The growth in the number and size of index funds has been explosive in recent years, thanks to the interest shown by pension funds, insurance companies, and other big institutional investors. More than $400 billion has been invested in index funds, and the overwhelming majority of that is invested in S&P 500-type index funds because it is still the benchmark most investors compare themselves against. All of this "smart" money going into index funds shows how difficult it can be to outperform the market. If it were a simple matter to know how to invest in the right stocks (or bonds) at the right time, everyone would be wealthy.

An investment in an index fund is another way of saying, "It is so hard to consistently do better than the market averages! I'll give up the potential to make *more* than the overall market in return for knowing that I won't make *less*." Once you create your Just-the-Basics portfolios, there's nothing further to do (other than a few hours of annual paperwork) throughout the year except sit back, relax, and hopefully enjoy the ride. By using index funds, we keep pace with the markets virtually without effort. And, as seen in the graphs on page 155, by getting the same returns as the overall market (represented by the dotted line), we'll outperform the vast majority of professional investors. Ironically, we win by *not trying* to win.

Let's now take a look at the funds we'll be using to implement our Just-the-Basics strategy.

Many fund organizations offer index funds, but the ones from the no-load Vanguard Group are especially well suited to this approach. I'll explain the Just-the-Basics concept using the Vanguard funds, starting with the Vanguard Index Trust: 500 Portfolio. This fund attempts to duplicate the performance of Standard & Poor's 500 stock index. It invests in all 500 companies in the same proportion as the weight they carry in the index. It has been around since 1976 and has done an excellent job over the years of fulfilling its mandate. For the ten years ending in 1995, the fund gained 14.6% per year versus 14.9% per year for the S&P 500 index. The small difference is attributable to the costs of operating the fund.

Another Vanguard stock fund will also play an important role: Vanguard's Index Trust: Extended Market Portfolio. This fund attempts to provide investment results that correspond to the price and yield performance of 6,000 smaller-to-medium-sized U.S. companies. Naturally, it can't invest in all 6,000, but by using some fancy computer-driven statistical techniques, it buys about 1,800 stocks that, when taken together in the right proportions, act pretty much the same as if all 6,000 were present and accounted for. (It's sort of like when the news people take exit interviews at election time and tell us who the winners are going to be based on how a small number of people voted.)

PERFORMANCE HISTORY OF THE SIX JUST-THE-BASICS PORTFOLIOS

| | Individual Funds | | | | Just-the-Basics Portfolios | | | | | |
	Intl Growth	Extend Market	Index 500	Total Bond	All Stocks	80% 20%	60% 40%	40% 60%	20% 80%	All Bonds
1981	−1.5%	−1.5%	−5.2%	6.5%	−3.0%	−1.1%	0.8%	2.7%	4.6%	6.5%
1982	5.2%	13.6%	21.0%	31.5%	14.8%	18.4%	21.9%	25.2%	28.4%	31.5%
1983	43.1%	25.5%	21.3%	8.3%	27.0%	22.5%	18.5%	14.8%	11.4%	8.3%
1984	−1.0%	−1.7%	6.2%	14.9%	1.6%	4.4%	7.1%	9.8%	12.4%	14.9%
1985	57.0%	32.0%	31.2%	22.3%	36.8%	33.4%	30.3%	27.4%	24.8%	22.3%
1986	56.7%	11.8%	18.1%	15.5%	24.8%	22.8%	20.9%	19.0%	17.2%	15.5%
1987	12.5%	−3.5%	4.7%	1.5%	4.3%	3.7%	3.2%	2.6%	2.1%	1.5%
1988	11.6%	19.8%	16.2%	7.3%	15.9%	14.2%	12.5%	10.8%	9.1%	7.4%
1989	24.8%	24.0%	31.4%	13.7%	27.0%	24.6%	22.0%	19.3%	16.5%	13.7%
1990	−12.0%	−14.0%	−3.3%	8.7%	−9.3%	−6.2%	−3.0%	0.6%	4.4%	8.7%
1991	4.7%	41.9%	30.2%	15.3%	26.2%	24.1%	21.9%	19.7%	17.5%	15.3%
1992	−5.8%	12.5%	7.4%	7.1%	5.9%	6.1%	6.4%	6.6%	6.9%	7.1%
1993	44.7%	14.5%	9.9%	9.7%	19.0%	17.3%	15.5%	13.7%	11.7%	9.7%
1994	0.8%	−1.8%	1.2%	−2.7%	0.1%	−0.4%	−0.9%	−1.4%	−2.0%	−2.7%
1995	14.9%	33.8%	37.4%	18.2%	30.3%	28.3%	26.1%	23.7%	21.0%	18.2%
15 Yrs	15.1%	12.7%	14.4%	11.6%	13.9%	13.5%	13.1%	12.6%	12.1%	11.6%
10 Yrs	13.6%	12.7%	14.5%	9.2%	13.7%	12.9%	12.0%	11.1%	10.2%	9.2%
5 Yrs	10.6%	19.1%	16.4%	9.3%	15.7%	14.6%	13.4%	12.1%	10.7%	9.3%

The 5/10/15 year annualized returns are for the periods ending December 31, 1995.

Now, here's the neat thing about these two funds: *none of their holdings over-lap!* This means that if you invest in both of them, you are essentially investing in 6,500 different stocks ranging from the very small to the very large. *The end result is that you've pretty much invested in the entire American stock market.*

To gain a global flavor, we'll use a third Vanguard stock fund — its International Growth fund. This fund is authorized to invest in stocks anywhere in the world outside the U.S. It's the one fund in our portfolio that is not an index fund (Vanguard doesn't offer a foreign stock index fund that invests worldwide); however, it has an excellent long-term track record. It usually ranks in the upper one-fourth of foreign stock funds, and it finished in the top 5 percent for the three years ending in 1995.

Finally, we need to add the Vanguard Bond Index: Total Bond Portfolio to our arsenal. This fund does in the world of bonds what the first two stock funds do in the world of stocks: acts as if it owns them all. It's designed to track the Lehman Brothers Aggregate Bond Index of more than 6,000 high quality corporate, government, and mortgage-backed bonds of varying maturities. The Vanguard Bond Market Fund has an average bond quality rating of AAA and weighted maturity of around eight years.

We'll put together these funds in different combinations . . .

. . . so as to produce six portfolios of varying degrees of risk. The portfolio at the low end of the risk scale is invested 100% in the bond fund. This one is designed to incur minimum risk in an attempt to preserve capital while generating current income. As we learned in chapter 11, investing by lending is the lowest risk kind of investing.

By increasing the stock allocation in incremental steps of 20%, we begin moving up the risk scale until we reach the high end — a portfolio invested 100% in the stock funds. I suggest that the stock portion of the portfolio be invested one-fifth in International, two-fifths in the Extended Market, and two-fifths in the S&P 500 (see blackboard on page 178). The graphs at right show the six Just-the-Basics portfolios and their historical performance over the past fifteen years.

When you combine the four Vanguard funds in these various ways, you get the potential rewards of stock ownership along with a reduction in risk due to the less volatile bond portion. Sometimes the funds will move together, but it will often be the case that the bond fund will move opposite the stock funds, and the international stock fund will behave differently from the two U.S. stock funds. When that happens, the price changes somewhat cancel each other out. The effect of this is to increase the price stability of the overall portfolio. Thus, although you are less likely to score a huge gain in any one year when holding a combination of the four funds, you are also unlikely to incur a huge loss. This improved price stability (which equates to lower risk) is one of the primary

SIX JUST-THE-BASICS PORTFOLIOS

Risk is usually defined in terms of the potential an investment has for wild swings up and down in its market value. The term "volatility" refers to the extent of these price swings. An investment with high volatility (meaning very wide, often abrupt, swings in its market value) is defined as high risk. An investment with low volatility (meaning narrow, usually gradual, swings in its market value) is thought of as having low risk. The graphs below were designed to give you an idea of how much volatility and risk to expect with each of the six Just-the-Basics portfolios. They show the total returns for each twelve-month period which begins on a calendar quarter for the years 1981 through 1995. Notice the extreme ups and downs of the top graph versus the one at the bottom. This graphically illustrates what we have been learning about the risks of investing by lending versus owning: bonds are lower risk than stocks. Standard deviation is a measure of risk that we will be learning more about in chapter 17. All you need to know now is the lower the standard deviation, the lower the risk.

Portion Allocated to Stocks:	Portion Allocated to Bonds:	Your Need for Growth of Capital:	Your Need for Current Income or Protecting Capital:	Average Annualized Return:	Best 12 Month Return:	Worst 12 Month Return:	Standard Deviation (Risk):	
100%	0%	Maximum	None	15.4%	66.4%	−16.3%	17.3	
80%	20%	High	Little	14.6%	57.3%	−11.0%	14.6	
60%	40%	Moderate	Modest	13.9%	49.2%	−7.1%	12.2	
40%	60%	Modest	Moderate	13.3%	42.0%	−2.7%	10.3	
20%	80%	Little	High	12.7%	35.6%	−2.0%	9.0	
0%	100%	None	Maximum	12.1%	34.7%	−3.4%	8.6	

advantages for the average investor of diversifying through mutual funds.

The portfolio that is best for your situation depends on two factors—your emotional tolerance for risk and the season of life you are now in. In the next chapter, I'll give you some guidelines you can use to select which of the six portfolios is best for you.

The use of index funds as your core holdings merits your serious consideration. Here are several of the advantages they offer:

◆ **A correct emphasis.** Your most far-reaching investing decision involves how you allocate your money between stocks, bonds, and cash reserves. In *Bogle on Mutual Funds*, Vanguard chief John Bogle claims "that decision has accounted for an astonishing 94% of the differences in total returns achieved by institutionally managed pension funds." In other words, if Fund A out-performs Fund B, the difference can almost entirely be explained in terms of how each fund allocated its portfolio rather than by looking at the individual securities each fund owned. Bogle's conclusion: "The 94% figure suggests that long-term fund investors might profit by concentrating more on the alloca-tion of their investments between stock and bond funds and less on the ques-tion of *which particular* stock or bond funds to hold" (emphasis added). An indexing strategy forces the investor to focus on the most relevant issue.

"Studies show that the performance of overall markets in stocks and bonds, rather than individual selections of securities, determines more than 90% of your investment return. Therefore, your biggest decisions will be how to divide your portfolio among asset classes."

Fortune magazine

◆ **To guard against sub-par investment returns.** Index funds help assure that your results are in line with those of the general market. They can be counted on to closely track the market at which they're targeted. Since the stocks in the S&P 500 represent about 80% of the value of the entire U.S. stock market, an index fund based on the S&P will correlate very well with the market as a whole. Thus, if the market continues its historical 10% rate of annual growth over the next decade, it is predictable that an S&P 500 index fund will also gain roughly 10% per year during the period.

◆ **Lower expenses.** One of the reasons it's difficult for mutual funds to con-sistently outperform the averages is that they have to overcome the costs of running the fund. The operating expenses (for management fees and certain marketing expenses) for the average fund amount to about 1.25% a year. Plus, money spent on commissions when the fund does its buying and selling adds another 0.5% to 1.0% per year (depending on how active the portfolio manager is in buying and selling). Thus, the shareholders' profits in the typical fund are reduced by about 2.0% per year due to operating and transaction costs. Index funds, on the other hand, have very low expenses. Management fees are nomi-nal because the fund can essentially be run by a computer, and transaction costs are quite low because index funds require relatively little buying and selling within the portfolio. The expenses of Vanguard's index funds run less than 0.25% per year, about one-eighth of what a typical stock fund might incur.

◆ **Fewer taxable distributions**. Like individual investors, mutual funds aren't taxed on their "paper profits." A taxable event takes place only when securities are sold and the paper gains are realized. The fact that index funds require fewer transactions means there are fewer occasions when stocks are sold and the paper profits converted to taxable profits. This reduces the amount of capital gains taxes, a significant advantage if you're investing taxable dollars, i.e., outside a tax-deferred retirement account.

◆ **Easy accessibility**. Many readers have written concerning the difficulty they're having in applying the SMI strategy to their retirement accounts where they have a limited number of investment options. Index funds, especially those based on the S&P 500, are increasingly being offered in 401(k)s and variable annuities. That makes it easier to include your retirement assets in your overall allocation strategy.

If indexing is so great, why doesn't everybody do it?

Index funds have long been used by large pension funds in a major way, yet they account for only about 5% of the assets of stock mutual funds. Obviously, individual investors have not embraced them despite their many advantages. Here are some guesses as to why that has been the case.

Index funds conflict with our desire for security. The most significant drawback is that index funds offer no protection during periods of market weakness. They are fully invested in a portfolio of stocks that reflects the index they are designed to mimic, and they *stay* fully invested at all times. If the next bear market takes stocks down 30%, index funds will fall 30% right along with it. This is a scary thought. As long as we're actively buying and selling, we hope to somehow have the insight, impulse, or just plain luck to stand aside in time to avoid the carnage.

Because they're on automatic pilot, index funds are said to be "passively managed" funds. The managers of "actively managed" stock funds, on the other hand, can take defensive measures like increasing their holdings of cash or high-dividend-paying stocks. Such efforts may or may not help cushion the fall, but at least the managers are trying.

Our Just-the-Basics strategy deals with these drawbacks by combining several index funds into one portfolio. By adding a bond fund, we hope to provide a cushion to bear market weakness. By adding Vanguard's Extended Market index fund and the International Growth fund, we increase our diversification by adding small company and foreign stocks to the mix. These additional funds will not enhance performance every year, but they do add safety and stability to the portfolio over the long haul.

Index funds conflict with the financial interests of the investing industry. Indexing threatens the profits of most investment advisers, stockbrokers,

"The Risks of Index Funds"
by Austin Pryor.
Excerpted from the
Sound Mind Investing
newsletter.
See Briefing 15,
page 476.

and financial magazines and newsletters. These companies, for the most part, prosper from the public's interest in above-average returns. That's why there's always a sense of urgency surrounding their advertising—the emphasis is always on what's new and changes you should make *now*. If their customers began relying on indexing, buying and selling activity would greatly diminish and their profits would as well. It's no coincidence that none of the major full-service brokerage firms even offers an index fund.

Index funds conflict with common sense. The success of index funds is not something you'd expect. How can doing nothing be better than doing something? How can expert advice consistently be worse than no advice at all? And more mysteriously, how can you win by refusing to even play? Yet, the facts speak for themselves. Beating the market for a single year or two is not too hard. Beating it consistently over many years, as Charles Ellis points out, "is so very difficult to do—and it's so easy, while trying to do better, to do worse." Here's another example of this: Of the twenty-four investment newsletters tracked by Hulbert that have track records of at least ten years, *only four* did better than the S&P 500 over the past decade.

Index funds conflict with human nature. Who wants to settle for "average" when being "above average" doesn't really seem that hard? Most people are optimistic and see themselves as having a good chance of being in that select group who can consistently outperform the market—either through their own skills or by selecting and relying on the right advisers. Contrary to their ambitions and best efforts, however, most investors are not beating the market. The market is beating them. Anyone who invested in the S&P 500 ten years ago would have earned 14.4% per year compared to 12.6% for the average stock mutual fund. In the process, such an investor would have outdistanced about 80% of the mutual fund managers and investment newsletter writers who are the "experts."

I encourage you to give the Just-the-Basics strategy a serious look, and consider using it as the foundation of your long-term strategy.

Of course, indexing need not be an "all or nothing" proposition. Many of my newsletter readers use the Just-the-Basics funds as "core" holdings to anchor their portfolios. For example, you might invest two-thirds of your portfolio in a Just-the-Basics mix of funds, and then use the other one-third to be a little more flexible. With the remaining third, you could either be more adventurous (by investing in selected stock funds or individual stocks) or more conservative (by adding Treasuries, CDs, or other money market holdings). In Section Four, you'll find helpful information on how to evaluate risk and potential reward as you shop for bond and stock funds if you wish to supplement your Just-the-Basics strategy. ◆

CHAPTER PREVIEW

Selecting the Portfolio Mix Best Suited to Your Risk-Taking Temperament and Current Season of Life

I. **All of us have "money personalities" that reflect our attitudes toward earning, spending, saving, and investing money.**

   A. Psychologist Kathleen Gurney has conducted nationwide surveys and found that people have a financial self and use money as a means to gain security, freedom, love, respect, power, and happiness.

   B. Gurney notes nine distinct money personality types, but I have combined several in developing the four investing temperaments in this chapter.

II. **Meet the Preserver, Researcher, Explorer, and Daredevil.**

   A. Each of these investing personalities reflects a different emotional reaction to risk taking.

   B. A series of "attitudinal snapshots" should enable you to select the one that is closest to the way you feel about financial security and the tradeoffs between risk and reward.

III. **For financial planning purposes, life can be divided into four phases.**

   A. Laying the foundation: Typically runs up into your forties.

   B. Accumulating assets: Your forties and fifties.

   C. Preserving assets: Your sixties and seventies.

   D. Distributing assets: Age eighty and beyond.

IV. **These two factors — your temperament and your current "season of life" — come together to determine how much risk is appropriate for your situation.**

   A. The "controlling your risk" matrix shows how I suggest dividing your investments between stocks (investing-by-owning) and bonds (investing-by-lending).

   B. This matrix provides a rational basis for dealing with the constant tension between the need for capital growth and the fear of capital loss that confront every investor.

"I'm trying to find myself."
Common quest of
popular culture

"If you don't know who you
are, the markets are an
expensive place to find out."
Adam Smith
The Money Game

"Not only do we have a physical self, an emotional self, and a social self, but we have a financial, or money, self.

"This money self is an integral part of our behavioral repertoire and influences the way we interact with our money. In other words, your money personality is a major factor in how you utilize your money. Most of us fail to realize the extent to which our money personality impacts our financial habits and affects the degree of satisfaction we get from what money we have. There is an inseparable link between our unconscious feelings about money and the way in which we earn it, spend it, save it, and invest it."

This observation is made by Kathleen Gurney in her book *Your Money Personality*. She adds that psychologists believe that money is a kind of "emotional currency" that symbolizes many of our unconscious needs and desires, among them:

◆ **security** (If I have enough money, I'll always be safe. No person and no catastrophe can harm me.)

◆ **freedom** (If I have enough money, I can freely choose my jobs or choose not to work; my options are open.)

◆ **love** (If I have enough money, more people will care about me. Money makes relationships a lot easier.)

◆ **respect** (If I have enough money, everyone will recognize that I have merit, that I accomplished what I set out to do.)

◆ **power** (If I have enough money, nobody will ever push me around. I will be strong and have total control over my life.)

◆ **happiness** (If I have enough money, I will truly be happy. I can finally relax and enjoy life.)

Dr. Gurney suggests that as many as nine different investment personality types exist (which she discusses in detail). To simplify matters, I have combined them in order to consider just four. There's nothing "official" about these. I devised them simply to help make this process easier and perhaps a little more fun. We all probably have some elements of each of the four types within us, so don't think I'm saying that any one type will fit you perfectly. But you may find that you identify with one temperament more than the other three. If so, you can learn something about yourself from this exercise.

I call the most aggressive investors "Daredevils."
They enjoy the investment "fast lane" . . .

. . . and are often found playing the markets on a short-term basis. They have plenty of self-confidence. The new issues market, stock and index options, and commodity futures would be areas of interest due to the opportunities they offer to make a lot of money quickly.

They often resist advice to diversify into more prudent, less colorful investments. Yet, even Daredevils need a solid, conservative base to counter their occasional impulsiveness and higher-risk tendencies. If they're not careful, they'll reach their retirement years with little to show for a lifetime of wheeling and dealing.

Daredevils could really benefit from the Just-the-Basics approach where we emphasize putting first things first. The use of highly diversified mutual fund portfolios, while not as high-stakes as some of their other investments, would bring a much-needed balance to their overall investment picture. It would go a long way toward countering their natural inclinations to "go for it."

"Explorers" are fascinated by the money-making potential of investing . . .

. . . but if they lack confidence in choosing the best path, they often take refuge in the safety of following the crowd. They are attracted to the latest trendy investments that are dominating the news. The "thrill of the hunt" is the fun part for them.

Explorers can be impetuous and often hop aboard a new investment without fully understanding just how serious the risks might be. As a result, their holdings are frequently a random assortment of moderate- to high-risk "good deals" collected over the years. Such a portfolio likely lacks balance and has no long-term focus. Explorers would benefit from a systematic, controlled-risk way of moving toward their long-term goals.

"Researchers" also tend toward caution, but their self-confidence enables them to overcome their concerns . . .

. . . if they feel they have done sufficient investigation. Simply reading in this book that a certain mutual fund is recommended may not be good enough for Researchers; they may want to know more about that mutual fund and why I recommend it. They are willing to immerse themselves in facts and figures in order to get a thorough understanding of the strengths and drawbacks of the investments they are considering.

They can easily postpone making commitments because they want more information. Up to a point, this caution serves them well. If overdone, their ability to make decisions is paralyzed because they will never know for sure that they have all the relevant information. Researchers appreciate the self-discipline imposed by following an objective set of guidelines. In addition, they have the long-term mind-set and patience necessary to stay with their game plan for many years in spite of occasional setbacks.

"Preservers" tend to worry about their investments . . .

. . . because the risk of losing their capital is very real to them. As a result, they are usually quite cautious, favoring CDs, government bonds, and only the highest quality blue-chip stocks. This approach helps them to preserve their wealth but may not provide enough growth to achieve reasonable performance goals.

Sometimes their desire to be cautious makes it difficult for them to make any investment decisions at all. If they can find advisers in whom they have confidence, they are frequently willing to rely on them heavily to assist with investment decisions. Realizing that they are safety conscious and must accept lower returns as part of the trade-off for safety, they usually have realistic expectations with regard to how much they can reasonably hope to make.

If you're a Preserver, the basic philosophy underlying all of your investing decisions is to preserve capital. You would agree with Warren Buffett, a legendary investor of our time, when he said there were only two really important rules of investing. Rule #1 is "Don't lose any money," and Rule #2 is "*Never* forget Rule #1."

You're now ready to select the investment temperament that best describes your attitudes toward . . .

. . . monetary risk-taking and its possible rewards. On the following two pages, you'll find each of the four investment temperaments listed along with their corresponding attitudes on risk and profit expressed in a variety of ways. Read each of them carefully and thoughtfully. You might want to pencil in checkmarks next to the statements that you identify with. Which of the four temperaments has the most check marks? (If you're married, you should ask your spouse to study them as well.)

It's been my experience that most people have little trouble seeing themselves in one of the four. The identification is usually almost instantaneous. However, if you narrow it down to two and have trouble deciding between them, my suggestion is to select the one on the right, the more conservative one (risk decreases as you move from left to right). Err on the side of safety and prudence rather than risk-taking.

Once you identify your money personality, I encourage you to stay within the boundaries it implies if at all possible. James Dale Davidson and Sir William Rees-Mogg, in their best-selling investment book, *Blood in the Streets*, stated well what usually happens to those who play a high-stakes game for which they are temperamentally unsuited:

> *Nothing is more surely condemned to failure than a high-risk strategy pursued by a low-risk man; he will always flinch at the point before the strategy has succeeded, and*

will throw away his potential gains in an attempt to leap back to the security he actually prefers. . . . To be a successful investor you have to be right, but in your own way. It is not only a matter of knowing yourself. It is even more important to be yourself.

There's always a tension between our *need for capital growth* and our *fear of capital loss.*

Obviously, it would be great if we could make all that we need on our investments without taking any risk. A relatively small number of multimillionaires might be able to live comfortably off the interest paid by their T-bills, but the rest of us aren't so fortunate. Without taking away from the importance of "being yourself" as stated above, we must sometimes learn how to live with a little more risk than we would like.

Many readers of my newsletter became so committed to their comfort levels that they were not making sufficient progress in building their capital. To remedy this, I developed guidelines for helping them decide how to balance their holdings between stocks and bonds. They're based on the "seasons of life" through which we all travel. The four temperaments still play an important role, but a new dimension has been added—the need for capital growth at various phases of life:

Phase 1: Laying the foundation. This is the starting point for most of us. We spend the greater part of our twenties and thirties acquiring transportation and a residence, paying off student and other loans, and building a contingency reserve. There may not be much in the way of monthly surplus left to invest for retirement (which is still twenty-five or more years away). The money we do put aside can be invested aggressively because we have a very long time frame in which to work. This is the phase where we can afford to take our greatest risks.

Phase 2: Accumulating assets. Most of us experience our peak earning years during our forties to fifties. At the same time, our expenses should be

CONTROLLING YOUR RISK MATRIX

| | NEED FOR GROWTH | | FEAR OF LOSS | | | | | | |
| | | | Daredevil | | Explorer | | Researcher | | Preserver | |
Financial Phase	Characterized by	Typical Age	Stock	Bond	Stock	Bond	Stock	Bond	Stock	Bond
Phase 1	Laying foundation	Under 45	100%	0%	80%	20%	60%	40%	40%	60%
Phase 2	Accumulating assets	45 to 60	80%	20%	60%	40%	40%	60%	20%	80%
Phase 3	Preserving assets	60 to 75	60%	40%	40%	60%	20%	80%	0%	100%
Phase 4	Distributing assets	Over 75	40%	60%	20%	80%	0%	100%	0%	100%

The Daredevil

The Explorer

The Daredevil	The Explorer
❏ If I believe an investment has a chance of really paying off big, I'm willing to take the chance that I could lose a large part (maybe even all) of my money.	❏ I'm willing to take a greater-than-average amount of risk in return for the possibility of having my portfolio grow substantially.
❏ I can accept losses in the value of my investments, even if they continue for several consecutive years. The end result is all that really matters!	❏ I can accept an occasional year where I lose money on my investments, but I wouldn't like it if I had two of them back-to-back.
❏ I almost always prefer to make my investing decisions on my own.	❏ I occasionally make my investing decisions all on my own, but usually I prefer to let my broker bring me what he thinks are his best ideas.
❏ The amount of current income I receive from an investment is not a factor in my decision making.	❏ It would be desirable to receive some current income from my investments, but I don't insist upon it in every case.
❏ Inflation is the number one threat. I think it's essential that you beat inflation, and that means you don't have the luxury of playing it safe all the time.	❏ Inflation is a genuine concern, so I'm willing to invest where there's a good chance of getting a "real" return even though there's a little more risk.
❏ I've had some super results on a few high-risk situations. Of course, I've had my share of big losers, too. To really make money, you've got to risk money.	❏ I think exploring new financial territory is exciting. When I hear about the latest "hot" investment area, I like to take a look.
❏ For me to risk 10% of my net worth in an investment that seemed to have a 90% chance of success, the potential profit would have to be at least equal to the amount I put at risk.	❏ For me to risk 10% of my net worth in an investment that seemed to have a 90% chance of success, the potential profit would have to be at least twice as much as the amount I put at risk.
❏ I suppose I'm optimistic (and a tad impulsive at times), but I don't usually worry about my investment decisions once they're made.	❏ I don't have time to bury myself in the details like some people. I keep my ear to the ground and think I have pretty good intuitive insights.
❏ It's important to me, perhaps even a source of pride, that my portfolio does better than the stock market over the course of an economic cycle.	❏ I do tend to compare the results in my portfolio with what the overall stock market did. It's a good feeling to know that you "beat" the market.
❏ If a stock doubled in price a year after I bought it, I'd buy some more shares in that company.	❏ If a stock doubled in price a year after I bought it, I'd hold on and hope for still more gains.

The Researcher

The Preserver

The Researcher	The Preserver
❏ I'm fairly conservative, but am willing to take a greater-than-average amount of risk with part of my portfolio in order to boost its growth potential.	❏ I'm very conservative, and am much more concerned about protecting what I already have than in taking risks to make it grow.
❏ I can handle the month-to-month ups and downs of investing, but I wouldn't want to end up losing any money for the entire year.	❏ It's important to my peace of mind to have stable, consistent year-to-year results.
❏ I prefer to make my own investing decisions, but am always open to ideas from the "experts" which I search out in magazines, books, and television/radio.	❏ Making investing decisions all on my own makes me a little nervous. I tend to rely a lot on others to help me.
❏ It's fairly important that I receive current income from my investments, but I'm willing to accept some uncertainty as to the amount.	❏ The amount of current income I receive from an investment is important to me; if possible, I'd like to know the amount in advance.
❏ Inflation is a genuine concern, but gains lower than the rate of inflation are acceptable if it means I can keep my risk down.	❏ Preserving my capital and knowing how much current income I'll receive are much more important to me than beating inflation.
❏ I want to make my decisions based on a solid understanding of all the facts. I don't believe in investing in something just because everyone else is doing it.	❏ News about such things as the savings and loan closings, our trade deficits, or the losses in "junk bonds" are a little scary and confusing.
❏ For me to risk 10% of my net worth in an investment that seemed to have a 90% chance of success, the potential profit would have to be at least four times as much as the amount I put at risk.	❏ No amount of potential profit is worth risking the loss of 10% of my net worth.
❏ Once I make a decision, I have a lot of confidence in it, which enables me to stay with it even if others around me are changing their minds.	❏ Making investment decisions is hard for me; I'm never quite sure I have all the facts. I wish I could be sure what the best investments are for me.
❏ I keep an eye on what the overall stock market is doing during the year. Naturally, I'd like to do even better, but it's not a major factor in my thinking.	❏ It's irrelevant to me whether my portfolio does better than the stock market over the course of an economic cycle.
❏ If a stock doubled in price a year after I bought it, I'd sell half my shares and lock in part of my profits.	❏ If a stock doubled in price a year after I bought it, I'd sell all my shares.

falling as the house gets paid for and the kids are raised. Retirement is now more than a distant concept; we see it as an economic reality that we will actually experience. Fine-tuning our financial plans and following a workable strategy takes on a new importance. We should begin reducing risk because our time horizon has shortened.

Phase 3: Preserving assets. Unbelievably, retirement is just around the corner (or already here)! Our need for preserving capital and generating current income has risen, and if we've done our job well, our need for additional growth in our capital base has abated. Our time horizon, which used to allow us the luxury of decades to bounce back from bear market losses, has shrunk dramatically. The situation calls for more fixed income investments and fewer stocks.

Phase 4: Distributing assets. We're in the home stretch of life, and can envision it won't be too long before we'll experience the joy of what Scripture means when it teaches that "to be away from the body" is to be "at home with the Lord." As much as prudently possible, we'll want to give away our surplus capital to our children and the Lord's work. At this point, unnecessary risk-taking should be avoided.

Locate your investing personality in the "controlling your risk" matrix on page 167. Then, select the financial phase of life that best describes your situation. Use the ages as guidelines, not laws. You might be age thirty-five and already in Phase Two, or fifty and still laying your Phase One foundation. If your recommended stock/bond mix requires a greater commitment to stocks than you've been comfortable with in the past, you've got a judgment call to make. You can use a dollar-cost-averaging approach (see chapter 16) for making the transition from where you are now to where you want to go.

The matrix reflects my personal sense of risk. Other investment advisers might feel more comfortable with less restrictive guidelines. For example, they might feel that a mix of 80% stocks and 20% bonds is acceptable even when you move into Phase 3 of life. All of us are being arbitrary to a degree. The point is that as the time to begin drawing on the investments draws ever nearer, you should move increasingly to a more conservative approach. If you've got ten or more years, you can afford to take more risk if you want to—but do you want to? It's up to you.

THE PERSONALITY TRAITS UNDERLYING THE FOUR TEMPERAMENTS

The temperaments were developed by factoring in one's willingness to lose money in the quest to make more money. You might say it's a question of whether optimism or caution is the governing emotion.

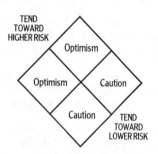

Then, we divide the diamond to show the levels of self-confidence in making one's own financial decisions versus the tendency to rely on others.

Another very important reminder: After you select guidelines that you feel comfortable with, *stick with them!* There will be many temptations from your broker, well-meaning friends, the media, and your own desires for higher returns that will encourage you to "make an exception" or abandon your guidelines altogether. You do so at your own peril.

Being realistic in your expectations is an important part . . .

. . . of your investment planning process. Making assumptions (often known as "wild guesses") about the future is an unavoidable part of planning and budgeting. One fundamental question that needs answering is: "How much of a return can I reasonably expect from my investment portfolio?" It's important that your answer be grounded in reality and not wishful thinking.

To this end, on page 157 I provided annual performance data for the Just-the-Basics portfolios. I could only go back to 1981 because that's as far as the index data went. The 1980s were an unusual time of economic growth and prosperity. The decade was hardly typical. After all, the stock market's average historical return over the past quarter century is about 12% per year, and the bond market's is about 8% a year. You can see that the performance numbers shown are slightly higher than that. So, in order to provide a more realistic guide as to what you might expect in the future, I would suggest that you have performance expectations that are 1%-2% lower than those shown.

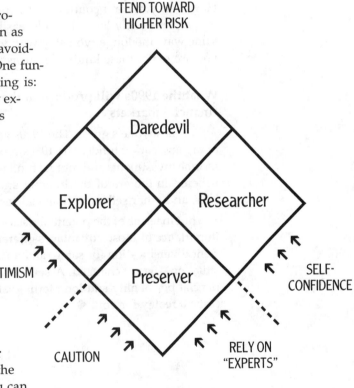

THE RESULT IS FOUR RISK PROFILES WITH DISTINCT STYLES OF INVESTMENT DECISION-MAKING

TEND TOWARD HIGHER RISK

Daredevil

Explorer   Researcher

OPTIMISM   Preserver   SELF-CONFIDENCE

CAUTION   RELY ON "EXPERTS"

TEND TOWARD LOWER RISK

Interestingly, the high-risk "all stocks" portfolio didn't do all that much better than the cautious "all bonds" portfolio over the *entire fifteen-year period.* There's only about a 2% per year difference in average returns between the highest and lowest risk portfolios! This is unlike the long-term performance history of stocks and bonds (see table on page 28). Bonds have performed above their long-term average due to the fact that interest rates have been in an extended decline from the lofty heights they reached in the early 1980s. As a result, the returns from stocks and bonds have been sufficiently similar that the percent invested in each type turned out to not make a big difference during many of the past fifteen years. For shorter periods, the amount allocated to stocks can make a huge difference, as you can see in the five-year returns.

Bear in mind that the results shown are merely averages. We know that if a penny is tossed 1,000 times, it's likely to land heads up about half the time. However, you can't count on these probabilities asserting themselves if you toss a penny *only twice*. It could easily come up tails twice in a row. In the same way, the longer you stay with your investing program, the more likely you are to get these kinds of returns.

What the 1990s will produce in the way of dramatic change in the financial markets . . .

. . . is anyone's guess. The 1970s gave us listed stock options and the birth of money market funds. The 1980s produced a veritable explosion in the fixed income investments and mutual fund industries. And the 1990s have — so far — ushered in the era of the Internet and on-line transactions with banks, brokers, and other sellers of financial services.

But in terms of the potential risks and rewards for the average investor, the importance of those advantages offered by the Just-the-Basics strategy — sufficient diversification for safety and a risk level designed to fit your individual situation — hasn't changed. Assemble a portfolio tailored to your individual financial personality and long-term goals, and peace-of-mind investing can become a reality for you. ◆

15

Getting Started on the Road to Financial Security

I. There are six key principles I believe should be incorporated into every investment strategy, all of which are reflected in the Just-the-Basics strategy.

   A. The foremost principle is to diversify in order to protect your capital against unexpected economic developments.

   B. Other principles include having clear-cut, objective rules for your decision making, staying within your emotional comfort zone, acknowledging your current financial limitations, and having a provision for investing in small amounts so you can get an early start.

II. The Just-the-Basics strategy requires you to open an investing account with the no-load Vanguard Group.

   A. I will walk you through the steps of how to do this, leading to the launch of your personalized Just-the-Basics portfolio.

   B. Tables are provided to show you how to divide your money among the Vanguard funds in order to achieve the portfolio mix and level of risk that you desire.

III. Just-the-Basics avoids the four "red flag" traps discussed in chapter 9.

IV. After your Just-the-Basics portfolio is in place, it requires you to take further action only once a year.

   A. This annual rebalancing process restores your desired portfolio allocations to their correct levels.

   B. It can be done at any time during the year which is convenient to you, but I usually recommend January as being a good time because it tends to coincide with other financial planning activities.

"The spontaneous tendency of our culture is to inexorably add detail to our lives: one more option, one more problem, one more commitment, one more expectation, one more purchase . . .

. . . one more debt, one more change, one more job, one more decision. We must now deal with more 'things per person' than at any other time in history. Yet one can comfortably handle only so many details in his or her life. Exceeding this threshold will result in disorganization or frustration. It is important to note here that the problem is not in the 'details.' The problem is in the 'exceeding.' This is called overloading."

I've been reading in Dr. Richard Swenson's interesting book *Margin*. He says that margin is the space that once existed between us and our limits. It's the gap between rest and exhaustion, between peace and anxiety. He thinks most of us don't have enough margin, and he has written his book to provide a prescription for the dangers of overloaded lives. I've found it fascinating so far, and intend to finish it as soon as I can find the time.

Swenson lists twenty-three specific types of overload. I was struck by how many of the items could also appear on a list of frustrations that often overwhelm average people as they attempt to manage their financial lives. A few of them include: choice overload (too many possible investments clamoring for attention), education overload (too much to learn), expectation overload (we're told we can have "wealth without risk"), hurry overload (investing ads are presented as if it's essential to "act now"), information overload (research, articles, and opinions coming at us faster than we can possibly absorb them), and media overload (thousands of experts writing thousands of books and appearing on tens of thousands of radio and TV programs).

It was to help eliminate this sense of overload and the paralysis it can cause that I created the Four Levels process and Just-the-Basics investing strategy. To get a perspective as to where we now stand on our journey toward sound mind investing, let's briefly review what we've covered thus far.

◆ In Section One, we laid a foundation of basic principles to guide you as you set your financial priorities. We looked at what investing is, and why it's actually quite simple (chapter 1). Next, we considered two financial fitness tests you should pass before using your monthly surplus to invest in the stock and bond markets. The first was to get debt-free (chapter 2). We also discussed where paying off a house mortgage fit in (chapter 3). The second test was that of saving for future needs by building a contingency reserve (chapters 4 and 5). Finally, we considered the rising costs of college and how to plan for them (chapter 6).

◆ In Section Two, we looked at the world of mutual funds. This included the advantages they offer the average investor (chapter 7), how they're sold and the best way to buy them (chapter 8), necessary cautions that should be understood about their risks (chapter 9), and the tax consequences of owning mutual funds (chapter 10).

◆ Thus far in Section Three, we've looked at some basic things you should know about the nature of bonds (chapter 11) and stocks (chapter 12). Next, I introduced you to a "no muss, no fuss" approach to putting together a long-term stock and bond portfolio that I've dubbed Just-the-Basics because of its simplicity and low maintenance requirements. In chapter 13, I explained how it works and why it gives better results than the majority of professional money managers can achieve. And in chapter 14, I gave you some guidelines for personalizing the all-important decision as to how much of your Just-the-Basics portfolio should be invested in stocks versus bonds.

In this chapter, I'm going to equip you with the remaining specifics you need to launch your own Just-the-Basics strategy. I'd like to start by showing how Just-the-Basics reflects the six principles that I believe every investment strategy should follow. Whether you're single or married, young or nearing retirement, investing for college or buying your first house, this strategy is flexible enough to work well for you! Here are the six principles.

Principle #1: Success in investing comes not in hoping for the best, but in knowing how you will handle the worst.

Always remember: nobody *really* knows what's going to happen next. Some things can be predicted; most things can't. The tide tables, for example, can be prepared far ahead of time because they are governed by physical laws. The investment world is a colossal engine fueled by human emotions. Millions of people make billions of decisions all reflecting their feelings of fear or security, hardship or prosperity. To attempt to make reliable forecasts in the face of this staggering complexity is foolhardy.

Therefore, since nobody really knows what is going to happen next year, next month, or even next week, your plan must allow for the fact that the investment markets will experience some unexpected rough sledding every now and then. That's where diversification comes in. The idea is to pick investments that "march to different drummers." This means your strategy involves owning a mix of investments that are affected by different economic events. For example, you might invest in both a bond fund and a gold fund. When inflation really heats up, bonds go down (due to rising interest rates) while at the same time gold goes up (because investors want a secure "store of value"). To the extent that the price changes in the two funds offset each other, you have added stability to your overall portfolio.

Surprisingly, it is possible to assemble some lower-risk investment combinations that give pretty much the same returns over time as higher-risk ones. When that is done, such a mix of investments is said to be more "efficient" because it accomplishes the same investment result while taking less risk. Just-the-Basics offers you portfolios that combine stocks and bonds in various combinations in order to reduce volatility and risk while still achieving attractive long-term returns.

Principle #2: Your investing plan must have easy-to-understand, clear-cut rules.

There must be no room for differing interpretations. You must be able to make your investing decisions quickly and with confidence. This means reducing your decision making to numerical guidelines as much as possible. A strategy that calls for a "significant investment" in small company stocks is not as helpful as one that calls for "30% of your portfolio" to be invested in small company stocks.

Insofar as possible, your strategy should not only tell you *what* to invest in but also offer precise guidance in telling you *how much* to invest and *when* to buy and *when* to sell. With Just-the-Basics you'll always know exactly where you stand and what you need to do to stay on course.

ATTITUDE CHECK

When Saddam Hussein launched his surprise invasion of Kuwait, the Dow Jones Industrials fell 130 points in three days. After stabilizing for a few sessions, it dropped almost 200 more points in another three-day period. Imagine yourself watching the value of your hard-earned investment portfolio losing more than 10% of its value so quickly! Not only that, but there was no way of knowing how long the weakness would last or what the final outcome would be. Which of these statements do you think would best reflect your reaction to what was happening in the financial markets? Your choice reflects your investment temperament (shown in parentheses).

❑ "You never know when something like this could happen. That's why I don't put much of my money in the stock market. I'm very conservative and am more interested in holding on to what I have than in taking risks that might make my money grow" (Preserver).

❑ "I realize that things like this are going to happen from time to time. That's why I'm careful to investigate before I invest. I'm fairly conservative but am willing to accept some risk of loss in return for greater growth potential. My long-term plan is still sound. I'm going to stay calm and ride this out" (Researcher).

❑ "My broker called and said he was recommending that his clients buy some call options on oil. I've never invested in options before, but this sounded like a good time. I'm willing to risk losing a fair amount of my capital in return for the possibility of having my money grow substantially" (Explorer).

❑ "What a great opportunity! Oil prices are skyrocketing, gold is moving up, and stocks are really taking a beating. By jumping in quickly, a person has a chance to double his money pretty fast. I'm willing to risk losing all of the money I put at risk if I'm convinced that the investment has a chance of paying off really big" (Daredevil).

Principle #3: Your investing plan must reflect your current financial limitations.

Your plan should effectively prevent you from taking risks you can't financially afford. The words "higher risk" mean that there's a greater likelihood that you can actually lose part or all of your money. Every day, people who mistakenly thought "it will never happen to me" find just how wrong they were. Investing in the stock market is not a game where gains and losses are just the means of keeping score. Money is not an abstract commodity. For most of us, it represents years of work, hopes, and dreams. Its unexpected loss can be devastating.

That's why the sound mind approach sets getting debt-free and building your emergency reserve as your two top priorities. Only then are you financially strong enough to bear the risk of loss that is an ever-present reality in the stock market. I encourage you: do not invest any discretionary funds in the stock and bond markets until your debt and savings goals are fully met. At that time, you can refer to the "controlling your risk" matrix for guidelines that reflect the growth needs appropriate for your current season of life.

Principle #4: Your investing plan must keep you within your emotional "comfort zone."

Your investing plan should prevent you from taking risks that rob you of your peace. Consider the four responses given in the Attitude Check (far left). These are likely reactions from our four investment temperaments. The amount of risk you take should be consistent with your temperament. You shouldn't adopt a strategy that takes you past your good-night's sleep level! If you do, you will tend to bail out at the worst possible time. A Just-the-Basics portfolio, used in conjunction with the risk matrix shown on page 167, will reflect your investing personality and current season of life.

Principle #5: Your investing plan must be realistic concerning the level of return you can reasonably expect.

I receive letters asking me to recommend safe investments that will guarantee returns of 12%, 14%, and more. If by "safe" it is meant that there's absolutely no chance of the value of the investment falling, then I must answer that I don't know of any investments like that. The ones that I do know about that are "safe" in that sense usually pay much less than 12%.

The reason any investment offers a potentially higher rate of return is that *it has to* in order to reward investors for accepting a higher level of risk. My goal is to help you get started in the right direction, incurring the least risk possible that will still get you to your destination safely. The tables on page 157 provided the historical performance results of each of the Just-the-Basics portfolios in order to let you know ahead of time what are reasonable expectations with respect to rates of return.

"How to Calculate Your Rate of Return" by Austin Pryor. Excerpted from the Sound Mind Investing newsletter. See Briefing 16, page 477.

Principle #6: Your investment plan must allow you to begin investing in small amounts so that you can get started right away and take full advantage of the tremendous power of compound interest.

Remember the story of Jack and Jill in chapter 4? Who would you have expected to have the larger retirement fund at age sixty-five—Jack, who put $6,600 in as a young paperboy, or Jill, who put in $80,000 over the forty years of her working life? Weren't you surprised to learn that Jack was the winner? His fund had grown to more than $1,078,000, an amount 162 times more than he put in as a child! Jack's earlier start, even with much smaller amounts and for far fewer years, was too much for Jill to overcome, thanks to the tremendous power of compounding.

That's why it's important to start investing early and to add to your program regularly. The Vanguard mutual funds recommended in this strategy offer automatic savings programs, some of which will accept amounts as low as $50 per month. Even such small amounts can grow to substantial sums over many years. Every dollar makes a difference!

Here's how to open your Just-the-Basics account at Vanguard.

Vanguard is one of the largest and most respected no-load mutual fund organizations in the investment industry. It offers an exceptional variety of funds from which you can choose, and you can move your money from one of its funds into another via the telephone at no cost. Vanguard has a reputation for giving excellent service while keeping administrative costs low. Accounts can be opened with as little as $3,000.

As with all no-load funds, there are no commissions charged, either when you invest or when you take your money out. However, Vanguard does levy an 0.5% transaction fee when you purchase the Extended Market index fund. Although I wish it didn't feel a need to do this, I can understand the reasoning. An index fund attempts to achieve the same rate of return as the index which it follows. To do this, the fund manager tries to weight the securities in the portfolio so they closely mirror the weight they're given in the underlying index. If the portfolio manager receives $1 million in new money, he can't just buy one or two stocks with it. He has to spread it out so that the correct portfolio mix is being maintained. For indexes that contain a great many stocks, the trading commissions can get pretty steep if investors move in and out of the fund a lot. One way to discourage this and keep operating costs down is to charge investors an entry fee each time they deposit money in the fund. If it makes you feel any better, Vanguard doesn't keep the fee for itself. It goes back into the index fund to help offset commission expenses.

HOW I SUGGEST DIVIDING YOUR MONEY UNDER THE JUST-THE-BASICS STRATEGY

(SEE RISK MATRIX ON PAGE 167)

Percentage of stocks:	100%	80%	60%	40%	20%	0%
Percentage of bonds:	0%	20%	40%	60%	80%	100%
International Growth	20%	16%	12%	8%	4%	0%
Index: Extended Market	40%	32%	24%	16%	8%	0%
Index: S&P 500	40%	32%	24%	16%	8%	0%
Index: Total Bond Market	0%	20%	40%	60%	80%	100%

Call Vanguard toll-free at (800) 662-7447. Ask them to send information on their money market funds and the four funds used in Just-the-Basics. To reduce confusion over similar sounding names, Vanguard assigns each of its funds a number—see headings, page 182. It helps if you will specify each fund by its number when asking for information or buying and selling shares. (It's possible to move your current IRA, SEP-IRA, Keogh, or 403(b) account to Vanguard. If interested, request the necessary forms at this time as well.)

In the package that you will receive is an account registration form for opening a money market fund account. This is a simple form that can be completed in a few minutes. Some of the questions request that you make choices (which can be changed at any time) among different convenience options. You can call Vanguard toll-free, if you need to, for help in completing the form.

The automatic investment plan is especially helpful for automating your program. By providing the information about your local bank, you can have your bank send the amount you choose directly to your Vanguard money market account every month. Vanguard will take care of the arrangements. I also suggest that you sign where indicated and apply for check-writing privileges. Vanguard will send you checks, which will come in handy in case you need to quickly transfer your money from Vanguard to your home bank.

Initially, I suggest you deposit all of your money into the Vanguard Money Market Prime Portfolio.

It pays excellent short-term interest rates with virtually no risk. Once your account is established, your initial deposit will be sitting in your new money market account. Then, you can make a phone call with instructions to move the money out of the money market fund and into our recommended funds in accordance with the portfolio mix you have selected.

There are many different ways to achieve the various portfolio mixes. The ones shown on the chalkboard (far left) are offered as guidelines. While I've made an effort to provide a proper balance on the stock side, they are still arbitrary to a certain extent. For example, you might want to invest less in international stocks and more in the small company stocks represented by the Extended Market index fund. It's fine to make some small adjustments. In fact, in my newsletter, I fine-tune them a little going into each new year. So, don't feel like you have to follow them to the letter of the law. Also, don't worry about being super-precise ("My S&P 500 fund is only 29% and it should be 32%"). If you're off a little one way or the other, it's OK.

To simplify your tax accounting, I suggest that you tell Vanguard that you do not wish to have all income and capital gains distributions reinvested; instead, ask that they be deposited into your money market account, where you can reallocate them among the four funds at a convenient time.

Keep in mind that the minimum for investing in any of the Vanguard funds is initially $3,000. This makes it difficult for smaller accounts to diversify among the four funds according to the portfolio allocation guidelines I've suggested. To help you reach the approximate mix you're looking for, I prepared the tables on pages 182-183. (I didn't include suggestions for portfolios with 80% and 100% bond allocations because it's unlikely anyone who is in the process of getting started with a long-term strategy would want to be that conservative.) In addition to the four Just-the-Basics funds, you'll temporarily be using a few other Vanguard funds which will help you come close to achieving the mix you desire. They include:

Index Trust: Total Stock Market. The goal of this fund is to imitate the performance of the Wilshire 5000 index (see pages 145-146 for basics on Wilshire and other stock indexes). Stocks in the S&P 500 index represent about 70% of the Wilshire 5000, leaving 30% of this fund invested in smaller companies. This "small cap" component has enabled the Wilshire to outpace the S&P 500 in twelve of the past twenty years.

◆ **Star LifeStrategy Portfolios.** These are funds that invest in *other* Vanguard funds. For example, 50% of the Star Growth portfolio is invested in the Total Stock Market index, 15% is split between two regional foreign indexes (Vanguard doesn't offer a worldwide stock index fund), 10% is divided among four bond funds, and 25% is placed in Vanguard's Asset Allocation Fund. The latter fund divides its investments between a stock and bond index, altering the mix between the two as the portfolio manager thinks best; therefore, the amount of the Star portfolios invested in bonds varies depending on what's happening in the Asset Allocation fund. These portfolios are relatively new, and so have only a brief track record (except for what can be deduced from the history of the other Vanguard funds in which they invest). Due to Vanguard's low expenses, these funds seem like an attractive option for the beginning investor who wants to pursue an indexing strategy.

Keep in mind that the advantages of indexing—keeping costs low, for example—manifest themselves over time. Don't focus too much on short-term performance. Carefully review the material Vanguard sends in order to be sure you clearly understand the pros and cons of investing in index funds.

Remember the cautions concerning many of today's mutual funds which I alerted you to back in chapter 9?

At the end of that chapter, I promised to "introduce you to a special breed of mutual funds . . . that, by their very nature, avoid the red flag traps we've just discussed." Let's briefly look at how index funds and the Just-the-Basics strategy protect you from the abuses explained in chapter 9.

◆ Red Flag #1: You can't necessarily accept a fund's "investment objective" at face value.

You don't have to worry about an index fund broadening its investing horizons (and taking on more risk in the process), because that would be self-defeating. An index fund doesn't have any investment objective other than to replicate the performance of the index it's based on.

◆ Red Flag #2: You can't necessarily accept a fund's diversification claims at face value.

Recommended Resource

One of the advantages of investment newsletters is their ability to target their message to readers with highly specialized interests. Since the 1970s there have been newsletters that concentrated on no-load mutual funds, but in recent years a new breed of newsletter has come along with a much more limited focus—the funds of a single organization.

If you have an account at Vanguard (or are considering opening one), you might find The Independent Adviser for Vanguard Investors of interest. While it contains some market commentary and a variety of investing articles, it's primarily devoted to writing about the mutual funds offered by Vanguard. It reviews each one, giving it a buy, hold, or sell recommendation. It provides monthly updates on performance, current yields, and when distributions will be paid. It discusses Vanguard's policies, and critiques its annual reports to shareholders.

Bear in mind that every investment adviser has his or her own philosophy about how best to diversify and how to select the funds in your portfolio. All the recommendations in the Vanguard Adviser won't necessarily be in accord with what I'm saying in this book, but I trust that you're growing sufficiently in your knowledge and comfort level that a second opinion will be helpful rather than confusing!

For more information on subscribing to this newsletter, call (800) 211-7642.

For an index fund to concentrate its holdings in a relatively few stocks would also be self-defeating. Unless, of course, the fund is based on an index, like the Dow Industrials, which itself encompasses a small number of stocks. In that case, the fund would be doing exactly what it is supposed to do.

◆ Red Flag #3: You can't necessarily accept a fund's implied performance excellence at face value.

There's no incentive for an S&P 500 index fund to claim a gain of 15% in a year when the S&P 500 gained just 10%. It would only serve to reveal that the fund manager had done a poor job of tracking the index and make the manager look inept rather than insightful.

◆ Red Flag #4: You can't necessarily accept a fund's rankings at face value.

Performance rankings are a function of which peer group a fund is in and how well it performs in that group. There's no disagreement among industry observers as to which peer groups the various index funds should be placed in. Relative rankings of index funds may not always be in the top quartile, but they will at least be honest.

The four red flags are all symptoms of the same problem: Mutual funds function in a highly combative marketplace, and their managers are under tremendous pressures to outperform the competition. Take away the need to outperform, and you take away the stimulus for the abuses. Index funds have the luxury of being appreciated for the fact that, while they never outperform the markets, neither do they have the misfortune of underperforming it.

One of the periodic housekeeping chores investors must deal with from time to time is "rebalancing" their portfolios. It's like four people playing a game of Monopoly.

Everybody starts out with 25% of the money, but after a few rounds of play, some are richer and some poorer. To get back where you started, you'd have to "rebalance" by taking money from some players and giving it to others. Here's how that applies here.

Assume you invest along the lines recommended for those desiring a portfolio mix of 80% stocks and 20% bonds. You divide your money among the four Vanguard funds as shown in the first column of the graphic on page 184. In the months that follow, as some funds do better than others, the percentages you started with begin to change. If Index Extended Market does better than International Growth, for example, it may soon represent 35% of your total holdings while International Growth falls to just 12%. How long do you let this continue before you step in and sell some Extended Market in order to return its value to just 32% of your portfolio? How long, in other words, before you rebalance? I suggest the first week of each new year. Emotionally, January is a good time for new beginnings and fresh starts. Also, if you have taxable gains, waiting until

LAUNCHING A JUST-THE-BASICS PORTFOLIO
WITH A MIX OF 100% STOCKS AND 0% BONDS

Amount of Money You Have Available to Invest	Vanguard International Growth Stocks (Fund 81)	Vanguard Index Trust: Extended Market (Fund 98)	Vanguard Index Trust: S&P 500 (Fund 40)	Vanguard Bond Index: Total Bond Market (Fund 84)	Vanguard Total Stock Market (Fund 85)	Vanguard Star Growth Portfolio (Fund 122)	Vanguard Star Moderate Growth (Fund 914)	Vanguard Star Conservative Growth (Fund 724)
$3,000					$3,000			
$6,000		$3,000	$3,000					
$9,000	$3,000	$3,000	$3,000					
$12,000	$3,000	$4,500	$4,500					
$15,000	$3,000	$6,000	$6,000					
$20,000	$4,000	$8,000	$8,000					
$25,000	$5,000	$10,000	$10,000					
$30,000	$6,000	$12,000	$12,000					
$35,000	$7,000	$14,000	$14,000					
$40,000	$8,000	$16,000	$16,000					
$45,000	$9,000	$18,000	$18,000					
$50,000	$10,000	$20,000	$20,000					
Additional	20%	40%	40%					

LAUNCHING A JUST-THE-BASICS PORTFOLIO
WITH A MIX OF 80% STOCKS AND 20% BONDS

Amount of Money You Have Available to Invest	Vanguard International Growth Stocks (Fund 81)	Vanguard Index Trust: Extended Market (Fund 98)	Vanguard Index Trust: S&P 500 (Fund 40)	Vanguard Bond Index: Total Bond Market (Fund 84)	Vanguard Total Stock Market (Fund 85)	Vanguard Star Growth Portfolio (Fund 122)	Vanguard Star Moderate Growth (Fund 914)	Vanguard Star Conservative Growth (Fund 724)
$3,000						$3,000		
$6,000						$6,000		
$9,000						$9,000		
$12,000						$12,000		
$15,000	$3,000	$3,000	$3,000	$3,000	$3,000			
$20,000	$3,200	$6,400	$6,400	$4,000				
$25,000	$4,000	$8,000	$8,000	$5,000				
$30,000	$4,800	$9,600	$9,600	$6,000				
$35,000	$5,600	$11,200	$11,200	$7,000				
$40,000	$6,400	$12,800	$12,800	$8,000				
$45,000	$7,200	$14,400	$14,400	$9,000				
$50,000	$8,000	$16,000	$16,000	$10,000				
Additional	16%	32%	32%	20%				

LAUNCHING A JUST-THE-BASICS PORTFOLIO WITH A MIX OF 60% STOCKS AND 40% BONDS

Amount of Money You Have Available to Invest	Vanguard International Growth Stocks (Fund 81)	Vanguard Index Trust: Extended Market (Fund 98)	Vanguard Index Trust: S&P 500 (Fund 40)	Vanguard Bond Index: Total Bond Market (Fund 84)	Vanguard Total Stock Market (Fund 85)	Vanguard Star Growth Portfolio (Fund 122)	Vanguard Star Moderate Growth (Fund 914)	Vanguard Star Conservative Growth (Fund 724)
$3,000							$3,000	
$6,000							$6,000	
$9,000							$9,000	
$12,000							$12,000	
$15,000	$3,000	$3,000	$3,000	$6,000				
$20,000	$3,000	$4,500	$4,500	$8,000				
$25,000	$3,000	$6,000	$6,000	$10,000				
$30,000	$3,600	$7,200	$7,200	$12,000				
$35,000	$4,200	$8,400	$8,400	$14,000				
$40,000	$4,800	$9,600	$9,600	$16,000				
$45,000	$5,400	$10,800	$10,800	$18,000				
$50,000	$6,000	$12,000	$12,000	$20,000				
Additional	12%	24%	24%	40%				

LAUNCHING A JUST-THE-BASICS PORTFOLIO WITH A MIX OF 40% STOCKS AND 60% BONDS

Amount of Money You Have Available to Invest	Vanguard International Growth Stocks (Fund 81)	Vanguard Index Trust: Extended Market (Fund 98)	Vanguard Index Trust: S&P 500 (Fund 40)	Vanguard Bond Index: Total Bond Market (Fund 84)	Vanguard Total Stock Market (Fund 85)	Vanguard Star Growth Portfolio (Fund 122)	Vanguard Star Moderate Growth (Fund 914)	Vanguard Star Conservative Growth (Fund 724)
$3,000								$3,000
$6,000								$6,000
$9,000								$9,000
$12,000								$12,000
$15,000								$15,000
$20,000	$3,000	$3,000	$3,000	$11,000				
$25,000	$3,000	$3,800	$3,800	$14,400				
$30,000	$3,000	$4,500	$4,500	$18,000				
$35,000	$3,000	$5,500	$5,500	$21,000				
$40,000	$3,200	$6,400	$6,400	$24,000				
$45,000	$3,600	$7,200	$7,200	$27,000				
$50,000	$4,000	$8,000	$8,000	$30,000				
Additional	8%	16%	16%	60%				

January postpones paying the tax for a year.

The graphic below shows how the rebalancing computation is made. The initial purchases were made based on a portfolio mix of 80% stocks, 20% bonds as shown in column one. At the end of the year, the account balances have changed due to market fluctuations (and possibly because you added some new money during the year). Going into the new year, you want to get your portfolio back to the desired 80/20 levels. To do this, you simply multiply the percentage in column one for each fund times the new total value of your holdings (circled). In the example, the new target level for International Growth is $9,271 (16% x $57,942). To restore the fund to its proper level, you must buy $2,059 in new shares ($9,271 minus $7,212). This purchase (as well as the smaller one for the bond fund) is paid for by selling off shares in the Extended Market and S&P 500 funds.

AN EXAMPLE OF THE ANNUAL REBALANCING PROCESS

	Desired Mix	Initial Purchases	End Of Period	Desired Balances	Changes Needed
International Growth	16%	$8,000	$7,212	$9,271	+2,059
Index: Extended Market	32%	16,000	20,379	18,541	–1,838
Index: S&P 500	32%	16,000	19,564	18,541	–1,023
Index: Total Bond Market	20%	10,000	10,787	11,588	+801
Total Holdings	100%	$50,000	$57,942	$57,942	

You will notice that rebalancing takes money away from your star performers and gives it to the poorer performing groups.

A common question is: "Why are we buying more shares in last year's losers at the expense of last year's winners? Since they've done so poorly, wouldn't it be better to put less emphasis on them for the coming year?" If "better" means "more profitable," then the answer is that some years it would be better; but I think most years it would not. Market performance leaders change as the economy goes through the various stages of its cycle.

For example, in 1990, the worst performance among the four Vanguard Just-the-Basics funds was the Extended Market fund, which lost 14.0% (see page 157). If you had not rebalanced and built that portion of your portfolio back up to its recommended percent allocation, you would have been underinvested in that fund in 1991 when it turned in the best performance of the four (+41.9%). Similarly, in 1992, the worst performer was the International Growth fund, which lost almost 6%. If you had not rebalanced at the end of 1992, you would have missed out on having a full allocation in 1993's top performer among Just-the-Basics funds when International Growth soared 44.7%.

I assure you, this kind of thing happens all the time. If it didn't, wouldn't the markets be a great place to make easy money? ◆

CHAPTER PREVIEW

Systematic Strategies for Meeting Long-Term Investment Goals (Even if You're Starting from Scratch)

I. **Dollar-cost-averaging is a widely practiced formula strategy for investing that automates your decision making.**

    A. Dollar-cost-averaging requires investing the same amount of money in the same investment at regular time intervals. This approach forces you to do what every investor seeks to do: buy more shares when prices are low and fewer shares when prices are high.

    B. Dollar-cost-averaging is an excellent way to gradually invest a large sum.

II. **Value-averaging is an innovative improvement in the traditional dollar-cost-averaging strategy that helps assure you will reach your long-term goals on time.**

    A. Rather than making your monthly investment based on a fixed amount, value-averaging has you make whatever investment amount is necessary in order to get your account to rise in value by $100 (or some other goal) each month, after taking into consideration the market gains or losses in the account for that month.

    B. This strategy generates better returns than dollar-cost-averaging, as the investor buys more than usual when prices move lower. It does, however, involve greater complexity and requires more effort on the part of the investor.

III. **A strict buy/sell discipline, as provided by formula strategies, is essential for successful investing.**

    A. Formula strategies need not be "perfect" to be highly profitable.

    B. A disciplined strategy is essential to protect you from unexpected swings in the market and your own emotions.

One knowledgeable writer called dollar-cost-averaging a long-term investment technique that "beats the market . . . by ignoring the market."

A consistent theme of this book from the introduction forward has been the importance of taking charge of your own financial future by becoming an "initiator" rather than a "responder." The responder is passive until dramatic news events or a persuasive sales presentation prompts him to act. Often, after taking action, responders still can't articulate exactly how the particular decision they've just made serves to advance them toward their long-term investment goals. Initiators, on the other hand, don't let others shape their course; *they* set the pace. Action is taken as a result of specific guidelines from a specific strategy coming into play. They "plan their work and work their plan."

That's where systematic "formula" strategies come in. A formula strategy can be quite useful because it requires that you make your buying and selling decisions based solely on mechanical guidelines. There is no judgment involved; it's all automatic. They are helpful because they protect you against your own emotions and the tendency to go along with the crowd. Such strategies fit well into the disciplined framework for decision making desired by initiators.

Probably the best-known formula strategy is dollar-cost-averaging (DCA). It's neither complicated nor time-consuming; in fact, it is simplicity personified. Here's all you do: (1) invest the *same amount* of money (2) at *regular time intervals*. The amount and frequency are up to you. You could invest $1,000 every three months. Or $100 every month. The important thing is to pick an amount you can stick with faithfully over many years.

The benefits of DCA can best be illustrated with a simple example. (I'm going to exaggerate the amount of market volatility in order to show the mathematical effects.) Let's assume you can afford to invest $100 every month in your stock fund program. At the time of your first new investment, the fund shares sell for $10. The next month, the market soars and you pay $14 for your shares. Finally, the third month the market falls back, and your fund retreats to $12, midway between your two buying levels. Ordinarily, that would put you at break-even. But look at what has happened. The first month you were able to buy ten shares at $10 per share. The second month you acquired only 7.1429 shares at $14 per share. Now, at $12 each, your 17.1429 shares are worth $205.71. Instead at being at break-even, you have a small profit.

This improvement occurred *because your constant dollar investment forced you to buy more shares when the price was low and to buy fewer shares when the price was high.* In effect, you are buying more at bargain prices and relatively little at what might be considered high prices. Of course, only when you look back years from now will you know when prices really were bargains and when prices were too high.

The beauty of DCA is that it frees you from . . .

. . . the worry of whether you're buying stocks at the "wrong" time. *It is critically important to ignore all market fluctuations when employing a dollar-cost-averaging strategy.* Most investors who obtain poor returns in the market are victims of their own emotions. Only after stock prices have been rising sharply do responders work up enough courage to buy stock fund shares. And about the only time they ever sell shares is when they become especially fearful after prices have plunged. The consequence is that they buy high and sell low, the very opposite of their ambition. It is important, then, not to let your emotions control you. You must exercise the discipline of maintaining your systematic investment program.

You can make your dollar-cost-averaging investments as frequently as you wish: weekly, monthly, or even quarterly. However, for best results, it is better to make more frequent investments. The reason for this is that market lows may not occur near the time you are scheduled to make an investment. The more frequently your program calls for reinvestment, the greater likelihood the program will enable you to buy shares near intermediate-term lows. As you can see, this strategy almost makes you hope that the market will fall so you can accumulate more shares for your money!

One reminder. Dollar-cost-averaging is a two-edged sword.
It can lower your potential profits as well as losses.

If your fund's share prices had risen all year long, you would obviously show greater gains if you had made a single large investment early on. In fact, academic studies have appeared in recent years purporting to show that DCA is a bad idea. Why? Because the market has a long-term upward bias. Over time, the market always moves higher. The implication is that, on average, you're going to be paying more for your shares if you stretch your buying out than if you go ahead and invest as much as you can as soon as possible.

That's all well and good when you're looking back over a forty-year period with 20/20 vision. It ignores the fact that there are bear market periods along the way when it's quite easy for investors to be frightened out of the markets altogether. If you invest your $50,000 inheritance just before a bear market wipes out $10,000 of it, who's to say you're going to have the stomach for staying around and waiting for the next bull market to recoup your losses and then some? The academics may have it right in theory, but in the real world, DCA makes it easier for investors to overcome their fears and make the difficult decision to put their limited (and therefore, precious) savings at risk.

In summary, DCA is the systematic investing of a fixed amount of money on a regular basis (usually monthly). I especially like it when used in conjunction with no-load funds for these reasons:

◆ It eliminates the need to ask the question, "Is this a good time to buy stocks?" As far as DCA investors are concerned, every month is a good month.

◆ It imposes a discipline, forcing you to make regular "installment" payments on your future financial security.

◆ It will cause you to buy relatively more fund shares when prices are low and fewer shares when prices are high.

◆ Using no-load funds allows the purchase of fractional shares, eliminates commission costs, and provides sufficient diversification to reflect the stock market at large.

These advantages also make DCA a good way to "ease" into the stock market if you have a windfall or other lump sum to invest.

It's not at all unusual for people who have never been responsible for investing to suddenly find themselves confronted with the responsibility for making important decisions regarding a large amount of money. The money might have come from the sale of a home, an unexpected inheritance, an IRA rollover, or from aging parents who no longer can handle the investing of their own funds. Here's how they can use the Sound Mind strategy to develop a prudent plan:

❶ Deposit the money into one of the leading money market mutual funds in order to put it to work right away. (See chapter 5 for shopping tips.) This removes any pressure on you to make decisions quickly. When you open your account, be sure to ask for check-writing privileges, which will enable you to later make your long-term investments more conveniently.

❷ Review the suggestions for making "right" investment decisions given in chapter 17. Follow the principles given as closely as possible.

❸ Refer to the "controlling your risk" matrix in chapter 14 for help in dividing your money between lower-risk lending-types of investments and higher-risk owning-types.

"Stock Market Seasonality" by Austin Pryor. Excerpted from the Sound Mind Investing newsletter. See Briefing 17, page 478.

❹ Decide whether you will be following Just-the-Basics or attempting some of the fine-tuning strategies. *I would suggest the most conservative approach of combining Just-the-Basics with end-of-month seasonality* (see Briefing 17) to time your investments. It's much simpler, which means it will be easier to understand, easier to implement, and easier to monitor over time. You can always move to greater complexity later if you feel it's justified.

❺ Decide to invest a certain number of dollars every month until it's all deployed the way you want it. If you have $50,000, you can invest $25,000 per month for two months, or $10,000 per month for five months, or whatever seems comfortable. There is no particular rule of thumb as to which is best. Here's one way to decide. Which sounds worse to you — moving in quickly in two steps only to find that you paid more for your shares than necessary, or moving slowly in ten steps and missing most of the gains from what turned out to be a good period for the market?

Here's my perspective: It's better to lose an *opportunity* than to lose *money*. Dividing your money into five to ten parts and investing it over the same number of months strikes me as a good balance. If you're doing DCA with more than one mutual fund, ideally you should add to each of the funds each month. Investing in several funds over ten months involves many different transactions, but it has the advantage of being the more cautious approach.

Let's now address one problem presented by the typical DCA strategy: you have no way of knowing ahead of time . . .

. . . what your DCA portfolio will be worth in five, ten, or twenty years. For planning purposes, you know how much you expect to be putting in each month, but you *don't know* what it will grow to over the years. The solution to this dilemma has been suggested by Michael Edleson in his interesting book called *Value Averaging, The Safe and Easy Strategy for Higher Investment Returns*.

A professor at Harvard's Graduate School of Business Administration (with a Ph.D. from the Massachusetts Institute of Technology), Edleson suggests a simple change in the traditional DCA formula. Rather than making your monthly investment based on a fixed amount (say $100 each month), he suggests making *whatever investment amount is necessary* in order to get your account to rise in value by $100 (or some other amount) each month. The focus is on the resulting value in your account instead of on how much you put in. He calls his approach "value averaging" (VA) and offers several different variations of how you might tailor it to your situation.

In his book (which you will want to purchase and study if you think value averaging would be a good approach for your situation), Edleson says that his research indicates that VA is consistently superior to the traditional DCA approach. To whet your appetite, I'm going to walk you through an example of the simplest VA strategy, the one Edleson calls the "no-sell" variation.

First, you must set up your "value path." You know how much you are starting with and how much you'd like to end with; your value path is merely the value in your account at each month's end along the way. A very simple one would be that if you started with $2,000 and wanted to have $8,000 in two years, your value path would increase by $250 each month (see first two columns in "Value Averaging Worksheet" on next page).

Once you know your value path, it's simply a matter of adding enough each month to make your portfolio value conform to your value path.

Gains and losses in the investment account each month are reflected in the Portfolio Value column. At the end of the first month, the portfolio has gained

Recommended Resource
Value Averaging:
The Safe and Easy Strategy
for Higher Investment Returns
by Michael Edleson

If you're not naturally a "math" person, Professor Edleson's book will walk you through the process and give you the answers you need. If you have any experience with computer spreadsheets, Edleson includes the Lotus cell formulas in the book as an additional convenience for his readers. Once you create a template, you're all set. The purchase price is worth the insights and help you will receive.

$42, taking the account value up to $2,042. But since the value path calls for $2,250 at the end of month one, we need to add $208 to the investment account. That gives us the desired $2,250 total. In month two, we add $216 to build the account to $2,500; in month three, we add $240 to build it to $2,750, and so on.

That's all there is to it: depositing enough extra money into the account so as to preserve the value path. When the two years are up, the goal will have been reached. In the example shown, the $8,000 breaks down as follows: $2,000 of it was the starting amount, $813 was earned in the investment account, and $5,187 represents the monthly additions along the way.

VALUE AVERAGING WORKSHEET

End of Month	Value Path	Portfolio Value	Need to Deposit	After Deposit
	$2000			
1	2250	$2042	$208	$2250
2	2500	2284	216	2500
3	2750	2510	240	2750
4	3000	2783	217	3000
5	3250	3042	208	3250
6	3500	3244	257	3500
7	3750	3591	159	3750
8	4000	3814	186	4000
9	4250	3948	302	4250
10	4500	4322	178	4500
11	4750	4586	164	4750
12	5000	4707	293	5000
13	5250	5035	215	5250
14	5500	5366	134	5500
15	5750	5418	332	5750
16	6000	5900	100	6000
17	6250	5982	268	6250
18	6500	6306	194	6500
19	6750	6611	139	6750
20	7000	6831	169	7000
21	7250	7021	229	7250
22	7500	7170	330	7500
23	7750	7613	137	7750
24	8000	7688	312	8000

Next, let's do something about the way the monthly deposit varies so much.

A drawback you may have noticed is the way the monthly amount is constantly changing. How can you do your planning when there's no telling how much you'll need to put into your VA account each month? The solution is to select a fixed amount that you will deposit each month (just like in regular DCA). With this variation, you only put as much into your investment account as the VA formula calls for; the rest goes into a money market account at the same fund organization.

Study the graphic on the next page as I walk you through the process (notice the two new columns on the right). Let's start with the decision to set aside a fixed $225 a month for our VA strategy. The $2,000 we have on hand to start with plus the twenty-four planned monthly deposits of $225 equals total capital of $7,400. We're counting on the investments to earn at least $600 over the coming two years in order to meet our $8,000 target.

At the end of month one, we put $208 into the investment account just as before. That leaves $17 of the $225 that wasn't needed this month; it gets deposited into the money market account. In month two, $216 is required for the investment account; the remaining $9 goes into the money market. In month three, the VA formula calls for $240 being added to the investment account. We put all of the $225 monthly deposit there, *plus we move $15 from the surplus we've built in the money market account.* We continue in the same way throughout the two years. At the end of the two years, the $8,000 goal has been reached, plus there's another $211 in the money market fund (not including the interest that would have been earned during the period). Notice that once again we made $813 in market gains: the $600 we were counting on when we began plus the $213 in the money fund.

The VA strategy generates better returns than conventional DCA because it doesn't just "buy more when prices are low" as with DCA. It buys even more than usual when prices move lower during the month.

Consider months nine and fifteen when much more than the "normal" $225 goes into the stock fund account. And conversely, it doesn't just "buy less when prices are high" as with DCA. It *buys even less than usual* when prices are unusually strong during the month. Months seven and fourteen are two examples of this. So VA does an even better job of providing mechanical guidance to your buying than traditional DCA.

Let's move on to see how value averaging would have worked in recent years. Assume you began your value-averaging program . . .

. . . at the worst possible time—near the highs just before the crash of 1987. The assumption is that you have saved up $3,000 for college for your oldest child and invest it in the Vanguard Index 500 Fund at the end of June 1987. Furthermore, you are able to put aside

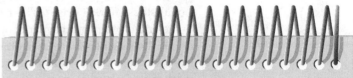

VALUE AVERAGING WORKSHEET

End of Month	Value Path	Portfolio Value	Need to Add	After Addition	Left for MoneyMkt	MoneyMkt Balance
	$2000					
1	2250	$2042	$208	$2250	$17	$17
2	2500	2284	216	2500	9	26
3	2750	2510	240	2750	−15	11
4	3000	2783	217	3000	8	19
5	3250	3042	208	3250	17	36
6	3500	3244	257	3500	−32	4
7	3750	3591	159	3750	66	70
8	4000	3814	186	4000	39	109
9	4250	3948	302	4250	−77	32
10	4500	4322	178	4500	47	79
11	4750	4586	164	4750	61	140
12	5000	4707	293	5000	−68	72
13	5250	5035	215	5250	10	82
14	5500	5366	134	5500	91	173
15	5750	5418	332	5750	−107	66
16	6000	5900	100	6000	125	191
17	6250	5982	268	6250	−43	148
18	6500	6306	194	6500	31	179
19	6750	6611	139	6750	86	265
20	7000	6831	169	7000	56	321
21	7250	7021	229	7250	−4	317
22	7500	7170	330	7500	−105	212
23	7750	7613	137	7750	88	300
24	8000	7688	312	8000	−87	213

another $75 per month into your VA strategy. Your value averaging work-sheet looks like the one at the right. The notes will help you track your VA strategy through highlights of the first five years, including how it fared after the crash of 1987 and the sell-off following the invasion of Kuwait.

Given enough time, you will survive (and even prosper from) the occasional stock market crises. The problem occurs if the sell-off comes too close to the end of your multi-year program. If you had been ending your program in late 1987 rather than just getting started, you would almost certainly not have attained your value path goal. That's why the threat posed by a poor market environment increases as you get ever closer to your investment goal; there's not enough time to recoup your losses. To help offset this risk, here are a few ways you can be more conservative in your VA strategy: (1) plan on meeting your target a year or two ahead of schedule; (2) set your dollar goal at a higher level than actually needed; or (3) put in more money monthly than the formulas call for. Make a point to reevaluate your program every year or two. Are your market growth assumptions still valid? Does your dollar goal still appear sufficient for your needs? Should you increase the amount of your monthly contribution?

Reviewing the market lessons of years gone by only renews my commitment to the discipline . . .

. . . imposed by having a specific, well-researched strategy in place—a strategy that has *objective* decision-making criteria. Such discipline is essential to your investment survival for four reasons.

❶ **Every investment strategy involves some capital risk.** There's no way around it: to live is to take risks. In the same way, financial life has risks. Investing your capital involves accepting some risk of losing part or all; not investing invites the risk of losing buying power to inflation. Unfortunately, all investing is, to varying degrees, speculation.

❷ **Nobody really knows what's going to happen next.** Nobody. There are things that can be predicted. We know precisely when the sun is going to come up each morning, for instance. The investment world, on the other hand, is about people and their attitudes about money. It's primarily a world governed by human emotions and behavior and, as such, cannot be predicted with certainty by anyone or any method.

❸ **The market won't present a clear warning when it's time to act.** The reality is that you cannot know in advance how long a good thing is going to last. It might last a long time. On the other hand, it might end tomorrow. Systematic investing will help balance the up and down swings in your portfolio.

❹ **Our emotions naturally cause us to postpone committing ourselves.** First, there's our natural optimism. Second, there's simple greed. And third,

❶ We invest our entire $3,000 nest egg at the outset. At the time, we don't know whether it's a "good" time or a "bad" time to buy stocks. It soon turns out to be a very bad time.

❷ At the end of the first month, the gains in the stock fund have us "ahead of schedule" versus where the value path says we should be. That means we can put the entire monthly addition of $75 into the money market fund for use in the future.

❸ To our horror, the crash of '87 takes place during the fourth month. Our stock fund drops more than 20% in value, and we are now $757 behind our value path. We invest our monthly $75 plus the entire $223 from the money market fund in the stock fund account.

❹ For the past nine months, we've been investing our entire $75 each month into the stock fund, and we are now only $190 behind the value path. In the process, we've been loading up on shares at some pretty low prices.

❺ At the end of year two, gains in the stock fund portfolio (from all those shares we bought at bargain prices after the crash) have now enabled the stock fund to surpass our value path goal. We also have a nice $488 additional cushion in the money market fund.

❻ You can't tell it from looking at the stock fund value, but the market sold off heavily in month thirty-eight due to the Iraqi invasion of Kuwait. While other investors were selling in panic, we calmly invested our normal $75 plus an additional $378 pulled from the money market fund. In month thirty-nine, we invested another $75 plus $316. By month forty-two we were once again comfortably ahead of schedule.

VALUE AVERAGING WORKSHEET

End of Month	Value Path	Portfolio Value	Add to Portfolio	After Addition	Left for MoneyMkt	MoneyMkt Balance
	$3000					
1	3073	$3147	$0	$3147	$75	$75
2	3134	3268	0	3268	75	150
3	3196	3194	2	3196	73	223
4	3259	2502	298	2800	-223	0
5	3322	2511	75	2586	0	0
6	3387	2775	75	2850	0	0
12	3791	3601	75	3676	0	0
18	4230	4193	37	4230	38	38
24	4704	4925	0	4925	75	488
30	5218	5556	0	5556	75	938
36	5772	6082	0	6082	75	1058
42	6372	6742	0	6742	75	539
48	7019	7696	0	7696	75	989
54	7717	8780	0	8780	75	1439
60	8470	8714	0	8714	75	1889

❼ At the end of year five of our ten-year plan, we are $2,133 ahead of schedule (a $244 "surplus" in our portfolio plus $1,889 in the money market fund). This provides a solid cushion (and a little extra courage) to confidently face the uncertain years ahead.

COLUMN HEADINGS

◆ VALUE PATH: Amount we should have at the end of each month if we are to reach $10,000 by the end of the tenth year (calculated by using the formula given in Dr. Edleson's book). ◆ PORTFOLIO VALUE: The month-end market value of the stock fund account. ◆ ADD TO PORTFOLIO: The amount used to purchase more stock fund shares. ◆ AFTER ADDITION: Value of the stock fund after the month-end purchase of new shares is made. ◆ LEFT FOR MONEY MARKET: The amount deposited in the money market fund due to the fact that the entire $75 monthly contribution wasn't needed in the stock fund. ◆ MONEY MARKET BALANCE: Month-end balance after all transactions, excluding interest earned.

there is an enormously powerful influence felt by every investor: the "fear of regret." It's this fear of doing the wrong thing that can paralyze us and prevent us from taking prompt action.

The key to successful investing is in having the self-discipline to adhere to your strategy.

It's not that any strategy is perfect: there's no such thing. But a strategy doesn't have to be perfect in order to be highly profitable over time. The value of discipline and how it can protect us, from the markets and from ourselves, cannot be overstated. Please keep that in mind as you risk your capital in what is basically a high-risk endeavor. ◆

17

Making the Transition:
How to Get from Where You Are Now to Where You Want to Go

I. **The "right" portfolio moves can't be evaluated simply in terms of maximizing profits.**

   A. No investment portfolio can be consistently positioned to maximize profits from coming events.

   B. The "right" portfolio move looks ahead to your goal and has a high probability of reaching it (and may have to occasionally settle for lower gains along the way in order to protect capital).

II. **The "right" investment portfolio takes into account the spiritual, intellectual, and emotional aspects of the investor.**

   A. The right portfolio moves are consistent with a specific, biblically sound, long-term strategy you've developed. They come after giving sufficient time to prayer and seeking Christian counsel.

   B. The right portfolio moves should be reasonable, explainable, and prudent under the circumstances.

   C. The right portfolio moves are consistent with your investing temperament.

III. **A remodeling worksheet can provide an overview of how you go about making the transition.**

   A. The remodeling worksheet will list current equity and fixed-income holdings and allow you to conveniently calculate the percentage allocations between the two.

   B. The worksheet will show you what changes in holdings are necessary to change your portfolio from its present structure to one that matches your investment temperament and long-term goals.

"Future shock is the disorientation that affects an individual when he is overwhelmed by change and even the prospect of change. It is the consequence of having to make too many decisions . . .

. . . about too many new and unfamiliar problems in too short a time. . . . We are in collision with tomorrow. Future shock has arrived." — *Alvin Toffler*

Do you ever feel like that? As if the decisions you are required to make, especially about your finances, are coming at you at an ever faster and more confusing rate? A great many people today are finding it increasingly difficult to know which is the "right" step to take. They wonder:

"Is this a good time to buy stocks?"

"Which money market mutual fund would be best?"

"Should I sell some of my employer's stock in order to diversify?"

"My CDs mature soon. Should I renew them for thirty days, ninety days, a year?"

"How much of my retirement plan at work should I put in stocks versus bonds?"

"If I sell this losing investment and buy something else, will I be better off?"

Since we cannot know the future with certainty, it's obvious that no investment portfolio that any of us comes up with will ever be *perfectly* positioned to profit from upcoming events. As the future unfolds, it will always be possible to point to ways we could have made more money than we did — and some of them will appear incredibly obvious in retrospect! *This means that it's pointless to think of the "right" investment portfolio simply in terms of maximizing profits. If that is your approach, you will always be frustrated and second-guessing your decisions.*

The "right" portfolio is one that realistically faces where you are right now, looks years ahead to where you want to go, *and has a very high probability of getting you there on time.* As you consider "remodeling" your current holdings, let's look at some of the characteristics of the "right" steps to take.

> The plans of the diligent lead to profit as surely as haste leads to poverty.
> Proverbs 21:5

❶ The right portfolio move is one that is consistent with a specific, biblically sound long-term strategy you've adopted.

One common trait that I find among many of those I counsel is that their current investment portfolio tends to be a random collection of "good deals" and assorted savings accounts. Each investment appears to have been made on its own merits without much thought of how it fit into the whole.

I find savings accounts (because the bank was offering a "good deal" on money market accounts), company stock (because buying it at a discount is a "good deal"), a savings bond for the kids' education (because they read an article that said they were a "good deal" for college), a universal life policy (because their insurance agent said it was a "good deal" for someone their age), a real-estate partnership (which their broker said was a "good deal" for people in their tax bracket), and 100 shares of XYZ stock (because their best friend let them in on this *really* "good deal").

As we've discussed, I want you to become an *initiator* (one who develops an individual investing strategy tailored to your personal temperament and goals) rather than a *responder* (one who reacts to sales calls, making decisions on a case-by-case basis. Then you can select the appropriate investments accordingly. The right investment step is the one that *you* seek out purposefully, knowing where it fits into the overall scheme of things.

❷ The right portfolio move is one where you've taken plenty of time to pray and to seek trusted, experienced Christian counsel.

Because your decisions have long-term implications, you should take all the time you need to become informed. Don't be in a hurry; there's no deadline. A good friend once commented to me: "The Christian life isn't a destination; it's a way of travel." Likewise, you're not under pressure to predict the best possible portfolio for the next six months or make this year's big killing. You're remodeling in order to settle in for a comfortable investing lifestyle that will serve you well for decades.

Besides, prayer takes time. You need time to pray, ask for the counsel of others, and reflect. You should consider the alternatives, examine your motives, and continue praying until you have peace in the matter. If you're married, you should pray with your partner and talk it out until you reach mutual agreement. You're in this together and, rain or shine, you both must be willing to accept responsibility for the decision. The right investment step is the one that results from careful and prayerful consideration. This will add to your steadfastness during the occasional rough sledding along the way.

❸ The right portfolio move is one that you understand.

This typically involves at least two things. First, it's relatively simple. It's not likely that your situation requires exotic or complicated strategies. In fact, the single investment decision of greatest importance is actually pretty easy to understand. Do you know what it is? (Hint: we covered it in the first chapter.) It's deciding what percentage of your investments to put in stocks (where your return is uncertain) as opposed to bonds and other fixed income investments (where your return is relatively certain). *This one decision has more influence on your investment results than any other.*

And second, you've educated yourself on the basics. When you're able to give a simple explanation of your strategy to a friend and answer a few ques-

> The way of a fool seems right to him, but <u>a wise man listens to advice</u>.
> Proverbs 12:15

> The <u>heart of the discerning acquires knowledge</u>; the ears of the wise seek it out.
> Proverbs 18:15

tions, you've probably got at least a beginner's grasp. The right investment step is the one where you understand what you're doing, why you're doing it, and how you expect it to improve matters. That's the least you should expect of yourself before making decisions that can dramatically affect your life and the lives of those you love.

A simple man believes anything, but a _prudent man gives thought to his steps_. Proverbs 14:15

❹ The right portfolio move is one that is prudent under the circumstances. Does it pass the "common sense" test?

How much of your investing capital can you afford to lose and still have a realistic chance of meeting your financial goals? The investments that offer higher potential returns also carry correspondingly greater risks of loss. The right portfolio for you is not always the one with the most profit potential.

For example, it's usually best not to have a majority of your investments in a single asset or security. For that reason, people who have large holdings of stock in the company they work for often sell some of it in order to diversify. If the stock doubles after they sell it, does that mean they did the "wrong" thing? No, they did the right thing. After all, the stock could have fallen dramatically as well as risen. What would a large loss have done to their retirement planning? The right investment step is the one that protects you in the event of life's occasional worst-case scenarios. Generally, this moves you in the direction of increased diversification.

Do not be anxious about anything, but in everything, by prayer and petition, with thanksgiving, present your requests to God. And the peace of God, which transcends all understanding, will guard your hearts and your minds in Christ Jesus. Philippians 4: 6–7

❺ The right portfolio move is one that is consistent with your investing "self" — will it fit comfortably?

I originally developed the structure of the four Sound Mind Investing temperaments to illustrate that, as part of our separate God-given identities, we each have different capacities to accept risk and uncertainty. Some people actually seem to be energized by the thrill of adventure, whereas others prefer more secure, predictable surroundings. If you make investments that violate your natural temperament, you are much more likely to react emotionally when the occasional setbacks occur and objective decision making is needed.

When someone presents me with two investing alternatives and invites my opinion, I often ask, "Which one would you like to do, and why?" This is my way of learning more about that person's investing temperament. Unless I find a grievous flaw in people's financial logic, I encourage them to take the course of action they intuitively prefer. They are more likely to stick with their strategy over the long term and exercise the self-discipline needed to be successful if they are comfortable with their portfolio. The right investment step is the one that enhances your ability to make calm and well-reasoned decisions.

With these points in mind, it's time to walk through a "remodeling" project that revamps an investment portfolio. I have designed it . . .

. . . to teach by example. Carefully follow the steps taken by Tom and Marilyn Randolph as they adjust their portfolio to achieve the mix that they have decided is best for them given their tolerance for risk and current stage of life—40% invest-by-owning and 60% invest-by-lending. In developing this example, I assumed that Tom's 401(k) plan offers the typical choices: company stock, blue-chip stock fund or S&P 500 index fund, long-term bond fund, and money market fund.

As you begin, keep in mind these two guiding principles:

◆ You don't need to *perfectly* achieve the recommended percentages for the various risk categories. It's good enough to come close; when in doubt, go with less risk.

◆ You don't have to change things all at once. Take it in steps over many months (or even a few years) as your comfort level grows.

Step 1: List the current values of your assets.

Basically, this means writing down the investments over which you exercise control. Divide them into two groups: investments where you are an owner and investments where you are a lender (see the notepad at right). There are two exceptions. Do not count the savings set aside for your Level Two contingency fund—they are not part of your long-term risk-taking strategy. Also, do not include money set aside for the children's education. These assets should go through their own remodeling process once you understand how to do it.

If you're married, put down both spouses' investments. Married partners are in this together—I discourage attempts to keep "his" money separate from "her" money. Also, as you can see from Tom and Marilyn's list, you don't need to distinguish between retirement or current savings, or when you bought them or what you paid. Nor do you care whether the investment is held in a normal brokerage account, an IRA, a 401(k), a variable annuity, or any other legal structure in which investments are placed. The goal is to list on paper your

INVESTMENT HOLDINGS OF TOM AND MARILYN RANDOLPH

INVESTMENTS WHERE WE ARE OWNERS

$6,000	Marilyn's pension plan invested in a growth fund
8,300	Tom's 401(k) at work invested in the "S&P 500" portfolio
15,800	Tom's 401(k) at work invested in G.E. stock
4,300	Goodyear shares inherited from Marilyn's mother
3,300	Utility shares inherited from Marilyn's mother
$37,700	Equity portion is 62% of total holdings

INVESTMENTS WHERE WE ARE LENDERS

$1,900	Tom's 401(k) at work invested in long-term govt bonds
6,200	Marilyn's pension plan invested in long-term corp bonds
3,000	IBM bond inherited from Marilyn's mother
4,600	Tom's 401(k) at work that's invested in the money market
2,400	Credit union passbook joint savings account
2,600	Tom's IRA invested in a bank money market account
2,600	Marilyn's IRA invested in a bank money market account
$23,300	Fixed income portion is 38% of total holdings
$61,000	Total Investment Holdings

various investments and the amount you would expect to receive if you sold or exchanged them.

When you're finished, add up the totals and calculate what percentage each group represents in your total holdings. This is your first insight into how much risk you're taking in your portfolio. If you're like most people, your investments carry a higher overall risk level than you expected.

Step 2: Determine what dollar changes are needed.

Now that the Randolphs know their current mix (62% equity and 38% fixed income), they can compute the dollar amount of the change needed to achieve the mix they seek (40% equity and 60% fixed income). Obviously, they will need to decrease the equity portion and increase the fixed income portion.

Here's how they calculate the dollar amount. They take the total value of their holdings of $61,000 and multiply it times 40% to arrive at the equity portion goal—$24,400. They then subtract this from their current equity portion of $37,700 to learn how much of a decrease is needed.

This tells them that they need to sell $13,300 worth of securities from the equity side and reinvest it over on the fixed income side. This will decrease their equity portion to $24,400 (current $37,700 less sales of $13,300) while increasing the fixed income portion to $36,600 (current $23,300 plus new investments of $13,300). Once this is done, their desired mix will have been accomplished.

Step 3: Decide which holdings to sell in order to meet your dollar goal.

They say that "timing is everything." When it comes to investing, the timing of buy orders gets all the attention. Many forces work to incline us toward making an investment (e.g., friends, relatives, brokers, and financial planners), but very few of these sources return with the message "It's time to sell that stock I told you about!"

The Randolphs now know they need to liquidate $13,300 worth of their equity holdings—but which ones? Here are a few rules of thumb that might be of help in deciding.

◆ Keep in mind any limitations imposed by your pension holdings. For example, if Tom sells some of his 401(k) equity holdings, he can only reinvest the money in *other* 401(k) offerings. This limits the number of possible ways he can accomplish his goal.

◆ Move toward increased diversification. This means that Tom's large holding in his employer's stock (G.E.) could prudently be reduced.

◆ Sell the losers. The alternative is to sell the winners—the strong companies that have fulfilled your hopes and expectations. Why would you want to unload the winners and hang on to the disappointments? Go ahead and acknowledge that they didn't work out. If the stock is not being held in a tax-deferred account, you can take advantage of the loss for tax purposes.

◆ Sell a stock when the reason you bought it is no longer valid. For whatever reason (the expected new product didn't pan out, the merger was called off, they didn't land the big government contract, etc.), the original case for investing in the stock no longer holds true.

◆ Sell stocks whose earnings have fallen. Any company looks bad if it reports lower earnings, so its management will go to great lengths (and accounting mischief) to avoid doing so. Only when they exhaust all their options for disguising their deteriorating profits will management generally report earnings that are down (for the most recent twelve-month period compared with the previous twelve months). It may be a good time to exit.

◆ Don't worry. Many people fear "being wrong" and selling something that later goes higher. They're right to expect it, but wrong to think there's anything they can do about it. You can't know the future, so be realistic and accept your limited vision—don't let it paralyze you.

The Randolphs decide to sell their Goodyear and utility stocks plus however many of Tom's G.E. shares are necessary in order to reach a total of $13,300. These moves are steps toward achieving greater diversification.

Step 4: Decide in which risk categories to make your new purchases.

Now that they have raised the $13,300 to add to their fixed income portion, how do they decide *exactly* where to put it? Again, there are no absolute rules that govern this. There is no single "right" way to do your portfolio fine-tuning.

Let's assume the Randolphs decide to deal with the risk of rising interest rates by having

LEVELS OF INVESTMENT RISK

Investing by Lending (your fixed income holdings)	Investing by Owning (your equity holdings)
Zero coupon bonds	Oil and gas partnerships
High yield "junk" bond funds	Gold/silver coins/bars
Long-term high quality bond funds	Real-estate partnerships
Long-term tax-free bond funds	Individual shares in small companies
High yield "junk" tax-free bond funds	Sector funds
Fixed annuities	Small company/growth funds
Medium-term high quality bond funds	International stock funds
Medium-term tax-free bond funds	Rental property
Govt-backed mortgage bond funds	Small company/value funds
Short-term high quality bond funds	Small company index funds
Short-term tax-free bond funds	Individual shares in large companies
Money market mutual funds	Large company/growth funds
Bank CDs/money market accounts	Large company/value funds
U.S. Treasury bills	S&P 500 index fund
Volatility and risk is lowest at the bottom.	Volatility and risk is lowest at the bottom.

roughly equal portions of their fixed income holdings in long-term bonds (over ten years), medium-term bonds (over four years but less than ten years), and money market funds and savings accounts. That means allocating $12,200 (one-third of their fixed income portfolio of $36,600) to each of the three categories. The targets were attained as follows:

❶ They raised $7,600 by selling the Goodyear and utility stock, then invested in a new medium-term no-load bond fund at Vanguard.

(Note that once the Randolphs knew the *kind* of investments they wanted to make, they selected a no-load mutual fund organization *that offered funds with demonstrated performance excellence in their area of interest*—bonds.)

❷ The $3,000 IBM bond was sold and the proceeds were added to the new Vanguard bond fund account also. This increases the diversification.

❸ They withdrew $1,600 from their credit union savings and also added to the new Vanguard bond fund account, making the total $12,200.

❹ In Tom's 401(k) plan, he sold $5,700 worth of G.E. shares, transferring $4,100 of it into the long-term bond fund and $1,600 into the money market fund. Note that none of this money actually left the 401(k), but it was moved around *within* it.

The "remodeling" worksheets the Randolphs used are shown on pages 204-205. Each of the above numbered steps is shown in the "changes needed" columns. The final result is summarized on the notepad at the far right. Notice they didn't feel they needed to follow my allocation suggestions "to the letter of the law." They had the flexibility of adjusting their bond holdings to fit their personal situation and preference.

It's at this stage that investors often "freeze up." Many people seem to find investing to be a nerve-racking . . .

. . . if not downright scary experience. Making investment decisions, and then watching the results unfold, can be stressful. Do you become anxious when circumstances compel you to make important investing decisions? Most of us do to one degree or another. If my mail is any indication, a great degree of financial fretting is common. Three recurring comments lead the list of ways my readers express their concerns.

◆ There's so much at stake. I'm afraid I'll make the wrong decision.

◆ I don't have much experience. I'm afraid I'll make the wrong decision.

◆ My savings aren't making enough now, but if I make a change I'm afraid I'll make the wrong decision.

What is the "wrong" decision, anyway? If you feel a wrong decision is like saying 2+2=5, then you're off track; such thinking implies investing decisions can be made with mathematical certainty. They can't. This doesn't mean the economy and investment markets are completely random, only that you're dealing with *probabilities*, not certainties and predictable events. Scientists can predict with great accuracy when the next eclipse of the sun will occur decades into the future, yet they can't tell you if the sun will be eclipsed by clouds and ruin next week's picnic.

All of this is actually good news. It means anybody can play. It's like learning to drive a car. After a couple of lessons, you know enough to travel around town if you follow a few basic safety guidelines. After all, you're not trying to qualify for the Indy 500—you just want to reach your destination. In the same way, once you understand the concepts in this book, you're fairly well equipped for making whatever decisions you face.

Pretend you're in a contest where . . .

. . . you are to travel from coast to coast before the current interstate system was built. You can choose any route (but they're almost all two-lane roads), travel any speed, and take as much time as you want. There are no extra bonus points for getting there first—the only goal is to arrive safely. Everybody who does that "wins."

As you drive along, you constantly must make decisions. Should you take the route to the left or to the right? Is there construction or traffic up ahead? Will there be a motel with a vacancy? There are no scientific answers to these questions. Every decision requires some powers of observation, the ability to learn from your experiences, and a little common sense. You rarely come to a point where the decision is obvious. It would always be helpful to have "just a little more" information—but the challenge of the trip is the necessity of making choices *without having all the information. Nobody ever has all the relevant information.*

Investing is a lot like such a contest. You can't know for certain what lies ahead; anyone who would have you believe otherwise is lying to you. It's *because* we can't know the future that we diversify and stay flexible. This brings us to one of the few rules that investing has: protect your capital! That's the only prerequisite for "arriving safely." When in doubt, take the safe route.

INVESTMENT HOLDINGS OF TOM AND MARILYN RANDOLPH AFTER REBALANCING

INVESTMENTS WHERE WE ARE OWNERS

$6,000	Marilyn's pension plan invested in a growth fund
8,300	Tom's 401(k) at work invested in the "S&P 500" portfolio
10,100	Tom's 401(k) at work invested in G.E. stock
$24,400	Equity portion is 40% of total holdings

INVESTMENTS WHERE WE ARE LENDERS

$6,000	Tom's 401(k) at work invested in long-term govt bonds
6,200	Marilyn's pension plan invested in long-term corp bonds
12,200	Vanguard intermediate-term corporate bond fund
6,200	Tom's 401(k) at work that's invested in the money market
800	Credit union passbook joint savings account
2,600	Tom's IRA invested in a bank money market account
2,600	Marilyn's IRA invested in a bank money market account
$36,600	Fixed income portion is 60% of total holdings
$61,000	Total Investment Holdings

INVEST-BY-OWNING (Risk Generally Decreases as You Move Down the Page)				
What Goes Here	Your Current Holdings	Current Value	Changes Needed	After Rebalancing
Include in this section any investments that are not specifically named in the SMI strategy				
Total				
Special purpose equity investments				
Total				
International equity investments				
Total				
Investments that fall into Stock Risk Category 4: Small companies + "growth" characteristics	Marilyn's pension plan	6,000		6,000
Total		$6,000 9.8%		$6,000 9.8%
Investments that fall into Stock Risk Category 3: Small companies + "value" characteristics				
Total				
Investments that fall into Stock Risk Category 2: Large companies + "growth" characteristics	Tom's 401(k) S&P 500 portfolio	8,300		8,300
	Tom's 401(k) G.E. stock	15,800	❹ −5,700	10,100
	Goodyear shares	4,300	❶ −4,300	
Total		$28,400 46.6%		$18,400 30.2%
Investments that fall into Stock Risk Category 1: Large companies + "value" characteristics	Utility shares	3,300	❶ −3,300	
Total		$3,300 5.4%		
	INVESTING BY OWNING	$37,700 61.8%	−13,300	$24,400 40.0%

INVEST-BY-LENDING
(Risk Generally Decreases as You Move Down the Page)

What Goes Here	Your Current Holdings	Current Value	Changes Needed	After Rebalancing
Include in this section any investments that are not specifically named in the SMI strategy				
	Total			
Special purpose bond investments				
	Total			
Investments that fall into Bond Risk Category 4: Lower quality high-yield (junk) bonds				
	Total			
Investments that fall into Bond Risk Category 3: Long-term bonds of generally high quality	Tom's 401(k) long-term govts	1,900	❹ +4,100	6,000
	Marilyn's pension plan	6,200		6,200
	Total	$8,100 13.3%		$12,200 20.0%
Investments that fall into Bond Risk Category 2: Medium-term bonds of generally high quality	Vanguard Intermed-term Corp		❶ +7,600	
	Vanguard Intermed-term Corp		❷ +3,000	
	Vanguard Intermed-term Corp		❸ +1,600	12,200
	Total			$12,200 20.0%
Investments that fall into Bond Risk Category 1: Short-term bonds of generally high quality	IBM bond (matures 6/2000)	3,000	❷ −3,000	
	Total	$3,000 4.9%		
Cash-equivalent investments like savings accounts, CDs, T-bills, and money market funds	Tom's 401(k) money market	4,600	❹ +1,600	6,200
	Credit union joint savings	2,400	❸ −1,600	800
	Tom's IRA bank money market	2,600		2,600
	Marilyn's IRA bank money market	2,600		2,600
	Total	$12,200 20.0%		$12,200 20.0%
	INVESTING BY LENDING	$23,300 38.2%	+13,300	$36,600 60.0%

You control the level of risk you take by deciding how you divide your money between the two choices—to invest by lending (lower risk) and to invest by owning (higher risk). Don't make decisions in isolation (e.g., should I renew this CD? or, should I change the mix in my 401(k) plan?) without taking into account *how the decision affects your overall mix.*

Scripture teaches that "to the Lord your God belong the heavens, even the highest heavens, the earth and everything in it" (Deuteronomy 10:14). God has ownership rights; we have management responsibilities. That's why, whether you have many or few investments, doing your best to manage them in a God-pleasing manner is a task that must be taken seriously. It's a lifelong calling.

You've come to a fork in the road.
The next section of the book is optional.

In Section Four, you'll learn more about mutual funds and a technique for assessing the risks of investing in them. We'll look at methods for attempting to select top-performing mutual funds. We'll go out into the marketplace and look at specific ones, including their track records of risk and reward.

There's also material on foreign investing and a primer to help you gain a better understanding of the currencies markets. Chapter 23 addresses what I call "earthquake watch" topics like inflation and investing in precious metals and other hard assets.

If you're content with adopting a Just-the-Basics strategy, all of this material can wait for a future time. Although it's interesting and helpful, it's not material you *need to know* at present. And keeping with my promise in the preface, I don't want to bury you under an avalanche of new information that's not basic to your developing a viable long-term plan. If you prefer, feel free to move on from here to Section Five, which covers retirement-related topics.

On the other hand, if everything we've covered up to this point has merely whetted your appetite for a greater understanding of investing principles and the fund industry, welcome to Section Four! ◆

A More Ambitious Strategy

Going Out into the Marketplace and
Assembling a Diversified Portfolio
of No-Load Mutual Funds

"Let's try it one more time. The stock fund managed by Fulcher apparently owns
all the shares of Koch's growth fund, which is fully invested in the Mosher stock
fund, which seems to have put all its money into the Fulcher fund..."

Understanding Volatility and Risk

I. **There is no such thing as "wealth without risk."**

    A. In any investment opportunity, the risk goes up as the potential for gain goes up.

    B. There are many different kinds of risk other than that of losing your capital. Among them are: purchasing power risk, liquidity risk, opportunity risk, and reinvestment risk.

II. **Volatility equates to risk.**

    A. The greater the month-to-month price volatility of an investment, the greater the risk.

    B. Your risk of losing money in the stock and bond markets goes down the longer you hold your investments.

III. **Standard deviation is a tool for measuring risk.**

    A. The lower the standard deviation of month-to-month performance, the lower the risk.

    B. Standard deviation is useful when comparing mutual funds because it reveals the degree of volatility (and therefore of risk) over time.

IV. **The Sharpe Ratio and scattergram are tools for comparing the potential reward versus the potential risk of various investments.**

    A. The higher the Sharpe Ratio, the greater the reward in relation to the risk taken.

    B. The scattergram gives a visual representation as to whether funds are doing a better job than an index fund with similar objectives in terms of risks taken and rewards received.

V. **Risks can't be avoided.**

    A. Economic uncertainty is certain.

    B. Following scriptural principles for managing one's financial affairs offers the surest protection against economic uncertainty.

Susie and I really plan for St. Valentine's Day. It's a special time for us, a kind of midwinter pick-me-up.

We usually fence off some private time in our schedule, close the gate to our home in the woods, take the phone off the hook, and enjoy being alone together for three or four days. Last year, we thought it was time to do something a little different, so we began considering various mini-vacation options.

As we sat and read through the brochures from the travel agent, it certainly was reassuring to learn we were going to have an absolutely wonderful travel experience. The brochures promised we'd be headed for a vacation paradise where the breezes are "fragrant and relaxing" and the beaches "beautiful, pristine and secluded." The surrounding "azure seas are breathtaking," and the sunsets are "spectacular." The island landscape is "lush, a place of protected quiet beauty."

This all sounded wonderful, but what kind of accommodations would we have? Fortunately, our hotel was "luxurious" and rendered "impeccable service." Our room would be "spacious and comfortable, a masterpiece of design and craftsmanship." And we were assured the food was nothing less than "exquisite," "sumptuous," and "tantalizing."

We'd heard that not every island paradise appreciates being trodden by the American masses. That may be true some places, we learned, but not on *our* island. The local people are not only friendly, but "gentle," "honest," and "enchanting" as well. Their culture is "rich in history and charm."

It sounded great to "find respite among such peaceful shores" as we looked forward to enjoying a pace that was "tranquil and lazy." But what if we got bored after a few days of finding respite? More great news. We'd be going to an island where the recreation is superlative—the kind of place where "divers delight," bird watchers "marvel," and hikers "climb skyward." Plus, the shopping adventures that awaited promised to be "colorful and beguiling."

This is what we were looking for—a vacation free of worry or disappointment! The brochures were telling us what we wanted to hear, that it could all be ours. Now let me pose a hypothetical question: If we took the trip, relying on the advertising claims made in the brochures, do you think our island vacation would have been as wonderful as we hoped? I very much doubt it, given that we would have acted on a set of highly optimistic expectations.

In the same way, millions of people hold unrealistic expectations concerning their investments.

They mistakenly believe it's not too difficult to make 25% a year consistently, or that annual gains of 20% are practically a given for the informed investor. This optimism is reinforced by: (1) a brief period during the eighties when gains of 20% per year and more were common; (2) financial magazines

---

Purchasing Power Risk is the chance that the value of your current income and investments will be eroded because of an increase in the prices of the things you purchase. This risk is faced by all members of society, not just stock and bond investors.

Liquidity Risk is the chance that you will not be able to sell your investments quickly enough because selling opportunities are limited. This risk is faced by all investors, but is typically not as great a concern for popularly traded securities and mutual funds as it is for real estate, oil and gas partnerships, and other investments that lack a daily trading market.

Opportunity Risk is the chance that, while your money is tied up in your current investments, you will lose the opportunity to make better returns in other investments that have better growth potential.

Reinvestment Risk is the chance that, due to a change in the financial environment, you will not be able to reinvest your interest and dividend income at the same rate of return you are enjoying today. This is most often associated with fixed income investing.

that run accounts of how everyday folks like the "Johnsons gained 32% in global funds last year and are going to earn at least 15%" this year; and (3) financial newsletters whose advertising claims promise returns of 30%, 40%, and more. Charles Givens's best-selling books notwithstanding, however, there's no such thing as "wealth without risk."

It's easy to smile at the naïveté of anyone who would take a travel brochure at face value. As it turned out, Susie and I did a reality check and opted for a cabin in the Great Smoky mountains. I suggest you apply that same healthy skepticism when you're offered a risk-free trip to a money-making paradise. It's a fantasy island.

In chapter 13, I offered another kind of reality check (see "It's Tough to Beat the Market" on page 155). In this chapter, we're going to continue in that vein with a look at the reality of risk. We'll examine what it is, how to measure it, how to relate it to performance, and, finally, how to cope with it from both a practical and emotional perspective.

Brokers and media commentators routinely encourage you to seek higher returns but downplay the rote reminder that "higher risk" is always involved.

The real possibility that you could ever have to deal with the consequences of accepting greater risk is presented as an abstraction, not related to what you can expect your everyday experience to be like. Actually losing part or all of your money in an investment is something that happens to the "other guy," sort of like getting cancer or dying in a plane crash. I want to be certain that when you consider accepting a higher risk, you mentally translate that in your mind to: "Hey, I'd better stop and think. This means I stand a very real chance of actually losing some of my money. Can I afford that?" A discussion of risk should not come across as academic and impersonal.

Most investors tend to think of risk in terms of quality considerations. For example, low-quality junk bonds are "risky" and high-quality U.S. Treasuries are "safe." If only it were that simple! There is another critically important component to the risk equation: *time*. It's not just a question of whether an investment will ultimately be rewarding (say after ten years); you must also consider what is likely to happen to its value *during* the ten-year period. Circumstances may dictate a change in your long-term plan, and you might not be able to hold the investment for the full ten years. This is why a long-term Treasury bond can be a higher-risk holding than a very short-term junk bond (see chapter 11 for why bond values are hurt by rising interest rates).

There are many kinds of risks facing investors (see sidebars), but the one on which we'll be focusing in this chapter is "volatility." This term refers to the extent to which an investment experiences dramatic price swings.

Principal Risk
is the chance that your investments will drop in value. All of the following types of risk reflect different ways that can happen.

Credit Risk
is the chance that whoever you lend money to will not repay it as promised. This is most often associated with investing in bonds.

Interest Rate Risk
is the chance that interest rates will go up, causing the market value of fixed income securities to fall. This is most often associated with investing in bonds.

Market Risk
is the chance that the entire market falls (taking your investment with it) due to changes in economic conditions such as interest rates, inflation rates, earnings expectations, and the business cycle. This is most often associated with investing in stocks.

Business Risk
is the chance that the financial prospects of a particular company will suffer due to poor management, technological advances, new competition, demographic and lifestyle changes among its customers, and so on. This is most often associated with investing in stocks.

**To illustrate why high volatility translates into high risk,
let's look at a new kind of graph I developed for this book.**

Most mutual fund performance graphs that you see in financial magazines and newsletters show "calendar year" returns (meaning they start in January and run through December). That really doesn't give you a clear picture because investors don't buy only on January 2 and sell only on December 31. I have created graphs that use the concept of a "rolling" year. That is, they also include twelve-month periods that run from February through the following January, March through the following February, and so on. This gives you an idea of the worst you might expect during any twelve-month period, regardless of which month of the year you begin your investment. I call them "worst-case scenario" graphs.

I've prepared an illustration using two stock mutual funds that had similar average gains over the past fifteen years. Mutual Shares is a value-oriented, relatively low risk stock fund. From 1981-1995, it averaged 16.5% per year. To get a good contrast, I chose Delaware Trend, an aggressive growth fund. It recorded averaged returns of 16.9% per year during the same period. If you had to choose which to invest in and all you knew were their fifteen-year performance numbers, you might be inclined to think there wasn't much difference between them.

But our worst-case scenario graphs (far right) tell a different story. They show that the fifteen years was a real roller coaster ride for Delaware Trend's shareholders compared to the steady trip enjoyed by Mutual

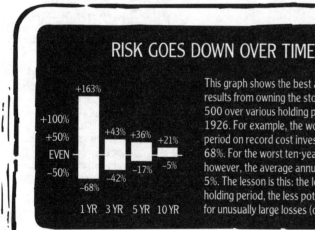

RISK GOES DOWN OVER TIME

+163%
+100%
+50%
EVEN
–50%
–68%

+43% +36% +21%
–42% –17% –5%

1 YR   3 YR   5 YR   10 YR

This graph shows the best and worst results from owning the stocks in the S&P 500 over various holding periods since 1926. For example, the worst one-year period on record cost investors a loss of 68%. For the worst ten-year period, however, the average annual loss was just 5%. The lesson is this: the longer your holding period, the less potential there is for unusually large losses (or gains).

Shares's investors. Each of the vertical bars in the graphs represents the return over a different twelve-month period. The more violent ups and downs (or volatility) indicate a much higher degree of risk *because it's always possible that circumstances (or your emotions!) will cause you to sell after a major sell-off.*

Don't pass too quickly over those down periods. You might look at a graph like this and only "see" the times you could have doubled your money in a single twelve-month period. You think you'll tough it out during the bad times, but when they actually arrive and the media reinforce the negatives at every opportunity, your fears may cause you to throw in the towel and sell at the worst possible time.

Students of the markets have a way to measure the price volatility of an investment. They call it "standard deviation."

That is, based on an investment's past, how much would you expect the investment to deviate—either up or down—from its historical norm in any one month in the future? The higher the standard deviation, the more it would be expected to vary from its norm and the higher the perceived risk associated with holding that investment. By measuring expected volatility in this way, you can evaluate and compare the potential risk of different investments using the same yardstick.

I'll be using the concept of standard deviation as a way to measure risk throughout this section. You don't need to understand how it's calculated in order to use it. Just remember that the higher the standard deviation, the higher the risk. But for those who are interested in the "number crunching" behind the data, I'll walk you through an example using Vanguard's S&P 500 index fund.

The graph on the next page is a picture of the monthly returns of the Vanguard Index 500 Fund for a recent ten-year period. Each column represents a different monthly result, and each "x" represents a particular month in which the fund experienced that result. For example, the column indicated by the number ❶ tallies the number of times the fund lost between 2% and 3% in a single month. As you can see, there were ten months during the 1985-1994 period when the fund lost between 2% and 3%.

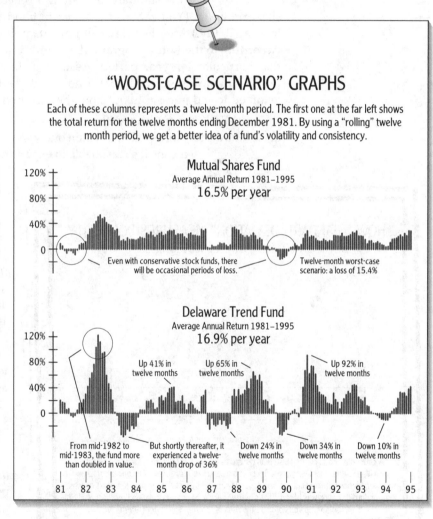

"WORST-CASE SCENARIO" GRAPHS

Each of these columns represents a twelve-month period. The first one at the far left shows the total return for the twelve months ending December 1981. By using a "rolling" twelve month period, we get a better idea of a fund's volatility and consistency.

Mutual Shares Fund
Average Annual Return 1981–1995
16.5% per year

Even with conservative stock funds, there will be occasional periods of loss.

Twelve-month worst-case scenario: a loss of 15.4%

Delaware Trend Fund
Average Annual Return 1981–1995
16.9% per year

Up 41% in twelve months

Up 65% in twelve months

Up 92% in twelve months

From mid-1982 to mid-1983, the fund more than doubled in value.

But shortly thereafter, it experienced a twelve-month drop of 36%

Down 24% in twelve months

Down 34% in twelve months

Down 10% in twelve months

81 82 83 84 85 86 87 88 89 90 91 92 93 94 95

By adding up all 120 of the monthly results and dividing by 120, I found that the *average* monthly result over the ten-year period was a gain of 1.2%. This, therefore, is considered the norm for this fund. Usually, but not always, the tallest column in the graph will be the one containing the monthly norm. That's what happened here. Column ❷, where I recorded the seventeen times that the fund's monthly gain ranged between 1% and 2%, turned out to be the tallest.

To compute the standard deviation, I relied on my Lotus 1-2-3 spreadsheet program. (You can also use certain hand-held calculators which have that capability.) After keying in all 120 data points, I used the @STD function. According to the Lotus program, the monthly standard deviation was 4.4 for that particular ten-year period. Assuming the future is similar to the past (which it won't necessarily be), I now had the information I needed to develop educated guesses about how the fund will behave in years to come.

Statistical theory—bear with me here—says that approximately two-thirds of all future data points will fall within one standard deviation of the norm. That means it's reasonable to expect (no guarantees!) that the results from about two-thirds of future months will fall between -3.2% (arrived at by subtracting 4.4 from 1.2) and +5.6% (arrived at by adding 4.4 to 1.2). In other words, based on past behavior we might expect that two of every three months in the future will see results that range between -3.2% and +5.6%. This is a concept we'll come back to when we discuss lowering your investment risk as you approach retirement in chapter 30.

But what if you wanted a higher degree of certainty—a range that would include *more than* two-thirds of future data points? Statistical theory says that approximately 95% of all future points will fall within *two* standard deviations of the norm. Here's how we apply that to project the lower part of the expected range for the Van-

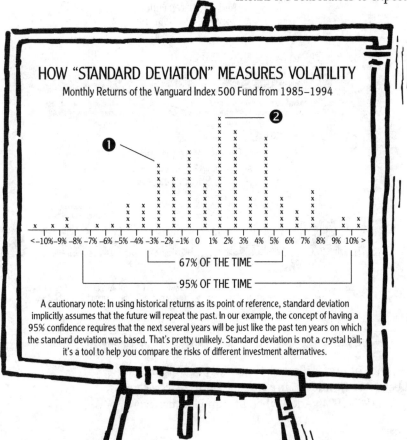

HOW "STANDARD DEVIATION" MEASURES VOLATILITY
Monthly Returns of the Vanguard Index 500 Fund from 1985–1994

❶   ❷

<-10% -9% -8% -7% -6% -5% -4% -3% -2% -1% 0 1% 2% 3% 4% 5% 6% 7% 8% 9% 10% >

67% OF THE TIME

95% OF THE TIME

A cautionary note: In using historical returns as its point of reference, standard deviation implicitly assumes that the future will repeat the past. In our example, the concept of having a 95% confidence requires that the next several years will be just like the past ten years on which the standard deviation was based. That's pretty unlikely. Standard deviation is not a crystal ball; it's a tool to help you compare the risks of different investment alternatives.

guard fund. Start with the norm (1.2) and subtract two times the standard deviation (2 x 4.4). You get -7.6%. Or, to get the upper limit of the range, take the norm (1.2) and add two times the standard deviation (2 x 4.4). You get +10.0%. Thus, we have a reasonable expectation that 95% of all future monthly returns from this fund will fall between -7.6% and +10.0%.

There might be times when you will want to use an annualized version of standard deviation rather than the monthly version we've just discussed. In fact, it's the more commonly cited statistic; if you see a standard deviation number quoted and the version isn't specified, you can usually assume it's the annualized computation being given. Later in this chapter we'll be looking at two more ways of assessing risk—the Sharpe Ratio and a "scattergram." Both require an annualized standard deviation measurement. For do-it-yourselfers, the annual number can be calculated by taking the monthly standard deviation and multiplying it times the square root of twelve (which is 3.464). In the above example, you would multiply the monthly standard deviation of Vanguard's S&P 500 fund of 4.4 times 3.464 to arrive at an annualized standard deviation of 15.2.

If you're not inclined to tackle the math yourself, you can get the most recent three-year, five-year, and ten-year annual standard deviation calculations from the standard mutual fund reports that Morningstar sells. Remember, a standard deviation calculation applies only to the specific period being measured. Just like a moving average, it will change slightly each month as the new month is added and the old month is dropped off the back end. If a fund experienced a lot of volatility in 1991 and 1992, and then calmed down from 1993 through 1995, the five-year standard deviation would be higher (show more volatility) than the three-year one. Morningstar offers the calculation over three different time periods to give you a better long-term perspective.

So, why is it good to know all this? It's good because it enables you to measure the volatility and better understand the relative degrees of risk between different investments.

Let's do that now by returning to Mutual Shares and Delaware Trend, the two funds for which we constructed the worst-case scenario graphs. In the graphs at right, the top one shows an "ideal" investment in terms of risk. There is no volatility at all. It's the essence of consistency. Like clockwork, this theoretical fund turns in reliable gains month after month after month. In the real world, the investments that behave the most like this are bank certificates of deposit and U.S. Treasury bills. The problem with those investments is they don't offer a high enough return. That's why we have to accept more risk.

Mutual fund reports are available from Morningstar OnDemand at (800) 876-5005. These reports are only one page in length, but they pack a lot of statistical and analytical data into them. Reports are available on more than 1,500 funds. The cost is $5 per report, and they will either fax it to you or send it via first class mail.

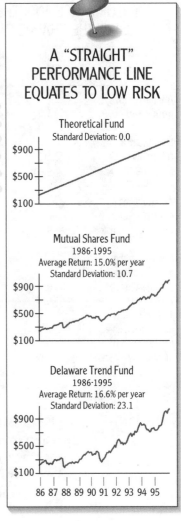

A "STRAIGHT" PERFORMANCE LINE EQUATES TO LOW RISK

Theoretical Fund
Standard Deviation: 0.0

Mutual Shares Fund
1986-1995
Average Return: 15.0% per year
Standard Deviation: 10.7

Delaware Trend Fund
1986-1995
Average Return: 16.6% per year
Standard Deviation: 23.1

86 87 88 89 90 91 92 93 94 95

The bottom two graphs provide another way of looking at the difference in volatility between Mutual Shares and Delaware Trend that we saw earlier. This time, the most recent ten-year period is shown. Mutual Shares' performance line, while not as flat as that of the theoretical fund, is nevertheless admirably consistent for a growth stock fund. It obviously has less volatility, and therefore less risk, than the Delaware Trend fund, which shows many pronounced ups and downs. But *how much* less risk?

That's where standard deviation can help us. Turning to Morningstar, I learn that Mutual Shares' annual standard deviation for the ten years ending in December 1995 was 10.7, and that Delaware Trend's was 23.1.

From this, we see that Mutual Shares carried less than half as much risk during the period. In other words, Mutual Shares was less than half as risky because its performance deviated from its norm, on average, less than half as much as did the performance of Delaware Trend. Thus, two funds that initially looked similar on the basis of their historical returns look quite different when you take their volatility into consideration.

To combine these two factors — gains recorded and risk taken — we turn to the Sharpe Ratio . . .

. . . (named after its inventor, economist and Nobel Laureate William Sharpe). The Sharpe Ratio is a risk measurement tool that is gaining prominence in the financial industry because it does a good job of tying performance and risk together in an understandable fashion. To aid in our learning as we go along, we'll apply the Sharpe Ratio to the performance records of the two funds we've been studying. The starting point for Sharpe's analysis is the risk-free return available from Treasury bills. Since the return on T-bills is available free of any risk, Sharpe reasoned that it only makes sense to incur risk to the degree you are able to earn more than the T-bill yield. The average annual compounded rate of return from T-bills from 1986-1995 was 5.6%. By subtracting this amount from the ten-year performance numbers of the two funds, we learn how much investors were "rewarded" by each fund for taking on risk.

The concluding step is to see if the "reward" is reasonable in light of the risks

TYING RISK AND PERFORMANCE TOGETHER BY USING THE SHARPE RATIO

	Mutual Shares	Delaware Trend
Annual return from 1986–1995	15.0%	16.6%
Less the risk-free return available from U.S. T-bills	– 5.6%	– 5.6%
Additional gains earned in return for accepting risk	= 9.4%	= 11.0%
Divided by the amount of risk taken (standard deviation)	10.7	23.1
The amount of additional gain earned for each unit of additional risk taken	= .88	= .48

taken. We do this by dividing the amount of the reward by the amount of risk (that is, by the standard deviation). The result is a Sharpe Ratio of .88 for Mutual Shares and .48 for Delaware Trend. The higher the Sharpe Ratio, the better. The number itself doesn't mean anything in an absolute sense; it's useful only for comparing investments to one another. In this case, it shows a dramatic difference in favor of Mutual Shares. In light of the Sharpe Ratios, some experts would say that Mutual Shares was much more "efficient" in managing risk. Others would say the fund did a better job of "exploiting" risk. In more familiar terms, you might just say that Mutual Shares gave investors "more bang for the buck."

It's important to keep in mind that it's not only how much money you make. It's how much risk you take to make the money you make.

Consider the stock mutual funds shown at the right. Their performance and risk scores are shown for the five-year period ending December 1995. Before you read this chapter, you might have looked at this list and concluded that the 20th Century Ultra Fund easily did the best job over that time period. But with the help of our two new tools—standard deviation and the Sharpe Ratio—you can now see that the fund was

Fund Name	5 Year Annualized Return	5 Year Standard Deviation	Sharpe Ratio
20th Century Ultra Investors	25.0%	20.5	1.01
20th Century Vista Investors	22.4%	20.4	0.89
Fidelity Equity-Income II	22.0%	8.9	2.00
Third Avenue Value	21.2%	10.1	1.67
Fidelity Value	20.8%	9.4	1.75
Founders Frontier	20.3%	14.6	1.10
Founders Special	19.7%	15.3	1.01
Mutual Shares	19.1%	7.5	1.97
Safeco Growth	19.0%	18.1	0.81
Janus Twenty	17.8%	14.4	0.94

the riskiest in the group (standard deviation of 20.5) and that shareholders weren't sufficiently rewarded for that extra risk (Sharpe Ratio ranked in the bottom half of the group). For my money, the standout was Fidelity Equity-Income II. It combined the third best performance with the second lowest risk, leading to the best Sharpe Ratio of the bunch. Mutual Shares also did better than you might initially have thought. Its performance was achieved with quite a low risk score—almost two-thirds less than the high-flying Ultra Fund—leading to the second highest Sharpe Ratio. Mutual Shares' investors got a high return in light of the relatively small amount of risk they took.

The last risk assessment tool we'll look at is a visual representation of a fund's risk and reward in relation to a comparable market index. It's a special kind of graph called a scattergram.

In chapter 13, I explained a strategy which I called Just-the-Basics. It's easy to understand, has an excellent track record, and requires almost no maintenance once it's in place. There's no reason to pursue a more complicated, time-consuming strategy unless you can consistently earn greater rewards while experiencing the same or lower levels of risk.

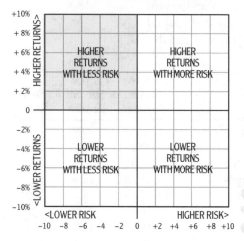

USING A SCATTERGRAM TO ASSESS FUND PERFORMANCE IN RELATION TO AN INDEX FUND

Fund Name	5 Year Annualized Return	Vs. Index Fund	5 Year Standard Deviation	Vs. Index Fund
Vanguard Index 500	16.4%		10.0	
❶ 20th Century Ultra	25.0%	8.6%	20.5	10.6
❷ Fidelity Equity-Income II	22.0%	5.6%	8.9	−1.1
❸ Mutual Shares	19.1%	2.7%	7.5	−2.5
❹ Janus Twenty	17.8%	1.4%	14.4	4.4
❺ AARP Capital Growth	14.9%	−1.5%	13.3	3.3
❻ Safeco Income	14.8%	−1.6%	7.6	−2.4

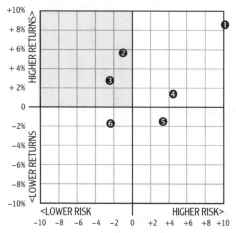

To the left are two scattergrams. The top one contains no fund plot points; it's shown just to illustrate the graph conceptually. We'll use the bottom scattergram to provide a snapshot of whether any of six selected mutual funds accomplished the above goal of higher-returns-with-lower-risk over a given period of time.

Along the vertical axis of the scattergram, we'll plot a fund's annualized performance in relation to the corresponding fund in the Just-the-Basics strategy. In this example, I'll be assessing the performance of several stock funds which invest in large companies. Therefore, I'm using Vanguard's large cap S&P 500 index fund as the benchmark. Along the horizontal axis, we'll plot a fund's risk (i.e., annual standard deviation) in relation to the risk of the S&P 500 index fund.

Our goal, as I've stated, is to identify funds that turn in higher performance numbers while simultaneously taking on similar or lower levels of risk. Such funds, if any are in our sample, will appear in the upper left-hand quadrant. The worst performance, on the other hand, would be to earn lower returns than the passive index fund while taking greater risks. Such funds will show up in the lower right-hand quadrant. Hopefully, this will become more clear as we walk through the example.

The funds shown in the table are ranked in order of their five-year performance from 1991-1995. If all we were taking into consideration was the rate of return, 20th Century Ultra would be the obvious winner. Its plot point in the scattergram reflects this by being the nearest the top. It outperformed the benchmark index fund by more than 8%. But should it be selected on that basis alone? After all, Ultra's very high volatility also gave it the highest risk score, placing it furthermost to the right with a plot point of 10.6.

Funds designated ❷, ❸, and ❹ also outperformed the S&P 500 index fund (as can be seen by their plot points above the horizontal zero line). Only Fidelity Equity-Income II and Mutual Shares, however, accomplished this while taking on less risk than the benchmark fund. Thus, they placed in the highly desirable upper left-hand quadrant.

AARP Capital Growth, alone in the lower right-hand quadrant, experienced the worst of both worlds—it experienced higher volatility than the S&P 500 index fund yet earned lower returns. Investors were not rewarded for the extra risks they took.

The scattergram is not saying that funds ❶ and ❹ are necessarily bad. They took extra risks, but they paid off with higher returns. The question each investor has to answer is whether the extra volatility is an acceptable price to pay for the incremental gains. Your personal risk-taking temperament will play a large role in settling that question in your own mind.

The volatility of returns should be taken into account, even for investors who have a long-term (ten years and more) commitment in mind.

There are at least three reasons for this.

◆ Unforeseen circumstances could arise that would force you to liquidate part or all of your holdings earlier than planned. If that occurs while your strategy is temporarily in a losing position, you'll incur losses that could have been avoided if you had been allowed more time.

◆ During periods of dramatic market weakness, the fear of further losses often causes investors to abandon their strategies rather than stay the course. It is less likely you will abandon a strategy which involves lower levels of volatility. Peter Lynch, legendary manager of the Magellan fund, has expressed the opinion that more than half of those who invested in the Magellan fund lost money despite its superior track record. Why? Because they sold during periods of market weakness only to buy back in when the market moved higher.

◆ Past performance is more indicative of future results when it is based on a low volatility strategy. Mark Hulbert, publisher of the leading publication that evaluates investment newsletters, has discovered in his research: "*As a general rule, of two advisers with the same performance, the one who achieved his performance with lower risk is more likely to be able to do it again.*" That's because a high volatility portfolio might be reflecting the success of a few big winners. A low volatility portfolio requires monthly consistency, which means that luck alone is unlikely to have played a prominent role in the outcome.

We can't avoid taking risks.

Life is filled with uncertainties. Even getting out of bed in the morning and driving to work is not without its risks. But we can manage our financial affairs so that when the unexpected comes along, we can isolate the damage it does. The blueprint for planning in this manner is given to us in the Scripture, and it is incorporated into the strategies taught in this book. Know where you're going. Avoid debt. Spend less than you earn. Save for the future. Diversify your investments. Exercise self-control and stay with your plan.

In his book *Storm Shelter*, financial planner Ron Blue points out that while economic uncertainty is certain, God's principles are adequate for our protection. They've been tested through the centuries and never found wanting.

Standard deviation is one of the measures of risk which the Securities and Exchange Commission is considering for use in new regulations that would require mutual funds to disclose more information about potential risk to their investors.

"Investors are hungry for ways to assess the risks in mutual funds. The Securities and Exchange Commission has received 1,500 comments since it asked the public for ideas on informing investors about fund risks. The flood of comments will probably 'eclipse whatever our record has been for the most comments' at the agency's division of investment management, says Barry Barbash, the division's director.

"If the SEC eventually imposes some form of risk disclosure, the results will depend heavily on how it measures risk. Funds that seem risky by one measure often appear sedate by another. To some fund-industry people, this means the SEC should stay out of the risk-measurement business altogether, because any 'magic number' it mandates is bound to be misleading. Mr. Barbash says the SEC won't necessarily mandate a single measure. But he adds that just because risk is hard to measure, that doesn't mean that individuals shouldn't be given more information about the risks of funds that they're considering, or that they own."

The Wall Street Journal 7/5/95

The picture is as clear in my mind as it was nearly thirteen years ago. As I pulled off the interstate en route to my office, I did not see the road markers; instead my eyes swam with the signs of the times.

The year was 1982. Interest and inflation rates had soared to all-time highs, investors faced crushing 70 percent tax brackets, and the price of gold leapfrogged daily. Taking stock of the situation, most analysts warned of a devastating financial explosion within the next few years.

As I drove to work that day, the economic consequences seemed both crippling and inevitable. I had just launched our investment and financial counseling firm. How, I wondered, were we supposed to respond to the clients who came to us for advice? Could anyone afford to purchase a home with 15 to 20 percent interest rates? Which kinds of investments and tax plans could stand up to double-digit inflation? And if the predicted monetary collapse did occur, would the resulting political turmoil uproot even the best-laid financial plans?

One of my fears as I navigated the interstate highway that day was that we faced a "worst-ever" economic climate. Yet economic uncertainty — and its accompanying effects on our sense of security and well-being — are nothing new.

Ten years earlier, in 1972, we had been saddled with Watergate and an oil crisis that threatened to throttle the world's economy. Who can forget the lines at the gas stations or the rationing of fuel oil that winter? Then, too, I remember being hit with wage and price controls for the first time since World War II. And for the first time in my memory, the prime rate hit ten percent. Economic security seemed an elusive, if not impossible, dream.

Ten years before that, in 1962, the specter of economic and political uncertainty had hovered in every corner of the world. Our amazement at seeing a shoe-pounding Nikita Khrushchev vow to "bury" us turned to horror as the Cuban missile crisis unfolded. At that point a nuclear holocaust seemed at least possible, if not imminent. And Vietnam lay just around the corner . . .

In 1952, in the shadow of the spread of Communism, amid the mud and blood of the Korean War, bomb shelters were among the best-selling items in the United States. In 1942, we faced Pearl Harbor and felt the full force of our entry into World War II. In 1932 we awoke to the nightmare of the Great Depression.

And on and on and on. The point is that we will always face uncertainty. Suddenly, I felt the subconscious click of the proverbial light bulb: The biblical principles of money management I had been teaching and using for years would work under any economic scenario. Armed with these concepts, I knew exactly how to help our clients weather the coming storm, no matter how hard the financial winds blew.

The predicted financial blowout never did occur. Yet as our business grew in the years that followed, we faced a thousand different financial situations that seemed specially tailored to test the worth and endurance of the money-management concepts our firm espoused. But in each and every case the biblical principles held fast, strengthening our clients' economic positions — and bringing them peace and security in the bargain. [1] ◆

[1] Excerpted from Storm Shelter, Protecting Your Personal Finances by Ron Blue. Copyright 1994 by Ronald W. Blue. Published by Thomas Nelson, Inc. Used by permission. All rights reserved.

CHAPTER PREVIEW

Understanding Bond Fund Risk

I. **By using the two main influences on risk, we can create a "risk profile" for categorizing bond funds that will greatly simplify the process of selecting the bond funds that are best for you.**

    A. First, I will divide all bond funds into two groups: those that invest only in bonds of the highest quality (which includes government and high quality corporate bonds) and those that are willing to invest in lesser-rated bonds in a search for higher yields (the so-called "junk bond" group).

    B. Second, I'll subdivide the first group further: those funds with short-term maturities in their portfolios (less than four years), those funds with medium-term maturities in their portfolios (from four to ten years), and those with longer-term maturities (over ten years).

    C. This results in four distinct categories (or "peer groups"), each having its own risk characteristics in terms of quality and average maturities.

II. **The risk profile enables us to build a "risk ladder."**

    A. In our bond "risk ladder," I provide ten-year performance histories based on an average of all the funds in each of the four risk categories. I also point out risk characteristics you should understand.

    B. For each of the four risk categories, I provide a sampling of ten no-load bond funds.

        1. The data include each fund's ticker symbol, the minimum you need to open an account, its 800 information number, risk information based on standard deviations and the Sharpe Ratio, and ten years of performance histories.

        2. These funds are not recommended for purchase per se, but are offered as a starting point for your own research.

        3. Mutual fund policies, performance, and portfolio characteristics are constantly subject to change. Contact the fund for current information before you invest.

III. **Although they have advantages, investing in bond funds has two drawbacks that don't apply to investing in individual bonds: they never reach maturity, and, under certain conditions, they may have tax disadvantages.**

How do you distinguish among the large number of bond mutual funds and select the ones most appropriate for you?

There are many varieties of bond funds. They differ in whether they're committed to investing in high quality bonds or will specialize in higher-risk, higher-yielding ones of lower quality. They differ in the maturities of their portfolios—some seek to keep their average weighted maturities at three years or less, others want to keep theirs at no less than twenty years. Some generate taxable dividends, others tax-free dividends. Some limit themselves to the U.S. market, whereas others are permitted to invest overseas. Now imagine that you started mixing and matching all these possibilities to see how many different combinations are possible. The answer? A lot! More than you want to read about—one writer on the bond market published a book spanning 1,426 pages!

To bring some kind of order out of this chaos, I've grouped bond funds in a way that should be most helpful for beginners.

These aren't the "official" groupings used for comparing risk and performance among mutual funds. In fact, there's no such thing. The Investment Company Institute, which is the trade association for the mutual fund industry, has its way of grouping funds (see sidebar at left). Morningstar and Lipper, the two major mutual fund reporting services, have their own ways—and each is different from the other. Their classification systems are rather complicated; they have from fourteen to twenty-seven different bond fund categories, depending on whose system you use. I wouldn't even consider trying to explain them to you or using them in this book. Instead, I have created my own way of classifying bond funds that I believe you will find relatively easy to understand and use. Here's how it works.

First, I divide all the bond funds (other than international funds, which I'll talk about in chapter 21) into two groups. One group is composed of those funds that invest in a diversified portfolio of bonds that are taxable and have no unusual features. These are the funds I regard as primary when assembling a bond portfolio and are the ones we'll be focusing on in this chapter. The other group includes what I call "special purpose" bond funds because they invest in bonds with distinctive features. This group includes mortgage-backed bonds, zero coupon bonds, and tax-exempt bonds. We'll look at special purpose bond funds in chapter 22.

I'll illustrate bond fund risk for you by using a graphic device that I call a "risk profile," and dividing it into four diamond-shaped compartments.

As we've discussed, there are two major threats facing lenders. The first is the risk that the bonds will go into default. The extensive diversification you

---

Bond funds as classified for risk by the Investment Company Institute

Here are the definitions used by the mutual fund industry's trade association. You will note how vague they are compared to the highly specific approach recommended in this book.

U.S. Government Income Funds

seek income by investing in a variety of U.S. Government securities, including Treasury bonds, federally guaranteed mortgage-backed securities, and other government-backed issues.

Income-Bond Funds

seek a high level of income by investing in a mixture of corporate and government bonds.

Corporate Bond Funds

seek a high level of income by purchasing primarily bonds of U.S.-based corporations; they also invest in other fixed-income securities such as U.S. Treasury bonds.

High-yield Bond Funds

maintain at least two thirds of their portfolio in noninvestment-grade corporate bonds (those rated Baa or lower by Moody's rating service and BBB or lower by Standard and Poor's rating service). In return for potentially greater income, high-yield funds present investors with greater credit risk than do higher-rated bond funds.

achieve in a bond mutual fund virtually eliminates this risk as a meaningful threat. Bonds are issued by borrowers from all across the "credit-worthiness" spectrum. The U.S. government is regarded as the borrower highest on the quality scale. Even there, many experts make a distinction between direct obligations of the U.S. Treasury versus those of government agencies, the latter being considered as ever so slightly lower in quality.

Then come corporate bonds issued by financially strong companies that receive "investment grade" ratings (AAA, AA, A, and BBB—see page 132 for definitions of bond ratings). The subtle credit distinctions among investment grade bonds may be of interest if you're buying only a few issues, but they are less important when buying into a mutual fund portfolio. Defaults are rare events at this level of quality, and even if one should come along, the investor is well protected by the diversification.

For purposes of assessing the credit risk, I don't make a distinction between a fund invested only in U.S. government-backed bonds versus one that also invests in BBB-rated corporate bonds. Taken individually, of course, the government bonds are of higher quality. But, as a practical matter, in a diversified portfolio that includes a sampling of BBB-rated bonds, the differences in risk are insignificant. Even the so-called "general corporate" bond funds will invest to some extent in Treasury securities (in order to balance out some of their risk as well as put idle cash to good use in case they can't find enough of the lesser grade bonds they like). Since they obviously can own large amounts of governments, we shouldn't think of them as buying only bonds issued by businesses. Therefore, I'm treating funds that invest in any of the above kinds of bonds the same. Their overall credit quality will range from AAA to BBB, and they will be placed in one of the three lower diamonds in our risk profile (see step one in sidebar on next page).

That leaves the bonds of weaker companies, the so-called "junk" bonds that must pay higher yields to attract investors.

Junk bonds are corporate bonds that have been given low ratings by independent grading firms such as Moody's and Standard & Poor's. The ratings are intended to evaluate a company's financial strength and, accordingly, its ability to pay both the principal and interest on its debts as they come due. Generally, bonds rated in the top four categories are considered "investment grade" quality. Only several hundred of the strongest companies qualify for these high ratings.

That leaves several thousand companies stuck with the "junk" label, although naturally there are differences in financial strength even here. There are distinctions between those companies that just barely failed to qualify for an investment grade rating and those that have problems so severe that they

---

How can junk bonds suffer through defaults and still come out ahead?

Here's how it might work. Say the average yield in the fund portfolio is 12% on junk bond holdings of $1 million. That means the fund would receive $120,000 in interest payments throughout the year. Assume that the fund experiences a 2.5% default rate ($25,000 of their bond holdings). Even in a default, bonds don't typically become worthless; bondholders usually recoup 40%–50% of the principal value of the bonds. If the fund recouped 40% of its investment in the bad bonds, it would get $10,000 of its capital back. That means the fund lost $15,000 on the defaulting bonds, which would be offset against the interest income. After all is said and done, the fund would still come out $105,000 ahead for the year.

A healthy economy is very important to buyers of junk bonds because it helps maintain a positive cash flow that enables even weaker companies to keep up with their interest payments. While a recession spells trouble for everybody, it can be especially devastating for companies with high debt loads. It's the same problem faced by families with high credit card and other consumer debt.

With this dynamic in mind, it's easy to see why junk bond funds often respond to economic events more like stock funds do. Stockholders really need a company to continue growing in order for their investments to succeed; so do junk bondholders. If things go wrong, stockholders can lose most of their investment; so can junk bondholders.

have already filed for bankruptcy protection. If you want the higher yields that these companies offer (in order to entice investors to buy their bonds), the trick is to sort through these lower-rated offerings and pick the strongest of the weak. That's the task of the fund manager.

The junk bond fund group often marches more with the average stock fund than it does with other bond funds. In 1991, high-quality bond funds returned about 15%, and stock and junk bond funds, even though the economy was in a recession, returned a surprisingly strong 33% and 37%, respectively. Why? Because, like the stock market, junk bonds are valued based on *anticipated events* in the economy six to nine months away. Investors began expecting the recovery to kick in and greatly improve the cash flow of the companies that had issued the bonds. (Junk bonds flourished during the strong economies of 1986 and 1988.) This appeared to lower the risk, and the high yields looked great in comparison to other savings-type investments, which had fallen to extremely low levels. And so the rush was on.

Junk bond investors are realistic enough to expect some of their holdings to eventually default. Studies have shown that it's normal for 1.5% to 2.5% of junk bonds to default in any given year. That's why the diversification provided by the fund is so essential—it spreads out this risk over a sufficiently large number of bonds to reasonably assure that its default experience will be in this range. The higher yields paid by junk bonds compensate investors for this expected small loss of capital. Due to their high risk, funds that invest in junk bonds will be placed in category four, the uppermost of the four diamonds in the risk profile. Step one (upper left) summarizes the placement of funds based on the risk of default.

The second major threat facing bond owners is that of rising interest rates—as rates go up, bond prices go down.

BUILDING A RISK PROFILE FOR BOND FUNDS: STEP #1

Separate funds according to the credit-worthiness of their portfolios

Mixed Quality — ④
High Quality — ③
High Quality — ②
High Quality — ①

BUILDING A RISK PROFILE FOR BOND FUNDS: STEP #2

Separate funds according to the average maturities of their portfolios

Various Maturities — ④
Long Term — ③
Medium Term — ②
Short Term — ①

BUILDING A RISK PROFILE FOR BOND FUNDS: STEP #3

Combine criteria to create four distinct risk categories based on overall credit quality and average portfolio maturities

Mixed Quality Various Maturities — ④
High Quality Long Term — ③
High Quality Medium Term — ②
High Quality Short Term — ①

A bond fund's average portfolio maturity tells us more about the risk of that fund than just about any other factor. As you move toward longer maturities, the risk of being hurt by rising interest rates increases. The sooner the bonds in your portfolio mature, the sooner your fund manager can go out and buy bonds paying the new higher rates. It follows, therefore, that the shorter the average portfolio maturity of a bond fund, the less its price volatility.

We reflect this in the second step of building our risk profile. Because the short-term portfolios pose the least risk, we assign them to the lowest diamond; the medium-term funds go into category two; and the long-term portfolios, which have the highest risk among high quality bond funds, are placed in category three.

Now to put all this together. As you can see in step three, the two fundamental risk considerations combine to create four distinctive risk categories. The diamond that is positioned lowest in the profile (category one) is also the category with the lowest risk because it combines the safety of high quality bonds with shorter maturities. The category that is positioned highest in the profile (category four) is the category with the highest risk because it features bonds of mixed quality that also have medium-to-long-term maturities. The two diamonds in the center are for bond funds with risk in between the two extremes. Once you know which of these four risk categories a bond fund falls in, you know a lot about that fund's likely volatility as well as its potential for gain or loss.

Let's apply the lessons you've learned about bonds (chapter 11) and fund risk (chapter 18) as we study the "risk ladder" for bond funds below.

It's called a risk ladder because it's safest at the bottom, and each step up to the next rung increases your risk. The statistics were compiled from the Morningstar OnDisc database for the year ending December 1995.

❶ Notice that the actual risk scores (standard deviation) and five-year annualized returns for each group show the kind of pattern we'd expect—bond funds in category four have the highest numbers, and they gradually decrease as you move down the

RISK LADDER FOR BOND FUNDS

SOURCE: MORNINGSTAR ONDISC

Risk Category	Standard Deviation	5 Year Annualized	1995 Return	1994 Return	1993 Return	1992 Return	1991 Return	1990 Return	1989 Return	1988 Return	1987 Return	1986 Return
4 Invest by Lending: Bond Risk Category 4 — Bond funds that invest in high-yield junk bonds, typically of medium-term maturities	5.8	16.6%	17.1%	–3.3%	18.8%	17.2%	36.7%	–10.1%	–0.7%	13.1%	2.0%	13.5%
3 Invest by Lending: Bond Risk Category 3 — Bond portfolios of generally high quality with long-term average maturities (over 10 years)	5.7	10.4%	21.5%	–5.7%	12.7%	7.7%	17.0%	5.8%	13.0%	9.4%	0.9%	16.8%
2 Invest by Lending: Bond Risk Category 2 — Bond portfolios of generally high quality with medium-term average maturities (4–10 years)	4.1	8.5%	16.5%	–3.9%	9.6%	6.7%	15.2%	7.9%	11.9%	7.3%	1.8%	14.3%
1 Invest by Lending: Bond Risk Category 1 — Bond portfolios of generally high quality with short-term average maturities (4 years or less)	2.6	6.6%	10.4%	–0.7%	6.1%	5.5%	12.1%	7.8%	10.5%	6.7%	3.9%	14.3%

ladder. The ladder was devised based on theory as to how risk and return relate to each other in bond investing, and the experience of the different risk categories during the 1991-1995 period demonstrates that the theory holds up in actual practice.

❷ Notice that the short-term category-one funds did better (as expected) in years like 1994 when rising interest rates hurt bond prices. Conversely, the more volatile long-term funds were the performance winners during years like 1995 when rates were falling.

❸ Notice that the high-yield category-four funds march to a different drummer. There is a relatively consistent pattern that shows up when comparing the year-by-year results of the funds in categories one through three; however, the performance of the category four funds seems almost random. That's because, as I pointed out earlier in this chapter, junk bonds often behave more like stocks due to their sensitivity to the strength in the economy.

On the following pages, you'll find listings of no-load bond funds from the four different risk categories we've discussed in this chapter.

To further familiarize you with what you can expect in terms of risk and performance, I've assembled a sampling of ten no-load funds from each risk category. Beginning on page 228, you'll find data tables that include:

◆ Each fund's ticker symbol. The ticker symbol is a five letter code that is assigned to every fund by the National Association of Security Dealers. No two funds have the same ticker symbol. Using this code when placing buy and sell orders will assure that you are not misunderstood.

◆ The minimum you need to open a regular account. Each organization sets its own policies in this regard. Most mutual funds have lower minimums for IRA accounts, commonly set at $500, than they do for regular accounts. Also, many organizations will lower their minimums further (or waive them altogether) if you will sign up for their automatic investment program, which transfers at least $50 monthly from your bank account into your new fund account. Check with each fund for specific details.

◆ Their 800 numbers. Many organizations staff their help lines twenty-four hours a day. Whether you want to request general information, sales literature, or account forms, this is the number to call. Most no-load organizations also have helpful materials on planning for college, retirement planning, and other financial topics of interest to the beginning investor. They will send it free of charge and without obligation.

◆ Three-year risk data based on standard deviations and the Sharpe Ratio. The column headed "Versus Index" shows how volatile the fund was in contrast to the comparable Vanguard index fund used in our Just-the-Basics strategy. A positive number means the fund was more volatile (higher risk) than the Vanguard index fund during 1993-1995, and a negative reading means it was less volatile (lower risk).

◆ Three-year annualized returns for each fund, and how that performance measured up against the comparable Vanguard index fund. A positive number means the fund outperformed the Vanguard index fund, and a negative reading means it underperformed. We keep making comparisons to the Vanguard funds because they represent what was available to investors with no research and very little effort via the Just-the-Basics strategy. The three-year risk and return numbers versus the Vanguard fund provide the plot points for the scattergram. See pages 213-218 for a review of how to use this data in making comparisons among competing funds.

◆ Ten years of performance histories. This is helpful when trying to get an idea of how consistent the returns have been. The numbers shown are the returns received by shareholders after all expenses. All the funds shown are no-load, so there are no sales commissions to take into account.

These funds are not necessarily recommended for purchase per se, but are offered as a starting point for your further investigation. Remember, fund managers and portfolios can change quickly, so don't use these listings without also carefully reviewing the literature the fund sends you to make sure it has the kind of quality and maturities you're looking for.

In concluding this chapter on the risks of owning bond funds, let's look at how investing in a bond fund differs from investing in a portfolio of individual bonds that you put together yourself.

Investing in a pre-assembled portfolio via a bond fund offers convenience and professional management, but there are some drawbacks.

1. Bond funds never reach maturity. The job of the bond fund manager is to maintain the fund's average maturity at the level stated in its prospectus. For example, the Vanguard Long-Term Corporate Bond Fund (see listings for category three on pages 232-233) is committed to keeping the average weighted maturity of its portfolio between fifteen and twenty-five years. As time goes by and maturities shorten, the manager will need to replace some of the shorter-term bonds with longer-term ones in order to stay within the stated range. Although time is passing, the fund never gets closer to the day when the entire portfolio matures and every shareholder will cash out whole.

This is different from what takes place if you buy an individual bond. Assume you invest in one which has a fifteen-year maturity. Each year, it moves closer to the date when it will be paid off. That means the tendency of your bond to experience wide price swings in its market value is reduced year by year. Eventually, there will come a time when you will receive all your money back. This is not an assurance that investors in bond funds (continued on page 236)

THE CHARACTERISTICS OF A
CATEGORY ONE SHORT-TERM BOND PORTFOLIO

☒ High quality bonds with an average weighted portfolio maturity of less than four years. Risk is low.
☐ High quality bonds with an average weighted portfolio maturity of four to ten years. Risk is moderate.
☐ High quality bonds with an average weighted portfolio maturity of greater than ten years. Risk is high.
☐ Lower quality bonds with an average weighted portfolio maturity of four to ten years. Risk is high.

Name of Fund	Stated Investment Objective	Nasdaq Ticker Symbol	Minimum Initial Purchase	Minimum IRA Purchase	Maximum Sales Charge	Number to Call for Information	3 Year Risk Data		
							Sharpe Ratio	Standard Deviation	Versus Index
❶ Dreyfus 100% U.S. Treas S-T	Govt Treasury	DRTSX	$2,500	$750	No Load	800-648-9048	0.82	2.2	−2.0
❷ Dreyfus Short-Intermed Govt	Govt General	DSIGX	$2,500	$750	No Load	800-645-6561	0.83	2.6	−1.6
❸ Dreyfus Short-Term Income	Corp General	DSTIX	$2,500	$750	No Load	800-645-6561	1.12	2.3	−1.9
❹ Loomis Sayles S-T Bond	Corp General	LSSTX	$2,500	$250	No Load	800-633-3330	1.27	1.8	−2.4
❺ Montgomery S-T Govt Bond	Govt General	MNSGX	$1,000	$1,000	No Load	800-572-3863	1.45	1.9	−2.3
❻ Sit U.S. Government Secs	Govt General	SNGVX	$2,000	None	No Load	800-332-5580	1.56	1.7	−2.5
❼ Strong Advantage	Corp General	STADX	$1,000	$250	No Load	800-368-1030	2.59	0.9	−3.3
❽ Strong Short-Term Bond	Corp General	SSTBX	$1,000	$250	No Load	800-368-1030	0.89	2.5	−1.7
❾ Vanguard S-T Corporate	Corp General	VFSTX	$3,000	$500	No Load	800-662-7447	0.99	2.3	−1.9
❿ Vanguard S-T Federal	Govt General	VSGBX	$3,000	$500	No Load	800-662-7447	0.76	2.4	−1.8

Data source: Morningstar Mutual Funds OnDisc. Copyright by Morningstar, Inc., 53 West Jackson Blvd., Chicago, IL 60604. (800) 876–5005. Although gathered from reliable sources, data accuracy and completeness cannot be guaranteed. Performance numbers reflect periods ending 12/31/95 unless otherwise stated. Mutual fund performance and policies are constantly subject to change. Contact the fund for current information before you invest.

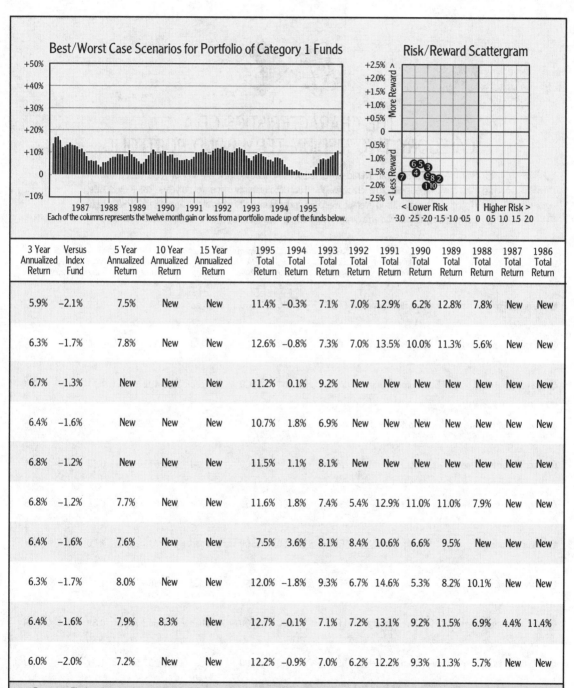

Best/Worst Case Scenarios for Portfolio of Category 1 Funds

Each of the columns represents the twelve month gain or loss from a portfolio made up of the funds below.

Risk/Reward Scattergram

3 Year Annualized Return	Versus Index Fund	5 Year Annualized Return	10 Year Annualized Return	15 Year Annualized Return	1995 Total Return	1994 Total Return	1993 Total Return	1992 Total Return	1991 Total Return	1990 Total Return	1989 Total Return	1988 Total Return	1987 Total Return	1986 Total Return
5.9%	−2.1%	7.5%	New	New	11.4%	−0.3%	7.1%	7.0%	12.9%	6.2%	12.8%	7.8%	New	New
6.3%	−1.7%	7.8%	New	New	12.6%	−0.8%	7.3%	7.0%	13.5%	10.0%	11.3%	5.6%	New	New
6.7%	−1.3%	New	New	New	11.2%	0.1%	9.2%	New	New	New	New	New	New	New
6.4%	−1.6%	New	New	New	10.7%	1.8%	6.9%	New	New	New	New	New	New	New
6.8%	−1.2%	New	New	New	11.5%	1.1%	8.1%	New	New	New	New	New	New	New
6.8%	−1.2%	7.7%	New	New	11.6%	1.8%	7.4%	5.4%	12.9%	11.0%	11.0%	7.9%	New	New
6.4%	−1.6%	7.6%	New	New	7.5%	3.6%	8.1%	8.4%	10.6%	6.6%	9.5%	New	New	New
6.3%	−1.7%	8.0%	New	New	12.0%	−1.8%	9.3%	6.7%	14.6%	5.3%	8.2%	10.1%	New	New
6.4%	−1.6%	7.9%	8.3%	New	12.7%	−0.1%	7.1%	7.2%	13.1%	9.2%	11.5%	6.9%	4.4%	11.4%
6.0%	−2.0%	7.2%	New	New	12.2%	−0.9%	7.0%	6.2%	12.2%	9.3%	11.3%	5.7%	New	New

Footnotes: The best/worst columns reflect "rolling" twelve month periods from the 1981–1995 period, or for the life of the fund, whichever is shorter (see chapter 18). Portfolio characteristics are subject to rapid change at the fund manager's discretion. By the time you read this, these funds may have characteristics different from those shown. These are not recommended funds per se, but are offered here as worthy of your consideration.

THE CHARACTERISTICS OF A
CATEGORY TWO MEDIUM-TERM BOND PORTFOLIO

☐ High quality bonds with an average weighted portfolio maturity of less than four years. Risk is low.
☒ High quality bonds with an average weighted portfolio maturity of four to ten years. Risk is moderate.
☐ High quality bonds with an average weighted portfolio maturity of greater than ten years. Risk is high.
☐ Lower quality bonds with an average weighted portfolio maturity of four to ten years. Risk is high.

Name of Fund	Stated Investment Objective	Nasdaq Ticker Symbol	Minimum Initial Purchase	Minimum IRA Purchase	Maximum Sales Charge	Number to Call for Information	Sharpe Ratio	Standard Deviation	Versus Index
❶ Columbia Fixed-Income	Corp High Quality	CFISX	$1,000	$1,000	No Load	800-547-1707	0.92	4.5	+0.3
❷ Fidelity Intermediate Bond	Corp High Quality	FTHRX	$2,500	$500	No Load	800-544-8888	0.95	3.4	−0.8
❸ Harbor Bond Fund	Corp General	HABDX	$2,000	$500	No Load	800-422-1050	1.13	4.2	0.0
❹ Invesco Intermediate Govt	Govt General	FIGBX	$1,000	$250	No Load	800-525-8085	1.01	3.6	−0.6
❺ Legg Mason Investment Grade	Corp General	LMIGX	$1,000	$1,000	No Load	800-577-8589	0.87	4.7	+0.6
❻ Loomis Sayles U.S. Govt Secs	Govt General	LSGSX	$2,500	$250	No Load	800-633-3330	0.88	6.8	+2.6
❼ SteinRoe Income	Corp General	SRHBX	$2,500	$500	No Load	800-338-2550	1.10	4.6	+0.4
❽ Strong Government Secs	Govt General	STVSX	$1,000	$250	No Load	800-368-1030	1.13	4.6	+0.4
❾ Vanguard Interm-Term U.S.	Govt Treasury	VFITX	$3,000	$500	No Load	800-662-7447	0.89	5.1	+0.9
❿ Warburg Pincus Fixed-Income	Corp General	CUFIX	$2,500	$500	No Load	800-257-5614	1.21	3.4	−0.8

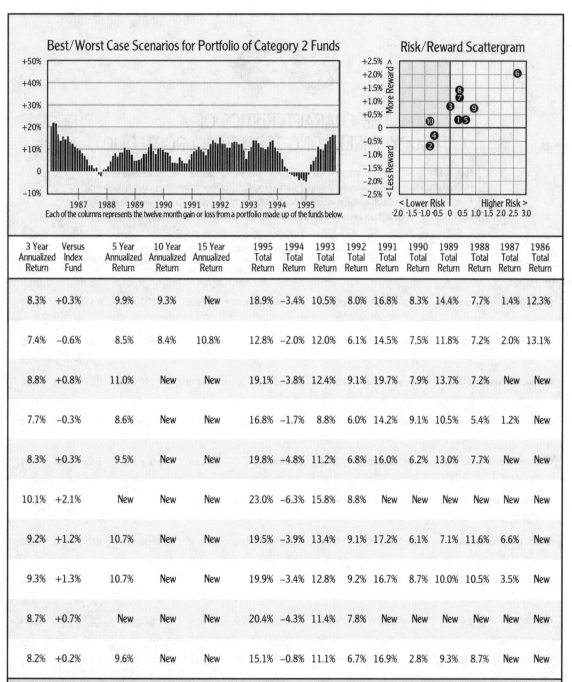

Best/Worst Case Scenarios for Portfolio of Category 2 Funds

Each of the columns represents the twelve month gain or loss from a portfolio made up of the funds below.

Risk/Reward Scattergram

3 Year Annualized Return	Versus Index Fund	5 Year Annualized Return	10 Year Annualized Return	15 Year Annualized Return	1995 Total Return	1994 Total Return	1993 Total Return	1992 Total Return	1991 Total Return	1990 Total Return	1989 Total Return	1988 Total Return	1987 Total Return	1986 Total Return
8.3%	+0.3%	9.9%	9.3%	New	18.9%	–3.4%	10.5%	8.0%	16.8%	8.3%	14.4%	7.7%	1.4%	12.3%
7.4%	–0.6%	8.5%	8.4%	10.8%	12.8%	–2.0%	12.0%	6.1%	14.5%	7.5%	11.8%	7.2%	2.0%	13.1%
8.8%	+0.8%	11.0%	New	New	19.1%	–3.8%	12.4%	9.1%	19.7%	7.9%	13.7%	7.2%	New	New
7.7%	–0.3%	8.6%	New	New	16.8%	–1.7%	8.8%	6.0%	14.2%	9.1%	10.5%	5.4%	1.2%	New
8.3%	+0.3%	9.5%	New	New	19.8%	–4.8%	11.2%	6.8%	16.0%	6.2%	13.0%	7.7%	New	New
10.1%	+2.1%	New	New	New	23.0%	–6.3%	15.8%	8.8%	New	New	New	New	New	New
9.2%	+1.2%	10.7%	New	New	19.5%	–3.9%	13.4%	9.1%	17.2%	6.1%	7.1%	11.6%	6.6%	New
9.3%	+1.3%	10.7%	New	New	19.9%	–3.4%	12.8%	9.2%	16.7%	8.7%	10.0%	10.5%	3.5%	New
8.7%	+0.7%	New	New	New	20.4%	–4.3%	11.4%	7.8%	New	New	New	New	New	New
8.2%	+0.2%	9.6%	New	New	15.1%	–0.8%	11.1%	6.7%	16.9%	2.8%	9.3%	8.7%	New	New

Footnotes: The best/worst columns reflect "rolling" twelve month periods from the 1981–1995 period, or for the life of the fund, whichever is shorter (see chapter 18). Portfolio characteristics are subject to rapid change at the fund manager's discretion. By the time you read this, these funds may have characteristics different from those shown. These are not recommended funds per se, but are offered here as worthy of your consideration.

THE CHARACTERISTICS OF A
CATEGORY THREE LONG-TERM BOND PORTFOLIO

☐ High quality bonds with an average weighted portfolio maturity of less than four years. Risk is low.
☐ High quality bonds with an average weighted portfolio maturity of four to ten years. Risk is moderate.
☒ High quality bonds with an average weighted portfolio maturity of greater than ten years. Risk is high.
☐ Lower quality bonds with an average weighted portfolio maturity of four to ten years. Risk is high.

Name of Fund	Stated Investment Objective	Nasdaq Ticker Symbol	Minimum Initial Purchase	Minimum IRA Purchase	Maximum Sales Charge	Number to Call for Information	3 Year Risk Data		
							Sharpe Ratio	Standard Deviation	Versus Index
❶ Benham L-T Treasury/Agency	Govt General	BLAGX	$1,000	$1,000	No Load	800-331-8331	0.83	8.6	+4.4
❷ Dreyfus A Bonds Plus	Corp High Quality	DRBDX	$2,500	$750	No Load	800-645-6561	0.83	5.9	+1.8
❸ Fidelity Investment Grade	Corp General	FBNDX	$2,500	$500	No Load	800-544-8888	0.87	4.8	+0.6
❹ Invesco Select Income	Corp General	FBDSX	$1,000	$250	No Load	800-525-8085	1.49	3.9	−0.3
❺ Loomis Sayles Bond	Corp General	LSBDX	$2,500	$250	No Load	800-633-3330	1.82	6.3	+2.1
❻ Managers Bond	Corp General	MGFIX	$2,000	$500	No Load	800-835-3879	0.95	6.9	+2.7
❼ Price US Treasury L-T	Govt Treasury	PRULX	$2,500	$1,000	No Load	800-638-5660	0.99	7.0	+2.8
❽ Strong Corporate Bond	Corp General	STCBX	$1,000	$250	No Load	800-368-1030	1.73	5.2	+1.0
❾ Vanguard L-T Corp Bond	Corp High Quality	VWESX	$3,000	$500	No Load	800-662-7447	1.07	6.5	+2.3
❿ Vanguard L-T U.S. Treasury	Govt Treasury	VUSTX	$3,000	$500	No Load	800-662-7447	1.01	8.0	+3.8

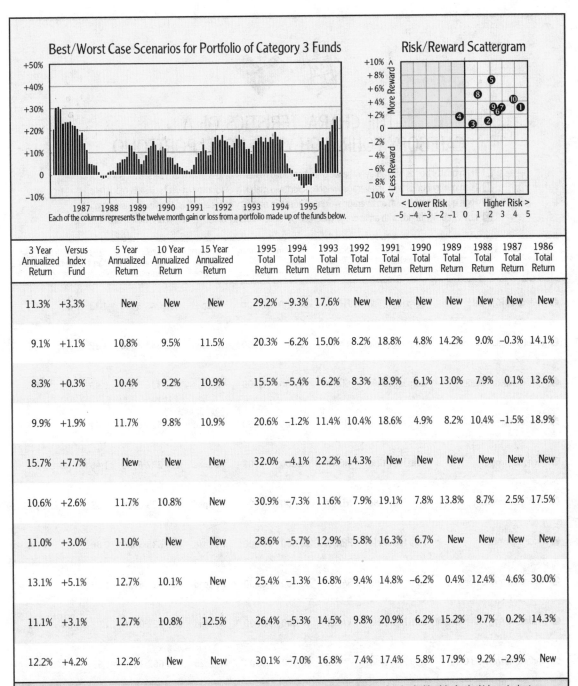

Best/Worst Case Scenarios for Portfolio of Category 3 Funds

Each of the columns represents the twelve month gain or loss from a portfolio made up of the funds below.

Risk/Reward Scattergram

3 Year Annualized Return	Versus Index Fund	5 Year Annualized Return	10 Year Annualized Return	15 Year Annualized Return	1995 Total Return	1994 Total Return	1993 Total Return	1992 Total Return	1991 Total Return	1990 Total Return	1989 Total Return	1988 Total Return	1987 Total Return	1986 Total Return
11.3%	+3.3%	New	New	New	29.2%	–9.3%	17.6%	New	New	New	New	New	New	New
9.1%	+1.1%	10.8%	9.5%	11.5%	20.3%	–6.2%	15.0%	8.2%	18.8%	4.8%	14.2%	9.0%	–0.3%	14.1%
8.3%	+0.3%	10.4%	9.2%	10.9%	15.5%	–5.4%	16.2%	8.3%	18.9%	6.1%	13.0%	7.9%	0.1%	13.6%
9.9%	+1.9%	11.7%	9.8%	10.9%	20.6%	–1.2%	11.4%	10.4%	18.6%	4.9%	8.2%	10.4%	–1.5%	18.9%
15.7%	+7.7%	New	New	New	32.0%	–4.1%	22.2%	14.3%	New	New	New	New	New	New
10.6%	+2.6%	11.7%	10.8%	New	30.9%	–7.3%	11.6%	7.9%	19.1%	7.8%	13.8%	8.7%	2.5%	17.5%
11.0%	+3.0%	11.0%	New	New	28.6%	–5.7%	12.9%	5.8%	16.3%	6.7%	New	New	New	New
13.1%	+5.1%	12.7%	10.1%	New	25.4%	–1.3%	16.8%	9.4%	14.8%	–6.2%	0.4%	12.4%	4.6%	30.0%
11.1%	+3.1%	12.7%	10.8%	12.5%	26.4%	–5.3%	14.5%	9.8%	20.9%	6.2%	15.2%	9.7%	0.2%	14.3%
12.2%	+4.2%	12.2%	New	New	30.1%	–7.0%	16.8%	7.4%	17.4%	5.8%	17.9%	9.2%	–2.9%	New

Footnotes: The best/worst columns reflect "rolling" twelve month periods from the 1981–1995 period, or for the life of the fund, whichever is shorter (see chapter 18). Portfolio characteristics are subject to rapid change at the fund manager's discretion. By the time you read this, these funds may have characteristics different from those shown. These are not recommended funds per se, but are offered here as worthy of your consideration.

THE CHARACTERISTICS OF A
CATEGORY FOUR HIGH-YIELD BOND PORTFOLIO

☐ High quality bonds with an average weighted portfolio maturity of less than four years. Risk is low.
☐ High quality bonds with an average weighted portfolio maturity of four to ten years. Risk is moderate.
☐ High quality bonds with an average weighted portfolio maturity of greater than ten years. Risk is high.
☒ Lower quality bonds with an average weighted portfolio maturity of four to ten years. Risk is high.

Name of Fund	Stated Investment Objective	Nasdaq Ticker Symbol	Minimum Initial Purchase	Minimum IRA Purchase	Maximum Sales Charge	Number to Call for Information	3 Year Risk Data		
							Sharpe Ratio	Standard Deviation	Versus Index
❶ Federated High Yield	Corp High Yield	FHYTX	$2,500	$2,500	No Load	800-245-5040	1.33	4.9	+0.7
❷ Fidelity Capital & Income	Corp High Yield	FAGIX	$2,500	$500	No Load	800-544-8888	1.32	5.7	+1.5
❸ GIT Maximum Income	Corp High Yield	GITMX	$2,500	$500	No Load	800-336-3063	0.96	4.7	+0.5
❹ Invesco High-Yield	Corp High Yield	FHYPX	$1,000	$250	No Load	800-525-8085	1.04	4.7	+0.6
❺ Nicholas Income	Corp High Yield	NCINX	$500	$500	No Load	414-272-6133	1.46	3.6	−0.6
❻ Northeast Investors	Corp High Yield	NTHEX	$1,000	$500	No Load	800-225-6704	1.68	5.9	+1.7
❼ Price High-Yield	Corp High Yield	PRHYX	$2,500	$1,000	No Load	800-638-5660	0.86	5.8	+1.6
❽ Safeco High-Yield Bond	Corp High Yield	SAFHX	$1,000	$250	No Load	800-426-6730	1.39	4.0	−0.2
❾ Value Line Aggressive Income	Corp High Yield	VAGIX	$1,000	$1,000	No Load	800-223-0818	1.52	4.5	+0.3
❿ Vanguard High-Yield Corp	Corp High Yield	VWEHX	$3,000	$500	No Load	800-662-7447	1.53	4.8	+0.6

Data source: Morningstar Mutual Funds OnDisc. Copyright by Morningstar, Inc., 53 West Jackson Blvd., Chicago, IL 60604. (800) 876–5005. Although gathered from reliable sources, data accuracy and completeness cannot be guaranteed. Performance numbers reflect periods ending 12/31/95 unless otherwise stated. Mutual fund performance and policies are constantly subject to change. Contact the fund for current information before you invest.

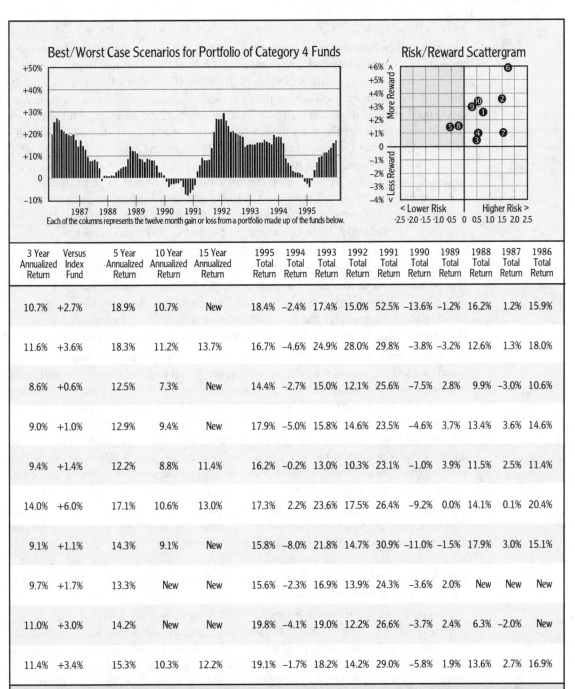

Best/Worst Case Scenarios for Portfolio of Category 4 Funds

Each of the columns represents the twelve month gain or loss from a portfolio made up of the funds below.

Risk/Reward Scattergram

3 Year Annualized Return	Versus Index Fund	5 Year Annualized Return	10 Year Annualized Return	15 Year Annualized Return	1995 Total Return	1994 Total Return	1993 Total Return	1992 Total Return	1991 Total Return	1990 Total Return	1989 Total Return	1988 Total Return	1987 Total Return	1986 Total Return
10.7%	+2.7%	18.9%	10.7%	New	18.4%	–2.4%	17.4%	15.0%	52.5%	–13.6%	–1.2%	16.2%	1.2%	15.9%
11.6%	+3.6%	18.3%	11.2%	13.7%	16.7%	–4.6%	24.9%	28.0%	29.8%	–3.8%	–3.2%	12.6%	1.3%	18.0%
8.6%	+0.6%	12.5%	7.3%	New	14.4%	–2.7%	15.0%	12.1%	25.6%	–7.5%	2.8%	9.9%	–3.0%	10.6%
9.0%	+1.0%	12.9%	9.4%	New	17.9%	–5.0%	15.8%	14.6%	23.5%	–4.6%	3.7%	13.4%	3.6%	14.6%
9.4%	+1.4%	12.2%	8.8%	11.4%	16.2%	–0.2%	13.0%	10.3%	23.1%	–1.0%	3.9%	11.5%	2.5%	11.4%
14.0%	+6.0%	17.1%	10.6%	13.0%	17.3%	2.2%	23.6%	17.5%	26.4%	–9.2%	0.0%	14.1%	0.1%	20.4%
9.1%	+1.1%	14.3%	9.1%	New	15.8%	–8.0%	21.8%	14.7%	30.9%	–11.0%	–1.5%	17.9%	3.0%	15.1%
9.7%	+1.7%	13.3%	New	New	15.6%	–2.3%	16.9%	13.9%	24.3%	–3.6%	2.0%	New	New	New
11.0%	+3.0%	14.2%	New	New	19.8%	–4.1%	19.0%	12.2%	26.6%	–3.7%	2.4%	6.3%	–2.0%	New
11.4%	+3.4%	15.3%	10.3%	12.2%	19.1%	–1.7%	18.2%	14.2%	29.0%	–5.8%	1.9%	13.6%	2.7%	16.9%

Footnotes: The best/worst columns reflect "rolling" twelve month periods from the 1981–1995 period, or for the life of the fund, whichever is shorter (see chapter 18). Portfolio characteristics are subject to rapid change at the fund manager's discretion. By the time you read this, these funds may have characteristics different from those shown. These are not recommended funds per se, but are offered here as worthy of your consideration.

have (zero coupon bond funds are an exception to this—see chapter 22).

2. Bond funds may rob Peter to pay Paul. Typically, bond fund investors are seeking regular income. This leads most bond funds to distribute income to their shareholders on a monthly basis. Because their portfolios are constantly undergoing change, bond funds don't receive the same amount of interest income on their holdings every month. That means that the amount of income they distribute varies slightly from month to month. Or at least it should. But shareholders prefer that the amount of the monthly check they receive be predictable and consistent. Some bond funds have responded to this by paying out a set amount. The problem arises when the set amount turns out to be more than the fund actually earned. Assume the portfolio manage finds it reasonable to believe that the fund's earnings will be approximately $1.20 a share over the coming year. Accordingly, he sets a monthly payout of 10¢ per share.

Now, suppose his estimate is off. Perhaps interest rates have fallen, and the new money coming into the fund can't be invested at the formerly high rate. At this point, the fund manager has two options. One, he can invest the new money at the lower rates. If he does this, the fund's income per share will come in below expectations. Ultimately, the monthly payout will have to be reduced (because the earnings won't be there to support it) and shareholders will be disappointed.

Alternately, he can invest the new money in "premium" bonds. These are bonds which were issued a year or two earlier when interest rates were still high, and because they carry such attractive coupon rates, they sell in the marketplace at a premium over par value (say $1,150 for a $1,000 bond). The trade-off is obvious—in order to have more income now (i.e., maintain the high payout rate), the manager will have to settle for less later (because he is guaranteed to lose $150 in value per bond between now and the maturity date). If he chooses this course, the losses in the premium bonds will gradually eat away at the price per share of the fund and shareholders will be disappointed.

Individual bonds, on the other hand, don't require any special action in order to assure that the interest income received is predictable and consistent. They're that way by design. Most bonds make regular interest payments at six month intervals, and the amount of the payment is always the same. A thirty-year $1,000 bond with an 8% coupon rate will make payments of $40 every six months for the next thirty years.

Buying premium bonds is not a "bad" strategy per se. After all, you have a higher level of income to offset the losses in market value. The significance has more to do with the taxes paid by investors. Buying premium bonds has the effect of adding to current income and taking away from capital gains. As long as income is taxed at higher rates than capital gains, this works to the detriment of the shareholder. This problem is neutralized if the shares are held in a tax-sheltered account like an IRA, 401(k), or 403(b) plan. ◆

20

Understanding Stock Fund Risk

I. **Investors in the stock market can be emotional as well as objective; that's why the markets do not always behave rationally.**

   A. The market is financially driven and therefore subject to many of the pressures of crowd psychology, including investors' false bravado, greed, and hysteria.

   B. Because of its susceptibility to crowd influences, the market and stock prices at times can become overvalued (and undervalued). Long-term investors may need to be cautious about the timing of their initial investments.

II. **When assessing risk, knowing the average size of the companies in which a fund invests as well as the investing "style" used by the manager provides helpful guidance.**

   A. *Large* companies are generally safer to invest in than *small* companies, although they don't have the capital gain potential.

   B. Two of the major styles of investing are *value* and *growth*. The value approach is the more conservative because of its emphasis on getting your money's worth.

III. **By categorizing funds according to their actual portfolio holdings, we can create a helpful guide to risk using the characteristics of *value* versus *growth* and *large* versus *small* companies.**

   A. The funds with the lowest risk/reward characteristics will be those that follow a large company/value strategy.

   B. The highest risk/reward potential is found among funds that employ a small company/growth strategy.

IV. **We take a look at the volatility and historical performance of stock funds in four basic risk categories.**

   A. Stock funds that employ a value strategy to invest in larger companies.

   B. Stock funds that employ a growth strategy to invest in larger companies.

   C. Stock funds that employ a value strategy to invest in smaller companies.

   D. Stock funds that employ a growth strategy to invest in smaller companies.

I hope you won't be disillusioned when I say that you shouldn't expect the markets to always behave rationally.

Because the financial markets constantly speak a language of numbers, we get the impression that investing is like scientific research—when you add up all the proven facts, you can arrive at the "correct" answer. We assume that investing decisions can be made with mathematical certainty.

None of this is the case. Investing is more of an art than a science. There are very few rules, and decision making is almost entirely subjective. The markets are merely collections of people who act according to their emotions and desires of the moment. We've all observed (and probably contributed to) how people act differently when they are part of a crowd than they do when acting alone. Gustave Le Bon wrote his classic study of "crowd psychology" in 1895, but it's always been a part of human nature—from the behavior of Joseph's brothers thousands of years ago to the L.A. riots of 1992. We see people exhibiting false bravado, greed, and hysteria when they are part of a group that they would be quite unlikely to show as individuals acting alone. Peer pressure also plays a major role. In the same way, the herd mentality in the stock market often leads investors to actions they later regret.

Fifty years before Le Bon's work, an Englishman named Charles Mackay became interested in the psychological aspects of crowd behavior with respect to people's investment decisions. After analyzing several early widespread financial manias (such as the Dutch Tulipmania and the South Sea Bubble), he wrote a book that has become a classic: *Extraordinary Popular Delusions and the Madness of Crowds*. When you hear the details of these infamous financial episodes, it's hard to believe that otherwise rational people could get so caught up in a mass delusion. After these bubbles burst, the participants themselves are hard pressed to explain their own behavior. Although published in 1841, the lessons the book teaches are still instructive today. Because of human nature and our susceptibility to crowd influences, it isn't unusual for markets and stock prices to become overvalued (or undervalued) from time to time.

Should this matter to long-term investors? If you're willing to invest in stocks and maintain your commitments over the long haul (ten to fifteen years), does it really make a difference if you pay a little too much at the outset? The answer to that depends on how much is "too much" and what the following decade is like. Consider the fate of investors during the early 1970s who didn't mind paying top dollar for shares in quality companies.

After the crash of the high-flying stocks of the 1960s, money managers made a dramatic turn toward quality. No more speculative stuff . . .

. . . only the best would do. They sought out blue chip companies with proven growth records. Four dozen or so companies soon became regarded

---

The Psychology of Investing

Most people are willing to invest time and expense in gaining a good understanding of market fundamentals (knowledge) and work at assembling that knowledge into a proven strategy (technique). Unfortunately, these are not the only attributes needed for success—if they were, we'd all be millionaires!

The quality that separates the top professionals from the rest of us is one that takes years to develop: emotional self-control. Our emotions interact with news and market events in ways that incline us to act at exactly the wrong time. We all want to "buy low and sell high," but experience shows that most investors do the opposite. That is likely because, emotionally, it's quite difficult to "buy low." The reason that prices are low is that the news is bad and people are pessimistic. They become fearful about the future and have no interest in taking on new risks. Investors feel pressured, and under pressure, emotions tend to dictate our actions. As our fears increase, so do our anxieties, and we can become paralyzed. We know what we should do, but we "tighten up." Athletes call it "choking." A short putt to a golfer or free throw to a basketball player is no big deal in a friendly pick-up game. But with huge television audiences looking on and millions of dollars at stake, it's a far different story. Why? Emotions.

The graph on the next page shows the movement of stock market prices in the years leading up to and following the "crash" of 1987. I've labeled various points along the way that characterized as the premier growth stocks of the day. The list included familiar names such as IBM, Xerox, Kodak, Disney, Polaroid, and Avon to name a few. They became known as the "Nifty Fifty" and were thought to be stocks that could be bought and—due to their stature, profitability, and future prospects—held virtually for a lifetime if investors so wished. And since you had such a long-term view, what did it matter if the price you paid per share was on the expensive side? *Forbes* magazine said, "The delusion was that these companies were so good that it didn't matter what you paid for them; their inexorable growth would bail you out."

investors' attitudes as events unfolded. They each reflect a different aspect of two very powerful emotions: fear and greed. Your investing temperament has a lot to do with how you react under the pressure of making investment decisions.

It seemed everyone wanted to own these same high-quality stocks. The prices kept going higher and higher, but the buyers kept coming. In fact, the more the prices pushed higher, the more they seemed to validate the excellence of the Nifty Fifty. By late 1972, these stocks were selling for prices that could not be justified by the earnings and future prospects of the companies. Eventually, of course, the mania for the Nifty Fifty ended. It ended as all bubbles do—when demand was finally exhausted. This occurred when the last buyer who just "had" to own the Nifty Fifty satisfied his desire. After that, the only investors left were those who, although they might admire the quality of the Nifty Fifty companies, were unwilling to pay exorbitant prices.

EMOTIONS AND THE MARKETS
S&P 500 AT MONTH-END 1983-1988

If you'd like to know more about the psychological side of investing, you might enjoy a book by market veteran Justin Mamis called The Nature of Risk (published by Addison Wesley, 1991). It offers interesting insights into why we behave as we do in making investing decisions. For example, he explains why our desire to "be sure" before we invest actually *increases* our risk. This is not casual reading, so be prepared for your thinking to be stimulated and challenged.

**At that point, prices can only go in one direction: down.
Let me use the story of the Mazda Miata to illustrate . . .**

. . . why it must be this way. In 1990, Mazda's new two-seater sports convertible hit the market and received rave reviews. Dealers found that because interest in this new car was so intense and supplies were still limited, they could charge more than the $16,000 sticker price and still sell all they could get their hands on. There were reports of consumers paying a dealer $18,000 and immediately selling the car to another eager buyer for a quick profit. As Miata-mania grew, the cars were changing hands for as much as $30,000 and more. The buyers were people who just "had" to have one—even if it meant paying absolutely top dollar.

As you might expect, there is only a limited number of such carefree spenders (even among fad-conscious, buy-now-and-pay-later baby boomers). When the last determined buyer finally acquired his Miata, the upward pressure on prices disappeared. So, when the next Miata owner decided to sell—because

the novelty of cramped, noisy, and rough-riding transportation had worn off —
there was no one left who would pay $30,000. There were still people who would
like to own one, but not for $30,000! To attract a buyer, sellers needed to drop
the asking price until someone was enticed off the sidelines. The balance of
power then shifted from the sellers to the buyers. Once this happened, it was
only a matter of time before the price returned to its former fair value range.
Two years later, you could buy a 1990 Miata for $12,000-$13,000.

With similar forces at work on the Nifty Fifty, prices began to plunge in the beginning of 1973.

When the dust settled eighteen months later, the Standard & Poor's 500
Stock Index had fallen 45% in price. Many of the Nifty Fifty did much worse
(for example, Avon and Polaroid fell an amazing 87% and 91% respectively).
Many highly respected stock mutual funds also fell dramatically from their 1972
highs. Imagine Magellan dropping 59%, Mathers 56%, Nicholas 69%, Price New
Horizons 64%, 20th Century Growth 46%, and Explorer Fund 52%! Eventually
the funds would rise back to their former heights, but many investors couldn't
endure the uncertainty of a long wait and sold at a loss. For those who stuck it
out, twelve long years went by before they caught up with those cautious souls
who had resisted the lure of the Nifty Fifty in the first place and remained in
Treasury bills the entire time. Obviously, even for long-term investors there's a
limit to what is a reasonable price to pay for stock shares.

Did investors understand the risks they were taking? In chapter 9, I
pointed out why the standard definitions used to place mutual funds into risk
groupings leave a lot to be desired. That's why, when writing this book for a
lay audience, I felt it was necessary to try to develop a system that would
both simplify matters and also offer better insights into the risks that fund
managers were taking with their shareholders' money.

In this chapter, stock mutual funds are assigned to one of four risk categories based on two portfolio characteristics: (1) whether the fund invests primarily in larger, stronger companies versus investing in smaller, newer ones, and
(2) whether the portfolio manager tends to use a growth or value strategy when
selecting companies for the portfolio. These characteristics must be defined in
numerical terms in order to make the assignments, and this is where a degree
of subjectivity enters in. Just how big must a company become before it moves
from the small to the large category? And how do you decide if the portfolio is
more growth- or value-oriented? Let me take each of these questions in turn.

There's a tendency to view the stock market as moving in lockstep, but behind the scenes . . .

. . . there are performance differences among various groups. The rally in the stock market in 1995 was led by strength in the shares of large companies. What is a "large" company? Is size measured by the number of employees? The most sales? Or profits? Or perhaps the largest amount of assets? All of these are meaningful indications, but the measure most commonly used by investing professionals is "market capitalization" (or "market cap" for short). This merely refers to the current market value of all a company's outstanding stock. In other words, how valuable is the company? If you could buy every one of its shares at today's closing price, how much would it cost you? By this criteria, America's largest company is General Electric, which had a recent market capitalization of more than $100 billion.

Larger companies, like those in the Dow Jones Industrial Average and the S&P 500 index, are usually stronger in terms of market penetration and financial muscle. Their earnings might be temporarily affected by competitive pressures, technological developments, or a recession, but they are expected to survive and prosper. They have limited potential to grow quickly in size, however; their glory "growth" days are largely behind them.

Smaller companies (sometimes called "small caps") carry higher risk because they are more easily devastated by economic setbacks. On the other hand, they have the potential to grow to ten, twenty, or fifty times their present size. The time to "get in on the ground floor" is when they're still small. A study of the historical performance data reveals that the average returns from small companies exceed those of large companies over most time periods measured, with their best-case scenarios dramatically superior. Of course, the worst-case loss scenarios from investing in smaller companies is greater, especially for one-year holding periods. For holding periods of ten years and more, two-thirds of the time the range of results clearly favors smaller companies over large ones.

One group is not "better" than another. They offer different strengths which are suitable for different investing needs. Large companies typically offer higher dividends and greater price stability; smaller companies offer higher long-term growth potential. Many factors influence whether large companies or smaller companies are popular with investors at a given time.

◆ **Interest rates.** In order to grow, small companies need (1) money and (2) a healthy economy. Larger companies are financially stronger. Smaller companies are more easily devastated by high interest rates or a recession; they need a healthy economy and affordable interest rates to prosper.

◆ **The strength of the U.S. dollar.** In 1994-1995, a weak dollar helped the large multinational companies that have business abroad (often 20%–40% of total sales). A rebounding dollar cuts the other way. Lower profits for large companies make small companies look relatively more attractive. According to an analyst quoted in *The Wall Street Journal*, there have been three periods over the

HISTORICAL RETURNS FROM MUTUAL FUNDS INVESTING IN LARGE COMPANIES VERSUS SMALL COMPANIES

SOURCE: MORNINGSTAR ONDISC

Year	Large	Small
1995	31.7%	27.2%
1994	−1.3%	−1.0%
1993	10.8%	17.0%
1992	7.3%	14.2%
1991	33.6%	46.0%
1990	−4.1%	−11.4%
1989	25.8%	22.4%
1988	13.9%	20.0%
1987	2.9%	−4.1%
1986	16.2%	9.4%
5 Year Annualized	15.5%	19.0%
10 Year Annualized	12.8%	12.2%

past decade when the dollar rallied 10% or more. Each time, the Russell 2000, a small company index, significantly outperformed the S&P 500.

◆ **A potential cut in the capital gains tax.** If a capital gains cut passes, investors who have been reluctant to cash in their profits (because they did not want to pay the tax) would have a new freedom to sell. The amount of so-called "captive" assets has been estimated to be as high as $6 trillion! A large portion of this selling would be in appreciated stock of larger companies—an obvious negative for that group. But according to a Merrill Lynch study reported in the *National Review*, small cap stocks would benefit. "During 1968-88, small and medium-sized firms outperformed large companies in the year following a capital-gains tax cut. . . . Smaller capitalization stocks have greater sensitivity to tax changes because they tend to be capital-gains rather than income oriented."

Let's begin building our risk profile for stock funds. As before, we'll divide a large diamond into four smaller diamond-shaped compartments. The idea is to place all stock funds into one of the four compartments using criteria that we feel have the greatest bearing on risk. In this way, we can get a quick insight into the general riskiness of a fund just by seeing in which of the four compartments it is placed. In step one, we'll take the size of the companies in the portfolio into consideration.

There is no "official" size criterion for categorizing a company as being large. Determining exactly where the dividing line should be drawn between the small and large category is somewhat arbitrary. Many market professionals put it at $1 billion. That's a little low for my purposes. In my risk system, if a company's market value is under $2 billion, I treat it as a small company. Accordingly, "large company" mutual funds in SMI are those that invest in companies that have market values, *on average*, that are greater than $2 billion. Those funds are placed in categories one and two. "Small company" mutual funds are those that invest in companies with market values, *on average*, of less than $2 billion. They go in the higher risk categories three and four (see graphic at far right).

For the most part, investing strategies (or "styles") used by portfolio managers of stock funds can be grouped into two major camps—value investing and growth investing.

The "value" camp emphasizes how much you're getting for your investment dollar. This kind of manager primarily considers the present state of a company's assets, earnings, and dividends in arriving at an assessment of its stock's intrinsic value. They prefer to bargain-hunt, and often end up buying unglamorous, unappreciated companies (because that's where the bargains are). Value managers are serious about getting their money's worth. If a bear market comes along, they shouldn't get hurt too badly

HISTORICAL RETURNS FROM MUTUAL FUNDS INVESTING WITH A VALUE STRATEGY VERSUS A GROWTH STRATEGY

SOURCE: MORNINGSTAR ONDISC

Year	Value	Growth
1995	28.3%	35.0%
1994	−1.1%	−1.6%
1993	15.4%	12.8%
1992	12.9%	7.5%
1991	31.1%	51.3%
1990	−8.5%	−4.9%
1989	21.8%	30.3%
1988	18.1%	14.7%
1987	−0.1%	1.9%
1986	15.1%	13.9%
5 Year Annualized	16.5%	19.1%
10 Year Annualized	12.3%	14.5%

because many of the stocks they buy have already been beaten down in price (which is when *they* bought them) and hopefully won't fall much further. The drawback is that the reason a stock is bargain priced in the first place is that it either has operating problems or is simply out of favor with investors. It often takes *years* for such stock purchases to bear fruit. This approach is the more conservative, but requires great p-a-t-i-e-n-c-e.

The other style of stock investing is the *growth* camp. The managers with this strategy act on future expectations. They would say, "Look at all the great things the company has going for it! It has a tremendous future ahead." A great deal of their success hinges on the ability to accurately predict corporate earnings a few years into the future. When measured in terms of the company's current earnings and dividends, the stock may appear expensive at present, but if the company can achieve its potential, today's share price will look like a bargain a few years from now. When they're right in their projections and they've got a good economy to work with, they can hit home runs. These are the funds that can gain 50% to 100% in a single good year. But this approach carries more risk because growth stocks typically *are already priced* on the assumption that all the future good news will come to pass. As we saw in our look at the Nifty Fifty, if there are disappointments along the way, the share prices of growth stocks have a lot of room to fall.

BUILDING A RISK PROFILE FOR STOCK FUNDS: STEP #1

Separate funds according to the average size of the companies in which they invest

Small Companies ❹
Small Companies ❸
Large Companies ❷
Large Companies ❶

How are you to know which style of investing a particular fund is following?

Morningstar Mutual Funds suggests using a fund's price/ earnings and price/book ratios (which you can obtain from the fund with a phone call) as a guide. Value stocks are typically priced at below normal levels based on earnings, dividends, and book values while growth stocks are priced at higher-than-average levels.

Since valuation is relative, the fund's ratios should be compared to benchmark ratios like those of the S&P 500 in order to be more meaningful. Morningstar uses these ratios to assign every fund to one of three different style categories: value, growth, and a combination of the two. I've adapted this concept to our risk profile approach by eliminating the "combination" category.

BUILDING A RISK PROFILE FOR STOCK FUNDS: STEP #2

Separate funds according to whether they use a value- or growth-oriented philosophy of investing

Growth Strategy ❹
Value Strategy ❸
Growth Strategy ❷
Value Strategy ❶

BUILDING A RISK PROFILE FOR STOCK FUNDS: STEP #3

Combine criteria to create four distinct risk categories based on the size of companies in the portfolio and the investing style

Small Co. Growth Strategy ❹
Small Co. Value Strategy ❸
Large Co. Growth Strategy ❷
Large Co. Value Strategy ❶

Popular benchmarks useful for deciding if a stock is reasonably priced

The price-to-earning ratio (P/E) is calculated by dividing the price of a stock by its reported earnings for the past four quarters. If your favorite stock, Can't Miss, Inc., is selling for $32 a share and has reported earnings for the past twelve months of $2 per share, it is said to have a P/E of 16 ($32/ $2). Historically, a P/E ratio between 10 and 20 has been considered "normal." The problem with using earnings as a guide to stock valuation is that they are very susceptible to manipulation by the company. Accounting principles and IRS rules offer a variety of ways to deal with depreciation, research and development expenses, marketing expenses, inventory costs, and so on. Other problems with using earnings is that optimistic investors often tend to justify higher stock prices by using projected future earnings rather than current earnings when computing the P/E.

The price-to-book ratio (P/B) relies on the size of a company's assets (rather than its earning power) to determine what would be a fair price to pay for its shares. The book value is theoretically what you get if you were to sell all the company's assets, pay off all its liabilities, and pay what's left to the shareholders. If Can't Miss, Inc., has a book value of $10 per share, its P/B is 3.2 ($32/$10). This ratio suffers from the same failing as the P/E: it's highly subject to variation depending upon the accounting practices of the company. The actual value of the company assets might be much higher than reported (e.g., if land owned in downtown Dallas

(continued on next page)

This makes the guidelines somewhat less precise but gains in simplicity and ease of use. Here is how it works. (If you don't care for number crunching, you can skip the next two paragraphs.)

First, I look up the price/earnings ratio of the S&P 500 index (in *Barron's* Market Week section), which will serve as my definition of "normal." For example, at the end of 1995 it was 17.5. Next, using the Morningstar OnDisc database, I look up the average P/E ratio of the stocks being held in the XYZ fund's portfolio. Let's say it's 26.8. I then compare these two numbers by dividing the fund's average P/E by that of the S&P 500. The result is 1.53. This means that the XYZ fund's P/E ratio is 53% higher than the norm.

I repeat the process for the price/book ratio. Let's assume I come up with a reading of 1.13 for that, meaning that the XYZ fund's P/B ratio is 13% higher than the norm. Finally, I add the two together to get what I call the "value index," in this case 2.65. If a fund's value index equals 2.00, that means the fund has the same valuation characteristics as the market as a whole (that is, as the S&P 500, which is generally used as a proxy for the overall market by investing analysts). If the value index is above 2.00, I regard that fund's portfolio as more growth-oriented because it includes stocks with above-average prices in relation to earnings and book value. Funds with a value index below 2.00 indicate the opposite, and are regarded as more value-oriented.

Historically, both value and growth philosophies have made money, but no investment style results in top performance year after year. As we go through the recurring growth-recession cycle, economic events favor different styles at different times. Leading value funds like Windsor Fund, Mutual Shares, and Lindner Fund were all top performers in the mid-1980s only to fall to the bottom 25% of stock funds at the end of the decade. So, the point is not necessarily to try to pick one style over the other—both will have their "day in the sun" at various times. In fact, structuring your portfolio so as to include stock funds using each philosophy is a sensible diversification move.

When we put it all together, we have four distinct types of fund portfolios from which we can choose . . .

. . . with some degree of confidence that we understand the investment strategy and risk of loss associated with each (see sidebar on previous page). The risk is lowest at the bottom of the profile (funds that invest in large companies and use a value strategy) and greatest at the top (funds that invest in small companies and use a growth strategy). One last point. Bear in mind that when using this technique, we assign each fund to one of the four groups based on its actual portfolio holdings using the most current information available. Mutual fund portfolios change on a daily basis, so it's possible for a fund to move to a different risk category periodically as its portfolio holdings change.

The risk ladder below shows the historical risks and rewards from investing in mutual funds assigned to each category. The numbers reflect the average of all the funds in each group; individual funds will vary. That's the trick, of course—picking the funds *in advance* that will be above average in their respective risk categories. It's a very tough thing to do well on a consistent basis. We'll discuss this further in chapter 24.

"Never pack anything of such great value that its loss would devastate you."

These words of advice are given by a writer of travel books in the opening scene of the movie *The Accidental Tourist*. He's telling his readers what to take, and not take, in suitcases that often disappear into cargo areas of airports, never to be seen again.

Given what we all know about the rude treatment frequently given luggage by airlines, that just seems like common sense, doesn't it? Who would pack valuable, possibly irreplaceable, jewelry in a suitcase and then hope for the best? Yet, we frequently hear of otherwise sensible people who have lost their life savings by investing it all in one place with the wrong person, or at the wrong time, because they were trying to make just a little bit more.

Starting on the next page, I have provided a sampling of stock funds from each of the four categories on our risk ladder. They are arranged in the same fashion as those that covered the bond fund categories in (continued on page 254)

is carried on the books at the low price paid for the land 30 years ago), or much lower than reported (e.g., deferred expenses for research are carried on the books of the company as having value when in fact the research proved fruitless).

Only the price-to-dividend ratio (P/D) reflects the actual reality experienced by shareholders. The reported earning per share or book value per share may be subject to manipulation by the company, but there is no doubt surrounding the amount of dividends it is paying out. Either you received dividends in a certain amount, or you didn't. If you received $1.60 per share from Can't Miss over the past twelve months, then the P/D ratio is 20 ($32/$1.60). Historically, the P/D ratio for the Standard & Poor's index has tended to range between 22 and 34.

RISK LADDER FOR STOCK FUNDS

SOURCE: MORNINGSTAR ONDISC

Risk Category	Standard Deviation	5 Year Annualized	1995 Return	1994 Return	1993 Return	1992 Return	1991 Return	1990 Return	1989 Return	1988 Return	1987 Return	1986 Return
Invest By Owning: Stock Risk Category 4 Stock funds that invest in smaller companies and employ a growth-oriented strategy	16.7	22.1%	35.4%	even	16.7%	9.6%	59.1%	–9.5%	29.3%	19.3%	–3.5%	10.3%
Invest By Owning: Stock Risk Category 3 Stock funds that invest in smaller companies and employ a value-oriented strategy	11.1	17.7%	22.5%	–0.4%	17.4%	18.4%	36.5%	–14.1%	17.9%	22.0%	–4.4%	10.2%
Invest By Owning: Stock Risk Category 2 Stock funds that invest in large companies and employ a growth-oriented strategy	12.6	16.0%	33.0%	–1.7%	7.2%	4.5%	45.7%	–1.4%	30.3%	11.8%	5.2%	14.8%
Invest By Owning: Stock Risk Category 1 Stock funds that invest in large companies and employ a value-oriented strategy	10.3	15.9%	31.4%	–1.6%	14.4%	9.4%	29.9%	–6.8%	23.8%	15.7%	0.5%	17.3%

THE CHARACTERISTICS OF
A LARGE COMPANY / VALUE STRATEGY

☒ Invests primarily in established companies that are leaders in their industries. This lowers risk.
☒ Commitment to buying at bargain prices caused by temporary market factors. This lowers risk.
☐ Invests primarily in up-and-coming companies with superior growth potential. This raises risk.
☐ Willingness to pay more for companies with above-average growth potential. This raises risk.

Name of Fund	Stated Investment Objective	Nasdaq Ticker Symbol	Minimum Initial Purchase	Minimum IRA Purchase	Maximum Sales Charge	Number to Call for Information	3 Year Risk Data		
							Sharpe Ratio	Standard Deviation	Versus Index
❶ Babson Value Fund	Growth+Income	BVALX	$1,000	$250	No Load	800-422-2766	1.83	7.8	−0.4
❷ Crabbe Huson Equity	Growth	CHEYX	$2,000	$2,000	No Load	800-541-9732	1.56	8.5	+0.3
❸ Dodge & Cox Stock	Growth+Income	DODGX	$2,500	$1,000	No Load	800-621-3979	1.63	8.8	+0.6
❹ Fidelity Equity-Income II	Equity+Income	FEQTX	$2,500	$500	No Load	800-544-8888	1.46	8.0	−0.2
❺ Fidelity Value	Growth	FDVLX	$2,500	$500	No Load	800-544-8888	1.84	8.0	−0.2
❻ Homestead Value	Growth+Income	HOVLX	$1,000	$1,000	No Load	800-258-3030	1.72	7.9	−0.3
❼ Mutual Shares	Growth+Income	MUTHX	$5,000	$2,000	No Load	800-553-3014	1.73	7.9	−0.4
❽ Oakmark Fund	Growth	OAKMX	$2,500	$1,000	No Load	800-625-6275	1.99	9.0	+0.7
❾ Safeco Equity	Growth+Income	SAFQX	$1,000	$250	No Load	800-426-6730	1.85	9.5	+1.3
❿ Schafer Value Fund	Growth	SCHVX	$2,000	$2,000	No Load	800-343-0481	1.38	9.1	+0.9

Data source: Morningstar Mutual Funds OnDisc. Copyright by Morningstar, Inc., 53 West Jackson Blvd., Chicago, IL 60604. (800) 876–5005. Although gathered from reliable sources, data accuracy and completeness cannot be guaranteed. Performance numbers reflect periods ending 12/31/95 unless otherwise stated. Mutual fund performance and policies are constantly subject to change. Contact the fund for current information before you invest.

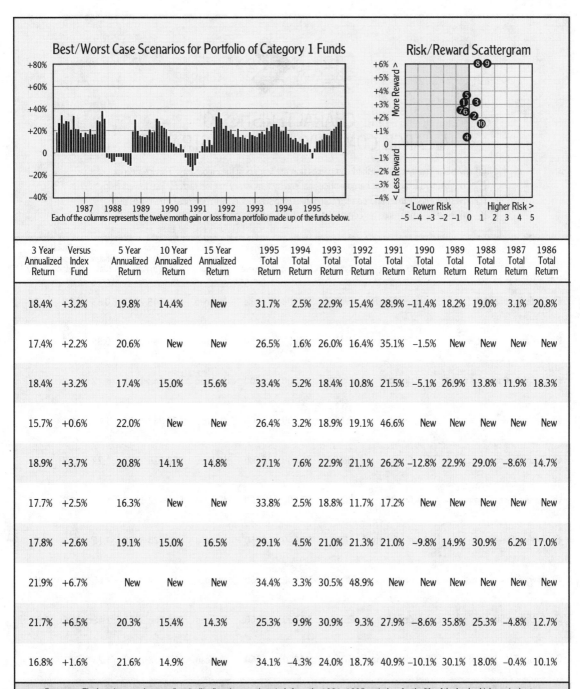

Best/Worst Case Scenarios for Portfolio of Category 1 Funds

Each of the columns represents the twelve month gain or loss from a portfolio made up of the funds below.

Risk/Reward Scattergram

3 Year Annualized Return	Versus Index Fund	5 Year Annualized Return	10 Year Annualized Return	15 Year Annualized Return	1995 Total Return	1994 Total Return	1993 Total Return	1992 Total Return	1991 Total Return	1990 Total Return	1989 Total Return	1988 Total Return	1987 Total Return	1986 Total Return
18.4%	+3.2%	19.8%	14.4%	New	31.7%	2.5%	22.9%	15.4%	28.9%	–11.4%	18.2%	19.0%	3.1%	20.8%
17.4%	+2.2%	20.6%	New	New	26.5%	1.6%	26.0%	16.4%	35.1%	–1.5%	New	New	New	New
18.4%	+3.2%	17.4%	15.0%	15.6%	33.4%	5.2%	18.4%	10.8%	21.5%	–5.1%	26.9%	13.8%	11.9%	18.3%
15.7%	+0.6%	22.0%	New	New	26.4%	3.2%	18.9%	19.1%	46.6%	New	New	New	New	New
18.9%	+3.7%	20.8%	14.1%	14.8%	27.1%	7.6%	22.9%	21.1%	26.2%	–12.8%	22.9%	29.0%	–8.6%	14.7%
17.7%	+2.5%	16.3%	New	New	33.8%	2.5%	18.8%	11.7%	17.2%	New	New	New	New	New
17.8%	+2.6%	19.1%	15.0%	16.5%	29.1%	4.5%	21.0%	21.3%	21.0%	–9.8%	14.9%	30.9%	6.2%	17.0%
21.9%	+6.7%	New	New	New	34.4%	3.3%	30.5%	48.9%	New	New	New	New	New	New
21.7%	+6.5%	20.3%	15.4%	14.3%	25.3%	9.9%	30.9%	9.3%	27.9%	–8.6%	35.8%	25.3%	–4.8%	12.7%
16.8%	+1.6%	21.6%	14.9%	New	34.1%	–4.3%	24.0%	18.7%	40.9%	–10.1%	30.1%	18.0%	–0.4%	10.1%

Footnotes: The best/worst columns reflect "rolling" twelve month periods from the 1981–1995 period, or for the life of the fund, whichever is shorter (see chapter 18). Portfolio characteristics are subject to rapid change at the fund manager's discretion. By the time you read this, these funds may have characteristics different from those shown. These are not recommended funds per se, but are offered here as worthy of your consideration.

THE CHARACTERISTICS OF
A LARGE COMPANY / GROWTH STRATEGY

☒ Invests primarily in established companies that are leaders in their industries. This lowers risk.
☐ Commitment to buying at bargain prices caused by temporary market factors. This lowers risk.
☐ Invests primarily in up-and-coming companies with superior growth potential. This raises risk.
☒ Willingness to pay more for companies with above-average growth potential. This raises risk.

Name of Fund	Stated Investment Objective	Nasdaq Ticker Symbol	Minimum Initial Purchase	Minimum IRA Purchase	Maximum Sales Charge	Number to Call for Information	3 Year Risk Data		
							Sharpe Ratio	Standard Deviation	Versus Index
❶ 20th Century Ultra	AggressGrowth	TWCUX	$2,500	None	No Load	800-345-2021	0.83	16.0	+7.8
❷ Berger 100	Growth	BEONX	$250	$250	No Load	800-333-1001	0.55	12.7	+4.4
❸ Cappiello-Rushmore Growth	Growth	CRGRX	$2,500	$500	No Load	800-343-3355	1.22	11.3	+3.1
❹ Columbia Growth	Growth	CLMBX	$1,000	$1,000	No Load	800-547-1707	1.01	10.1	+1.8
❺ Founders Growth	Growth	FRGRX	$1,000	$500	No Load	800-525-2440	1.22	13.8	+5.5
❻ Harbor Capital Appreciation	Growth	HACAX	$2,000	$500	No Load	800-422-1050	1.02	12.5	+4.3
❼ Invesco Dynamics	AggressGrowth	FIDYX	$1,000	$250	No Load	800-525-8085	1.15	11.3	+3.1
❽ Mairs & Power Growth	Growth	MPGFX	$1,000	$1,000	No Load	612-222-8478	1.65	10.1	+1.9
❾ Robertson Stephens Value+Grth	Growth	RSVPX	$5,000	$1,000	No Load	800-766-3863	1.48	16.6	+8.4
❿ Strong Total Return	Growth+Income	STRFX	$250	$250	No Load	800-368-1030	1.23	9.1	+0.9

Data source: Morningstar Mutual Funds OnDisc. Copyright by Morningstar, Inc., 53 West Jackson Blvd., Chicago, IL 60604. (800) 876–5005. Although gathered from reliable sources, data accuracy and completeness cannot be guaranteed. Performance numbers reflect periods ending 12/31/95 unless otherwise stated. Mutual fund performance and policies are constantly subject to change. Contact the fund for current information before you invest.

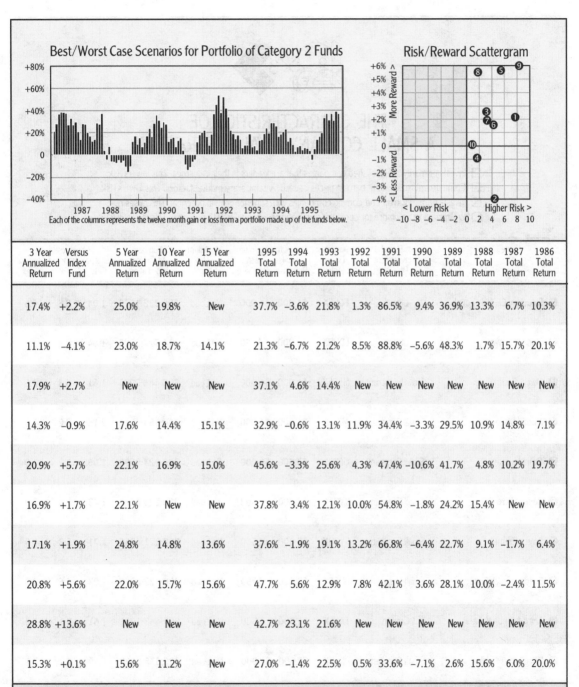

Best/Worst Case Scenarios for Portfolio of Category 2 Funds

Each of the columns represents the twelve month gain or loss from a portfolio made up of the funds below.

Risk/Reward Scattergram

3 Year Annualized Return	Versus Index Fund	5 Year Annualized Return	10 Year Annualized Return	15 Year Annualized Return	1995 Total Return	1994 Total Return	1993 Total Return	1992 Total Return	1991 Total Return	1990 Total Return	1989 Total Return	1988 Total Return	1987 Total Return	1986 Total Return
17.4%	+2.2%	25.0%	19.8%	New	37.7%	−3.6%	21.8%	1.3%	86.5%	9.4%	36.9%	13.3%	6.7%	10.3%
11.1%	−4.1%	23.0%	18.7%	14.1%	21.3%	−6.7%	21.2%	8.5%	88.8%	−5.6%	48.3%	1.7%	15.7%	20.1%
17.9%	+2.7%	New	New	New	37.1%	4.6%	14.4%	New	New	New	New	New	New	New
14.3%	−0.9%	17.6%	14.4%	15.1%	32.9%	−0.6%	13.1%	11.9%	34.4%	−3.3%	29.5%	10.9%	14.8%	7.1%
20.9%	+5.7%	22.1%	16.9%	15.0%	45.6%	−3.3%	25.6%	4.3%	47.4%	−10.6%	41.7%	4.8%	10.2%	19.7%
16.9%	+1.7%	22.1%	New	New	37.8%	3.4%	12.1%	10.0%	54.8%	−1.8%	24.2%	15.4%	New	New
17.1%	+1.9%	24.8%	14.8%	13.6%	37.6%	−1.9%	19.1%	13.2%	66.8%	−6.4%	22.7%	9.1%	−1.7%	6.4%
20.8%	+5.6%	22.0%	15.7%	15.6%	47.7%	5.6%	12.9%	7.8%	42.1%	3.6%	28.1%	10.0%	−2.4%	11.5%
28.8%	+13.6%	New	New	New	42.7%	23.1%	21.6%	New	New	New	New	New	New	New
15.3%	+0.1%	15.6%	11.2%	New	27.0%	−1.4%	22.5%	0.5%	33.6%	−7.1%	2.6%	15.6%	6.0%	20.0%

Footnotes: The best/worst columns reflect "rolling" twelve month periods from the 1981–1995 period, or for the life of the fund, whichever is shorter (see chapter 18). Portfolio characteristics are subject to rapid change at the fund manager's discretion. By the time you read this, these funds may have characteristics different from those shown. These are not recommended funds per se, but are offered here as worthy of your consideration.

THE CHARACTERISTICS OF
A SMALL COMPANY / VALUE STRATEGY

☐ Invests primarily in established companies that are leaders in their industries. This lowers risk.
☒ Commitment to buying at bargain prices caused by temporary market factors. This lowers risk.
☒ Invests primarily in up-and-coming companies with superior growth potential. This raises risk.
☐ Willingness to pay more for companies with above-average growth potential. This raises risk.

Name of Fund	Stated Investment Objective	Nasdaq Ticker Symbol	Minimum Initial Purchase	Minimum IRA Purchase	Maximum Sales Charge	Number to Call for Information	3 Year Risk Data		
							Sharpe Ratio	Standard Deviation	Versus Index
❶ Fiduciary Capital Growth	Growth	FCGFX	$1,000	$1,000	No Load	800-338-1579	1.04	8.8	−0.5
❷ Lindner Growth	Growth	LDNRX	$2,000	$250	No Load	314-727-5305	1.04	8.2	−1.1
❸ Maxus Equity	Growth+Income	MXSEX	$1,000	$1,000	No Load	800-446-2987	1.61	6.8	−2.5
❹ Mutual Discovery	Small Company	MDISX	$1,000	$1,000	No Load	800-553-3014	2.16	8.2	−1.1
❺ .Omni Investment	Small Company	OMNIX	$3,000	$1,000	No Load	800-223-9790	1.06	11.2	+1.9
❻ Royce Micro-Cap	Small Company	RYOTX	$2,000	$500	No Load	800-221-4268	1.49	7.3	−2.0
❼ Royce Premier	Small Company	RYPRX	$2,000	$500	No Load	800-221-4268	1.71	5.3	−4.0
❽ Shadow Stock Fund	Small Company	SHSTX	$2,500	$250	No Load	800-422-2766	1.03	6.6	−2.7
❾ Third Avenue Value	Growth	TAVFX	$1,000	$500	No Load	800-443-1021	1.61	8.1	−1.2
❿ Price Small-Cap Value	Small Company	PRSVX	$2,500	$1,000	No Load	800-638-5660	1.69	7.2	−2.1

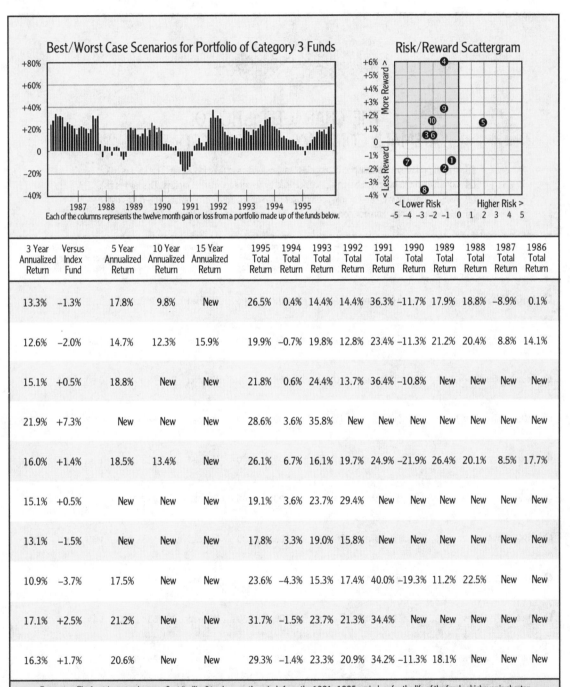

Best/Worst Case Scenarios for Portfolio of Category 3 Funds

Each of the columns represents the twelve month gain or loss from a portfolio made up of the funds below.

Risk/Reward Scattergram

3 Year Annualized Return	Versus Index Fund	5 Year Annualized Return	10 Year Annualized Return	15 Year Annualized Return	1995 Total Return	1994 Total Return	1993 Total Return	1992 Total Return	1991 Total Return	1990 Total Return	1989 Total Return	1988 Total Return	1987 Total Return	1986 Total Return
13.3%	−1.3%	17.8%	9.8%	New	26.5%	0.4%	14.4%	14.4%	36.3%	−11.7%	17.9%	18.8%	−8.9%	0.1%
12.6%	−2.0%	14.7%	12.3%	15.9%	19.9%	−0.7%	19.8%	12.8%	23.4%	−11.3%	21.2%	20.4%	8.8%	14.1%
15.1%	+0.5%	18.8%	New	New	21.8%	0.6%	24.4%	13.7%	36.4%	−10.8%	New	New	New	New
21.9%	+7.3%	New	New	New	28.6%	3.6%	35.8%	New	New	New	New	New	New	New
16.0%	+1.4%	18.5%	13.4%	New	26.1%	6.7%	16.1%	19.7%	24.9%	−21.9%	26.4%	20.1%	8.5%	17.7%
15.1%	+0.5%	New	New	New	19.1%	3.6%	23.7%	29.4%	New	New	New	New	New	New
13.1%	−1.5%	New	New	New	17.8%	3.3%	19.0%	15.8%	New	New	New	New	New	New
10.9%	−3.7%	17.5%	New	New	23.6%	−4.3%	15.3%	17.4%	40.0%	−19.3%	11.2%	22.5%	New	New
17.1%	+2.5%	21.2%	New	New	31.7%	−1.5%	23.7%	21.3%	34.4%	New	New	New	New	New
16.3%	+1.7%	20.6%	New	New	29.3%	−1.4%	23.3%	20.9%	34.2%	−11.3%	18.1%	New	New	New

Footnotes: The best/worst columns reflect "rolling" twelve month periods from the 1981–1995 period, or for the life of the fund, whichever is shorter (see chapter 18). Portfolio characteristics are subject to rapid change at the fund manager's discretion. By the time you read this, these funds may have characteristics different from those shown. These are not recommended funds per se, but are offered here as worthy of your consideration.

THE CHARACTERISTICS OF
A SMALL COMPANY / GROWTH STRATEGY

☐ Invests primarily in established companies that are leaders in their industries. This lowers risk.
☐ Commitment to buying at bargain prices caused by temporary market factors. This lowers risk.
☒ Invests primarily in up-and-coming companies with superior growth potential. This raises risk.
☒ Willingness to pay more for companies with above-average growth potential. This raises risk.

Name of Fund	Stated Investment Objective	Nasdaq Ticker Symbol	Minimum Initial Purchase	Minimum IRA Purchase	Maximum Sales Charge	Number to Call for Information	3 Year Risk Data		
							Sharpe Ratio	Standard Deviation	Versus Index
❶ Baron Asset	Small Company	BARAX	$2,000	$2,000	No Load	800-992-2766	1.58	11.0	+1.7
❷ Columbia Special	Small Company	CLSPX	$2,000	$2,000	No Load	800-547-1707	1.24	10.5	+1.2
❸ Founders Frontier	Small Company	FOUNX	$1,000	$500	No Load	800-525-2440	0.90	13.0	+3.7
❹ IAI Emerging Growth	Small Company	IAEGX	$5,000	$2,000	No Load	800-945-3863	0.92	17.0	+7.7
❺ Janus Enterprise	Growth	JAENX	$1,000	$250	No Load	800-525-8983	1.12	11.5	+2.2
❻ Kaufmann	AggressGrowth	KAUFX	$1,500	$500	No Load	800-237-0132	1.19	14.0	+4.7
❼ PBHG Growth	Small Company	PBHGX	$2,500	$2,000	No Load	800-433-0051	1.49	18.9	+9.6
❽ SteinRoe Cap Oppor	AggressGrowth	SRFCX	$2,500	$500	No Load	800-338-2550	1.49	13.6	+4.3
❾ Price New Horizons	Small Company	PRNHX	$2,500	$1,000	No Load	800-638-5660	1.44	13.8	+4.5
❿ Warburg Pincus Emerg Gr	Small Company	CUEGX	$2,500	$500	No Load	800-257-5614	1.20	12.7	+3.4

Data source: Morningstar Mutual Funds OnDisc. Copyright by Morningstar, Inc., 53 West Jackson Blvd., Chicago, IL 60604. (800) 876–5005. Although gathered from reliable sources, data accuracy and completeness cannot be guaranteed. Performance numbers reflect periods ending 12/31/95 unless otherwise stated. Mutual fund performance and policies are constantly subject to change. Contact the fund for current information before you invest.

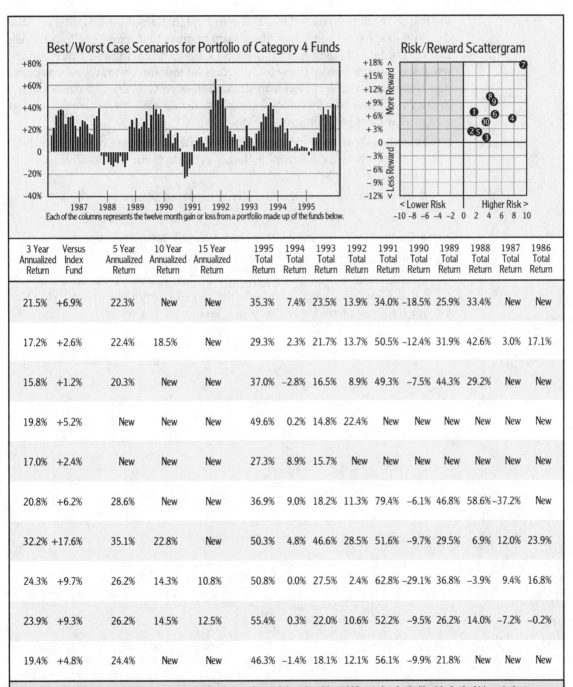

Best/Worst Case Scenarios for Portfolio of Category 4 Funds

Each of the columns represents the twelve month gain or loss from a portfolio made up of the funds below.

Risk/Reward Scattergram

3 Year Annualized Return	Versus Index Fund	5 Year Annualized Return	10 Year Annualized Return	15 Year Annualized Return	1995 Total Return	1994 Total Return	1993 Total Return	1992 Total Return	1991 Total Return	1990 Total Return	1989 Total Return	1988 Total Return	1987 Total Return	1986 Total Return
21.5%	+6.9%	22.3%	New	New	35.3%	7.4%	23.5%	13.9%	34.0%	–18.5%	25.9%	33.4%	New	New
17.2%	+2.6%	22.4%	18.5%	New	29.3%	2.3%	21.7%	13.7%	50.5%	–12.4%	31.9%	42.6%	3.0%	17.1%
15.8%	+1.2%	20.3%	New	New	37.0%	–2.8%	16.5%	8.9%	49.3%	–7.5%	44.3%	29.2%	New	New
19.8%	+5.2%	New	New	New	49.6%	0.2%	14.8%	22.4%	New	New	New	New	New	New
17.0%	+2.4%	New	New	New	27.3%	8.9%	15.7%	New	New	New	New	New	New	New
20.8%	+6.2%	28.6%	New	New	36.9%	9.0%	18.2%	11.3%	79.4%	–6.1%	46.8%	58.6%	–37.2%	New
32.2%	+17.6%	35.1%	22.8%	New	50.3%	4.8%	46.6%	28.5%	51.6%	–9.7%	29.5%	6.9%	12.0%	23.9%
24.3%	+9.7%	26.2%	14.3%	10.8%	50.8%	0.0%	27.5%	2.4%	62.8%	–29.1%	36.8%	–3.9%	9.4%	16.8%
23.9%	+9.3%	26.2%	14.5%	12.5%	55.4%	0.3%	22.0%	10.6%	52.2%	–9.5%	26.2%	14.0%	–7.2%	–0.2%
19.4%	+4.8%	24.4%	New	New	46.3%	–1.4%	18.1%	12.1%	56.1%	–9.9%	21.8%	New	New	New

Footnotes: The best/worst columns reflect "rolling" twelve month periods from the 1981–1995 period, or for the life of the fund, whichever is shorter (see chapter 18). Portfolio characteristics are subject to rapid change at the fund manager's discretion. By the time you read this, these funds may have characteristics different from those shown. These are not recommended funds per se, but are offered here as worthy of your consideration.

the last chapter. See pages 226-227 for an explanation of how to interpret the data and graphs. As you study them, keep in mind that removing your money from the safety of savings accounts and CDs in order to invest in the stock market is always a risky thing to do. Don't let low interest rates on your savings tempt you to invest money in stocks unless you can afford to take a much greater risk. Just because stocks are going up doesn't mean they're a good buy or that they will continue to rise.

Take the advice of *The Accidental Tourist:* never, repeat *never*, put yourself in a position where a catastrophic loss is even theoretically possible. Among other things, this means to:

◆ Invest from a specific, carefully considered plan.

◆ Diversify, diversify, diversify.

◆ Choose investments on their merits and not for their tax benefits.

◆ Assume nothing; verify everything.

◆ Remember Will Rogers's perspective: "It is not the return *on* my investment that I am concerned about; it is the return *of* my investment." Don't be too quick to leave familiar territory in search of higher returns elsewhere. ◆

21

CHAPTER PREVIEW

Understanding International Fund Risk

I. **There are two primary ways you hope to profit when investing outside the U.S.**

   A. The value of your foreign portfolio could rise. That's all we usually focus on when investing in the U.S.

   B. The value of the dollar could go down versus the local currency of the country in which you're investing.

II. **Currency fluctuations play an important role when you invest internationally.**

   A. A primer on currencies shows the dollar's long-term downtrend against other major currencies and explains what factors cause the dollar to weaken and what the implications are for American investors.

   B. Performance data is provided for six mutual funds that specialize in currency-related investments.

III. **Investing outside the U.S. is a more complicated undertaking, but it offer several benefits.**

   A. Investing internationally offers protection against hyperinflation and a weak dollar.

   B. Investing internationally offers a potentially lower level of risk.

   C. Investing internationally offers additional profit opportunities.

IV. **A risk ladder is given that will help you understand the risk and reward characteristics of four categories of stock funds that invest in foreign companies. Performance data is provided for twelve funds in each of the four categories.**

**When investing overseas, changes in the strength of the
local currency versus the U.S. dollar will affect your total returns.**

There are two primary ways you hope to profit when investing outside the U.S. Your first hope, naturally, is that the value of the stocks or bonds in your portfolio will go up in value. That's all we usually think about when investing in our own market. But in buying overseas, another important factor is the value of the foreign country's currency relative to the U.S. dollar. That's because the prices of shares overseas are expressed in terms of the local currency. Here's how it works.

❶ Let's say you want to invest $10,000 in the French market. To do that, you need to exchange your dollars for French francs. In mid-1996, a franc was worth a little over 19 cents in our currency. Stated another way, one U.S. dollar could be exchanged for about 5.2 francs. That means you could swap 10,000 U.S. dollars for 52,000 French francs.

❷ You take the 52,000 francs and invest them in a portfolio of French stocks.

❸ Later, you sell your French shares for 57,200 francs. You make a tidy 10% profit.

❹ Now it's time to convert your francs back into dollars so you can use them here in the States. The dollar-franc relationship changes slightly on a daily basis; the dollar is continually either gaining or losing strength with respect to other currencies in response to normal demand/supply forces.

◆ **You're helped by a weak dollar.** It sounds strange to think that bad news for America's currency is good news for you. But, remember—you want to be able to buy as many dollars as possible with your francs. If the dollar has dropped (say, to 4.8 francs), your 57,200 francs are worth $11,920. You not only made money on your stocks ($1,000) but on the weakness of the dollar as well ($920). That's why investing overseas can be a good strategy *if* it appears the dollar is going to get weaker (as it typically does during periods of high inflation).

This is a picture of the value of the dollar versus 18 different currencies as measured by the J.P. Morgan Index. Each currency is weighted in the index according to the amount of trade we do with that country (base year is 1990). Apart from a brief resurgence in the first half of the 1980s, the dollar has been gradually losing strength over the past quarter century.

The Morgan Index, being an average, masks the dollar's value against individual currencies. The German mark was one of the currencies that gained value against the dollar. This is the same as saying the dollar weakened against the mark. Worth just 27¢ in 1970, the mark had climbed to 70¢ by 1995. This equates to an average gain of 3.7% per year.

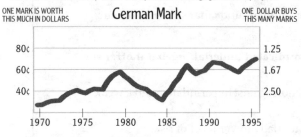

The Japanese yen, likewise, has become more valuable in relation to the dollar. Its graph shows a more consistent pattern of strength. In 1970, one dollar could be exchanged for 358 yen. In 1995, a dollar would buy just 100 yen (i.e., a yen is now worth about the same as a penny). This equates to an average gain of about 4.9% per year.

Having your foreign stock go up *and* the local currency rise against the dollar is the best of both worlds. That's why constant monitoring of the dollar is important to international investors.

◆ **You're hurt by a strong dollar.** But what if the currency exchange rate has gone the other way? If the dollar has gotten stronger versus the franc during the time you owned your French shares (say it's now worth 5.8 francs), your 57,200 francs can be exchanged for only $9,860. Although you made money in French stocks, you lost back more than you made due to a strong dollar.

Many mutual funds prefer to avoid this "currency" risk. They're willing to give up the potential extra gains they might make from a weak dollar. In return, they gain the assurance there won't be unexpected losses due to a strong dollar.

To accomplish this, they "hedge" their positions in the currency futures markets. You don't need to understand the mechanics of hedging. The important point is that hedging activities, if done properly, neutralize the currency risk. Some mutual funds that invest in other countries use hedging, and some do not. If they do hedge, then changes in the dollar should not affect them. If they don't hedge, their returns will be enhanced by a weak dollar (as in our example), and they will be decreased by a strong one.

If you are investing overseas *primarily* as a way of protecting yourself against a weak dollar, make sure the fund(s) you use do not employ hedging strategies, which neutralize the effects of fluctuating currency exchange rates. How can you tell if they are? Call and ask them.

Currency fluctuations play an important role when investing internationally. Let's pause for a brief primer on exchange rates.

The Swiss franc has a long tradition as a "hard" currency (a currency in which there is widespread confidence due to the economic and political stability of the country, often associated with a history of low inflation). Such currencies hold their value well. Since 1970, the Swiss franc has gained an average of 5.2% per year against the dollar.

Although the dollar has lost ground against strong currencies like those of Germany, Japan, and Switzerland, it has gained ground against many other currencies. The British pound is one. The world's strongest currency in the last century, the pound has been hurt by England's move toward socialism since the 1920s.

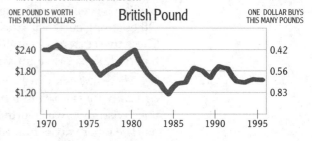

Have you ever noticed that the prices that appear on U.S. products (like magazines) are higher if you pay in Canadian money? That's because the Canadian dollar is equal to only about 73¢ in U.S. dollars. That's down about 15% since 1990, and 25% since 1975. At the end of 1995, it took $1.36 Canadian to equal $1.00 U.S.

It can be confusing when we hear that "the dollar is strong" or "the dollar is weak." It sounds as if the dollar is gaining or losing ground in an absolute sense. But actually the dollar is in a long-distance race with dozens of other currencies, and during any given stretch of the race it gains against some of its competitors while losing ground to others. That's the nature of a "floating rates" system where rates of exchange are determined by market forces of supply and demand instead of being set by international agreements between countries. This is illustrated by the graphs on pages 256-257.

The graph of the U.S. dollar is a picture of the *average* change in value of the dollar in comparison to eighteen other leading currencies. *On average,* the dollar has gotten weaker over a long period of time. But that's of limited help because we invest overseas *in specific countries,* and our success is affected by how the dollar changes in value *against specific currencies for shorter periods* of time. For example, all other things being equal, an investment made in Japan in 1995 did worse for Americans than an investment in Germany. That's because the mark gained strength against the dollar during the year (meaning your mark will buy more dollars when you convert back) while the yen lost some ground (meaning your yen will buy fewer dollars back).

The point is that it's difficult to generalize about the value of the dollar versus other currencies. When you hear it said that "the dollar is weak," ask the question "weak against *which* currencies?" In the graphs on the previous two pages, you can see that the currencies of Switzerland, Germany, and Japan have been quite strong versus the dollar over the past quarter century. Other strong currencies include the Austrian schilling and the Dutch guilder. These five currencies would be expected to be most attractive should there be a period of excessive inflation in the U.S.

There are two ways currency values are quoted. One is *how much the foreign currency is worth* in terms of the dollar. For example, at the end of 1995, one Swiss franc was worth about 87¢, one British pound about $1.55, and so on. The other way is to turn the question around and ask *how many of the foreign currency units it would take to buy* $1 U.S. It would take 1.15 francs ($1.00/87¢) but just .64 pounds ($1.00/$1.55). This can be confusing at first, but you'll eventually get the hang of it.

What causes the dollar to weaken?

Exchange rates on currencies move up and down daily based on the supply and demand in the marketplace. When there is too much supply (or too little demand), sellers are forced to lower their asking prices if they want to transact business.

The largest demand comes from foreign investors—individuals, institutions, and governments—who want dollars to use for purchasing our stocks and bonds. To a large degree, their demand for dollars depends on how attractive our interest rates are and the outlook for inflation in our country. When our interest rates are moving up, that's a plus as far as they're concerned. The primary problem seems to be a growing anxiety about our ability to avoid a re-newed round of inflation. Before they will exchange their own currencies for more dollars and use them to invest further in our markets, they need to be-lieve that the dollars they will get back (when they sell their stocks or bonds many years down the road) will still have close to the purchasing power they have today. This means they're very sensitive to our economic policies that af-fect inflation, especially our inability to get our budget deficits under control.

Ultimately, the dollar is a commodity. When we create more of them than is needed in the world marketplace to perform normal transactions, the value of the commodity falls. We have run huge federal budget deficits for years and financed it by printing dollars. Also, we buy more from the rest of the world than the rest of the world buys from us. In 1995, this "trade deficit" amounted to $174 billion, the worst level on record! That means every month we're net sellers of huge amounts of dollars in order to obtain the currencies we need to buy the imports we want. The world is drowning in dollars, and with more sellers than buyers, its price falls. This weakness begets further weakness—a mind-set among currency traders develops that a further fall in the value of the dollar is likely. This becomes a self-fulfilling prophecy as another round of speculative dollar selling does indeed drive its value down, and the downward spiral continues.

PERFORMANCE DATA FOR FOREIGN CURRENCY FUNDS

SOURCE: MORNINGSTAR ONDISC

Fund	Nasdaq Ticker Symbol	Minimum Initial Purchase	Maximum Sales Charge	5 Year Standard Deviation	5 Year Annualized Return	1995 Total Return	1994 Total Return	1993 Total Return	1992 Total Return	1991 Total Return	Number To Call For Information
Fidelity Deutsche Mark Invests in Germany's money market	N/A	$5,000	0.4%	11.9	6.4%	11.0%	16.4%	−1.2%	1.1%	5.9%	800-544-8888
Fidelity Sterling Performance Invests in England's money market	N/A	$5,000	0.4%	11.7	1.8%	3.9%	9.9%	2.4%	−12.2%	6.2%	800-544-8888
Fidelity Yen Performance Invests in Japan's money market	N/A	$5,000	0.4%	10.8	7.7%	−3.6%	12.6%	13.1%	2.5%	15.0%	800-544-8888
Franklin/Templeton Hard Currency Invests in low inflation currencies	ICPHX	$100	3.0%	9.8	7.2%	6.6%	14.4%	4.6%	2.2%	8.3%	800-342-5236
Franklin/Templeton Global Currency Invests in low inflation currencies + U.S.	ICPGX	$100	3.0%	5.3	6.1%	5.0%	8.1%	6.0%	3.6%	7.6%	800-342-5236
Franklin/Templeton High Income Currency Invests in high-yielding currencies + U.S.	ICHIX	$100	3.0%	7.9	5.0%	9.3%	10.2%	−2.6%	−2.9%	12.0%	800-342-5236

What's so bad about a weak dollar?

It discourages foreign investments in U.S. assets. The primary implications have to do with interest rates. For example, a Japanese investor who bought $10,000 of our bonds in 1982 had to pay 2,500,000 yen. If the bond matured today, the $10,000 would convert back into less than 1,000,000 yen—a 60% loss! If foreign investors believe the dollar will continue to fall, they will demand much higher yields to offset this risk. This drives up interest rates. Also, there are inflationary implications. When the value of the dollar goes down, the cost of imported goods (like Hondas) goes up. This ripples through the economy because it allows domestic competitors (like Ford) to raise their prices also without the fear of losing market share.

If all this sounds pretty complicated, that's because it is.

Investing overseas has many complexities. You shouldn't proceed until you understand the basic dynamics. (The fund data on pages 262-265 is presented merely to familiarize you with the breadth of funds available.) You're dealing with currency fluctuations, different accounting procedures that make an accurate evaluation more difficult, local political situations, and foreign stock exchanges with different regulations (usually more lax) than those we're accustomed to in this country. In light of these potential difficulties, what are the benefits?

◆ **Investing internationally offers protection against hyperinflation (see chapter 23) and a weak dollar.** As we've just seen, currency movements can have a great impact on the profitability of your foreign holdings. From the perspective of an American investor, a 15% increase in the value of the German mark versus the U.S. dollar would make the same profit contribution to an international fund invested in German stocks as if the German market itself had risen 15%. The *Mutual Fund Forecaster* newsletter published an interesting article showing that currency fluctuations are often the overriding influences on international portfolios.

Let's consider the performance of international funds versus U.S. funds in three completely different currency environments. During the four-year period 1981-1984, the U.S. dollar was very strong. The result was that the average

DIVERSIFYING INTO FOREIGN STOCKS LOWERS RISK

As a further small test of the effects of adding international stocks to a portfolio, I compared two Just-the-Basics strategies. Portfolio A doesn't invest internationally. Its stock holdings are split evenly between the two domestic funds—Vanguard's Index 500 and Index Extended Market. Portfolio B adds Vanguard's International Growth fund, using it for 20% of the stock portfolio (the remainder being split evenly between the two U.S. funds).

For the five-year period ending in 1995, the portfolio with the international fund underperfomed. This was due to 1991 and 1995 being very strong years for the U.S. market. Over longer periods, however, Portfolio B came in ahead. Of greater interest, the standard deviation (and therefore the risk) was less for Portfolio B for every time frame.

	(A) Stock Portion of Just-Basics With U.S. Stocks Only	(B) Stock Portion of Just-Basics With International Growth Fund
1981	–3.4%	–3.0%
1982	17.3%	14.9%
1983	23.4%	27.3%
1984	2.2%	1.6%
1985	31.6%	36.7%
1986	14.9%	23.3%
1987	0.6%	3.0%
1988	18.0%	16.7%
1989	27.7%	27.1%
1990	–8.7%	–9.3%
1991	36.0%	29.8%
1992	9.9%	6.8%
1993	12.2%	18.7%
1994	–0.3%	–0.1%
1995	35.6%	31.5%
5 Yr Avg Return	17.81%	16.66%
5 Yr Standard Dev	5.0	4.3
10 Yr Avg Return	13.70%	13.95%
10 Yr Standard Dev	7.8	7.2
15 Yr Avg Return	13.62%	14.14%
15 Yr Standard Dev	8.0	7.7

U.S. fund rose 50%, while the typical international fund rose only three-fifths as much. Then came the three-year weak-dollar period from 1985 to 1987 when the typical international fund doubled, vastly outdistancing U.S.-invested funds. Finally, from 1988 to mid-1992, the dollar has been relatively flat versus the typical foreign currency and, not surprisingly, the returns of U.S. and international funds have been relatively similar; international funds rose 63% in the period, while the average U.S. equity fund gained 85%. If you combine all three periods, international funds rose 13.9% per annum compounded, not much different from the 12.8% gain of the average U.S. fund. As the dollar was essentially unchanged on balance over these 11½ years, that is not a particularly surprising result.

Thus, currency fluctuations are a significant factor underlying the performances of international funds. In fact, in some instances, it is the overriding consideration. For example, spectacular portfolio gains of 14,600% achieved by Brazil Fund in just a two-year period were all but totally wiped out by concurrent losses in the value of the Brazilian cruzeiro. During the same period, all of the net gain in Swiss Helvetia fund was attributable to strength in the Swiss franc, not the fund's portfolio.

Of course, some international funds will perform well owing to good security selection and being invested in the right countries at the right time. But currency fluctuations often dominate over market performance. If you believe the U.S. dollar will be strong and foreign currencies weak, avoid international funds. On the other hand, if you look for a weak dollar and strong foreign currencies, internationals may be just the place for your investment dollars.[1]

[1]Used by permission. Mutual Fund Forecaster is published by The Institute for Econometric Research, 3471 North Federal, Fort Lauderdale, FL 33306; telephone (800) 442-9000; one year subscription $49.

RISK LADDER FOR FOREIGN STOCK FUNDS

SOURCE: MORNINGSTAR ONDISC

Risk Category	Number of Funds	Standard Deviation	5 Year Annualized	1995 Return	1994 Return	1993 Return	1992 Return	1991 Return	1990 Return	1989 Return	1988 Return	1987 Return	1986 Return
Emerging Markets Funds Focus on developing economies in Asia, Africa, and Latin America	36	17.0	10.8%	–8.4%	–12.9%	65.6%	–0.6%	15.5%	–14.2%	28.1%	10.5%	0.2%	20.6%
Regional Funds Typically limit their investing to either Europe or the Pacific	82	15.1	9.6%	7.8%	–4.5%	44.0%	–3.2%	10.8%	–15.4%	27.1%	16.1%	17.1%	55.3%
Foreign Funds Can invest worldwide *except* in the United States	128	12.5	10.2%	9.8%	–2.0%	38.7%	–4.4%	12.8%	–11.2%	23.3%	17.4%	8.7%	51.0%
Global Funds Can invest worldwide *including* the United States	90	12.1	12.8%	16.2%	–2.6%	31.4%	0.3%	25.2%	–9.1%	23.0%	16.8%	2.3%	27.1%

Performance Histories of Selected Global Stock Funds

Name of Fund	Nasdaq Ticker Symbol	Minimum Initial Purchase	Maximum Sales Charge	Number to Call for Information	Sharpe Ratio	3 Year Data Standard Deviation	Annualized Return	1995 Total Return	1994 Total Return	1993 Total Return
API Growth Fund	APITX	$500	No Load	800-544-6060	0.76	10.6	12.2%	23.7%	–3.4%	18.3%
Fidelity Worldwide	FWWFX	$2,500	No Load	800-544-8888	1.08	9.7	14.6%	7.2%	3.0%	36.5%
Founders Worldwide Growth	FWWGX	$1,000	No Load	800-525-2440	0.93	12.0	15.3%	20.6%	–2.2%	29.9%
Janus Worldwide	JAWWX	$1,000	No Load	800-525-8983	1.26	10.6	17.5%	21.9%	3.6%	28.4%
Keystone Global	KAGOX	$1,000	5.75%	800-343-2898	1.24	13.2	20.5%	23.7%	2.7%	37.7%
New Perspective	ANWPX	$250	5.75%	800-421-4120	1.27	9.6	16.3%	20.4%	3.0%	27.0%
Scudder Global	SCOBX	$1,000	No Load	800-225-2470	1.14	9.4	14.8%	20.5%	–4.2%	31.1%
Scudder Global Small Company	SGSCX	$1,000	No Load	800-225-2470	0.89	11.7	14.6%	17.8%	–7.7%	38.2%
Templeton Global Community	TEGOX	$100	5.75%	800-292-9293	0.85	12.0	14.3%	12.8%	–4.0%	38.1%
Templeton Growth I	TEPLX	$100	5.75%	800-292-9293	1.30	9.6	16.6%	18.4%	0.8%	32.7%
Templeton Smaller Growth	TEMGX	$100	5.75%	800-292-9293	1.00	9.8	14.0%	17.6%	–4.6%	31.8%
Templeton World	TEMWX	$100	5.75%	800-292-9293	1.35	10.2	17.9%	21.6%	0.9%	33.6%

Data source: Morningstar Mutual Funds. Copyright by Morningstar, Inc., 53 West Jackson Blvd., Chicago, IL 60604. (800) 876–5005. Although gathered from reliable sources, data accuracy and completeness cannot be guaranteed. Performance numbers reflect periods ending 12/31/95. These are not recommended funds per se, but are offered here as worthy of your consideration. Mutual fund policies are subject to change. Contact the fund for current information before you invest.

Performance Histories of Selected Foreign Stock Funds

Name of Fund	Nasdaq Ticker Symbol	Minimum Initial Purchase	Maximum Sales Charge	Number to Call for Information	3 Year Data			1995 Total Return	1994 Total Return	1993 Total Return
					Sharpe Ratio	Standard Deviation	Annualized Return			
Acorn International	ACINX	$1,000	No Load	800-922-6769	1.07	11.2	16.0%	8.9%	−3.8%	49.1%
Fidelity Diversified International	FDIVX	$2,500	No Load	800-544-8888	1.13	12.0	17.7%	18.0%	1.1%	36.7%
Harbor International	HAINX	$2,000	No Load	800-422-1050	1.31	13.0	21.2%	16.1%	5.4%	45.4%
Hotchkis & Wiley International	HWINX	$5,000	No Load	800-346-7301	1.27	11.9	19.3%	19.9%	−2.9%	45.8%
Ivy International A	IVINX	$1,000	5.75%	800-456-5111	1.23	13.0	20.2%	12.6%	3.9%	48.4%
Managers International Equity	MGITX	$2,000	No Load	800-835-3879	1.37	10.1	17.9%	16.3%	2.0%	38.2%
Sit International Growth	SNGRX	$2,000	No Load	800-332-5580	0.90	13.6	16.3%	9.4%	−3.0%	48.4%
Strong International Stock	STISX	$1,000	No Load	800-368-1030	0.88	13.5	16.0%	7.8%	−1.6%	47.1%
Templeton Foreign I	TEMFX	$100	5.75%	800-292-9293	1.15	9.6	15.1%	11.2%	0.4%	36.8%
T. Rowe Price International Stock	PRITX	$2,500	No Load	800-638-5660	0.91	12.8	15.7%	11.4%	−0.8%	40.1%
Vanguard International Growth	VWIGX	$3,000	No Load	800-662-7447	1.17	12.6	18.8%	14.9%	0.8%	44.7%
Warburg Pincus Intl Eq Comm	CUIEX	$2,500	No Load	800-257-5614	0.94	15.5	18.7%	10.4%	0.2%	51.3%

Data source: Morningstar Mutual Funds. Copyright by Morningstar, Inc., 53 West Jackson Blvd., Chicago, IL 60604. (800) 876–5005. Although gathered from reliable sources, data accuracy and completeness cannot be guaranteed. Performance numbers reflect periods ending 12/31/95. These are not recommended funds per se, but are offered here as worthy of your consideration. Mutual fund policies are subject to change. Contact the fund for current information before you invest.

Performance Histories of Selected Foreign Regional Stock Funds

Name of Fund	Nasdaq Ticker Symbol	Minimum Initial Purchase	Maximum Sales Charge	Number to Call for Information	Sharpe Ratio	3 Year Data Standard Deviation	3 Year Data Annualized Return	1995 Total Return	1994 Total Return	1993 Total Return
Alliance New Europe A	ANEAX	$250	4.25%	800-227-4618	1.26	11.5	18.6%	18.6%	4.6%	34.6%
EuroPacific Growth	AEPGX	$250	5.75%	800-421-4120	1.11	10.4	15.7%	12.9%	1.1%	35.6%
Fidelity Europe	FIEUX	$2,500	3.00%	800-544-8888	1.18	11.0	17.1%	18.8%	6.3%	27.2%
Invesco Pacific Basin	FPBSX	$1,000	No Load	800-525-8085	0.79	14.8	15.8%	4.0%	4.7%	42.6%
Normura Pacific Basin	NPBFX	$1,000	No Load	800-833-0018	0.68	15.0	14.3%	2.5%	5.3%	38.3%
Pacific European Growth	PGPEX	$250	4.00%	800-866-7778	0.81	14.1	15.6%	6.0%	–3.6%	51.3%
Prudential Pacific Growth A	PRPAX	$1,000	5.00%	800-225-1852	0.80	16.0	17.0%	5.4%	–8.8%	66.6%
Putnam Asia Pacific Growth A	PAPAX	$500	5.75%	800-225-1581	0.98	15.0	18.8%	2.8%	–0.5%	64.0%
Putnam Europe Growth A	PEUGX	$500	5.75%	800-225-1581	1.35	11.1	19.1%	21.2%	6.4%	31.1%
T. Rowe Price European Stock	PRESX	$2,500	No Load	800-638-5660	1.19	11.1	17.3%	21.9%	4.1%	27.2%
T. Rowe Price New Asia	PRASX	$2,500	No Load	800-638-5660	0.46	22.4	14.5%	3.8%	–19.2%	78.8%
Vontobel EuroPacific	VNEPX	$1,000	No Load	800-527-9500	0.76	12.8	13.9%	10.9%	–5.3%	40.8%

Data source: Morningstar Mutual Funds. Copyright by Morningstar, Inc., 53 West Jackson Blvd., Chicago, IL 60604. (800) 876–5005. Although gathered from reliable sources, data accuracy and completeness cannot be guaranteed. Performance numbers reflect periods ending 12/31/95. These are not recommended funds per se, but are offered here as worthy of your consideration. Mutual fund policies are subject to change. Contact the fund for current information before you invest.

Performance Histories of Selected Emerging Markets Stock Funds

Name of Fund	Nasdaq Ticker Symbol	Minimum Initial Purchase	Maximum Sales Charge	Number to Call for Information	3 Year Data			1995 Total Return	1994 Total Return	1993 Total Return
					Sharpe Ratio	Standard Deviation	Annualized Return			
Biltmore Emerging Markets	BTEMX	$250	4.50%	800-462-7538	New	New	New	7.9%	New	New
Fidelity Emerging Markets	FEMKX	$2,500	3.00%	800-544-8888	0.39	22.6	13.0%	–3.2%	–17.9%	81.8%
Govett Emerging Markets A	GIEMX	$500	4.95%	800-225-2222	0.44	20.3	13.1%	–7.9%	–12.7%	79.7%
G.T. Global Emerging Markets A	GTEMX	$500	4.75%	800-824-1580	0.35	19.5	10.9%	–13.9%	–3.8%	64.5%
Ivy New Century A	IVCAX	$1,000	5.75%	800-456-5111	New	New	New	6.4%	New	New
Lexington Worldwide Emerging Mkts	LEXGX	$1,000	No Load	800-526-0056	0.32	17.9	9.8%	–5.9%	–13.8%	63.4%
Merrill Lynch Mid East / Africa	MDAFX	$1,000	5.25%	800-637-3863	New	New	New	10.2%	New	New
Montgomery Emerging Markets	MNEMX	$1,000	No Load	800-572-3863	0.35	17.0	10.0%	–9.1%	–7.7%	58.7%
Scudder Latin America	SLAFX	$1,000	No Load	800-225-2470	0.33	25.1	12.5%	–9.8%	–9.4%	74.3%
Templeton Developing Markets I	TEDMX	$100	5.75%	800-292-9293	0.94	13.7	17.0%	0.4%	–8.6%	74.5%
USAA Emerging Markets	USEMX	$1,000	No Load	800-382-8722	New	New	New	3.7%	New	New
Warburg Pincus Emerg Mkt Com	WPMEX	$2,500	No Load	800-257-5614	New	New	New	17.4%	New	New

Data source: Morningstar Mutual Funds. Copyright by Morningstar, Inc., 53 West Jackson Blvd., Chicago, IL 60604. (800) 876–5005. Although gathered from reliable sources, data accuracy and completeness cannot be guaranteed. Performance numbers reflect periods ending 12/31/95. These are not recommended funds per se, but are offered here as worthy of your consideration. Mutual fund policies are subject to change. Contact the fund for current information before you invest.

◆ **Investing internationally offers a potentially lower level of risk.** Numerous studies have shown risk is actually *reduced* by allocating 15%–20% of one's portfolio to stocks not primarily tied to the American economy or currency. In a non-diversified portfolio, all the investments tend to move in the same direction at the same time. Overseas stocks, however, don't march in lockstep with our markets, so their ups and downs can somewhat offset our ups and downs. According to research by the respected Frank Russell Company, "the diversification benefits of international stocks are even greater than previously estimated; placing a higher percentage of one's portfolio overseas dramatically increases the efficiency of the portfolio mix."

◆ **Investing internationally offers additional profit opportunities.** In the 1990s, many countries in Europe and Asia are likely to continue having faster economic growth than the United States. Although most overseas markets are influenced to some degree by the U.S. market, they are first and foremost going to reflect conditions and expectations concerning their local economies. For example, the Hong Kong market was quite strong in 1992, reflecting the anticipated boom in business with mainland China. Meanwhile, in another part of the Pacific, the Japanese market was down in 1992 for the third straight year, and eventually fell more than 55% from its late-1989 high. Your success at investing overseas very much depends on which markets you choose to participate in.

"Emerging markets" is a term that applies to those developing countries whose economies are relatively small but growing quickly. They are scattered around the globe, but are found in greatest number in Asia (China, Malaysia, Indonesia, Singapore, Thailand, and the Philippines) and Latin America (Argentina, Brazil, Chile, Peru, Venezuela, and Mexico).

Such markets typically have a relatively small investor base within the country. That means they are not large enough to take it in stride when huge sums of money from foreign investors suddenly pour into the country in search of profit opportunities—and then often retreat just as quickly. Although they offer tantalizing potential, emerging markets are often characterized by unusual volatility due to the effects of the large money flows which come and go in response to political instability, social unrest, and currency fluctuations. For example, Turkey's market more than tripled in 1993, but was down by half in 1994! Or, look at the problems of the Mexican peso, which have cost U.S. investors dearly and dominated the headlines in 1995. Large profit potential notwithstanding, it takes a *really* long-term perspective to ride these financial roller coasters. One international fund manager recommends you have at least a ten- to fifteen-year time horizon when investing in emerging markets. ◆

22

CHAPTER PREVIEW

Special Purpose Funds

I. **In addition to the bond funds in our risk ladder, other "special purpose" bond funds have a specialized emphasis.**

    A. Mortgage bonds backed by the Government National Mortgage Association are called Ginnie Maes. They offer attractive yields and pay monthly dividends. The disadvantage of Ginnie Maes is the "prepayment risk" experienced when homeowners refinance their mortgages at lower rates.

    B. Zero coupon bonds make no interest payments to investors. Instead, the interest is accumulated and added to the market value of the bond. The current market values of zeros react dramatically to changes in interest rates.

    C. Tax-free bonds are issued by state and local governments. The interest received from tax-free bonds is exempt from federal income tax and also exempt from state income tax in the state where the bond is originally issued. Because city and state governments are under increasing financial strains, it's important to stay with bonds that have quality ratings of A and better.

II. **Some mutual funds invest in both bonds and stocks rather than limiting themselves to one or the other.**

    A. "Balanced" funds typically place limitations on the manager's freedom in regard to the maximum percentage of the fund's assets (typically 60%–65%) he can invest in either bonds or stocks. The managers of these funds tend to primarily focus their efforts on their securities selection rather than adjusting the ratio of stocks to bonds.

    B. "Asset allocation" funds place top priority on adjusting the ratio of stocks to bonds, often based on an analysis of business cycle trends. This means the managers of these funds will shift their portfolio allocations among stocks, bonds, and cash frequently and aggressively.

III. **Sector funds are special purpose stock funds that limit their investing to a specific segment of the marketplace.**

    A. They are higher in risk because of their lack of diversification and flexibility, but when their particular industry is in favor, such funds can have unusually strong performance.

    B. The most popular kinds of sector funds include such specialized investing themes as: communications, financial services, health services, natural resources, precious metals, real estate, technology, and utilities.

We've gone *beyond* abundance in this country!

Whether I go to buy breakfast cereal, pet food, light bulbs, or a tennis racket, I'm dazed by the array of options I face. It's easy to stress out trying to deal with the option glut. Of course, a nice selection is a good thing up to a point. But when you try to process all the pros and cons that confront you for just about everything you want to buy or do, it's overwhelming!

During our annual trek to the ocean, I like to relax by sitting on the beach and soaking up the sun as I read. But if I took the time to shop for the best combination of ingredients from among a skillion tanning lotions (". . . this one has the best protection but you've got to reapply it every 30 minutes, that one has great moisturizer but it feels like pure grease, this one does everything but it smells like a fruit market . . ."), I'd *never* get to the beach. So, I do what most of us do at one time or another. I take the path of least resistance — I use Susie's lotion.

THE FAMILY TREE OF MORTGAGE-BACKED INVESTMENTS

Fixed-Rate Mortgages

are the typical home mortgage, with a set rate for a fifteen or thirty year period. Their most serious drawback is that you never know when they'll mature because homeowners have the right to prepay their mortgages whenever they can find a better deal. Funds that specialize in these have long track records for you to consider.

Adjustable-Rate Mortgages

are the kind where the interest rate is moved up or down periodically to more closely match the rates that are prevailing at that time. Funds that specialize in these are fairly new; it's too soon to see how they'll fare during a period of rising interest rates. I would suggest waiting and watching.

Collateralized Mortgage Obligations

are an attempt to eliminate some of the uncertainty caused by the prepayment risk. They do this by "putting you in line" as to when you receive principal back from mortgage prepayments rather than distributing the prepaid principal proportionately to all the shareholders at once. Don't invest in these unless you thoroughly understand what happens to the CMO's payback rate and yield if rates change by two or three points. And plan to hold them until maturity—they're not designed for easy resale.

Fortunately, when it comes to mutual fund investing, the path of least resistance leads you to our Just-the-Basics strategy, which has a pretty good track record. For once, you're not hurting yourself by taking the easy way out. But there may be situations where you want to throw another fund or two into your portfolio in order to achieve special goals associated with increasing your potential for current income, capital growth, tax reduction, or inflation protection.

The mutual funds in this chapter have special characteristics that make it inappropriate to include them in the risk ladders for stock and bond funds we created in chapters 19 and 20. I'll briefly discuss each type of fund and close the chapter with risk and performance data for selected funds in each group.

You may think your local lender is on the receiving end of those monthly mortgage checks you write . . .

. . . but guess again. Most likely the ultimate recipients are shareholders in a special kind of bond fund. Because they invest in fixed-rate mortgages which meet the standards of the Government National Mortgage Association (GNMA), such funds are often called Ginnie Mae funds.

Ginnie Mae funds behave somewhat differently than normal bond funds due to the right that homeowners have to prepay their mortgages whenever they can find a better deal. Here's how a typical mortgage investing cycle affects the Ginnie Mae investor.

❶ Let's say your neighbor Jim takes out an FHA or VA insured mortgage. The local bank or savings and loan that made the loan doesn't keep it on its books. Instead, it's combined with others that have similar terms (say fifteen-year loans with an 8% rate). When the bank has at least $1 million of these loans, it sells them as a package to big institutional investors. In this way, it makes a quick, small profit and has its money back to go out and make more loans.

❷ The buyers take the package to the Government National Mortgage Association to be sure it meets certain standards. Then, it is assigned a pool number to show that the timely payment of the interest and principal on every mortgage in the package is guaranteed by the "full faith and credit" of the U.S. government.

❸ A mortgage-oriented bond fund, like Vanguard's GNMA fund, buys the pool of mortgages and is thereafter entitled to have the monthly mortgage payments, minus a small servicing and insurance charge, "passed through" to it from the original lenders (the local banks and mortgage companies) who are receiving the homeowners' monthly checks. And what does Vanguard do with the money when they get it? They pay the interest portion out to their shareholders every month and reinvest the principal portion in more pool certificates. If you're a shareholder in the Vanguard fund, you'd end up with a portion of Jim's monthly mortgage payment!

❹ The reward from investing in Ginnie Maes is that they offer slightly higher yields—approximately .75% to 1% per year—than are usually available with short- or medium-term bonds of high quality. During the 1991-1995 period, the average Ginnie Mae fund returned 8.0% per year.

❺ Their biggest drawback is that if interest rates *fall*, the homeowners in the pool will take out new lower-rate mortgages and pay off their old high-rate mortgages. Then, instead of receiving interest from a pool of higher-yielding mortgages for years to come, the Vanguard fund gets its money back all at once and must reinvest it. Of course, by this time rates have fallen and yields are much less attractive. Bummer. This dilemma is called the "prepayment risk."

On the other hand, if rates *rise*, the fund is left with a pool of mortgages that has become a low-rate investment (relatively speaking), and fund shares will fall in value like other bond funds.

Also, bear in mind that the government guarantee doesn't protect investors in these funds against declines in either the yield (as mortgage rates fall) or the value of their fund shares (which fluctuates daily). And their monthly dividend checks, which vary in amount as interest rates change, are fully taxable. From my perspective, the drawbacks outweigh the potential benefit. Ginnie Mae funds are much ado about nothing.

When it comes to bonds that carry a high interest-rate risk, zero-coupon bonds are the ultimate!

Would you be interested in buying bonds that pay "zero" interest? That's right, no interest at all. Doesn't sound very appealing, does it? But what if I was willing to sell you a three-year $1,000 zero-coupon bond for $760? Invest $760 for three years and get $1,000 back. If you said yes, good move! Although you would be receiving no interest for three years, when you finally got your $1,000 it would represent an effective yield of +9.58% per year before taxes.

Zeros are a special breed of bond that do not pay current interest. Instead, they retain the interest you earn and automatically reinvest it. When the bond matures, you receive all the interest and principal at one time.

Here's an example of how they work. Suppose you buy a $1,000 zero-coupon bond that matures in 2006. The price you pay will

PERFORMANCE DATA FOR SPECIAL PURPOSE BOND FUNDS

SOURCE: MORNINGSTAR ONDISC

Risk Category	Standard Deviation	5 Year Annualized	1995 Return	1994 Return	1993 Return	1992 Return	1991 Return	1990 Return	1989 Return	1988 Return	1987 Return	1986 Return
Invest by Lending: Ginnie Mae Mortgage Bonds Bond portfolios of very high quality invested in government-backed home mortgages	3.7	8.0%	16.0%	–3.2%	7.1%	6.5%	14.6%	9.5%	13.0%	7.9%	2.2%	11.2%
Invest by Lending: Zero Coupon Bonds This is the track record of the no-load Benham Target Maturity 2010 bond fund	11.9	15.3%	42.1%	–12.0%	23.5%	8.8%	21.0%	–1.4%	27.0%	18.7%	–11.9%	80.2%
Invest by Lending: Tax-Free Bond Risk Category 4 Bond funds that invest in tax-free high-yield bonds, typically of medium-term maturities	5.0	8.4%	17.5%	–6.3%	12.2%	8.2%	11.8%	5.3%	10.2%	11.8%	1.3%	19.8%
Invest by Lending: Tax-Free Bond Risk Category 3 Bond portfolios of generally high quality with long-term average maturities (over 10 years)	5.5	8.3%	17.0%	–6.2%	12.3%	8.6%	11.7%	6.3%	9.6%	11.3%	–0.6%	18.3%
Invest by Lending: Tax-Free Bond Risk Category 2 Bond portfolios of generally high quality with medium-term average maturities (4-10 years)	3.8	7.5%	12.6%	–3.3%	9.9%	7.8%	10.7%	6.8%	8.2%	6.9%	2.3%	13.7%
Invest by Lending: Tax-Free Bond Risk Category 1 Bond portfolios of generally high quality with short-term average maturities (4 years or less)	1.7	5.6%	7.6%	0.1%	6.1%	6.0%	8.1%	6.5%	7.3%	6.1%	3.2%	8.9%

be at a deep discount from its $1,000 face value, say $510. That means you pay out $510 now, receive no interest until maturity, and then get $1,000 back after ten years. Such an investment would yield an effective +6.96% annual compounded rate of return before taxes.

Zeros were created in the early 1980s by the brokerage community and were sold primarily to large pension investors who needed to know exactly how much they would be getting back at specific times. Zeros make this possible by hedging what is called the "reinvestment risk." With normal bonds, when you receive your semi-annual interest payments, you are faced with the task of reinvesting. But if interest rates have fallen, as they have in recent years, you won't get as attractive a rate on your reinvested amounts as you did on the original bond. That's the reinvestment risk. Zeros eliminate this concern because the issuer, in effect, makes you this offer: "I promise to let you reinvest at the initial rate throughout the life of the bond. But to keep things simple, rather than mail you a check and have you mail it back, I'll just keep the interest money here."

Zeros are especially suited for those investors who plan on holding their bonds to maturity. Because you know up front the rate at which your money will be reinvested over the life of the bond, you can calculate a predictable rate of return for the entire period. This makes planning easier and explains why many individuals buy zeros for their children's education. Taking the above example, parents who wanted to have $20,000 available in 2006 for a child's college expenses could pretty much assure their goal would be met by buying $20,000 face value of zero-coupon bonds. It would cost them $10,200 ($510 cost today multiplied by twenty bonds).

Zeros have two unpleasant drawbacks. First, the IRS taxes you on the interest you earn from your zeros each year even though you won't actually receive it until they mature. That makes them better choices for tax-sheltered accounts like IRAs and Keoghs. Second, zeros are very sensitive to changes in interest rates. In fact, they are the ultimate in high "interest-rate risk" bonds. Their market prices rise and fall much more dramatically than regular bonds as rates fluctuate. If all goes well with the issuer, the bonds will be worth their full face value when they mature, but if you need to sell them prior to maturity in a climate of rising interest rates, you might be shocked at how much they have dropped in value.

As you can probably tell, I'm not that excited about zeros. But if you truly desire to buy some, here are my suggestions: (1) wait until you have reason to believe that interest rates are at or near a peak; (2) buy only the U.S. treasury kind; (3) buy only as many as you are fairly certain you can afford to hold until they mature; and (4) buy them only in your IRA or Keogh in order to escape the income taxes.

Tax-free bonds: they're not for everybody.

Here's the deal. You work hard, live frugally, save your money, and invest it carefully. Then, when the fruit of your labor and sacrifice—your interest check—arrives, state and federal tax agents show up and demand their cut. Their combined share (for most families) starts at about one-third and can climb to almost one-half of your investment earnings. Obviously, any investment that can avoid such a heavy penalty is worth knowing about.

Tax-free bonds (also called "municipal" bonds) are debt securities issued by state and local governments. By law, the interest earned on such bonds is exempt from federal taxes. If the issuer is a city in your state, or the state itself, the interest is also exempt from the state income tax. Because of the value of these tax benefits, issuers of tax-free bonds can borrow money at interest rates lower than those paid by other borrowers. That means they won't pay as much in interest, but what tax-free funds do pay, you can keep entirely!

Would you benefit from investing in tax-free bonds? That depends on your "marginal" tax bracket. At present, the federal tax law provides for several tax brackets—15%, 28%, 31%, 36%, and 39.6%—to be applied against "adjusted gross income." Different rates apply for singles and married persons. See the graphic on page 274 for the tax brackets as they were in 1996. The brackets are adjusted annually for inflation. How high up the tax ladder does your income take you? The highest rate you pay is called your marginal rate.

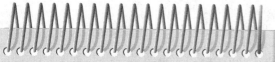

WOULD TAX-FREES GIVE YOU A BETTER RETURN?

Assume you have a choice between a bank CD that is offering a yield of 5.5% and a tax-free bond fund that is yielding 3.8%. Which would be better for you?

For a 28% Marginal Tax Bracket Investor
1 minus .28 = .72
The 3.8% tax-free rate divided by .72 = equivalent to a 5.28% pre-tax rate

For a 31% Marginal Tax Bracket Investor
1 minus .31 = .69
The 3.8% tax-free rate divided by .69 = equivalent to a 5.51% pre-tax rate

For a 36% Marginal Tax Bracket Investor
1 minus .36 = .64
The 3.8% tax-free rate divided by .64 = equivalent to a 5.94% pre-tax rate

In this example, the tax-free fund is the better option for high tax-bracket investors. This will not always be the case. Bond yields can change quickly, so it pays to run the numbers regularly.

Here's an easy calculation you can make to see if you're better off receiving a higher rate of interest that is taxable or a lower return that is tax-free.

First, subtract your marginal rate from "1." Second, divide the yield of the tax-free bond by the resulting number. This formula converts the after-tax yield of the tax-free bond to its *equivalent before-tax yield*. Then you can compare apples with apples. Let's walk through an example. Assume that one-year bank certificates of deposit (CDs) are paying 5.5%, and you can buy a high-quality tax-free bond that is yielding 3.8%. Which would give you the higher after-tax return? Using the two-step calculation, we can convert the 3.8% tax-free yield to its equivalent before-tax yield (see graphic at left).

Since the CD pays a taxable 5.5% yield, it's clearly a better deal for tax-payers in the 28% (and lower) marginal tax brackets. For the 31% tax-bracket investor, however, there's not much difference. Only for the 36% (and higher) taxpayers is it clearly more profitable to take the 3.8% tax-free bond.

(Due to a provision in the tax code that affects the deductibility of itemized deductions, tax-frees are even more attractive than the formula would imply if your adjusted gross income rises above the $100,000 area.)

There is even more incentive to switch to tax-frees if you live in a high-tax state. There are so-called "single state" tax-exempt funds . . .

. . . that invest solely in tax-free securities issued from within that one state. This means the interest income is *double tax-free:* from state income taxes as well as federal ones. This brings us to another factor that complicates the computation. New Yorkers, for example, could have combined federal, state, and local taxes totaling as high as 48%. For such a taxpayer, investing in a New York-only tax-free fund yielding 3.8% would generate an equivalent before-tax return of 7.31%. Since this is significantly higher than the hypothetical 5.5% bank CD, such a bond fund makes sense from a tax point of view for some investors.

Be aware, however, that a huge amount of diversification protection is lost with this approach. It seems to me this is a significant drawback— you'll have all your muni investments riding on the financial condition of only your state and its financial strength. For example, the state of Massachusetts's well-publicized financial difficulty in 1990 led to a lowering of its credit rating. Bond buyers would no longer pay the same price for Massachusetts tax-free bonds—they demanded additional discounts, and bond values plunged. With concerns mounting about the financial health of several of our major cities and states, many analysts question the wisdom of placing much of one's savings at higher risk merely to save a percent or so on taxes.

TAX-EXEMPT BONDS

Issue	Coupon	Maturity	Price	YTM
Allegheny Co Hospital Dv Pa	5.375	12-01-25	90	6.10
Chicago Board of Education	6.000	12-01-26	98	6.15
Dade Co Fla Ser	5.750	10-01-26	95	6.12
Dade Co Fla School Board	5.500	05-01-25	92 3/8	6.06
Dade Co Fla Water & Sewer	5.500	10-01-25	93	6.01
Delaware River Pa Revenue	5.500	01-01-26	92 7/8	6.02
Denver Colo Airport Sys	5.600	11-15-25	91 3/4	6.21
Houston Tx Water & Sewer	5.250	12-01-25	89	6.05
Mass Bay Transit	5.625	03-01-26	93 5/8	6.09
Murray City Utah Hosp	4.750	05-15-20	81 1/2	6.23
NC Muni Power Agency	5.375	05-15-20	91 1/2	6.05
New Orleans La Exhibit Hall	5.600	07-15-25	93 1/8	6.11

Issuer
is the city, state, or government agency that borrowed the money initially.

Coupon Rate
is the rate of interest paid by the issuer. The owner of this bond will receive $5.50 per year for each $100 of face value of bonds owned.

Maturity Date
is the date when the bond's issuer is scheduled to pay investors the full face value of the bond.

Current Market Value
is the last price at which the bond was traded for the day. This bond is valued at $92.875 for each $100 of face value.

Yield to Maturity
This is the return an investor would earn by buying this bond at the quoted price and holding it until it matures in 2026.

When it comes to the safety of tax-free bonds, let the buyer beware!

It is estimated that individuals already own $450 billion of these tax-exempt securities, and, with taxes creeping higher nationwide, the popularity of municipal bonds seems sure to grow. Unfortunately, this growing attraction to munis comes at a time when many states and cities are under increasingly difficult financial pressures. Years of overspending have combined with reduced federal revenue-sharing and regional recessions to drastically weaken the finances of state and local governments. The result is a lowering of the overall quality of the tax-free bond market. One expert estimates that about one-third of the muni market is on its way to becoming the junk bonds of the 1990s.

If you believe you would benefit from investing in tax-frees, I strongly encourage you to diversify widely to minimize the risk of defaults. This can easily be accomplished by investing in three no-load muni funds rather than putting all your money into just one.

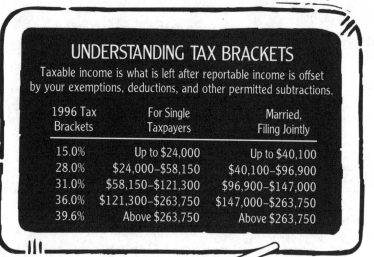

UNDERSTANDING TAX BRACKETS

Taxable income is what is left after reportable income is offset by your exemptions, deductions, and other permitted subtractions.

1996 Tax Brackets	For Single Taxpayers	Married, Filing Jointly
15.0%	Up to $24,000	Up to $40,100
28.0%	$24,000–$58,150	$40,100–$96,900
31.0%	$58,150–$121,300	$96,900–$147,000
36.0%	$121,300–$263,750	$147,000–$263,750
39.6%	Above $263,750	Above $263,750

Many funds have purchased insurance policies that cover their portfolios—the interest and principal are both guaranteed to be paid by the insurer should the issuer default. This insurance earns them AAA ratings for quality. To "play it safe," should you limit yourself to only insured funds?

That's up to you, but let me explain a few of the drawbacks. First, remember that the guarantee is only as strong as the insurance company behind it. When Mutual Benefit Life went into receivership in 1991, it temporarily played havoc with the value of many insured bond funds that had coverage with Mutual Benefit, because their portfolios had lost their AAA status overnight.

Second, insured funds are pure interest-rate plays, which makes them somewhat more volatile than uninsured funds. Higher volatility is the opposite of what you're trying to achieve. Third, it's the portfolio manager's job to know the market and select quality holdings—why pay for that expertise and then insure the portfolio too?

If you can find an insured fund that is yielding more than a normal one, that would seem to be a good deal. But you have to ask yourself: If the insurance has value and is actually adding to the safety of the portfolio, why is the market paying me *more* to invest in it rather than less? Shouldn't higher quality go hand in hand with somewhat lower returns?

When it comes to tax-frees, I suggest you stay with top-quality bonds rated A or better all the way. When you call a fund that you're considering, ask for a breakdown of the quality ratings of their holdings. This is often called a credit analysis, and it will tell you what percent the fund has in AAA-rated bonds, AA-rated bonds, and so on. I wouldn't restrict myself to only the "insured" funds.

So far, we've been talking about special purpose bond funds. Now let's turn to a type of mutual fund that throws some stock into the portfolio as well. These funds are called "balanced" funds . . .

. . . because they own both bonds and stocks rather than limiting themselves to one or the other. The former give interest income and stability to the portfolio, whereas the latter offer dividend income and some growth potential. How much of each is in the portfolio? That's for the fund manager to decide, although some balanced funds place limitations on the manager's freedom in this regard. Most balanced funds I surveyed at the end of 1995 showed stock holdings greater than 50%, and quite a few held more than two-thirds of their assets in stocks. Some managers emphasize investing in large companies, while others prefer small-to-medium-sized ones. Some balanced fund managers are value-oriented, others growth-oriented in their stock selections. In short, it's difficult to generalize about what kind of portfolio you'll end up with. For purposes of controlling risk and fine-tuning your portfolio between stocks and bonds, such funds can present problems because you don't know how your money will be invested from month to month.

A special kind of balanced fund is called an "asset allocation" fund. Morningstar defines them as "funds that seek total returns by placing top priority on the decision as to which types of securities will be held, often based on an analysis of business cycle trends." This means the managers of these funds will shift their portfolio allocations among stocks, bonds, and cash frequently and

PERFORMANCE DATA FOR BALANCED FUNDS

SOURCE: MORNINGSTAR ONDISC

Risk Category	Standard Deviation	5 Year Annualized	1995 Return	1994 Return	1993 Return	1992 Return	1991 Return	1990 Return	1989 Return	1988 Return	1987 Return	1986 Return
Balanced Funds												
Primary emphasis on security selection; allocations between stocks and bonds relatively slow to change	7.3	13.0%	24.9%	−2.5%	11.6%	7.7%	26.0%	−0.9%	18.9%	13.1%	1.4%	16.7%
Asset Allocation Funds												
Primary emphasis on moving between stocks and bonds in response to changing economic conditions	6.9	12.5%	24.6%	−2.2%	12.0%	8.5%	22.2%	1.2%	16.6%	10.3%	3.0%	14.0%

aggressively. These funds are much more unpredictable because so much depends on how well the portfolio manager is handling this demanding chore.

In short, balanced funds have significant differences in strategy, portfolio allocations, and investing styles. That's why they don't fit neatly into my risk classification system. I think they are most useful for: (1) investors who don't have enough money to meet the fund minimums in order to diversify into several funds and fine-tune their own stock/bond mix; (2) dollar-cost-averaging strategies where you want to get both your stock and bond investing in one easy monthly purchase; and (3) investors who simply don't want to make the investment allocation decisions and are content to leave them with a portfolio manager.

Sector funds are special purpose stock funds that limit their investing to a specific segment of the marketplace.

Rather than gaining broad diversification, which is one of the main reasons for investing in mutual funds, investors in sector funds are buying into a restricted portfolio that restricts its reach to a particular industry or investing theme. When their particular industry is in favor, such funds really shine. But they have greater risk than regular stock funds because when tough times hit the industry in which the fund specializes, the fund manager can't switch into something else.

The most popular kinds of sector funds include such specialized investing themes as:

◆ Communications: Companies involved with communications, entertainment, publishing, and media industries; companies that are involved in the development, manufacture, or sale of communications equipment or services, including local or long-distance telephone service, or cellular, microwave, or cable businesses; companies that are engaged in and developing, constructing, or operating infrastructure projects; and companies that participate in technological advances in interactive services and products accessible through consumer-electronics devices.

◆ Financial services: Companies with significant lending operations, including money-center banks with international connections as well as regional banks that may benefit from changes in the banking industry; insurance companies; full-service and discount brokerages; and leasing companies.

◆ Health services: Companies that offer health-care services or produce health-related products, including medical research, pharmaceutical manufacturers, hospital management companies, nursing centers, medical and dental equipment manufacturers and suppliers, and hospital suppliers.

◆ Natural resources: Companies that primarily own, explore, mine, process, or otherwise develop natural resources, including minerals, timber, oil, natural gas, coal, uranium, water, and other such industries; suppliers of goods and services to such companies; oil exploration, refining, and marketing; natural gas production; and companies that may develop energy-efficiency technologies and other processing systems.

◆ Precious metals: Companies involved in mining, processing, fabricating, distributing, or otherwise dealing in gold, silver, or platinum; many also invest in gold and silver bullion, diamonds, and other precious metals and minerals.

◆ Real estate: Companies that derive revenues from the ownership, construction, management, or sales of residential, commercial, or industrial real-estate; companies whose products and services are related to the real-estate industry; companies whose securities consist of shares of real-estate investment trusts.

(continued on page 284)

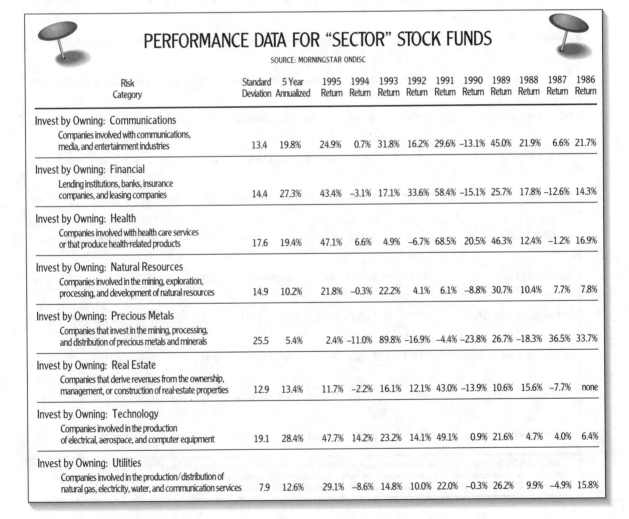

PERFORMANCE DATA FOR "SECTOR" STOCK FUNDS

SOURCE: MORNINGSTAR ONDISC

Risk Category	Standard Deviation	5 Year Annualized	1995 Return	1994 Return	1993 Return	1992 Return	1991 Return	1990 Return	1989 Return	1988 Return	1987 Return	1986 Return
Invest by Owning: Communications Companies involved with communications, media, and entertainment industries	13.4	19.8%	24.9%	0.7%	31.8%	16.2%	29.6%	–13.1%	45.0%	21.9%	6.6%	21.7%
Invest by Owning: Financial Lending institutions, banks, insurance companies, and leasing companies	14.4	27.3%	43.4%	–3.1%	17.1%	33.6%	58.4%	–15.1%	25.7%	17.8%	–12.6%	14.3%
Invest by Owning: Health Companies involved with health care services or that produce health-related products	17.6	19.4%	47.1%	6.6%	4.9%	–6.7%	68.5%	20.5%	46.3%	12.4%	–1.2%	16.9%
Invest by Owning: Natural Resources Companies involved in the mining, exploration, processing, and development of natural resources	14.9	10.2%	21.8%	–0.3%	22.2%	4.1%	6.1%	–8.8%	30.7%	10.4%	7.7%	7.8%
Invest by Owning: Precious Metals Companies that invest in the mining, processing, and distribution of precious metals and minerals	25.5	5.4%	2.4%	–11.0%	89.8%	–16.9%	–4.4%	–23.8%	26.7%	–18.3%	36.5%	33.7%
Invest by Owning: Real Estate Companies that derive revenues from the ownership, management, or construction of real-estate properties	12.9	13.4%	11.7%	–2.2%	16.1%	12.1%	43.0%	–13.9%	10.6%	15.6%	–7.7%	none
Invest by Owning: Technology Companies involved in the production of electrical, aerospace, and computer equipment	19.1	28.4%	47.7%	14.2%	23.2%	14.1%	49.1%	0.9%	21.6%	4.7%	4.0%	6.4%
Invest by Owning: Utilities Companies involved in the production/distribution of natural gas, electricity, water, and communication services	7.9	12.6%	29.1%	–8.6%	14.8%	10.0%	22.0%	–0.3%	26.2%	9.9%	–4.9%	15.8%

Performance Histories of Selected
Mortgage-Backed Bond Funds and Zero Coupon Bond Funds

Name of Fund	Nasdaq Ticker Symbol	Minimum Initial Purchase	Maximum Sales Charge	Number to Call for Information	Sharpe Ratio	3 Year Data Standard Deviation	Annualized Return	1995 Total Return	1994 Total Return	1993 Total Return
Benham GNMA Income	BGNMX	$1,000	No Load	800-331-8331	0.75	3.4	6.7%	15.8%	–1.7%	6.6%
Dreyfus Basic GNMA	DIGFX	$10,000	No Load	800-645-6561	1.08	3.5	7.9%	16.7%	–1.1%	8.8%
Fidelity Ginnie Mae	FGMNX	$2,500	No Load	800-544-8888	0.70	3.6	6.7%	16.6%	–2.0%	6.2%
Fidelity Mortgage Securities	FMSFX	$2,500	No Load	800-544-8888	1.47	2.9	8.4%	17.0%	1.9%	6.8%
T. Rowe Price GNMA	PRGMX	$2,500	No Load	800-638-5660	0.82	3.7	7.1%	17.8%	–1.6%	6.1%
USAA GNMA	USGNX	$3,000	No Load	800-382-8722	1.12	3.2	7.7%	16.8%	0.0%	7.1%
Vanguard F/I GNMA	VFIIX	$3,000	No Load	800-662-7447	0.85	3.5	7.1%	17.0%	–1.0%	5.9%
Wright Current Income	WCIFX	$1,000	No Load	800-888-9471	0.59	4.2	6.6%	17.5%	–3.3%	6.6%
Benham Target Maturity 2005	BTFIX	$1,000	No Load	800-331-8331	0.75	10.4	11.8%	32.6%	–9.4%	16.5%
Benham Target Maturity 2010	BTTNX	$1,000	No Load	800-331-8331	0.90	12.7	15.6%	42.1%	–12.0%	23.5%
Benham Target Maturity 2015	BTFTX	$1,000	No Load	800-331-8331	0.73	16.6	16.2%	52.7%	–14.2%	19.6%
Benham Target Maturity 2020	BTTTX	$1,000	No Load	800-331-8331	0.87	18.7	20.4%	61.3%	–17.7%	31.6%

Data source: Morningstar Mutual Funds. Copyright by Morningstar, Inc., 53 West Jackson Blvd., Chicago, IL 60604. (800) 876–5005. Although gathered from reliable sources, data accuracy and completeness cannot be guaranteed. Performance numbers reflect periods ending 12/31/95. These are not recommended funds per se, but are offered here as worthy of your consideration. Mutual fund policies are subject to change. Contact the fund for current information before you invest.

Performance Histories of Selected Tax-Free Municipal Bond Funds

Name of Fund	Nasdaq Ticker Symbol	Minimum Initial Purchase	Maximum Sales Charge	Number to Call for Information	Sharpe Ratio	3 Year Data Standard Deviation	Annualized Return	1995 Total Return	1994 Total Return	1993 Total Return
T. Rowe Price Tax-Free Short-Intm	PRFSX	$2,500	No Load	800-638-5660	0.38	1.9	4.9%	8.1%	0.3%	6.3%
USAA Tax Exempt Short-Term	USSTX	$3,000	No Load	800-382-8722	0.38	1.7	4.8%	8.1%	0.8%	5.5%
Vanguard Muni Limited-Term	VMLTX	$3,000	No Load	800-662-7447	0.40	2.0	4.9%	8.5%	0.1%	6.3%
T. Rowe Price Tax-Free Interm-Term	PTIBX	$2,500	No Load	800-638-5660	0.73	4.5	7.4%	13.0%	−2.6%	12.7%
USAA Tax Exempt Interm-Term	USATX	$3,000	No Load	800-382-8722	0.62	4.9	7.2%	15.1%	−4.0%	11.5%
Vanguard Muni Interm-Term	VWITX	$3,000	No Load	800-662-7447	0.74	4.5	7.4%	13.6%	−2.1%	11.6%
Schwab Long-Term Tax-Free	SWNTX	$1,000	No Load	800-526-8600	0.52	6.7	7.6%	18.1%	−6.9%	13.4%
Scudder Managed Muni Bonds	SCMBX	$1,000	No Load	800-225-2470	0.53	6.5	7.5%	16.8%	−6.0%	13.3%
Vanguard Muni Long-Term	VWLTX	$3,000	No Load	800-662-7447	0.60	6.9	8.3%	18.7%	−5.8%	13.5%
SteinRoe High-Yield Munis	SRMFX	$2,500	No Load	800-338-2550	0.63	5.5	7.6%	17.5%	−4.0%	10.5%
T. Rowe Price Tax-Free High Yield	PRFHX	$2,500	No Load	800-638-5660	0.77	5.0	8.0%	16.6%	−4.4%	13.0%
Vanguard Muni High-Yield	VWAHX	$3,000	No Load	800-662-7447	0.60	6.6	8.1%	18.1%	5.1%	12.7%

Performance Histories of Selected Balanced Funds and Asset Allocation Funds

Name of Fund	Nasdaq Ticker Symbol	Minimum Initial Purchase	Maximum Sales Charge	Number to Call for Information	Sharpe Ratio	3 Year Data Standard Deviation	3 Year Data Annualized Return	1995 Total Return	1994 Total Return	1993 Total Return
Dodge & Cox Balanced	DODBX	$2,500	No Load	800-621-3979	1.64	6.6	14.9%	28.0%	2.1%	16.0%
Dreyfus Balanced	DRBAX	$2,500	No Load	800-645-6561	1.92	4.6	13.0%	25.0%	4.0%	10.8%
Founders Balanced	FRINX	$1,000	No Load	800-525-2440	1.73	6.7	15.6%	29.4%	−1.9%	21.8%
Janus Balanced	JABAX	$1,000	No Load	800-525-8983	1.34	5.7	11.8%	27.3%	−0.8%	10.6%
Vanguard/Wellesley Balanced	VWINX	$3,000	No Load	800-662-7447	1.24	6.5	12.2%	28.9%	−4.4%	14.6%
Vanguard/Wellington Balanced	VWELX	$3,000	No Load	800-662-7447	1.42	7.3	14.5%	32.9%	−0.5%	13.5%
Crabbe Huson Asset Alloc	CHAAX	$2,000	No Load	800-541-9732	1.30	6.1	12.1%	20.2%	−0.8%	18.2%
General Securities Asset Alloc	GSECX	$500	No Load	800-577-9217	1.66	5.2	12.7%	27.9%	5.4%	6.2%
Invesco Total Return Asset Alloc	FSFLX	$1,000	No Load	800-525-8085	1.58	6.2	14.0%	28.6%	2.5%	12.4%
Strong Asset Allocation	STAAX	$250	No Load	800-368-1030	1.38	5.1	11.2%	22.0%	−1.5%	14.5%
Valley Forge Asset Alloc	VAFGX	$1,000	No Load	800-548-1942	1.51	4.6	11.1%	10.6%	5.9%	17.1%
Vanguard Asset Allocation	VAAPX	$3,000	No Load	800-662-7447	1.41	7.4	14.5%	35.5%	−2.3%	13.5%

Performance Histories of Selected
Communications, Financial Services, and Health Services Sector Funds

Name of Fund	Nasdaq Ticker Symbol	Minimum Initial Purchase	Maximum Sales Charge	Number to Call for Information	3 Year Data Sharpe Ratio	Standard Deviation	Annualized Return	1995 Total Return	1994 Total Return	1993 Total Return
Fidelity Select Develop Communic	FSDCX	$2,500	3.00%	800-544-8888	0.93	18.3	21.2%	17.4%	15.1%	31.8%
Fidelity Select Multimedia	FBMPX	$2,500	3.00%	800-544-8888	1.66	12.1	24.3%	33.7%	4.0%	38.0%
Fidelity Select Telecommunications	FSTCX	$2,500	3.00%	800-544-8888	1.45	11.4	20.6%	29.7%	4.3%	29.7%
UST Master Commun & Entertmt	UMCEX	$500	4.50%	800-446-1012	1.15	14.2	20.5%	24.9%	1.2%	38.2%
Fidelity Select Home Finance	FSVLX	$2,500	3.00%	800-544-8888	1.63	13.5	26.1%	53.5%	2.7%	27.3%
Fidelity Select Regional Banks	FSRBX	$2,500	3.00%	800-544-8888	1.08	12.6	17.8%	46.8%	0.2%	11.2%
Hancock Regional Bank A	FRBAX	$1,000	5.00%	800-225-5291	1.73	10.2	21.8%	48.6%	0.5%	21.1%
PaineWebber Regional Finance	PREAX	$1,000	4.50%	800-647-1568	1.28	10.4	17.4%	47.7%	−0.8%	10.3%
Fidelity Select Health Care	FSPHX	$2,500	3.00%	800-544-8888	1.25	14.3	22.0%	45.9%	21.4%	2.4%
Franklin Global Health Care	FKGHX	$100	4.50%	800-342-5236	1.17	16.3	23.3%	54.6%	14.2%	6.2%
Medical Research Investment	MRIFX	$200	No Load	800-262-6631	1.44	14.0	24.3%	61.2%	−6.4%	27.3%
Vanguard Specialized Health Care	VGHCX	$3,000	No Load	800-662-7447	1.37	12.4	21.1%	45.2%	9.5%	11.8%

Data source: Morningstar Mutual Funds. Copyright by Morningstar, Inc., 53 West Jackson Blvd., Chicago, IL 60604. (800) 876–5005. Although gathered from reliable sources, data accuracy and completeness cannot be guaranteed. Performance numbers reflect periods ending 12/31/95. These are not recommended funds per se, but are offered here as worthy of your consideration. Mutual fund policies are subject to change. Contact the fund for current information before you invest.

Performance Histories of Selected
Natural Resources, Precious Metals, and Real Estate Sector Funds

Name of Fund	Nasdaq Ticker Symbol	Minimum Initial Purchase	Maximum Sales Charge	Number to Call for Information	3 Year Data Sharpe Ratio	3 Year Data Standard Deviation	3 Year Data Annualized Return	1995 Total Return	1994 Total Return	1993 Total Return
Fidelity Advisors Global Resources	FAGNX	$2,500	4.75%	800-522-7297	1.33	12.0	20.1%	28.7%	–2.3%	37.9%
Fidelity Select Paper & Forest	FSPFX	$2,500	3.00%	800-544-8888	0.86	16.4	18.2%	22.0%	14.1%	18.6%
T. Rowe Price New Era Fund	PRNEX	$2,500	No Load	800-638-5660	1.11	8.5	13.6%	20.8%	5.2%	15.3%
Vanguard Specialized Energy	VGENX	$3,000	No Load	800-662-7447	0.77	15.4	15.9%	25.3%	–1.6%	26.4%
Fidelity Precious Metals	FDPMX	$2,500	3.00%	800-544-8888	0.81	27.6	26.5%	–3.3%	–1.1%	111.6%
Midas	EMGSX	$500	No Load	800-400-6432	0.95	28.3	31.1%	36.7%	–17.1%	98.8%
Scudder Gold	SCGDX	$1,000	No Load	800-225-2470	0.67	21.5	18.6%	13.2%	–7.4%	59.4%
United Services World Gold	UNWPX	$1,000	No Load	800-873-8637	0.64	28.2	22.3%	15.9%	–16.9%	89.8%
Vanguard Specialized Gold	VGPMX	$3,000	No Load	800-662-7447	0.62	26.4	20.4%	–4.5%	–5.4%	93.4%
Cohen & Steers Realty Shares	CSRSX	$10,000	No Load	800-437-9912	0.65	13.0	12.6%	11.1%	8.3%	18.8%
Fidelity Real Estate Investments	FRESX	$2,500	No Load	800-544-8888	0.36	11.9	8.4%	10.9%	2.0%	12.5%
Templeton Real Estate Securities	TEMRX	$100	5.75%	800-292-9293	0.57	8.9	9.2%	6.0%	–7.7%	33.0%

Performance Histories of Selected
Advanced Technology and Utilities Sector Funds

Name of Fund	Nasdaq Ticker Symbol	Minimum Initial Purchase	Maximum Sales Charge	Number to Call for Information	3 Year Data			1995 Total Return	1994 Total Return	1993 Total Return
					Sharpe Ratio	Standard Deviation	Annualized Return			
Fidelity Select Computers	FDCPX	$2,500	3.00%	800-544-8888	1.59	18.2	33.0%	51.7%	20.5%	28.9%
Fidelity Select Electronics	FSELX	$2,500	3.00%	800-544-8888	1.80	18.8	37.9%	69.4%	17.2%	32.1%
Fidelity Select Software & Comp	FSCSX	$2,500	3.00%	800-544-8888	1.18	17.6	24.9%	46.1%	0.4%	32.7%
Invesco Strategic Technology	FTCHX	$1,000	No Load	800-525-8085	1.15	14.5	20.9%	45.8%	5.3%	15.0%
T. Rowe Price Science & Technology	PRSCX	$2,500	No Load	800-638-5660	1.55	17.2	30.8%	55.5%	15.8%	24.2%
United Science & Technology	UNSCX	$500	5.75%	800-366-5465	1.23	15.1	22.8%	55.6%	9.8%	8.5%
Fidelity Select Utilities Growth	FSUTX	$2,500	3.00%	800-544-8888	0.86	9.0	11.9%	34.4%	−7.4%	12.5%
Fidelity Utilities	FIUIX	$2,500	No Load	800-544-8888	0.98	8.7	12.7%	30.6%	−5.3%	15.6%
Global Utility A Fund	GLUAX	$1,000	5.00%	800-225-1852	0.95	8.1	11.8%	23.4%	−7.9%	22.9%
Invesco Strategic Utilities	FSTUX	$1,000	No Load	800-525-8085	0.88	7.8	11.0%	25.3%	−9.9%	21.2%
MFS Utilities A Fund	MMUFX	$1,000	4.75%	800-637-2929	1.39	7.8	14.9%	32.5%	−4.9%	20.5%
Vanguard Specialized Utilities	VGSUX	$3,000	No Load	800-662-7447	0.96	8.4	12.1%	34.0%	−8.6%	15.1%

◆ Technology: Companies involved in aerospace components, electrical equipment, computer electronics, and precision instruments; companies that provide systems-level software, applications software, time-sharing services, computer consulting services, or other related goods and services; companies that may be engaged in providing information services, or the development, manufacture, sales, or servicing of information-age products; and companies expected to benefit from technological advances and improvements.

◆ Utilities: Companies which produce and deliver electricity, natural gas, telephone, and telecommunication services.

Due to their occasionally eye-popping results, these funds continue to grow in popularity, surpassing $60 billion in assets in 1995. Because of their lack of flexibility, however, sector funds are considered to carry high risk. For that reason, I suggest that only experienced investors should consider sector funds for inclusion in their portfolios.

Utility funds are sector funds. Are they high risk?

In light of their reputation for being conservative investments, should utility funds be lumped in with the volatile precious metals funds? Obviously not all sector groups carry equal risk, but utilities may have more risk than you think. Due to deregulation, they've slowly been losing their protected status. Competition is doing what it always does in free markets—offering better service and pricing for consumers and a more challenging and threatening environment for the producers.

There are three major kinds of utility companies, each with its own risk profile. *Electric companies* pay the highest dividends but have the weakest growth prospects. Standard & Poor's recently raised the standards that it uses in its debt-ratings formula for electric utilities, saying the sector is in a long-term decline. It will be difficult for their historically high dividend rates to be maintained in the face of increased competition. *Natural gas* stocks offer average dividends and good long-term growth. Natural gas is clean-burning and in abundant supply—seemingly well positioned to be the energy source of the future. *Telecommunications companies* generally pay the lowest dividends but have the greatest growth potential. Many are on the cutting edge of the "information highway" and have share prices that act more like high-tech stocks than the utilities of old.

This should help you understand why all utility funds are not alike in terms of risk or reward. For the ten years ending December 1995, the best performing utility fund gained 13.1% versus just 4.1% per year for the worst. So, as in other risk categories, fund selection is still the key element in investing success. ◆

CHAPTER PREVIEW

Earthquake Watch:
Staying Ahead of Inflation

I. **Inflation is the greatest long-term threat to your financial well-being.**

   A. Inflation can be caused either by imbalances in supply and demand in the marketplace, or — as in the case in the U.S. over the past quarter century — by a government's mismanagement of the currency.

   B. Inflation is a subtle form of taxation where the government gains spendable funds at the expense of the citizens, whose money and savings decline in value.

   C. The most commonly cited measure of inflation is the consumer price index.

II. **If there is a financial crisis ("economic earthquake"), it will take one of two forms — either a deflationary depression or a hyperinflationary collapse.**

   A. An investment portfolio that is well suited for a deflationary depression would be devastated by hyperinflation, and vice versa.

   B. The best way to prepare for a crisis is to progress through the Four Levels and build your financial strength, flexibility, and understanding of which kinds of investments do best under each scenario.

III. **"Tangible" assets generally perform well during periods of accelerating inflation. Investors prefer them when the future is uncertain.**

   A. Tangible assets are things you can own that *have practical uses in daily life.* This group includes farmland, housing, commercial real estate, crude oil, precious metals, and diamonds.

   B. We take a look at the historical performance of various categories of assets in relation to inflation over the past quarter century. Among them are: Treasury bills, long-term corporate bonds, common stocks, gold, silver, commercial real estate, single-family homes, and farmland.

   C. The merits of investing in gold and real estate are discussed in greater detail.

IV. **Many experts believe that deflation is as likely as inflation. Investors should remain alert for either scenario.**

What is inflation? That's easy—it's when your money doesn't buy as much as it used to. What causes it? That's not so easy.

Few questions in the field of economics give rise to as much disagreement and heated discussion. There are two competing schools of thought. One view sees inflation as resulting from the usual supply and demand forces in the marketplace. For example, if supply can be controlled, then a monopoly (the post office) or trade cartel (OPEC oil) can raise prices as it wishes. Occasionally the supply is limited by natural events, like when a flood or drought devastates food crops. Or, perhaps the cost of producing the supply is increased (unions demand higher wages or costly environmental regulations are imposed) and the cost gets passed on to the consumer.

On the demand side, intense consumer interest (Mazda Miata, see pages 239-240) means prices are gradually bid up. One recurring example is the demand for tickets to high-profile sporting events like the Super Bowl or the NCAA Final Four Basketball Championship, which is so strong that scalpers are able to charge outrageous prices to determined, cash-carrying fans.

The opposing view sees the problem of inflation as caused primarily by the amount and kind of currency in circulation. Nobel Laureate Milton Friedman, the best-known spokesman for the "monetarist" school, has said, "Inflation is always and everywhere a monetary problem." In other words, over the long term, the problem lies not in the marketplace but in the manner in which the government manages the currency.

In addition to Friedman, who's concerned primarily about *increases in the quantity* of money, there are those who are concerned about the *poor quality* of our money. They are opposed to government-printed paper money that is not convertible into anything else. They consider our currency to be "fiat" money because it has no intrinsic value. Nor is it convertible into anything else (like silver or gold) that does have intrinsic value. Dollars are "money" only because the government says they're money. This group would like to return to a form of the gold standard where there is an anchor that provides the discipline needed to keep the price of the currency stable.

History has several compelling accounts that give credence to the concerns of the monetarists. Here's an excerpt from one such episode as retold in John Train's fascinating and highly instructive little book *Famous Financial Fiascos:*

> By 1789 France was once again in financial straits because of military costs, royal extravagance, and the chaos that came with the Revolution. Gold and silver currency was disappearing from circulation, as the public hoarded it in fear of some new catastrophe. After passionate discussion the Assemblee finally decreed the issuance of 400 million livres' worth of assignats — government notes secured by the estates of the Church. They bore a three percent interest rate. Under the impact of this stimulus, business did pick up. Unfortunately the government, as always, instantly found a thousand uses for

its financial windfall, and within only five months was back clamoring for more. By a close vote, in September 1789 the Assemblee decreed the issue of another 800 million livres, this time in noninterest-bearing notes. It was solemnly specified that the total of notes in circulation must never, never exceed 1.2 billion livres.

Alas, easy money is addictive. Only nine months after this issue a new one was voted, of 600 million livres, and in December 1791 another, of 300 million. The following April came another, of 300 million, making a total of 2.4 billion in circulation. As the torrent of paper poured out of the presses, silver and gold coins vanished, goods were hoarded, and prices flew upward. Price controls were instituted, under the so-called Law of the Maximum. In response, as always, farmers and manufacturers decreased their output. As a result many towns had to initiate rationing. In 1794, assignats in circulation reached 7 billion; by May 1795, 10 billion; two months later, 14 billion — ten times over the 1.2 billion limit set four years earlier. Finally, in 1797, all assignats and mandats were repudiated and became essentially worthless. At Bonaparte's first cabinet meeting after he became consul he was asked what was to be done. "I will pay cash or pay nothing," he replied. And so he did. He never went back to paper money.

The phenomenon described by Train is called hyperinflation. It is caused by an extremely rapid growth in the supply of paper money. Hyperinflation happens when a government regularly issues large quantities of new money in order to pay for ever-increasing levels of government spending. If all of this sounds too familiar for comfort, you now understand why some in our country are sounding the alarm and trying to arouse a lethargic American public concerning the dangers of our governments' out-of-control spending habits. Inflation, generally speaking, is a subtle form of taxation where the government gains new money at the expense of the citizens whose money and savings decline in value. Hyperinflation has the effect, therefore, of an incredibly large and devastating tax.

Inflation is not well understood by the general public.
We think of it as meaning things cost more. Actually, it happens . . .

. . . when our currency is worth less. As the government "inflates" the number of dollars being passed around by printing billions and billions more than is justified by America's real economic growth, the value of each individual dollar is diluted. This is what decades of federal government deficit spending have accomplished. So the problem is more accurately described as one of "shrinkage."

Shown on the next page is a picture of the purchasing power of the dollar as it has changed over the past 200 years. When the line is falling, the dollar is buying less. In other words, we're experiencing inflation. When the line is rising, the dollar buys more — we're experiencing deflation. A quick look at the

Gold Standard
is a monetary system under which units of currency, in our case dollars, are convertible into fixed amounts of gold. That means that for every dollar printed and put into circulation, the U.S. government theoretically has gold in storage to back it up (in case someone wants to exchange his paper money for "the real thing"). Of course, since not everyone holding dollars is likely to show up on the same day and ask to swap paper currency for gold, governments always have a little room to cheat by printing more money than the amount of gold on hand justifies. Even so, the fact that there is a finite, measurable, limited amount of gold in storage means there are limits even to this form of "inflating" the currency. Eventually, there can be no further increase in printed money without a meaningful increase in the amount of gold in storage.

For the first 140 years of our history, the U.S. was on a gold standard. In 1933, Roosevelt got Congress to pass legislation that made it illegal for American citizens to even own gold, let alone try to swap paper dollars for it. The greatly reduced demand for gold that resulted cleared the way for the government to irresponsibly print even more paper currency (now called "federal reserve notes" rather than gold certificates). The U.S. government continued to allow foreign governments to exchange any dollars they might have for gold, but even this practice was discontinued in 1971. The last restraint on the government's unrestricted use of its money printing presses was gone.

graph shows that inflation clearly runs in cycles. There are times when it's a problem and times when it disappears altogether. In fact, there are periods spanning decades where deflation is the rule. It's also obvious, beginning with the War of 1812 and following through all the way to the Vietnam era, that the economic strains caused by fighting wars consistently lead to high inflation.

It is instructive to divide the 200 years of inflation data into three parts.

(1) 1792–1933: Over the course of our first 140 years, during which time we were on some form of gold standard, we experienced overall price stability. Despite the occasional disruptions caused by wars, prices eventually returned to "normal." Inflation averaged a mere 0.3% per year.

(2) 1933–1971: FDR and his policymakers believed that raising the Treasury's gold price (in effect, devaluing the dollar) would help stimulate the economy. In effect, they thought an unusually high level of government spending could lead us out of the Great Depression. To facilitate this, laws were passed that called in all the gold coins in circulation, eliminated the convertibility of paper currency into gold, made the hoarding of gold illegal, and prohibited the exporting of gold. This gave the Federal Reserve monopoly control of the printing presses

THE DECLINE AND FALL OF THE AMERICAN DOLLAR
200 YEARS OF THE INFLATIONARY/DEFLATIONARY CYCLE
SOURCE: THE MYTHS OF INFLATION AND INVESTING BY STEVEN LEUTHOLD / 1792 = $1.00

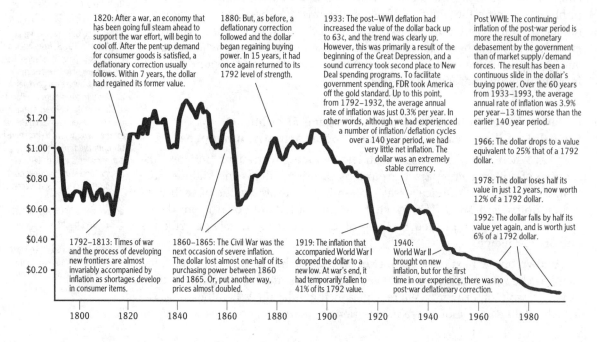

1820: After a war, an economy that has been going full steam ahead to support the war effort, will begin to cool off. After the pent-up demand for consumer goods is satisfied, a deflationary correction usually follows. Within 7 years, the dollar had regained its former value.

1880: But, as before, a deflationary correction followed and the dollar began regaining buying power. In 15 years, it had once again returned to its 1792 level of strength.

1933: The post–WWI deflation had increased the value of the dollar back up to 63¢, and the trend was clearly up. However, this was primarily a result of the beginning of the Great Depression, and a sound currency took second place to New Deal spending programs. To facilitate government spending, FDR took America off the gold standard. Up to this point, from 1792–1932, the average annual rate of inflation was just 0.3% per year. In other words, although we had experienced a number of inflation/deflation cycles over a 140 year period, we had very little net inflation. The dollar was an extremely stable currency.

Post WWII: The continuing inflation of the post-war period is more the result of monetary debasement by the government than of market supply/demand forces. The result has been a continuous slide in the dollar's buying power. Over the 60 years from 1933–1993, the average annual rate of inflation was 3.9% per year–13 times worse than the earlier 140 year period.

1966: The dollar drops to a value equivalent to 25% that of a 1792 dollar.

1978: The dollar loses half its value in just 12 years, now worth 12% of a 1792 dollar.

1992: The dollar falls by half its value yet again, and is worth just 6% of a 1792 dollar.

1792–1813: Times of war and the process of developing new frontiers are almost invariably accompanied by inflation as shortages develop in consumer items.

1860–1865: The Civil War was the next occasion of severe inflation. The dollar lost almost one-half of its purchasing power between 1860 and 1865. Or, put another way, prices almost doubled.

1919: The inflation that accompanied World War I dropped the dollar to a new low. At war's end, it had temporarily fallen to 41% of its 1792 value.

1940: World War II brought on new inflation, but for the first time in our experience, there was no post-war deflationary correction.

$1.20
$1.00
$0.80
$0.60
$0.40
$0.20

1800 1820 1840 1860 1880 1900 1920 1940 1960 1980

while simultaneously taking away the right of U.S. citizens to exchange the Fed's paper money for gold. During this period, inflation averaged 3.0% per year.

Although U.S. citizens could not exchange dollars for gold, foreign governments still could—one ounce of gold for every $35. The "gold window" was the place where these dollar redemptions took place. However, throughout the 1960s, the U.S. found itself increasingly burdened by the costs of: serving as the primary military defender of the West, the space program, the Great Society social welfare programs, and the war in Vietnam. The country could not afford them all. To pay our bills, we either borrowed or printed what we needed. The result was that we were sending billions of gold-backed dollars overseas *for which we had no gold.*

(3) 1971–the present: By 1971, foreigners held over $300 billion, but the U.S. had just $14 billion in gold reserves to back them up. In his fascinating book *The Death of Money*, economist Joel Kurtzman gives this account of our "solution" to this problem and the ramifications that followed:

> *President Nixon announced that he had closed the gold window. This represented the biggest challenge to the world economy since the Great Depression; it meant the value of the dollar was no longer linked to the amount of gold in Fort Knox. It was a change of monumental proportions. . . .*
>
> *By closing the gold window, Nixon destroyed the carefully crafted Bretton Woods system. His actions also precipitated a monetary crisis around the world and threw the world's credit markets into chaos. Within a week the value of the dollar decreased by more than 17% against the world's other major currencies. At the same time, prices on the world's stock and bond markets gyrated up and down as the world's money managers tried to assess the consequences of the new floating non-system. For the world's finance ministers the new uncertainty and financial volatility was too much. Within one day of Nixon's announcement they temporarily shut down the world's largest foreign-exchange markets. . . .*
>
> *On August 15, 1971, money — in the old sense, the traditional sense — was repealed. Nixon transformed it into something totally new, a currency without any underlying value whatsoever and without any limitations on the government's ability to create it. Nixon turned money — traditionally a symbol of real, tangible wealth — into a twisted abstraction. "The dollar has become a circular argument," said R. David Ranson, chief economist of Wainwright Economics in Boston. "It is still a promise to pay. But to pay what to whom?" That remains a vexing question to this day.*[1]

Without the discipline imposed by the gold standard, there was nothing left to prevent the federal government from printing as much money as it could dream up ways to spend (which is more or less what it has been doing ever since). The picture has been one of continual inflation (i.e., a continual decline in the purchasing power of the dollar). During the 1972-1995 period, inflation averaged 5.6% a year. The dollar bought about one-fourth as much at the end of this period as it did at the beginning.

[1] Joel Kurtzman, The Death of Money, [New York: Simon & Schuster, 1993], pp. 51–60.

INFLATION IN THE U.S.
OVER THE PAST 50 YEARS

This table is based on the 1982–84 series of consumer prices. That means the index uses the number "100" to represent the average cost of living during those years. One way of expressing the 1995 CPI reading of 153.5 is to say, "In 1995, it cost $153.50 to purchase what $100.00 would buy in mid-1983." Or, "In 1956, you could pay $27.60 to get what cost $100.00 in mid-1983."

End of	C.P.I 1982–84	Rate of Inflation	
1955	26.8	0.4%	
1956	27.6	3.0%	
1957	28.4	2.9%	**Deflation**
1958	28.9	1.8%	is when prices are
1959	29.4	1.7%	moving lower. This is
1960	29.8	1.4%	what many over-built
1961	30.0	0.7%	housing markets
1962	30.4	1.3%	experienced in the
1963	30.9	1.6%	1980s.
1964	31.2	1.0%	
1965	31.8	1.9%	In 1971, President
1966	32.9	3.5%	Nixon closed the gold
1967	33.9	3.0%	window, removing the
1968	35.5	4.7%	last restrictions on the
1969	37.7	6.2%	government's ability to
1970	39.8	5.6%	increase the supply of
1971	41.1	3.3%	money at will. Serious
1972	42.5	3.4%	inflation problems
1973	46.2	8.7%	began soon thereafter.
1974	51.9	12.3%	
1975	55.5	6.9%	Accelerating inflation
1976	58.2	4.9%	is when the rate of
1977	62.1	6.7%	inflation is growing.
1978	67.7	9.0%	Prices are moving
1979	76.7	13.3%	higher each year at an
1980	86.3	12.5%	ever-increasing pace.
1981	94.0	8.9%	
1982	97.6	3.8%	
1983	101.3	3.8%	
1984	105.3	3.9%	
1985	109.3	3.8%	
1986	110.5	1.1%	
1987	115.4	4.4%	
1988	120.5	4.4%	
1989	126.1	4.6%	
1990	133.8	6.1%	**Disinflation**
1991	137.9	3.1%	is when the rate of
1992	141.9	2.9%	inflation is slowing.
1993	145.8	2.7%	Prices are still moving
1994	149.7	2.7%	higher, but not as
1995	153.5	2.5%	rapidly as they had been.

How is inflation measured?

We know that inflation means prices are going up, but *which* prices? Are we talking about the inflation facing the average household (a narrow measure) or the country as a whole (a very broad measure)? There are many ways inflation is measured and reported by the government.

The inflation indicator that is probably most familiar to us is the consumer price index (CPI). The government begins by choosing an assortment of items that the average household in urban areas is likely to buy during a year of spending. Economists call this a "fixed basket of goods and services." More than 100,000 items are in the basket, and it includes such everyday necessities as food, clothing, housing, transportation, medical care, education, and recreation. Each item in the basket doesn't carry equal weight, but is weighted according to estimated "spending patterns," that is, in proportion to the way households are thought to actually spend their money (e.g., housing costs count a lot more in the index than recreation costs).

The last time the government went through this start-up process was 1982-84 (which is referred to as the "base period"). Its inspectors hit the streets, visiting retail stores and service establishments to see what all the items in the basket were going to cost. The prices used are the actual transaction prices that consumers pay at the cash register, taking into account such factors as discounts and sales taxes. The prices were then tallied, and the total dollar cost of the basket was established. This dollar cost serves as *the basis of comparison* for all future price surveys.

Rather than report the actual dollar cost, however, the CPI for the base period is set at 100. (That's why you often see the notation associated with the CPI that "1982-84=100.") Each month thereafter, the government returns to the same businesses to obtain the current prices for the items in the basket. Those prices are then converted into their index equivalent. For example, at the end of 1995, the CPI was reported at 153.5. That means the fixed basket of goods and services that cost $100.00 in 1982-84 would cost $153.50 at the end of 1995.

By keeping the basket constant for years at a time, apples-to-apples comparisons can be made. A drawback of this, however, is that the CPI is not a true "cost-of-living" indicator. In real life, people's spending patterns are continually undergoing change. When consumers tighten their belts by substituting items whose prices have stayed low in place of items whose prices have risen, their cost-of-living goes down even though inflation may have gone up.

Unfortunately, the accuracy of the CPI has become suspect.

In 1995, members of Congress maintained that the CPI overstates inflation by anywhere from 0.5% to 1.0%. Bear in mind, however, that the government has a vested interest in keeping the "official" inflation rate as low as possible. That's because increases in the CPI cause changes in payments under all sorts of agreements ranging from labor contracts to Social Security and other pension benefits. Also, because higher inflation leads to higher interest rates, the cost of interest on the national debt can rise dramatically, making the federal budget deficit problem even worse.

These pressures may be the reason that government officials occasionally change the way the CPI is computed. Of course, they do this under the guise of making it more accurate or "representative." However, the changes always have the effect of lowering, rather than raising, the numbers. For example, in the 1980s they stopped including the cost of new automobiles in the CPI. The justification was that since new models always have improvements, you can't really compare a new car to last year's model. Besides, you don't buy a new car every year. Likewise, when housing payments began to rise, they took them out. Not everyone has a mortgage, they said.

This kind of tampering means that your "personal" inflation experience might be much higher than the "official" inflation rate. In fact, it is the contention of many in the private sector that the CPI understates the rate of inflation. Some economists maintain that the true rate of inflation has actually been much higher than the CPI numbers shown at the far left. For the decades of the 1970s and 1980s, one consulting firm calculated it to be 6% per year higher than reported by the government, the editor of the nation's largest financial newsletter for retirees placed the inflation rate at about 7.5% higher, and a national accounting firm came up with a number that was about 9% per year higher.

I don't know which view of the accuracy of the CPI is closer to the truth, but for the sake of consistency, I have used the CPI rate as released by the government when discussing and measuring inflation in this book.

In Larry Burkett's best-selling book of 1991, *The Coming Economic Earthquake*, he pointed out . . .

. . . that due to the explosive growth of our national debt over the previous fifteen years, a crisis was certain to come if the federal government didn't put

A Better Measure of Inflation
There is another inflation indicator that is more technical in nature and tracked primarily by economists. It's called the Gross Domestic Product implicit price deflator. What the CPI does at the household level, the price deflator attempts to do at the level of the entire economy. This is the most broadly based indicator of price changes. It includes not only the goods and services purchased by consumers, but also outlays having to do with government spending, capital investment, and international transactions as well.

Furthermore, rather than using the CPI technique of tracking a basket of goods and services that is fixed, this indicator reflects the changes in spending patterns from year to year. For example, if there is a shift in consumer spending this year where a greater proportion of resources are spent on health care than on transportation, and health care costs rise more than transportation costs do, then the price deflator will rise more sharply than the CPI. This is because the price deflator recognizes the shift in spending patterns and gives greater weight to health care while the CPI would keep the health care weighting constant.

This indicator comes closer to reflecting day-to-day experience because it reflects changes in the way money is being spent as well as price increases.

its financial house in order. He pointed out that there are two primary forms that any eventual crisis would take. One is a deflationary depression, similar to the 1930s. The other is a hyperinflationary collapse, similar to what happened in Germany in the early 1920s (and in France in the late 1700s, as we saw earlier in this chapter).

Ever since I read Larry's book, I have been building a library on this topic. I now have accumulated twenty-four books that discuss our current problems and theorize as to which kind of crisis we'll have. Of the books I have on hand, thirteen lean toward depression as the likely outcome, and eight lean toward hyperinflation. (Three say we will have neither, that boom times are in store!)

What I've read in these books reinforces what I already expected, namely that: (1) for every persuasive argument, there is a reasonable counter-argument by those who disagree, (2) the crisis, if it comes, is still several years away, and (3) it involves the entire global economy, not just America.

Inflation

Since 1972, inflation has averaged 5.6% per year. If you project this inflation rate over an extended period of time, say forty years, an hourly wage of $6 in 1995 would have to increase to $53 an hour in the year 2035 to be an equivalent wage. A $30,000 annual income would rise to $265,000, but that wouldn't get you very far toward your first house—the average cost of a new home would have risen to $1.2 million.

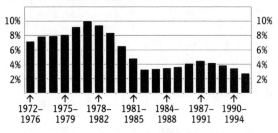

The world economy is presently undergoing massive structural changes. Will these changes have inflationary or deflationary consequences?

In my leisure time, I like to read "whodunit" mysteries to relax. But they pale in comparison to the complexity of one of the biggest mysteries in the world right now: What will be the economic effects of the fall of communism and the resultant rise of new free markets involving *billions* of people?

Core Rate of Inflation is the CPI with the volatile food and energy items removed because they tend to create short-term distortions. In 1990, for example, the core rate was lower than the CPI. This means that food and energy costs rose faster in price than the other CPI items, probably due to the Gulf War. The next year, after the war, the trend reversed.

Many observers consider it inflationary, that is, it will have the effect of raising prices worldwide. For example, consider the implications for the price of crude oil. The populations of poor Asian countries use less than one barrel of oil per person per year. The usage in industrialized countries typically falls into the ten to fifteen barrels per person range. As poorer nations prosper under capitalism, they will be able to afford more of the conveniences and industrial uses that oil offers. If the economies of China and India could grow over the next decade so as to afford just four barrels per person—only half of what Mexico uses—that would add more than *six billion barrels per year* to world demand. Similar projections could be centered around other categories like housing, cars, and consumer durables. The new demand coming on-stream for the raw materials needed to produce these items will be enormous, and it's reasonable to expect their prices to rise in response.

On the other hand, most experts seem to be focusing on the strong deflationary effects. The labor costs in these emerging markets are extremely low relative to those in the West. When combined with the rapid advances in technology we're seeing on so many fronts, the costs of labor in our "global village" are under relentless downward pressure. We already see this in the computer industry price wars, where the costs of purchasing raw computing power continue to spiral downward. This has ominous implications for traditional forms of employment both in factories and offices.

If we knew how these conflicting pressures will work themselves out, it would greatly simplify our planning!

An investment portfolio that is well suited for a deflationary depression would be devastated by hyperinflation, and vice versa. That means you can't institute changes *now* that will protect you "no matter what." There is no short-term fix; there is only long-term commitment. You must progress through the Four Levels and build your financial strength, flexibility, and understanding of which kinds of investments do best under each scenario.

Up to this point in the book, I've primarily focused on "financial" assets (also called "paper" assets) like stocks and bonds. Financial assets can be valuable *only because of what they represent*. If you own stock or a bond issued by a company that goes out of business, your investment "isn't worth the paper it's written on."

Now let's turn to "tangible" assets (also referred to as "hard" assets). Tangible assets are things you can own that *have practical uses in daily life*. This group includes farmland, housing, commercial real estate, crude oil, precious metals, and diamonds. When you acquire ownership of something that has a practical usefulness, that asset becomes your new "money." Unlike paper dollars, it has intrinsic value that stems from the practical ways it can be used. Land can grow crops, a house can provide shelter, metals have industrial uses, and oil is needed worldwide on a massive scale. You have broken the chain that linked you to the fate of the dollar. When you convert a tangible asset back into dollars, it will be valued in terms of what the dollar is worth *at that time*. If you have invested wisely, the amount of dollars you get back when you sell your ownership rights will have at least as much, and hopefully more, *purchasing power* as the dollars you spent to acquire it in the first place.

HOW DIFFERENT KINDS OF INVESTMENTS HOLD THEIR VALUE

TYPE OF INVESTMENT	HYPERINFLATION	DEPRESSION
Cash assets like bank savings, CDs, money market funds, and bonds	Generally poor	Generally good
Common stocks	Some good, some poor	Generally poor
Foreign currencies	Generally good	Some good, some poor
Tangible assets like real estate, farm land, gold, silver, oil, and diamonds	Generally good	Generally poor

Investors hold financial assets when they have confidence in the future; they tend to prefer tangible assets when the future is less certain. The graphs below compare the two groups over various five-year periods. You'll see that when inflation was high in the 1970s, tangible assets outperformed financial assets; the reverse was true after inflation was brought down in the 1980s. Adding a portion of tangible assets to a traditional stock and bond portfolio makes the returns more consistent (i.e., lowers the risk) while also providing a more effective insurance policy against inflation.

Too many investors spend the bulk of their time focusing on which *individual* investments to buy. This is a mistake. If inflation begins heating up, spend more time reading and thinking about *how you want to divide your assets among the broad categories* rather than on which specific investments are best *within* those categories. Your allocation is the more strategic decision.

The rest of this chapter will be spent looking at various categories of investments and how good a job they have done over the past quarter century in keeping ahead of inflation.

Let me begin by explaining the graphs that will accompany our discussion. Each column in the graphs represents a five-year period. I construct them this way because price behavior can change quickly from year to year. Such volatility makes graphs based on one-year periods more difficult to interpret because they seem so erratic. Using multi-year periods evens things out,

TANGIBLE ASSETS AND INFLATION

Adding a small percentage of tangible assets to one's portfolio can improve the likelihood of keeping ahead of inflation over a five-year period, while reducing overall risk. In the three graphs below, each column represents a five-year period, beginning on the far left with the period 1973–1977 and continuing across to the 1988–1992 period on the far right. The shaded area that appears in the background represents the rate of inflation during the various five-year periods. Note that while the average rates of return for the "financial assets" and "mixed assets" portfolios are comparable, the risk of the mixed portfolios is less than half that of the financial portfolios (standard deviation of 2.3 versus 4.8—see pages 213–215).

FINANCIAL ASSETS	TANGIBLE ASSETS	MIXED
50% STOCKS 50% BONDS	25% GOLD ◆ 25% SILVER 25% OIL ◆ 25% FARMLAND	40% STOCKS ◆ 40% BONDS ◆ 5% GOLD 5% SILVER ◆ 5% OIL ◆ 5% FARMLAND
AVERAGE 5 YEAR COMPOUNDED RATE OF RETURN: +12.1%	AVERAGE 5 YEAR COMPOUNDED RATE OF RETURN: + 7.2%	AVERAGE 5 YEAR COMPOUNDED RATE OF RETURN: +12.1%
STANDARD DEVIATION: 4.8	STANDARD DEVIATION: 10.2	STANDARD DEVIATION: 2.3

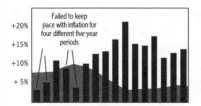

Failed to keep pace with inflation for four different five-year periods

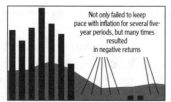

Not only failed to keep pace with inflation for several five-year periods, but many times resulted in negative returns

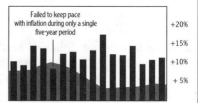

Failed to keep pace with inflation during only a single five-year period

and makes the longer-term trends and characteristics more apparent. Five years is a commonly used time frame among professionals.

The first graph in the series (which appears on page 292) is a picture of inflation as measured by the Consumer Price Index. The first column is for the five-year period that ran from the beginning of 1972 through the end of 1976. Inflation climbed at an average rate of 7.2% per year during this period (the individual years can be seen in the table on page 290). The graph shows the high rates of inflation we experienced in the 1970s, which peaked in 1979 at the previously unimaginable level of 13.3%.

It took strong action by the Federal Reserve—which led to a prime rate over 20% and the recession of 1981–1982—to break the inflationary spiral. It's surprising how quickly an inflationary environment can come to an end. For example, in 1919 and 1920 inflation ran 15% and 16% respectively. But this was followed by *deflation* the next two years as the excesses of the war economy were corrected. The disappearance of major inflation in 1981 was similarly sudden. By 1982, inflation was down to 3.8%. For the 1991–1995 period, inflation averaged 2.8% per year.

90 Day Treasury Bills

The baseline represents the rate of inflation. For example, a reading of 5% means 5% per year *better than inflation*, and so on. Fixed income investments have a spotty record against inflation. Treasury bills, the ultimate in safety and liquidity, returned an average of 7.3% per year from 1972–1995. Overall, this was 1.7% higher than inflation, but it masks an extended period in the 1970s when T-bills failed to generate any real returns.

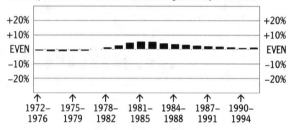

The remaining graphs in the series show the performance histories of various investment categories after taking inflation into account.

Such after-inflation returns are called "real" returns. Stated another way, a real return of zero means that an investment earned exactly the same return as the rate of inflation.

The two graphs at right picture the inflation-adjusted returns of two popular fixed-income investments. Generally speaking, they do best when inflation and interest rates are relatively low, which has been the situation for most of the past fifteen years. The graphs show that they do poorly during periods of rising rates and inflation, as we experienced from 1973-1981.

Long-Term Corporate Bonds

Longer maturities, although more volatile, produced overall better results. That's only true, however, for those bond investors who were able to hold onto their bonds until the inflationary spiral ended and interest rates returned to lower levels. Investors who bought in 1977 and sold at the end of 1981 would have lost 11.4% per year. However, when inflation is low, as it's been in recent years, long-term corporates have provided acceptable real returns.

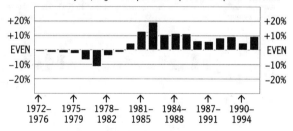

The next two graphs (page 296) show the after-inflation returns for common stocks. You can immediately see that stocks have been more consistently effective in protecting investors against inflation. Not only were there fewer five-year periods that failed to show real returns, but the magnitude of those returns was consistently greater, especially in the large stock category as represented by the S&P

500 index. The under-performing years on the left side of the graphs reflect the devastating 1973–74 bear market. Even the Crash of '87 failed to make a lasting dent in the stock market's long-term effectiveness as an inflation fighter.

These first four graphs depict the performance of paper assets against inflation. The remaining five (on pages 298-299) look at various tangible asset categories. Let's take a more in-depth look at two of these categories—gold and real estate.

It's important to understand that gold is not a particularly outstanding hedge against inflation per se.

The price of gold has essentially moved sideways since 1982 as it has moved up and down between $300 and $500 a troy ounce. (Troy weights are European in origin and still commonly used when weighing precious metals and gems. A troy ounce is about 10% heavier than a regular ounce.) We've had continuous inflation each and every year for the past three decades, and gold has barely kept pace. Gold is actually cheaper now than it was during most of 1980–1983, despite continuous inflation during this period.

The point I want to make is that it is a dramatic change in the *rate* of inflation that really brings gold to life. A consistent *level* of inflation, whether at 4% or 12%, will not put upward pressure on gold prices. As long as investors feel that they have a good handle on what inflation will be like two and three years down the road, they will rely on their customary savings and investing strategies. But when there is uncertainty, such as exists during periods of *rapidly accelerating changes* in the rate of inflation, confidence in conventional holdings is shaken and there is a flight to gold for safety. Gold appreciates in value when inflation is *worsening*.

As an illustration of this, the dramatic upmove in gold in the late 1970s corresponded almost identically with the accelerating growth in the rate of inflation at that time. When inflation rose from 6.5% to 13.5% in just three years, there was great concern as to how high it might go. As a result, gold moved from an average yearly price of $148 to $613 during the same period. When inflation peaked out in 1980, the price of gold did also. Once investors saw that the worst was over and that ever-

Stocks in Large, Blue Chip Companies

After failing terribly during the 1970s to outpace inflation, blue chip stocks (shown here as measured by the S&P 500 index) rebounded strongly during the 1980s and 1990s. The real returns shown here assume that all dividends were reinvested in additional shares. For the entire period, these stocks averaged 12.0% per year. Adjusting for annual inflation of 5.6%, that leaves average real returns of 6.4%.

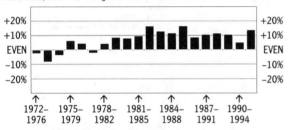

Stocks in Smaller, Growing Companies

There is a big difference between investing in established companies and smaller, newer ones. The risks are greater, but in recent years the big payoffs have been there. For the entire period, smaller company stocks (as measured by the Nasdaq Composite index) averaged just 9.7% per year. But over the past five years (1991–1995, column on far right), the average annual gain has been 23.0% before inflation, 20.2% after inflation.

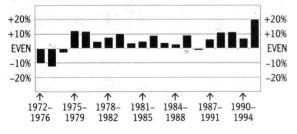

increasing changes in the rate of inflation (hyperinflation) were not a threat, the flight to gold ended.

We've just discussed what some analysts call the "macroeconomic" aspect to gold analysis. It focuses on the demand for gold only in terms of its role as a haven of safety during economic upheaval. But gold can also be evaluated just like corn, lumber, or any other commodity — based on its own "supply/demand" factors. How much is being produced from the mines? How much is being melted down from scrap? How much inventory is in warehouses? Then you consider the demand side. Who is doing the buying? How much do they want/need? Is it reasonable to believe they'll continue buying?

As this is being written in the summer of 1996, many longtime observers of the gold markets are very bullish because of their reading of these supply/demand factors. Among their arguments favoring higher gold prices, here are the ones most commonly cited.

◆ *Mine production appears to have peaked.* After a period of expanding production through the 1980s, production growth has recently slowed as old mines are becoming exhausted or rising costs make them unprofitable at today's gold price. Estimates indicate that it might take prices in the $500-$600 range to make it profitable for many mines to either continue in operation or increase their production.

◆ *Demand is growing.* In the developing nations of the Far East, there is often little confidence in a country's currency. Demand for gold is growing dramatically in countries like South Korea, Thailand, and Singapore. The Republic of China, where the currency is rapidly depreciating, is now the world's largest consumer of gold. Most experts agree that annual new demand will far exceed annual new supply for the next several years.

For More on Precious Metals

I rely on Silver and Gold Report for specific investment recommendations and "where-to-shop" information concerning the precious metals markets. For subscription information, telephone (800) 289-9222.

PRICE OF GOLD PER TROY OUNCE
BASED ON MONTH-END CLOSING PRICES DURING 1976–1996

◆ *The total market is relatively small compared to other assets.* The trading in gold futures, for example, is about a $6-$7 billion market. Compare this to $35-$40 billion each for both treasury and S&P 500 futures. Or consider that there is $3 trillion in CDs in the United States. Just a 1% shift in investors' thinking would send billions into gold, an impressive amount in such a relatively small market.

There are several unknowns that could throw a monkey wrench into the bulls' arguments for higher prices. It's the nature of investing that the most profitable plays come before all the pertinent information is known. Obtaining accurate information about all the factors concerning gold is particularly difficult. So keep in mind that gold is a volatile, high risk investment. No one has consistently forecasted gold prices correctly, and there have been many false starts along the way.

Many investors who bought gold as a hedge against inflation are disappointed and dispirited.

When the subject comes up, the conversation usually goes like this:

"Austin, I bought some gold years ago and it's gone nowhere since. Do you think I should sell it and invest the money somewhere else?"

"Well, that depends. Tell me, do you carry insurance on your house?"

"Of course. What's that have to do with it?"

"How many years have you carried homeowners insurance?"

"Since we bought our first home."

"Have you ever lost your home to a fire or any other catastrophe?"

"No, we've been fortunate. What's all this have to do with gold?"

"Don't you feel a little foolish having wasted thousands of dollars over the years by buying insurance that you ended up not needing?"

"Of course not. How was I to know I wouldn't need it?"

"Precisely! And gold is the same way. Think of it as financial insurance. You buy it because you want some protection against the economic catastrophe of hyperinflation. The good news is that you haven't needed it—yet. But that doesn't mean you've been foolish to hold it."

"But you haven't answered my question. You said whether I should sell it 'depends.' On what?"

"On whether you look at gold as insurance or an investment. If it's insurance, hold on to it. It still offers some protection, and unlike your homeowners insurance, it still has value. If you look at it as an investment, then you're on your own. I don't know what the price of gold will do in the next few years, and neither does anyone else."

Gold

Gold reached its highest price ever in 1980 when it sold for $850 per ounce. Following the 1980 rise and collapse, the price of gold has been on an erratic sideways course. Ironically, as a hedge against inflation (which is its primary investment attraction), gold has done poorly. It rallies in the face of *accelerating* inflation, not merely high inflation. It should be considered more as "insurance" against economic chaos than as an investment.

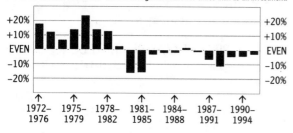

Silver

Silver was a great hedge against inflation throughout the 1970s, but a disaster through-out the 1980s, turning in a worse performance than gold. Silver experienced one of the greatest collapses in investment history in 1980 when it fell from an all-time high of over $50 per ounce in January to just over $10 an ounce two months later! Not until midway through the '90s has it even matched the rate of inflation (see 1991–1995 below).

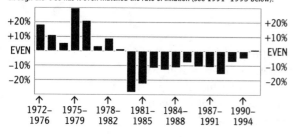

If you're interested in adding gold to your portfolio, I suggest you consider the following guidelines:

1. Use no-load funds to invest in mining companies rather than gold bullion itself.

2. Select gold funds that have low minimums (say $1,000) so you can more easily diversify into two or more funds. See page 282 for data on five precious metals funds worth investigating.

3. Read their prospectuses so you are familiar with their respective strengths and weaknesses.

4. Limit your eventual commitment to no more than 5%–10% of your total Level Four portfolio.

5. Expect volatility. Settle in for a long-term commitment.

Real estate is another tangible investment that can do well during periods of rising inflation.

Investors are on a real estate binge! Real estate investment trusts, known as REITs, are being formed and sold at a record pace. What are REITs, and should you consider them for your portfolio? Let's take a look.

Shares in REITs are traded like stocks (either on one of the major exchanges or in the over-the-counter market) and are bought and sold through brokers. Similar to mutual funds, REITs allow small investors to combine their money into a pool that will be invested by a team of real estate professionals. REITs typically invest in rental properties like apartments, retail shopping centers and malls, hotels, office buildings, and industrial parks, typically owning 20 to 100 properties in total. (About one of every ten invests primarily in mortgages where they loan money to others who take the ownership risks.) Most REITs have no predetermined life span; if a property is sold, another one is purchased to take its place.

The value of all properties held in REITs was estimated to exceed $100 billion at the end of 1995, five times what it was at the end of 1992. The growth has been fueled by the convergence of several factors.

Commercial Real Estate

Shortly after their introduction to the financial community, real estate investment trusts, on average, lost about 60% of their value during the recession of 1973–74. After their poor start, REITs turned in excellent returns over the next decade until the real estate slump that swept the country in the mid-1980s hit them for losses. Over the past five years (1991–1995), the average annual gain has been 16.6% before inflation, 13.8% after inflation.

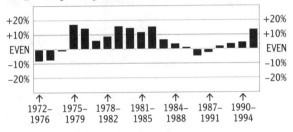

Single Family Housing

What a pleasant surprise to learn that our old friend, the family homestead, comes quite close to providing a consistent inflation hedge. Many experts feel the housing market shows promise but must be viewed only from a long-term perspective. For the entire period shown, the cost of the median new house climbed at an average rate of 6.0% per year. Adjusting for annual inflation of 5.6%, that leaves average real returns of 0.4%.

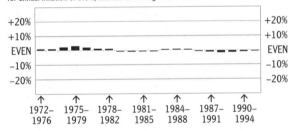

Farmland

Renting farmland for the growing of crops can yield as little as 1% or as high as 8%. The land's potential for appreciation will be the key determinant for the overall return of your investment. For the years shown, prices grew at a rate of 6.1% per annum, barely more than the rate of inflation. From 1983–1987, prices dropped about 25%. Only in 1995 did prices regain their 1982 levels. After inflation, however, they are only back up to 1974 levels.

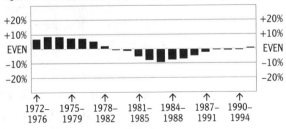

◆ The economy has been strengthening, which is good for occupancy rates. A robust economy can eventually lead to higher rents due to inflation adjustments as well as less available space on the market.

◆ Low interest rates meant that REITs could raise capital for about 6%-7% and deploy it into properties that returned 9%-10%. The resulting spread of 3% was high by historical standards.

◆ The weak real estate market of the 1987–1990 period resulted in many insurance companies and banks selling properties they had taken in foreclosure. It has been a buyer's market with bargains aplenty.

REITs offer several advantages.

Experienced management. As with any discipline that requires specialized skills, this is extremely important.

Diversification. Real estate doesn't move up and down in sync with the stock and bond markets. Thus, by adding a real estate component, you reduce the volatility in your overall holdings. Plus, with REITs you own a small piece of a large real estate portfolio that is invested in many different properties. This diversification spreads out the risk within your real estate component.

Liquidity. Unlike actual real estate, you can sell your holdings at any time.

Flexibility. Because share prices tend to be under $20, you can fine-tune your investment to the amount you desire.

High yields. REITs don't pay taxes as long as they pass at least 95% of their earnings through to their shareholders. This means they typically generate attractive yields of 6% and more while also offering the potential for capital gains when properties are sold.

Tax advantages. Those dividends typically include a substantial return of capital (say 30%) that is not taxable as current income. Rather, it reduces the investor's basis and is eventually taxed as a capital gain when the asset is sold.

For all their positives, REITs nevertheless carry considerable risk. Here are some potential problem areas.

Lateness of the hour. Because the boom has been going on for some time, the prices for some REITs have been driven to overvalued levels. Are there any "good deals" left?

Troubled properties. A large number of weak projects were bought with the expectation of a quick turnaround that didn't work out as expected. A great many of them are owned by REITs.

Inflation hedge is not automatic. Real estate prices will rise along with inflation *assuming* the real estate market is in equilibrium. If inflation hits at a time when the supply of real estate properties has outpaced the demand, landlords will not be able to pass rising costs along in the form of higher rents.

☞ High fees. Underwriting fees and brokers' commissions for new REITs can run 7%-10% of the amount raised. Plus, there are management fees as well.

☞ Amount and type of debt. REITs borrow to leverage their holdings, but too much debt lessens their stability. Also, if they've borrowed under low cost adjustable-rate agreements, rising interest rates can hurt their dividend payout.

Evaluating the merits of a REIT can be a daunting task. Is the management capable? Are the properties sound? Are they valued realistically? Is the debt load acceptable? Is the yield to investors sustainable? As you can see, there is a lot of homework associated with intelligently investing in real estate! That's why I believe the smartest way to go for the average investor is to turn the task over to a mutual fund that specializes in investing in REITs.

There are more than three dozen real estate funds. The three largest, shown in the table on page 282, are a good place to start your search. As with gold, I recommend holding real estate to no more than 5%-10% of your total investments. If the equity in your house represents a significant portion (one-third to one-half) of your net worth, you already have a major commitment to real estate and may not want to add any more for now. Remember, these are long-term investments suitable only for investors who are able to accept above-average risk. Although real estate is staging a comeback, it has a highly volatile price history.

Millions of baby boomers had to fight for their economic lives during the double-digit inflation of the seventies.

As inflation robbed the family paycheck of its purchasing power, household budgets were stretched to the breaking point. This led to dramatic changes in the financial landscape:

◆ Savers became market players. To get a better return, people moved their savings from low-paying bank savings accounts to the higher yields available through money market mutual funds. The brokerage and fund industries gained millions of new customers who would gradually be enticed into the investment markets.

◆ Houses became investments. As inflation made home ownership ever more costly, the family shelter became the financial asset of greatest value to most families. Buyers were encouraged to acquire the biggest house they could afford in order to maximize their gains.

◆ Thrift became foolish and debt became wise. Why save for next year when your dollars will buy 15% less? "Buy now and pay later" seemed smart because paying later meant paying with cheaper dollars. Consumer borrowing increased by a stunning 60% during the three years ending in 1978.

It's been almost fifteen years since inflation was a problem. But many of us, including financial professionals, are still expecting its unwelcome return.

Consider these headlines from recent years: "Get Ready for Inflation" *(Forbes,*

4/26/93); "Inflation Makes U.S. Markets No Place to Be" *(Barron's,* 4/4/94); and "The Growing Threat of Inflation" *(Fortune,* 1/16/95). Yet, there's a lot of economic data accumulating that suggests that deflation, not inflation, may be an equally serious risk in the U.S. economy. Commercial real estate prices have collapsed. The average-size house of today is 15% less expensive (after adjusting for inflation) than in 1979. Downsizing and layoffs have contributed to declining wages in real terms. At the time of this writing, growth prospects for 1996 were questionable. Auto sales are weak, leading Ford and Chrysler to cut back production. Gold prices have flattened out.

Should deflation develop, we would see a reversal of the trends just mentioned. Market players would return to being savers (1) in order to preserve capital and (2) because cash is king during a recession. Houses would lose their status as shrewd investments (as has already happened in many parts of the country) and would once again be priced primarily for their utility as dwelling places. And thrift would be wise and debt once again recognized as foolish. High debt loads during periods of recession can be devastating. If you would be at financial risk should these reversals take place, it may be time to review your long-term assumptions and financial strategy.

I have added the above reminder at the end of this chapter only because many people can't imagine that deflation is even a possibility.

We're all familiar with the fear of poverty that characterizes millions who lived through the Great Depression. Decades later, people who have since become millionaires are still stockpiling money because they "never want to go through that again." The experience left them psychologically scarred. It's easy to see when others are controlled by their fears, but can we see it in ourselves?

Many of those who had a financially difficult time during the high inflation of the late 1970s (myself included) are still concerned with fighting the last war. Let's not become so preoccupied with the threat of inflation that we forget there are *two* equally plausible scenarios for a major financial earthquake — the U.S. is caught between the current global deflation and the inflationary pressures brought on by an undisciplined federal government that is debasing our currency. Which force will prove the stronger, and the timing on how this will ultimately play out, is anyone's guess. ◆

24

CHAPTER PREVIEW

Selecting Your Funds

I. There are many theories about how to pick winning mutual funds.

A. To be useful, any fund selection method should result in performance better than the S&P 500 over most time frames tested. Otherwise, an S&P 500 index fund is a better choice.

B. The "best of the past five years" theory and the *Forbes* magazine theory are based on funds' long-term track records. They are discussed and shown to consistently underperform the S&P 500 index.

C. There are competing theories about the usefulness of funds' most recent one-year performance. Several studies, which reach opposite conclusions, are listed.

D. Sheldon Jacobs and Dan Wiener have each developed methods of using one-year performance numbers that generate results superior to those of an S&P 500 index fund. Their strategies are explained, and recommended as worthy diversification moves for the long-term investor.

E. Burton Berry's "upgrading" strategy is briefly discussed. It has an excellent long-term track record and is worthy of consideration by those seeking a more active strategy.

F. The star ratings given by the Morningstar organization are discussed and shown to be primarily useful in gauging a fund's risk/reward characteristics rather than having predictive value as to future performance.

G. The fund selection method used in the *Sound Mind Investing* newsletter is briefly discussed.

II. As important as it is to make good fund selections, it is actually third in importance in terms of the impact it will have on your long-term investment results.

A. How you allocate your portfolio between stocks and bonds is of primary importance.

B. How you further divide your holdings among the various stock and bond risk categories is of secondary importance. Suggestions are offered for six different portfolio allocations.

III. Don't place any confidence in market experts and commentators. They don't know what's best to invest in now anymore than you do.

At the start of the 1980s, the reigning media investment superstar was Joe Granville. When he told his followers to sell everything . . .

. . . many of them stampeded to the exit door, causing the Dow Jones Industrial Average to fall more than 3% — a loss equivalent to over 100 Dow points today — on the heaviest volume of trading in the 188-year history of the New York Stock Exchange up to that time. At the peak of his popularity, he once began an investment speech by walking across a swimming pool on a plank hidden just below the surface. Turning to the crowd, he exulted, "And now you know! I can walk on water!" But he failed to predict the start of the great 1980s bull market. As the rally began, he advised his followers to "go short" (selling shares with the expectation of buying them back later at lower prices) in expectation of profiting when the market collapsed. After missing the major market advance of the early 1980s, he finally turned bullish — right at the top of the market before the crash of 1987. By being one of the few analysts to recommend buying *after* the crash, his record over the past few years is once again one of the better ones.

Granville was replaced by Robert Prechter. He captured center stage with forecasts based on a rather mysterious theory of market movements and mass psychology called the Elliott Wave. He was the first to call for a Dow move to the then-incredible heights of 2700+, a forecast that was widely derided as absurdly optimistic. As that goal was approached, he raised his sights to the 3600+ area. There is some controversy as to whether he changed his mind in time to get his followers out before the 1987 crash. In any event, he has lost the great influence he once commanded and now spends his time writing articles and publishing books by other Elliott Wave scholars. He expected the nineties to be disastrous for the stock market and advised, "The 1990s will be the decade of cash. Stay in U.S. treasury bills." To date, that has proven to be poor advice, indeed — the S&P 500 more than doubled from the beginning of 1991 through mid-1996.

And we shouldn't forget Henry Kaufman, then the chief economist for Salomon Brothers. He came to be known as "Dr. Doom" because his accurate forecasts of rising interest rates repeatedly sent shudders through the financial markets. His following gradually evaporated when he was too slow to recognize the sharp drop in interest rates that launched the bull market in bonds in the early eighties. Rarely quoted these days, he runs a money management firm that specializes in bonds.

One respected Wall Streeter says: "Investors are always looking for a messiah. The system will always produce a new superstar, and inevitably, the star will fall flat on his or her face."

Market gurus come and go because it is impossible to predict future market movements with consistent accuracy. This is one of the reasons . . .

. . . that a majority of stock mutual funds have underperformed the general market averages (see pages 154-155). That's why I devised the Just-the-Basics strategy and devoted chapter 13 to explaining its virtues. It combines rates of return that are better than the average diversifed stock fund with modest risk and virtually no upkeep.

If you're not willing to settle for that, your other option is to put together your own portfolio of funds. In making your selections, you are faced with many decisions. How much emphasis should you place on a fund's past performance? How far back is a fund's performance relevant—one year, two, three, five? How will you know when the time has come to sell your fund and move on to something else? How will you know you are effectively dealing with the red flags I warned you about in chapter 9? How will you know how much risk you're taking? Making these decisions is not easy.

There are many *theories* about how to pick winning mutual funds. What does that tell you?

You don't read theories on why airplanes fly. That's because the laws governing aerodynamics are known and certain. You do read theories on what holds the atom together, because it's still a mystery. No one has yet devised a foolproof method for selecting next year's top performers. There are no rules you can rely on that will guarantee the result you want.

I'm telling you this so you'll have realistic expectations about what you're up against. In this chapter, we're going to look at several of the leading methodologies concerning stock fund selection. Where possible, I'll share the results of studies that tend to either support or undermine them. If you find the conflicting claims a little confusing, that's OK. At times, I do too.

♦ **The "best of the past five years" theory.** An oft-heard piece of advice is that you should select your funds based on their long-term track records (typically five years is suggested) rather than on who had the hot hand last year. Performance leadership among mutual funds is constantly rotating. The market is so volatile that this year's fund winners may very well be next year's losers, or so the thinking goes. So, rather than focus on a fund's recent history, seek out funds with good long-term records that have proven themselves through many kinds of market environments.

Burton Berry, publisher of a helpful mutual fund ranking newsletter which he calls *NoLoad Fund∗X*, performed an interesting study of mutual fund performance. He identified the twenty funds that had the best track records over a recent five-year period and posed this question: how many of these funds will be in the top performing group again next year? The surprising answer was only one. He tried it again for a different five-year period, and the answer was none. Altogether, he checked out twenty-one different five-year periods and found that, on average, *only two* of the top twenty-five performers of the past five years made the list again the following year.

Well, you might say, isn't it asking too much to expect these funds, which have the best records over the past five years, to be top performers in the sixth year as well? Shouldn't you give them more than just one year to prove themselves? Good point, and one that Berry thought of. He also followed up to see how well the funds did if you held them for five years. For example, of the top twenty-five stock funds in the 1971-1975 period, how many of them were among the top twenty-five for the 1976-1980 period? Only one, which turns out to be about average for all the periods Berry studied between 1966 and 1992.

Berry's work stimulated me to try a slightly different approach. Rather than test to see if a top performing five-year record was indicative of a future "top twenty-five" ranking, I tested to see if it was at least indicative of future results that would be better than investing in an S&P 500 index fund. Since I already have my Just-the-Basics strategy in place, the first requirement of any new approach I might adopt is that it surpass my index fund strategy. If it could also be a top twenty-five performer, so much the better. But that would be icing on the cake.

Using the Morningstar database, I structured my test with the assumptions that I would only be investing in no-loads and that I didn't want to have to spread my investments over more than ten funds. Starting with the 1976-1980 period (which is as far back as the data went), I ranked the diversified stock funds according to their five-year track records. Next, I selected the top ten performers and calculated their returns for the 1981-1985 holding period. I assumed that I divided my investment equally among the ten. Finally, I compared the result with what I would have made in the S&P 500 index fund. The results are shown at the bottom of the page. For the eleven periods tested,

A FIVE-YEAR TRACK RECORD ISN'T PREDICTIVE

Ten top-performing funds were taken from this five-year period	Their average annual performance during this period	The funds were then held during this five-year period	Their average annual performance during this period	Performance of S&P 500 index fund during this period	How much better or worse did the top performers do than the S&P 500?
1976-1980	36.0%	1981-1985	12.0%	14.2%	−2.2%
1977-1981	28.4%	1982-1986	15.5%	19.3%	−3.8%
1978-1982	30.1%	1983-1987	12.6%	15.9%	−3.3%
1979-1983	30.0%	1984-1988	10.3%	14.9%	−4.6%
1980-1984	22.3%	1985-1989	17.6%	19.9%	−2.3%
1981-1985	22.0%	1986-1990	9.2%	12.8%	−3.6%
1982-1986	23.9%	1987-1991	12.2%	15.0%	−2.8%
1983-1987	19.2%	1988-1992	14.3%	15.6%	−1.3%
1984-1988	17.2%	1989-1993	13.4%	14.3%	−0.9%
1985-1989	22.6%	1990-1994	10.3%	8.5%	1.8%
1986-1990	15.0%	1991-1995	20.8%	16.4%	4.4%

the portfolio of top performers failed my test nine times. Thus, funds selected this way couldn't even meet the less demanding standard of simply outperforming a passive index fund.

As an afterthought, I went back and performed the same test with the top five funds from each period rather than the top ten. Perhaps if I stayed with the very best ones, I'd have better results. This approach turned out to be slightly worse than using all ten funds. In addition to my research and that of Berry, the uselessness of five-year performance histories as guides to future performance has also been reported in articles in *Investment Vision* (June 1991) and *Worth* (November 1994).

◆ **The *Forbes* theory.** *Forbes* magazine is well known for its annual "honor roll" of mutual funds. Publishing such a list has been an annual practice at *Forbes* dating back to 1973. In assembling its annual list, the magazine does some heavy-duty number crunching. Their process takes into account how funds have done in past market cycles, emphasizing a fund's performance in both up and down markets. This requires looking at performance data that may go as far back as ten years. They also apply several other criteria which they believe are relevant to investors. (I won't include them here because they change their "rules" every few years.)

In the introduction to its September 1989 list, *Forbes* offers this haughty we-know-what's-best lead-in:

This list of first-class stock funds isn't at all like a list of the best gainers over the past five years. Good performance is a little more subtle than that. . . . We consider the simpleminded straight-line measurements used by most surveys to be virtually worthless. . . . To get on the Forbes honor roll, a fund had to deliver excellent long-term results and do so without exposing investors to excessive risk. . . . It is hard to get on, harder still to stay on.

Forbes's goal is to select funds that can be bought and held for several years, through good times and bad. In its 1991 annual mutual fund issue, *Forbes* suggests that "this year's hot performer will be next year's laggard." But instead of acknowledging that some ongoing routine maintenance is therefore necessary to keep your portfolio running smoothly, they lead you on a search for all-weather performers that you can supposedly buy and forget about.

Unfortunately, the results simply don't produce as advertised. In the exhibits on pages 308–309, I've listed the results of a study I performed on the *Forbes* honor roll funds over a wide variety of time periods. For purposes of my test, I assumed that (1) an investor divided his capital equally among the diversified U.S. stock funds—some load, some no-load—on the honor roll; (2) the investment was made on the last day of the year; (3) the portfolio was held for periods of one year, three years, or five years; and (4) because the goal was to compare the returns with those turned in by the S&P 500 index fund used in my Just-the-Basics strategy, international funds, balanced funds, and closed-end funds that may have been listed on the honor roll were excluded.

I performed the test ten times—that is, on ten different honor roll lists—beginning with the honor roll of August 1981. The instances in which the honor roll funds, as a group, were superior to the Vanguard index fund are circled. As you can see in the graphic below (left), *Forbes*'s approach proved superior in only nine out of the thirty time frames tested. In other words, more than two-thirds of the time, some of the best portfolio managers in the country (according to *Forbes*) failed to outperform an unmanaged index fund. Is this supposed to be outstanding and sophisticated fund selection?

In the graphic on the right, the loads charged by some of the honor roll funds were factored into the calculations. These numbers more closely reflect what an investor's experience might have been. With the addition of the loads, the honor roll portfolios outperformed the no-load Vanguard index fund only in three instances—only 10% of the time frames tested. The average margin of superiority for the index fund approach was a hefty 6.5% for a one-year holding period due to the dramatic effects of paying the sales commission. When the costs of the loads are spread over several years, their burden is gradually lessened. Even so, the average annual margin of superiority for Vanguard's "no-brainer" S&P 500 index fund was 3.6% for the average three-year holding period, and 2.3% for the average five-year period.

In the 1994 honor roll issue, *Forbes* conceded (for the first time that I'm aware of) that "Tough though it is to make the honor roll, we make only modest claims for its predictive power." They should have started the article with that admission rather than begin, as they did, with another of their slams at the "run

THE <u>FORBES</u> HONOR ROLL ISN'T PREDICTIVE / PART ONE

Date Recommended in <u>Forbes</u>	8/81	8/82	8/83	8/84	9/85	9/86	9/87	9/88	9/89	9/90
Following Year	1982	1983	1984	1985	1986	1987	1988	1989	1990	1991
Average performance of Honor Roll funds the following year	28.2%	24.7%	–3.2%	27.4%	11.8%	3.7%	15.5%	28.3%	–5.4%	33.0%
Performance of S&P 500 index fund the following year	21.0%	21.3%	6.2%	31.2%	18.1%	4.7%	16.2%	31.4%	–3.3%	30.2%
Superiority of the <u>Forbes</u> Honor Roll versus the S&P 500 index fund	(7.2%)	(3.4%)	–9.4%	–3.8%	–6.3%	–1.0%	–0.7%	–3.1%	–2.1%	(2.8%)
Following Three Years	82-84	83-85	84-86	85-87	86-88	87-89	88-90	89-91	90-92	91-93
Average annual performance of Honor Roll funds the following 3 years	14.9%	16.6%	11.1%	14.1%	9.9%	14.6%	10.9%	19.1%	11.2%	17.4%
Average annual performance of S&P 500 fund the following 3 years	15.9%	19.1%	18.1%	17.5%	12.8%	16.9%	13.9%	18.3%	10.6%	15.4%
Superiority of the <u>Forbes</u> Honor Roll versus the S&P 500 index fund	–1.0%	–2.5%	–7.0%	–3.4%	–2.9%	–2.3%	–3.0%	(0.8%)	(0.6%)	(2.0%)
Following Five Years	82-86	83-87	84-88	85-89	86-90	87-91	88-92	89-93	90-94	91-95
Average annual performance of Honor Roll funds the following 5 years	16.9%	13.8%	10.3%	17.4%	9.4%	14.9%	15.0%	16.3%	9.2%	16.5%
Average annual performance of S&P 500 fund the following 5 years	19.3%	15.9%	14.9%	19.9%	12.8%	15.0%	15.6%	14.3%	8.5%	16.4%
Superiority of the <u>Forbes</u> Honor Roll versus the S&P 500 index fund	–2.4%	–2.1%	–4.6%	–2.5%	–3.4%	–0.1%	–0.6%	(2.0%)	(0.7%)	(0.1%)

Several of the stock funds listed on the <u>Forbes</u> honor roll carry load charges that range from 3.0% to 8.5%. Those sales commissions <u>have not</u> been taken into account in the above table in order to assess the <u>Forbes</u> system strictly in terms of the excellence of the fund managers recommended.

of the mill surveys" published by competing magazines.

The moral is this: don't look down on an investment strategy just because it's simple and straightforward. The way *Forbes* makes its honor roll selections is so complicated and time-consuming that you could never do it on your own. Its writers tend to give the impression that investing is so complicated and difficult—a kind of first cousin to quantum physics—that you need experts (like them) to constantly guide you. Well, it's not and you don't. All you really need is a prudent, understandable plan and a reasonable amount of self-discipline. "Sophisticated" approaches aren't necessarily more effective. Legendary investor Warren Buffett says it well: "There seems to be some perverse human characteristic that likes to make easy things difficult."

The next time you hear an "expert" advise selecting stock funds based on their five-year track records, I hope you'll remember the foregoing evidence to the contrary. Maybe five years is going back too far . . .

. . . how about using mutual funds' recent one-year records instead? There is a real battle in the investing community over the extent to which performance excellence during the most recent year is indicative of excellence during the coming year. Here are a few of the combatants.

✍ *Kiplinger's Personal Finance Magazine*, in its September 1992 issue, ran an article titled "Should You Buy This Year's Winners?" Here's what they had to say:

Recommended Resource

Despite what you might think from my assessment of its annual mutual fund honor roll, <u>Forbes</u> is my favorite financial/investing magazine. It has interesting and informative articles on a broad range of topics. The regular investing columns which appear in the back, including Mark Hulbert's, are worth the cost of admission.

THE <u>FORBES</u> HONOR ROLL ISN'T PREDICTIVE / PART TWO

Date Recommended in <u>Forbes</u>	8/81	8/82	8/83	8/84	9/85	9/86	9/87	9/88	9/89	9/90
Following Year	1982	1983	1984	1985	1986	1987	1988	1989	1990	1991
Average performance of Honor Roll funds the following year	24.2%	19.1%	–8.0%	21.1%	6.9%	–0.7%	10.5%	21.9%	–9.8%	27.2%
Performance of S&P 500 index fund the following year	21.0%	21.3%	6.2%	31.2%	18.1%	4.7%	16.2%	31.4%	–3.3%	30.2%
Superiority of the <u>Forbes</u> Honor Roll versus the S&P 500 index fund	(3.2%)	–2.2%	–14.2%	–10.1%	–11.2%	–5.4%	–5.7%	–9.5%	–6.5%	–3.0%
Following Three Years	82-84	83-85	84-86	85-87	86-88	87-89	88-90	89-91	90-92	91-93
Average annual performance of Honor Roll funds the following 3 years	13.7%	14.8%	9.1%	12.2%	8.3%	12.9%	9.3%	17.1%	9.5%	15.7%
Average annual performance of S&P 500 fund the following 3 years	15.9%	19.1%	18.1%	17.5%	12.8%	16.9%	13.9%	18.3%	10.6%	15.4%
Superiority of the <u>Forbes</u> Honor Roll versus the S&P 500 index fund	–2.2%	–4.3%	–9.0%	–5.3%	–4.5%	–4.0%	–4.6%	–1.2%	–1.1%	(0.3%)
Following Five Years	82-86	83-87	84-88	85-89	86-90	87-91	88-92	89-93	90-94	91-95
Average annual performance of Honor Roll funds the following 5 years	16.2%	12.7%	9.2%	16.2%	8.4%	13.9%	14.0%	15.1%	8.2%	15.6%
Average annual performance of S&P 500 fund the following 5 years	19.3%	15.9%	14.9%	19.9%	12.8%	15.0%	15.6%	14.3%	8.5%	16.4%
Superiority of the <u>Forbes</u> Honor Roll versus the S&P 500 index fund	–3.1%	–3.2%	–5.7%	–3.7%	–4.4%	–1.1%	–1.6%	(0.8%)	–0.3%	–0.8%

Several of the stock funds listed on the <u>Forbes</u> honor roll carry load charges that range from 3.0% to 8.5%. Those sales commissions <u>have</u> been taken into account in the above table in order to assess the <u>Forbes</u> system strictly in terms of its profitability to investors versus an S&P 500 index fund.

Consider the annual winners within categories, such as aggressive growth, long-term growth, growth and income, and international. Chances are these categories' top funds will reward you even after the year they finished first. How do we know? We examined historical mutual fund performance records to determine how one-year winners within a certain category did during the subsequent five years. The result: Funds that top the chart for a one-year period more often than not end up with above-average records for the next five years. In other words, go ahead and buy this year's winners.

Phrases like "chances are" and "more often than not" don't inspire confidence. Also, my goal is to find a method for picking funds that will outperform the S&P 500—funds that are "above average" may or may not accomplish this. Still, here is a respectable voice saying that last year's winners (notice they only took the top-ranked fund in each category) are likely to continue enjoying a measure of success.

👎 John Bogle, chairman of the Vanguard Group of no-load funds, has long maintained that picking last year's top funds is a poor way to make your selections. In his book, *Bogle on Mutual Funds,* he reports a study that examined fund performance between 1972 and 1982. It showed that the top twenty stock funds for each year had an average rank of 284 (among 681 funds) in the subsequent year. Vanguard's investor newsletter, *In the Vanguard,* reported: "Numerous studies reached the same conclusion: selecting yesterday's top performers does not appear to increase your chances of selecting tomorrow's winners."

👍 An article in *The Wall Street Journal* in early 1993 was headed "Buy Last Year's Hot Funds." The *Journal's* study was designed to learn which was the better criterion—last year's winners, leaders over the past five years, or ten-year performance. The data covered the period from 1970 to 1992, and concluded that investors do well by picking last year's hot funds.

👎 Not so fast, says Mark Hulbert, columnist for *Forbes* and publisher of the respected *Hulbert Financial Digest,* which monitors the performance of investment advisory letters. "The Journal study is shot full of holes. Professor Josef Lakonishok of the University of Illinois at Urbana-Champagne points out that the study suffers severely from what statisticians call a survivorship bias" (*Forbes*, March 15, 1993). Hulbert then goes on to explain the technical deficiencies in detail. He concludes: "One-year sprinters rarely go the distance."

👍 Later in 1993, three Harvard professors published their work in the *Journal of Finance.* They studied past performance histories that were as brief as the most recent ninety days up to as long as two years, and concluded that the one-year "hot hand" approach was the way to go. This study was widely reported in the financial press.

👎 Not so fast (part two), says Mark Hulbert. In his *Forbes* column of December 20, 1993, he names professors from NYU and Columbia who claim that the Harvard study is—you guessed it—statistically flawed. "All the Harvard study really showed, then, was that buying the hot hands would keep you ahead of the fund average— which is not the same by any means as beating the market." I agree with Mark on

Recommended Resource
The Hulbert Financial Digest is available via subscription only. Currently, the annual cost is $59 for fourteen issues. For subscription information, call (800) 485-2378.

that point, which is the same one I made regarding the Kiplinger study.

I could also mention a study done by professors from Yale and Columbia (👍) and another one sponsored by the Brookings Institute (👎), but you should have the picture by now. The outcome seems to depend on how you define the "top" performers (is it just the number one fund, or the top twenty, or the top 10%, or what?) and your goal (is it to beat the average mutual fund or to beat the S&P 500?).

If using last year's performance as a key to this year's winners intrigues you, here are three easy "hot hands" strategies that have excellent track records.

◆ **Sheldon Jacobs's theory.** A bona fide expert on mutual funds and publisher of *The No-Load Fund Investor* newsletter, Jacobs developed a strategy based on "persistency of performance." Here's how he explains it:

> *Suppose that at the end of each year, you had bought that year's top-ranked fund, held it for one year, then switched to the next year's top-ranked fund. Suppose, too, that you had continued this strategy for a number of years. If you had adopted this strategy nineteen years ago, you would have done four times as well as if you had invested in the average equity fund. . . .*

> *Here's how I choose each year's winning fund. I go down the list of top no-load funds until I find the best diversified equity fund available for sale. (Because the performance of specialized gold and sector funds are notoriously inconsistent, I exclude them from consideration.) The selected fund is purchased, and held for twelve months . . . .*

> *Many studies, including our own, prove the value of the persistency of performance factor. Although my research was on a calendar-year basis, you can begin the strategy at any time. One caution. This is a long-term high-risk strategy. There is no guarantee that it will work every year. Indeed, each year's winning fund is likely to be volatile, so a serious bear market could sharply reduce your profits. To obtain the benefits of this strategy, you need to continue it for several years.*

◆ **Dan Wiener's theory.** Another longtime observer of the mutual fund scene and publisher of *The Independent Adviser for Vanguard Investors*, Wiener has come up with a similar approach for those who have accounts at Vanguard. (His entire newsletter is directed to those investors.) Dan's view:

> *I've discovered a great way for Vanguard investors to allocate at least a portion of their portfolios so they consistently beat the market over the long haul. I call it the "hot hands" strategy. This strategy doesn't work for all fund families. But it does at Vanguard, primarily because fund objectives and investment policies are so well defined. With Vanguard's funds there's little room for managers to change their tactics. . . .*

> *Here are the ground rules. I picked the best Vanguard equity fund each year between 1981 and 1995. The only funds I excluded were sector funds, as well as the two international index funds since they are somewhat akin to sector funds. However, I left the two diversified internationals in the mix. . . .*

Recommended Resource

The No-Load Fund Investor is available via subscription only. Currently, the cost is $129 for twelve monthly issues. For subscription information, call (800) 252-2042.

Recommended Resource

The Independent Adviser for Vanguard Investors is available via subscription only. Currently, the cost is $99.95 for twelve monthly issues. For subscription information, call (800) 211-7642.

Remember, however, that buying the "hot hands" fund for the following year doesn't guarantee you are going to beat the market every year. In fact, the hot fund only beats the S&P 500 index a bit more than half the time. But that's not the point. It's the accumulation of market-beating periods that really makes the difference. Or to put it another way, it's the long haul I'm really interested in.

The year-by-year results from these two hot-hands strategies are shown in the graphic below and on the next page. The years in which they outperformed the S&P 500 index fund have been circled. The important thing to notice is the consistency with which their systems generated above-market returns over various five-year holding periods. If you follow one of their strategies faithfully, although you won't do better than the market *every* year, you will likely do better than the market over a five-year period. This is due to the occasional year when their funds make up for lost time by comfortably outdistancing the S&P index. If you miss one of those key years, you'll lose a lot of the benefit their strategies offer.

A good use of these systems is to add diversification to your portfolio. For example, one scenario would be to invest 80% of your capital using the Just-the-Basics strategy, 10% using Jacobs's strategy, and 10% using Wiener's strategy. Tinker with the percentages to suit your goals and risk tolerance. These strategies could also be used when investing for college and other long-term needs that are funded outside your normal retirement investment portfolio.

◆ **Burton Berry's "upgrading" theory.** In his newsletter, *No-Load Fund∗X*, Burton Berry explains a way to measure fund performance that pinpoints which funds to buy, and when to sell them and buy something else. He

SHELDON JACOBS'S USE OF ONE-YEAR PERFORMANCE

For the year	Top performing domestic stock fund	The fund was then held during	Gain for that year	Gain for S&P that year	Versus the S&P 500	5 year period	Jacobs's system	S&P 500
1980	Hartwell Leverage	1981	−13.2%	−5.0%	−8.2%			
1981	Lindner Fund	1982	27.1%	21.4%	5.7%			
1982	Tudor Fund	1983	28.0%	22.4%	5.6%			
1983	Strong Investment	1984	9.7%	6.1%	3.6%			
1984	Vanguard High Yield Stock	1985	30.1%	31.6%	−1.5%	1981-1985	15.0%	14.5%
1985	Fidelity OTC	1986	11.4%	18.6%	−7.2%	1982-1986	20.9%	19.7%
1986	Strong Opportunity	1987	11.8%	5.1%	6.7%	1983-1987	17.9%	16.3%
1987	Mathers	1988	13.7%	16.3%	−2.6%	1984-1988	15.1%	15.1%
1988	Kaufmann	1989	46.8%	31.4%	15.4%	1985-1989	22.0%	20.2%
1989	Twentieth Century Vista	1990	−15.7%	−3.3%	−12.4%	1986-1990	11.9%	13.0%
1990	Founders Discovery	1991	62.5%	30.4%	32.1%	1987-1991	20.6%	15.2%
1991	Montgomery Small Cap	1992	9.6%	7.6%	2.0%	1988-1992	20.2%	15.7%
1992	Oakmark	1993	30.5%	10.0%	20.5%	1989-1993	23.5%	14.4%
1993	PBHG Growth	1994	4.8%	1.3%	3.5%	1990-1994	15.5%	8.6%
1994	PBHG Emerging Growth	1995	48.5%	37.6%	10.9%	1991-1995	29.3%	16.6%

devised a strategy that he calls "upgrading." His basic assumptions, which my experience bears out, are that (1) performance results that are more than one year old are no longer very meaningful, and (2) more recent months should be weighted more heavily than distant months. These assumptions led Berry to develop a methodology for evaluating mutual fund performance based on each fund's most recent one-month, three-month, six-month, and twelve-month performance. His approach also involves awarding extra rating points for funds that place in the top of their peer group for each of the time frames being measured.

The results from Berry's newsletter recommendations have been excellent. According to the *Hulbert Digest*, his "higher quality growth funds" portfolio has returned 15.0% over the past ten years (1986-1995) and 16.7% over the past fifteen years (1981-1995). Both periods reflect performance results better than the S&P 500. The fifteen-year results were good enough to place *No-Load Fund*∗*X* among the top performing newsletters monitored by Hulbert during that period. If you'd like to know more about Burton Berry's system, his newsletter gives specific, easy-to-follow instructions. I have been a subscriber since the early 1980s, and recommend the newsletter to those interested in a more activist strategy.

Recommended Resource
No-Load Fund∗X is available via subscription only. Currently, the cost is $125 for twelve monthly issues. For subscription information, call (415) 986-7979.

If you've done any reading in the major financial publications, you've likely come across mention of the "star" system of rating fund performance invented by Morningstar Mutual Funds of Chicago.

A profile on the organization appeared in *Smart Money* magazine in May 1994, and contained this assessment of Morningstar's influence:

DAN WIENER'S USE OF ONE-YEAR PERFORMANCE

For the year	Top performing domestic stock fund	The fund was then held during	Gain for that year	Gain for S&P that year	Versus the S&P 500	5 year period	Weiner's system	S&P 500
1980	Explorer	1981	1.8%	−5.0%	6.9%			
1981	Windsor	1982	21.7%	21.4%	0.3%			
1982	Index: Small Cap	1983	18.2%	22.4%	−4.2%			
1983	International Growth	1984	−1.0%	6.1%	−7.1%			
1984	Windsor	1985	28.0%	31.6%	−3.5%	1981-1985	13.2%	14.5%
1985	International Growth	1986	56.7%	18.6%	38.2%	1982-1986	23.4%	19.7%
1986	International Growth	1987	12.5%	5.1%	7.4%	1983-1987	21.4%	16.3%
1987	Trustees International	1988	18.8%	16.3%	2.5%	1984-1988	21.6%	15.1%
1988	Windsor	1989	15.0%	31.4%	−16.4%	1985-1989	25.3%	20.2%
1989	U.S. Growth	1990	4.6%	−3.3%	7.9%	1986-1990	20.3%	13.0%
1990	U.S. Growth	1991	46.8%	30.4%	16.3%	1987-1991	18.7%	15.2%
1991	Explorer	1992	13.0%	7.6%	5.4%	1988-1992	18.8%	15.7%
1992	Convertible Securities	1993	13.5%	10.0%	3.5%	1989-1993	17.8%	14.4%
1993	International Growth	1994	0.8%	1.3%	−0.6%	1990-1994	14.7%	8.6%
1994	PRIMECAP	1995	35.5%	37.6%	−2.1%	1991-1995	20.8%	16.6%

Can this be the 800-pound gorilla of the mutual fund industry? Don't doubt it for a minute. . . . Flip through the pages of any finance magazine and there you'll see, in eye-arresting type, advertisements touting the five-star seal of approval Morningstar gives to about 350 mutual funds on any given month. Scan the stories about mutual funds in those same publications and you'll be confronted with the seeming omniscience of Morningstar. In 1993 alone, the company was cited 1,575 times — more than four times a day, each day of the year. . . . Turn on CNN or CNBC, and there you will likely spot Morningstar's baby-faced editor, John Rekenthaler, holding court about the state of the stock market as interviewers sit, rapt in attention. . . .

To some people in the industry, Morningstar's judgment of a mutual fund has taken on the aura of infallibility. "There's no getting around it," says Chris Holman, director of investment communications at Fortis Advisers. "People look at star ratings, and it is akin to sainthood.". . . That's what it all comes down to: those stars. There is no denying their effectiveness as a marketing tool, especially to people who buy funds directly. . . . According to Strategic Insight, a mutual fund research and consulting firm, two-thirds of the top-selling directly marketed funds last year carried four or five stars, while only seven percent of the new money going into mutual funds was placed in funds carrying three or fewer stars.[1]

[1]Reed Abelson, "The Only Game in Town," <u>Smart Money</u>, May 1994, 105–111.

Unfortunately, there are some characteristics of Morningstar's ratings that most investors appear to be unaware of.

◆ The star ratings were designed to quantify a fund's risk and reward characteristics. This is not the same as saying they do a good job of identifying next year's good performers. No less an authority on the subject than Joe Mansueto, Morningstar's founder, agrees: "The star system isn't meant to be predictive." Nor are ratings meant to substitute for an investor's own research. According to Morningstar's subscriber's guide, the stars are meant merely to "give people a way to narrow down the group of funds that they want to look at in more depth."

◆ The star ratings are transitory. They are adjusted monthly and will change as market cycles come and go. It's common to see hundreds of funds have their ratings move up or down by one star over the course of a year.

◆ The star ratings give heavy weight to a fund's ten-year track record. This means that today's ratings can be influenced, for example, by managers who aren't running a fund anymore and by investment numbers turned in when the fund had a different investment objective in the past.

◆ The star ratings are heavily influenced by a fund's price volatility. Fifty percent of a star rating is based on Morningstar's assessment of how risky it is to own that fund. Even granting that risk is important, there is controversy within the mutual fund industry over whether the methods used by Morningstar to measure it are correct.

These concerns wouldn't matter if the star system resulted in superior returns. Turning again to *The Hulbert Digest*, we find that for the three-year period from 1993-1995 (the longest period reported by Hulbert), Morningstar's portfolio of five-star "higher risk" stock funds gained 10.3% per year. This was better performance than that turned in by their "medium risk" and "lower risk" portfolios, which returned 10.0% and 9.4% per year respectively. During the same three years, the S&P 500 returned 15.3%. Furthermore, even if the results were great, it would be difficult to cash in—in any given month, about 25-30 funds in each risk group carry a five-star rating. You can't invest in all of them, and how would you know which to choose?

This is not to say Morningstar's reporting service isn't excellent. I pay $795 a year for their monthly updates, which arrive on a CD-ROM, and rely on it heavily for my research. According to the *Smart Money* article, more than 50,000 investors pay $395 a year for Morningstar's twice-a-month newsletter, so obviously the company is doing a lot of things right. The problem isn't so much with the star system; it's with fund organizations and investors using it in ways that were never intended. Don't be influenced to buy a fund just because it has a five-star rating from Morningstar.

The last fund selection method I want to mention is the one I use in my monthly *Sound Mind Investing* **newsletter.**

Building on Burton Berry's upgrading strategy, I have developed a ranking procedure that I compute monthly and use in the fine-tuning decisions I make when selecting no-load funds to recommend to my monthly readers.

In adapting the upgrading concept to SMI's framework, I've made changes in how I apply it. Here are some of the ways that the SMI newsletter strategy differs from the "pure" Burton Berry format: (1) The major difference is that I assign funds to risk categories based on the nature of their portfolio holdings (see pages 224-

A SAMPLE OF THE FUND RANKINGS FROM THE SOUND MIND INVESTING NEWSLETTER

Name of Fund	Morningstar Investment Objective	Schwab One Source	Fidelity Funds Network	MO	3 Mos Total Return	6 Mos Total Return	12 Mos Total Return	3 Year Avg Return	3 Year Standard Dev	3 Year Sharpe Ratio	Expense Ratio (%)	Price-to-Earnings Ratio	Value Index	Median Market Capital	Min Initial Purch	Max Sales Load
Category 1: Lowest Risk Stock Funds Portfolios Which Invest Primarily in Large Companies Using a Value-Oriented Strategy																
Kemper-Dreman High Return A	Growth-Inc	Yes	Yes	61.7	7.6%	15.1%	39.0%	18.7%	10.3	1.38	1.25	18.2	1.77	10,390	1,000	5.8%
T. Rowe Price Value	Growth	Yes	No	61.3	8.6%	18.3%	34.4%	new	new	new	1.10	23.6	1.87	2,552	2,500	NL
Neuberger&Berman Partners	Growth	NTF	No	50.9	5.8%	14.4%	30.7%	17.9%	9.9	1.35	0.83	20.6	1.82	3,656	1,000	NL
Tweedy, Browne American Val	Growth	Yes	Yes	49.9	6.4%	14.6%	28.8%	new	new	new	1.39	18.4	1.68	2,417	2,500	NL
Torray	Growth	Yes	No	49.3	1.8%	10.2%	37.3%	20.7%	8.7	1.87	1.25	20.2	1.97	4,940	10,000	NL
Fidelity Value	Growth	Yes	NTF	47.6	6.6%	13.4%	27.5%	18.5%	7.8	1.78	0.96	21.2	1.97	12,892	2,500	NL
Babson Value	Growth-Inc	NTF	NTF	46.4	6.7%	12.9%	26.7%	20.5%	7.6	2.10	0.98	16.3	1.48	5,605	1,000	NL
Dodge & Cox Stock	Growth-Inc	Yes	No	46.0	7.0%	13.1%	25.9%	18.0%	8.7	1.55	0.60	18.1	1.64	9,005	2,500	NL
Vanguard/Windsor II	Growth-Inc	Yes	Yes	45.3	4.0%	12.2%	29.1%	16.9%	8.4	1.47	0.39	19.7	1.91	17,907	3,000	NL
Harbor Value	Growth-Inc	Yes	No	45.0	5.5%	12.7%	26.8%	16.1%	8.0	1.44	0.90	20.1	1.73	5,398	2,000	NL
Benham Income & Growth	Growth-Inc	NTF	Yes	44.8	4.6%	11.9%	28.3%	16.6%	7.6	1.60	0.67	16.7	1.75	16,695	1,000	NL
Vanguard Quantitative	Growth-Inc	Yes	No	44.5	4.8%	11.3%	28.4%	16.6%	8.2	1.48	0.47	18.4	1.83	15,373	3,000	NL
Benham Equity Growth	Growth	NTF	Yes	44.0	4.3%	13.3%	26.4%	17.0%	7.7	1.63	0.71	16.9	1.65	11,028	1,000	NL
USAA Growth & Income	Growth-Inc	No	No	43.9	5.7%	11.4%	26.8%	new	new	new	1.01	21.8	1.94	9,046	3,000	NL

Which no-load mutual fund organization is best?

Well, it depends. Best for what purpose? How long do you expect to hold your investments there? What else do you own? Are you willing to monitor your funds' progress, or do you want to just buy a fund and forget it for the next few years? There can be no "best" in an absolute sense; the selection must take place within the context of your personal goals and risk tolerance. Here are some things to keep in mind as you prepare to build your portfolio.

1. Each fund organization has its own areas of excellence. For example, if you're primarily going to be investing in stock index or bond and money market funds, Vanguard is hard to beat. On the other hand, if you're interested in having access to stock funds across the entire risk spectrum, Price and Scudder are two organizations that have good selections. Or if a large selection isn't important, 20th Century's stock funds are super during periods of rising stock prices (but beware of them in a bear market!).

2. Consider opening more than one account. If you don't mind the paperwork and can manage the initial minimums, open accounts at two (or more) of the no-load organizations. Having an account at Vanguard so you can invest in my Just-the-Basics strategy or their fixed income funds, and one at Price or Scudder to have access to their stock funds, would be a good combination. Or, if you're moving two IRAs, put them at different organizations and enjoy a greater selection. Although it's important that you discipline yourself to have a long-term commitment to the diversification strategy, you need only make short-term commitments to individual funds and organizations.

225 for bond fund classifications and pages 243-245 for stock funds). Mr. Berry, for the most part, tries to work within the existing industry framework. (2) Mr. Berry's momentum calculation includes the most recent one month's performance, and extra momentum points are awarded to the top performing funds in each time period (one month, three months, etc.). My calculation includes neither of these two factors. (3) Mr. Berry replaces a fund when it drops out of the top five of its risk group; I apply looser standards in order to reduce the number of transactions. (4) I limit myself to those no-load funds available through Schwab and Fidelity; Mr. Berry does not. (5) The greatest deviation is that I inject my personal views about market risk into the decision-making process. For example, I have occasionally held funds even after they've fallen below the median in their group because I believed they would hold up better during a market reversal. Mr. Berry goes strictly by the numbers.

I did not sit down and decide on my adaptations all at once. They were each introduced over time as I attempted to make my strategy simple to understand and as easy to implement as possible (items one through four). Plus, because I've learned that most of my readers are risk averse, I've tried to make my recommended portfolios relatively safe (item five).

If you understand and approve of the rationale behind upgrading, and decide you want to apply the strategy in your portfolio, you have three choices. One, you can subscribe to Burton Berry's monthly newsletter and follow his lead. I make no claim that my approach is superior to his, and remain indebted to him for introducing me to the upgrading concept. Two, you can subscribe to my newsletter (see inside back cover) and let me do the work for you. Or three, you can do the research, data collection, and math calculations for yourself. You'll still need a source to provide you with the updated monthly performance data—which will likely cost you more than either of the above-mentioned newsletters. But it's a good way to build your understanding of the fund industry and increase your familiarity with the risks/rewards of owning the various kinds of funds.

As important as it is to make good fund selections, I hope you remember from Section Three that such decisions are third in importance . . .

. . . when it comes to the impact it will have on your long-term results. The decision of first importance is the asset allocation decision—what percentage of your investments should be in stocks and what percentage in bonds. In chapter 14, I provided a "controlling your risk" matrix to help you with this. It took into account both your current season of life and your emotional tolerance for risk (see pages 164-170).

Second in importance is deciding how much of your bond holdings to invest in each of the various bond risk categories (pages 224–225) and how much of your stock holdings to invest in each of the various stock risk categories (pages 243–245).

To help get you started, the table at right shows the suggestions I made to my newsletter readers in 1996 for each of six different stock-to-bond allocations. These suggestions reflect my particular sense of the markets at that time. They are not absolutes—other market professionals might consider them too conservative or risky. You should feel free to make adjustments as you think best for your situation and current market conditions.

A final reminder:
Don't misplace your confidence.

Recently a huge audience tuned in to a sporting event that takes place in my hometown every year on the first Saturday in May—the Kentucky Derby. In addition to the tens of millions who watch on television, 140,000 or so crowded into Churchill Downs in order to experience the tradition, wagering, and cheering firsthand. It's the most discussed and anticipated thoroughbred event of the year.

Before the race, a "vote" is taken as to which horse will win. Participants vote with their pocketbooks by placing their bets, and the horse on which the most money is wagered becomes the favorite. Rarely do the fans in any sport spend more time studying data, reading commentary, or listening to experts before reaching a decision. The eventual favorite reflects the collective wisdom of the racing world.

In 1996, *for the seventeenth year in a row*, the favorite failed to win the Kentucky Derby. Based on their knowledge of the horses' recent histories, people "in the know" make educated judgments about how the horses will perform on a given day. But they're just guessing, right? Nobody knows for sure. In that sense, it will always be a case of the blind leading the blind.

CHOOSING YOUR RISK LEVEL

Portion of Portfolio Allocated to Stocks:	100%	80%	60%	40%	20%	None
Portion of Portfolio Allocated to Bonds:	None	20%	40%	60%	80%	100%
Invest by Owning: International Stocks — Stock portfolios that invest worldwide; may be growth/value, invest in large/small companies	15%	10%	10%	10%	None	None
Invest by Owning: Stock Risk Category 4 — Stock funds that invest in smaller companies and employ a growth strategy ↑ / Invest by Owning: Stock Risk Category 3 — Stock funds that invest in smaller companies and employ a value strategy ↓	50% ↑↓	45% ↑↓	30% ↑↓	20% ↑↓	10% ↑↓	None ↑↓
Invest by Owning: Stock Risk Category 2 — Stock funds that invest in large companies and employ a growth strategy ↑ / Invest by Owning: Stock Risk Category 1 — Stock funds that invest in large companies and employ a value strategy ↓	35% ↑↓	25% ↑↓	20% ↑↓	10% ↑↓	10% ↑↓	None ↑↓
Invest by Lending: Bond Risk Category 4 — Bond funds that invest in high-yield junk bonds, typically of medium-term maturities	None	None	10%	10%	15%	15%
Invest by Lending: Bond Risk Category 3 — Bond portfolios of generally good quality with long-term average maturities (over 10 years)	None	None	None	None	None	None
Invest by Lending: Bond Risk Category 2 — Bond portfolios of generally good quality with medium-term average maturities (4–10 years)	None	10%	20%	35%	45%	60%
Invest by Lending: Bond Risk Category 1 — Bond portfolios of generally good quality with short-term average maturities (4 years or less)	None	10%	10%	15%	20%	25%

The financial markets are no different. When an investing professional offers stock, bond, and mutual fund recommendations, he doesn't know where the markets are going any more than you do. But he may know where they've been; that is, *he may know how they've behaved in the past under similar economic circumstances.* The expert knows more history, that's all. Based on that knowledge, he forms opinions as to how the markets will behave in the near future. Unfortunately, it's not that simple. As Warren Buffett has observed, "If you could simply extrapolate the past into the future, the richest people would all be librarians."

With this in mind, a certain humility is in order concerning one's ability to profit (and help others profit) from correctly anticipating coming economic events. Unfortunately, this does not seem to have occurred to the publishers of the three financial magazines I have sitting before me on my desk. The bold headlines, which claim the ability to know what's going to be best for you in the coming months, virtually shout from the covers.

◆ *Money* has photos of everyday people asking questions like: "Will stocks rebound? Will bonds come back big? What's the coolest bet for my future?" Fortunately, *Money* has the answer in the cover story: "Where to Make Money Today, Rewarding Answers to Your Most Urgent Questions."

◆ The May 1995 cover of *Smart Money* promoted the article "Where to Invest Now" with this subhead: "Growth or recession? Either way, here are five investments that will thrive."

◆ *Worth* magazine's cover article "New Outlook for Stocks" was hyped with this self-assured subhead: "Last year's strategies won't work in this market. Here's what will."

Notice how words like "today," "now," and "new" are used in the headlines to communicate a sense of urgency, as if last month's advice is already obsolete. When does such presumption become a form of fraud perpetrated on the consumer? This is harmful and misleading stuff. It incorrectly conveys a sense of predictability concerning the economy and markets. It downplays the reality of risk and encourages a false sense of security. And it undermines your ability to develop the long-term mind-set that is characteristic of most successful investors.

In writing SMI, my premise is that it's impossible to self-destruct financially if our decision-making is pointed in the direction of God's glory. (We'll talk more about this in Section Six.) One characteristic of investing that glorifies God is that it respects His wisdom, not man's. If it's your desire to have confidence in managing your finances rather than relying on the guesswork of others, ask God to help you learn the essential basics you need in order to become a faithful and effective steward. It's a prayer He's eager to answer. "If any of you lacks wisdom, he should ask God, who gives generously to all without finding fault, and it will be given to him" (James 1:5). ◆

Retirement Countdown

Preparing for the
High Cost of Prime Time

"The Social Security system calls it quits.
Details at 11:00. And now, sit back and enjoy tonight's movie..."

CHAPTER PREVIEW

The High Cost of Living in Prime Time

I. **As the baby-boomer generation moves into retirement, the sixty-five-and-over age group will grow from 12% at present to 20% of the total population. The need for adequate retirement planning will grow too.**

    A. Today's retirees are the wealthiest in U.S. history. With life expectancies of about fifteen years following retirement, the vast majority of them live out their lives quite comfortably.

    B. As life expectancies continue to increase, the baby-boomer generation can reasonably expect to live twenty to twenty-five years past retirement.

    C. Longer life expectancies and the increasing cost of health care indicate that today's workers must plan carefully to be sure of financial security during retirement.

II. **Projecting your financial needs for a secure and comfortable retirement involves making many financial assumptions concerning inflation, future rates of return, and your life expectancy. Worksheets are included that will help you through the process.**

    A. Project your post-retirement budget by making adjustments in your current budget to reflect the changes that accompany retirement.

    B. Allow for the effects of inflation.

    C. Estimate your "prime time wealth," the total amount of capital needed to carry you from the commencement of your retirement years though the rest of your life.

    D. Determine the income you'll receive from Social Security and other pensions.

    E. Project the value of your current long-term investments at retirement.

    F. Based on all the above, you can calculate how much you should be saving each year between now and retirement in order to reach your financial goals.

    G. Your projected income needs at retirement may appear daunting. You should be comforted by God's promise to meet all our needs "according to his glorious riches in Christ Jesus" (Philippians 4:19).

When I was a small child, perhaps five or so, it used to fascinate me to think that someday I'd be "old" like my parents.

My mother was twenty-one when I was born, and I used to say to her (proud of my newly acquired ability to add numbers), "Mom! When I'm twenty-one, you'll be forty-two!" And she'd answer back, "And when you're forty-two, I'll be sixty-three!" Knowing it was my turn to go next, I would usually begin giggling at what to me was a really silly idea; namely, that I would *ever* be sixty-three or that she would *ever* be eighty-four!

I could imagine being old enough to go to high school someday, and maybe college after that. I could almost imagine being old enough to get married, although I wasn't at all sure why I would ever want to. But picturing myself as being over sixty, like my grandparents, was simply incomprehensible, beyond the limits of my youthful imagination.

I recalled my little childhood game recently as I read some fascinating statistics on what has been called "the graying of America." Did you know that today's generation of retirees (I'll call them "prime-timers") are the wealthiest in U.S. history? They participated in the postwar economic boom, watched their homes greatly escalate in value during the inflationary 1970s, and paid far less into pension plans and Social Security than they are now taking out in indexed benefits. At the same time, the children are grown and out on their own, most mortgages are paid off, and work-related expenses are no longer a drag on the family budget.

The vast majority of Americans sixty-five and older are living comfortably. They have an average net worth . . .

. . . of around $100,000 per household. According to a report based on 1990 census data published in *American Demographics* magazine, 75% own their own homes, almost 80% have savings that average $20,000, and more than 20% have another $11,000 in stock and bond portfolios.

The number of those joining the ranks of the retired is increasing at twice the rate of the overall population. By the year 2030, the post-WWII "baby boomers" will raise the prime-timer population to 64 million. This translates to about one out of every five Americans, up from only one in every eight now. What will retirement be like for us newcomers? (Although I was born a year too early to officially be a boomer, I'm taking a little editorial license and including myself.) Will we have it as good? The trends are not encouraging.

Somewhat paradoxically, the problem has to do with the fact that life expectancy continues to make remarkable gains. This increasing longevity is due mainly to the continuing improvements in health care; also contributing to longer lives is the American public's discovery of the benefits of nutrition, physical fitness, and healthier lifestyles. About 80% of prime-timers consider their health excellent, good, or fair. A significant decline in activities and interests doesn't generally occur until age 85 and later.

It now seems that moving into the 85-plus group has the "elderly" connotation formerly associated with the 65-plus group. One expert refers to them as "old-olds" to distinguish them from the "young-olds" who are *only* 65 to 84. The old-olds population is growing fast, projected to exceed 8 million by 2030. The odds of living to age 100 are now down to just eighty-seven to one. The number of centenarians will triple in the next ten years; more than 35,000 are now at least age 100.

In short, we'll all be living longer. And let's face it: living costs money.

Of course, the longer the life, the greater the likelihood that support services will be needed; families now stand a greater chance than ever before of having a disabled elderly relative to support. More than 80% of us will enjoy reasonably good health, but even so, it's estimated that health care for prime-timers costs three to four times what it costs the rest of the population. Then there are the other niceties of everyday life, such as food, shelter, clothing, and recreation.

LIFE EXPECTANCIES		
Age	Men	Women
30	50 more years	55 more years
35	45 more years	50 more years
40	40 more years	45 more years
45	36 more years	40 more years
50	31 more years	35 more years
55	27 more years	31 more years
60	23 more years	26 more years
65	19 more years	22 more years
70	15 more years	18 more years
75	12 more years	14 more years
80	9 more years	11 more years
85	7 more years	8 more years
90	5 more years	6 more years
95	4 more years	4 more years

A fundamental fact of retirement life is that you don't want your money to run out before you do! For a reasonable guess as to how long you'll live in retirement, let's consider the case of 65-year-old males as shown in the table at right. On average, a man who lives to age 65 goes on to live another 19 years. Roughly half of this age 65 group will live more than 19 years and half will live less. To be on the safe side, financially speaking, you have to assume you'll be in the surviving group. If you make it to age 85, your expected life span is increased another seven years. That means, in the absence of health reasons to the contrary, your goal should probably be to have enough money to support yourself (and your spouse, if married) into your nineties.

So that brings us to the big question: how much is all this going to cost, anyway?

If you're feeling a sense of urgency about learning the answer, good! I've got your attention. Now you're ready to make the effort needed to come up with a reasonable approximation of how much you should be budgeting for your own prime-time experiences. My goal is to help you understand what it will take to get you "in shape" financially in preparation for your retirement years. The process will involve making a series of assumptions. As we go along, I will explain the reasoning for the ones I make, but feel free to change them to fit your own sense of what is appropriate.

Getting in shape is not a particularly enjoyable process. It requires us to consistently sacrifice *certain* enjoyments now in return for *uncertain* benefits in the future. Watching my diet and scheduling regular workouts is, for me, extremely easy to postpone. Retirement planning, and the goal of getting in shape financially, is similar. It's no fun, it requires short-term sacrifice with little immediate positive reinforcement, and the benefits can seem a long way off. That may explain why too many of us arrive in our sixties ill-prepared—in both body and bank account—to get the most from our retirement years. You need not let this happen to you and your family.

The remainder of this chapter is devoted to a step-by-step process that will help you see where you are now in relation to your long-term retirement needs.

The series of worksheets on the following pages is designed to serve only as a very general tool to help you think through your personal retirement planning responsibilities. It is based on a variety of assumptions concerning inflation and the rates of return you will earn on your investments. The closer you are to retirement, the more accurate it is likely to be. It's a good idea to run the numbers anew every two years or so to keep them reasonably on target.

"Should You Use a Financial Planner?" by Dan Hardt. Excerpted from the Sound Mind Investing newsletter. See Briefing 18, page 479.

Unless noted, I've made no special attempt to take one's normal annual income tax obligations into consideration. All the financial goals and standard of living assumptions are based on "before tax" dollars. My hypothetical couple, the Millers, have a current income of $50,000 before income taxes. The dollars they have remaining after they pay their income taxes are sufficient to support a certain standard of living. I assume the same will be true during their retirement. That is, they will have to pay their income taxes out of their projected retirement income just as they do their other living expenses. I took this approach because it was impossible to accommodate all of the various state and federal income tax rates currently in effect, let alone guess what they might be years into the future.

Let me warn you ahead of time that you might be tempted to feel discouragement when you complete step 11. That's the point at which you discover . . .

. . . based on assumptions you will have made regarding lifestyle costs, inflation, and your life expectancy, how much money you will need in order to live comfortably for the rest of your life once you retire. It will be a huge number. But don't stop there. By the time you factor in Social Security and your other pension and retirement assets, you'll likely find that the amount you need to save between now and retirement (step 45) is manageable.

Bear in mind that the projections in the worksheet are based on the assumption that you will live to a specific age. If the end of your (earthly) life comes earlier than you had assumed, there will be money on hand that you won't need. It can be left to your heirs and the Lord's work. If you die "on schedule," you and your money will run out at the same time. If you live longer than you had expected, you'll have a problem.

There are two ways to deal with this "risk." One is to pick a very long life expectancy (e.g., 95 or 100). That way, you would be less likely to outlive your money. A second way, assuming you own your house, is to sell it or take out a "reverse mortgage" in order to create additional cash flow.

If you don't like filling out forms such as those that follow, the Vanguard organization offers a very user-friendly computer program . . .

. . . that automates most of the retirement planning process and does all the math for you. *The Vanguard Retirement Planner* (version 3.0 for Windows) is an inexpensive tool that can help you plan realistically. It will assist you in answering such key questions as, "How much do I need to be saving now in order to have a comfortable retirement later?" and, "How should I allocate my savings among the different types of investments?" The interview process is simple and straightforward, and the color graphics are entertaining and informative. Since situations change frequently throughout our lives, *The Planner* makes it easy to make adjustments at any time and review how they affect your course.

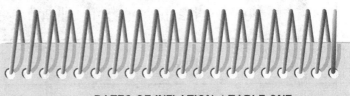

RATES OF INFLATION / TABLE ONE

YEARS UNTIL RETIREMENT

	3.0%	3.5%	4.0%	4.5%	5.0%	5.5%	6.0%
5	1.159	1.188	1.217	1.246	1.276	1.307	1.338
6	1.194	1.229	1.265	1.302	1.340	1.379	1.419
7	1.230	1.272	1.316	1.361	1.407	1.455	1.504
8	1.267	1.317	1.369	1.422	1.477	1.535	1.594
9	1.305	1.363	1.423	1.486	1.551	1.619	1.689
10	1.344	1.411	1.480	1.553	1.629	1.708	1.791
11	1.384	1.460	1.539	1.623	1.710	1.802	1.898
12	1.426	1.511	1.601	1.696	1.796	1.901	2.012
13	1.469	1.564	1.665	1.772	1.886	2.006	2.133
14	1.513	1.619	1.732	1.852	1.980	2.116	2.261
15	1.558	1.675	1.801	1.935	2.079	2.232	2.397
16	1.605	1.734	1.873	2.022	2.183	2.355	2.540
17	1.653	1.795	1.948	2.113	2.292	2.485	2.693
18	1.702	1.857	2.026	2.208	2.407	2.621	2.854
19	1.754	1.923	2.107	2.308	2.527	2.766	3.026
20	1.806	1.990	2.191	2.412	2.653	2.918	3.207
21	1.860	2.059	2.279	2.520	2.786	3.078	3.400
22	1.916	2.132	2.370	2.634	2.925	3.248	3.604
23	1.974	2.206	2.465	2.752	3.072	3.426	3.820
24	2.033	2.283	2.563	2.876	3.225	3.615	4.049
25	2.094	2.363	2.666	3.005	3.386	3.813	4.292
26	2.157	2.446	2.772	3.141	3.556	4.023	4.549
27	2.221	2.532	2.883	3.282	3.733	4.244	4.822
28	2.288	2.620	2.999	3.430	3.920	4.478	5.112
29	2.357	2.712	3.119	3.584	4.116	4.724	5.418
30	2.427	2.807	3.243	3.745	4.322	4.984	5.743
31	2.500	2.905	3.373	3.914	4.538	5.258	6.088
32	2.575	3.007	3.508	4.090	4.765	5.547	6.453
33	2.652	3.112	3.648	4.274	5.003	5.852	6.841
34	2.732	3.221	3.794	4.466	5.253	6.174	7.251
35	2.814	3.334	3.946	4.667	5.516	6.514	7.686
36	2.898	3.450	4.104	4.877	5.792	6.872	8.147
37	2.985	3.571	4.268	5.097	6.081	7.250	8.636
38	3.075	3.696	4.439	5.326	6.385	7.649	9.154
39	3.167	3.825	4.616	5.566	6.705	8.069	9.704
40	3.262	3.959	4.801	5.816	7.040	8.513	10.286

(continued on page 335)

RETIREMENT PLANNING WORKSHEET: SECTION 1			
How much annual income will you need during prime time?			
Overview	Step by Step	Millers	Yourself
In order to project the amount of annual income you are likely to need each year during retirement, we start by considering how your income needs will change as you enter retirement. The good news is that you can expect to maintain approximately the same standard of living you have now in spite of the fact you will have a lower income after you retire. There are several reasons for this: 1. You won't have work-related expenses such as commuting, eating away from home, and wardrobe maintenance. 2. You won't have the children to feed, clothe, transport, and educate. 3. You won't have to pay Social Security and other payroll taxes. 4. You won't be contributing to your personal and employer's retirement plans. 5. And, assuming you arrive at retirement debt-free, you won't have home mortgage payments, car payments, or credit card payments to make. Of course, as I've already pointed out, you'll be facing increased health care costs, and since you'll have more free time, you're also likely to spend more on recreation. But all in all, most experts say that if your retirement income is around 70%–80% of what you're earning now, you'll be in good shape; however, they warn that you're likely to face financial difficulties if it drops below 50% of what you're now making. Let's see how this works. I'm going to pick a family out of the mid-range of the census data and assume we are preparing a projection for them. Let's call them the Millers. The husband and wife are both thirty-five years old and have current income (before taxes) of $50,000 per year. What will their annual income needs be when they retire? To be on the conservative side, I'm going to use 80% as their "lifestyle maintenance" assumption; that is, the Millers' retirement income needs will be equal to 80% of their current level of income. By multiplying the lifestyle maintenance assumption times their current income (80% x $50,000), we learn that the Millers will need to generate $40,000 per year in income (before taxes) during their prime-time years. Of course, that's in today's dollars. How can we adjust this number so that it will have the same buying power during retirement that is does today? Continue on to the next page.	1. Enter <u>your current before-tax annual income</u>, or if you wish to plan for a higher standard of living than you now enjoy, enter an amount that you believe would provide that standard of living. 2. Enter <u>your lifestyle maintenance assumption</u>. 3. Multiply Item 1 by Item 2. This provides an estimate of how much <u>annual income (before taxes) you will need during retirement</u> to maintain your standard of living.	*$50,000* *x 80%* *= $40,000*	

	RETIREMENT PLANNING WORKSHEET: SECTION 2		
	What about the effects of inflation?		
Overview	Step by Step	Millers	Yourself
At the end of 1975, the consumer price index was 55.5. Twenty years later, it stood at 153.5. That translates to an average official inflation rate of +5.2% per year. Stated in terms that are more understandable, a 1975 dollar has officially shrunk to just thirty-six cents! Because your family's spending pattern is unique, your personal inflation experience will be different from any theoretical number computed for the "typical" American family.	3. From page 326.	$40,000	
	4. Enter the rate of inflation assumption which you are making for planning purposes.	4% inflation	
The Millers' $40,000 will not always buy for them what it can buy today. We need to take the $40,000 per year we projected as the Millers' annual income need during retirement and translate that to a higher number to allow for the fact that the value of the dollar shrinks a little every year.	5. Enter the number of years remaining until you retire.	30 years	
To do that, we refer to the inflation chart on page 325. I'm assuming that long-term inflation will average 4% per year. (You are free to change the inflation assumption. Choosing a higher rate, for example, is for the extra cautious person who wants to be doubly careful to arrive at retirement with a sufficient nest egg built up. Choosing a lower rate is for those who think I'm being too pessimistic—after all, inflation averaged just 3.5% annually for the ten years ending in 1995.)	6. Using the table on page 325, enter the inflation adjustment factor which reflects your assumption concerning the rate of future inflation and the years remaining until you retire.	x 3.243	
Since the Millers have thirty years to go before they retire at age sixty-five, we look down the left-hand column until we come to the number "30." Then, we go over three columns to find the number listed under the 4% heading.	7. Multiply Item 3 by Item 6. This is an estimate of the amount of income you will need during your first year of retirement to sustain your desired standard of living.	= $129,720	
The number we find is 3.243. Now, here comes the scary part. We multiply $40,000 times 3.243 to learn what the Millers' income will need to be when they retire in thirty years in order to maintain the standard of living they enjoy today. The answer is $129,720 per year! Sort of overwhelming, isn't it? It's difficult to imagine that the day will come when a family would need that much money every year just to maintain a modest lifestyle.			

RETIREMENT PLANNING WORKSHEET: SECTION 3

Will you have enough to sustain you through a normal life expectancy?

Overview	Step by Step	Millers	Yourself

An essential part of your planning is to come up with a reasonable estimate of how long you (and, if married, your spouse) will live. The table of life expectancies on page 323 is a good starting point. You can make adjustments based on your current state of health and family history.

We use this information to project how much income you'll need during the whole of your retirement years. This is a function of your standard of living, life expectancy, and the rate of inflation after you retire.

The table below has been designed to do the math for you. In the Millers' situation, I'm being cautious and assuming they will live to be ninety. This means their life expectancies after retirement at age sixty-five are another twenty-five years. Continuing to assume inflation of 4%, the table gives us a factor of 43.31.

RATES OF INFLATION / TABLE TWO

Years	3.0%	3.5%	4.0%	4.5%	5.0%	5.5%	6.0%
1	1.03	1.04	1.04	1.05	1.05	1.06	1.06
2	2.09	2.11	2.12	2.14	2.15	2.17	2.18
3	3.18	3.21	3.25	3.28	3.31	3.34	3.37
4	4.31	4.36	4.42	4.47	4.53	4.58	4.64
5	5.47	5.55	5.63	5.72	5.80	5.89	5.98
6	6.66	6.78	6.90	7.02	7.14	7.27	7.39
7	7.89	8.05	8.21	8.38	8.55	8.72	8.90
8	9.16	9.37	9.58	9.80	10.03	10.26	10.49
9	10.46	10.73	11.01	11.29	11.58	11.88	12.18
10	11.81	12.14	12.49	12.84	13.21	13.58	13.97
11	13.19	13.60	14.03	14.46	14.92	15.39	15.87
12	14.62	15.11	15.63	16.16	16.71	17.29	17.88
13	16.09	16.68	17.29	17.93	18.60	19.29	20.02
14	17.60	18.30	19.02	19.78	20.58	21.41	22.28
15	19.16	19.97	20.82	21.72	22.66	23.64	24.67
16	20.76	21.71	22.70	23.74	24.84	26.00	27.21
17	22.41	23.50	24.65	25.86	27.13	28.48	29.91
18	24.12	25.36	26.67	28.06	29.54	31.10	32.76
19	25.87	27.28	28.78	30.37	32.07	33.87	35.79
20	27.68	29.27	30.97	32.78	34.72	36.79	38.99
21	29.54	31.33	33.25	35.30	37.51	39.86	42.39
22	31.45	33.46	35.62	37.94	40.43	43.11	46.00
23	33.43	35.67	38.08	40.69	43.50	46.54	49.82
24	35.46	37.95	40.65	43.57	46.73	50.15	53.86
25	37.55	40.31	(43.31)	46.57	50.11	53.97	58.16
26	39.71	42.76	46.08	49.71	53.67	57.99	62.71
27	41.93	45.29	48.97	52.99	57.40	62.23	67.53
28	44.22	47.91	51.97	56.42	61.32	66.71	72.64
29	46.58	50.62	55.08	60.01	65.44	71.44	78.06
30	49.00	53.43	58.33	63.75	69.76	76.42	83.80

LIFE EXPECTANCY AFTER RETIREMENT (vertical label)

7. From page 327. — $129,720

8. Using the life expectancy table on page 323 as a guide, enter the number of years of life after retirement that you have decided to use for financial planning purposes. — 25 years

9. Enter the inflation assumption that you are making for planning purposes. It can be the same assumption you used in Item 4, or you can raise or lower it if you have a different outlook for the more distant years. — 4% inflation

10. Using the table at left, enter the inflation adjustment factor that reflects your inflation assumption as well as the years of life expectancy after retirement. — x 43.31

11. Multiply Item 7 by Item 10. This is the approximate total spending you anticipate during all of your retirement years. Let's call it your "prime time wealth." In the Millers' case, this would be the total expected spending for the twenty-five years following retirement. — $5,618,173

RETIREMENT PLANNING WORKSHEET: SECTION 4			
How much of your "prime time wealth" will Social Security provide?			
Overview	Step by Step	Millers	Yourself

Overview	Step by Step	Millers	Yourself
For years, workers have been paying much more in Social Security taxes than was needed to fund the current level of benefits. That's because a surplus was needed in order to take care of the baby boomers when they retire beginning around 2010. Projections made at the time of the 1983 "reforms" predicted the surplus would peak at a huge $16 trillion before the baby boomer drawdown began.	12. Enter the amount of <u>your combined annual Social Security benefits</u> as projected in your current Earnings and Benefit Estimate Statements (in today's dollars).	$23,544	
Critics at the time said this was based on several unrealistic assumptions having to do with birth rates, life expectancies, and economic growth. They were dismissed, of course, as hysterical "gloom and doomers." Yet, eleven years later the projected surplus had almost vanished. The 1994 annual report on Social Security projected a peak surplus of a little over $1 trillion! Obviously, the critics were correct, and the reality is that the benefits will have to be substantially scaled back. We'll look at Social Security in the next chapter.	13. Enter the <u>inflation adjustment factor</u> used in Item 6.	x 3.243	
	14. Multiply Item 12 by Item 13. This is the approximate amount of <u>your Social Security benefit during your first year of retirement</u>.	$76,353	
Call (800) 772-1213 and request a Personal Earnings and Benefit Estimate Statement. This is a form you can file with the Social Security Administration that will provide you with a record of the contributions credited to your account and an estimate of what your retirement benefit will be. (You should do this every three years to check the accuracy of SSA's records.) If you will be retiring in the next ten years, this number will likely be fairly accurate. The further you go beyond ten years, however, the more you might want to adjust the estimate downward to allow for economic and political realities.	15. Enter Social Security's annual cost-of-living increase. You might assume an increase less than the inflation assumption (made in Item 9) in order to reflect the possibility of benefit cutbacks.	3% annual increases	
APPROXIMATE SOCIAL SECURITY BENEFITS TABLE THREE	16. Using Table Two on the opposite page, <u>enter the inflation adjustment factor</u> that reflects the inflation assumption in Item 15 as well as the years of life expectancy shown in Item 8.	x 37.55	

APPROXIMATE SOCIAL SECURITY BENEFITS TABLE THREE

Until your statement arrives, you can estimate your benefits from the table below. The Millers are a one-income family. Mr. Miller's estimated benefit is circled. Mrs. Miller's estimated benefit as a non-working spouse is equal to 50% of her husband's.

Age in 1995	Income in 1994:			
	$30,000	$40,000	$50,000	$60,000
30	$12,564	$14,196	$15,696	$17,376
35	$12,564	$14,196	($15,696)	$17,340
40	$12,564	$14,196	$15,696	$17,196
45	$12,564	$14,196	$15,696	$17,016
50	$12,564	$14,184	$15,528	$16,596
55	$12,564	$14,016	$15,108	$15,900
60	$12,504	$13,776	$14,652	$15,204
65	$12,348	$13,404	$14,064	$14,388

17. Multiply Item 14 by Item 16. This is the approximate total amount of <u>Social Security you can anticipate receiving during all of your retirement years</u>.

$2,867,062

RETIREMENT PLANNING WORKSHEET: SECTION 5

How much of your prime time wealth will your company's pension provide?

Overview	Step by Step	Millers	Yourself
There are two different varieties of pension plans (which we'll review in chapter 27). One kind is called a "defined-benefit" plan because the focus is on the lifetime benefit you'll ultimately receive. These plans promise to pay you, when you retire, a certain dollar amount every month for as long as you live. If you participate in a defined-benefit plan, your employer is required by law to offer you a summary of the plan that's written in layman's terms. This is called a "summary plan description," and should be readily available from your personnel department. Many companies also provide a personalized employee benefit statement once a year that provides an estimate of how much your monthly retirement check will be.	18. Enter the amount of your annual pension benefit. See your most recent employee benefit statement.	$3,312	
(The other major category of employer-sponsored retirement plans are called "defined-contribution" plans because they place their emphasis on how much the employer will put into the plan for you each year. They should not be included in the worksheet at this point— we'll get to those on the next page.)	19. If your benefit is "indexed for inflation," enter the factor used in Item 16. Or, if your benefit is not "indexed for inflation," enter the factor used in Item 8.	25	
When you reach retirement and the time comes for your monthly pension benefit to be paid, you have several choices as to how you wish it to be calculated. See pages 356-358. If you are currently a participant in a defined-benefit plan, make an appointment with the appropriate person at your company to get your specific questions answered.	20. Multiply Item 18 by Item 19. This is the approximate total amount of pension income you can anticipate receiving during all of your retirement years.	$82,800	
If you have participated in such a plan in the past at another company, you may have earned vested benefits there as well. Be sure to include them here also unless you have already moved them into an IRA rollover. In that case, enter the value of that account on the next page.	21. Enter the amount of your spouse's annual pension benefit from his or her employee benefit statement.	none	
	22. If your spouse's benefit is "indexed for inflation," enter the factor used in Item 16. Or, if your spouse's benefit is not "indexed for inflation," enter the factor used in Item 8.	N/A	
	23. Multiply Item 21 by Item 22. This is the approximate total amount of pension income your spouse can anticipate receiving during all of his or her retirement years.	none	

RETIREMENT PLANNING WORKSHEET: SECTION 6

How much of your prime time wealth must you provide?

Overview	Step by Step	Millers	Yourself

<table>
<tr><td>

In step 27, we learn the amount that you must supply from your own retirement investment strategy. Of course, you don't need to have all your prime time wealth available on your first day of retirement. After all, it's going to take the rest of your life to spend it all. The question is: How much of your prime time wealth do you need to have <u>at the outset</u> (knowing that your investments will continue to earn a respectable rate of return after you retire)?

Table Four, shown below, will help you ascertain that amount. It assumes not only that your retirement capital earns a return (see headings which range from 6% to 10%), but also that withdrawals are made from your investment accounts each month to meet current spending needs. The withdrawals are designed to exhaust the investment account by the end of your life expectancy. For example, when you have a remaining life expectancy of twenty-five years, you can withdraw 4.00% of the account value during that year (1 divided by 25). The next year, when you have twenty-four years of life expectancy, you can withdraw 4.17% of the account value (1 divided by 24). And so on. In the Millers' example, I assumed a 7% long-term return during retirement. This is lower than the 9% expected return prior to retirement because they should be taking less risk at this stage of life.

You should understand that this provides only a rough blueprint of what each year's cash flow will be like. The 7% return is an average over a twenty-five-year period. You might start off with a 15% return the first year, or a loss. If a given year's scheduled withdrawal is insufficient to cover that year's needs, you might have to "borrow" from next year and wait for your investment returns to catch up.

</td></tr>
</table>

RATES OF RETURN DURING RETIREMENT
TABLE FOUR

Years	6%	7%	8%	9%	10%
5	0.8368	0.8126	0.7891	0.7665	0.7445
10	0.7157	0.6764	0.6392	0.6039	0.5704
15	0.6080	0.5579	0.5115	0.4687	0.4292
20	0.5129	0.4559	0.4047	0.3587	0.3175
25	0.4299	0.3694	0.3166	0.2708	0.2311
30	0.3580	0.2968	0.2452	0.2019	0.1658
35	0.2963	0.2366	0.1881	0.1489	0.1174
40	0.2438	0.1873	0.1430	0.1086	0.0822

(LIFE EXPECTANCY — left axis label)

Step by Step / Millers:

24. Enter the amount from Item 11. I've been calling this <u>your prime time wealth</u>. — $5,618,173

25. Enter the amount from Item 17. This is the approximate total amount of <u>Social Security</u> you anticipate receiving during all of your retirement years. — $2,867,062

26. Enter the sum of Items 20 and 23. This is the approximate total amount of <u>pension income</u> you anticipate receiving during all of your retirement years. — $82,800

27. Subtract Items 25 and 26 from Item 24. This is the total <u>amount of your prime time wealth that you must provide</u>. — $2,668,311

28. Enter the average annual rate of return you are assuming <u>your investments will earn during retirement</u>. — 7% rate of return

29. Enter the factor from Table Four that reflects the life expectancy during retirement (Item 8) and the expected return on investments (Item 28). — x .3694

30. Multiply Item 27 by Item 29. This is the amount of capital you should have on hand as you enter retirement. — $985,674

RETIREMENT PLANNING WORKSHEET: SECTION 7

How much will your current tax-deferred portfolio be worth when you retire?

Overview	Step by Step	Millers	Yourself

Overview

Now that we know your prime time wealth goal, let's see how far along you are toward achieving it. In this section, we project the current values in any tax-deferred accounts you may have into the future. For the Millers, I'm assuming a 9% average annual rate of return. If you'd like to use a different assumption, see the table below. Using a lower percentage assumption implies a more cautious view, and may require a higher level of savings between now and retirement.

RATES OF RETURN / TABLE FIVE

Years	6%	7%	8%	9%	10%	11%	12%
5	1.34	1.40	1.47	1.54	1.61	1.69	1.76
6	1.42	1.50	1.59	1.68	1.77	1.87	1.97
7	1.50	1.61	1.71	1.83	1.95	2.08	2.21
8	1.59	1.72	1.85	1.99	2.14	2.30	2.48
9	1.69	1.84	2.00	2.17	2.36	2.56	2.77
10	1.79	1.97	2.16	2.37	2.59	2.84	3.11
11	1.90	2.10	2.33	2.58	2.85	3.15	3.48
12	2.01	2.25	2.52	2.81	3.14	3.50	3.90
13	2.13	2.41	2.72	3.07	3.45	3.88	4.36
14	2.26	2.58	2.94	3.34	3.80	4.31	4.89
15	2.40	2.76	3.17	3.64	4.18	4.78	5.47
16	2.54	2.95	3.43	3.97	4.59	5.31	6.13
17	2.69	3.16	3.70	4.33	5.05	5.90	6.87
18	2.85	3.38	4.00	4.72	5.56	6.54	7.69
19	3.03	3.62	4.32	5.14	6.12	7.26	8.61
20	3.21	3.87	4.66	5.60	6.73	8.06	9.65
21	3.40	4.14	5.03	6.11	7.40	8.95	10.80
22	3.60	4.43	5.44	6.66	8.14	9.93	12.10
23	3.82	4.74	5.87	7.26	8.95	11.03	13.55
24	4.05	5.07	6.34	7.91	9.85	12.24	15.18
25	4.29	5.43	6.85	8.62	10.83	13.59	17.00
26	4.55	5.81	7.40	9.40	11.92	15.08	19.04
27	4.82	6.21	7.99	10.25	13.11	16.74	21.32
28	5.11	6.65	8.63	11.17	14.42	18.58	23.88
29	5.42	7.11	9.32	12.17	15.86	20.62	26.75
30	5.74	7.61	10.06	(13.27)	17.45	22.89	29.96
31	6.09	8.15	10.87	14.46	19.19	25.41	33.56
32	6.45	8.72	11.74	15.76	21.11	28.21	37.58
33	6.84	9.33	12.68	17.18	23.23	31.31	42.09
34	7.25	9.98	13.69	18.73	25.55	34.75	47.14
35	7.69	10.68	14.79	20.41	28.10	38.57	52.80
36	8.15	11.42	15.97	22.25	30.91	42.82	59.14
37	8.64	12.22	17.25	24.25	34.00	47.53	66.23
38	9.15	13.08	18.63	26.44	37.40	52.76	74.18
39	9.70	13.99	20.12	28.82	41.14	58.56	83.08
40	10.29	14.97	21.72	31.41	45.26	65.00	93.05

YEARS UNTIL RETIREMENT

Step by Step

31. Enter the current values of any tax-deferred investment accounts you and your spouse have:
   a. IRAs — *Millers:* $4,552
   b. 401(k) — *Millers:* $22,460
   c. 403(b)
   d. Variable annuity
   e. Other
   f. Other

32. Enter the sum of all the accounts listed in Item 31. This is the total amount of tax-deferred capital that you and your spouse currently have working for you. — *Millers:* $27,012

33. Enter the average annual rate of return you are assuming your investments will earn between now and the year you retire. — *Millers:* 9% rate of return

34. Using the table at left, enter the rate of return factor that reflects your assumption concerning the future annual rate of growth of your long-term capital (Item 33) over the period of time between now and retirement (Item 5). — *Millers:* x 13.27

35. Multiply Item 32 by Item 34. This is an estimate of the value of your current tax-deferred capital when you reach retirement. — *Millers:* $358,449

How much will your current taxable holdings be worth when you retire?

Overview	Step by Step	Millers	Yourself

Overview

Now, we calculate the current value in your taxable holdings and estimate their value at the time of your retirement. We will take into account the taxes due on your gains under the assumption they will be paid with funds from these accounts. For the Millers, I'll use the same estimated rate of return of 9% as before. You can use the table below to select another one if you wish. This table differs from the one on page 332 in that it assumes a 34% combined state/federal income tax rate.

RATES OF RETURN / TABLE SIX

Years	6%	7%	8%	9%	10%	11%	12%
5	1.21	1.25	1.29	1.33	1.38	1.42	1.46
6	1.26	1.31	1.36	1.41	1.47	1.52	1.58
7	1.31	1.37	1.43	1.50	1.56	1.63	1.70
8	1.36	1.44	1.51	1.59	1.67	1.75	1.84
9	1.42	1.50	1.59	1.68	1.78	1.88	1.99
10	1.47	1.57	1.67	1.78	1.89	2.02	2.14
11	1.53	1.64	1.76	1.89	2.02	2.16	2.31
12	1.59	1.72	1.85	2.00	2.15	2.32	2.50
13	1.66	1.80	1.95	2.12	2.30	2.49	2.69
14	1.72	1.88	2.06	2.24	2.45	2.67	2.91
15	1.79	1.97	2.16	2.38	2.61	2.86	3.14
16	1.86	2.06	2.28	2.52	2.78	3.07	3.39
17	1.94	2.16	2.40	2.67	2.96	3.29	3.65
18	2.01	2.25	2.52	2.83	3.16	3.53	3.94
19	2.09	2.36	2.66	2.99	3.37	3.79	4.26
20	2.17	2.47	2.80	3.17	3.59	4.06	4.59
21	2.26	2.58	2.95	3.36	3.83	4.36	4.96
22	2.35	2.70	3.10	3.56	4.08	4.67	5.35
23	2.44	2.83	3.27	3.77	4.35	5.01	5.77
24	2.54	2.96	3.44	3.99	4.64	5.38	6.23
25	2.64	3.09	3.62	4.23	4.94	5.77	6.72
26	2.74	3.24	3.81	4.48	5.27	6.19	7.26
27	2.85	3.39	4.01	4.75	5.62	6.63	7.83
28	2.97	3.54	4.22	5.03	5.99	7.12	8.45
29	3.08	3.71	4.45	5.33	6.38	7.63	9.12
30	3.21	3.88	4.68	(5.65)	6.80	8.19	9.84
31	3.33	4.06	4.93	5.98	7.25	8.78	10.62
32	3.47	4.24	5.19	6.34	7.73	9.42	11.46
33	3.60	4.44	5.46	6.71	8.24	10.10	12.37
34	3.75	4.64	5.75	7.11	8.79	10.84	13.35
35	3.89	4.86	6.05	7.54	9.36	11.62	14.41
36	4.05	5.08	6.37	7.98	9.98	12.47	15.55
37	4.21	5.32	6.71	8.46	10.64	13.37	16.78
38	4.37	5.56	7.07	8.96	11.34	14.34	18.11
39	4.55	5.82	7.44	9.49	12.09	15.38	19.54
40	4.73	6.09	7.83	10.06	12.89	16.50	21.09

YEARS UNTIL RETIREMENT

Step by Step

36. Enter the current values of any <u>taxable investment</u> accounts that you and your spouse may have that are not part of your contingency fund or set aside for a special purpose like college or house purchase:
  a. Bank savings/CDs
  b. Money market funds .... $ 3,188
  c. Mutual funds
  d. Brokerage accounts .... $ 8,524
  e. Other
  f. Other

37. Enter the <u>sum of all the accounts listed in Item 36</u>. This is the total amount of taxable investments that you and your spouse currently have working for you. ...... $ 11,712

38. Using the table at left, <u>enter the rate of return factor</u> that reflects your assumption concerning the future annual rate of growth of your long-term capital (Item 33) over the period of time between now and retirement (Item 5). ...... x 5.65

39. Multiply Item 37 by Item 38. This is an estimate of the <u>value of your current taxable holdings when you reach retirement.</u> $66,173

RETIREMENT PLANNING WORKSHEET: SECTION 9
How much should you save each year to meet your retirement goal?

Overview	Step by Step	Millers	Yourself

Overview

Your final step is to calculate how much you need to save in the future in order to arrive at retirement day with the amount of capital needed. If the amount computed in step 43 is a positive number, you're already in great shape. Unfortunately, most of us need to continue adding to our retirement savings. Table Seven will help you determine the annual amount which you need to add each year to a tax-deferred account (it assumes no taxes are paid on the returns earned).

RATES OF RETURN / TABLE SEVEN

Years	6%	7%	8%	9%	10%	11%	12%
5	17.22%	16.80%	16.39%	15.99%	15.60%	15.22%	14.85%
6	13.92%	13.51%	13.11%	12.72%	12.34%	11.98%	11.63%
7	11.57%	11.16%	10.78%	10.40%	10.04%	9.69%	9.35%
8	9.81%	9.42%	9.04%	8.68%	8.33%	7.99%	7.67%
9	8.45%	8.07%	7.70%	7.35%	7.01%	6.69%	6.38%
10	7.37%	6.99%	6.64%	6.30%	5.98%	5.67%	5.38%
11	6.48%	6.12%	5.78%	5.45%	5.14%	4.85%	4.57%
12	5.76%	5.40%	5.07%	4.75%	4.45%	4.17%	3.91%
13	5.14%	4.80%	4.47%	4.17%	3.88%	3.62%	3.37%
14	4.62%	4.28%	3.97%	3.68%	3.40%	3.15%	2.91%
15	4.17%	3.84%	3.54%	3.26%	3.00%	2.75%	2.53%
16	3.78%	3.46%	3.17%	2.90%	2.65%	2.42%	2.21%
17	3.44%	3.13%	2.85%	2.59%	2.35%	2.13%	1.93%
18	3.14%	2.84%	2.57%	2.32%	2.09%	1.88%	1.69%
19	2.88%	2.58%	2.32%	2.08%	1.86%	1.66%	1.49%
20	2.64%	2.36%	2.10%	1.87%	1.66%	1.48%	1.31%
21	2.43%	2.15%	1.91%	1.69%	1.49%	1.31%	1.15%
22	2.24%	1.97%	1.73%	1.52%	1.33%	1.17%	1.02%
23	2.07%	1.81%	1.58%	1.38%	1.20%	1.04%	0.90%
24	1.91%	1.66%	1.44%	1.25%	1.08%	0.93%	0.80%
25	1.77%	1.53%	1.32%	1.13%	0.97%	0.83%	0.71%
26	1.64%	1.41%	1.20%	1.03%	0.87%	0.74%	0.63%
27	1.52%	1.30%	1.10%	0.93%	0.79%	0.66%	0.56%
28	1.42%	1.20%	1.01%	0.85%	0.71%	0.59%	0.49%
29	1.32%	1.11%	0.92%	0.77%	0.64%	0.53%	0.44%
30	1.23%	1.02%	0.85%	(0.70%)	0.58%	0.48%	0.39%
31	1.14%	0.95%	0.78%	0.64%	0.52%	0.43%	0.35%
32	1.07%	0.88%	0.72%	0.58%	0.47%	0.38%	0.31%
33	1.00%	0.81%	0.66%	0.53%	0.43%	0.34%	0.28%
34	0.93%	0.75%	0.61%	0.49%	0.39%	0.31%	0.25%
35	0.87%	0.70%	0.56%	0.44%	0.35%	0.28%	0.22%
36	0.82%	0.65%	0.51%	0.41%	0.32%	0.25%	0.19%
37	0.76%	0.60%	0.47%	0.37%	0.29%	0.22%	0.17%
38	0.71%	0.56%	0.44%	0.34%	0.26%	0.20%	0.15%
39	0.67%	0.52%	0.40%	0.31%	0.24%	0.18%	0.14%
40	0.63%	0.48%	0.37%	0.28%	0.22%	0.16%	0.12%

YEARS UNTIL RETIREMENT

Step by Step / Millers

40. Enter the amount from Item 35. This is the estimated value of your current tax-deferred investments when you reach retirement. — $358,449

41. Enter the amount from Item 39. This is the estimated value of your current taxable investments when you reach retirement. — $66,173

42. Enter the amount from Item 30. This is the amount of your prime time wealth that you must provide from your retirement investment strategy. — $985,674

43. Add Items 40 and 41 and subtract Item 42. This is your estimated shortfall if you do not continue adding to your retirement savings in future years. — − $561,052

44. Using the table at left, enter the annual savings growth factor that reflects your assumption concerning the future rate of growth of your capital (Item 33) over the period of time between now and retirement (Item 5). — × .70%

45. Multiply Item 43 by Item 44. This is an estimate of the amount of new savings you need to add to your tax-deferred accounts each year. — $3,927

For those investing in the Just-the-Basics strategy explained in Section Three, it's even more useful. *The Planner* can show you the likely results from using Vanguard's index funds. In fact, all Vanguard funds are found within the program, showing their total return, investment characteristics of each, and their risk and reward potential. Through a "What if?" illustration, the program also allows you to see how your portfolio would look under different assumptions. For example, what would likely happen if you adopted a more aggressive asset allocation (retirement more than twenty years away), or became more conservative as you approach retirement? The price is right—under $25 as this is written in 1996. To order by credit card, or for more information, call (800) 876-1840.

Of course, neither this brief exercise nor generalized computer software is an adequate substitute for sitting down with a qualified tax adviser or financial planner to develop a more personalized strategy.

**If all this seems a bit overwhelming, don't despair.
Inflation can be harnessed to work for you . . .**

. . . as well as against you. Before Section Five is completed, you'll have been given enough information to enable you to overcome three of the four most common elements of financial failure:

❶ **A failure to inquire.** Many are ignorant of the serious financial implications of our changing society and how they will be affected.

❷ **A failure to learn.** Once made aware, they may still lack the know-how needed to begin putting their financial house in order.

❸ **A failure to plan.** Even informed, knowledgeable people can let years go by without formulating goals and a strategy for achieving them.

But after I inform you of the seriousness of the situation, teach you the basics of survival, and lead you through the planning process, there's still one element that only you can overcome:

❹ **A failure to act.** Procrastination can be the greatest deterrent to reaching your financial goals. If you're like I was as a child, acting as if you'll never grow old, you've been losing valuable time. Commit yourself now to making the sacrifices needed to put your family's finances on a solid foundation.

**A new organization you should know more about is the
Christian Association of PrimeTimers.**

In September 1994 I wrote "Breaking Faith," an editorial in my monthly *Sound Mind Investing* newsletter that decried the endorsements by the American Association of Retired Persons (AARP) of the Clinton and Gephardt/Mitchell health reform proposals. I detailed how the organization had evolved from its altruistic, consumer-oriented beginnings in 1958 to its current status as a major player in Washington politics. In the pursuit of profits, the AARP has compromised its commitment to provide cost-competitive insurance products to its members. Further, its support of socialized medicine is but one manifestation of an overtly liberal political agenda.

Shortly after my editorial appeared, I was pleased to learn of a newly formed group called the Christian Association of PrimeTimers (CAP). Concerned for millions of Christians, either retired or nearing retirement, the association "provides its members with products and services of exceptional value, and encourages them to use their God-given talents and acquired wisdom to restore decency, morality, and righteousness in our nation."

CAP also provides challenging and life-enriching opportunities for those who wish to engage in volunteer service. The individual skills of CAP members are matched with the needs of various Christian organizations both here and abroad.

Some of the products that CAP provides at significant savings are: prescription drugs; comprehensive major medical and Medicare supplement insurance; homeowners, auto, and RV insurance; Christian books, magazines, music, and gifts; individual and group travel; a bank CAP MasterCard; and Wayside, a bed and breakfast travel club between members.

Membership in CAP is open to anyone age fifty or older, whether retired, semi-retired, or still working. Dues, for an individual or a couple, are only $12.95 annually. For membership information, write to: Christian Association of PrimeTimers, P. O. Box 777, St. Charles, Illinois, 60174, or call (800) 443-0227.

**As you contemplate the challenges ahead, meditate
on the promises of God given to us in Philippians 4:**

> *Do not be anxious about anything, but in everything, by prayer and petition, with thanksgiving, present your requests to God. And the peace of God, which transcends all understanding, will guard your hearts and your minds in Christ Jesus. . . . I have learned to be content whatever the circumstances. I know what it is to be in need, and I know what it is to have plenty. I have learned the secret of being content in any and every situation, whether well fed or hungry, whether living in plenty or in want. I can do everything through him who gives me strength. . . . And my God will meet all your needs according to his glorious riches in Christ Jesus.* ◆

CHAPTER PREVIEW

The Outrageous Truth About Social Security

I.   **The truth about Social Security is that it is a wealth-transfer program, much like welfare. It takes money from one group of citizens (active workers) and gives it to another group of citizens (inactive workers).**

    A.   It is not an "insurance" program because the amount you put in has no correlation to the amount you receive back. It does not "entitle" you to benefits because Congress can legally reduce them any time it chooses.

    B.   There is no "trust fund" set aside to be invested for future retirees, and so there can be no "surplus." Part of the payroll taxes coming in are transferred directly to retirees, but the rest are "borrowed" and spent immediately on federal programs.

    C.   Workers do not make "contributions" that "earn" them protection. Workers pay taxes that earn them nothing.

II. **When the baby-boomer generation enters retirement, there will be an inadequate number of active workers to tax. To balance the books:**

    A.   Changes will be needed that require active workers to pay more in taxes each year as well as work for more years before retiring.

    B.   Changes will be needed that decrease the level of monthly income that retired workers can expect to receive.

    C.   There will be a national dialogue in coming years on the various reform proposals. It's in your financial interest to become educated on the issues and actively participate in the debate.

**OK, I admit it. I wasn't looking forward to writing this chapter.
As the deadline approached . . .**

. . . I had to force myself to sit down, gather the needed reference materials, and begin reading. I had always considered the subject of Social Security to be complicated and boring. To my surprise, I was only half right; boring, it isn't.

It's shocking ("causing intense surprise, disgust").

It's appalling ("horrifying, daunting, and disheartening").

And yes, it's outrageous ("grossly offensive to one's sense of right or decency").

But it's not boring. What I learned, and will document for you here, is the extent to which today's workers are laboring under burdensome payroll taxes imposed on them by yesterday's leaders to pay for benefits promised to yesterday's voters.

**That there has not yet been a popular uprising against
Social Security can only mean . . .**

. . . that most Americans don't understand what is going on. And that is due in large part to the fact that *the Social Security system has been misrepresented to the American people from the beginning*.

When George Orwell wrote his classic novel *1984*, he coined the expression "doublethink." The ruling government ("Big Brother") used doublethink language to make lies sound truthful and to give an appearance of virtue where there was none. Our own government has proven masterful at this in the words it has used to promote the Social Security program.

**Recommended
Resource**
Social Security, Medicare,
and Pensions:
The Sourcebook for
Older Americans

by Joseph L. Matthews

The sixth edition of this
helpful book guides you
through the maze of federal
income and benefit
programs. In plain
language, it explains how
to keep from missing out
on income and coverage
and how to collect all
benefits due. It describes
the changes in the
Medicare system now that
the Catastrophic Coverage
Act has been repealed, and
explains all the rules senior
citizens need to know.

From the very founding of our country, most Americans believed that caring for the elderly was a private matter between family members. While Christian charities, churches, and state and local governments would often assist those with special needs, the basic responsibility remained with the individual. This all changed with the passing of the Social Security Act of 1935. For the first time, it became morally acceptable for the government to confiscate money from one group of citizens for the sole purpose of giving it away to another group of citizens. *Responsibility for the elderly was being transferred from the individual/family to society.* In order to overturn our 150-year tradition of self-reliance, doublethink wording was used to make this transition more acceptable to the American people.

Doublethink Example #1: We're told we're buying "insurance."

To disguise the fact that Social Security is actually a wealth-transfer program, the government named it "Old Age and Survivors Insurance." After all, buying insurance is a prudent financial step every family should take, isn't it? But insurance involves making payments proportionate to the risk involved. That's why insurance companies hire actuaries—to help them set premiums based on reasonable life expectancies. Social Security isn't like insurance at all;

your payments have little direct correlation to your ultimate benefits.

This immediately became obvious with the case of Ida Fuller. Before retiring in 1939, she had paid a mere $22 into Social Security. In her first month, she recouped all that she had ever paid in! By the time she left this life thirty-four years later at the age of 100, she had collected over $20,000—almost 1,000 times more than she had put in!

In *Beyond Our Means*, Alfred Malabre shares a different, but equally compelling, scenario:

> *Consider a worker who began paying into the system in 1937, when it was launched, and worked until 1982. If he had paid the maximum in Social Security taxes each of the forty-five working years, his payments would have totaled $12,828. His benefits would have begun at $734 a month. If he were married, his wife would collect half of his benefit, or an additional $367 monthly, bringing their total first-year benefit to $13,217, or more than he had paid in the forty-five years of employment.*

Malabre goes on to show that if the couple live out normal life expectancies, their lifetime benefits would amount to some $375,000! You may wonder how all this lavish generosity is possible. We'll take that up shortly.

Doublethink Example #2: We're told we're "entitled" to benefits.

We're led to believe that, upon retirement, our years of payments give us specific entitlement rights. That is, the government is obligated to honor its commitments. Unfortunately, that's not the case. The fact is that the government can change the rules anytime it wants. For example, it used to be that you could retire at age sixty-five with "full benefits." In 1983, as part of a Social Security bailout plan, Congress decided to raise the age requirements on a graduated basis. Now, people (like me) who were born between 1943-1954 have to work until age sixty-six to get full benefits. That involves not merely waiting an additional year to collect, but also an additional year of paying in. So, what I had been promised for half of my working life was suddenly changed at the stroke of a pen. Congress giveth and Congress taketh away.

Is that fair? No less an authority than the U.S. Supreme Court has ruled that Congress can do whatever it wants with Social Security, saying,

> *The Social Security program is in no sense a federally-administered insurance program under which each worker pays premiums over the years and acquires at retirement an indefeasible [guaranteed] right to receive for life a fixed monthly benefit irrespective of the conditions which Congress has chosen to impose from time to time.*

Justice Black dissented, saying in part,

> *I cannot believe that any private insurance company in America would be permitted to repudiate its matured contracts with its policyholders who have regularly paid all their premiums in reliance upon the good faith of the company.*

Pastors and Social Security

"The decision to withdraw from the Social Security system must be made solely on the basis of a pastor's conscientious objection to Social Security as a form of government welfare or assistance, and is not allowed under any other circumstances. There are also financial ramifications from that decision, and although they cannot be part of the decision, must be dealt with as a result of withdrawing. A pastor needs to understand the requirements placed upon him as a good steward of the Lord's property and of his family. If he elects to withdraw from Social Security, he needs to discipline himself and save and invest in an alternate retirement plan, as well as provide disability insurance in case he becomes unable to perform his duties for medical reasons."

Larry Burkett

But Justice Black lost because Social Security is a tax, not insurance as it has been called.

Doublethink Example #3: We're told we're making "contributions" that "earn" us protection.

Money is automatically taken out of our paychecks and called a "contribution." But unlike voluntary payments into a private pension plan, there's nothing voluntary about these so-called contributions. Try to get the government to stop the withholding and see what happens. The simple fact is that Social Security is a tax.

A majority of working Americans *now pay more in Social Security withholdings than they do in federal income taxes.* What started out as a 1% payroll tax with a $30 per year maximum per person is now a 12.4% tax with an annual maximum of $7,774 (of which you pay $3,887 directly out of your paycheck, and $3,887 is paid on your behalf by your employer—see sidebar).

For many years, Social Security distributed a booklet that contained this statement: "Nine out of ten working people are earning protection for themselves and their families under the social security program." The truth is that the individual worker is not "earning" anything in the same sense as one who invests in an IRA or other private pension plan. Rather, as we have seen, what nine out of ten working people are actually doing is paying taxes, which are then given to persons who are not working.

Now, I might not consider this to be all that bad if I thought my own turn would come—if, like Malabre's worker, I would get back all that I had paid in during my very first year of retirement, and that I would eventually reap lifetime benefits that were almost thirty times more than the total taxes I paid. But, alas, I harbor no such illusions; I know the awful truth about the so-called trust fund.

Doublethink Example #4: We're told our money goes into a "trust fund."

For most of us, the expression "trust fund" means that a sum of money is being accumulated, invested safely, and is growing daily as it awaits the time when it will be needed. It sounds secure. So it would be understandable if you thought in those terms when you hear that your money is going into the Social Security trust fund. That's what you're *supposed* to think. Unfortunately, nothing could be further from the truth. The Social Security program has not set aside any trust money for our future use, and never has. Actually the program is more like the world's largest chain letter.

Remember the examples I gave you earlier about the people receiving huge sums in relation to what they put in? Since their withholdings couldn't possibly have grown that much purely from investments, how was it possible? Here's how they did it. From the millions of dollars of "contributions" coming into Social Security each morning from the younger workers, Social Security took what they

Although 50% of the tax appears to be charged to the employer, most economists regard the entire 12.4% tax as being paid by the employee. The employer's half comes out of the total compensation package it is willing to offer to the worker. In the absence of the tax, that money would presumably be available for an increase in salary or fringe benefits.

needed in order to pay the generous "benefits" in the afternoon to the older retired workers. What did they do with the rest? They "invested" it in Treasury bonds.
In other words, Social Security loaned what was left to the federal government to
spend on whatever it wanted. That money is long gone; only the IOUs remain.

No one can tell you with certainty where the government will get the money
to pay Social Security for these IOUs. Need I remind you that we're talking here
about a government that annually spends hundreds of billions of dollars more
than it takes in? It is very good at borrowing; it is very bad when it comes to
paying back. It is so bad, in fact, that America has now become the world's largest debtor nation. Where will the government come up with the money when
Social Security comes knocking at its door with trillions of dollars of government IOUs in hand? In the great doublethink tradition, what Congress likes to
call a trust fund is actually a gigantic future liability!

Doublethink Example #5: We're told that Social Security is running a "surplus."

You will hear that the Social Security "trust fund" is running a surplus. According to government figures, it was $496 billion at the end of 1995. This is sup-
posed to be reassuringly good news, but it's not. The surplus is a drop in the bucket
compared to the level of benefits already promised. Here's the coming scenario
according to the *1996 Annual Report of the Board of Trustees of the Federal Old-Age
and Survivors Insurance Fund.*

◆ **From now until 2012.** At the present time, the taxes being paid into the
system by current workers is more than enough to pay the promised benefits to
retirees. The money that's not needed for paying benefits gets carried over to
the next year, increasing the surplus. Think of it as a family that is able to live
within its income and save for the future.

◆ **From 2012 through 2018.** Matters are projected to continue in this way until
2012, at which time the money going out (to an ever-larger number of retirees)
will exceed the money coming in (from an ever-smaller number of workers). At
that point, Social Security will have to use some of the interest income it receives
from its Treasury IOUs to make up the difference. Our family is now spending all
its income, and needs to use part of its interest income to support its standard of
living.

◆ **From 2019 through 2029.** In 2019, the interest income is no longer sufficient
to make up the difference. To continue making payments, Social Security will need
to draw on the surplus. This has two important implications: (1) the Treasury will
need to begin paying off its IOUs, and (2) as the IOUs are paid off and the money
distributed to retirees, there are fewer IOUs to earn interest for the coming years.
Our family is now beginning to spend the capital that has been providing the essential interest income. A downward spiral has begun.

Recommended Resource

Social Insecurity

by Dorcas R. Hardy
& C. Colburn Hardy

In case you doubt some of
the issues I raise about Social
Security in this chapter,
here's your chance to get the
facts direct "from the horse's
mouth." This book is
coauthored by Dorcas Hardy,
the commissioner of Social
Security under both
Presidents Reagan and Bush.
Her own testimony is that the
program will be "in serious
trouble soon after the start of
the 21st century." The book
is informative, sobering, and
motivational (see page 344
for an excerpt). The authors
begin by shattering the seven
most common myths about
Social Security and then
provide a personal action
guide that outlines the steps
you need to take to protect
yourself from the coming
crisis. I sent this book to
Larry Burkett, and he liked it
enough to have the author on
his radio program. Highly
recommended to get you
more fully informed about
Social Security.

◆ **2029 and later.** The surplus is gone; the trust fund is empty. All the IOUs have all been paid (don't ask me where the Treasury got the money) and the money spent. There is no interest income. And the tax money coming in covers only about three-fourths of the need. Our spendthrift family is broke.

As bad as this sounds, it's probably worse.

In 1975, Nobel Prize-winning economist Paul Samuelson defended Social Security, saying: "Social Security is sound with a life expectancy that can be measured in the centuries." And yet a brief two years later, it was on the brink of collapse. Jimmy Carter initiated a major rescue effort by dramatically raising Social Security taxes and trimming benefits. We were then assured that the program was sound "for the rest of this century and well into the next one."

But by 1980, it was already in deep trouble. This time a commission headed by Alan Greenspan, currently head of the Federal Reserve, was appointed. In 1983, it proposed a second rescue package, this one consisting of even more severe tax increases and benefit cuts. They included: raising the Social Security tax from 10.8% to the present 12.4%; raising the amount of salary that was subject to the tax; gradually increasing the normal retirement age at which retirees qualify to receive full benefits from sixty-five to sixty-seven; requiring some recipients to pay income tax on their Social Security benefits. Although these changes were unpleasant, we were told they would keep Social Security healthy for the next seventy-five years. In 1992, presidential candidate Bill Clinton assured us concerning Social Security, "It's solid. It's secure. It's sound."

Yet in 1995, we're told the system is in trouble again. The Social Security trustees, along with other economists and presidents from both parties, have an unbelievably poor track record when it comes to projecting the future condition of the system. In their 1990 annual report, the trustees projected the trust fund would be fine until 2043. By 1993, the time of reckoning had moved forward seven years to 2036. Now it has moved another seven years to 2029. Why should we have confidence that they got it right this time?

Sounds pretty hopeless, doesn't it? Just *how* hopeless depends on . . .

. . . how close *you personally* are to the day you switch teams—leaving the ranks of the people paying in and joining those in that happy state of grace where you receive monthly income for life far in excess of your earlier contributions. If you are planning to retire in the next ten years, you're in pretty good shape. There may be minor adjustments to your benefits along the way, but congressional hypocrisy and cowardice is probably good for another decade of failure to face up to Social Security's monumental problems.

The rest of us are probably going to be pretty unhappy about whatever "fix" Congress finally comes up with, and the younger we are now, the more unhappy

---

A Few Trillion Here, A Few Trillion There

"For the past decade Americans have been paying more Social Security tax than was needed to pay benefits. The idea, enacted in the 1983 reforms, was to build up a $16 trillion treasure trove of savings that the country could draw upon to pay benefits when the Baby Boom generation retires. Forget it. The $16 trillion was just an estimate based on unrealistic assumptions about fertility rates, life expectancies, interest rates and economic performance. In the 1994 annual report of Social Security, we find a new estimate of $1.2 trillion."

Barron's
May 9, 1994

we're likely to be. In the past, each generation of workers was asked to support the benefits for the previous generation. But it is falling to the baby-boomer generation to pay for the retirement of not only the previous generation (the workers who supported Ida Fuller so generously) but also to provide trillions in additional taxes for their own retirement as well.

Numerous reforms are being floated as ways to remedy the system.

◆ **Increase payroll taxes again.** A former chief actuary for the Social Security Administration estimated that individual payroll taxes would have to be raised from their present 12.4% rate to more than 40% just to pay all the benefits currently being promised. Is it realistic to think that the next generation will tolerate increases of that magnitude? Should they? Not a chance.

◆ **Slowing benefit growth.** Social Security is already a terrible investment for today's workers under age fifty. Reducing benefits would make it even worse. According to the *Wall Street Journal*, eliminating the deficit without increasing taxes would require that "Social Security would pay out 14% less across-the-board compared with what is currently promised by 2020 and up to 30% less by 2070."

◆ **Means testing.** This involves requiring individuals to pass a test concerning their annual income before granting them full benefits. One such proposal suggests that benefits should start being reduced for anyone who enjoys an annual retirement income of $40,000, and eliminated entirely if the income exceeds $120,000. This is a truly terrible idea because it would: (1) undermine public support for the Social Security program by turning it into just another welfare program where only the "needy" would receive full benefits; (2) discourage hard work, saving, and an attitude of self-reliance because your other retirement accounts would be used against you to deprive you of benefits that would be available only to those who weren't as frugal or farsighted; and (3) summarily break the promises of the past sixty years, further undermining respect for the law. It's an evil thing to force people to pay all their working lives into such a system, continually reassuring them that their benefits will be there when they retire, and then defrauding them at the last minute.

◆ **Privatization.** There have been several proposals that would allow younger workers to divert part of their Social Security taxes to an account similar to an IRA where they would have control over how it is invested. In return, they would surrender part of their future Social Security benefits. Chile pioneered this years ago when faced with a similar dilemma, and it has worked well there. Many other countries are studying Chile's results with an eye toward applying a similar strategy. There are many variations on this theme, and while the details differ, it seems inevitable that some form of privatization will be included in any long-term solution. Since this is where the action will likely be, I encourage you to read carefully any articles you see on this topic in order to stay informed.

Only a Starter?
"When President Clinton pushed his big tax increase through Congress in 1993, 85% of a Social Security pension became taxable income to people with substantial amounts of other income. This despite the fact that they had already been taxed on the money they put in. If you have savings and a private pension, the U.S. government taxes your Social Security contributions twice—before they go in and when they come out.

That broken promise is probably only a starter. Congress will almost certainly do such things as raise the pensionable retirement age and make Social Security need-based— a safety net rather than a pension plan. In the end only the disabled and seriously needy 70-year-olds may get the pension we all paid for."

Forbes
October 9, 1995

Today's workers carry the triple burden . . .

. . . of (1) paying far more in Social Security taxes than any previous generation, (2) waiting longer to collect than any previous generation, and (3) retiring with lower after-tax benefits than any previous generation. As unfair as this is, tomorrow's workers, our children, might have to pay even more, wait even longer, and receive even less. And that's why the truth about Social Security is indeed outrageous.

In light of the uncertainties surrounding the level of Social Security benefits after 2010, receiving significant support from the private retirement plans sponsored by your employer is all the more critical. A basic understanding of their strengths and weaknesses is essential if you are to plan realistically. We begin our look at such plans in the next chapter. ◆

COPING WITH SOCIAL INSECURITY

From the Introduction to Social Insecurity, by Dorcas R. Hardy, the commissioner of Social Security for
three years under Presidents Reagan and Bush, and C. Colburn Hardy, noted financial author and adviser.
Copyright 1991 by The Stonesong Press, Inc. Reprinted by permission of Villard Books, a division of Random House, Inc.

We ought to call it Social Insecurity, not Social Security. The Social Security system is a ticking time bomb. In the next century, just a few years away, the United States will face a potentially devastating crisis: the retirement checks that should be sent to benefit millions of Americans will not be there. This crisis will not affect those now receiving Social Security, but to maintain benefits for future retirees, significant changes must be made by Congress. Reform will not be easy. Because of its politically unappealing nature, the most critical economic issue America will face in the 21st century continues to simmer unabated.

The hard demographic and financial facts are that future retirees are unlikely, under any circumstances, to benefit as much from Social Security as their parents have. . . . The bottom line is that there are going to be many more older people, and relatively fewer working people to support them. By 2030, there will be only two workers for every retiree compared to three workers for every retiree today.

This ratio is crucial because Social Security is a pay-as-you-go system. Current taxes pay for current benefits. If benefits for future retirees are to remain unchanged, some project that payroll taxes may have to go as high as forty percent. Despite window dressing, Social Security is not a funded pension system where workers' money is invested and then paid back, with interest, later. It is a straightforward transfer of wealth from workers to retirees.

As a practical matter, it is unlikely that the Social Security system will collapse completely, the way some private pension systems have. More likely the fallout will be a combination of reduced benefits for retirees and increased taxes for everyone. Fortunately, in the United States, the private sector usually develops effective alternatives, and retirement income should be no exception. The individual must assume greater responsibility for his or her own after-work income by personal savings directly and through pension plans, sometimes with support from the employer.

There are also actions Congress can take to minimize the potential damage. A start would be to restore the full tax deductibility of Individual Retirement Accounts, which was taken away in the 1986 tax reform. Other important measures should be to: (1) raise the limits of annual contributions to all types of pension programs; (2) revise the mandated withdrawal schedule now for the actuarial lives of the recipients, to permit beneficiaries of pension plans to meet the realities of a longer life span; and (3) privatize a portion of Social Security taxes so that the individual worker can be responsible for financing his or her own retirement.

All these actions would be very helpful, but the ultimate responsibility for retirement income is yours. If you plan to rely heavily on Social Security, as the average retiree now does, your golden years are going to be a time of want and financial anxiety. What you save, or fail to save, while working, will determine what you can, or cannot do, upon retirement. A program of serious and consistent savings, and wise investment, begun now will assure a financially secure retirement.

CHAPTER PREVIEW

Your Pension at Work

I. **Employer-sponsored pension plans that promise to pay a specific dollar amount when you retire are called "defined benefit" plans.**

A. There are usually eligibility requirements to be met in terms of the length of time you've been with the company before you can participate in the plan.

B. The amount of your retirement benefit is computed according to a formula that takes many variables into account. Among them are your: salary and age at retirement, years with the company, Social Security benefits, and the survivors' benefit you select.

C. You should understand fully the circumstances under which you will receive a retirement benefit and how the benefit will be computed.

1. You are entitled to receive annual financial reports from your company, which contain information about the plan as well as your personal benefit.

2. If your company goes bankrupt before you retire, there is a chance your benefit will be affected. The Pension Benefit Guaranty Corporation exists to insure your benefit, but your best defense is to maintain an active, informed interest in all affairs affecting your company plan.

II. **Employer-sponsored pension plans that pay specific dollar amounts into your retirement account each year are called "defined-contribution" plans.**

A. These plans make no promises as to how much your benefit will be when you retire. Your retirement benefit will ultimately be determined by the amount and frequency of annual contributions and the investment performance experienced in your account.

B. Under such plans the risk of poor investment returns rests with the employee rather than the employer. That's why employees generally have significant control over the investment portfolios.

C. There is a variety of these plans with differing contribution requirements, limitations, and employer matching features. We discuss the key features of the major kinds of plans.

D. When you are ready to withdraw your benefits, these plans provide three alternative methods. Each has its own advantages, depending on your personal income and tax situation at that time.

**Although the government itself can change its rules anytime
it wants and arbitrarily reduce . . .**

. . . the Social Security benefits you've been "contributing" to for a working lifetime, it won't let *your employer* do that to you. After all, that wouldn't
be fair. (Congress loves to apply one set of standards to itself and a completely
different set to the rest of us!) So let's look at employer-sponsored pension
plans to see what help you can expect from your company. First, you should
understand that there are two different kinds of pension plans. One kind promises only to put a certain amount aside for you each year and makes no projections as to the amount of your ultimate monthly benefit. This kind is called
a "defined-contribution" plan, and it comes in a bewildering array of alpha-
bet-like names such as SEP-IRA, MPP, 401(k), and 403(b). We'll look at these
plans later in the chapter.

For now, let's concentrate on the other type of pension plan, the kind that
has been the overwhelming preference of business, industry, and state and
local governments. Of American workers who were covered by an employer-
sponsored pension plan in 1990, about 70% of them had this plan as their
primary pension coverage.

**These plans promise to pay you, when you retire,
a certain dollar amount every month for as long as you live . . .**

. . . however, they promise nothing about how much money your company will put aside each year to accomplish this (other than to observe certain minimum federal requirements). These plans are called "defined benefit"
plans because the focus is on the *lifetime monthly benefit* you'll ultimately receive. Under this arrangement, the employer carries the burden of where the
money for the contributions comes from as well as how well the investments
do between now and your retirement.

The first barrier standing between you and your monthly pension check
is meeting the eligibility requirements. Just because you've been hired doesn't
mean you immediately qualify for a company's retirement plan. Usually they
require (1) that you've reached a certain age, and (2) that you have been with
the company for a certain period of time before you qualify to join the plan. It
is customary that an employee must be at least twenty-one years old and have
been with the company at least one year.

Once you're eligible, what you really want to know is . . .

. . . how much is my monthly benefit going to be when I retire? That depends on several factors. Each is fairly simple; let's take them one at a time.

◆ **Salary formula.** The goal of a monthly pension check is to help replace
the earnings lost when you retire. That means your benefit is based primarily

on the amount of your annual earnings while you were still working. Some formulas take an average of your earnings from all the years you worked for the company. Presumably, the earlier years were not as well paying, so this is not as favorable to you as a plan that uses a formula based on your final year(s) of service.

◆ **Years of service.** People who spend their entire career with the same company receive more than those who come along later. Your benefit is affected by the number of years you work for your employer. But how many hours are needed to constitute a "year of service"? Some plans may require 500 hours in a twelve-consecutive-month period, whereas others require 1,000 hours. Or what if you worked for twenty years, left for two years, and returned for another eighteen years? Do you get credit for thirty-eight years or just the last eighteen years? And does it matter why you left for those two years? There are countless variations on this theme that can affect your benefit.

◆ **Vesting requirements.** When can you know for sure that you're guaranteed to receive at least some pension benefit from your employer? The day you start to work? The year you qualify to join the plan? After three years with the company? That's where the concept of "vesting" comes in. It means you have an absolute right to receive some money from a retirement plan, even if you resign or are fired. You're entitled to it no matter what.

Some plans call for "graded vesting," where you receive a right to a pension gradually (for example, 20% after three years, 40% after four years, and so on). Others provide for what is called "cliff vesting," an all-or-nothing approach where, for example, you could become 100% vested after five years but be entitled to nothing if you leave before then. The most favorable is "vesting upon entry" where you must wait for two years before qualifying to participate in the plan, but are immediately 100% vested upon entry. This is especially helpful to working women who, on average, change jobs more frequently than men.

◆ **Normal retirement age.** Most plans use formulas that consider sixty-five as the normal retirement age. If you choose to work past sixty-five (federal law prohibits age discrimination rules that would *require* you to retire before age seventy), will your plan give you credit for the additional years worked? Or what if you wanted to take early retirement—how much will that reduce your monthly pension check? The rules governing these matters vary from plan to plan.

◆ **Social Security considerations.** So-called "integrated plans" deduct a portion of your monthly Social Security check from your monthly benefit check. Remember that your employer has already paid hefty Social Security taxes. From his point of view, it seems reasonable that the company retirement plan formula recognize that you are receiving Social Security benefits to which the company has already contributed.

Employee Stock Ownership Plans

ESOPs are similar to profit-sharing plans except you receive shares in your company's stock rather than a portion of company profits. The number of shares you receive is based on your salary, typically ranging in value from 5% to 25% of your annual compensation. Taxes usually aren't due until you leave the company or sell the shares.

Savings and Thrift Plans

Similar to 401(k) plans in that you elect to make contributions which your employer will match; however, unlike a 401(k), your contribution is made with *after-tax* dollars. The primary advantages are the matching funds put in by your company and the fact that earnings grow tax-deferred.

"Salary Reduction" SAR–SEP IRAs

These are not to be confused with the regular SEP IRAs described in the graphic on page 352. Under the Tax Reform Act of 1986, firms with twenty-five or fewer employees may elect SEPs with features similar to 401(k) plans. These are useful in situations where the employer is not willing to make annual contributions—all contributions are made by the employee. Under such plans, employee contributions are permitted up to $9,500 annually, or 15% of your compensation, whichever is less.

◆ **Survivors' benefits.** As an alternative to the basic "monthly check for life" benefit, federal law requires most plans to offer you another approach: a joint and survivor annuity. If this is selected, the monthly benefit check doesn't stop coming when you die; it goes instead to your spouse (or whoever you have named in the annuity). The trade-off is that your pension will be 10%–20% lower than it otherwise would be—after all, it has to last for two lifetimes now instead of just one—and the amount of the monthly check is cut in half when you pass on. Even so, it's good to know that your spouse will still be provided for.

Armed with this information, you might now be wondering how the plan at your company . . .

. . . measures up in these various areas. If you aren't sure, it's time to find out! And don't worry about how you'll ever get your thoughts together in order to ask the right questions. Your employer is required by law to offer every participant a summary of the plan that's written in layman's terms. This is called a "summary plan description" and should be readily available from your personnel department. Ask for one. It will explain all of the above and lots more.

Many companies also provide a personalized "employee benefit statement" once a year that explains the amount of benefits you've earned to date and provides an estimate of how much your monthly retirement check will be. Other items that you're entitled to receive upon request include: the "summary annual report" (your plan's balance sheet), the Form 5500 (your plan's tax return and an excellent source of information concerning its financial health), and the retirement plan document itself (in case you happen to enjoy digging through page after page of mind-numbing legalese).

OK, let's stop and see where we stand. You now know how to find out what your company's pension benefit would be for a person with your years of service and salary history. You also know what you need to do to qualify for it.

Assuming you do your part, there's only one thing (and I hate to bring it up but somebody needs to tell you) that can go wrong . . .

. . . your company could reach retirement before you do, that is, your company could go into bankruptcy. To understand the possible consequences, it's time you were introduced to ERISA.

For the pension world, 1974 was a watershed year because of the passage of the Employee Retirement Income Security Act. For the first time, there were uniform federal guidelines, which all employer pension plans were required to follow. The major emphasis was on setting standards concerning which employees would be eligible for coverage, when they would receive vesting rights, and how employers should go about funding their plans to make sure

Federal rules require that if your pension plan is more than 10% underfunded, your employer must tell you. Such a notice is likely to appear in the annual batch of material you receive that updates you on your plan and the benefits you've been promised. Review the material carefully.

the money was there to provide the benefits they promised. ERISA also set maximum limits for contributions and benefits, and made sure the employer didn't discriminate in favor of its managers and owners.

The new funding requirements revealed that many plans had inadequate reserves to meet the pension promises being made to their employees. These underfunded plans were required to build their reserves up to a fully funded position, but were given as long as forty years to do so. That's why, almost twenty years after ERISA was passed, there are still companies that have underfunded plans. As long as these companies survive and are able to continue following their pension funding programs, retirees will receive all of the benefits to which they're entitled.

But what if a company goes under? Congress planned for that, too.

At the same time it passed ERISA, Congress created the Pension Benefit Guaranty Corporation (PBGC) to insure pension benefits in much the same way the FDIC insures bank deposits. This protection is funded by employers, who must pay an annual premium for each participant. The PBGC guarantees that more than 41 million workers in more than 58,000 defined-benefit retirement plans will receive their basic pension benefits.

There is a shortfall between the level of benefits promised by all these plans and the money put aside by employers to pay for them. This "underfunding gap" was $10 billion in 1983, and the situation deteriorated consistently over the next decade. By 1993, the gap was a huge $71 billion. Then, for the first time since the early 1980s, the gap fell. At the end of 1994, the total underfunding of all pension plans insured by the PBGC was $31 billion. A significant portion of the underfunding that exists is in plans sponsored by firms with below-investment-grade ratings.

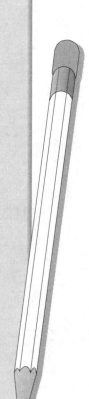

GOOD QUESTIONS TO ASK YOUR COMPANY ABOUT YOUR BENEFITS

❑ What do I have to do to participate in the plan?

❑ Do I contribute money, and if so, does the company match my contributions?

❑ How quickly is my contribution deposited in my account?

❑ Is the plan federally insured by the Pension Benefit Guaranty Corporation?

❑ When will I be fully vested?

❑ What are the investments in the plan?

❑ Do I get to decide how the investments in my account are allocated?

❑ Can I borrow or withdraw money before I retire?

❑ Does the plan include death or disability benefits?

❑ What happens if I take early retirement?

❑ What happens if I work past the normal retirement age?

OK, so that's the PBGC's problem (except it could become your problem too if taxes are raised to pay for all this). I know you're more interested for now in making sure your pension is secure. What can you do? Here's what I suggest.

❶ **Ask your company if its defined benefit plan is fully funded.** Unfortunately, even if you learn your plan is fully funded, you're still not home free (see item two below). You can also check with the PBGC, which annually releases a list of the fifty U.S. companies with the most seriously underfunded plans. The 1995 list included such familiar names as: Uniroyal Goodrich, Westinghouse, Bethlehem Steel, Northwest Airlines, Woolworth, American Standard, Del Monte Foods, Boise Cascade, Sears, USAir, and UPS.

❷ **Ask what assumptions your company is making about the kinds of investment returns it expects in the plan over the long term.** If a conservative number such as 7%-8% is being used, that's good because it's realistic. But if the company is counting on, as General Motors is, its plan investments to average 10% a year, it's on shaky ground. Unrealistically high assumptions make the plan's funding look better without improving the actual health of the plan.

❸ **If you have concerns about the adequacy of your plan's funding, contact the U.S. Department of Labor.** This agency serves as a watchdog of employee benefit programs and conducts inquiries into underfunded plans. The name and number of someone to contact should be listed in your plan's annual report. If you have questions about the PBGC's insurance program and retirement guarantees, contact its Technical Assistance Division at (202) 326-4000.

❹ **Recognize the limitations of the insurance coverage.** If your plan falls into the hands of the PBGC, the maximum benefit allowed in 1996 was approximately $31,700 a year (increased annually to allow for inflation). This could be less than your plan originally promised.

And one suggestion for retirees. If you've been provided with an annuity that your employer bought for you from an insurance company, keep close tabs on the financial health of the insurer. Many employers buy the annuities without regard to the financial strength of the insurer; low cost is often their primary criterion.

So far, we've looked at retirement plans that promise to pay, upon retirement, a certain dollar amount every month for as long as you live. Under that arrangement, the employer makes all the contributions into the plan plus carries the burden of how well the investments perform until your retirement.

There is another major category of employer-sponsored retirement plans. They are called "defined-contribution" plans because . . .

. . . they place their emphasis on how much (if any) the employer will put into the plan for you each year. No promises are made with respect to how much your account will be worth when you retire. In this respect, they are like IRAs.

The advantage to employers of this approach is that *you* bear the investment risk between now and retirement rather than your company. If the investments do great, you'll have a healthy amount in the plan at retirement; if they perform poorly, you must make do with a lesser amount. This shift of the investment risk from the employer to you is significant; you no longer can "count on" having a specific monthly income.

Some observers view this as a dastardly move on the part of employers. *Newsweek* magazine ran an article (December 6, 1993) with the title "Retirements at Risk." The subhead read: "The scare about cash-short pension plans is overstated. The bigger worry: firms that force workers to make their own choices." Oh, those heartless cads in corporate America! What could be worse, in the minds of the paternalistic editors of *Newsweek*, than to give workers the right to make their own decisions concerning their financial futures, and then having to live with the results? We're too stupid, you see, to be trusted with such responsibility.

Agreed, not everyone handles such decision-making well. It's also true that not everyone drives a car safely or eats the right foods. But we generally don't decry the unfairness of being "forced" to make our own choices in those areas. Why look at the negatives? The flip side of this change is that above-average investment performance in your account now benefits you and your heirs rather than your employer. Look at it as an opportunity! Here is another area that is now under your control where your Sound Mind strategy can help shape a balanced long-term portfolio that will be personalized to your specific goals and risk tolerance.

Over the years, Congress has created several varieties of defined contribution plans. I've listed them in a table on the next page to give you an overview of the possibilities. Many companies have more than one of these plans in place in order to help you take the fullest advantage of the tax-sheltering possibilities. Though I cannot review all the complexities, the table will provide a general idea of the kinds of plans your employer may offer. Make an appointment with the appropriate person at your company to get your specific questions answered.

By far the most popular of these is the 401(k) plan.

The 401(k) is becoming the bedrock of our private pension system. According to a study published in *Worth* magazine (March 1996), about 75% of those eligible to participate in a 401(k) do so. Within five years, the average 401(k) account will be worth $45,000 and represent 40% of a typical family's retirement capital. At that time, an estimated $1 trillion will be invested through 401(k) plans.

AN OVERVIEW OF THE MAJOR KINDS
OF DEFINED-CONTRIBUTION PLANS

Your company may offer one or more of the following defined-contribution pension plans. These are the most common types; however, there are many variations depending on the way your company's plan was initially structured. This is a highly technical area, and this table is merely intended to provide an overview. For more information on your specific rights and benefits, contact your company's human resources department.

Type of Plan	Money Purchase	Profit Sharing	SEP IRA	401(k) Plan	403(b) Plan
Brief summary	Your company agrees to contribute a certain percentage of your salary every year (even in unprofitable years). Can be either a corporate plan or, if employer is not incorporated, can be a Keogh plan.	Your company annually contributes a portion of its profits, if any, into a fund for employees. Can be either a corporate plan or, if employer is not incorporated, can be a Keogh plan.	Simplified Employee Pensions use a form of employee IRAs rather than set up a separate company plan. Primarily funded by your employer, these accounts are highly portable if you change jobs.	A salary reduction plan where you decide how much of your salary to put in (up to a maximum level that is raised annually for inflation). The amount you contribute is not counted as taxable income.	Similar to the 401(k) plan, but limited to employees of public schools, government agencies, hospitals, religious organizations, and other nonprofit institutions.
What is the most you can put in each year?	You don't contribute.	You don't contribute.	Your normal $2,000 IRA contribution.	$9,500	$9,500
What is the most your employer can put in each year?	25% of compensation or $30,000, whichever is less.	15% of compensation or $22,500, whichever is less.	15% of compensation or $22,500, whichever is less.\n\nSee sidebar on page 347 for mention of a second kind of SEP IRA that has salary reduction features similar to a 401(k).	Can match a percentage of your salary deferral up to 100%. Your contribution plus employer's can't exceed $30,000 or 25% of your salary (after deducting your contribution), whichever is less.	Can match a percentage of your salary deferral up to 100%. Your contribution plus employer's can't exceed $30,000 or 25% of your salary (after deducting your contribution), whichever is less.
Are annual contributions fixed at a certain amount?	Yes. The salary contribution formula must be followed each year.	No. The amount contributed can change from year to year.	No. The amount contributed can change from year to year.	No. The amount contributed can change from year to year.	No. The amount contributed can change from year to year.
When do you receive ownership rights to your pension?	Typically 3-7 years.	Typically 3-7 years.	Immediately.	Immediately on your contributions, but at the employer's discretion on any matching amounts.	Immediately on your contributions, but at the employer's discretion on any matching amounts.
Can you borrow from your account?	Some plans allow borrowing at the employer's discretion.	Some plans allow borrowing at the employer's discretion.	No.	At the employer's discretion.	At the employer's discretion.

Yet, according to the same article, 95% of those who participate in a 401(k) plan contribute less than they are allowed. The benefits of participation are clear: You receive a tax deduction for your contributions, tax deferral on all gains and income, plus an immediate bonus if your employer elects to match your contribution. I encourage you to participate to the maximum allowed, *especially* if yours is an employer-matching plan.

Here are two additional points of interest with respect to getting the most from your 401(k) or 403(b) plan.

◆ **Don't overcommit to your company's stock.** One study indicated that 30% of all 401(k) assets were invested in company stock. You've already got your career riding on your company's continued health. Do you really want your retirement to depend on it too? If too high a percentage of one's total assets are tied up in the stock of just one company, the loss of diversification greatly increases the risk. There are pitfalls that arise from being dependent on a single company for one's income, health and life insurance, and retirement investments. Not only did many workers lose their jobs and health benefits during the 1991 recession, but they also watched the value of their retirement assets plunge as the stock market value of their company's stock fell. How much company stock is too much? There is no hard-and-fast rule concerning this because individual situations can vary widely. However, a general range that is useful is to limit (if possible) your investing in any one stock—whether it's your company or not—to 10%-25% of your total investable assets, and that the smaller the value of your total portfolio, the more you should gravitate to the lower end of the range.

◆ **Do understand what a good 401(k) plan looks like.** New federal regulations, known as 404(c) standards, provide that a plan should: offer at least three investment options, not counting your company's stock; offer a program to educate you on the pros and cons of the various choices; and offer the opportunity to adjust your choices once a quarter at the time of your choosing. These standards are actually quite minimal. See sidebar for more information.

Federal workers participate in a retirement plan . . .

. . . similar to a 401(k) arrangement—the Thrift Savings Plan. Those hired after 1983 are covered by the Federal Employees Retirement System (FERS), which means, among other things, that the government will match employees' contributions to the Thrift plan in a very generous way.

First, the government automatically contributes an amount equal to 1% of salary. Second, for every dollar employees contribute up to 3% of their salary, the government matches it with a dollar. Third, for every dollar employees contribute above 3% of salary (up to 5%), the government puts in 50 cents. By contributing 5%, therefore, employees have doubled their money

---

A 401(k) Top Ten List

"The following are characteristics of a first-rate retirement savings plan, along with the percentage of 401(k) plans that offer the feature.

1. A 50-cent or larger employer match on every dollar you set aside. (55%)

2. The ability to direct investment of employer contributions as well as your own. (65%)

3. At least six investment options to choose from. (45%)

4. No forfeiture of employer contributions, regardless of how briefly you work for the company. (35%)

5. Daily updates of account balances, and the flexibility to transfer funds between options at any time. (36%)

6. The ability to borrow from the plan. (75%)

7. Plan administrative fees paid by the employer rather than by participants. (73%)

8. Account statements delivered within two weeks at the end of the month or quarter. (18%)

9. A system for checking account balances and making transactions by phone. (75%)

10. The option to make both pretax and after-tax contributions. (30%)"

Kiplinger's Personal Finance Magazine (March 1996)

Source: HR Investment Consultants and Access Research, Inc.

just by virtue of the government's matching funds. Finally, employees can contribute another 5% of salary (raising their total contribution to 10%) which, although not matched by the government, does provide an additional tax deduction and long-term tax-deferred compounding of investment returns.

According to a report in *Kiplinger's* in 1995, one out of four FERS participants doesn't contribute to the Thrift plan. In light of the generous matching provisions, this is surprisingly shortsighted behavior. Their goal should be to contribute 3% of salary at a minimum, and 5% if at all possible. Federal workers hired in 1983 and earlier fall under the Civil Service Retirement System (CSRS). While that plan doesn't offer matching funds for the Thrift plan, it does allow workers to contribute to it. Check to see when the next open season for signing up or raising your contribution arrives.

Other points of interest concerning the Thrift plan: You can borrow from your account for purposes of buying a house, paying education or medical expenses, or alleviating a temporary financial hardship. When you leave your job with the government, you can roll your Thrift account assets into your personal IRA. To make sure you're getting the most from your Thrift plan opportunities, get a copy of *Your Thrift Savings Plan,* a privately produced, comprehensive guidebook for both FERS and CSRS employees. The cost is $16.95 postage-paid. Call (800) 989-3363.

MANAGING 401(K) OR 403(B) ALLOCATIONS

Investment Choices	For Purposes of Assessing Risk When Rebalancing Portfolio
International Stock Fund Invests primarily in foreign stocks, but many also allow some U.S.	Treat as International Stock
Growth Fund Invests primarily in stocks chosen for their potential to rise in price.	Treat as Stock Category 2 or 4.
Stock Index Fund Usually designed to give results identical to S&P 500 stock index.	Treat as Stock Category 2.
Equity Income Fund Invests primarily in stocks chosen for their dividend-paying potential.	Treat as Stock Category 1.
Balanced Fund Invests in a fixed combination of stocks and bonds.	Treat as Stock Category 1.
Government Bond Fund Invests primarily in long-term IOUs of U.S. Treasury.	Treat as Bond Category 3.
Money Market Fund and Guaranteed Investment Contracts Short-term IOUs of businesses, banks, government, insurance companies	Treat as Bond Category 1.

For purposes of controlling risk, it's important to include your retirement plan investments as part of your overall portfolio.

This requires that you understand where the various choices in your retirement plan fit in terms of SMI's risk categories (see graphics below, as well as pages 199-206, 225, 245, and 317 for review). The Thrift plan currently offers just three investment choices. The government is considering the addition of two excellent new options (also shown), but such changes take a long time because they must be approved by Congress. To encourage things along, you can voice your opinion to the Thrift Retirement Board by calling (202) 942-1600. If you want to change the way your money is currently allocated, you can authorize transfers by phoning (504) 255-8777. You're allowed to make changes four times a year.

You should consider all of the investments over which you have decision-making authority, including those in your retirement accounts, as you analyze how best to diversify your portfolio to achieve the portfolio allocation strategy you have elected to follow. By shifting some of your retirement plan holdings from stocks to bonds or vice versa, you can achieve the desired balance between equity and interest-earning investments.

Much has been said concerning the tendency of investors to be too conservative in their retirement plan investments. The SMI philosophy is that you

MANAGING THRIFT PLAN ALLOCATIONS

For Federal Workers	For Purposes of Assessing Risk When Rebalancing SMI Portfolio
Proposed New Fund To invest in common stocks of foreign companies. Would be similar in performance to: Morgan Stanley EAFE Index	Treat as International Stock
Proposed New Fund To invest in common stocks of smaller, emerging growth companies. Would be similar in performance to: Vanguard Index Extended Market	Treat as Stock Category 4.
The C Fund Invests in common stocks of large, blue chip companies. Similar in performance to: Vanguard Index 500	Treat as Stock Category 2.
The F Fund Invests in corporate, government, and mortgage-backed securities. Similar in performance to: Vanguard Bond Index / Total Bond Market	Treat as Bond Category 2.
The G Fund Invests in short-term Treasury securities. Similar in performance to: Money market funds listed in Level Two column.	Treat as Bond Category 1.

should be guided by the mix appropriate to your season of life and investing temperament (see risk matrix on page 167). However, just so you'll know, many others recommend using a common rule of thumb: subtract your age from 100 and allocate at least that percentage to your holdings in stocks. This formula gives younger workers, who can afford to take more risk, a greater opportunity for long-term capital growth.

If you participate in a 401(k) retirement plan, don't let the "guarantee" fool you.

Chances are high that one of the options you have is to allocate a portion of your account to a "guaranteed investment contract" (GIC). These are investment contracts sold by insurance companies to retirement plans that promise a specified rate of return over a one- to five-year period. They have been very popular because they usually offer yields up to 1% higher than those available from money funds or U.S. Treasury securities.

However, the money is not guaranteed at all. The contracts are backed only by the insurance companies that sell them. They're just IOUs. The word "guarantee" refers to the rate of return that's agreed upon at the outset, as in "rather than take your chances in the stock market, we'll guarantee you 9% per year." That's all dandy as long as the insurance company prospers and is financially strong enough several years from now to honor its commitments. But because of bad investments in junk bonds and real estate, the credit-worthiness of many insurance companies is now being questioned.

Employers are dealing with this concern in a variety of ways. One cosmetic change is that many have removed the word "guaranteed" in favor of calling these investments "stable value" contracts. Some are now buying GICs only from the highest rated insurance companies. Others are increasing the number of insurers with whom they do business in order to spread the risk around. Others have returned to Treasury securities, abandoning the GIC market completely. These changes are likely to mean that the fixed-income portions in many 401(k) and other retirement plans will offer slightly lower returns. If this happens to you, don't complain about the lower rates; instead, thank your employer for protecting your retirement assets.

All of these plans have one thing in common: at some point, you're going to want to take your money out!

Your decision as to how to do this will be one of the most important and far-reaching ones of your financial life. You shouldn't make it hurriedly; in fact, you should begin thinking about it years ahead of time. Make sure you understand the laws (which Congress has succeeded in making complicated and confusing by changing them from time to time) and how they affect your range of options.

Getting Your Money Out Early

Withdrawing funds from your tax-deferred plans prior to turning $59\frac{1}{2}$ should be a last resort. The tax consequences are severe—a 10% premature withdrawal penalty plus income taxes on the amount you take out. There are other ways to meet a temporary cash squeeze:

◆ Stop contributing to the plan. This may sound obvious, but many workers become so accustomed to having their contribution automatically deducted from each paycheck that they forget it's their choice.

◆ Borrow from your account. Most profit-sharing and 401(k) plans permit employees to borrow against their retirement account, often up to 50% of its value. Repayments typically must begin immediately and be completed within three to five years.

◆ If you have made after-tax contributions, withdraw them first. You'll have to pay the 10% penalty and income tax only on the interest earned while your money was in the plan.

Some of the factors that will influence your decision include your age at retirement, birth year, health and life expectancy, income tax bracket, other sources of retirement income, inflationary expectations, desire for certainty versus desire for greater potential future income, and the list goes on.

Basically, you have three choices: to take all your money out in one large payment, to transfer your account value to an IRA rollover where you can continue to invest it on a tax-deferred basis, or to take it in the form of monthly payments spread over the remainder of your life. Here are some guidelines to consider as you go about making your decision. After finding out from your employer the amounts of both your lump-sum benefit and your monthly income benefit, ask yourself these questions:

◆ *How long do I expect to live?* Obviously, you can only make a guess based on your health at the time and your family history. The reason this comes into play is that the monthly payment option is usually computed based on a life expectancy of age eighty. The longer you live past eighty, the greater the value of your total monthly pension and the better off you are versus taking the lump-sum.

◆ *How dependent are my spouse or heirs on my estate?* If your spouse is dependent on you, you might prefer

THE THREE PRIMARY CHOICES FOR RECEIVING YOUR RETIREMENT BENEFITS

	Take your money in one large payment	Transfer your money to an IRA rollover account	Take your money in monthly payments
How do you receive your money?	Your employer pays your retirement benefit to you all at one time.	Your employer sends your entire retirement benefit directly to your new IRA account.	You choose the combination of amount and duration of guaranteed monthly payments.
What taxes will you pay?	The entire amount is taxed at ordinary income rates in the year it is received.	None until you begin making withdrawals (which will be taxed as income the year they are received).	The money you receive will be taxed as income the year it is received.
What other factors come into play?	A special tax formula that can reduce your taxes may apply. Depending on your birth year, income averaging over five- or ten-year periods may be permitted. Early withdrawal penalty could apply if you are under age 59½.	You lose the option of reducing your tax burden by income averaging over a five- or ten-year period. Your investments continue to grow tax-deferred and are under your direct supervision.	Early withdrawal penalty could apply if you are under age 59½ and do not choose the lifetime income option. If your employer provides your monthly payments by buying an annuity for you, a financially strong insurance company is of great importance.

the "joint and survivor" pension. It provides a monthly payment to you for life (about 10%–20% lower than it would otherwise be), with an ongoing monthly payment (reduced by half) to your spouse after your death. If providing for your spouse is a primary consideration, these and other options should be explored fully with your pension administrator. If providing for heirs is important, then the lump-sum option is the way to go.

◆ *How do I feel about inflation?* Unless your monthly benefit provides for adequate cost-of-living increases, you may find it difficult keeping up with inflation over the longer term. The lump-sum approach burdens you with the responsibility and risk of investing, but following our Sound Mind portfolio recommendations should keep you ahead of inflation.

◆ *What other sources of income will I have?* Both options have their risks: the lump-sum the risk of doing your own investing, and the monthly payment the risk of keeping ahead of inflation. You should also consider what additional help you can expect from Social Security and your investments.

The table on page 357 summarizes the tax implications and other important features of each of the three alternatives. For additional help, I encourage you to contact some of the leading no-load organizations. Just tell them you are facing this very important decision of whether to take your retirement in a lump-sum or roll it into an IRA. They've developed some user-friendly explanatory material (Schwab, Fidelity, Price, and Vanguard have done especially good jobs), which will walk you through the technical aspects. No-load fund organizations offer their help free of charge because they're hoping to win you over as a long-term customer during your retirement years.

Be careful when "rolling out" of your company's pension plan.

Prior to 1993, you were given sixty days to deposit your lump-sum benefit check into an IRA rollover in order to avoid any tax bite and preserve your tax-deferred program. Under a new law, your benefit check will be hit with a 20% withholding rate *if it's made out to you*. This is a form of withholding similar to what your employer takes out of your paycheck. The amount withheld will be included on your annual income tax return where it will be applied as a credit against your total tax liability for the year.

You can avoid the withholding by removing yourself from the transfer process. Arrange in advance for your employer to send your money directly to your new IRA rollover account. This is called a trustee-to-trustee transfer (see page 364).

Why change the old way, which was working fine? Under the guise of wanting to encourage workers not to elect the lump-sum option (where they might spend it rather than save it), the new law seems to be primarily motivated by a need to help raise new tax revenues. The government says it expected to gather in more than $2 billion from those unsuspecting citizens who were unaware that the rules have been changed. Again. ◆

CHAPTER PREVIEW

Your Personal Pension: The Ins and Outs of IRAs

I. **The Individual Retirement Account can play a key role in your retirement investing strategy. Its appeal is twofold.**

   A. You might qualify for a tax deduction for your IRA contribution, up to a maximum of $2,000 a year.

   B. All the earnings in your IRA compound tax-deferred until you begin taking them out at retirement.

II. **The control you have over your IRA makes it very flexible.**

   A. You select the financial organization with which you do business.

   B. You control how its assets are invested.

   C. You decide whether to contribute each year, and if so, how much.

   D. You select the timing and amount of your withdrawals.

III. **In this chapter, I answer several general questions concerning the use of IRAs.**

   A. When should you make it a priority to put money into an IRA?

   B. Under what circumstances can you write off your IRA contributions?

   C. What are some of the drawbacks of investing through an IRA?

   D. What is an IRA rollover?

   E. What is an IRA asset transfer?

   F. What are the rules for taking money out of an IRA?

   G. Which financial firms offer the most attractive terms for opening an IRA?

Your retirement income rests on what has been referred to as a three-legged stool.

Social Security has traditionally been regarded as the first of the three legs (see chapter 26); however, the problems with Social Security make it impossible to project with confidence the level of monthly benefits twenty years and more into the future. Historically, the program has provided 35%-45% of retirees' monthly income; to be on the conservative side, investors under age fifty should use a lower assumption to reflect the uncertainty.

Private employer-sponsored pension plans are the second leg (see chapter 27) and provide about 15%-20% of retirees' monthly income on average, according to the Social Security Administration. But there's a lot of room for variation here. For workers who spend most of their careers with the same company, it would not be unusual for them to receive a pension equal to 30%-40% of what they were making at the time of retirement. On the other hand, there's been a move away from defined-benefit plans in recent years, so your employer might not even offer a plan that pays a guaranteed monthly pension.

IRA Laws May Change
The material in this chapter was correct as of mid-1996. Proposals for changing aspects of the laws governing IRAs were announced during the 1996 presidential campaign. Be sure to familiarize yourself with the current regulations before making important planning decisions.

In any event, it is obvious that the third leg of personal savings and retirement funds will continue to play a very important role in providing adequate retirement incomes. And one of the best ways to go about building your personal retirement funds is by using the tax-deferred Individual Retirement Account (IRA).

The IRA first appeared on the financial scene in 1981 when Congress voted to allow working persons to put away up to $2,000 a year for retirement *and deduct it* from their federal income tax return. Not only did they enjoy immediate tax-savings, but they also were excused from paying any income taxes on the investment profits they made. Until they began withdrawing the money upon retirement, they had the pleasure of watching their money grow tax-deferred. After the deductibility of home mortgage interest, it was the best tax break available to the middle class.

Congress soon decided it had been too generous in allowing middle-class taxpayers to keep so much of their own income. In passing the 1986 Tax Reform Act, the law was changed to limit the deductibility of IRA contributions to those folks who were not participating in retirement plans at work *unless* their income fell below certain levels. Although the 1986 tax law changes made IRAs less attractive for some, it has been estimated that 75% of IRA owners were unaffected by the changes. Therefore, despite the modifications, the Individual Retirement Account plays a key role in the retirement planning of most families.

How should you invest the money you put into your IRA?

An IRA is not, in and of itself, an investment. It's merely a tax shelter that you put your investments in. IRAs can contain a wide variety of investments of your choosing. To get the most from the tax-deferred advantage, put your fixed-income higher-yielding investments in your IRA (because a large part of their total returns is interest income, which is taxed at your highest marginal tax rate). Investments where you expect a large part of your total return will be from growth should be put in your regular accounts because the tax on capital gains is limited to 28%.

Don't invest in tax-exempt securities like municipal bonds and annuities in your IRA. There's no point in putting investments that are already tax-exempt into an IRA; there's no additional tax savings. With municipal bonds, you're lowering your investment potential as well as, ironically, turning the interest from them (which would ordinarily be tax-free) into income that is taxable. Why? Because all your earnings are taxed when you withdraw them, even the earnings that come from otherwise tax-exempt investments.

I would encourage you to make it a priority to fully fund your IRA each year if:

◆ You've paid off all credit card and other consumer debt (chapter 2);

◆ You have an adequate contingency fund set aside (chapter 4);

◆ Neither you *nor your spouse* is an "active participant" in a pension plan at work, in which case your IRA contributions remain fully tax deductible.

This assumes you have already saved enough to make a down payment on a house. If you haven't, you might wish to make that a higher priority. Or, you might want to delay funding your IRA in order to make additional principal payments on your mortgage. That would also be a reasonable decision, although not one that I personally would make. See the story about Rob and Dan on pages 46-48 for more on this subject.

The maximum amount any one person can contribute to his or her IRA is equal to the lesser of (1) $2,000, or (2) his or her total compensation. In other words, you can contribute an amount equal to your total earnings, up to a maximum of $2,000.

What does it mean to be an "active participant"?

Special rules apply to determine whether you are considered to be an active participant for any given tax year. These rules differ depending on whether the plan is a defined benefit or a defined contribution plan. They also differ depending on your marital status.

For a defined benefit plan, you are considered to be an active participant if you have attained eligibility for coverage by the plan. If your company plan calls for a waiting period before you are eligible, you may make a deductible IRA contribution provided that: (1) you weren't eligible at any time during the tax year in question, and (2) your spouse was not an active participant in a company plan at his or her place of employment.

For a defined contribution plan, such as a 401(k) or 403(b), you are considered to be an active participant if you or your employer contributed to your account during the tax year in question.

THE TAX DEDUCTIBILITY OF YOUR IRA CONTRIBUTIONS

The tax deduction for making an IRA contribution is phased out as your income increases <u>unless</u> you do not belong to a retirement plan at work. In that case, you are entitled to a full deduction regardless of your income level. Note: For simplicity, the phase-out of the tax deduction for making a contribution to an IRA account is shown in $1,000 income increments. Actually, the phase-out is calculated in $10 increments.

Deduction	Singles	Married
$200	$35,000	$50,000
	$34,000	$49,000
$400	$33,000	$48,000
$600	$32,000	$47,000
$800	$31,000	$46,000
$1,000	$30,000	$45,000
$1,200	$29,000	$44,000
$1,400	$28,000	$43,000
$1,600	$27,000	$42,000
$1,800	$26,000	$41,000
$2,000 Deduction	$25,000	$40,000

THE VALUE OF STARTING YOUNG

Age	Jack's Amount Deposited	Jack's Interest Earned	Jack's Year-End Value	Jill's Amount Deposited	Jill's Interest Earned	Jill's Year-End Value
8	$600	$ 60	$ 660	0	0	0
9	600	126	1,386	0	0	0
10	600	199	2,185	0	0	0
11	600	278	3,063	0	0	0
12	600	366	4,029	0	0	0
13	600	463	5,092	0	0	0
14	600	569	6,262	0	0	0
15	600	686	7,548	0	0	0
16	600	815	8,962	0	0	0
17	600	956	10,519	0	0	0
18	600	1,112	12,231	0	0	0
19	0	1,223	13,454	0	0	0
20	0	1,345	14,799	0	0	0
21	0	1,480	16,279	0	0	0
22	0	1,628	17,907	0	0	0
23	0	1,791	19,697	0	0	0
24	0	1,970	21,667	0	0	0
25	0	2,167	23,834	0	0	0
26	0	2,383	26,217	$2,000	$ 200	$ 2,200
27	0	2,622	28,839	2,000	420	4,620
28	0	2,884	31,723	2,000	662	7,282
29	0	3,172	34,895	2,000	928	10,210
30	0	3,490	38,385	2,000	1,221	13,431
31	0	3,838	42,223	2,000	1,543	16,974
32	0	4,222	46,446	2,000	1,897	20,872
33	0	4,645	51,090	2,000	2,287	25,159
34	0	5,109	56,199	2,000	2,716	29,875
35	0	5,620	61,819	2,000	3,187	35,062
36	0	6,182	68,001	2,000	3,706	40,769
37	0	6,800	74,801	2,000	4,277	47,045
38	0	7,480	82,281	2,000	4,905	53,950
39	0	8,228	90,509	2,000	5,595	61,545
40	0	9,051	99,560	2,000	6,354	69,899
41	0	9,956	109,516	2,000	7,190	79,089
42	0	10,952	120,468	2,000	8,109	89,198
43	0	12,047	132,515	2,000	9,120	100,318
44	0	13,251	145,766	2,000	10,232	112,550
45	0	14,577	160,343	2,000	11,455	126,005
46	0	16,034	176,377	2,000	12,800	140,805
47	0	17,638	194,015	2,000	14,281	157,086
48	0	19,401	213,416	2,000	15,909	174,995
49	0	21,342	234,758	2,000	17,699	194,694
50	0	23,476	258,234	2,000	19,669	216,364
51	0	25,823	284,057	2,000	21,836	240,200
52	0	28,406	312,463	2,000	24,220	266,420
53	0	31,246	343,709	2,000	26,842	295,262
54	0	34,371	378,080	2,000	29,726	326,988
55	0	37,808	415,888	2,000	32,899	361,887
56	0	41,589	457,476	2,000	36,389	400,276
57	0	45,748	503,224	2,000	40,228	442,503
58	0	50,322	553,547	2,000	44,450	488,953
59	0	55,355	608,901	2,000	49,095	540,049
60	0	60,890	669,791	2,000	54,205	596,254
61	0	66,979	736,770	2,000	59,825	658,079
62	0	73,677	810,447	2,000	66,008	726,087
63	0	81,045	891,492	2,000	72,809	800,896
64	0	89,149	980,641	2,000	80,290	883,185
65	0	98,064	1,078,706	2,000	88,519	973,704

That means most singles can contribute up to $2,000, and working married couples up to $4,000 (husband and wife each have their own separate IRAs). For couples where only one spouse works outside the home, the limit is $2,250. That amount can be divided between their two IRA accounts however they wish, as long as neither account gets more than the $2,000 maximum. This opportunity is available to everyone under age 70½ who earns income from employment (including self-employment).

Can you write off your IRA contribution on your tax return?

Under the rules, you get a full tax deduction provided *neither* spouse is an active participant in a tax-advantaged retirement plan, like a 401(k), at work. Even if one of you is, however, you might still qualify for a tax deduction if your income is below a certain amount. A sliding scale, based on income, comes into play to determine how much of your contribution is deductible.

◆ If your family income is less than $40,000 ($25,000 for singles), you can take the full deduction.

◆ If your family income is more than $40,000 but less than $50,000 (between $25,000 and $35,000 for singles), only a portion of your contribution is tax-deductible (see graph on page 361).

◆ If your family income is $50,000 or more (more than $35,000 for singles), you receive no deduction.

(Income as used here actually refers to the tax concept of "modified adjusted gross income." This involves taking the adjusted gross income from your federal income tax return and adding back certain items. Chief among them is the deduction you took for your IRA contribution.)

In chapter 4, I shared the story of Jack and Jill (pages 57-58). The table at left shows the year by year results of their IRA investments. Every time I look at these numbers, they look wrong to me. It just doesn't seem possible that Jack came out ahead, let alone became a millionaire. But that's what an early start and a 10% annual compounded return can do for you.

You may be thinking, after working so hard on his paper route, how likely is it that a youngster is going to want to put his hard-earned money out of reach for the next half century? Not very likely. That's why IRAs make nice presents for your children or grandchildren (if they have W-2 or 1099 income). Jack's relatives can use *their* money to start *Jack's* IRA up to the limit of Jack's earnings. They get no tax deduction, of course.

What are some of the drawbacks of investing through an IRA?

It's easy to become so impressed with the power of tax-deferred compounding that we can overlook a few of the disadvantages of the IRA. The most obvious one is that your money is generally unavailable for other uses for several decades. You can't borrow against it. When you finally do qualify to begin taking your money back out, it all gets taxed as ordinary income even though a sizable portion of your growth came in the form of capital gains. There are specific rules governing how much you must take out each year, and if you run afoul of them, the penalties are unbelievable (see page 366).

Then, there's a truly awful tax (dubbed the "success tax" in the financial media) that applies to those who have accumulated a large sum to carry them through retirement. The government wants you to do well, but not *too* well. According to IRS Publication 590: "If you received retirement distributions during the year of more than $150,000, you may have to pay a 15% tax on the distributions exceeding that amount. The term retirement distributions means your distributions from any qualified employer plan, tax-sheltered annuity plan, or IRA." So after we've spent a lifetime of saving, investing, and playing by the rules, the government comes along and once again feels entitled to pick our pockets.

Of course, no discussion of our government's tax atrocities would be complete without mentioning estate taxes. These are the taxes we Americans pay for the privilege of dying and leaving what wealth we may have attained to our loved ones. (The first $600,000 is exempt.) This tax has always struck me as outrageous because the estate that we leave behind is comprised of wealth that, by and large, has already been taxed at the local, state, and federal level. It seems criminal for the government to come back for more. Yet, federal estate taxes start at 18% and gradually rise to 50%. Thus, in the lives of some taxpayers the government demands for itself an equal standing with their heirs—one-half for the family, and one-half for the government. This drives me crazy . . . but I digress.

The question is: How do IRAs fit into all this? They suffer the same fate as other tax-deferred retirement accounts. According to the *Wall Street Journal*:

> Death is brutal for retirement accounts, because the government still insists on collecting all the income taxes owed. Sure, your heirs may be able to delay the impact, but eventually a combination of income taxes, estate taxes, and the 15% tax penalty will wreak their havoc.

[1] Jonathan Clements, "Here's an Unconventional Idea: Don't Fund Your IRA This Year," Wall Street Journal, March 14, 1995.

With larger estates, you can get 75% or 80% of the retirement plan going to taxes. . . . By contrast, if you die with your money in a regular taxable account, only estate taxes get levied.[1]

What is an IRA rollover?

A rollover is a tax-free distribution to you of cash or other assets from one retirement program that you then contribute to another retirement program. The money always passes through your hands, albeit temporarily, during a rollover. The amount you roll over tax-free is generally taxable later when the new retirement program makes distributions to you (or your beneficiary).

There are two kinds of IRA rollovers. In one, the money you're putting into your new IRA comes from a qualified employer plan (like those discussed in chapter 27). In the other, the money you're putting into your new IRA comes from another IRA. In this second kind of rollover, you must complete the transaction within sixty days of receiving the check (although completing it within sixty days of the date on the check is safer because you can prove you complied with the time limit). If you miss the sixty-day deadline, you might be assessed income tax and early withdrawal penalties on the full amount of the check.

Also, such a change can be done only once in any one-year period (the period begins on the date you receive your money from the old IRA, not on the date you roll it over into your new one). You may, however, roll over assets from separate IRAs during a one-year period. In other words, each "old" IRA has its own one-year period, and if you have several IRA accounts, it's OK if they overlap. You must roll over into your new IRA the same amount (the same "property") you received from your old one.

What is an IRA asset transfer (sometimes called a trustee-to-trustee transfer)?

There's another way to move your IRA that's easier than a rollover—have the trustee/custodian of your new IRA do it for you. A transfer of funds at your request from your old IRA *directly* to your new one is technically *not* a rollover because there is no distribution to you—the money never passes through your hands. Since it is not a rollover, it is not affected by the one-year waiting period mentioned above.

> For more on the technical aspects of IRAs, request IRS Publication 590. To obtain a free copy, call the IRS Forms Distribution Center at (800) 424-3676.

I recommend using either a no-load fund organization or one of the leading discount brokers that also offer no-load mutual funds (see shopping comparisons on page 368). Once you sign the authorization forms they provide, they will take care of the paperwork in what is called a trustee-to-trustee transfer. It couldn't be easier!

> Many advisers suggest that you pay any fees associated with your IRA account directly rather than allowing them to be deducted from the account. This preserves the capital in the IRA for futher tax-deferred growth.

If you have more than one IRA account, you might consider combining them into one. It's not unusual for people to have many different IRAs spread around various places that were offering the "best deal" at the time their contribution was made. By combining them into one account at a no-load mutual fund organization, you'll save on annual account fees and cut your paperwork. More important, you'll have a much easier time managing your investments and tracking their performance.

It's worth moving your IRA where it can get better returns even if they amount to only 2%-3% a year. For example, someone with $10,000 in his IRA who earns 8% a year will have $68,485 in twenty-five years. But if he could earn 10% instead, he'd have $108,347. That extra $40,000 provides additional months of income once he retires.

The longer you wait before withdrawing money from your IRA, the longer it can continue to grow tax-deferred.

Since it's your money, you might think that it's up to you to decide when to start tapping your IRA account and how much to withdraw each year. Naturally, because the federal government is involved, you'd be wrong.

The IRS imposes very strict rules that dictate how long you can postpone making withdrawals from your IRA, as well as the minimum amount you must withdraw each year. (They want you to start taking your money out so you will begin paying some of those long deferred income taxes.) The minimum withdrawal amounts are called "required minimum distributions," and the latest you can wait to begin making them is April 1 of the year after you reach age 70½. If you violate the IRS guidelines, there are some horrendous penalties awaiting you. Here are the basics.

◆ **Up to age 59½ — Take it and pay a penalty.** The general rule is that IRA withdrawals are taxed as ordinary income in the year you receive them. If you withdraw money before reaching age 59½, you are also hit with a 10% penalty that is in addition to any income tax you owe. The penalty does not apply if you have a disability, or if you begin a series of scheduled annuity payments based on your life expectancy (more on this annuity aspect on page 367).

Things get slightly more complicated if you've made nondeductible contributions, because they've already been taxed. In that case, part of your withdrawal is taxed and part of it is treated simply as a return of your nondeductible contribution. The 10% penalty is applied to the taxable amount of your withdrawal.

◆ **Age 59½ to age 70½ — Take it or leave it.** You have the greatest flexibility in your sixties. You can take out as much as you like, or nothing at all. The amounts you withdraw are no longer subject to the 10% penalty tax, although it is still possible to run afoul of the 15% success tax mentioned above. Of course, normal income taxes apply. If they can afford it, most people are inclined to make no withdrawals during this period in order to make the most of the benefits of tax-deferred growth.

"Securities regulators issued a warning to investors to beware of phony 'IRA-approved' investments that promise solid retirement income from investments touted as having been endorsed by the Internal Revenue Service for individual retirement accounts. More than 170 enforcement actions have been brought and investigations are underway in 20 states by state regulators. Tips for avoiding scamsters who prey on IRA investors:

▶ Never transfer IRA or other retirement funds directly to an investment promoter.

▶ Don't buy an investment touted in a TV infomercial or a radio advertisement.

▶ Beware of "general partnerships" and "limited liability companies."

▶ Don't be pressured into quick decisions.

▶ Remember that you, not your bank or other IRA custodian, are the one responsible for checking out investments."

From "IRA Money May Attract Shady Deals," by Ellen E. Schultz. Wall Street Journal, December 7, 1994

◆ **Age 70½ and over—Leave it and pay a penalty.** You've gotten the most from the tax deferral, and the IRS now insists you make a withdrawal whether you need the money or not. Listen carefully: The law says that you must take your first minimum annual distribution no later than April 1 of the year *after the year* you reach 70½. The IRS calls this your "required beginning date." Furthermore, you must take additional minimum annual distributions no later than December 31 of each year after you attain age 70½.

For example, if you were born on March 15, 1950, you'll turn 70½ on September 15, 2020. You must make your first minimum withdrawal on or before April 1, 2021. Then you must make your second minimum withdrawal by December 31, 2021. These deadlines are for people who have resisted taking their distributions. You don't have to wait this long. If you wish, you can begin making penalty-free withdrawals as soon as you turn 59½. Remember that when you begin withdrawing IRA funds, you'll pay taxes at that time. *Being tax-deferred is not the same as being tax-free.* Don't think of your IRA in the same category as a truly tax-free investment like municipal bonds.

How is the minimum annual withdrawal calculated?

We've been discussing the concept of "required minimum distributions," but don't let that give you the impression that you are restricted to taking small amounts out of your IRA. You're free to empty the entire account anytime you want (of course, the penalty tax applies before age 59½, and the income tax applies regardless of your age). But assuming you want to minimize your withdrawals, how is the required minimum calculated?

The law requires that withdrawals must be made in "substantially equal amounts" over a period that does not extend beyond your life expectancy (as determined according to IRS tables). Or, you may elect a longer period—which would result in smaller withdrawals—that involves using the "joint life and last survivor" expectancy of you and the beneficiary that you name.

The minimum amount that must be withdrawn annually is calculated by dividing your account balance (as of December 31 of the previous year) by the applicable life expectancy. The table at left shows the value to use if the calculation is based on the life expectancy of the owner of the IRA. For example, a 67-year-old person with a year-end IRA value of $250,000 would be required to withdraw at least $13,587 the following year (250,000 divided by 18.4).

What if you fail to withdraw the minimum? That's where the "horrendous" penalty I referred to previously comes in—a 50% nondeductible excise tax is assessed on the shortfall, that is, on the difference between what you should have withdrawn and what you actually withdrew. If the 67-year-old retiree in the above example withdrew $5,000 the following year, the excise tax would amount to $4,293 (50% of the difference between $13,587 and $5,000). And the excise tax would not be deductible on that year's income tax return.

LIFE EXPECTANCIES FROM IRS TABLES

Age	Expectancy
35	47.3
36	46.4
37	45.4
38	44.4
39	43.5
40	42.5
41	41.5
42	40.6
43	39.6
44	38.7
45	37.7
46	36.8
47	35.9
48	34.9
49	34.0
50	33.1
51	32.2
52	31.3
53	30.4
54	29.5
55	28.6
56	27.7
57	26.8
58	25.9
59	25.0
60	24.2
61	23.3
62	22.5
63	21.6
64	20.8
65	20.0
66	19.2
67	18.4
68	17.6
69	16.8
70	16.0
71	15.3
72	14.6
73	13.9
74	13.2
75	12.5
76	11.9
77	11.2
78	10.6
79	10.0
80	9.5

The moral of this is that it's really important to pay close attention to the details when you're planning how you want to use your IRA during retirement. The rules can be complicated, especially those that relate to what's best in terms of naming a beneficiary. The articles I've read on this subject make clear that the choices you make prior to your "required beginning date" have important long-term implications. As that date approaches, make sure you have adequate tax planning counsel and plenty of time to make your decisions.

If you experience a cash crunch and need to tap your IRA before reaching age 59½, there is a way around the 10% early withdrawal penalty. It involves invoking the annuity option.

You don't read much about the strategy I'm about to describe. Possibly it's because financial advisers don't want to encourage the investing public to spend their IRA funds prematurely. I certainly can understand that. On the other hand, on those occasions where the need for cash is so great that a decision to withdraw it from an IRA has already been made, wouldn't it be good to know there's a way to do it without paying the 10% penalty? Here's the key as explained in IRS Publication 590:

> *Generally you cannot withdraw assets from your IRA until you reach age 59½ without having to pay a 10% additional tax. However, there are a number of exceptions to this rule. . . . You can receive distributions from your IRA that are part of a series of substantially equal payments over your life . . . without having to pay the 10% additional tax even if you receive such distributions before you are age 59½. You must use an IRS-approved distribution method and you must take at least one distribution annually for this exception to apply. . . . The payments under this exception must continue for at least five years, or until you reach age 59½, whichever is the longer period.*

In essence, you can decide to temporarily treat your IRA as an annuity. The amount of your annual withdrawal depends on your life expectancy at the time, and all withdrawals are taxable as income in the year you receive them. Once you begin your withdrawals, you must continue taking them for at least five years, or until you reach 59½ if that period is longer. The table at right illustrates how this could work for a 52 year old who is temporarily unemployed, but has a $300,000 IRA that resulted from a rollover out of his previous employer's retirement plan.

His withdrawal schedule is designed so that, even though his payments increase each year as he ages, they are calculated based on his life ex-

Age	Value of IRA	IRS factor	Annuity withdrawal	IRA after withdrawal	Assume 9% return	IRA at end of year
52	$300,000	31.3	$9,585	$290,415	$26,137	$316,553
53	316,553	30.4	10,413	306,140	27,553	333,692
54	333,692	29.5	11,312	322,381	29,014	351,395
55	351,395	28.6	12,287	339,109	30,520	369,628
56	369,628	27.7	13,344	356,284	32,066	388,350
57	388,350	26.8	14,491	373,859	33,647	407,507
58	407,507	25.9	15,734	391,773	35,260	427,032
59	427,032	25.0	17,081	409,951	36,896	446,847
60	446,847	24.2	18,465	428,382	38,554	466,936

pectancy so as to last the remainder of his lifetime. Upon reaching age 59½, he has the option of stopping the payments and once again working to rebuild his IRA account with additional tax-deductible contributions.

There are other IRS-approved distribution methods that result in higher yearly withdrawals for a fixed number of years, at the end of which his IRA would have been completely emptied. Consult a professional for guidance and a discussion of your options.

All the major banking, brokerage, and mutual fund institutions offer self-directed IRA accounts.

Self-directed means you decide how to invest the money you put in the account. To help you find a home for your IRA, I've surveyed several organizations to find out which ones are currently offering the most attractive terms (see table below). The competition for your IRA business is fierce, as can be seen by the willingness of the firms to waive their annual fees if your account is large enough. Scudder has gone all the way—no fees ever. The "deals" being offered change frequently, so these may be outdated by the time you read this. Check with these and other no-load fund organizations for their current policies.

Investors are fee-sensitive, as evidenced by the fact that financial organizations give such great emphasis to their low fees in their advertising. However, I would suggest that you give greater weight to having a large number of investment alternatives from which you can choose. After all, what good are low fees if you have only a few average-performing funds to select from? ◆

WHO'S OFFERING THE MOST FAVORABLE TERMS ON IRAs?

Group	Annual Fee	Minimum to Avoid Annual Fees	Minimum to Open IRA Account	Minimum Subsequent Deposit	Minimum Automatic Deposit [1]	For More Information
Fidelity	$12 for each fund owned [2]	$2,500 per fund	$500	$250	$100	(800) 544-8888
Janus	$12 for each fund owned [3]	No way to avoid fee	$500	$50	$50	(800) 525-8983
Schwab	$29	$10,000 total account	$1,000	None	$10	(800) 472-4922
Scudder	No annual fees	No annual fees	$500	$100	$50	(800) 225-2470
Strong	$10 for each fund owned [4]	$25,000 total account	$250	$50	$50	(800) 368-1030
T. Rowe Price	$10 for each fund owned	$5,000 per fund	None [5]	$50	$50	(800) 541-6592
Vanguard	$10 for each fund owned	$5,000 per fund [6]	$1,000	$100	$50	(800) 847-2999

FOOTNOTES: [1] Monthly automatic investments can be made directly from your checking or savings account, a good way to be sure you save as well as benefit from dollar-cost-averaging. [2] However, the maximum fee is $60 regardless of how many funds you own. Also, if you enroll in the automatic investment program, the $12 fee is waived regardless of the balance in the account. [3] However, the maximum fee is $24 regardless of how many funds you own. [4] However, the maximum fee is $30 regardless of how many funds you own. [5] You must set up automatic monthly deposits to qualify; otherwise the minimum is $1,000. [6] If your combined IRA assets at Vanguard total $50,000 or more, all fees are waived regardless of the balances in your individual fund accounts.

CHAPTER PREVIEW

Understanding Annuities:
How Fixed and Variable Annuities
Fit into Your Retirement Planning

I. **A fixed annuity is like a long-term, tax-sheltered CD.**

   A. Advantages: It pays a fixed rate of return agreed upon up front and offers the tax-deferred compounding of your investment income. You know what to expect in terms of investment return.

   B. Disadvantages: You are "loaning" your money to an insurance company, and you could lose part or all of your investment if the company fails. There are also significant surrender charges if you cash your annuity in early.

   C. The financial rating services offer some guidance as to the relative safety of doing business with an insurance company, but they aren't foolproof. Limit yourself to insurers with only the highest ratings from two or more services.

II. **A variable annuity (VA) is like a long-term, tax-sheltered mutual fund.**

   A. Advantages: You control the investments. If you choose the right investment mix and a good performing product, variable annuities can be far more profitable than fixed annuities.

   B. Disadvantages: You don't know what your annuity will eventually be worth; risk/reward is a two-edged sword. Further, the layers of fees make them more costly than simply buying mutual funds outright. There can be tax complications down the road, especially if you die and leave a sizable amount of money still in your VA account. And like fixed annuities, there are usually surrender charges if you decide to cash out early.

   C. There are a few no-load VAs that have low annual fees and no surrender charges. They are included in a listing of two dozen variable annuities that shows the annual expenses, surrender charges, and investment options of each.

In its simplest form, an annuity is a payment from an insurance company. You give the insurance company your money now . . .

. . . and they promise to give it back (plus a return on your investment) to you in the future. They credit your account as time goes along, but you don't actually get your money until later. As long as the insurance company has your money, any gains credited to your account aren't taxable. When you finally start getting it back, any gains you receive are taxed at the tax rate you are paying in the year you get it back. This tax deferment on your gains is the primary reason for considering an annuity.

Annuities get complicated because of all the choices you have. The first and biggest decision you have to make is:

(a) Do you want to know in advance exactly how much your investment return will be (a fixed annuity), or

(b) Are you willing to let the return vary depending on certain investment choices you make (a variable annuity)?

A fixed annuity is like a long-term, tax-sheltered CD.

It pays a fixed rate of return for an agreed-upon period of time, just like a CD. The reason to buy a fixed annuity instead of just buying a CD is because you want the tax shelter. But there are some drawbacks.

CHARACTERISTICS OF FIXED VERSUS VARIABLE ANNUITIES

	Fixed	Variable
Guaranteed rate of return	Yes	No
Hedge against inflation	No	Yes
Control over investments	No	Yes
Possible to lose on investments	No	Yes

◆ Bank CDs are fully backed by the federal government up to $100,000, but fixed annuities are "guaranteed" only by the insurance company. The guarantee is only as strong as the financial strength of the company behind it. Many insurers have invested their own money in too many junk bonds (First Executive Life) and troubled real estate projects (Mutual Benefit). The collapse of five large insurers in 1991 jeopardized more than 500,000 annuity holders. If your insurer fails, you could be just like any other creditor trying to get his money back. And it doesn't matter where you buy your annuity; not even those sold by banks are federally insured.

◆ The "early withdrawal" penalty for cashing in a CD early is relatively mild (usually you forfeit a portion of the interest you've earned), but the "surrender charges" on annuities can be horrendous. The amount you receive if you cash in early is reduced by charges that can start as high as 7% of your capital the first year, typically dropping 1% per year until they disappear after the seventh year.

Some companies have no surrender charges, instead assessing "deferred sales charges," which you pay whether you take your money out or not. Thanks a lot. Others promise that you won't lose any of your principal if you cash in early — that means that the most you can lose is all the income you've earned. Still pretty steep. But all companies waive surrender charges in the event of your death; your beneficiary receives the total amount accumulated in your annuity.

◆ If you take your money out of an annuity before age 59½, the IRS hits you with a 10% penalty tax on your earnings. This is in addition to the normal income tax. Remember: Just because the insurer is willing to forgo surrender charges *doesn't mean* you won't have to pay the IRS's penalty tax for cashing in early.

◆ Here are some points to consider when comparing rates offered by various fixed annuities: (1) The fixed rate promised is only good for so many years; after that the insurer can lower the rate at its discretion; (2) so-called "bonus" and "tiered-rate" annuities, which promise high returns during the first year, usually pay either lower rates down the road or impose unpleasant restrictions on when and how you can get your money back; and (3) tax *deferred* is not the same as tax *free*. Don't fall for promotions that imply that a 7% return on an annuity is like an 11% pre-tax return on a CD. You do *eventually* have to pay taxes on your annuity earnings; they're not tax-free.

Don't forget to consider the credit risk when investing in a fixed annuity. Such contracts are just another way for insurance companies to borrow money.

Fixed annuities, guaranteed investment contracts, and cash value life insurance policies are all products where it's possible for you to lose part or all of your money. The publicity that surrounded the problems of several insurers in 1991 made clear to investors the importance of dealing with a financially strong insurance company. Given that insurance companies have the image of being stodgy, conservative, and safe, it's sometimes difficult to understand how many of them got into financial difficulty. Here's how it happened.

The high interest rates in the early 1980s made the low returns offered by life insurance policies unattractive to individuals. Rather than looking at their life insurance as *protection*, buyers increasingly regarded it as an *investment*. The industry was forced to redesign its products in order to stay competitive. Companies came out with new kinds of cash value policies and annuities that promised better returns. The "guaranteed investment contract" (GIC) was invented so the industry would have a more appealing product to offer employer-sponsored retirement plans. These products were successful, but their very success had a dramatic impact on the industry's mix of policies. Whereas

"Choosing Life Insurance That's Right for You" by Michael Cave.
Excerpted from the Sound Mind Investing newsletter. See Briefing 19, page 480.

How Annuities Are Bought

Single Payment is when you make one lump sum deposit into your annuity account.

Periodic Payments are a series of regularly scheduled deposits over a period of time.

When Your Income Begins

Deferred Annuity is the most common form of annuity. The insurance company holds your money for years before you annuitize, that is, before you start receiving payments. Can be purchased on either a single payment or periodic payments basis.

Immediate Annuity is where you pay the insurance company a single lump sum and begin receiving your monthly lifetime payments right away.

in 1969, only 26% of the policies written were annuities and pensions, twenty years later this number had grown to 67%.

The problem with this is the pressure it put on the insurers to earn higher returns on their own investment portfolios in order to pay the higher rates they were promising investors. This ultimately led them into higher risk areas, most notably the "junk" bond market and the commercial real estate market. Both of these areas are high risk, but they differ in the seriousness of the consequences if problems arise.

◆ **Junk bond losses.** Money lost in the junk bond market through defaults is usually gone forever. A survey of insurance companies showed an average of 24% of their portfolio in junk bonds; critics suggest a 5%-10% ceiling is in order. One reason the Executive Life failure was so costly is that the company had about two-thirds of its assets in junk, a dangerous level by almost any standard.

◆ **Real estate losses.** A soft economy increases office vacancies and decreases retail spending. This pushes some of the marginal commercial developments over the edge. Still, real estate loans in foreclosure, given sufficient time to find a buyer, usually have a reasonable expectancy of recouping some or most of the money at risk. Mutual Benefit Life's troubles were due to its real estate portfolio. Whereas the industry average is less than 25% of invested assets, Mutual Benefit had committed 40% to real estate loans. This need not have become a problem, but Mutual Benefit took other steps that greatly increased its risk. Not only did it concentrate its loans in relatively fewer developments than prudent diversification would require, but the company also invested in some of the bigger projects as well as loaned money to them. So if a project got into trouble, there was a conflict between Mutual Benefit's interests as a lender versus its interests as an owner. The owner side won, leading the company to continue loaning funds to the problem developments in order to keep them going. By the time regulators took charge of Mutual Benefit, about 10% of its $5 billion real estate and mortgage-loan portfolio was in trouble.

You can't necessarily count on state regulators, who are often overworked and understaffed, to protect you.

Most state funds are not capable of handling large-scale problems, so the hope is that by giving these insurers more time, their problems will eventually be corrected. That's why they allow problem companies to continue to operate. Delay is the accepted strategy.

When regulators come in to reorganize or sell an insurer, their first responsibility is to protect the present policyholders as much as possible. In order to do this, they usually "freeze" the company assets in order to keep control of as much of the money as possible while they sort out the damage. This

---

Are You Protected If Your Insurance Company Fails?

Deposits in bank and S&L accounts are insured by the FDIC against loss up to $100,000. There is no comparable federal program that protects customers of insurance companies. Regulating the insurance industry has traditionally been handled at the state level.

Every state has a fund designed to protect its residents. The money in the state funds is not government money, but comes from the insurers licensed in the state. They pay into the fund based on their premium income. If the fund is inadequate to pay claims caused by a major failure, it could take several years for residents to receive their full payments.

The amount of coverage differs from state to state. Typically, the cash values of life policies and annuities are protected up to $100,000, with a total limit of $300,000–$500,000 per person (which includes death benefits). Some states include GIC protection in this, some don't. And if your insurer is not licensed to do business in your state (say you bought your policy elsewhere before moving to your present home), you may not be protected.

One way to find out where you stand is to call your state office and ask. They're paid to serve you, so don't be hesitant to call.

means that, for the time being, policyholders are no longer allowed to cash in their life insurance policies or annuities, move them to another insurer, or even borrow against them. The most important activities, like paying death benefits and mailing out the payments on annuities and GICs, usually continue in the normal fashion.

Will policyholders in investment-type products eventually receive 100% of what they're entitled to after the regulators sort things out? According to Joseph Belth, publisher of *The Insurance Forum*:

> *Despite the existence of guaranty associations, policyowners of failed companies face substantial uncertainties, delays, and potential losses. In most cases where life companies were seized by regulators, moratoriums were placed on cash surrenders and policy loans, and policyowners were not able to obtain access to their funds for long periods of time. Although benefits, in most cases, have been paid in full, there have been instances in which death benefits were delayed and annuity benefits reduced.*

Only limited protection is offered by the various insurance rating organizations.

There are five major ratings services.

The A.M. Best Company offers the oldest service. It rates a very large number of firms (around 1,750), for which it charges each firm a fee that is typically under $1,000. Best is *known for its leniency* and releases its ratings only with the insurance company's permission. As a result, the highly publicized Best ratings are looking increasingly meaningless. For example, Executive Life carried an A+ from Best until it disclosed massive junk bond losses in early 1990. Even then, it was only downgraded to an A. And Mutual Benefit enjoyed an A+ from Best until just ten days before state regulators moved in.

In many ways, Weiss Research is the opposite of the Best Company. It's the newest service, is known for having the toughest guidelines, and accepts no rating fees from the insurance companies. Weiss rates about 1,450 insurers. Reflecting its stricter standards, only 6% of the life insurance companies covered in its current directory get the B+ or higher grades necessary to land on Weiss's recommended list.

Three other companies—Duff & Phelps, Moody's, and Standard & Poor's—take up the middle ground. They charge insurers $25,000 to $30,000 a year to include them in their ratings, which explains why there is a much smaller number of insurance firms in their databases. Their ratings are based on meetings with each company and highly detailed financial information they provide. Using this methodology, Moody's has assigned ratings to 137 companies, Duff & Phelps to 187 companies, and Standard & Poor's to 288 companies (as of the end of 1995). If a life insurance company does not agree with the rating given it, the company may request that it not be published. Like

State Insurance Departments

Your state department of insurance can be a helpful source of information on the companies doing busines in your state. Don't be bashful about calling.

Alabama	(334) 241-4126
Alaska	(907) 465-2578
Arizona	(602) 912-8470
Arkansas	(501) 371-2750
California	(916) 322-3555
Colorado	(303) 894-7495
Connecticut	(860) 297-3845
Delaware	(302) 739-4254
Florida	(904) 922-3137
Georgia	(404) 656-2100
Hawaii	(808) 586-2790
Idaho	(208) 334-4339
Illinois	(217) 782-6366
Indiana	(317) 232-2410
Iowa	(515) 281-4038
Kansas	(913) 296-7862
Kentucky	(502) 564-6004
Louisiana	(504) 342-0860
Maine	(207) 624-8475
Maryland	(410) 333-4056
Massachusetts	(617) 521-7794
Michigan	(517) 373-0234
Minnesota	(612) 296-6319
Mississippi	(601) 359-3582
Missouri	(573) 751-3518
Montana	(406) 444-2539
Nebraska	(402) 471-2201
Nevada	(702) 687-4276
New Hampshire	(603) 271-2261
New Jersey	(609) 292-4390
New Mexico	(505) 827-4552
New York	(518) 474-6630
North Carolina	(919) 733-7487
North Dakota	(701) 328-3548
Ohio	(614) 644-2665
Oklahoma	(405) 521-3916
Oregon	(503) 378-4511
Pennsylvania	(717) 787-3840
Rhode Island	(401) 277-2223
South Carolina	(803) 737-6110
South Dakota	(605) 773-3513
Tennessee	(615) 741-2693
Texas	(512) 322-3503
Utah	(801) 538-3855
Vermont	(802) 828-3301
Virginia	(804) 371-9631
Washington	(360) 407-0341
Washington, D.C.	(202) 727-8000
West Virginia	(304) 558-0610
Wisconsin	(608) 266-8699
Wyoming	(307) 777-7310

A.M. Best, Duff & Phelps and Standard & Poor's will suppress the rating (and not publish the fact that this has been done). Moody's, on the other hand, refuses to suppress a rating.

To find out if your insurer is in good financial health . . .

. . . put your agent to work. You paid him a sizable commission not only to sell you the annuity policy, but also to service it. Tell him you want to know the ratings on your insurer from Weiss and any of the others that publish a rating for it.

If your agent fails to satisfy your concerns, here are two other options. Standard and Poor's offers a free service where they will tell you over the phone the current ratings on the 450 insurers they cover. There is a limit of five ratings per call. Call their Ratings Information Line at (212) 208-8000. Alternately, Weiss Research will send you a one-page "safety brief" on your insurer, which contains their latest rating and an easy-to-understand update of the major factors behind it. There is a $25 charge for this service. Call (800) 289-9222. Remember, due to the different ratings systems devised by these two firms, you cannot compare them to one another — a B rating from Weiss might be comparable to an AA rating from S&P. Be sure you get a copy of the definitions describing what the ratings mean.

If you're considering moving your fixed annuity to another insurer . . .

. . . here are some costs to keep in mind. First, there are surrender penalties that routinely cost 7% during the first year of a policy, dropping 1% per year until they finally stop. Second, there are also tax consequences if you cash out of a policy and receive more back than you paid in premiums. If you decide that a move is best, be sure to do a 1035 exchange. This will continue the tax deferral on the earnings in your cash-value policies and annuities. Your agent can provide the form you need.

Although the reports of several insurance failures in the early 1990s was unsettling, it hopefully will lead to a positive long-term result. As Americans shift to the stronger firms, the result will be a healthier insurance industry and economy. At the same time, those insurers that have remained strong by taking their fiduciary responsibilities seriously and following a prudent investment course will be rewarded.

Variable annuities (VAs) are the other kind of annuity we're going to look at. They circumvent the insurance company credit risk by giving you control of the investments.

Think of them as mutual funds wrapped up in a tax-sheltered package. Unlike a fixed annuity, where you are essentially loaning money to the insurance

Recommended Resource
The Insurance Forum annually publishes a "special ratings issue." This report carries listings of more than 3,000 ratings assigned to about 1,500 life insurance companies by four rating firms (A.M. Best ratings not included). It also includes explanations of the four ratings systems and how they differ.

This is an excellent resource at a reasonable price. In addition to the listing tables, helpful additional research is also provided. For example, the October 1995 report suggested:

"If a person wants to be conservative, he or she might select a company which has very high ratings from at least two of the four ratings firms. For the purposes of this criterion, these are very high ratings:

S&P: AAA, AAAq, AA+, AA, AAq
Moody's: Aaa, Aa1, Aa2, Aa3
Duff and Phelps: AAA, AA+
Weiss: A+, A, A-, B+, B

When this issue was assembled, 142 life-health companies met the criterion."

The names of those companies were then listed.

Reprints of the "special ratings issue" are $15 (Indiana residents add 5% sales tax). To order, send your check to: Insurance Forum, Post Office Box 245, Ellettsville, IN 47429-0245.

company and, in return, agree upon a rate of return up front, the returns in a variable annuity aren't locked in ahead of time. They vary depending on how well the investments perform—that's why they're called "variable."

The VA has one major advantage over the fixed kind—*you* have control over the investments. Insurance companies typically offer several investment choices in their variable annuities, including a blue-chip stock fund, a bond fund, an international fund, and a money market fund. They let you decide how much of the money you give them goes into each category. Your eventual return is affected by three things.

❶ **Your allocation decisions.** If you decide to put all your money into the stock market just before a major sell-off, you'll get off to a slow start. On the other hand, if you play it safe in the money market fund, you're giving up the reason for choosing a VA in the first place—greater profit potential.

❷ **Investment fund performance.** It could be that even though you make excellent allocation decisions, the funds offered by your particular insurer just don't perform well. Just like mutual funds, some finish in the top ranks year after year, whereas others are perennial also-rans. Check out the track records of the funds in the variable annuity being offered to you. How do they compare with other variable annuity funds over the same period?

❸ **Fees, fees, and fees.** There are three kinds of fees you have to pay with most VA products. First, there are the sales fees, usually disguised as "surrender charges." In the most common arrangement, there are no up-front sales charges; instead, the cost of commissions paid to the brokers and insurance agents is recovered by penalties paid if investors take their money out of the annuity in the first seven years.

Next come the "contract fees," which include annual administrative and insurance fees. Among their other purposes, these fees guarantee that your beneficiaries won't get back less than you put in, regardless of how poorly your investment choices perform. According to Morningstar, these fees average about 1.3% per year. You pay these every year you own the annuity.

Finally there are the fees paid to the investment managers who make the portfolio decisions in the funds. These are similar to the management fees paid by shareholders of regular mutual funds and typically run about 0.9% per year. These also are ongoing.

So, you can see how the overhead expenses cut into your returns by about 2.2% each and every year, even assuming you hold your annuity longer than seven years and avoid the surrender charges. Another drawback is the loss of liquidity. Annuities are designed for retirement planning and are intended as long-term investments. Once you put your money into one, you're supposed to leave it there until at least age 59½. If you take it out sooner, you get hit with a 10% penalty from the government, just as with IRAs.

Are variable annuities worth the cost, red tape, and possible tax headaches down the road?

Because of the high costs and the possible tax disadvantages (see graphic below), many financial planners recommend VAs only as a "last resort," that is, after all the other options have been explored and exhausted. Their unique characteristics create a situation where it's difficult to decide which kinds of investments would be appropriate within a variable annuity:

On the one hand, if you invest in equities with growth potential, you're going to end up paying ordinary income tax rates on what would otherwise qualify for long-term capital gains tax treatment. If the capital gains rate is lowered from its present 28% level, the problem becomes even worse.

On the other hand, if you put your VA money in fixed income investments, then the high fees become particularly burdensome. Do you really want to pay 2% a year and more just to invest in bonds (which have historically returned about 8% a year)? The same investment in a low-cost, no-load mutual fund (like those at Vanguard) would cost only about 0.3% per year.

INVESTING IN VARIABLE ANNUITIES VERSUS MUTUAL FUNDS

Advantages	Disadvantages
You're insured against losses.	On average, annual fees are about twice as high as those for mutual funds.
The taxes on your gains are deferred.	If you want to move your money elsewhere, there may be surrender charges.
	When you take your money out, any profits will be taxed at ordinary income rates. This includes capital gains, which otherwise might have been taxed at lower capital gains rates.
	If you take your money out before reaching age 59½, you'll face a 10% tax penalty on your profits. This is in addition to the usual income taxes.
	Even when you take your money out after age 59½, you could still run into the "success tax" (see page 363).
	For estate tax purposes, annuities offer no "step-up" in your cost basis. Should you die with money still in your annuity, your heirs will owe income taxes on the profits in your variable annuity as well as estate taxes on its market value.

From a planning point of view, a VA makes the most sense if:

◆ You are in one of the higher tax brackets now (28% and up) and have a reasonable expectation that your tax bracket will be lower after you retire.

◆ You expect to make withdrawals in regular, systematic payments to supplement your other retirement income.

◆ You anticipate that your regular monthly withdrawals will exhaust the assets in your annuity in your lifetime. (Due to tax laws, an annuity is not a good vehicle for accumulating capital to leave to your heirs.)

◆ You got a late start contributing to other tax-deferred retirement accounts and are using an annuity as a means for making up lost ground.

Before investing in a VA, I suggest you should be able to pass all the following tests:

◆ You're already making the full tax-deductible contribution to your IRA.

◆ You're already paying the maximum permitted into an employer-sponsored 401(k) plan.

◆ You've got investment money you're willing to lock away for at least ten years, which is the time needed to make up for the fees.

◆ You've set aside an amount of cash sufficient to cover major expenses and emergency needs so that you'll have no need to withdraw your money before age 59½.

After considering the above, if you think a variable annuity makes a good fit in your situation, great. That means it's time to look at specific alternatives.

The first decision to make is whether to contact your favorite insurance agent or stockbroker . . .

. . . or to go the do-it-yourself route. I recommend you consider the latter, mainly because you'll save a lot on either front-end commissions or the redemption charges (exit fees) on withdrawals. VAs come with a variety of frills, some helpful, others merely confusing the issue. When you're shopping, three questions worth asking are:

❶ "How many subaccount choices do you offer, and what are they?" (In annuity lingo, "subaccount" is another name for what you ordinarily call a mutual fund.) This question lets you know what kind of variety you will have to select from as you make the investment decisions in your annuity.

❷ "Do you allow telephone switching? If so, how often? Is there a charge?" Telephone switching allows you to transfer your money between the various investments offered with a simple phone call.

❸ "Do you offer a dollar-cost-averaging option?" This enables you to set up a schedule for automatically moving your money into stock and bond funds at regular intervals over time (in order to reduce the risk of moving at the wrong time).

To help get you started, on the next two pages you'll find cost and performance information . . .

. . . on two dozen reputable VA products. I've included several no-loads as well as some of the leading competition. Here are some pointers on how to interpret the various columns within the tables.

Since cost is such an important consideration, the annuities are ranked according to the amount of the total annual expense they charge investors (see "Fees, fees, and fees" on page 375). Expenses were calculated for each annuity by taking an average of all its stock, bond, and balanced investment subaccounts that had been in existence for at least one year as of the end of 1995. The average expense will change slightly over time, but (continued on page 380)

"How to Turn $10,000 into $20 Million" by Paul Merriman.

Excerpted from the Fund Exchange newsletter. See Briefing 20, page 483.

Recommended Resource
What would be the results from investing in a tax-deferred VA versus its taxable cousin, the mutual fund? Computer software offered by T. Rowe Price and Security Benefit Life Insurance lets investors compare hypothetical variable annuity accounts to the performance in no-load funds. Using a database of T. Rowe Price products, this Windows software helps you see the trade-offs under a variety of "what if" situations. It's educational, and once you learn your way around the program, you can change the assumptions to reflect funds and VAs other than those offered by Price. It's free for the asking. Call (800) 469-5304 and request a copy of the Variable Annuity Analyzer.

Investment Options and Expense Features
of Selected Variable Annuities

Name of Variable Annuity	Total Annual Expense	Maximum Surrender Charge	Years Charge Applies	Annual Contract Charge	How Many Stock Funds to Choose From?	How Many Ranked in Top 25% in 1995?	How Many Bond Funds to Choose From?	How Many Ranked in Top 25% in 1995?	Phone Number to Call
1. Vanguard Variable Annuity Plan	0.85%	0	N/A	$25	4	4	1	0	(800) 462-2391
2. Scudder Horizon Plan	1.45%	0	N/A	0	3	0	1	0	(800) 242-4402
3. VALIC Independence Plus	1.51%	5%	5 years	$15	5	2	3	1	(800) 448-2542
4. Dreyfus/Transamerica	1.64%	6%	7 years	$30	5	1	2	1	(800) 258-4260
5. Fidelity Retirement Reserves	1.64%	5%	5 years	$30	4	1	2	1	(800) 634-9361
6. Schwab Investment Advantage	1.81%	0	N/A	$25	10	1	2	0	(800) 838-0650
7. Prudential VIP-86	1.81%	8%	8 years	$30	4	2	3	2	(201) 802-6000
8. Mutual of America Sep Acct 2	1.82%	0	N/A	$24	7	2	4	0	(800) 468-3785
9. Lincoln National Multi Fund	1.83%	7%	7 years	$25	7	2	1	0	(800) 348-1212
10. Bankers Security USA Plan	1.95%	7%	8 years	$30	7	2	3	0	(800) 338-7737
11. MONYMaster	2.01%	7%	8 years	$30	3	2	4	1	(800) 487-6669
12. Travelers Universal Annuity	2.03%	5%	5 years	$30	10	5	8	3	(800) 842-9493

Data source: Morningstar Mutual Funds. Copyright by Morningstar, Inc., 53 West Jackson Blvd., Chicago, IL 60604. (800) 876–5005. Although gathered from reliable sources, data accuracy and completeness cannot be guaranteed. Performance numbers reflect periods ending 12/31/95. These are not recommended funds per se, but are offered here as worthy of your consideration. Variable annuity policies are subject to change. Contact the insurer for current information before you invest.

Investment Options and Expense Features
of Selected Variable Annuities

Name of Variable Annuity	Total Annual Expense	Maximum Surrender Charge	Years Charge Applies	Annual Contract Charge	How Many Stock Funds to Choose From?	How Many Ranked in Top 25% in 1995?	How Many Bond Funds to Choose From?	How Many Ranked in Top 25% in 1995?	Phone Number to Call
13. Janus Retirement Advantage	2.06%	0	N/A	$30	4	2	2	1	(800) 504-4440
14. Dean Witter Variable Annuity II	2.12%	6%	6 years	$30	6	3	2	1	(800) 654-2397
15. Hartford Putnam Cap Manager	2.12%	6%	7 years	$30	4	3	3	1	(800) 862-6668
16. Best of America IV/Nationwide	2.12%	7%	7 years	$30	14	2	5	1	(800) 848-6331
17. Life of Virginia Commonwealth	2.12%	6%	6 years	$30	12	4	7	3	(800) 352-9910
18. New England Zenith Accum	2.14%	8%	10 years	$30	10	4	3	1	(800) 333-2501
19. Templeton Investment Plus	2.20%	6%	6 years	$35	2	2	1	0	(800) 243-4840
20. Ameritas Overture II	2.20%	6%	7 years	$30	8	4	2	1	(800) 734-1112
21. Aetna Marathon Plus	2.22%	7%	7 years	$30	15	3	5	1	(800) 531-4547
22. Pacific Mutual Select VA	2.30%	6%	5 years	$30	5	2	3	1	(800) 722-2333
23. American Skandia Advisors	2.47%	8%	7 years	$30	16	4	6	0	(800) 752-6342
24. PaineWebber Milestones D	3.06%	0	N/A	$30	4	0	3	0	(800) 552-5622

Data source: Morningstar Mutual Funds. Copyright by Morningstar, Inc., 53 West Jackson Blvd., Chicago, IL 60604. (800) 876–5005. Although gathered from reliable sources, data accuracy and completeness cannot be guaranteed. Performance numbers reflect periods ending 12/31/95. These are not recommended funds per se, but are offered here as worthy of your consideration. Variable annuity policies are subject to change. Contact the insurer for current information before you invest.

this will provide a good estimate as to who the low-cost operators are. I suggest you begin your shopping with those VAs listed on page 378.

The maximum surrender charge shows the penalty you will pay to the insurance company for cashing out in the early years. The adjacent column shows how many years must pass before the surrender charges no longer apply. It's a common practice for surrender charges to decrease 1% per year. For example, the surrender charges on the VALIC annuity (ranked third) begin at 5% during the first year, drop to 4% the second year, to 3% the third year, and so on. After five years, there are no surrender charges. For maximum flexibility, you want low numbers in these columns.

No-load variable annuities, like the ones offered by Vanguard, Scudder, Schwab, and Mutual of America, assess no surrender charges. Note that PaineWebber (ranked twenty-fourth) attempts to position itself as a no-load, but they more than make up for it with very high annual expenses.

You want to have a variety of investment options in your VA. I have included columns that show how many stock and bond subaccounts each VA offers. New ones are being added continually, so check with the insurance company for the latest information. I have only included subaccounts that were up and running on or before January 1, 1995.

Of course, having a lot of choices isn't much help if they are all poor performers. That's why I've included columns to show how many of a VA's subaccount offerings were top performers in 1995. (For our purposes here, a top performer is one that finishes in the top 25% of all the funds having the same investment objective. Thus, growth funds are measured against other growth funds, and so on.) Although VALIC offered only five stock subaccounts versus Schwab's ten, VALIC had twice as many top performers. This is just a single year's data, so perhaps too much shouldn't be made of it. I included it primarily to impress upon you that it's not just the quantity of subaccount offerings that you should consider; quality of performance is important as well. After all, it is the total return from your annuity that will ultimately determine your degree of satisfaction. ◆

Recommended Resource

If you're looking for current performance data on a variable annuity, Morningstar's OnDemand service might be of interest.

Full page reports are available on about 900 variable annuity subaccounts. Each report is $5, and will be faxed immediately (or if you prefer, sent via first class mail). To order, call (800) 876-5005.

If all you're looking for is an update on a VA subaccount's performance over the past four-week and one-year periods, you can find it listed in the Market Week section of Barron's. Published every Saturday, this respected financial newspaper is available at any bookstore that carries the daily Wall Street Journal. The price is $3.00.

CHAPTER PREVIEW

Lowering Your Investment Risk as You Approach Retirement

I. **Because nobody knows what the future holds for the investment markets, we can never know in advance which combination of investments will minimize our risk while maximizing our gains.**

   A. This uncertainty makes it difficult to decide with confidence how much to cut back your investment risk as you near retirement. To a large extent, your decision will reflect your personal investing temperament.

   B. The risk matrix contains my suggestions as to what is an appropriate allocation between stocks (higher risk) and bonds (lower risk) given your age and temperament. Other professionals may offer different suggestions. There is no universally agreed upon "right" allocation for a retired person.

II. **A study of historical returns since 1926 shows how various combinations of stocks and bonds have performed in the past.**

   A. A table is presented that is useful for gaining an understanding of the potential risks and rewards from holding six different stock/bond allocations over various time periods ranging from one year to thirty years.

   B. A similar table is presented that is useful for gaining an understanding of the potential risks and rewards from holding shares in large companies versus those of small companies.

   C. There are no "sure things." It is inevitable that you must make decisions that involve trade-offs between the risks you're willing to take and the rewards you hope to reap.

Like all the other kids, I wanted to see *Jurassic Park* when it came out in the summer of 1993.

As I expected, it turned out to be an action-packed, nerve-wracking tale overflowing with amazing special effects. What I didn't expect was the intellectual stimulation and the way the film got me to thinking about the critical importance of boundaries.

Boundaries exist for safety reasons; breaking through them can be dangerous. The film is scary because the prehistoric creatures break through *physical boundaries* and attack the people. And it provokes us to weigh the risks before breaking through *scientific boundaries* and playing with the building blocks of life. It may even have something to say to societies that are breaking through *moral boundaries* and removing limits on personal freedoms that have characterized civilized societies for thousands of years.

Because I'm a person who thinks a lot about how to help people invest more successfully, the film caused me to also reflect on the risks taken by those who willfully ignore *time boundaries*. We are quite limited as to what we can know of the future with certainty.

My favorite character in *Jurassic Park* is Malcolm, the "chaos theory" scientist. I particularly liked the passage in the book where he is describing to a co-worker why many events are inherently, inescapably unpredictable:

"Computers were built because mathematicians thought that if you had a machine to handle a lot of variables simultaneously, you would be able to predict the weather. Weather would finally fall to human understanding. And men believed that dream for the next forty years. They believed that prediction was just a function of keeping track of things. If you knew enough, you could predict anything.

"Chaos theory throws it right out the window. It says that you can never predict certain phenomena at all. You can never predict the weather more than a few days away. All the money that has been spent on long-range forecasting is money wasted. It's a fool's errand. It's as pointless as trying to turn lead into gold. We've tried the impossible — and spent a lot of money doing it. Because in fact there are great categories of phenomena that are inherently unpredictable."

"Chaos says that?"

"Yes, and it is astonishing how few people care to hear it."

Consider that last line: "*. . . it is astonishing how few people care to hear it.*" How well that applies to people when they're making investment decisions! We refuse to believe that the markets, like the weather, cannot be accurately predicted. Throughout my advisory career I've seen people suffer financially because they look to the forecasts and opinions of gurus and experts to guide their decisions.

I was slow in accepting this limitation myself. But it's very important we learn to admit, "I don't know what the future holds. The financial commentators in the media don't know. Investment experts don't know. Nobody knows. So, I must face

"Are Living Trusts for You?"
by Busby, Barber, and Temple.
Excerpted from The Christian's Guide to Worry-free Money Management,
See Briefing 21, page 485.

"Charitable Remainder Trusts: A Win-Win Proposition"
by Busby, Barber, and Temple.
Excerpted from The Christian's Guide to Worry-free Money Management,
See Briefing 22, page 486.

"Leave a Guide so They Don't Get Lost"
by Robert Frank.
Excerpted from the No-Debt Living newsletter.
See Briefing 23, page 487.

the fact that I can never know in advance which investment alternatives will make the most money, lose the most money, or do little at all."

This uncertainty makes it difficult to know how much to cut back our investment risk—and the potential gains we're hoping for—as we near retirement.

In chapter 14, I offered my opinion on how this might best be done. The risk matrix (see pages 167–170) balances the two competing influences in your investment planning—your fear of loss and your need for growth. On the one hand, I believe that insofar as possible, you should "be yourself" as you make investing decisions. The quiz I designed helps you select the investing temperament best suited to your personality by probing the intensity of your fear of losing money (an ever-present possibility in the markets). It's important that you be emotionally comfortable with your strategy. Otherwise, it's questionable if you'll develop the confidence and discipline needed to hang in there when the periodic storms of market turbulence blow through.

On the other hand, your investing strategy must face the realities of your present stage of life—how much time remains before you reach retirement, and what financial goals do you hope to achieve by that time? If you structure your portfolio too conservatively, your investment capital may not grow by the needed amount. But if you take too great a risk, you could suffer a large loss just before you need to withdraw capital for living expenses.

In the matrix, I offer suggestions on how much to invest-by-owning (typically in stocks and stock funds) versus how much to invest-by-lending (in savings accounts, bonds and bond funds, and other fixed income holdings). As I pointed out at the time, however, "This matrix reflects my personal sense of risk. Other investment advisers might feel more comfortable with less restrictive guidelines." In fact, most do.

After reviewing several of the books in my library on the subject of how to adjust your stock-to-bond mix as you grow older, it's clear that the guidelines I offer are somewhat conservative.

For example, if you're sixty years old (in what I call "phase three" of your financial life), the matrix indicates that the stock portion of your holdings not exceed 60% in stocks. The recommendations of other advisers called for portfolios with stock allocations ranging from 40% to as high as 75%. Their argument for higher stock holdings is that, although stocks are subject to occasional major setbacks, they are needed to keep ahead of inflation.

The response to that argument is that, while it's true that stocks have always recovered from previous bear markets, older investors may have a need to withdraw their money before stocks have time to rebound. Interest income from bonds is certain; good returns from stocks in the short run are not. So, it's a matter of balance. You need stocks for growth and bonds for income, but, putting your emotions aside,

HISTORICAL INVESTMENT RETURNS
OF VARIOUS PORTFOLIO COMBINATIONS

Portfolio Consists of >>>	Stocks: 100% Bonds: 0%	Stocks: 80% Bonds: 20%	Stocks: 60% Bonds: 40%	Stocks: 40% Bonds: 60%	Stocks: 20% Bonds: 80%	Stocks: 0% Bonds: 100%
Average of 805 1-Year Periods	12.8%	11.4%	10.0%	8.6%	7.3%	5.9%
Best 1-Year Period	**①** 163.0%	**②** 134.2%	**③** 105.5%	**④** 76.7%	**⑤** 48.0%	**⑥** 46.8%
Worst 1-Year Period	−67.6%	−55.6%	−43.7%	−31.8%	−19.8%	−18.2%
Result two-thirds of the time	−9.7% to 35.2%	−7.1% to 29.9%	−4.8% to 24.8%	−2.9% to 20.2%	−2.0% to 16.5%	−2.8% to 14.6%
Average of 781 3-Year Periods	10.8%	10.0%	9.1%	8.0%	6.8%	5.5%
Best 3-Year Period	**⑦** 43.3%	**⑧** 38.5%	**⑨** 32.9%	**⑩** 27.1%	**⑪** 24.9%	**⑫** 23.8%
Worst 3-Year Period	−42.4%	−32.5%	−23.2%	−14.3%	−5.6%	−6.9%
Result two-thirds of the time	−1.1% to 22.7%	0.3% to 19.7%	1.2% to 16.9%	1.7% to 14.3%	1.4% to 12.3%	0.0% to 11.1%
Average of 757 5-Year Periods	10.2%	9.5%	8.7%	7.8%	6.7%	5.4%
Best 5-Year Period	**⑬** 36.1%	**⑭** 31.7%	**⑮** 27.0%	**⑯** 24.0%	**⑰** 23.4%	**⑱** 23.9%
Worst 5-Year Period	−17.4%	−11.8%	−6.8%	−2.7%	−1.7%	−2.3%
Result two-thirds of the time	1.5% to 18.9%	2.6% to 16.5%	3.1% to 14.4%	3.1% to 12.5%	2.3% to 11.0%	0.7% to 10.1%
Average of 697 10-Year Periods	10.6%	9.8%	8.8%	7.7%	6.4%	5.0%
Best 10-Year Period	**⑲** 21.4%	**⑳** 18.7%	**㉑** 18.1%	**㉒** 17.7%	**㉓** 17.4%	**㉔** 16.9%
Worst 10-Year Period	−4.9%	−2.0%	0.6%	1.3%	1.4%	0.6%
Result two-thirds of the time	5.0% to 16.1%	5.4% to 14.2%	5.2% to 12.4%	4.5% to 10.8%	3.2% to 9.6%	1.4% to 8.6%
Average of 637 15-Year Periods	10.5%	9.6%	8.5%	7.3%	6.0%	4.5%
Best 15-Year Period	**㉕** 19.0%	**㉖** 16.2%	**㉗** 15.2%	**㉘** 13.9%	**㉙** 12.7%	**㉚** 11.7%
Worst 15-Year Period	−0.4%	1.4%	2.8%	3.6%	2.6%	1.0%
Result two-thirds of the time	6.0% to 15.0%	6.1% to 13.1%	5.8% to 11.2%	5.0% to 9.6%	3.7% to 8.3%	1.7% to 7.2%
Average of 577 20-Year Periods	10.6%	9.6%	8.4%	7.2%	5.7%	4.2%
Best 20-Year Period	**㉛** 17.1%	**㉜** 14.4%	**㉝** 12.0%	**㉞** 11.5%	**㉟** 11.0%	**㊱** 10.4%
Worst 20-Year Period	1.9%	2.9%	3.8%	4.4%	3.2%	1.3%
Result two-thirds of the time	7.3% to 13.9%	7.1% to 12.1%	6.6% to 10.3%	5.6% to 8.7%	4.0% to 7.5%	1.9% to 6.5%
Average of 517 25-Year Periods	10.8%	9.7%	8.5%	7.1%	5.6%	4.0%
Best 25-Year Period	**㊲** 16.1%	**㊳** 14.2%	**㊴** 12.0%	**㊵** 10.0%	**㊶** 9.6%	**㊷** 9.2%
Worst 25-Year Period	5.6%	5.8%	5.8%	5.0%	3.6%	1.5%
Result two-thirds of the time	8.6% to 13.1%	8.1% to 11.3%	7.3% to 9.6%	6.0% to 8.2%	4.2% to 6.9%	2.1% to 5.8%
Average of 457 30-Year Periods	11.0%	9.8%	8.5%	7.1%	5.6%	3.9%
Best 30-Year Period	**㊸** 14.8%	**㊹** 13.1%	**㊺** 11.2%	**㊻** 9.2%	**㊼** 8.5%	**㊽** 7.7%
Worst 30-Year Period	7.8%	7.4%	6.7%	5.6%	3.9%	1.8%
Result two-thirds of the time	9.6% to 12.3%	8.8% to 10.8%	7.7% to 9.3%	6.2% to 8.0%	4.4% to 6.7%	2.3% to 5.5%

Notes: The source for performance data was <u>Stocks, Bonds, Bills, and Inflation 1996 Yearbook</u> published by Ibbotson Associates in Chicago. The data for stocks are based upon total returns (capital appreciation and dividend income) of the Standard & Poor's 500 Index. The data for bonds are based on Ibbotson's "long-term corporate bonds" total return (capital appreciation and coupon interest income) index, which uses bonds of 20 years' maturity. The period covered runs from 1926 (where the Ibbotson data begins) through 1993. Portfolios were rebalanced to their original allocations every twelve months.

how much of each would be best given your current age?

To help put that question into historical perspective, I've prepared the table of performance data on the previous page. The six columns correspond to the different approaches for organizing your investments that are found in the risk matrix. They range from a very aggressive strategy of investing all your money in blue chip stocks to a more conservative strategy of investing only in bonds.

For each of the six portfolio combinations, the historical results for a variety of holding periods are shown. Let's start at the top (scenarios one through six) with a look at "rolling" one-year periods. Market results are usually stated in terms of calendar years. For instance, an analyst might claim that a search of the historical data since 1926 revealed that the single worst twelve-month performance for a portfolio of twenty-year corporate bonds was a loss of 8.1%. What the analyst has done is to look at the year-by-year results and picked 1969 as the twelve months with the worst performance. But investors don't buy bonds only on January 1, so that report is somewhat misleading as to the potential risk. That's where the use of "rolling" periods can be helpful. Here's how I ran the calculations.

After looking at the results from buying on January 1, 1926, and holding for twelve months, I then "rolled" to the next month to see what happened if the bonds had been purchased on February 1 and held for twelve months. Then I moved to March 1 and did the same thing. And so on. Continuing in this way, I computed the results for a total of 805 different twelve-month holding periods. This is in contrast to just sixty-eight periods when only calendar years are considered. Using this more exhaustive process provides a more accurate picture of the degree of volatility and level of returns that can be expected from different blends of stocks and bonds. In our example, I found that the worst-case one-year performance for twenty-year corporate bonds was actually a loss of 18.2% (April 1979–March 1980), as shown in scenario 6.

The forty-eight different scenarios shown in the table reflect the basic risk-reward relationships we have discussed in previous chapters.

If you study the numbers you'll see once again that:

◆ **The shorter your holding period, the higher the risks and potential rewards.** Over a thirty-year holding period (scenarios 43-48), the range of *likely* results is relatively narrow. They are shown on the line where it says "result two-thirds of the time." Even in an all-stock portfolio (such as scenario 43), this range of likely results is less than three percentage points per year from low to high. As you move up the table to shorter holding periods, the range broadens, that is, it becomes more volatile. By the time you get to a one-year holding period in the all-stock portfolio (scenario 1), there is a 45 percentage point difference from low to high in the range of likely results.

◆ **The more you allocate to stocks, the higher the risks and potential rewards.** As you move from right to left across the table, the "best" and "worst" results become more exaggerated. These extremes don't come along very often, so you can't weigh them too heavily in your decisions, but it's good to keep in mind the full range of possibilities (as unlikely as they may seem). The numbers illustrate the extent to which blue chip stocks carry greater risks than long-term bonds.

◆ **There's no sure thing.** Imagine having a holding period as long as ten years and still losing, on average, 4.9% a year *every year for ten years* (scenario 19). That's what happened during the 1930s. In the post-war era, the worst ten-year period for an all-stock portfolio saw average returns of less than 1% per year (October 1964–September 1974). While not in the minus column, this is hardly what investors were expecting from a market that had returned an average of 14% per year during the immediately preceding ten-year period (October 1954–September 1964).

Let me share with you how I might apply the data in the table to come up with an allocation strategy for my personal retirement investing.

I'm presently fifty years old. Based on normal life expectancies, an argument could be made for assuming a retirement age of seventy or even seventy-five, but in keeping with tradition, let's assume I select a time frame of fifteen years, which coincides with my reaching age sixty-five.

Since my goal is to earn average returns of 10% per year, the all-stock portfolio (scenario 25) appears to be the best choice. The range of 6.0% to 15.0% represents what actually happened two out of three times in the past. The remaining one-third of the time, the result was outside the "likely" range. That means I have roughly one chance in six of averaging less than 6.0% per year (that's the scary part), and a one in six chance of doing better than 15.0% per year (too good to be true).

Emotionally, the difficult part of this will be to stay with my 100% stock allocation as I get closer to age sixty-five. As I consider the probable results for the final three years, I will need to remind myself that those negative one- and three-year numbers (scenarios 1 and 7) are *already reflected* in the fifteen-year calculations that I based my asset allocation strategy on initially. So, even if I lose money during those final few years, hopefully my overall fifteen-year results will still fall within the likely range.

If I were now age fifty-five, however, I would probably go with an 80/20 mix for the next ten years (scenario 20). The low end of the likely range is 5.4%, which is a little closer to my 10% per year goal than the comparable number in the all-stock portfolio (scenario 19). For the same reason, I would select a 60/40 mix (scenario 15) if I were now age sixty, and a 40/60 mix (scenario 10) if I were at age sixty-two. Also, I might decide to shorten the maturities of the bonds, from the twenty years used in the table to maturities under five years, as a way to lessen the risk during the one- and three-year holding periods.

One way to deal with the risk of a heavy stock allocation as you enter retirement is to invest a portion of your capital in a money market fund. Pick an amount that, along with your Social Security and any pension you receive, will ensure you can live comfortably over the next five years. Knowing your liquidity needs are met, you can then commit to a five-year holding period and reduce the risks of short-term fluctuations.

How much should you invest in small company stocks versus those in larger companies?

Because the table on page 384 uses the Standard & Poor's 500 index to represent stock market returns, it implicitly assumes that all of your stock investing is done in larger companies. But as we saw in chapter 20 (page 241), shares in smaller companies have the potential to grow to ten, twenty, or fifty times their present size. They're the ones that offer the greatest profit potential. Of course, they also carry higher risk because they are more easily devastated by economic setbacks. Let's look at the historical risks and rewards of investing in small companies versus large ones.

The first data column in the table below shows the historical results from the S&P 500 index, and the column on the far right shows similar data for a portfolio consisting solely of small company stocks. The middle column shows the results from having your stock allocation split evenly between large and small companies. You can observe that:

◆ Average returns from small companies exceed those of large companies over every time period measured, with their best-case scenarios dramatically superior.

◆ The risk of loss from investing in smaller companies is greater (see lower end of the range of results that occur two-thirds of the time) than for investing in large ones, but other than for one-year holding periods, the increase in risk is not as high as I expected.

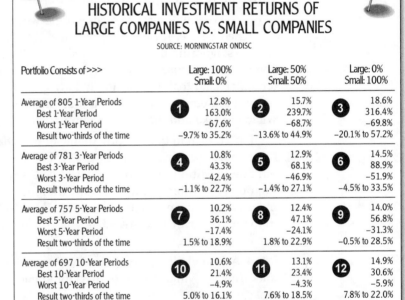

HISTORICAL INVESTMENT RETURNS OF LARGE COMPANIES VS. SMALL COMPANIES
SOURCE: MORNINGSTAR ONDISC

Portfolio Consists of >>>		Large: 100% Small: 0%		Large: 50% Small: 50%		Large: 0% Small: 100%
Average of 805 1-Year Periods	**1**	12.8%	**2**	15.7%	**3**	18.6%
Best 1-Year Period		163.0%		239.7%		316.4%
Worst 1-Year Period		−67.6%		−68.7%		−69.8%
Result two-thirds of the time		−9.7% to 35.2%		−13.6% to 44.9%		−20.1% to 57.2%
Average of 781 3-Year Periods	**4**	10.8%	**5**	12.9%	**6**	14.5%
Best 3-Year Period		43.3%		68.1%		88.9%
Worst 3-Year Period		−42.4%		−46.9%		−51.9%
Result two-thirds of the time		−1.1% to 22.7%		−1.4% to 27.1%		−4.5% to 33.5%
Average of 757 5-Year Periods	**7**	10.2%	**8**	12.4%	**9**	14.0%
Best 5-Year Period		36.1%		47.1%		56.8%
Worst 5-Year Period		−17.4%		−24.1%		−31.3%
Result two-thirds of the time		1.5% to 18.9%		1.8% to 22.9%		−0.5% to 28.5%
Average of 697 10-Year Periods	**10**	10.6%	**11**	13.1%	**12**	14.9%
Best 10-Year Period		21.4%		23.4%		30.6%
Worst 10-Year Period		−4.9%		−4.3%		−5.9%
Result two-thirds of the time		5.0% to 16.1%		7.6% to 18.5%		7.8% to 22.0%
Average of 637 15-Year Periods	**13**	10.5%	**14**	13.2%	**15**	15.2%
Best 15-Year Period		19.0%		21.7%		27.5%
Worst 15-Year Period		−0.4%		1.5%		0.5%
Result two-thirds of the time		6.0% to 15.0%		9.0% to 17.4%		10.3% to 20.1%
Average of 577 20-Year Periods	**16**	10.6%	**17**	13.1%	**18**	15.0%
Best 20-Year Period		17.1%		20.3%		24.0%
Worst 20-Year Period		1.9%		5.4%		7.4%
Result two-thirds of the time		7.3% to 13.9%		10.3% to 16.0%		11.9% to 18.0%

Notes: The source for performance data was Stocks, Bonds, Bills, and Inflation 1996 Yearbook published by Ibbotson Associates in Chicago. The data for large company stocks are based upon total returns (capital appreciation and dividend income) of the Standard & Poor's 500 Index. The data for small company stocks are based on the total returns of those companies listed on the New York Stock Exchange that fall in the bottom 20% in terms of market capitalization. The period covered runs from 1926 (where the Ibbotson data begins) through 1993. Portfolios were rebalanced to their original allocations every twelve months.

◆ For holding periods of ten years and more, the range of results that occur two-thirds of the time clearly favors smaller companies over large ones.

◆ A reasonable case is made for having a significant portion of your stock allocation, perhaps 50% for starters, diversified among small caps or mutual funds that specialize in them.

One group is not "better" than another. They offer different strengths that are suitable for different investing needs. Large companies typically offer higher dividends and greater price stability; smaller companies offer higher long-term growth potential.

How you react to this data largely depends on your temperament.

Preservers will tend to focus on the worst-case scenarios, thinking if it has happened before, it might happen again. Daredevils will look at the best-case numbers, ignoring the downside risks. Nothing in this chapter is meant to sway you toward a certain class of investments. Rather, it was written to help you better understand that there is no single "right" way to arrange your portfolio when nearing retirement, and that you must make trade-offs between the risks you're willing to take and the rewards you hope to reap.

Let's return to the opening theme of this chapter—nobody knows what the future holds or which investments will do best in the coming year. That's why our Sound Mind portfolios are based on a strategy of diversification—spreading out your money into several different areas so that you won't be over-invested in any single hard-hit area *and* you'll have at least some investments in the more rewarding areas. As you consider your investing strategy, let me encourage you to:

◆ **Acknowledge your limited vision.** "Now listen, you who say, 'Today or tomorrow we will go to this or that city, spend a year there, carry on business and make money.' Why, you do not even know what will happen tomorrow. . . . As it is, you boast and brag. All such boasting is evil" (James 4:13-14, 16).

◆ **Look to God, not man, for wisdom.** "If any of you lacks wisdom, he should ask God, who gives generously to all without finding fault, and it will be given to him" (James 1:5).

◆ **Diversify your risks and stay flexible.** "Give portions to seven, yes to eight, for you do not know what disaster may come upon the land" (Ecclesiastes 11:2).

◆ **And above all, let the Lord be your treasure.** "Delight yourself in the Lord and he will give you the desires of your heart" (Psalm 37:4).

This counsel from Scripture is a guide for all of us, not just during these uncertain economic times but as a way of life. It is my belief that it's ultimately impossible to self-destruct financially if our decision-making is pointed in the direction of God's glory. It's to that theme we turn in the next section. ◆

Investing That Glorifies God

A Biblical Blueprint for Building Your Financial House on Solid Rock

The awesome beauty of nature. The innocence of childhood. The security of a world at peace. The exuberance of romantic love. The joy of living life freely and fully.

All of these are noble themes. Great literature, art, and music have all been inspired by them. They capture our emotions and imaginations. They challenge our values and influence our priorities. They reflect universal longings of the human spirit. But although uplifting, they fall short of the noblest and greatest theme of all.

A grander theme runs through all of human history, from the beginning of recorded history to this very moment. This theme explains why we're here, why things happen as they do, where the world is headed, and why the world, as we know it, must eventually end. It underlies everything that is, and is the reason for everything that is not.

It is the incomparable glory of our God, surely the greatest theme in all the universe! In his book *Keys to Spiritual Growth*, John MacArthur describes it this way:

> *God possesses intrinsic glory by virtue of who He is. This is not given to Him. If man had never been created, if the angels had never been created, would God still be a God of glory? Certainly! If no one ever gave Him any glory, any honor, or any praise, would He still be the glorious God that He is? Of course! That is intrinsic glory — the glory of God's nature. It is the manifestation and combination of all His attributes. . . . It is His being, as basic as His grace, His mercy, His power, and His knowledge. All we do is recognize them. So we say, "Yes, it's true; God is glorious!"*

The theme of God's glory is a continuous golden thread which is woven throughout Scripture. We see it operative from the opening story of creation through the triumphal establishment of Christ's kingdom. The infinite worth of God's glory is emphasized over and over again. We should, therefore, be mindful that in all of our daily decision-making, including that small part that has to do with our financial and investing decisions, our primary goal must always be kept uppermost in mind — that of glorifying our wonderful God. In this section, we will explore what investing "for the glory of God" might involve.

31

Investing That Glorifies God Acknowledges His Sovereignty

David praised the Lord in the presence of the whole assembly, saying, "Praise be to you, O Lord, God of our father Israel, from everlasting to everlasting. Yours, O Lord, is the greatness and the power and the glory and the majesty and the splendor, for everything in heaven and earth is yours. Yours, O Lord, is the kingdom; you are exalted as head over all. Wealth and honor come from you; you are the ruler of all things. In your hands are strength and power to exalt and give strength to all. Now, our God, we give you thanks, and praise your glorious name."
(1 Chronicles 29:10-13)

"Who has known the mind of the Lord? Or who has been his counselor? Who has ever given to God, that God should repay him?" For from him and through him and to him are all things. To him be the glory forever! Amen. Therefore, I urge you, brothers, in view of God's mercy, to offer your bodies as living sacrifices, holy and pleasing to God—this is your spiritual act of worship. Do not conform any longer to the pattern of this world, but be transformed by the renewing of your mind. Then you will be able to test and approve what God's will is—his good, pleasing and perfect will.
(Romans 11:34-12:2)

Shortly after my twenty-fifth birthday, my father passed away and I inherited my share in a million-dollar restaurant business. Think about it . . .

. . . only twenty-five and already having just about everything you could reasonably hope for in life. I was financially secure and young enough to enjoy it! I was married to my college sweetheart, the girl of my dreams, and we had two healthy boys. In a world that values position, I was the head of six businesses employing two hundred people. In a world that values freedom, I could go places I wanted to go, pursue interests I wanted to pursue, be any kind of person I wanted to be. And yet, somehow, in some way, something was missing. In spite of it all, I wasn't really fulfilled.

Well, why not? If you had asked me, I couldn't have told you. Instead of feeling peace, I felt pressure to achieve further success in a business I didn't really enjoy. Instead of feeling happy, I felt guilt. In looking back, I can now identify two major areas of stress.

First, there was my time. Eighty-hour weeks are common in the restaurant business; I awoke at 4:30 A.M., arrived at the store by 5:30, and worked through breakfast, lunch, and dinner, leaving around 8:00 P.M. after taking the evening inventory. I would do this six days a week and take Tuesday off. When my friends with regular jobs would call on weekends to see if I could play, I'd say "No, I've gotta work. Would you like to do something on Tuesday?" No one ever did.

So, when I had two weeks off, I really appreciated it. But before I could really catch my breath, the two weeks were up and it was time to go back. What if you're twenty-five with a life expectancy of seventy-five and you've got fifty years to fill? Did I want to spend them running restaurants? For the first time, I began thinking about not only what I would do with my life, but also about what was *worth* doing.

I started really wondering about such things as . . .

. . . What's life all about? Where did I come from and where am I going? Where do I fit in now that I'm here? Mortimer Adler, the famous educator, said that the driving force behind human behavior is a search for significance. I could relate to that. Don't we all want it to somehow matter that we were born, that we worked and played, that we laughed and cried, that we visited this place? I wanted a purpose that had credibility, that would be adequate to take me all the way in life. Though a Christian, I did not realize my key purpose in work and play was to glorify God.

Then, there was my inheritance. I really hadn't made peace with it. My pride said I should make it on my own! Have you ever read the life story of a real financial achiever—someone who started out with nothing much, but who through force of will and intellect and creativity and courage established a business empire? When you finished reading, your response probably was respect, perhaps inspiration. That's how I felt.

I wanted to feel adequate in my own right—not just as the caretaker of my father's business. Years earlier, I had graduated in the upper tenth of my class with a major in banking and finance. Now I found myself attracted to the investment world. I thought that if I could set meaningful goals, and achieve them, in an area where my father had not been very proficient, at least I'd feel better about myself and maybe some of the other pieces would fall into place.

So I'll tell you what I did. I decided to try to make my fortune in the stock market.

(You can see what an original thinker I was.) But, hey—this was 1970, one of the exciting "go-go" years on Wall Street. Everyone seemed to be making money, even amateur upstarts like me. Well, I threw myself into it all the way! I subscribed to all the leading investment industry publications and began reading. Although I was working hard running the family business, I made time to teach myself the various trading and charting techniques. I began trading, and I kept meticulous records of my successes and failures. At one point, I had four brokers—simultaneously! (They loved me because I churned my accounts continuously. A few more like me and they would have been the office superstars.) Eventually I had a ticker installed right there in my office so I could get instant quotes from the New York and American Stock Exchanges. It was great! I was trading, making a little money in spite of myself, and having fun at it.

Then, one of my brokers introduced me to . . . (imagine the ominous soundtrack to *Jaws* playing in the background) . . . commodities futures. Given my propensity for trading, this was probably a criminal act on his part. In those volatile and emotional markets, I was soon swimming with the sharks. Surveys have indicated that nine out of ten commodities speculators lose money. It was said that you needed ice water in your veins to stay calm under the daily pressures. The leverage, the risks, and the rewards are great.

Think of the attraction this held for me as I sought to prove myself: I could make more money, make it faster, and make it under greater stress. What an arena! If you're up for playing Russian roulette with your self-esteem and your bank account, you should check it out. Personally, I loved it!

For a time, commodities became my driving purpose. You know, everyone has a driving purpose.

Everyone is driven by something. What drives you? I'll tell you how to find out. Ask yourself these questions. How do you spend your most precious resource, your time? What successes excite and exhilarate you the most? What defeats irritate and frustrate you the most? The ones tied to your driving purpose.

Well, for a time, commodities was it for me. I remember making and losing $10,000 (in 1970 dollars!) in a single day of trading. I remember driving along the Pennsylvania Turnpike on a summer getaway with Susie and ruining the whole effect by stopping every seventy-five miles to call my broker back in Louisville. Every hour I stopped. Can you believe it? Susie couldn't: "You don't mean we're stopping again?!" But she just didn't understand. I had left town still holding a heavy short position in frozen pork bellies and I had to be careful. (Now for you laymen, that means that I had sold 200 tons of bacon I didn't own to a buyer I had never met for a price one of us would regret. I was hoping it wouldn't be me!)

I remember that I made more money in commodities than I ever made in stocks.

But to my surprise, in spite of this success, I was not any deep-down happier. The up and down emotions . . .

. . . from running a restaurant chain and speculating in the markets was no foundation upon which to build a fulfilling life or a healthy marriage. I was searching, trying to fill the emptiness but not really knowing how. Pascal, the scientist and philosopher, said: "There's a God-shaped vacuum in the heart of every man placed there by God that only He can fill."

But I didn't know that. To be sure, Susie and I had Christian upbringings. I have a loving mom who took me to church when I was a boy, and I learned about God: how He had visited earth in the person of Jesus Christ, had died on a cross and in so doing had somehow accepted the penalty for my own personal sins, and had come back to life again and was seen by more than five hundred people. At least that's what they taught me, and I accepted those teachings. But somehow, in the process, I never developed a full picture of a personal God.

In the Sunday school where I grew up, there were all these colored drawings of Jesus and His disciples. They were walking through the desert, and He was teaching and healing people and feeding the multitudes. Miraculous things! And I used to think: *Boy, I wish I could have been there and seen* that! *To see an honest-to-goodness miracle!* Did you ever wish that? To see something undeniably supernatural? Well, I did. But Jesus lived two thousand years ago—a long, long, *long* time ago. So remote, so far away, that it almost wasn't even real. And it made God seem far away, because you never hear of those kinds of miracles anymore.

So I had gradually gotten the impression that you couldn't really know God now. He was there, but . . .

. . . seemed too far away. I didn't see any way to relate to Him in any meaningful, practical, relevant way. When I got to heaven, whatever and wherever that is, I could learn more about God. But until then, in this life, I assumed it was completely up to me to find my own way, to make my life count.

About this time, one of my very best friends came to town for a visit. We'd gone through high school together and were as close as brothers. He'd gone off to Ohio State to study engineering and had become involved with one of those Christian student organizations. He married a girl he met there, and they became really enthusiastic about spiritual things.

They came home about once a year and always wanted to talk about the Bible and the Christian life when we were together. Now you know, when you're not into that, a little bit goes a long way—so once a year was just about right for them!

Well, sure enough, Bob and Carole called to ask if they could stop by. I really wasn't up for it. I asked Susie, and she wasn't up for it. But he was a dear friend, so what can you do? After reluctantly concluding there was no gracious way out of it, I returned to the phone and said, "Great, we'd love to see you! How soon can you get over here? How about staying for dinner?"

After dinner, it wasn't long before Bob shifted the conversation to spiritual matters. He saw us living the comfortable life and asked Susie at one point: "Susie, are you happy?"

And she answered, "We've really got a lot to be thankful for." He said: "I can see that. But are you happy?" And she paused, then simply said, "No."

Well, I was surprised. I didn't know she was unhappy. And I was embarrassed! You just don't want your wife . . .

. . . to go around admitting she's unhappy. Before I could jump in and try to salvage the situation ("What Susie really meant by that was . . ."), Bob asked one of the most surprising questions I'd ever heard. He asked: "Have you ever considered asking Jesus Christ to take control of your life?"

Bob really took me off guard, because no one had ever suggested to me that Jesus was even remotely interested in assisting in the everyday management of my life, let alone asked if I would be willing to let Him. Anyway, Susie responded: "This may sound egotistical, but I don't think I want anyone running my life or telling me what to do."

The question scared her because, in our limited understanding of what it meant to give God "control" of our lives, it might mean that we had to go to the mission fields of Africa or something else equally traumatic. As for me, I certainly wasn't attracted to the idea of God telling me what to do. I suppose I imagined that He would rob my life of any fun, or joy, or excitement.

Besides, as a man I felt it would be a sign of weakness to depend on anyone else. Is there a higher, more masculine ethic . . .

. . . than absolute self-sufficiency? Isn't that why James Bond and Indiana Jones are so appealing—they're overwhelmingly adequate for any conceivable situation. As a man, I especially wanted to be completely in control of my own destiny. Remember William Henley's words from "Invictus"?

> It matters not how strait the gate, How charged with punishments the scroll, I am the master of my fate: I am the captain of my soul.

But even so, Bob and Carole shared some things that night that shed new light on the basics of the Christian faith that we had learned as children. The first point they made was that God is, after all, a personal God, that He loves us as individuals, and that He offers a wonderful plan for our lives. Christ said, "I have come that they may have life, and have it to the full [that it would be abundant and meaningful]" (John 10:10). I said this was hard to understand because it was obvious that the world is terribly messed up and that everyone is not experiencing an abundant life.

They responded with words something like these: "The reason for that is that we are the ones who choose to go our own independent ways and separate ourselves from God, so how *can* we know or experience God's love and plan for our lives? Man doesn't love God, but it's not that he hates God. It's more likely that he just couldn't care less. God is irrelevant to the important decisions of his everyday life.

"Although we were created to have fellowship with God, we have chosen to pretty much do our own thing, and fellowship with God has been broken off. Our independence, which may be characterized by either active rebellion or just passive indifference, is evidence of what the Bible calls sin. The consequences of our living independently from God is that we have been spiritually separated from Him.

"It's obvious that we sense this and try to bridge the separation and reach God. But we usually want to return to Him on our own terms of reference: a relatively moral life, some charitable work here and there, going to church regularly, perhaps even giving some money to charity. But these things are not enough."

Bob continued: "The truth is, we must approach God on *His* terms of reference. That's fair, isn't it? After all, He is God. But what exactly. . .

. . . are God's terms of reference as to how we should bridge this gulf of separation? That's where Jesus comes in. He is God's special and only provision for our rebelliousness. It is through Him that we are reconciled to God. The Scriptures say, 'God demonstrates his own love toward us in this: while we were still sinners, Christ died for us.'

"There is nothing we can add to this—we can only accept Christ's work in our behalf as one would accept a gift. Ironically, that's the hardest part. Our pride says we should contribute our fair share to this arrangement. Unfortunately, in this transaction, we have nothing to negotiate with. God looks at our meager efforts at righteousness, compares them to His holiness, and says in His book, 'All have sinned and fall short of the glory of God.'

"Since we are helpless to save ourselves, God took the initiative and provided the way back in Jesus Christ, who died in our place to pay the penalty for our rebellion and gives us right standing with God once more."

As I was listening, I was thinking, *Bob, I've heard most of this since we were kids. We used to go to church together all the time. This isn't what I really want to know. What I really am curious about is why do you and I believe pretty much these same things about who Christ was, but you're so excited about it, so fired up, and I'm not? What has happened to make you so different now?*

After they left, Susie and I continued to talk. I can still remember lying on our bed with arms outstretched . . .

. . . reading a little blue booklet they had left us, and sharing how we felt about what they had said. We eventually came to a prayer at the end of the booklet, which read:

Dear Father, I need You. I acknowledge that I have been directing my own life and that, as a result, I have sinned against You. I thank You that You have forgiven my sins through Christ's death on the cross for me. I now invite Christ to again take His place on the throne of my life. Fill me with the Holy Spirit as You commanded me to be filled, and as you promised in Your word that You would do if I asked in faith. I pray this in the name of Jesus.

Then, right under the prayer was the suggestion that, if the prayer expressed the desire of our hearts, why didn't we pray "right now." I started to turn the page, but Susie said to wait, and asked, "What do you think of this prayer?" I said it was a nice prayer. She said,

"Why don't we pray it right now?" I was surprised that she was so intense.

But as we talked, my mind returned to Bob and how, to him, Christ was so real and so personal. It was obvious to me that his relationship with Christ was on a much more intimate level than mine. I recognized that Christ offered a significance and purpose to life that the world couldn't match; that, as God, He was truly worthy of first place in my life.

After all, when you think it through to its logical conclusion, if the claims of Jesus are true, knowing Him is worth everything. Think about it . . .

. . . If He's worth anything, He's worth everything! And I decided, lying there on the bed next to my wife, that I wanted to know Christ the way my friend did. I wanted to share in his excitement of knowing God personally if that were possible. If it required me to make Him sovereign in my life, so be it.

In my heart, I confessed my sins to God, and there were a whole lot of them. Maybe the greatest sin of all was being indifferent to God—being what you might call a casual Christian—professing some sort of belief in God but really not treating it seriously. So Susie and I prayed together that night. Not because we were in church, not because everyone else was praying, but because we wanted to know God as never before.

God is sovereign. Being sovereign means "possessed of supreme power that is unlimited in extent, enjoying autonomy, having undisputed ascendancy." We see this aspect of God portrayed in Scripture repeatedly.

> *Hear, O my people, and I will speak, O Israel, and I will testify against you: I am God, your God. I do not rebuke you for your sacrifices or your burnt offerings, which are ever before me. I have no need of a bull from your stall or of goats from your pens, for every animal of the forest is mine, and the cattle on a thousand hills. I know every bird in the mountains, and the creatures of the field are mine. If I were hungry I would not tell you, for the world is mine, and all that is in it. (Psalm 50:7-12)*

> *Remember the former things, those of long ago; I am God, and there is no other; I am God, and there is none like me. I make known the end from the beginning, from ancient times, what is still to come. I say: My purpose will stand, and I will do all that I please. (Isaiah 46:9-10)*

> *His dominion is an eternal dominion; his kingdom endures from generation to generation. All the peoples of the earth are regarded as nothing. He does as he pleases with the powers of heaven and the peoples of the earth. No one can hold back his hand or say to him: "What have you done?" (Daniel 4:34-35)*

Amazingly, although God is sovereign over all He has made and could dictate our every thought and movement, He tolerates pockets of resistance to His reign. He allows us to make a decision of monumental importance: whether to willingly embrace Christ's rule in our lives and affections or to continue exercising our own self-rule and independence. We are allowed the audacity of challenging His "undisputed ascendancy" in our own lives.

What makes the choice so difficult is that the results are counterintuitive.

If we should abdicate control of our lives and invite His Spirit to guide us according to His purposes, we would expect a loss of freedom, power, and happiness. *The actual result is just the opposite.* We are never more free, never have more strength to reach our potential, and never experience more fulfillment than when we acknowledge His sovereignty over our lives. The reason for this is that only when we place our faith in Christ does He come to live within us, and it is His actual presence—the personal presence of the omnipotent Creator God of the universe—that raises our daily existence to a higher, entirely new level of existence.

On the other hand, we can choose to continue living independently, doing as we think best. We expect that way of living to give us the best chance of building a future that will be the most satisfying. But again, the result is just the opposite of what we expect. We find that achieving our goals provides only short-lived fulfillment. The thrill of acquiring material possessions wears off. Fame has a short shelf life, and perversely it creates greater anxiety than emotional security. A famous Hollywood producer, when asked how fame, fortune, and immense popularity had changed his life, gave this startling reply: "Success means never having to admit you're unhappy." His success did not end his unhappiness; it just allowed him to deny it.

Investing that glorifies God has a requisite first step: first we must invest ourselves. We do this by . . .

. . . willingly trusting His sovereignty—not only over the physical universe, but over our very lives as well. We asked Christ to take our lives and make us the kind of people He wanted us to be. Susie and I gave Him our lives. God says: "If you'll give Me your life, I'll give you My life." It has been called "The Great Exchange." In light of who He is and all that He offers, what could be more reasonable?

"Who has known the mind of the Lord? Or who has been his counselor? Who has ever given to God, that God should repay him?" For from him and through him and to him are all things. To him be the glory forever! Amen. Therefore, I urge you, brothers, in view of God's mercy, to offer your bodies as living sacrifices, holy and pleasing to God – this is your spiritual act of worship. *Do not conform any longer to the pattern of this world, but be transformed by the renewing of your mind. Then you will be able to test and approve what God's will is* – *his good, pleasing and perfect will.* (Romans 11:34–12:2)

It should go without saying that when we present ourselves to God as "living sacrifices," our material possessions are included. After surrendering all that we are and ever hope to be to His eternal sovereignty, the idea that we're also acknowledging God's ownership of the world's wealth (including ours) shouldn't be surprising. When we made The Great Exchange, part of the transaction involved exchanging ownership privileges for management responsibilities. It's called stewardship.

At the beginning of the book, I suggested that investing means to give up the use of something now in order to have something you desire more later. The Christian gives up, surrenders, loses his earthly life now in order to receive something of far greater value later—the voice of the Lord saying, "Well done, good and faithful servant. You have been faithful over a little; I will put you over much. Enter in to the joy of your master." ◆

CHAPTER PREVIEW

Investing That Glorifies God Values His Majesty

O God, you are my God, earnestly I seek you; my soul thirsts for you,
my body longs for you, in a dry and weary land where there is no
water. I have seen you in the sanctuary and beheld your power and
your glory. Because your love is better than life, my lips will glorify
you. I will praise you as long as I live, and in your name I will lift up
my hands. My soul will be satisfied as with the richest of foods; with
singing lips my mouth will praise you. On my bed I remember you;
I think of you through the watches of the night. Because you are
my help, I sing in the shadow of your wings.

(Psalm 63:1-7)

The God who made the world and everything in it is the Lord of
heaven and earth and does not live in temples built by hands. And he
is not served by human hands, as if he needed anything, because he
himself gives all men life and breath and everything else. From one man
he made every nation of men, that they should inhabit the whole earth;
and he determined the times set for them and the exact places where
they should live. God did this so that men would seek him and perhaps
reach out for him and find him, though he is not far from each one of us.

(Acts 17:24-27)

I can remember only one time during my childhood when I was asked "the" question that all kids face . . .

. . . "What do you want to be when you grow up?" I was probably around ten years old and was out with my mom doing some routine shopping. We were riding along when suddenly she popped the big question. She was visibly amused when I immediately replied, "A disc jockey!" In my formative radio-listening, rock-and-roll years, being a disc jockey must have seemed like it would be all the fun in the world. Mom's reaction, however, communicated that while being a disc jockey might be fun, it didn't reflect a highly developed sense of ambition. Neither of my parents ever asked me the question again, and to play it safe, I never brought the subject up either.

So as I moved through my teen years, an only child and obvious "heir apparent," it became the accepted wisdom that I would someday run the family business. In many respects, this greatly simplified things. I always knew that I had a summer job and what it would be—learning some new facet of restaurant operations (from the ground up). When I enrolled in college, I didn't agonize over a major—I went to business school and majored in finance. When I graduated, I didn't worry about job interviews—I simply returned home and went to work.

There was only one problem with all of this. I hated the restaurant business! I had no interest in food or cooking. I had poor people skills and felt inadequate as a leader. Rare was the morning I didn't dread getting up and going to work. But get up I must, and that's exactly what I did the morning after Bob and Carole's visit. I went off to work without giving the events of the night before—the talking with Susie, the soul-searching, the prayer of surrender—much thought at all. We had a special evening, sure, but it was now Monday morning and my life in what I thought of as "the real world" had resumed.

For Susie, it was an entirely different story. The little booklet our friends had left with us said that faith was the "engine" of the Christian life and that "feelings" were the caboose. We should not be controlled by our feelings, but as we exercise faith and obedience, feelings would follow. So she had whispered her prayer of surrender on that basis, and we went to sleep not "feeling" any different.

The next morning, however, she awoke with great joy. She now understood—truly "knew"—for the first time . . .

. . . that her forgiveness was based on placing her faith in Christ alone. It was not a matter of her trying to be good and holy for God, but rather just giving every area of her life over to Him *so He could be holy through her*. He would supply the strength. She felt totally accepted by God and had peace beyond question that she would be with Him in heaven for eternity. This was the way to relate to God that she had been looking for her whole life! She was so joyous over this that she began calling her friends and family to tell them this incredibly great news.

You can imagine my surprise at coming home from another routine day at the office to find this exuberant evangelist in our house. I don't recall exactly what was said that evening; I only remember that Susie "took off" in her spiritual growth and that it took a long time for me to catch up.

(Perhaps if the truth be known, I never have. The Lord has blessed me with many wonderful friends and teachers who have guided, corrected, and encouraged me in my Christian growth—I am indebted to them all. But there is also a secret life of the believer where our fears and hopes, joys and sorrows are rarely made known to others. It is only in the intimacy of the daily life in Christ between husband and wife where these matters can be shared or exposed. The "outside world" has little grasp of how married partners refresh each other and provide a desperately needed source of balance, wisdom, role modeling, inspiration, and challenge. Susie has been all these things and more to me. Without question, she has been the greatest single influence in my Christian life. We've been married for more than thirty years, and I've never appreciated her more, respected her more, or loved her than I do today. That's the kind of marriage God has built in us as we have trusted daily in His plans and in His power to live the Christ-centered life.)

Through the years, I had put my work and other family-related demands ahead of her needs, yet she remained committed to me and the sacred aspects of our marriage. As I gradually developed a new awareness of God in my life, I began to learn how to love Susie in a deeper, purer, and more protective kind of way. I finally began to see that my wife and children have a higher call on my time and attentions than my bread-winning activities. Let me tell you—there's nothing finer that can happen to a man, a husband, a father, than to be able to sit and listen to his wife and children pray to a God whom they know in a personal way.

As we sought to know our God better, our interest in spiritual matters grew. We were introduced to Christian ministries that were devising creative new ways for taking the message of God's love and forgiveness to people in all walks of life. One of them was Campus Crusade for Christ. Through a series of events too lengthy to detail here, we received an invitation from Crusade's president, Dr. Bill Bright, to join his staff at the ministry's headquarters. It required a move to southern California, one that was made possible when the Lord answered our heartfelt prayers to send someone to run the family business in my absence. We loaded up the station wagon, our two boys, Tre and Andrew, the cat and bird, and headed west for a "mission trip" that was to last almost two years.

I can still remember what it was like "reporting for work" that first week in California. I was thrilled . . .

. . . that for the first time in my life I would be doing work that *I* had picked out, that I would enjoy, and that had a challenge and purpose that I found ful-

Recommended Resource

The Secret: How to Live with Purpose and Power

by Bill Bright

This book contains much of Campus Crusade's excellent teaching concepts, including the essence of the material that Bob and Carole left with us that night. In chapter four, "What Does It Mean to Be Filled with the Spirit?" you will find a simple way of understanding how God wants to work through the life of every one of His children. It will be a life-changing truth if you take God at His word and apply it. It was for us.

filling. It was an unforgettable, incredibly stimulating experience. We formed friendships that are warmly treasured to this day. We joined expository Bible studies that opened up Scripture in new and personally relevant ways. We saw answers to prayers that radically changed our views of God's willingness—no, make that eagerness—to meet the needs of His children. We went to give, yet received more back than we could have ever imagined.

In the summer of 1974, Susie and I traveled to Fort Collins, Colorado, for an annual event within Crusade known as staff training. The staff had gathered together for a week of vision-building workshops and seminars. We heard many inspirational speakers, but one in particular quickly captured everyone's attention. To say that Ronald Dunn's messages were well received would be to greatly understate his impact. I have talked with Crusade staff who, fifteen and twenty years later, still recall with great appreciation (as I do) how his words were so encouraging to them that summer.

It was one of those rare times in life when "you just had to be there" to understand why it was special. His messages were really quite basic, just reminders of some of the "old truths" that we might have forgotten along the way, yet they were so meaningful to his audience. I still remember, vividly, the question he posed as he set the stage for one of his primary points:

"What is it, do you believe, that God wants from you more than anything else?" It was a sobering question.

I knew God wanted my obedience, my service, my thanksgiving, and much more. But what did He want *the most?* I really didn't know how to answer. What would you have said? From my notes, Ron's answer went something like this:

> I believe it is the testimony of the word of God, in both the Old and New Testaments, that the primary thing, the ultimate thing, that God wants from us is not our service. He wants our searching! *That we would seek the Lord. That we would seek the Lord.*

In Acts 17, Paul leaves no doubt that *the* primary purpose behind all of God's creative work is that we would seek Him.

> The God who made the world and everything in it is the Lord of heaven and earth and does not live in temples built by hands. And he is not served by human hands, as if he needed anything, because he himself gives all men life and breath and everything else. From one man he made every nation of men, that they should inhabit the whole earth; and he determined the times set for them and the exact places where they should live. God did this *so that men would seek him and perhaps reach out for him and find him, though he is not far from each one of us.*

More than anything else, the Lord wants us to seek Him. He wants to be the object of our affection and the focus of our attention. He wants to draw us to seek Him. If this is the case, then it shouldn't be surprising to think that God will negotiate circumstances or engineer certain events in order to bring us to the place where we come to the end of ourselves and are compelled to seek Him.

Now some may ask how the idea of "seeking the Lord" applies to Christians who have already sought Him out and placed their faith in Him. Ron's response was tremendous:

> When the apostle Paul wrote to the church at Philippi, he recounted his conversion experience, saying: "But whatever was to my profit, I now consider loss for the sake of Christ. What is more, I consider everything a loss compared to the surpassing greatness of knowing Christ."
>
> If I'd been writing that I might have said "the surpassing greatness of serving Christ." You know, he's had about every experience a fellow could have. There's not been anybody that has been able to serve in the magnificent magnitude that the apostle Paul has. Yet he comes to the end of this life and he says "I am continually giving up everything and counting everything but loss that I may . . . know Him."
>
> Well, now Paul, I thought you already knew Him. You met Him on the road to Damascus thirty or forty years ago. What do you mean you're counting everything but loss that you may know Him?
>
> Paul would say: "Well, you can know Him, and then you can know Him some more." You can know Him, and you can know Him, and you can know Him, and you can know Him some more. You see, my friends, the Christian life is not starting with Jesus, and then graduating to something better. It is starting with Jesus, staying with Jesus, and ending up with Jesus.
>
> I tell you I get excited when I realize that the Bible over and over again makes it clear that Jesus Christ is God's "everything." In Colossians, we read that all the fulness of the Godhead dwells in Him bodily, and we are complete in Him. All the fullness of the Godhead dwells in Jesus bodily, and I like the way Williams translates it "And you are filled with it too through union with Him." I mean, Jesus is everything.
>
> He's the Means to the end, and He's the End. He's the Door, and He's what you find on the other side of the door. He's the Light of the world, and He's what you see when that light shines. He's the Fountain, and He's also the Living Water that comes out of the fountain. He's the Alpha and the Omega. He's all that you need.
>
> And so to seek the Lord means that we seek for nothing else. We find in Jesus Christ our all in all. And so Paul is saying that the quest of the Christian life is not "How can I trust Him more? or How can I serve Him more?" but "How can I know Him better?"
>
> The goal of the Christian life is not service. The goal of the Christian life is Jesus. And our service is the overflow of our fellowship with the Lord Jesus Christ. So it means we need seek for nothing else, but it also means that we should settle for nothing less.
>
> I'll tell you what I think is happening in evangelical circles today: that we are settling for something less than the Lord Jesus Christ. We were on our way with Jesus, and we met something else along the way that caught our attention, and we settled for that. I started out with the Lord. My heart was filled with the joy of the Lord. I just

Recommended Resource
Don't Just Stand There, Pray Something!
by Ronald Dunn

This is the most helpful and practical book about prayer that I've had the pleasure to read. Ron Dunn is a gifted teacher who is great at communicating through the use of stories about everyday life. Much of the material that I found so life-changing in the summer of 1974 is here. I enthusiastically recommend this book!

*wanted Him, that's all! I was seeking the Lord, but in my seeking the Lord, along the way
I found service. And I find that often I end up settling for that.*

*Let me encourage you in something. As you seek the Lord, if you meet service, or a gift,
or a doctrine along the way, don't stop and settle for that. Please, you must keep on going
and seek the Lord. Constantly seek the Lord. Don't settle for anything less than Jesus, and
the fullness of fellowship with Him day by day.*

**As I listened to Ron, it was immediately clear to me that I had
taken a wrong turn somewhere. My serving God was a . . .**

. . . well-intentioned "living sacrifice," which I desired would please Him,
but it also represented a kind of detour. I so desired to serve Him, to "invest"
my life for Him, *that I no longer had time to seek Him.* I resembled the workaholic
husband who had little time for his wife, and when she pointed this out he
claimed he was "doing it all for her." This error can be quite a subtle thing; it
seems to happen in the smallest of increments. You are not even aware of it until
one day God works through your circumstances to get your undivided attention, and you "awaken" to find yourself miles off course.

Bob Benson, one of my favorite writers, had a way of telling humorous stories in simple ways that revealed great truths. One of them, where he carries on
a conversation with the Lord, touched on this tendency many of us seem to have.

"If you had more time, Bob, we could be together more."

*"Well, yes, Lord, we could. But I'm president of the company – a ministry-oriented
company. And I have a big family. I travel and speak a lot on weekends for you. The
company is growing and needs much attention from me. These are not easy days in
which to live, much less make a company grow. I'm having a hard time keeping it all
together."*

*"I know, I'm not trying to crowd you. And I'm not trying to add to your burdens. I
do not want to make it harder for you. I was just reminding you that if you had more time,
we could be together more."*

Like Bob, I understood what it meant to let the noise and pressures of everyday life drown out the quiet, patient voice of God. Like many others, I discovered there is a "tyranny of the urgent" that, if not consciously resisted, will rob
me of the spirit-sustaining pleasure and privilege of spending time alone with
Him each day. I identified with Bob's conclusion:

*Life has come along with its usual mixture of the good and the bad and the monoto-
nous. As usual, I am not sure that I even knew which was which at the time. But I have
affirmed some things that I have known for a long time but tend to forget.*

*One of those is that the quest, the quest for a shared life with Him, is just what the
word implies. It is always a quest. The shared life is not a destination, it is a journey. It is
not an arrival, it is a departure.*[1]

[1]Bob Benson,
See You at the House
[Nashville: Generoux, 1986],
p. 18. Used by permission.

Investing that glorifies God has a requisite worldview:
It sees *Him* as the pearl of great price . . .

. . . and we joyfully sell all that we have so that we may experience the price-less treasure of fellowship with God in Christ Jesus. We value His majesty and our communion with Him above all earthly ambitions and wealth. There is no greater thrill, no greater joy than to walk away from a time of prayer and meditation *having met God*. It is as Jonathan Edwards has written:

[2]Jonathan Edwards, The Works of Jonathan Edwards [Edinburgh: Banner of Truth Trust, 1974], p. 244.

> *The enjoyment of God is the only happiness with which our souls can be satisfied. To go to heaven, fully to enjoy God, is infinitely better than the most pleasant accommodations here. . . . [These] are but shadows; but God is the substance. These are but scattered beams; but God is the sun. These are but streams; but God is the ocean.*[2]

To glorify God, we must see Him as our great treasure. Our hearts and lives must be kept centered in Him. Christian service, although done in His name, is no substitute. Obtaining, securing, and increasing our store of wealth, although used for family support and kingdom purposes, is no substitute.

To invest more time, thought, energy, research, and emotional energy
in these areas than we invest in enjoying His presence is to grieve His
Father's heart. There are at least three reasons this must be true.

❶ It reveals that our pleasures are misplaced.

To delight more in the companionship of the creation around us than in the Creator who made us is idolatry. Even to delight more in the gifts we offer Him than in the gift His presence offers us is to elevate our glory above His. Our pleasure is to be in Him.

> *O God, you are my God, earnestly I seek you; my soul thirsts for you, my body longs for you, in a dry and weary land where there is no water. I have seen you in the sanctuary and beheld your power and your glory. Because your love is better than life, my lips will glorify you. I will praise you as long as I live, and in your name I will lift up my hands. My soul will be satisfied as with the richest of foods; with singing lips my mouth will praise you. On my bed I remember you; I think of you through the watches of the night. Because you are my help, I sing in the shadow of your wings. My soul clings to you; your right hand upholds me. (Psalm 63:1-8)*

❷ It reveals that our confidence is misplaced.

Isn't our security, whether spiritual, physical, emotional, or material, to be found in His loving promises rather than our human efforts and disciplines? Our confidence is to be in Him.

> *One thing I ask of the Lord, this is what I seek: that I may dwell in the house of the Lord all the days of my life, to gaze upon the beauty of the Lord and to seek him in his temple. For in the day of trouble he will keep me safe in his dwelling; he will hide me in the shelter of his tabernacle and set me high upon a rock. (Psalm 27:4-5)*

Keep your lives free from the love of money and be content with what you have, because God has said, "Never will I leave you; never will I forsake you." So we say with confidence, "The Lord is my helper; I will not be afraid. What can man do to me?" (Hebrews 13:5-6)

❸ It reveals that our gratitude is misplaced.

To whom or what do we owe our successes? The free-enterprise system that rewards hard work? The company we labor for? The government programs that provided needed assistance? Our investment counselor or broker who helped us have a good year? No, God is the source of our blessings and "the giver of every good gift." Our gratitude should be toward Him.

David praised the Lord in the presence of the whole assembly, saying, "Praise be to you, O Lord, God of our father Israel, from everlasting to everlasting. Yours, O Lord, is the greatness and the power and the glory and the majesty and the splendor, for everything in heaven and earth is yours. Yours, O Lord, is the kingdom; you are exalted as head over all. Wealth and honor come from you; you are the ruler of all things. In your hands are strength and power to exalt and give strength to all. Now, our God, we give you thanks, and praise your glorious name." (1 Chronicles 29:10-13)

The kingdom of heaven, and the King who reigns over it, are "like treasure hidden in a field. When a man found it, he hid it again, and then in his joy went and sold all he had and bought that field."

Do our daily lives—the decisions we make and the dreams we pursue— reflect that Christ is our treasure?

It is my earnest hope and prayer that I would faithfully seek the majesty of His companionship daily. My practice is, however, that too often I settle for too little. Perhaps you can identify with me in this. If so, may God grant us that we increasingly glorify Him in our seeking. John Piper, in his book *The Supremacy of God in Preaching,* beautifully sums up the relationship between our desire to please God and His desire to be glorified in our lives.

[3] John Piper, The Supremacy of God in Preaching [Grand Rapids: Baker Book House, 1990], p. 26.

God's deepest commitment to be glorified and my deepest longing to be satisfied are not in conflict, but in fact find simultaneous consummation in his display of and my delight in the glory of God. Therefore the goal of preaching is the glory of God reflected in the glad submission of the human heart. And the supremacy of God in preaching is secured by this fact: The one who satisfies gets the glory; the one who gives the pleasure is the treasure.[3] ◆

33

Investing That Glorifies God Builds His Kingdom

Remember this: Whoever sows sparingly will also reap sparingly, and whoever sows generously will also reap generously. Each man should give what he has decided in his heart to give, not reluctantly or under compulsion, for God loves a cheerful giver. And God is able to make all grace abound to you, so that in all things at all times, having all that you need, you will abound in every good work. As it is written: "He has scattered abroad his gifts to the poor; his righteousness endures forever." Now he who supplies seed to the sower and bread for food will also supply and increase your store of seed and will enlarge the harvest of your righteousness. You will be made rich in every way so that you can be generous on every occasion, and through us your generosity will result in thanksgiving to God.

(2 Corinthians 9:6-11)

Godliness with contentment is great gain. For we brought nothing into the world, and we can take nothing out of it. But if we have food and clothing, we will be content with that. People who want to get rich fall into temptation and a trap and into many foolish and harmful desires that plunge men into ruin and destruction. For the love of money is a root of all kinds of evil. Some people, eager for money, have wandered from the faith and pierced themselves with many griefs. . . . Command those who are rich in this present world not to be arrogant nor to put their hope in wealth, which is so uncertain, but to put their hope in God, who richly provides us with everything for our enjoyment. Command them to do good, to be rich in good deeds, and to be generous and willing to share. In this way they will lay up treasure for themselves as a firm foundation for the coming age, so that they may take hold of the life that is truly life.

(1 Timothy 6:6-10, 17-19)

In 1848, his mother worked as a shoemaker to support the family. At the age of thirteen . . .

. . . Andrew went to work in a textile mill to help ease the financial burdens. He worked twelve hours a day; he was paid $1.20 a week. He decided to go to night school to learn bookkeeping so he would qualify for a better job.

The next year Andrew got a job as a messenger for a telegraph company. Wanting to advance, he returned to night school to study telegraphy. His diligence paid off with a promotion to telegraph operator two years later. He continued to improve at his work and soon became one of the few people who could "read" the sound of telegraph clicks without looking at the readout. This brought him to the attention of a railroad executive who offered him a job as his personal telegrapher and secretary. He was seventeen years old and earning $8.10 a week.

Andrew continued to study as he worked, learning how railroads operated. He borrowed money to invest in the first "sleeping car" company; then he convinced his boss to buy sleeping cars for the railroad. By the time he was twenty-eight, Andrew's earnings had risen to $1,250 a week from his salary and investment income.

In 1865, he left his job and went to Europe to sell securities in the new American railroad companies. While in England, he learned of Bessemer's new process of steelmaking. When he returned to the U.S. in 1872, he gave up his other businesses and concentrated on steel. He was eventually able to persuade railroad managers to replace iron rails with steel ones. By 1889, his mills were producing more than a half-million tons of steel per year. At the turn of the century, he employed more than twenty thousand people. His was the largest industrial concern the world had ever known. When he sold his company to J. P. Morgan in 1901, he netted more than $200 million. On that day, Andrew Carnegie became the richest man in the world.

He was fond of saying, "The man who dies rich, dies disgraced." Once he retired, he spent the rest of his life trying to give away his entire fortune, most of it for educational purposes. He largely succeeded. How different a view from today's philosophy of life, which is so forthrightly proclaimed on bumper stickers saying: "Whoever dies with the most toys wins."

What is a proper motivation for our ambition and hard work? Carnegie, although a generous man, nevertheless devoted his life to building his own kingdom. Christians follow One who is building another kind of kingdom.

Jesus went through all the towns and villages, teaching in their synagogues, preaching the good news of the kingdom and healing every disease and sickness. . . . Then he said to his disciples, "The harvest is plentiful but the workers are few. Ask the Lord of the harvest, therefore, to send out workers into his harvest field." (Matthew 9:35-38)

And what is the mission of these workers? Consider the final command Jesus gave to His disciples just before His ascension. It has been called "The Great Commission."

All authority in heaven and on earth has been given to me. Therefore go and make disciples of all nations, baptizing them in the name of the Father and of the Son and of the Holy Spirit, and teaching them to obey everything I have commanded you. And surely I am with you always, to the very end of the age. (Matthew 28:18-20)

It couldn't be much clearer. Whose kingdom are you building?

I was completely unqualified for the task I was asked to undertake for Campus Crusade. I had no previous hands-on experience. I lacked . . .

. . . the innate personal temperament that it seemed to call for. I had no sphere of influence that could be tapped for guidance or assistance. In short, I was in over my head.

What was my job? I was to bring all of Crusade's fund-raising efforts under one umbrella. The goal was to make staff members more sensitive to the feelings and interests of the ministry's supporters, which would (hopefully) also make the process of raising financial support more productive over the longer term. When I started, my department had one person in it—me! This indicated to me that, far from Crusade spending too much time and attention on fund-raising (a charge made against many parachurch ministries), it spent very little.

Bill Bright operates under the principle that God will supply everything needed, including the money and manpower, to accomplish that to which the ministry is called. If there are insufficient resources, then we should take a second look at the project—perhaps we are going about it the wrong way, or it need not be a priority at the present time.

(While I'm on the subject of working with Bill, it's probably time I make a confession. Part of the reason that I wanted to serve with Crusade was the opportunity of working closely with Bill because, among other things, it would give me the opportunity to see if the private life and public persona were one and the same. I had often wondered about some of our best-known Christian leaders—are they truly the kind of people they appear to be? Would an honest "behind the scenes" look that caught their unguarded moments enhance or diminish my respect for them? Cynical of me, I know, but what can I say? It was something I wondered about. I discovered that Bill and Vonette Bright *are* authentic. When I think of them, the characteristic that comes to mind first is the love they have for our Savior and for His people. That is what motivates their passions for reaching the world for Him. Susie and I left our time of service with great affection for them personally and deep respect for their faithful role modeling of the life in Christ and their sincere commitment to bring glory to His name and to His name alone.)

**So there I was in a job for which I was ill-equipped.
As a businessman back home, I had experienced what
it was like to be asked to make large contributions . . .**

. . . but I had no experience in doing the asking. It required me to think through what biblical principles should guide me in formulating a strategy. Eventually, I saw the challenge primarily as one of evangelism and discipleship. Here's why.

It had been my experience that, as a donor, I would tend to make a token contribution to help others with "their" favorite causes while I thought nothing of making much larger gifts to *my* favorite causes. I was now volunteering time with Crusade because the Great Commission had become one of my favorite causes. How had this happened? As I had grown in my faith, my desires to tell everyone about the abundance of the Christian life had greatly increased, as had my desires to be obedient to the Lord's commands. Both of these desires found consummation in the Great Commission. Therefore I reached this conclusion: lead others to Christ and help them grow, and in due course they will also want to see the Great Commission being fulfilled. To the extent they see that happening through the ministries of Campus Crusade, they will happily and generously give. The strategy also aligned our motivations properly (how can we help these people grow?) rather than as manipulators (how can we get these people to give to us?).

The primary strategy I proposed led to a series of Executive Seminars for business and professional couples. These events featured a heavy emphasis on knowing Christ, understanding the Spirit-filled life, and the importance of sharing your faith with others. Fully one-fourth of the program was devoted to building healthy marriage relationships. There was also free time for recreation, socializing, or just plain relaxing. In the entire four-day seminar, we presented the financial needs of the ministry in only one forty-five-minute session. We trusted the Lord to prompt people to give—only He knew who was spiritually ready and how large a gift was appropriate for them. It was an exceptionally low-key approach.

Was it successful? Absolutely! We saw hundreds of men and women give their lives to Christ. Marriages were healed; parents and children were reconciled. Christians were emboldened to share their faith as a way of life in their home communities. Thousands of participants looked back on the event as a meaningful stepping-stone in their spiritual growth.

The strategy also was successful in raising money, though in ways we did not anticipate. When Christians develop a conviction about relinquishing their lives for Christ and His gospel, they do give generously as never before. But large amounts did not stream into Campus Crusade. Most of the people who began giving more did so back where they lived—to their churches, mission boards, and local parachurch outreaches. It's to Bill Bright's credit that he continued to enthusiastically support the Executive Seminar ministry for many years, far beyond the time when it had become apparent that Crusade was not the primary financial beneficiary. He had often said publicly that he wanted Crusade, whenever possible, to be a servant to local churches and other Christian ministries. Privately, he was as good as his word.

"God loves a hilarious giver." How hilarious are we?

I placed this chapter third in this section because you can't become a hilarious giver until you've settled two other issues. We are made in God's image for God's glory, and our lives should be pointed in the direction of that foundational truth. The only way we can reflect His glory is by making The Great Exchange, giving Him our lives so that He can give us His life—so that it is His life in us that is shining forth (chapter 31). God is the treasure hidden in a field—we joyously go and surrender all that we have in order that we might know Him (chapter 32).

Only now is it possible to begin seeing ourselves as God sees us. We are citizens of His heavenly kingdom (Philippians 3:20). We are Christ's ambassadors who are here to represent the interests of our King (2 Corinthians 5:20). We are not here to befriend the world, which would be treasonous (James 4:4). On the contrary, we are to live our lives as aliens and strangers (1 Peter 2:11). We are just passing through, like pilgrims on a journey. Randy Alcorn, in his excellent book *Money, Possessions, and Eternity*, describes it this way.

> *The pilgrim is unattached. He is a traveler—not a settler—acutely aware that the excessive accumulation of things can only distract him from what he is and does. Material things are valuable to the pilgrim, but only as they facilitate his mission. He knows they could become a god to grip him, and that if his eyes are on the visible they will be drawn away from the invisible.*

> *If you were traveling through a country on foot or on bicycle, what would your attitude be toward accumulating possessions? You would not hate possessions or think them evil—but you would choose them strategically, regarding most of them as encumbrances, unnecessary things that could slow your journey or eventually even make it impossible. Travelers do not build houses, amass furniture, and invest in the economy.*

> *Of course, many of us are called to stay in one place and will naturally become "settlers" in the temporal sense, living in houses, building barns, owning furniture, tools, crops, and businesses. There is nothing wrong with this. But we must nonetheless maintain the pilgrim mentality of detachment, the traveler's utilitarian philosophy concerning things. We need to be able to live in a house without owning it. If God so directs us, we need to be able to leave behind a farm or a business without having to go back. . . .*

> *Does the pilgrim mentality lead to a sour or cynical view of this present world? Precisely the opposite! It is the materialist, not the Christian pilgrim, who is the cynic. The typical citizen of this world doesn't derive true satisfaction from it. Materialists can't fully appreciate the joys and wonders of creation. It is the believer who can see his Creator's handiwork*

Recommended Resource
Money, Possessions, and Eternity
by Randy Alcorn
I found this book challenging on many levels and have received excellent comments back from others to whom I have recommended it. Warren Wiersbe said about it, "The Christian who wants a balanced survey of the Bible's philosophy of wealth will not be disappointed. The pastor who wants to teach his people and parents who want to train their children will get great help from it."

everywhere, who can truly see the beauty of mountains and rivers and waterfalls. No one appreciates creation like he who knows the Creator. No one can appreciate a good meal like those who love the one who provided it. No one can enjoy marriage like the one who knows its Architect and who understands what intimacy is.

Those in love with this world do not get the best it has to offer. They expect the world to deliver them from the emptiness within, so they are forever disillusioned. The Christian pilgrim has no such illusions about the world. He appreciates it for what it is — a magnificent creation of the one who does fill the emptiness of the heart. . . .

[1]Randy Alcorn, <u>Money, Possessions, and Eternity</u> [Wheaton: Tyndale House, 1989], pp. 196–198. Used by permission.

One of the greatest joys the Christian pilgrim finds in this world is in those moments it reminds him of the next, his true home. He has not seen this place, but he has read about it, and he lives with the exhilarating assurance that his beloved is making it ready for him this very moment (John 14:2-3).

In the truest sense, Christian pilgrims have the best of both worlds. We have joy whenever this world reminds us of the next, and we take solace whenever it does not. We have the promise of a new heaven and new earth, where the worst elements of this world — sorrow, pain, death, and the tears they produce — will be gone forever (Revelation 21:4). Yet we also know that the best elements of this world, the love, joy, wonder, worship, and beauty we have experienced here, will not be gone, but intensified and perfected in the remade world. . . .

In the last book of the Chronicles of Narnia, *when the unicorn reaches Aslan's country he exclaimed, "I have come home at last! This is my real country! I belong here. This is the land I have been looking for all my life, though I never knew it till now. The reason why we loved the old Narnia is that it sometimes looked a little like this."*[1]

Investing that glorifies God is motivated solely by a desire to see *His* kingdom grow. May I share with you some of the truths from Scripture that . . .

. . . I try to keep in mind as I plan my small role in the growth of God's kingdom and the accomplishment of His purposes? Consider these truths with me:

◆ **God is the absolute owner of everything in the universe. Period.**

To the Lord your God belong the heavens, even the highest heavens, the earth and everything in it. (Deuteronomy 10:14)

Who has a claim against me that I must pay? Everything under heaven belongs to me. (Job 41:11)

Yours, O Lord, is the kingdom; you are exalted as head over all. Wealth and honor come from you; you are the ruler of all things. (1 Chronicles 29:11-12)

◆ **God's ownership of all things includes me. God is never less than the sovereign/creator; I am never more than His steward/creature.**

The earth is the Lord's, and everything in it, the world, and all who live in it; for he founded it upon the seas and established it upon the waters. (Psalm 24:1-2)

Do you not know that your body is a temple of the Holy Spirit, who is in you, whom you have received from God? You are not your own; you were bought at a price. Therefore honor God with your body. (1 Corinthians 6:19-20)

◆ **Since I have nothing that was not given to me, I have no basis for pride, only gratitude.**

For who makes you different from anyone else? What do you have that you did not receive? (1 Corinthians 4:7)

For we brought nothing into the world, and we can take nothing out of it. But if we have food and clothing, we will be content with that. (1 Timothy 6:7-8)

And my God will meet all your needs according to his glorious riches in Christ Jesus. (Philippians 4:19)

◆ **Wealth comes with management responsibilities, not ownership rights. Being a steward is a lifelong calling that requires me to continually live with one eye on eternity.**

So if you have not been trustworthy in handling worldly wealth, who will trust you with true riches? And if you have not been trustworthy with someone else's property, who will give you property of your own? (Luke 16:11-12)

If anyone would come after me, he must deny himself and take up his cross and follow me. For whoever wants to save his life will lose it, but whoever loses his life for me will find it. What good will it be for a man if he gains the whole world, yet forfeits his soul? (Matthew 16:24-26)

◆ **My primary management responsibility is to be available to God for Him to think, act, speak, write, and give through me so that His will is accomplished and His name is glorified.**

If you remain in me and my words remain in you, ask whatever you wish, and it will be given you. This is to my Father's glory, that you bear much fruit. (John 15:7-8)

So whether you eat or drink or whatever you do, do it all for the glory of God. (1 Corinthians 10:31)

◆ **God has provided me with guidelines for how best to manage His wealth for His glory. For the most part, they are general rather than specific, which means I need to seek His wisdom continually in order to make wise choices.**

If any of you lacks wisdom, he should ask God, who gives generously to all without finding fault, and it will be given to him. But when he asks, he must believe and not doubt, because he who doubts is like a wave of the sea, blown and tossed by the wind. (James 1:5-6)

For God did not give us a spirit of timidity, but a spirit of power, of love and of self-discipline. (2 Timothy 1:7)

All Scripture is God-breathed and is useful for teaching, rebuking, correcting and training in righteousness, so that the man of God may be thoroughly equipped for every good work. (2 Timothy 3:16-17)

◆ **My giving, insofar as possible, is done primarily in the sight of God rather than in view of men. It belongs to the "secret life" of the believer so that God will receive the glory.**

Be careful not to do your "acts of righteousness" before men, to be seen by them. If you do, you will have no reward from your Father in heaven. . . . But when you give to the needy, do not let your left hand know what your right hand is doing, so that your giving may be in secret. Then your Father, who sees what is done in secret, will reward you. (Matthew 6:1, 3)

◆ **Wealth is exceedingly dangerous and has a history of spiritually devastating those who seek it. It must be handled with great care.**

People who want to get rich fall into temptation and a trap and into many foolish and harmful desires that plunge men into ruin and destruction. For the love of money is a root of all kinds of evil. Some people, eager for money, have wandered from the faith and pierced themselves with many griefs. (1 Timothy 6:9-10)

Command those who are rich in this present world not to be arrogant nor to put their hope in wealth, which is so uncertain, but to put their hope in God, who richly provides us with everything for our enjoyment. (1 Timothy 6:17)

◆ **I'm called to live fully in each day, not in the future. Therefore, God evaluates the faithfulness of my management based on what I do with what I have now, not what I might do someday if I had more.**

But seek first his kingdom and his righteousness, and all these things will be given to you as well. Therefore do not worry about tomorrow. (Matthew 6:33-34)

His master replied, "Well done, good and faithful servant! You have been faithful with a few things; I will put you in charge of many things. Come and share your master's happiness!" (Matthew 25:21)

◆ **I should manage with a sense of urgency. This inclines me toward giving what I can now rather than saving up in order to give more later. Later may be too late. This has implications for how much of my wealth I leave my children or put aside in charitable foundations.**

Do you not say, "Four months more and then the harvest"? I tell you, open your eyes and look at the fields! They are ripe for harvest. Even now the reaper draws his wages, even now he harvests the crop for eternal life. (John 4:35-36)

As long as it is day, we must do the work of him who sent me. Night is coming, when no one can work. (John 9:4)

The Lord is not slow in keeping his promise, as some understand slowness. He is patient with you, not wanting anyone to perish, but everyone to come to repentance. But the day of the Lord will come like a thief. (2 Peter 3:9-10)

◆ **God has built the law of sowing and reaping into the fabric of the universe. He can be trusted to pay me the perfectly appropriate wage for my work.**

Recommended Resource
A Biblical Theology of Material Possessions

by Gene Getz

Through an extensive search of Scripture, Gene Getz has formed more than 120 biblical principles that can be applied by any person in any culture. His book is practical as it searches the thoughts and intents of the heart on material matters. Larry Burkett called it "extremely informative as well as a practical tool for the local church." This is an excellent reference book to add to your Christian library.

Remember this: Whoever sows sparingly will also reap sparingly, and whoever sows generously will also reap generously. (2 Corinthians 9:6)

We speak of God's secret wisdom, a wisdom that has been hidden and that God destined for our glory before time began. None of the rulers of this age understood it, for if they had, they would not have crucified the Lord of glory. However, as it is written: "No eye has seen, no ear has heard, no mind has conceived what God has prepared for those who love him." (1 Corinthians 2:7-9)

◆ **Giving is an affair of the heart. God looks at our earnest intentions, not our gifts.**

The Lord does not look at the things man looks at. Man looks at the outward appearance, but the Lord looks at the heart. (1 Samuel 16:7)

Each man should give what he has decided in his heart to give, not reluctantly or under compulsion, for God loves a cheerful [hilarious] giver. And God is able to make all grace abound to you, so that in all things at all times, having all that you need, you will abound in every good work. (2 Corinthians 9:7-8)

◆ **It is not difficult to lay aside earthly wealth when you have God as your treasure.**

Do not be afraid, little flock, for your Father has been pleased to give you the kingdom. Sell your possessions and give to the poor. Provide purses for yourselves that will not wear out, a treasure in heaven that will not be exhausted, where no thief comes near and no moth destroys. For where your treasure is, there your heart will be also. (Luke 12:32-34)

"God's Plan for Systematic Giving" by Bill Bright. Excerpted from As You Sow. See Briefing 24, page 488.

God owns it all. He doesn't need our help or our money. The fact is we have nothing He needs . . .

. . . and He has everything that we need. Once again, I'm grateful to Bob Benson for putting things into perspective for us:

Do you remember when they had old-fashioned Sunday School picnics? I do. As I recall, it was back in the "olden days," as my kids would say, back before they had air conditioning.

They said, "We'll all meet at Sycamore Lodge in Shelby Park at 4:30 on Saturday. You bring your supper and we'll furnish the iced tea."

But if you were like me, you came home at the last minute. When you got ready to pack your picnic, all you could find in the refrigerator was one dried up piece of baloney and just enough mustard in the bottom of the jar so that you got it all over your knuckles trying to get to it. And just two slices of stale bread to go with it. So you made your baloney sandwich and wrapped it in an old brown bag and went to the picnic.

When it came time to eat, you sat at the end of a table and spread out your sandwich. But the folks who sat next to you brought a feast. The lady was a good cook and she had worked hard all day to get ready for the picnic. And she had fried chicken and baked beans

**Recommended
Resource**
<u>See You at the House,
The Stories Bob Benson
Used to Tell</u>

Selected & Edited by
R. Benson

God gifted Bob Benson
with a skill for communi-
cating great truths in
simple and humorous
ways. This book is a
collection of stories from
among his several books,
gathered by his son after
his father went to be with
the Lord. It is out-of-print
now, but don't let that
stop you. Many book-
stores belong to a
nationwide search system
for used books. It's worth
going to some trouble, if
necesary, to get a copy.
You'll laugh, and perhaps
shed a tear, and learn a
few new ways to think
about our God.

[2]Bob Benson,
<u>See You at the House,</u>
[Nashville: Generoux,
1986], pp. 68-69.
Used by permission.

and potato salad and homemade rolls and sliced tomatoes and pickles and olives and celery. And two big homemade chocolate pies to top it off. That's what they spread out there next to you while you sat with your baloney sandwich.

But they said to you, "Why don't we just put it all together?"

"No, I couldn't do that. I couldn't even think of it," you murmured in embarrassment, with one eye on the chicken.

"Oh, come on, there's plenty of chicken and plenty of pie and plenty of everything. And we just love baloney sandwiches. Let's just put it all together."

And so you did and there you sat, eating like a king when you came like a pauper.

One day, it dawned on me that God had been saying just that sort of thing to me. "Why don't you take what you have and what you are, and I will take what I have and what I am, and we'll share it together." I began to see that when I put what I had and was and am and hope to be with what he is, I had stumbled upon the bargain of a lifetime.

I get to thinking sometimes, thinking of me sharing with God. When I think of how little I bring, and how much he brings and invites me to share, I know that I should be shouting to the housetops, but I am so filled with awe and wonder that I can hardly speak. I know that I don't have enough love or faith or grace or mercy or wisdom, but he does. He has all of those things in abundance and he says, "Let's just put it all together."

Consecration, denial, sacrifice, commitment, crosses were all kind of hard words to me, until I saw them in the light of sharing. It isn't just a case of me kicking in what I have because God is the biggest kid in the neighborhood and he wants it all for himself. He is saying, "Everything that I possess is available to you. Everything that I am and can be to a person, I will be to you."

When I think about it like that, it really amuses me to see somebody running along through life hanging on to their dumb bag with that stale baloney sandwich in it saying, "God's not going to get my sandwich! No, sirree, this is mine!" Did you ever see anybody like that — so needy — just about half-starved to death yet hanging on for dear life. It's not that God needs your sandwich. The fact is, you need his chicken.

Well, go ahead — eat your baloney sandwich, as long as you can. But when you can't stand its tastelessness or drabness any longer; when you get so tired of running your own life by yourself and doing it your way and figuring out all the answers with no one to help; when trying to accumulate, hold, grasp, and keep everything together in your own strength gets to be too big a load; when you begin to realize that by yourself you're never going to be able to fulfill your dreams, I hope you'll remember that it doesn't have to be that way.

You have been invited to something better, you know. You have been invited to share in the very being of God.[2] ◆

CHAPTER PREVIEW

Investing That Glorifies God Upholds His Righteousness

I will listen to what God the Lord will say; he promises peace to his people, his saints—but let them not return to folly. Surely his salvation is near those who fear him, that his glory may dwell in our land. Love and faithfulness meet together; righteousness and peace kiss each other. Faithfulness springs forth from the earth, and righteousness looks down from heaven. The Lord will indeed give what is good, and our land will yield its harvest. Righteousness goes before him and prepares the way for his steps.

(Psalm 85:8-13)

What man is wise enough to understand this? Who has been instructed by the Lord and can explain it? Why has the land been ruined and laid waste like a desert that no one can cross? The Lord said, "It is because they have forsaken my law, which I set before them; they have not obeyed me or followed my law." . . . This is what the Lord says: "Let not the wise man boast of his wisdom or the strong man boast of his strength or the rich man boast of his riches, but let him who boasts boast about this: that he understands and knows me, that I am the Lord, who exercises kindness, justice and righteousness on earth, for in these I delight," declares the Lord.

(Jeremiah 9:12-13, 23-24)

The commencement speaker at the University of California School of Business had these words of advice: *"Greed is all right. Greed is healthy.*

"You can be greedy and still feel good about yourself. Greed works." The comments reportedly were received with laughter and applause by the new graduates. The speaker was Ivan Boesky, a man of vast wealth. Not too many months later, he was sent to prison for violating securities laws in his relentless quest to acquire even more.

How much is enough, anyway? Obviously, for some, there's no such thing as ever having "enough." It's not because they have material wants that are left unmet; Ivan Boesky couldn't possibly have spent, no matter how extravagant his personal lifestyle, all the money he had. There are those for whom money represents success, status, superiority, and power. They are pursuing it in a doomed attempt to fill an inner emptiness. But that emptiness is like a black hole; no matter how much you put in, it never fills with light. Ironically, Boesky's very life gave the lie to his words. Greed, it turns out, doesn't work after all.

Fortunately, we Christians already understand this. Greed may be something to watch out for . . .

. . . when doing business with "the world," but followers of Christ are not like that. We can relax with them. *They* would never take advantage of us, right? . . . Right? . . . Hello? . . .

Perhaps I imagine that my question is being received with less than thunderous agreement because I routinely receive letters from readers of my newsletter that contain horror stories of the various financial atrocities committed against them by people they trusted to have their best interests at heart. They met these people at church, in a couples' Bible study, through a Christian friend, or through some other association that would lead them to believe the person was trustworthy. Unfortunately, limiting your business transactions solely to Christians is no assurance that everything will work out happily ever after.

That reminds me, have I ever told you about my $100,000 tennis racket?

During my tenure with Campus Crusade, the idea struck me how great it would be if I found competent Christian people to invest with. They would perform the day-to-day work of the investment projects, and eventually we could live off the income and be free to continue devoting our time to ministry pursuits.

Well, it wasn't long (wouldn't you know it?) before I was approached about investing in a real estate project. I was introduced by a co-worker to a friend of his who was a developer (let's call him Dugan) in the greater San Diego area. He and his partner Roberts needed temporary financing on one of their projects until their permanent construction loan was approved. They were willing to pay a healthy rate of interest, personally guarantee the loan, plus pledge some stock Dugan owned as additional collateral. They had done other projects previously and had development experience. I verified with the lending institution that their loan request had, indeed, received approval, pending receipt of their pro forma financial statements.

Dugan and his wife were super people; you couldn't help but like them. They entertained us at their country club. They invited us over for friendly tennis (Dugan gave me one of his rackets so I could practice regularly). Since we were living away from Kentucky, they even included us in their plans for Thanksgiving dinner. We were practically family! So everything seemed to line up pretty well. And what seemed to confirm it was that the opportunity to invest with a Christian had come along just when it seemed the natural direction to go.

You know something went wrong, or I wouldn't own a tennis racket that cost me $100,000. Here's the sorry sequence of events.

◆ Through negligence, Dugan missed the deadline for submitting the financial statements to the lender, and they lost their construction loan.

◆ The economy was going through a downturn, and they could not get another loan commitment. The project never got off the ground. Fortunately, I still had the personal guarantees of the Dugans and the Robertses.

◆ Roberts died suddenly of a heart attack. Being a sensitive guy who doesn't want to invade a widow's grief, I let some time go by before asking for her share of my money. While I was being noble, her late husband's attorney was helping her hide her assets; she eventually produced a financial statement that made her appear penniless. Curiously, six months after the sudden departure of Mr. Roberts, the former Mrs. Roberts overcame her grief and married the helpful attorney.

◆ Mr. Dugan and his wife filed for protection under the bankruptcy laws and moved to northern California. I never heard from them again.

◆ The stock Dugan pledged was in a land development company that was operated and controlled by his brother. The brother later told me that things were going so well that my stock holdings would be worth $1 million within three years. This was a little optimistic; the company expanded too quickly, eventually lost its land holdings, and disappeared into bankruptcy never-never land. I never heard from the brother again.

What did I learn from this misadventure? I learned not to make certain unwarranted assumptions . . .

. . . when dealing with fellow Christians. First, I assumed that because Dugan had experience and seemed to know what he was doing, he was competent. I didn't really check him out. It turned out that his personable style made him competent only as a promoter. It was little help in the nitty-gritty of day-to-day details. Second, I assumed that these were people of integrity. They seemed so *sincere!* Yet they readily hid behind the bankruptcy laws to avoid repaying the money they had so earnestly besought me to loan them. Boy, had I learned an important lesson! I wouldn't make *those* mistakes again. I would make *new* ones.

This brings me to the story of my $50,000 Swiss army knife key ring.

Jack, a good Christian friend, brought it back as a souvenir from one of the frequent business trips to Europe he made for a business deal we were in together. I won't go into all the

PRYOR'S RULES FOR EVALUATING INVESTMENTS THAT SEEK YOU OUT

Rule #1
Assume the investment is being offered to you by a representative of Ivan Boesky. It's not that the person soliciting your investment is likely to be as greedy or dishonest as Boesky. I just want to help you to stay alert and not repeat the mistake of making unwarranted assumptions. All the remaining rules logically follow from this one.

Rule #2
Apply all decision-making guidelines for making the "right" decisions that I gave in chapter 17 (pages 196-198). All of them.

Rule #3
Ask the individual to put everything of importance (like representations of risk, how much money you're guaranteed to make, how long it's all going to take) in written form. Assume nothing; verify everything.

Rule #4
Check his facts out thoroughly. Ask someone you trust, who has nothing to do with the deal, to help you. Assume nothing; verify everything.

Rule #5
Investigate his track record. Contact other investors with whom he's done business. Assume nothing; verify everything.

Rule #6
Ask for personal character references, including one from his pastor. Then call the people and talk with them personally. Assume nothing; verify everything.

Rule #7
If you decide to go ahead, put the entire deal in writing, signed by all concerned, so that you have a legally enforceable position. Handshake deals are out.

Rule #8
Make absolutely, positively no exceptions to Rules #1 through #7. And, oh yes, assume nothing and verify everything.

details here. I'll just skip to the new lessons I learned about *other* unwarranted assumptions you shouldn't make. First, I assumed that all the facts of the deal were exactly as Jack had represented them to me. (By the way, note that I no longer needed go-betweens to introduce me to people like Dugan—by this time I was going directly to my close personal friends to lose my money.) I know that Jack truly believed—evidently too optimistically—everything he was telling me. The point is that I would never have accepted the story just on the word of a stranger. I would have expected documented proof of all the facts. With Jack, my guard was completely down.

Second, I assumed that because I could trust my friend, the usual precautions didn't apply. In chapter 17, I gave you five guidelines for making investment decisions (see pages 196-198). In this one deal, I broke the first four of the guidelines without hesitation.

Guideline 1: The deal wasn't consistent with my long-term strategy because I didn't have one.

Guideline 2: I didn't take much time to pray about it or seek counsel from others.

Guideline 3: I never really understood the logistics of the deal or why it was supposed to work the way it was.

Guideline 4: The investment totally failed the common sense test of prudence.

In retrospect, it's so improbable that it could have worked that I'm too embarrassed to even tell you what it was about.

In short, my trust was totally in the knowledge and experience of my friend. The reason I didn't give the guidelines a thought is that I hadn't learned to apply biblical principles to financial decision making at that point. (Larry Burkett was just getting his ministry started in those days. Larry, where were you when I needed you?) This happened in 1976, and I was still flying on gut instinct.

I hope you appreciate the "school" I went to in learning these lessons that I'm passing on to you for the unbelievably low price of whatever is printed on the back of this book. The tuition for this one cost me $50,000 (or just $49,990 if you want to count the $10 value of my Swiss army knife key ring).

Well, enough about evaluating an investment opportunity that is seeking *you* out. Let's look at the flip side—investments where you are the one taking the initiative.

This matter of taking heed of the ethical implications of where we invest our money has been popularly called "socially responsible" investing.

Socially responsible investing (SRI) continues to gather momentum as a force in the investment world. According to research from the Social Investment Forum, the amount invested in the U.S. under various forms of SRI totaled approximately $640 billion in 1995.

All practitioners of SRI create a set of portfolio guidelines, called "screens," which reflect the ethical values they wish to see represented in their investments. It's generally agreed that SRI falls into three main camps:

❶ **Avoidance investing.** Investors in this category develop screens designed to weed out companies engaged in activities or practices that they find objectionable. This is probably the most common approach, and is what most individual investors mean when they say they are interested in "ethical" investing.

❷ **Advocacy investing.** This is the opposite of avoidance investing because it seeks to invest in companies with the intention of changing objectionable corporate behavior by exercising one's ownership privileges. Because this strategy calls for an ongoing effort after the investment is made, it is sometimes known as activist or interventionist investing.

❸ **Alternative investing.** This is a proactive strategy where investment opportunities are sought in companies that are working to achieve those societal goals that the investor believes are important. Companies that underwrite community housing projects, search for alternative energy sources, manufacture pollution-control products, or have "nondiscriminatory" employment and promotion practices are examples of areas targeted for proactive investing.

Historically, SRI proponents have generally been in favor of: affirmative action, animal rights, environmental protection, gay and lesbian rights, gun control, low income housing, so-called women's issues, and nondiscrimination against people with AIDS. They have generally opposed: air pollution, alcohol, defense and weapons contractors, gambling, nuclear power, tobacco products, and South Africa.

This list shows that SRI activists hold, for the most part, "liberal" views concerning the way society, business, and government should be organized and operated. This is slowly changing, however, as greater numbers of investors from the "conservative" ranks are using their influence in support of values they believe are important.

The ethical screens used by SRI mutual funds are designed to reflect the moral values of those investors . . .

. . . that the fund hopes to attract. To help you see how each of the leading SRI mutual funds defines "responsible" behavior, I have prepared the table on the next page. The funds are grouped according to their primary portfolio emphasis, and are ranked within each group according to their 1995 performance. As you can see, the ethical screens being used today are, at long last, beginning to more fully reflect the diverse moral, cultural, and political views of the American people.

There has been an ongoing debate within investing circles as to whether an SRI strategy hurts performance.

The data presented in the table on the opposite page shed some light on this question as it pertains to mutual fund investors. In the first six data columns, each fund's performance over the past six years is shown (sales loads, if any, are not included). The second set of data columns lists each fund's year-by-year performance as compared to the average of all mutual funds that have the same investment objective. For example, the Citizens Emerging Growth fund gained 40.7% last year. This was 8.0% higher than the average for *all* aggressive growth funds. Positive numbers in these columns mean a fund outperformed its peers for the year in question, whereas negative numbers mean the fund underperformed. Unfortunately, only Parnassus has consistently had

THE SCREENING CRITERIA OF "SOCIALLY RESPONSIBLE" FUNDS

Source: Telephone Survey by Sound Mind Investing Newsletter Staff in April 1996

Fund Name	Primary Portfolio Emphasis	Morningstar Investment Objective	Abortion Concerns	Alcoholic Beverages	Animal Welfare	Casinos+ Gambling	Defense+ Weapons	Environment Concerns	Nuclear Energy	Pornography Concerns	Tobacco Products	Phone
Citizens Emerging Growth	Stocks	AggressGro		x	x		x	x	x	x	x	(800) 223-7010
Neuberger&Berman Soc Resp	Stocks	Growth		x		x	x	x	x		x	(800) 877-9700
Calvert Capital Accumulate A	Stocks	Growth		x			x	x	x		x	(800) 368-2748
Dreyfus Third Century	Stocks	Growth						x			x	(800) 645-6561
Aquinas Equity Income	Stocks	Equity-Inc	x				x	x	x	x	x	(214) 233-6655
Domini Social Equity	Stocks	Growth-Inc		x		x	x	x	x		x	(800) 762-6814
MMA Praxis Growth	Stocks	Growth	x	x		x	x	x	x	x	x	(800) 977-2947
Aquinas Equity Growth	Stocks	Growth	x				x	x	x	x	x	(214) 233-6655
Bridgeway Social Responsblty	Stocks	Growth-Inc		x	x	x	x	x	x		x	(800) 661-3550
Laidlaw Covenant	Stocks	Growth-Inc		x		x	x	x	x		x	(800) 275-2683
Rightime Social Awareness	Stocks	Growth-Inc		x			x	x	x		x	(800) 242-1421
Amana Income	Stocks	Equity-Inc		x		x				x	x	(800) 728-8762
Ariel Appreciation	Stocks	Growth					x	x	x		x	(800) 292-7435
Calvert Social Inv Equity A	Stocks	Growth		x	x	x	x	x	x		x	(800) 368-2748
New Alternatives	Stocks	Growth			x		x	x	x		x	(800) 423-8383
Ariel Growth	Stocks	SmallComp					x	x	x		x	(800) 292-7435
Timothy Plan	Stocks	Growth	x	x		x				x	x	(800) 846-7526
Calvert Strategic Growth A	Stocks	AggressGro		x			x	x	x		x	(800) 368-2748
Parnassus	Stocks	Growth		x		x	x	x	x		x	(800) 999-3505
Pax World	Both	Balanced		x		x	x	x	x		x	(800) 767-1729
Calvert Social Inv Managed A	Both	Balanced		x	x	x	x	x	x		x	(800) 368-2748
Aquinas Balanced	Both	Balanced	x				x	x	x	x	x	(214) 233-6655
Green Century Balanced	Both	Balanced					x	x	x		x	(800) 934-7336
Parnassus Income Fixed-Inc	Bonds	CorpGeneral		x		x	x	x	x		x	(800) 999-3505
MMA Praxis Intermediate Inc	Bonds	CorpGeneral	x	x		x	x	x	x	x	x	(800) 977-2947
Calvert Social Inv Bond A	Bonds	CorpHiQuality		x		x	x	x	x		x	(800) 368-2748
Citizens Income	Bonds	CorpHiQuality		x	x		x	x	x	x	x	(800) 223-7010
Aquinas Fixed-Income	Bonds	CorpHiQuality	x				x	x	x	x	x	(214) 233-6655

more "good" years than "bad" ones in this regard (although it turned in an uncharacteristically poor showing in 1995).

The center column shows how each fund compared with a corresponding Vanguard index fund over the past three-year period (the stock funds were compared to a stock index fund, and so on). You'll note that all the numbers are negative. As I pointed out in chapter 13, only about 20% of mutual funds have outperformed the market over time, so I was expecting SRI funds, as a group, to show similar results. Surprisingly, not a single one of the SRI funds surpassed its index fund counterpart over the past three years. Generally mediocre performance, however, has not been a factor in why I have not placed a major emphasis on SRI funds (which primarily engage in "avoidance investing" strategies) in my monthly investment newsletter. There are two reasons that are more fundamental.

ANNUAL RETURNS OF SRI FUNDS CONTRASTED WITH THEIR PEER GROUPS

Source: Morningstar Mutual Funds Ondisc

Fund Name	Annual Return 1995	Annual Return 1994	Annual Return 1993	Annual Return 1992	Annual Return 1991	Annual Return 1990	Versus Index 3 Yrs	Versus Peers 1995	Versus Peers 1994	Versus Peers 1993	Versus Peers 1992	Versus Peers 1991	Versus Peers 1990	Max Sales Charge	Min Initial Purch	Ticker Symbol
Citizens Emerging Growth	40.7%	new	new	new	new	new	new	8.0%	new	new	new	new	new	None	$2,500	WAEGX
Neuberger&Berman Soc Resp	38.9%	new	new	new	new	new	new	8.1%	new	new	new	new	new	None	1,000	NA
Calvert Capital Accumulate A	36.2%	new	new	new	new	new	new	5.4%	new	new	new	new	new	4.75%	2,000	CCAFX
Dreyfus Third Century	35.8%	−7.5%	5.2%	1.9%	38.1%	3.5%	−5.4%	5.0%	−5.7%	−6.6%	−6.8%	0.7%	8.4%	None	2,500	DRTHX
Aquinas Equity Income	35.6%	new	new	new	new	new	new	6.7%	new	new	new	new	new	None	1,000	AQEIX
Domini Social Equity	35.2%	−0.4%	6.5%	12.1%	new	new	−2.4%	4.3%	1.1%	−5.0%	3.6%	new	new	None	1,000	DSEFX
MMA Praxis Growth	33.8%	new	new	new	new	new	new	3.0%	new	new	new	new	new	4.00%	500	MMPGX
Aquinas Equity Growth	30.3%	new	new	new	new	new	new	−0.6%	new	new	new	new	new	None	1,000	NA
Bridgeway Social Responsblty	30.3%	new	new	new	new	new	new	−0.6%	new	new	new	new	new	None	2,000	NA
Laidlaw Covenant	29.6%	3.0%	4.0%	new	new	new	−3.6%	−1.3%	4.4%	−7.5%	new	new	new	4.50%	500	LLCFX
Rightime Social Awareness	28.7%	1.5%	−2.3%	12.6%	23.4%	new	−6.7%	−2.2%	3.0%	−13.8%	4.1%	−5.6%	new	4.75%	2,000	RTAWX
Amana Income	25.5%	−6.5%	11.6%	1.9%	23.6%	−3.4%	−5.8%	−3.5%	−4.8%	−2.4%	−7.7%	−3.2%	2.6%	None	100	AMANX
Ariel Appreciation	24.2%	−8.4%	8.0%	13.2%	33.2%	−1.5%	−8.1%	−6.7%	−6.6%	−3.9%	4.5%	−4.2%	3.4%	None	1,000	CAAPX
Calvert Social Inv Equity A	21.5%	−12.1%	2.1%	8.4%	21.9%	−4.9%	−12.2%	−9.4%	−10.3%	−9.7%	−0.3%	−15.5%	0.0%	4.75%	1,000	CSIEX
New Alternatives	19.5%	−3.7%	2.9%	4.9%	25.5%	−7.6%	−9.4%	−11.4%	−2.0%	−9.0%	−3.8%	−11.8%	−2.7%	4.75%	2,500	NALFX
Ariel Growth	18.5%	−4.2%	8.8%	11.7%	32.7%	−16.1%	−7.9%	−12.4%	−3.9%	−8.8%	−2.7%	−16.3%	−5.8%	None	1,000	ARGFX
Timothy Plan	7.9%	new	new	new	new	new	new	−22.9%	new	new	new	new	new	1.75%	1,000	TPLNX
Calvert Strategic Growth A	2.9%	new	new	new	new	new	new	−29.8%	new	new	new	new	new	4.75%	2,000	CSGFX
Parnassus	0.6%	12.0%	17.3%	36.8%	52.6%	−21.2%	−5.4%	−30.2%	13.7%	5.4%	28.1%	15.2%	−16.2%	3.50%	2,000	PARNX
Pax World	29.2%	2.6%	−1.1%	0.6%	20.6%	10.5%	−2.2%	4.1%	5.4%	−12.5%	−6.7%	−6.0%	11.2%	None	250	PAXWX
Calvert Social Inv Managed A	25.9%	−4.7%	6.0%	7.5%	17.8%	1.8%	−3.4%	0.8%	−2.0%	−5.5%	0.1%	−8.8%	2.4%	4.75%	1,000	CSIFX
Aquinas Balanced	23.1%	new	new	new	new	new	−2.0%	new	new	new	new	new	None	1,000	AQBLX
Green Century Balanced	18.3%	−4.3%	−0.5%	new	new	new	−7.6%	−6.8%	−1.5%	−12.0%	new	new	new	None	2,000	GCBLX
Parnassus Income Fixed-Inc	21.6%	−6.8%	11.0%	new	new	new	−0.1%	4.6%	−2.8%	0.2%	new	new	new	None	2,000	PRFIX
MMA Praxis Intermediate Inc	17.5%	new	new	new	new	new	new	0.5%	new	new	new	new	new	4.00%	500	MMPIX
Calvert Social Inv Bond A	17.4%	−5.3%	11.7%	6.7%	15.7%	8.3%	−0.6%	3.1%	−3.1%	3.1%	0.3%	0.9%	1.0%	3.75%	1,000	CSIBX
Citizens Income	17.4%	−3.1%	10.0%	new	new	new	−0.3%	3.1%	−0.8%	1.4%	new	new	new	None	2,500	WAIMX
Aquinas Fixed-Income	16.3%	new	new	new	new	new	new	2.0%	new	new	new	new	new	None	1,000	AQFIX

Reason #1: Because most investors tend to idealize their goals, ethical investing becomes an impossible mission.

I receive more questions asking for suggestions on where to find ethical investments than on any other single topic. I believe that the people writing have a genuine desire to please the Lord in the way they handle their finances. They are seeking investments that adhere to the righteous standards of Scripture. They sincerely strive to be faithful stewards, and they believe they have a responsibility to be sure they do not lend economic support to those forces in opposition to what they see as biblical values. I respect their heartfelt concerns. Unfortunately, I must tell them I can't be of help. Why not? Because I know of no investments that are guaranteed to meet their criteria. There are no morally pure investments, either in the mutual fund world or anywhere else. Consider:

◆ **Bank savings accounts and certificates of deposit.**

It's possible that your bank has loaned money to help build such businesses as the local newspaper that aggressively attacks Christian home-schooling in its editorials, the chemical company that illegally dumps its waste, or the bookstore that has several racks of pornographic magazines right by the front door where even young children can see them. Or your bank may have loaned money to the abortion clinic that has become the largest in your state, the engineering company whose PAC contributions perpetuate corruption in local government, or the music store in the local mall that promotes music and videos that glamorize sexually destructive and drug-addicting lifestyles. The possibilities are almost limitless; let your imagination run a little. Almost every business has bank loans to some degree. The question is not *if* your bank has made loans to businesses engaged in practices abhorrent to you, but rather *how many and for how much*. And where do the banks get the money to make these loans? From the savings put on deposit by trusting folks like you and me.

◆ **United States government bonds, notes, and Treasury bills.**

These are the investments that make it possible for our government to run the huge budget deficits that make inflation an ever-present fact of American life. Many who write on economics from a biblical perspective consider inflation to be a great evil because it constitutes theft by the government. Much has been written on that subject alone. In addition, however, start considering the many ways that government spends our money. Whether promoting abortion, supporting artists who produce blasphemous or pornographic exhibits, or undermining traditional family values through humanistic education and welfare programs, there is much for Christians to be concerned about. The one exception would be the bond mutual funds that invest only in government-backed GNMA mortgages (which provide capital for people to purchase homes). Other than these, are government securities ethical investments?

Helping Others While Saving at South Shore Bank

Established in 1973 as the country's first "community development" bank, the mission of South Shore Bank has been to lend financial support to those in its community (an inner-city neighborhood of Chicago) who are willing to help themselves by obtaining skills, jobs, and better housing.

South Shore Bank welcomes investors from all over the country. Here are a few of the ways you can participate in this mission while at the same time satisfying your own financial needs.

1. Money Market Max Savings and Checking. With a minimum of $2,500 each, these FDIC-insured savings or checking accounts offer competitive money market rates and flexibility.

2. Certificates of Deposits. Five different CDs are offered. Depending on length of maturity and investment amount, they are linked to providing special housing, job retention, and environment programs.

3. South Shore Bank Mastercard℠ and Visa℠. Both regular and gold are available with competitive interest rates and no annual fee. A portion of the bank's profits will be shared with five nonprofit affiliates, including The Neighborhood Institute, which offers services on the south side of Chicago. The affiliates use the funds to create jobs in their communities.

For more information on South Shore or any of the services mentioned, call (800) 669-7725.

◆ **Common stocks.**

How many of the Fortune 500 companies do you believe are operated according to Christian principles from top to bottom? That would mean the application of a biblical moral ethic in *all* of the following: their hiring and firing decisions, employee pay schedules, environmental impact policies, the way they price their products or services, their borrowing and lending decisions, and the whole of their advertising and marketing strategies. I doubt you can find even one.

It's interesting to me that many investors have a difficult time with the ethics of investing in stock mutual funds, yet don't give a second thought to the morality of building sizable bank savings account and Treasury bill holdings. Consistency would call for demanding ethical purity in those investments as well.

Let's look at your bank, for example. Assume that it has $100 million in loans outstanding, and that you would find $2 million of them seriously objectionable if you knew about them. Further assume that you have a $5,000 CD on deposit there. Your CD represents 1/200 of 1% of the bank's total loans outstanding. That means that for every $10,000 your bank loans out, you "contribute" 50¢ to the loan. Is your CD an ethical investment? If you are looking for absolute purity, then it doesn't qualify, because 2% of the loan portfolio fails your ethics test. But is your meager role statistically meaningful? Obviously not. That's why I would consider the CD investment acceptable.

I won't spend time reviewing the extent to which investing in U.S. securities (T-bills, notes, bonds, and government-only money market funds) support the federal government's spending programs. The relatively miniscule size of an individual's holdings in relation to the absolutely massive size of the federal budget is obvious.

My point is that investors have limited choices. Whether you invest in a bank certificate of deposit, U.S. Treasury securities, or selected common stocks, you have virtually no control over the specific uses to which your money is put *once you turn it loose*. We are "in the world" and must function in it. Paul writes in 1 Corinthians 5:9-10, "I have written you in my letter not to associate with sexually immoral people—not at all meaning the people of this world who are immoral, or the greedy and swindlers, or idolaters. In that case you would have to leave this world." Paul recognizes the impossibility of completely avoiding contact with the corrupt world we inhabit. My conclusion: You can't altogether avoid incidental financial contact with disagreeable causes in the course of your investing.

Well, perhaps not, you might be thinking, *but we can at least avoid giving them meaningful support*. True, which brings me to the second reason I have not emphasized avoidance investing.

Reason #2: Because companies don't directly profit when you buy their shares through a mutual fund, ethical investing becomes an ineffective mission.

Many investors are under the false impression that companies benefit when you buy their stock (or invest in mutual funds that own their stock). It's important that you understand that the money spent by a mutual fund to acquire shares in, say, a tobacco company did *not* go to the tobacco company. The shares were purchased in what's called the "secondary market," and the money paid for them went to the previous owners. It's the same as if you bought a used Pontiac from a friend. Your money would not go to General Motors, which got its money a long time ago and couldn't care less whether you buy the Pontiac or whether your friend continues to own it. SRI funds are no different from "regular" funds in this regard.

I believe that mutual funds are acceptable investing vehicles for the same reason that bank savings accounts and T-bills are acceptable: The role your investment plays is absolutely insignificant in relation to the size of the problem areas. In fact, it is too small to even be called "support" at all in the usual sense. Consider this. A mutual fund rarely owns even one-tenth of 1% of a given company's stock. Furthermore, few investors would ever hold as much as one-tenth of 1% of any one mutual fund's assets. Therefore, owning a mutual fund limits the average investor to holding *less than one one-millionth of any one company's shares.* The ownership effect is nil.

Here's an example of how this works. One of the Vanguard funds recommended in my newsletter held 366,000 shares of stock in Philip Morris, the huge tobacco company with more than 925 million shares outstanding. This means that the fund owns about 1/2,500 of Philip Morris. Let's assume you invest $5,000 in this Vanguard fund; how much ownership in Philip Morris would this give you? You would own 1/70,000 of a fund which owns 1/2,500 of Philip Morris. Congratulations! That makes you the owner of 1/175,000,000 (that's one part in 175 million!) of Philip Morris. Such investment hardly qualifies as support.

We want our drinking water to be clean, but we don't demand that it be sterile. We all would like clean air, but we don't walk around wearing oxygen masks. If we accept 99.9% purity when it comes to matters of life and health, doesn't it seem reasonable to apply the same standards to material pursuits like investing?

You may be concluding that I am unconcerned about corporate ethics and using one's economic influence to battle immoral forces. If so, you misunderstand my point. It's not that I want you to be less radical in this area. I want you to become *more* radical.

To do an effective job of withholding support from objectionable companies, we must be ready to boycott — *not their securities, but their products and services.*

In November 1990, *The Wall Street Journal* ran an article captioned "Facing a Boycott, Many Companies Bend." It reported that boycotts "have become increasingly common as more and more groups (representing consumers, environmentalists, religions and others) have targeted individual companies" requesting them to change their policies. Boycotters are finding increasingly receptive listeners at major corporations for two reasons. First, it only takes a modest decline in sales (5%-10%) to adversely affect their profits. And second, boycotters often come from two-income families in the high-spending "nest building" stage of life — a highly desirable demographic group of customers.

One of the most influential consumer organizations is Christian Leaders for Responsible Television, a coalition of approximately 1,600 denominational and parachurch groups. Finding the major television networks completely indifferent to the concerns of Americans who hold traditional biblical values of morality, this coalition turned its attention to the corporate sponsors who make the programming possible. The effectiveness of their approach was demonstrated in 1990 when Burger King was boycotted as the leading sponsor of sex, violence, profanity, and anti-Christian stereotyping on television. The boycott was concluded successfully when Burger King amended its advertising standards and ran half-page ads in more than 550 daily newspapers across the country stating its support for traditional values on television.

Frankly, I doubt that Burger King would have cared in the least if the Christian community decided not to buy any mutual funds that might own some minute fraction of one percent of the stock in its parent company. But when Christian consumers said it would be a year before they would eat their next Whopper, management could envision lost revenues running into tens of millions of dollars. They decided it was good business to give proper respect to the cherished values of the families upon whom they depend for their success.

There have been other successes in recent years. Movie theaters across the country refused to show *The Last Temptation of Christ*. Clorox changed its advertising practices, which had previously been in support of some terribly objectionable television programming. Meanwhile, more than 25,000 retail stores across the country have reportedly discontinued stocking the pornographic *Playboy* and *Penthouse* magazines, costing these publishers vast revenues and profits. Boycotts work!

This coalition was an outgrowth of the pioneering work done by the Rev. Don Wildmon, founder of the American Family Association. The AFA is right to be concerned about the moral decline of our society and its contribution to the destruction of the family. Falsely accused by some of "censorship," it has a boycotting philosophy that I find right on target: The networks are free to show whatever programming *they* wish, companies are free to sponsor whatever programming *they* wish, and consumers are free to support and patronize whomever *we* wish.

Companies primarily profit from our spending, not our investing.

Targeting our routine daily spending can be a potent force for change, as we saw in the five-year battle with Kmart over its subsidiary's pornography sales. I encourage you to spend strategically in order to reward those companies that enhance the quality of life from a Judeo-Christian perspective and avoid rewarding those whose activities undermine the health of the family and children. If a company's behavior is offensive to your deeply held convictions, why reward it with your patronage?

For *most* of us, strategic thinking regarding our routine daily spending is a more potent force for change than the threat of withholding our investing. Let me explain why, using the boycott of Disney by the AFA and the 16 million-strong Southern Baptists (see sidebar) as an example:

❶ **Everyone can participate.** All of us are consumers; not all of us have investment portfolios. Even if we do, they might not hold shares in the offending companies we are trying to influence. If you believe the value of your involvement is directly tied to the size and makeup of your investment portfolio, what do you do if your investments are modest in size and/or include no holdings, directly or indirectly, in Disney? You may conclude that there's no role for you to play.

❷ **Ease of recruitment.** There are millions of families who would be quite upset with Disney if they knew the facts. But in our society it can be quite awkward to talk to your friends about personal money matters concerning their investments and how they can/should use them to stand for biblical values. On the other hand, it's relatively easy to hand them an article on the subject and ask that they take this information into account before doing any further business with Disney or its many entertainment subsidiaries.

❸ **Ease of implementation.** To work for change through your investing requires adding an activity to already busy schedules: research who holds the shares and communicate your requests that they divest their holdings. But to work for change through your spending adds no new time demands. It merely requires a change in one's spending patterns. This makes it easier for each of us to get involved as well as making it easier to ask others.

❹ **Concentration of forces.** We can more readily join together and make our influence felt when we are all directing our efforts at a single decision-maker—Disney's top officer. In contrast, consider the challenge of influenc-

---

Excerpts from the SBC Disney Resolution

WHEREAS, Southern Baptists and their children have for many decades enjoyed and trusted the Disney Co.'s television programming, feature-length films, and theme parks which have reinforced basic American virtues and values; and

WHEREAS, The virtues promoted by Disney have contributed to the development of a generation of Americans who have come to expect and demand high levels of moral and virtuous leadership from the Disney Co.; and

WHEREAS, In recent years, the Disney Co. has given the appearance that the promotion of homosexuality is more important than its historic commitment to traditional family values and has taken direction which is contrary to its previous commitment; and

WHEREAS, In recent years, we have watched the world's largest entertainment company with growing disappointment as Disney Co.'s moral leadership has been eroded by a variety of corporate decisions which represent a significant departure from Disney's family-values image, and a gratuitous insult to Christians and others who have long supported Disney and contributed to its corporate profits; and

(continued on next page)

34 ◆ Upholds His Righteousness   429

ing hundreds of fund managers and institutional investors, who do not share the same concerns, to sell a significant amount of their Disney stock.

❺ Disney needs our spending, not our investing, for its success. Even if a million like-minded families decided to sell their mutual fund shares in protest, Disney would have only a *public relations* problem. The influence of those families is diluted because their investments are scattered across thousands of mutual funds and pension accounts. But if a million families who previously supported Disney's movies, videos, theme parks, etc., took their Disney spending elsewhere, Disney would begin to notice a decline in *profits*. That's a far more serious problem.

Don't let anyone tell you your opposition, as expressed through a boycott, is censorship. Censorship takes place only when the force of government is used to prevent or punish publication. Publishers are free to publish what they wish within the obscenity laws upheld by the Supreme Court. In the above example, Disney is free to make the movies, videos, and television programming it wishes to make, and to generally conduct its business in a way it believes will most advance its sales and profits. And you are free to do business with the companies you choose. While the First Amendment guarantees freedom of expression, it does not guarantee that every form of expression will meet with public acceptance or commercial success.

Let me make it clear that I am also in favor of taking action on the investment side as well. I am not saying that divestiture of Disney stock by Christian institutions is not desirable. These are important symbolic gestures that make a statement about our values and concerns. The drawback is they have no direct effect on Disney's finances. In a typical week, $4-$5 *billion* of Disney stock changes hands. The market can swallow up sales of Disney shares—even those amounting to tens of millions—with ease and little effect on the price.

Investing that glorifies God upholds His righteousness.

So far in this section, we have discussed why investing that glorifies God acknowledges His sovereignty (God owns it all), values His majesty (He is the treasure), and builds His kingdom (we are to manage His wealth for achieving God-given goals). If you are committed to making money-management decisions that reflect your firm convictions about those first three truths, you will have no problem understanding why our investing should also uphold His righteousness.

This, then, is how you should pray: "Our Father in heaven, hallowed be your name, your kingdom come, your will be done on earth as it is in heaven." (Matthew 6:9-10)

It naturally follows that you will feel a solemn obligation to use your financial leverage to the maximum in order that His righteousness is revealed and upheld. No one will need to persuade you that it is a good thing. You will be grieved to think it would be otherwise.

WHEREAS, Previous efforts to communicate these concerns to the Disney Co. have been fruitless; and

WHEREAS, Boycotts are a legitimate method for communicating moral convictions; Now, therefore,

BE IT RESOLVED, We as Southern Baptist messengers meeting in annual session on June 11–13, 1996, go on record expressing our deep disappointments for these corporate actions by the Disney Co.; and

BE IT FURTHER RESOLVED, That we affirm the employees of the Disney Co. who embrace and share our concerns; and

BE IT FURTHER RESOLVED, That we encourage Southern Baptists to give serious and prayerful reconsideration to their purchase and support of Disney products and to boycott the Disney theme parks and stores if they continue this anti-Christian and anti-family trend;

FINALLY, BE IT RESOLVED, That the Convention requests the Executive Committee to send a copy of this resolution to Michael Eisner, CEO of the Disney Co., and to encourage the Southern Baptist family to support this resolution with our purchasing power, letters and influence.

Righteous are you, O Lord, and your laws are right. The statutes you have laid down are righteous; they are fully trustworthy. My zeal wears me out, for my enemies ignore your words. Your promises have been thoroughly tested, and your servant loves them. (Psalm 119:137-140)

Far be it from us as Christians, who are responsible for handling God's wealth for God's glory, that we should provide essential financial support to the very people and institutions whose activities are undermining the biblical values we hold dear. Consider how the moral foundations of our society have been shaken in recent decades—can you doubt that we are under attack? We are in a war over whose values will prevail in America, not only for the rest of this century but for the next. Not just for our children, but for their children. Yet some of us routinely and indifferently subsidize those who most despise us.

Our God is righteous. He does not need to conform to a righteous standard; He is the standard. Because He is righteous, we must regard what belongs to Him, such as the money we manage, as consecrated for righteous purposes. The thought of turning God's wealth over to His enemies, to use against His glorious name and His church, should be abhorrent to the faithful steward. We must take care to avoid financing activities that lead others into temptation and sin.

Whoever welcomes a little child like this in my name welcomes me. But if anyone causes one of these little ones who believe in me to sin, it would be better for him to have a large millstone hung around his neck and to be drowned in the depths of the sea. Woe to the world because of the things that cause people to sin! Such things must come, but woe to the man through whom they come! (Matthew 18:5-7)

Because the Lord is righteous, we have an obligation to withhold support, insofar as possible, from those businesses whose corporate activities either actively mock or passively undermine the biblical values that God has given as the basis for righteousness in society. This can be done most effectively by boycotting their products and services. Withholding investment support from their stocks and bonds can also be helpful if done in a concerted fashion. I believe both of these strategies should play a central role in the spending and investing decisions of every follower of Christ. ◆

CHAPTER PREVIEW

Investing That Glorifies God
Seeks His Wisdom

The heavens declare the glory of God; the skies proclaim the work of his hands. Day after day they pour forth speech; night after night they display knowledge. There is no speech or language where their voice is not heard. Their voice goes out into all the earth, their words to the ends of the world. In the heavens he has pitched a tent for the sun, which is like a bridegroom coming forth from his pavilion, like a champion rejoicing to run his course. It rises at one end of the heavens and makes its circuit to the other; nothing is hidden from its heat.

The law of the Lord is perfect, reviving the soul.

The statutes of the Lord are trustworthy, making wise the simple.

The precepts of the Lord are right, giving joy to the heart.

The commands of the Lord are radiant, giving light to the eyes.

The fear of the Lord is pure, enduring forever.

The ordinances of the Lord are sure and altogether righteous.

They are more precious than gold, than much pure gold; they are sweeter than honey, than honey from the comb. By them is your servant warned; in keeping them there is great reward. Who can discern his errors? Forgive my hidden faults. Keep your servant also from willful sins; may they not rule over me. Then will I be blameless, innocent of great transgression. May the words of my mouth and the meditation of my heart be pleasing in your sight, O Lord, my Rock and my Redeemer.
(Psalm 19:1-14)

The last out. The eighteenth hole. The final buzzer. The checkered flag. The runner's tape. Match point.

In sports, all the players know where the "finish line" is. They can then train themselves and compete accordingly. But in the world of investing, very few clear rules are acknowledged by all the players. It's a kind of come-as-you-are, no-holds-barred event. You're free to participate without any preparation, training, or study of any kind. You don't need a doctor's certificate showing you're financially "fit" and able to afford the risk. Nor do you need a diploma as proof you've studied the disciplines involved and may actually know what you're doing. If you show up with a few dollars, you're almost invariably invited in.

This ease of entry usually makes people feel qualified to play. The financial media assure you that others with investment training similar to yours (that is, little or none) are making large sums with just minutes a day of effort. Surely, it can't be all that difficult. So you begin your playing days. That's what I was drawn to in the late 1960s, and it's what I returned to in the late 1970s.

Susie and I returned home to Kentucky just in time for Christmas 1974. We had reached a point in the growth and staffing of the new department I had helped build . . .

. . . that one of my assistants could now take over. The ministry-wide fund-raising activities, such as direct mail, had been brought together under one coordinated strategy, and the Executive Seminars were going very well. Meanwhile, we were getting a little homesick for family and friends, not to mention Kentucky's cold winters and green summers. I wasn't eager to return to the restaurant business, but industry trends and cultural changes were beginning to threaten our long-term profitability—a hard look at our future plans and prospects was in order. Bill and Vonette Bright thoughtfully gave us a "going away" party at their home. The pictures we still have of that evening always generate warm memories of the many friends we made on Crusade staff during our time there.

The next few years of my business life were primarily devoted to selling the family business. In one sense, it was a difficult decision to make. I was the third generation of our family to operate restaurants in Louisville; my grandfather had opened the first one in 1922. A family tradition that spans more than half a century is not easily abandoned. Yet, it was increasingly obvious that smaller "chains" like ours (we operated six restaurants) could not long survive against the money and marketing muscle of the large national companies. It was quickly becoming an uphill battle to maintain our market share. Add to the equation that my heart wasn't really in it, and it seemed the most prudent course was to sell the business while it was still performing well. With the consent of my mother (who owned one-half of the stock), we began a process that took almost three years to complete.

On the day in 1977 when I walked away from closing the final sale of the last of the restaurants . . .

. . . I was a happy man. I was young. I was deeply in love with my wife and three boys (God gave us Matthew while we were living in California). I still had a fair amount of money in the bank (despite my past errors of judgment). I was healthy. And I was unemployed.

I took advantage of my free time to pursue my ministry interests. I enjoyed serving on the founding board of directors of Crusade's Christian Embassy project in Washington, D.C. I was invited to be part of a group of businessmen and professional athletes who were starting a new training ministry—Pro Athletes Outreach—which was designed to "win, build, and send" pro players from our major sports. I started a Christian Business Men's Committee in Louisville. I had a lot of fun, and seeing the results from these efforts has been extremely satisfying. But our financial resources weren't so great that we could simply live off our investment income; I knew that I soon needed to make a career decision.

Initially, I didn't know what new direction my business life should take, but I did have a few thoughts as to the general framework. First, I recognized that my innate personality (according to the widely used Performax personal profile test) had a "perfectionist" bent. I'm the kind of person who gives attention to detail, has high quality standards, and likes to have an orderly working environment. Second, I considered my entrepreneurial background—I had always worked for my family or myself. Once I make a decision, I like to see it implemented quickly and efficiently. I wasn't sure how well I would function within a slow-moving bureaucracy. Third, I determined that I would never again participate in any project where my success or failure primarily resided with someone else. I would never forget my $100,000 tennis racket and other souvenirs. If I was going to fail, it would be entirely due to my own shortcomings. Finally, I still had an interest in finance and the investment markets. *Is that appropriate?* I wondered. *Last time I had gotten involved, it had almost taken over my life. Would I be like an alcoholic opening a tavern?*

As Susie and I prayed about these matters, our thoughts eventually came together in a decision that I should form an investment advisory firm . . .

. . . with one of my closest friends, Doug Van Meter, as my partner. After ten years as a stockbroker, he was ready to make a change. There were many reasons, both personal and professional, for this, but the one that most stands out in my mind after all these years is that he wanted to get away from the potential conflicts of interest he routinely faced.

Doug wanted to give his customers the very best service and investment counsel. He wanted to honor his commitment to Christ. And yes, he wanted to provide for his young and growing family. Often, he was thrust into situations where he felt these goals might be on a collision course. The primary culprit was a sys-

Why do you call me "Lord, Lord," and do not do what I say? I will show you what he is like who comes to me and hears my words and puts them into practice. He is like a man building a house, who dug down deep and laid the foundation on rock. When a flood came, the torrent struck that house but could not shake it, because it was well built. But the one who hears my words and does not put them into practice is like a man who built a house on the ground without a foundation. The moment the torrent struck that house, it collapsed and its destruction was complete.
Luke 6:46–49

All Scripture is God-breathed and is useful for teaching, rebuking, correcting and training in righteousness, so that the man of God may be thoroughly equipped for every good work.
2 Timothy 3:16–17

For the Lord gives wisdom, and from his mouth come knowledge and understanding.
Proverbs 2:6

tem that rewards stockbrokers based on their sales success (commissions earned) rather than their investment success (customers' profits). When my friend resigned his position in order to team up with me and launch our new company, Wall Street's loss was my gain. He taught me much about the technical aspects of investments and displayed a sincere interest in the welfare of our clients.

That was eighteen years ago. Since that time, my understanding of the investing process has been shaped by the books and financial periodicals I have read, the up and down markets I have experienced, and the mistakes I have made (will they never end?). Most of this book has been devoted to laying down for you a foundational understanding of how investments and the various markets work. Unavoidably, the emphasis has been on the technical and logistical basics. In this chapter, I want to focus almost exclusively on what is needed in terms of attitude and practice to be successful. It has been fascinating for me to discover that these principles, many of which I learned the hard way, were to be found in God's Word all along if only I had known where to look! Wisdom for investments, and all of life, can be found in the Bible.

Perhaps the most difficult aspect of applying what follows is trying to erase from your mind the preconceived ideas you have about what it means to be a "savvy" investor. If you're like most people . . .

. . . you have accumulated years of impressions concerning financial wizardry from the secular world. Most of them, however, are nothing more than a collection of contradictions, misconceptions, and false assumptions. You must try to forget what you *think you know* so you can learn what you *need to know*.

As you read this chapter, I am hoping to change more than your opinions; I am hoping to begin changing your convictions. An opinion is merely your preference when choosing among several alternatives. It's when you prefer one type of vacation over another or prefer one music style over another music style. An opinion is merely a personal preference. But a conviction is rooted in your moral value system. Your convictions will not change without your values changing also. And the values you hold are what you draw from when setting personal boundaries. In *Changes That Heal*, psychologist Henry Cloud describes boundaries this way:

> *Boundaries, in a broad sense, are lines or things that mark a limit, bound, or border. In a psychological sense, boundaries are the realization of our own person apart from others. This sense of separateness forms the basis of personal identity. It says what we are and what we are not, what we will choose and what we will not choose, what we will endure and what we will not, what we feel and what we will not feel, what we like and what we do not like, and what we want and what we do not want. Boundaries, in short, define us. In the same way that a physical boundary defines where a property line begins and ends, a psychological and spiritual boundary defines who we are and who we are not.*[1]

[1]Henry Cloud, Changes That Heal, [Grand Rapids: Zondervan, 1992], p. 92.

So when I say I want to help change your convictions, I'm talking about a foundational part of your identity—how you see yourself spiritually and your moral responsibilities. It all follows from the earlier chapters in this section: because God is the glorious Creator/Sovereign and we are the creature/stewards, we see knowing Him as the true treasure, and because we cherish Him, it is our heart's desire to build His kingdom and uphold His righteousness.

What convictions do I hope to change? The ones that have crept in from worldly "wisdom." Convictions that say it's OK . . .

. . . or merely a matter of personal preference whether you borrow to invest, invest in limited partnerships that involve cosigning for debt, frequently adjust your portfolio in response to changing world events, always seek the maximum return, or invest for short-term results. Such tactics may occasionally be profitable, but more often they are self-destructive. In any event, they go against God's wisdom as given to us in His Word. We need to learn to think with new minds in order to understand His will.

> *I urge you, brothers, in view of God's mercy, to offer your bodies as living sacrifices, holy and pleasing to God—this is your spiritual act of worship. Do not conform any longer to the pattern of this world, but be transformed by the renewing of your mind. Then you will be able to test and approve what God's will is—his good, pleasing and perfect will. (Romans 12:1-2)*

As we renew our minds, we not only see more clearly who God is; we also gain insight into our own natures.

As investors, we are our own worst enemies. This observation stems not only from my eighteen years of practical experience, but also is confirmed by God's Word. Given our fallen natures, it would be surprising if we *weren't* the primary problem we face when investing. Consider for a moment the kind of people we are. The failings of our wisdom, our motives, our emotions, and our clarity of vision are well documented in the Scriptures.

◆ **Our wisdom is flawed.**

> *Let no person deceive himself. If any one among you supposes that he is wise in this age—let him discard his [worldly] discernment and recognize himself as dull, stupid and foolish, without [true] learning and scholarship; let him become a fool that he may become [really] wise. For this world's wisdom is foolishness—absurdity and stupidity—with God. (1 Corinthians 3:18-19, Amplified)*

◆ **Our motivations are impure.**

> *The heart is deceitful above all things, and it is exceedingly perverse and corrupt and severely, mortally sick! Who can know it [perceive, understand, be acquainted with his own heart and mind]? (Jeremiah 17:9, Amplified)*

◆ Our emotions are powerful.

For I know that nothing good dwells within me, that is, in my flesh. I can will what is right, but I cannot perform it. I have the intention and urge to do what is right, but no power to carry it out. (Romans 7:18, Amplified)

◆ Our vision is limited.

Come now, you who say, Today or tomorrow we will go into such and such a city and spend a year there to carry on our business and make money. Yet you do not know [the least thing] about what may happen tomorrow. . . . You boast [falsely] in your presumption and your self-conceit. (James 4:13-14, 16, Amplified)

As we renew our minds, we can begin to put proper boundaries in place that not only define our Christian priorities and values but *will also serve to protect us from the markets and ourselves. The reason for having an individualized investment strategy is to provide these needed boundaries.*

You begin by acknowledging that you need help. Your financial life has no central focus. You make decisions as situations arise based on what you've read is best, what a friend says is best, or just by throwing a dart and hoping for the best. You find yourself pulled in all directions, looking something like this:

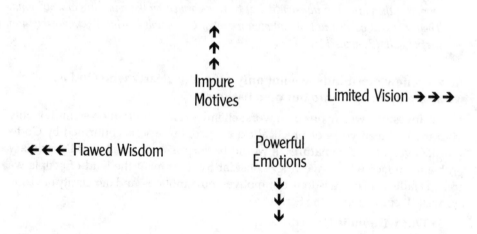

Having a specific strategy in place helps *contain and focus* your impulses by providing boundaries. It boxes you in and takes away your freedom to do what you might want. But it offers a new kind of freedom — the freedom to do what you should. It gives you a sense of perspective and a new way of knowing what's "right" for you. The illustration on the next page shows four biblically based boundaries to a focused investment strategy: objective, mechanical criteria for decision making; a portfolio that is broadly diversified; a long-term, get-rich-slow perspective; and a manager's (rather than owner's) mentality. Let's now look at how these boundaries come into play in practical ways in everyday situations.

Boundary One:
Using mechanical guidelines rather than your own intuition and judgment.

He who trusts in himself is a fool, but he who walks in wisdom is kept safe. (Proverbs 28:26)

But the fruit of the Spirit is . . . self-control. (Galatians 5:22-23)

Mechanical guidelines require that you develop objective criteria you follow for your buying and selling decisions. One example would be to use the risk matrix (pages 167-170) to select a specific mix of stocks and fixed income investments. The allocations that are laid out for you provide explicit, objective boundaries to help you diversify according to your risk tolerance and age. They help make your investment shopping purposeful. Such boundaries protect you from giving in to sales presentations on some "really attractive" investment that you don't need at present.

Another example would be setting value criteria for timing your stock buying and selling. Using the benchmarks explained on pages 244-245, you might decide to take profits in any stock once its price/earnings ratio reaches a certain predetermined level. Or you might look to buy underpriced stocks using the price/dividend or price/book ratios.

Guidelines can help you control your losses. When you buy a stock or fund that doesn't perform as you hope, it can be difficult emotionally to admit it didn't work out. People often hold onto weak companies for years hoping to sell when they can "get even." This is a form of denial; the loss has already taken place. This emotional trap can be avoided by a mechanical guideline that says, "I'll sell if it drops x% from where I bought it because if it gets that low, there's a probability I misjudged the situation."

The dollar-cost-averaging and value-averaging strategies (see chapter 16) use mechanical guidelines to help you know how much to invest and when. The discipline imposed by these programs is helpful because our judgment tends to be unduly influenced by news events of the moment. There will always be bad news, but news is rarely as bad or good as it might first appear. These guidelines protect you from overreacting (along with everyone else) to the crisis or euphoria of the moment.

The markets go to extremes because they are driven by emotions, not reason. Also, professional money managers are afraid of getting left behind and looking bad (they want job security too, you know), so they go along with the crowd and panic like everyone else. Mechanical guidelines help you harness the powerful emotions that often cause investors to do precisely the wrong thing at precisely the wrong time. Mechanical rules may appear dull, but that's actually a virtue—

the most successful market strategies tend to be dull because they are measured, not spontaneous.

Before leaving the subject of emotions, may I suggest another idea about how to remain objective? Don't give investment advice to friends and family, and don't tell them what your investment holdings are. It's not a question of secrecy; it's the tendency you'll have to lose your objectivity about the investments in question. It's important to remain flexible and follow your guidelines, right? But how can you take a loss in this great stock or fund that you've told everybody about? You might find yourself thinking, *This is humiliating. Everybody will think I'm an idiot. Better to at least wait until I can get out at "break-even" so I can save face.* Oops, that's exactly the kind of emotional decision-making you want to avoid.

Boundary Two:
Building a broadly diversified portfolio to protect against the uncertainties of the future.

> *Give portions to seven, yes to eight, for you do not know what disaster may come upon the land. (Ecclesiastes 11:2)*

> *But the fruit of the Spirit is . . . peace. (Galatians 5:22)*

Acknowledging our limited vision is to remember the reality check from Jurassic Park (page 382). Be honest with yourself and say, "Not only do I not know what the future holds, none of the experts do, either." Since we don't (and can't) know the future, we can never know in advance with certainty which investments will turn out most profitably. That is the rationale for diversifying—spreading out your portfolio into various areas so that you won't be overinvested in any hard-hit areas and you'll have at least some investments in the most rewarding areas.

Remember Ron Blue's analysis that I shared with you at the end of chapter 18? As far back as he could remember, there has been economic uncertainty and reasons to question our future prosperity. Yet, although business cycles come and go, we stand on the brink of the next century and the U.S. still has the strongest economy on the globe. Who was forecasting this even ten years ago? Our vision into the future is indeed limited!

Once you accept that "nobody knows," it makes a lot of sense to diversify and relax. Then, here are some of the things you're free to do:

◆ **Ask hard questions of anyone trying to sell you an investment.** Make them support and document every assertion, promise, or guarantee. You don't need to let them intimidate you anymore, because you know the truth: nobody knows for sure, no matter how confident they sound, whether what they're recommending will truly turn out to be the best for you. Then, before you act, review the decision-making guidelines I suggested on pages 196-198.

◆ **Ignore all forecasts by the "experts." They're guessing.** There's a kind of Newton's Law of Motion for economics: For every forecast by a group of experts with impressive credentials, there's an equal and opposite forecast by another group of experts with equally impressive credentials. Besides, if you've ever noticed, most forecasts seem to assume that the current trends (whatever they are) will continue. If they *were* to have any value, we'd need to know when the current trends will be reversed.

◆ **Ignore the media's explanations for why the markets are acting as they are. They're rationalizing.** Almost every item of economic news has both positive and negative implications, depending on what you want. For example, lower interest rates are good news if you're a borrower, bad news if you're a saver; a strong dollar is good news for importers, bad news for exporters. When the news is released, the media watch the markets' reactions. The next day, they merely emphasize *that aspect of the news* that the markets paid most attention to. If lower rates cause the stock market to go up, the media say it's because low rates are good for the economy; if the market goes down, the media say it's because low rates encourage renewed inflation. You should recognize that the media's explanations of market behavior are merely after-the-fact rationalizations.

◆ **Ignore most of the direct mail that you receive promoting an investment advisory letter. They're grossly exaggerating.** I'm talking primarily about the ones with the bold-letter "hype" that promise easy or guaranteed profits due to their consistent accuracy in making predictions about the markets. Such claims are meaningless—every newsletter writer is correct in some of his expectations and wrong about others. Some are right more than they're wrong, but nobody is consistently right. There's always a possibility that you can lose your money in the markets—it's irresponsible to imply otherwise. Such claims by any newsletter writer (or broker or anyone else) should immediately raise a red flag in your mind and call his credibility into question.

Boundary Three:
Developing a long-term, get-rich-slow perspective.

> *Dishonest money dwindles away, but he who gathers money little by little makes it grow. (Proverbs 13:11)*

> *But the fruit of the Spirit is . . . patience. (Galatians 5:22)*

Fewer things cause investors more losses than a short-term, get-rich-quick orientation to decision making. Patience, a fruit of the Spirit, is in short supply among investors today. Many have the attention span of a strobe light. A long-term view is extremely productive when investing; such a perspective has three major benefits:

❶ **It allows you time to do first things first.** I've already discussed the importance of being debt-free before proceeding into stocks, bonds, and other investments (other than those in your retirement plans). Once that foundation is laid, you can handle market risk with greater confidence. In the face of market setbacks, a long-term view says, "I'm investing with my surplus funds. This sell-off is no threat to my immediate well-being. I've got time to be patient and wait for the recovery."

❷ It allows you to let those "once-in-a-lifetime, you-don't-want-to-miss-this-one-but-you-must-act-now" deals go by. You've got plenty of time, and you don't want to invest in anything you haven't had time to carefully investigate and pray about. Trust me—there's always another day and another "great deal."

❸ It allows you to be more relaxed when your judgment turns out less than perfect (surprise!). For example, those times when the stock you just bought goes lower (which it always will) or the one you just sold goes even higher (which it always will). Why let that frustrate you? In your saner moments, you know it's extremely unlikely you're going to buy at the exact low or sell at the exact high. Taking the long view says, "It doesn't matter whether I bought at $14 when I could have bought at $12. The important thing is that I followed my plan. Over time, I know my plan will get me where I want to go."

Boundary Four:
Accepting management responsibility for your decisions, which leads you to acquire a knowledge of the basics and seek counsel when making important decisions.

> *Every prudent man acts out of knowledge, but a fool exposes his folly. (Proverbs 13:16)*
>
> *But the fruit of the Spirit is . . . faithfulness. (Galatians 5:22)*

Ultimately, you are accountable for what happens. You have been given a stewardship responsibility that you cannot delegate away. You can delegate authority to someone else to make certain investment decisions, but you cannot delegate your responsibility for the results that come from those decisions.

Once you "own" this fact, you will take your management obligations even more seriously. Many Christians do not see themselves as "investors" simply because they don't have large stock portfolios. I believe they have a misconception as to what investing involves. As I pointed out in the first chapter, *investing decisions involve deciding what you will do without today in order that you might have more of something later.*

Cutting back on your spending (sacrifice convenience/luxury) in order to get debt-free (gain peace of mind and freedom) is an investing decision. Buying a used car rather than a new one (sacrifice status and ego) in order to start saving for a house someday (gain shelter and security) is an investing decision. Keeping your savings in money market funds instead of bond funds (sacrifice yield) in order to have your principal safe (gain stability and flexibility) is an investing decision.

Knowing that managing this part of your life responsibly is a God-given task will help you to become more realistic about your needs in four areas:

◆ **More realistic about your need for additional knowledge.** You accept that you must learn certain financial and investing basics. You can't just say, "Oh, I don't have the time (or interest or intellect) for that." You understand that some study will be necessary.

◆ **More realistic about the limitations of what investing can accomplish for you.** As you study, you learn that rates of return over the long haul tend to be in the 8%-12% range, not 15%-20% as many imagine. The idea that you will readily make large returns to bail you out of your problems is a dream. And mixed in that 8%-12% average will be good years (gains of 20% to 30%) and bad years (losses of 10% to 20%). It's not a smooth road.

◆ **More realistic about the strengths and weaknesses of the investment industry.** It does not have your best interests, first and foremost, at heart. It is awash in conflicts of interest (brokers get paid for selling securities, publishers get paid for selling magazines, financial networks get paid for attracting viewers). Your naïveté will diminish as you develop a healthy skepticism. On the plus side, America is still a land of great economic opportunity for those who are willing to diligently apply themselves and who do not easily give up.

◆ **More realistic about the markets themselves.** You'll no longer believe that "the pros" know something you don't, and you'll see the widely erratic swings as being evidence of emotionalism rather than calm reason. You'll discover there are few absolutes, other than preservation of your capital and survival, to guide you as you navigate the tumultuous storms and cross-currents.

These doses of realism will be very, very good for you.

Investing that glorifies God seeks His wisdom.

The wisdom found in God's Word is there for our protection and His glory. In financial matters, it points to God Himself as our true treasure and helps us see that *we* are the ones who suffer when we seek our treasure elsewhere.

Let's not settle for the creation when we can have the Creator.

Let's not settle for the temporal when we can have the eternal.

Let's not settle for knowing man's wisdom when we can know God's wisdom— Christ Himself.

> *Where is the wise man? Where is the scholar? Where is the philosopher of this age? Has not God made foolish the wisdom of the world? For since in the wisdom of God the world through its wisdom did not know him, God was pleased through the foolishness of what was preached to save those who believe. Jews demand miraculous signs and Greeks look for wisdom, but we preach Christ crucified: a stumbling block to Jews and foolishness to Gentiles, but to those whom God has called, both Jews and Greeks, Christ the power of God and the wisdom of God. For the foolishness of God is wiser than man's wisdom, and the weakness of God is stronger than man's strength.*

> *Brothers, think of what you were when you were called. Not many of you were wise by*

human standards; not many were influential; not many were of noble birth. But God chose the foolish things of the world to shame the wise; God chose the weak things of the world to shame the strong. He chose the lowly things of this world and the despised things — and the things that are not — to nullify the things that are, so that no one may boast before him. It is because of him that you are in Christ Jesus, who has become for us wisdom from God — that is, our righteousness, holiness and redemption. Therefore, as it is written: "Let him who boasts boast in the Lord." (1 Corinthians 1:20-31)

May God grant us the grace to know Him. To seek for nothing else, and to settle for nothing less. ◆

Investing That Glorifies God Enjoys His Blessings

Delight yourself in the Lord and he will give you the
desires of your heart. Commit your way to the Lord; trust
in him and he will do this: He will make your righteousness
shine like the dawn, the justice of your cause like the noonday sun.
(Psalm 37:4-6)

As the Scripture says, "Anyone who trusts in him will never
be put to shame." For there is no difference between Jew and Gentile—
the same Lord is Lord of all and richly blesses all who call on him.
(Romans 10:11-12)

And my God will meet all your needs
according to his glorious riches in Christ Jesus.
To our God and Father be glory forever and ever. Amen.
(Philippians 4:19-20)

**I have concluded that I have very little ability to discern what
is valuable in life and what isn't.**

I don't always see clearly which experiences are blessings and which ones do me
harm. In fact, it's probably safe to say that I really don't even know — with complete certainty — what I truly want.

That being the case, one of the most exciting steps I can take is to pray and ask God
for things. I neither know which requests He'll grant nor have the slightest insight into
how He'll work through circumstances in granting those requests He does. But I'm learning it's usually in the most improbable and unexpected ways.

**After about five years of hard work, Doug and I had built our
advisory business to what could fairly be called a "successful" level.
Our investment performance results . . .**

. . . had frequently placed in the top 5% among advisers nationwide. Money goes
where it's treated best, and we had attracted enough clients to the point that we were
both taking home six-figure incomes. Plus, I still had time for my ministry interests. All
in all, things were working out pretty well.

Then, starting around 1985, I entered a period where I seemed to have the reverse Midas
touch. In about a three-year span, my financial roof fell in thanks to a variety of unrelated
events: a home that took three years to sell, unprecedented losses in my personal futures
trading account, and a costly business venture in South Carolina, to name a few.

The summer of 1987 was the worst period of my business life. In April, with the
Dow around 2300, we had sold all stock funds and placed our clients 100% into money
market funds. We did this because we felt the market had risen too far, too fast. The
environment had become one of high risk. As the Dow continued to make new highs
over the summer months (and everybody "knew" it was going to 3000), we began losing clients to other firms who had no such reservations about risk. Our warnings to our
departing clients fell on deaf ears. I'm sure many felt we were out of touch with the
realities of the market. In truth, they and their new money managers were the ones out
of touch, as the October crash violently demonstrated. In a single day, the Dow Jones
dropped more than 500 points, and it did not recover to its former level for two years.
The crash vindicated our caution, but it was too late to stabilize our client base. The
defections dealt a major blow to our company and required Doug and me to take dras-
tic salary cuts and make other expense-related adjustments.

**So there I was facing substantial business and personal financial pressures
that I would never have dreamed of a few years earlier. And I was asking . . .**

. . . "Lord, why is this happening to me? I travel and speak in Your name. I work
and give diligently for Your causes. How come You're treating me like this? Please get
me out of this mess. Please reassure me that everything's going to be all right. But most
of all, please let me know that You're still here with me."

You know what the Lord said to me? Nothing. I've never heard from the Lord *directly* in all my life. I know some people who have, but I never have. However, the Lord does speak to me by giving me ideas and impressions as I read and meditate in His Word. And, over time, the answer to my pleading question came. It was as if He said:

"You prayed that you could become mature, didn't you? I'm teaching you how to depend on Me more."

"You prayed for more faith, didn't you? I'm giving you a chance to trust Me more."

"You prayed that you could be used to minister to others, didn't you? I'm training you so you can serve Me more."

"You prayed that you might know Me better, didn't you? I'm helping you to seek Me more."

"You prayed that you might glorify Me with your life, didn't you? I'm refining you more."

When we pray prayers that contain such "spiritual" requests, we can have confidence we're praying according to God's will. We expect Him to grant us, in His own timing, these qualities of the Christian life we're seeking. But I think that subconsciously we must believe that God answers them with a kind of supernatural lightning bolt. Something like, "Well, bless your heart, child, here's all the faith, love, and Christlikeness you'll ever need." Zap!

Well, unfortunately, it doesn't usually work that way.

Do you want to mature in your Christian walk? Then expect some suffering.

Not only so, but we also rejoice in our sufferings, because we know that suffering produces perseverance; perseverance, character; and character, hope. And hope does not disappoint us, because God has poured out his love into our hearts by the Holy Spirit, whom he has given us. (Romans 5:3-5)

Do you want to have your faith strengthened? Then expect your faith to be tested.

Consider it pure joy, my brothers, whenever you face trials of many kinds, because you know that the testing of your faith develops perseverance. Perseverance must finish its work so that you may be mature and complete, not lacking anything. (James 1:2-4)

Do you want God to use you to minister to others? Then expect God to first comfort you during your own pain.

Praise be to the God and Father of our Lord Jesus Christ, the Father of compassion and the God of all comfort, who comforts us in all our troubles, so that we can comfort those in any trouble with the comfort we ourselves have received from God. (2 Corinthians 1:3-4)

Do you want to know God better? Then expect to give up the things of this world that are holding you back.

But whatever was to my profit I now consider loss for the sake of Christ. What is more, I consider everything a loss compared to the surpassing greatness of knowing Christ Jesus my Lord, for whose sake I have lost all things. I consider them rubbish, that I may gain Christ and be found in him. . . . I want to know Christ and the power of his resurrection and the fellowship of sharing in his sufferings. (Philippians 3:7-10)

Do you want to glorify Him with your life? Then expect to go through trials.

In this you greatly rejoice, though now for a little while you may have had to suffer grief in all kinds of trials. These have come so that your faith — of greater worth than gold, which perishes even though refined by fire — may be proved genuine and may result in praise, glory and honor when Jesus Christ is revealed. (1 Peter 1:6-7)

Most Christians, at one time or another, will ask God why He allows pain, suffering, and disappointment . . .

. . . to touch His children (in general) and touch *us* (in particular). When we meet the Lord face-to-face, we'll have an opportunity to ask Him in person (although seeing His glory may be all the answer we need). I wouldn't be surprised if part of the answer turns out to be: "Those things happened *because I was answering your prayers, in order to give you what you asked for."*

As I began to gain an insight into this, I found myself uplifted. Trials are all the more difficult if they seem to be needless or a waste. Once you begin to see that they are purposeful, it's a great thing because then you know that (1) they will come to an end when the purpose is accomplished, (2) you will somehow, in some way, have gained something of great value, and (3) you will have glorified God by trusting Him and giving Him time to work.

A passage that was very encouraging to me during this time was Jeremiah 29:10-14. God was revealing to the Israelites why they were having the excruciating experience of being taken as slaves into the Babylonian captivity.

[10]This is what the Lord says: "When seventy years are completed for Babylon, I will come to you and fulfill my gracious promise to bring you back to this place. [11]For I know the plans I have for you," declares the Lord, "plans to prosper you and not to harm you, plans to give you hope and a future. [12]Then you will call upon me and come and pray to me, and I will listen to you. [13]You will seek me and find me when you seek me with all your heart. [14]I will be found by you," declares the Lord, "and will bring you back from captivity."

Here are the encouraging truths I found in these verses:

◆ Trials eventually come to an end, and God can be absolutely counted upon to fulfill His promises (verse 10).

◆ God is still thinking about us, even when we're feeling lonely in our trials (verse 11). He is listening to our heartfelt prayers (verse 12).

◆ The only thoughts that God has toward us are thoughts of peace that include a future that is hopeful and good (verse 11).

◆ God allows our trials to come because they are necessary to accomplish His purpose in our lives (verse 11).

◆ God's purpose is that we would seek Him (verse 13).

◆ God allows Himself to be found when we search for Him with all our heart. He purposes to ultimately bring about our restoration (verses 13-14).

In this passage, the Israelites have been removed from their land and torn from their possessions, yet God does not tell them to seek the restoration of their land. He does not tell them to seek their possessions. He does not tell them to seek their freedom. He tells them to seek but one thing—Himself. And one way that God has of causing us to seek Him wholeheartedly is by allowing us to lose those other things that we highly prize.

So I knew I needed to seek God, be patient, and wait. I *wanted* to please God; I wanted to trust God. But the circumstances . . .

. . . around me were so utterly discouraging. It's not always easy to expect the best and believe that everything will work out for our good. To the Israelites in exile, seventy years must have seemed like an eternity, and three years can seem like seventy when you're badly hurting.

I concentrated my reading and devotional times in books that gave me hope, and I repeatedly read Job and the Psalms. In addition to Scripture, I read *The God of All Comfort* by Hannah Whitall Smith. I read Amy Carmichael. I read *Disappointment with God* by Philip Yancey. I read *Desiring God* by John Piper. They were all tremendously encouraging.

During this time, I discovered what it means to give to God out of my poverty rather than out of my surplus. The gift of two years of voluntary service in the 1970s paled in comparison to the effort of one week of walking with God during the tough times in the 1980s and saying to Him, "I still love You. I still trust You. I am not offended. I am doing the very best I can to believe You are working everything out together for my good." The two years were offered when I was on top and life was good; the week was given when I was on the bottom and circumstances were bleak. In a fashion similar to the widow and her mite, I believe a single week of "hoping against hope" can be more pleasing and glorifying to God than a two-year missionary journey.

Perhaps you have had occasion to survey the landscape of your life and found very little evidence that God has "plans to prosper you and not to harm you, plans to give you a hope and a future." May I encourage you . . .

. . . to immerse your mind daily in words that will help you to know God more intimately and that will remind you that your God is always present, invariably loving, inevitably faithful, and absolutely worthy of all your confidence. Consider the promises of God found later in Jeremiah: God is revealing in greater detail what it will be like when the trial His people are going through in Babylon has served its purpose. God declares in Jeremiah 32:

> They will be my people, and I will be their God. I will give them singleness of heart and action, so that they will always fear me for their own good and the good of their children after them. I will make an everlasting covenant with them: I will never stop doing good to them, and I will inspire them to fear me, so that they will never turn away from me. I will rejoice in doing them good and will assuredly plant them in this land with all my heart and soul. (Jeremiah 32:38-41)

Those are tremendous promises. In sharing His father's heart, God promises He will

Recommended Resource
The Pleasures of God: Meditations on God's Delight in Being God
by John Piper

This is one of my very favorite books! Starting with Scriptures that show our God is a happy God, John Piper goes on to look at various aspects of God's happiness. Chapters include:

◆ The Pleasure of God in His Son,

◆ The Pleasure of God in His Creation,

◆ The Pleasure of God in the Prayers of the Upright,

and the one I quote from on the next page,

◆ The Pleasures of God in Doing Good to All Who Hope in Him.

Understanding what gives God pleasure may enable you to know our glorious God better than you have ever known Him before.

"never stop doing good" to you. In *The Pleasures of God*, John Piper looks at the passage this way:

> *He will keep on doing good. He doesn't do good to his children sometimes and bad to them other times. He keeps on doing good and he never will stop doing good for ten thousand ages of ages. When things are going "bad" that does not mean God has stopped doing good. It means he is shifting things around to get them in place for more good, if you will go on loving him. He works all things together for good "for those who love him" (Romans 8:28). "No good thing does he withhold from those who walk uprightly" (Psalm 84:11). "Lo, it was for my welfare that I had great bitterness" (Isaiah 38:17). "It is good for me that I was afflicted, that I might learn your statutes" (Psalm 119:71). . . .*
>
> *But the promise is greater yet. Not only does God promise not to turn away from doing good to us, he says, "I will rejoice in doing them good" (Jeremiah 32:41). "The Lord will again take delight in prospering you" (Deuteronomy 30:9). He does not bless us begrudgingly. There is a kind of eagerness about the beneficence of God. He does not wait for us to come to him. He seeks us out, because it is his pleasure to do us good. "The eyes of the Lord run to and fro throughout the whole earth, to show his might in behalf of those whose heart is whole toward him" (2 Chronicles 16:9). God is not waiting for us, he is pursuing us. That, in fact, is the literal translation of Psalm 23:6, "Surely goodness and mercy shall pursue me all the days of my life." God loves to show mercy. He is not hesitant or indecisive or tentative in his desires to do good to his people. His anger must be released by a stiff safety lock, but his mercy has a hair trigger. . . .*
>
> *But still the promise is greater. First, God promises not to turn away from doing us good. Then he promises that he will do this good with rejoicing. Finally, he promises that this rejoicing over the good of his people will be with all his heart and with all his soul. . . . When God does good to his people it is not so much like a reluctant judge showing kindness to a criminal whom he finds despicable; it is like a bridegroom showing affection to his bride. And add to this, that with God the honeymoon never ends. He is infinite in power and wisdom and creativity and love. And so he has no trouble sustaining a honeymoon level of intensity; he can foresee all the future quirks of our personality and has decided he will keep what's good for us and change what isn't; he will always be as handsome as he ever was, and will see to it that we get more and more beautiful forever; and he is infinitely creative to think of new things to do together so that there will be no boredom for the next trillion ages of millenniums. . . .*
>
> *When we say that God exults over his people with loud singing, we mean that he exults over those who hope in his love. In this way God maintains his rightful place – the place we love for him to have – at the center of the gospel. There is a condition we must meet in order to know him as our God and be a part of the wonderful covenant in which he never turns away from doing us good but rejoices over us with all his heart and all his soul. That condition is to put our hope in him as the all-satisfying Refuge and Treasure. God takes pleasure in this response with all his heart, because it magnifies the glory of his grace and satisfies the longing of our soul.*[1]

[1] John Piper, The Pleasures of God, [Portland: Multnomah Press, 1991], pp. 189-209. Used by permission.

As I sought the Lord during those days, I opened my heart to whatever He had purposed for me. I had previously assumed I would continue in the investment advisory profession for the remainder of my career; now I wasn't so sure. Perhaps the Lord was using these difficult circumstances to change the direction of my working life. As long as I was financially comfortable and had a large client base, why would I consider anything else?

So, just in case this was part of the agenda (when you're seeking God's leading, you pray a lot of "just in case" prayers), I surrendered to the Lord all aspects of my professional life. If He wanted to rebuild my company, that would be fine. If He wanted me to take a job working for someone else, that would be fine. If He wanted me to leave the business world and go back into full-time ministry work, that would be fine. I was finally in the best place for a child of God to be: "Whatever You want, Lord, before You even reveal it, the answer is yes." I added a little P.S. "If You think it would be OK, I'd like work that's mentally challenging, emotionally satisfying, and which somehow involves a ministry to people."

The answer came unexpectedly (and unrecognized by me at the time) in October of 1989. I was having lunch with longtime friend Larry Burkett . . .

. . . and his ministry associate in charge of their counseling activities, Steve Humphrey. As we discussed the financial challenges facing the average Christian family, they felt what was lacking was a certain kind of monthly investment newsletter with a truly Christian perspective. Larry said there was a great need for a reliable source of information, written with easy-to-understand, "user-friendly" wording, which would guide readers through the investment process step-by-step with instruction and counsel from a biblical perspective. It would help Christians make the varied and often complex investment decisions they face, as well as continually attempt to help its readers "renew their minds" with God's principles.

My initial response was, "You're right. Sounds great—too bad nobody's doing anything like that." It didn't occur to me that *I* should undertake the task—after all, I was an investment manager, not a writer or publisher.

But as the weeks passed, the Lord seemed to keep bringing me back to Larry's comments. The number of investment services and products being offered today is mind-numbing in their variety. The tendency is to feel overwhelmed. The need was obvious. So I began to pray. Though I agreed he had a great idea, I wondered whether I should be the one to do it.

I began to pray for wisdom: "Lord, do You want *me* to try to do this? Well, it would certainly be mentally challenging—I don't have much experience as a writer and none as a publisher. If I could succeed in encouraging my readers, it would be emotionally satisfying because I know from my own experience how important encouragement is in sustaining our hope during the tough times. And to the extent Christians get their finances and investments straightened out and give more to Your work, it would certainly have a ministry component. But Lord, I don't have the experience or the start-up money or the wisdom to pull this off—*I'd have to depend totally on You.*" Hmm. . . .

After many other closed doors and much prayer, Susie and I felt the Lord was indeed orchestrating events so that I would begin moving in that direction. At a time when I was wondering if I should go into publishing, it "just happened" that Doug and Gena Cobb, two of our best friends, had built a successful publishing business centered on a lineup of monthly computer software journals. The Cobb Group is the national leader in its field. Their help, counsel, and prayers were invaluable. The first *Sound Mind Investing* journal was issued in July 1990.

More than six years have now come and gone since the day I bravely had 500 copies of the first issue printed. The start-up phase was physically demanding, emotionally satisfying, financially unprofitable, and spiritually fulfilling. The way in which events have unfolded have reminded Susie and me on several occasions that our God "is able to [carry out His purpose and] do superabundantly, far over and above all that we [dare] ask or think—infinitely beyond our highest prayers, desires, thoughts, hopes or dreams— To Him be glory in the church and in Christ Jesus throughout all generations, for ever and ever" (Ephesians 3:20-21, *Amplified*).

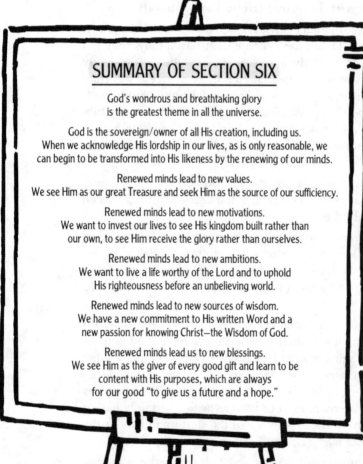

SUMMARY OF SECTION SIX

God's wondrous and breathtaking glory
is the greatest theme in all the universe.

God is the sovereign/owner of all His creation, including us.
When we acknowledge His lordship in our lives, as is only reasonable, we
can begin to be transformed into His likeness by the renewing of our minds.

Renewed minds lead to new values.
We see Him as our great Treasure and seek Him as the source of our sufficiency.

Renewed minds lead to new motivations.
We want to invest our lives to see His kingdom built rather than
our own, to see Him receive the glory rather than ourselves.

Renewed minds lead to new ambitions.
We want to live a life worthy of the Lord and to uphold
His righteousness before an unbelieving world.

Renewed minds lead to new sources of wisdom.
We have a new commitment to His written Word and a
new passion for knowing Christ—the Wisdom of God.

Renewed minds lead us to new blessings.
We see Him as the giver of every good gift and learn to be
content with His purposes, which are always
for our good "to give us a future and a hope."

One of the biggest surprises of my new publishing career has been the number of warm and encouraging letters I receive from my readers. They express appreciation for the fact that they are understanding certain financial and investing matters for the first time, and the new hope they have that they can really take control of their investment lives rather than relying on others. Their enthusiasm, and the number of them that say the journal "is an answer to prayer," is quite humbling. I never expected to feel such a sense of personal kinship with so many people I've never met.

I mention this only to point out how wonderfully God answered my prayer that He would give me a ministry as well as a business. He has, and I've never felt so gratified by anything I've done in my professional life.

Investing that glorifies God enjoys His blessings.

As I indicated at the beginning of this chapter, it's a tricky matter to accurately discern which experiences in life will ultimately work for our good. The reason for this is not that bad things are necessarily good things in disguise, but rather our God is so great that He can take the bad things and *transform* them into good things. He does this because He purposes to use everything in life that we might "be conformed to the likeness of his Son." Knowing that what appears good (wealth and success) can actually be bad for us, and that what appears bad ("trials of many kinds") can actually be good for us, gives one a certain humility in praying.

This truth is beautifully expressed in the *Prayer of an Unknown Confederate Soldier:*

I asked God for strength that I might achieve. I was made weak, that I might learn humbly to obey.

I asked for help, that I might do greater things. I was given infirmity, that I might do better things.

I asked for riches, that I might be happy. I was given poverty, that I might be wise.

I asked for power, that I might have the praise of men. I was given weakness, that I might feel the need of God.

I asked for all things, that I might enjoy life. I was given life, that I might enjoy all things.

I got nothing that I asked for but everything I hoped for. Almost despite myself, my unspoken prayers were answered.

I am, among all men, most richly blessed. (Source Unknown)

We're all looking for peace in an uncertain world. We don't know what the future holds, but we know who holds the future. Our trust in Him is never misplaced. Paul wrote: "For to me, to live is Christ, and to die is gain." *Paul* could say that because dying brought him even more of what he was living for. But today, if for us "to live is business success," then to die is loss. If for us "to live is financial riches," then to die is loss. If for us "to live is the praise of men," then to die is loss. Because dying takes all of those things away. On the day that we die, what wealth we may have will be of zero value to us, of no help or comfort whatsoever. But knowing Him will mean everything. And that's why He is our peace.

If you'll aim your life in the direction of God's glory, you'll enjoy His blessings. They may or may not be material blessings. But in whatever form God sends them, you can be sure they will satisfy your deepest longings. "Praise be to the God and Father of our Lord Jesus Christ, who has blessed us in the heavenly realms with every spiritual blessing in Christ" (Ephesians 1:3).

To conclude this section and my book, I've collected a few of the hundreds of promises God has made to you in His Word. Consider who you are and what you have, and give thanks!

◆ You are *a child of God.*
◆ You are *protected* by the name of Jesus.
◆ You have *peace* with God.
◆ You are *set free* by the truth.
◆ You are *kept* from the Evil One.

◆ You are *free from condemnation.*

◆ You have been *cleansed* by Christ's blood.

◆ You are a *joint heir* with Jesus Christ.

◆ You are *confident* that all things work together for your good.

◆ You are being *conformed* to the image of Christ.

◆ You are *inseparable from the love of God.*

◆ You are more than *a conqueror* through Jesus Christ.

◆ You have *eternal life* in Christ Jesus.

◆ You are *abiding in Christ;* Christ is abiding in you.

◆ You are the *image and the glory* of God.

◆ You are *free of the vicious cycle* of sin and death.

◆ You are *adequate* for anything because your adequacy comes from God.

◆ You are *a new creation* in Christ Jesus.

◆ You are *blessed with every spiritual blessing.*

◆ You are *chosen* by God to be holy and blameless.

◆ You are *eternally secure* in Christ.

◆ You have *wisdom* and insight to know His will.

◆ You are able to walk boldly *into Christ's presence.*

◆ You are *strengthened* with His power through His spirit in the inner man.

◆ You are receiving *exceedingly abundantly above all that you ask or think.*

◆ You are a *citizen* of heaven.

◆ You *don't have to be anxious* about anything.

◆ You are *guarded* by God's peace.

◆ You are *able to do all things through Christ* who strengthens you.

◆ You have *all your needs met* in Christ.

◆ You are *able to walk worthy* of the Lord, fully pleasing to Him.

◆ You've been *delivered* from the kingdom of darkness.

◆ You are *indwelt by Him* in whom all fullness dwells.

◆ You've been presented to God, *holy, blameless, and beyond reproach.*

◆ You are *filled with God's power*, which works mightily in you.

◆ You are *growing* because your nourishment and strength come from God.

◆ You are able to come boldly before His throne of grace and find *mercy* every time.

◆ *He who is in you is greater* than he who is in the world.

◆ You have not been given a spirit of fear, but of *power* and of *love* and of *a sound mind.*

◆ *You are complete in Christ!* ◆

"In your hearts set apart Christ as Lord. Always be prepared to give an answer
to everyone who asks you to give the reason for the hope that you have."
(1 Peter 3:15)

We would not be able to progress very far in our Christian faith apart from the kindnesses
shown to us by others of God's people who were "prepared to give an answer to everyone
who asks." I have been immeasurably helped, encouraged, and inspired along the way by
others who have lived out 1 Peter 3:15 to my benefit. Merely saying thank you, of course, is
an inadequate expression of deep gratitude. But not to say thank you would be to deny the
grace and power of God that reached out through them and changed my view of Him
forever. To the extent this book has been an encouragement to you, you owe thanks as well:

To Claudia Pryor
Thank you, Mom, for taking me to Sunday school at an early age
where I learned about the Savior who loves me.

To Bob and Carole McConnell
Thank you for coming and sharing the wonderful discovery
of the Spirit-filled life. You were faithful, and God honored it.

To Bill and Vonette Bright
Thank you for modeling the Christian life so powerfully that I knew, beyond ever
questioning again, that the gospel must be true. It is the only explanation for your lives.

To Arlis Priest
Thank you for taking a fatherly interest in me and showing me that because "the greatest ability is
avail-ability," even ordinary young businessmen can be used by a great God to minister in the world.

To Ron Dunn
Thank you for helping me realize I was settling for service and that I must continue to
seek Christ; that it was possible to know Him, and know Him, and know Him some more.

To John Piper
(whom I have never met, but would like to)
Thank you for helping me to rediscover that God is breathtaking
and to understand that He is most glorified in me when I am most satisfied in Him.

And Most of All to Susie
Other than our Lord, no one knows you like I do. Others don't know of your tenacity
and faithfulness in prayer. Or of the steadfast trust you have in His goodness even in the
face of crushing disappointments. Or of the deep love you have for His Word and the price
you have paid when standing firm in upholding it. But I know all these things and much more.
And so it is with great insight that I thank the Lord for giving me a wife of noble character.

"A wife of noble character who can find? She is worth far more than rubies.
Her husband has full confidence in her and lacks nothing of value."
(Proverbs 31:10-11)

Financial Briefings

Two Dozen Short Lessons that Can Help Guide Your Financial Planning and Shopping

"I'm relaxing in the jacuzzi watching t.v. when one of those financial interview shows comes on. They're talking about how easy it is to make a killing in high-tech stocks. By that time I've already sold my company and am pretty well set financially, ya know, but of course, who can't always use a little more? So..."

1

Ten Motivating Reasons to Get Debt-Free
By Wilson J. Humber

As appeared in the <u>Sound Mind Investing</u> newsletter in 1996.
Adapted from <u>The Financially Challenged: A Survival Guide for Getting Through the Week, the Month, and the Rest of Your Life</u>
by Wilson J. Humber. Copyright 1995. Published by Moody Press. Used with permission. All rights reserved.

Before we examine ten warnings against debt, let's look at the opposing theological positions concerning debt. One extreme is to assume that the passage "Owe nothing to anyone except to love one another" (Romans 13:8 NASB) is a command to avoid all debt at all times. A few even label debt as a sin. The opposite extreme assumes that debt is acceptable, normal, and often God's way of meeting our needs as He promised to do. My view is that debt is not a sin to avoid, but a dangerous tool which must be used with extreme caution due to its potential for enslaving people in financial bondage. Following are ten reasons I believe debt is extremely dangerous and should be used, if at all, with great care and after much prayer.

1. Debt presumes on the future. Scripture clearly says, "Do not boast about tomorrow, for you do not know what a day may bring forth" (Proverbs 27:1 NASB). When you commit yourself to payments over time, you are presuming: no pay reductions, no loss of job, and no unexpected expenses. That is a dangerous and improbable assumption.

2. Debt lowers your standard of living in the future. Money that you borrow today must be repaid over time along with the cost of renting the money, which is interest.

3. Debt avoids facing life-style decisions. It allows you to make the decision of whether you can afford to buy an item by focusing on the low payment rather than on the cost of the item. The question of whether you can afford it should include all the cost: purchase price, operational expense, and finance charges. Credit is dangerous because it is too easy to say yes to low payments over time and ignore the real decision—can I afford it, and do I need it?

4. Debt places the awesome power of compound interest at work against you. Here is an example for credit card debt. If you borrow $100 on your credit card and make only minimum payments, do you know how long it will take to repay the loan? Would you believe up to thirty years? Items charged on your Mastercard can cost you seven to eight times the purchase price!

5. Debt may delay God's plan for your life. Or it might cause you to forfeit a blessing God had planned to give. Before you obligate yourself to payments give God a chance to provide your needs.

6. Debt evades the necessity of distinguishing wants and desires from real "needs." In our home we have what we call the "I want list." The "I want list" has two rules. First, not more than five items are allowed on the list at one time. Second, we have to wait thirty days after the item is entered on the list before it can be purchased. You would be amazed how many wants and desires fade over the thirty days and the amount of impulse buying that is eliminated. This simple idea has helped to transform me from a chronic impulse buyer into a much better steward of His assets.

7. Debt encourages impulse buying and overspending. The chief financial officer of a national credit card company said that consumers will spend 27% more on plastic than they would with cash or check. Any merchant who accepts plastic will verify that consumers will spend 25% to 30% more with plastic. That is why businesses pay a fee of 1% to 7% of every purchase you make on plastic for the privilege of accepting your credit cards.

8. Debt and credit cards stifle creativity and resourcefulness. If we want something today, we charge it rather than "make do" with what we have. We feel entitled to what we want, when we want it, so we automatically head to the mall, never considering a simpler, less expensive choice: "doing without." It is not fashionable today to resole our shoes, repair our cars, or mend whatever wears out; we simply replace them.

9. Debt and credit cards eliminate margin in our lives. Plastic becomes our margin. Rather than planning what we need and allowing a margin for errors or overruns, we "charge" ahead and spend, thinking that if we must write a check that we don't have sufficient funds to cover, we have overdraft protection with our credit line. Your credit card is not an asset but a potential future liability which becomes a liability when you use it.

10. Debt teaches your children bad habits. Your children will have a casual regard for using credit cards, obtaining car loans, and applying for student loans. When I began counseling young people, I was astounded by the size of the debt load many had accumulated. They had graduated from college by borrowing the costs and living to the limit of their credit cards. They had never considered paying cash for transportation or anything else, and began adult life with a mountain of debt that creates years of financial bondage. ◆

Enjoying the Benefits of a Spending Plan
By Stephen and Amanda Sorenson

As appeared in the <u>Sound Mind Investing</u> newsletter in 1994.
Adapted from <u>Living Smart, Spending Less</u> by Stephen and Amanda Sorenson.

One of the best ways to save money is to allocate it wisely. With a wise spending plan (or a budget, as it is more commonly called) to guide you in spending your resources, you can plug money leaks and take steps to reduce debt. It's also easier to save money for wise purchases and just plain fun times with family and friends.

A spending plan is simply a helpful tool in financial planning. Some people view a spending plan as a whip-cracking slave driver that pushes them in ways they don't want to go. It's true that developing and living by a spending plan is not as much fun initially as spending money any way you want to. However, over time a good plan can give you much greater financial opportunities. Although everyone's financial situation is different, a spending plan offers advantages to everyone:

1. It reveals how you (and your spouse) spend money so you can accurately reduce or eliminate unnecessary spending.

2. It helps you use your current and estimated income more effectively.

3. It gives you accurate information so you can make wise choices, meet needs, satisfy wants, and attain desired goals.

4. It can help you prepare for uncertain economic times, since you will know where you stand financially and will be prepared to make adjustments when life throws curves at you.

5. It helps you measure your progress in saving money and reducing unnecessary spending.

6. It may improve your standard of living.

7. It gives you a base from which to discuss fun ideas and financial goals with your family.

8. It can lead to your having more money available for investments and charitable giving.

9. It is a key element in reducing debt—or eliminating it altogether.

10. It can give you the options to buy items you *want* as well as those you *need*.

11. It motivates others around you, including family members, to participate in the saving process.

12. It gives you the resources to take advantage of true "bargains."

Many excellent books have been written on how to develop and stick to a spending plan. [Note: *The Financial Planning Organizer* by Larry Burkett and *Taming the Money Monster* by Ron Blue are two excellent resources that will lead you through the process.] Here are some pointers we have found helpful.

◆ At the beginning, you (and your spouse) need to spend time each week evaluating how well your spending plan is working and making necessary adjustments.

◆ If you need to have everything accounted for perfectly, do it. If not, and you come close, that's OK, too. But if you don't come close, pay more attention to details.

◆ Gain the cooperation of key members. If your spouse isn't willing to follow a spending plan, conflicts will arise.

◆ Reflect the needs of individual family members in the spending plan. One child may need more money for sports equipment, for instance; another may need money for camp.

◆ Be conservative. If more money comes in than you expect, great. But if it doesn't, you'll be in stronger financial shape.

◆ Give each responsible family member a little money to spend that doesn't have to be accounted for.

◆ Set money aside for taxes when your income first comes in. We deposit all income into an account, but we set aside a percentage for taxes and don't consider that money to be "usable funds." Other people put tax money into a special savings account.

◆ Realize that your spending plan is a flexible planning tool. It should not be set in concrete. An unexpected expense, for example, may cause one or more other areas to shift. (For example, a forty-five-dollar doctor's visit may have to come out of "entertainment" if there are no more funds in the "medical" budget.)

◆ Be willing to revise the spending plan as your needs, goals, and wants change.

◆ As you cut spending, remove money from a number of categories instead of dramatically reducing one category (unless it is superfluous).

◆ Stick with your plan until you have your income and expenses well in hand and can follow the basic plan naturally. If at any time you begin to lose control of your spending, return to the basics again. ◆

◆ 3 ◆

Financial Deceptions
By Ron Blue

As appeared in the <u>Sound Mind Investing</u> newsletter in 1994.
Adapted from <u>Taming the Money Monster</u> by Ron Blue. Copyright 1993.
Published by Focus on the Family, Colorado Springs, CO. Used with permission. All rights reserved.

Often I am asked, "How do we get out of debt and stay out?" My advice is simple but not simplistic.

More deception (most of it unintended) is perpetrated by accountants, bankers, business schools, and businessmen regarding the use of debt than most of us realize. We tend to respect these professional people. Yet they only pass on what they've been taught, and in many cases they've been taught half-truths. Being a CPA, former banker, alumnus of a graduate business school, and businessman myself, I remember what I was taught and have in turn taught others in time past. And there are four major financial deceptions conveyed implicitly or explicitly by my peer group. They are as follows:

◆ Borrowed money is always paid back with cheaper dollars in the future.

◆ The tax deductibility of interest makes using debt a wise thing to do.

◆ Inflation is inevitable; therefore, it is always wise to buy now at a lower cost than in the future at a higher cost.

◆ Leverage (debt) is magic.

Perhaps I'm too critical in calling these deceptions, because they may or may not be true depending on certain assumptions. But the assumptions underlying the four statements are not adequately explained. So to better understand the whole issue of using debt wisely (if, in fact, you should use it at all), you must recognize these deceptions and evaluate them relative to your own circumstances.

Deception 1: Paying Back With Cheaper Dollars.

In the 1970s and early 1980s, inflation was at double-digit levels and was projected by almost everyone to be ever increasing. The "wisdom" then was that you would always be able to pay back borrowed money with dollars that were worth less in the future, because inflation eats away at the purchasing power of money. This wisdom was true as long as two basic assumptions were met. The first was that you were able to borrow at a fixed interest rate so your rate did not increase with inflation. The second was that inflation would continue.

The example used most frequently to sell this deception was the purchase of a home using a fixed-rate, long-term mortgage. This does in fact make sense in a time of inflation, because the dollars used to pay back the principal amount borrowed are worth less and less. In addition, when the interest rate is fixed for the life of the loan, you can't be hurt by the

increasing interest rates that go hand in hand with inflation. That approach continues to make sense if the two assumptions continue to be valid.

History proves, however, that there are economic cycles. They may not be geographically universal, but they do occur. For example, if you bought a home in the Southwest in the early 1980s, you would have paid a premium price. But when oil prices fell and the economy turned south in the Southwest, the assumption of continuing inflation proved to be wrong.

Other illustrations abound. Midwest farms in the early 1980s were selling as fast as they came on the market at prices that eventually reached $4,000 per acre. By the late 1980s, however, that same premium farmland could be purchased for $1,200 to $1,500 per acre. The point is that even if inflation were a valid assumption overall, it may not be valid for the region in which you live. When industries leave an area, inflation changes. There aren't as many people demanding the same goods and services, so prices tend to fall. Thus, what is true today regarding inflation may not be true tomorrow.

The idea of gaining an economic advantage by borrowing at fixed interest rates so your rate doesn't go up with inflation assumes that lenders are basically stupid and will continue to lend money at low, fixed rates for long terms even during times of inflation. That's not the case. In periods of inflation, interest rates rise, and lenders promote adjustable-rate mortgages. They also know that the average home loan will mature (be paid off) within eight years as borrowers sell or refinance. Then the money from the payoff of that mortgage can be reloaned on the same house at a higher interest rate.

Additionally, every time they make loans, lenders can charge points and fees that increase their income. Thus, they don't make bad decisions even when they're willing to make fixed-rate loans. They push as much of the risk to the borrower as they possibly can. And in times of inflation, they charge premium rates.

Whenever you borrow money at a premium interest rate, the fact of paying back with cheaper dollars in the future is mitigated by the high rate. In my twenty years of professional experience, interest rates on credit card and installment debt have never been lower than the inflation rate except for very short periods. So while you may repay the loan with cheaper dollars in the future, the premium interest rates charged more than offset the benefit.

Deception 2: The Tax Deductibility of Interest.

This deception says that because interest is tax deductible, it's a good idea to have interest expense in order to reduce income taxes. There's a certain amount of truth to that, but it doesn't present the whole picture. First, not all interest is 100% tax deductible. Consumer interest (credit cards, car loans, installment loans) isn't, and even investment interest has limitations. The only 100% deductible interest is home mortgage interest, and that has limits, too, when the mortgage goes above a certain amount.

Second, to say that an amount is deductible means only that it's deducted from income before computing the taxes owed. *It doesn't mean that taxes are offset dollar for dollar by the amount of interest.* For example, if you pay a total of 30% in state and federal income taxes, then for every dollar of fully deductible interest you pay, you reduce your taxes by $.30, not $1.00. Thus, the net cost of paying interest is $ .70 rather than $1.00, but it's still a net cost, and it's never a benefit.

To clarify whether you should borrow based on the fact that interest offers a tax deduction, I propose this agreement: If you'll loan me $1,000, I promise to never repay you. That way you can deduct the $1,000 as a bad debt expense and reduce your taxes accordingly. I, on the other hand, will keep the $1,000, report it as income, and pay the taxes. You tell me which of us will be better off. Interest deductions operate the same way.

Deception 3: It Will Cost More Later.

Again during the 1970s and early 1980s, when inflation rates were relatively high, a common advertising theme was "Buy now, because it will cost more later." In fact, it would cost more later. However, that ploy begs the true question, which is not "What will it cost later?" but "Do I really need it?"

The second aspect of this deception is the underlying assumption that everything will continue to go up in price. That's not always the case. Personal computer prices, for example, tend to start high when a new model is introduced and fall steadily. And almost everything goes on sale periodically.

The way to understand the real question when tempted by this deception is to ask, "So what?" In most cases, the answer is "I may not need it later" or "The future price makes no difference to me, because I have to have it." But making a purchase on the basis of its costing more later is a very short-term perspective and may well be a financial mistake.

Deception 4: The Magic of Leverage.

In graduate school, I was taught the value of OPM—the use of other people's money. The idea is that if you use debt to purchase something, you get a far greater return on your portion of the investment than you would if you paid all cash for it.

The classic example has again been the purchase of a home. If you were to purchase an $80,000 home and put 10% down, you would have a net investment of your own money of $8,000. If that home then appreciated 10% in one year (meaning you could sell the house for $88,000), you would have a 100% return on the money you invested (an $8,000 gain on an $8,000 investment). If, on the other hand, you paid cash for the home, you would have achieved only a 10% return (an $8,000 gain on an $80,000 investment). The difference between a 100% return and a 10% return is the magic of leverage.

This concept will work as illustrated if the underlying assumptions hold true. The basic assumption is that there will be appreciation rather than depreciation on whatever is purchased—an idea I've already shown to be false. The second assumption is that if you borrow money instead of paying cash, you have an alternative use for the money that will yield a return greater than your cost of money. Borrowing to buy a car at 12% interest, for instance, assumes that you can earn more than 12% by investing your money. But the only way you can earn that kind of return is to put your money at substantial risk.

Many people have gone bankrupt trying to take advantage of leverage. They didn't understand the real assumptions they were making. Even huge lending institutions all over this country have gone bankrupt because they lacked this understanding. Leverage can work for you, but it's like riding an alligator: It's a lot easier to get on than it is to get off safely.

The best way to conclude is to advise you that if a deal sounds too good to be true, it probably is. Second, be very careful when accepting counsel from anyone, including supposedly knowledgeable business and professional people. Truly successful people become well off not by using complex techniques or even by reducing their taxes to nothing. Instead, they become successful the old-fashioned way: They earn it. The key to financial success is to spend less than you earn and do it for a long time. There are no shortcuts to taming the money monster. ◆

Practical Guidelines to Control Spending
By Randy Alcorn

As appeared in the Sound Mind Investing newsletter in 1992. Adapted from Money, Possessions, and Eternity by Randy Alcorn. Copyright 1989. Published by Tyndale House. Used with permission. All rights reserved.

For many people, spending money becomes an addictive behavior similar to alcoholism or gambling. With compulsive spending, the true enemy is within. We need to replace our preoccupation with short-term gratification and make our spending decisions from the long-term perspective. We must replace our self-indulgence with self-control, which is a fruit of the Holy Spirit's work in our lives. *"Like a city whose walls are broken down is a man who lacks self-control"* (Proverbs 25:28). Without self-control on the inside, our lives are made vulnerable to an infinite variety of assaults from the outside. The following guidelines are designed to help you exercise self-control in your spending, that you may become a better steward of God's resources and free more funds to use for kingdom purposes:

◆ **Realize that nothing is a good deal if you can't afford it.** $60,000 sounds like an excellent price on a house worth $75,000. And $80 seems like a great deal on barely used skis that cost $250 new. But if you can't afford them, it simply doesn't matter. No thing is worth going into financial bondage.

◆ **Recognize that God isn't behind every good deal.** But suppose you *can* afford to buy this terrific item. Does that mean you should buy it? Not necessarily. Self-control often means turning down good deals on things we really want because God may have other and better plans for his money.

◆ **Understand the difference between spending money and saving money.** Money that is saved stays in your wallet or the bank and can be used for other purposes, including your needs or the needs of others that arise. On the other hand, money that is spent leaves your hands and is no longer at your disposal. Hence, when you buy a $55 sweater for $35, you do not save $20 — you spend $35. Whether the sweater was worth $35 or $200 is irrelevant. The point is, the $35 is gone, and you have saved nothing.

◆ **Look at the long-term cost, not just the short-term.** When you buy a nice stereo, you will end up buying lots of tapes. When you buy a new car you will pay for insurance or pay to have a dent fixed. When you are given a "free" puppy immediately you are spending $12 a month on dog food, and the next thing you know you are paying $250 to the veterinarian to stitch up his wounds from a dog fight. Count the cost in advance — almost everything ends up much more expensive than it first appears.

◆ **Pray before you spend.** When something is a legitimate need, God will provide it. How often do we take matters into our own hands and spend money impulsively before asking God to furnish it for us in some other way? Waiting eliminates most impulsive buying. Furthermore, the waiting period gives God the opportunity either to provide what we want, to provide something different or better, or to show us that we don't need it and would better use the money another way.

◆ **Examine every purchase in light of its ministry potential.** Every time I spend money, I gain something and lose something. What I lose is not merely money *but what could have been done with the money if used in another way.* Hence, money spent always represents lost opportunity. When I spend $100, I must weigh the value of my purchases against what the same amount of money could have done if used in another way — for instance, to feed the hungry or evangelize the lost. I don't say this to induce guilt trips. I sometimes choose to spend money on unnecessary things that still seem good and helpful and contributory to myself and my family. Sometimes I feel entirely good about this; sometimes it seems more borderline. Often, however, there is a clear line we feel would be wrong for us to cross.

◆ **Understand and resist the manipulative nature of advertising.** Responsible spending says yes to real needs and no to most "created needs." We have far fewer needs than we believe. Advertising thrives on instilling discontent. Its goal is to create a sense of need, to stimulate desire, to make you think you need and deserve more. We must consciously reject its claims and counter them with the Word of God, which tells us what we really do and do not need. Furthermore, to the degree possible, we need to withdraw ourselves from advertising that fosters greed or discontent. That may mean less television, less flipping through sales catalogs, and less aimless wandering in shopping malls.

◆ **Realize that the little things add up.** If a swimming pool is full of leaks, you can pump in more water, but it will never be enough until the leaks are fixed. We can take in more and more income, but until we fix the little leaks in our spending habits — the dollar here and ten dollars over there — we will never be able to divert the flow of money for higher purposes.

◆ **Set up and live by a budget.** I recommend you pick up one of the practical books on finances that deals specifically with budgeting. Such books show how to make a careful record of expenditures so you can find out where your money is going. It is not how much money we have, but how we handle it that really matters. A good budget is a tool to help us handle it wisely. ◆

5

How to Make Money the Easy Way
By C. Scott Houser

As appeared in the <u>Sound Mind Investing</u> newsletter in 1994.
Copyright 1990 by Ronald Blue & Co. Used with permission. All rights reserved.

One can get the same effect of increased investment return or a salary raise with absolutely no risk by spending wisely to reduce household cash outflow. If a family can budget, shop wisely, and follow the money saving tips outlined in this article, they could have $1,100 extra in the bank at the end of the year with no risk. In fact, the $1,100 saved on spending would be an after tax savings which is equivalent to much more than a $1,100 before tax investment return.

Many people are considered "cheap" if they pursue bargains or seek out the most economical sources in town for products or services. In fact, people who go to great lengths to save money on goods or services are often ridiculed by others. Yet, when people need advice on where to shop because of an unexpected major purchase or financial emergency, they run to the "cheapskates." Why? Because deep down inside, they see the wisdom of saving every possible dollar in order to use it for more productive ways.

The following list of money saving tips is not meant to be exhaustive, but it does represent ideas our family has used in order to allocate our resources efficiently, and accomplish our financial priorities. Give yourself a "raise" by spending wisely!

◆ **Buy used, especially for major purchases.** Contrary to popular belief, buying used is not risky and does not take a lot of expertise. It does take planning and a little bit of elbow grease. For example, when we moved to Atlanta fifteen years ago, we needed to buy a refrigerator. New refrigerators at that time cost about $750, way more than we had in cash after purchasing our first home. We decided that buying "used" was our best option. First, I studied refrigerators in *Consumer Reports*. Second, I began scanning the classified ads and made a lot of telephone calls. After you become adept at classified shopping, you soon learn how to screen people who are overselling or "hyping" their merchandise and those who sincerely have a genuine reason for wanting to sell. It has been my experience that you find the better buys in nice suburban areas. The result: I bought an almost new frost-free refrigerator for $250. There was nothing wrong with the refrigerator except that it was the wrong color for the seller's new home!

One of the main points in buying used is that, if at all possible, you should anticipate your need. If you know you are going to need a new appliance or a car, begin shopping three to four months before replacement becomes necessary. The following are items we have bought used: automobiles, television, stereo equipment, refrigerator, furniture (all types), children's clothing, and tools. One of the most obvious items to buy used is an automobile. Studies indicate that new cars depreciate as much as 20%-40% in the first year of ownership. Let someone else pay for that depreciation!

◆ **Rent.** Some things you just don't need to own: timesharing arrangements, boats, major tools, the list goes on. It amazes me how easy and cheap it is to rent state-of-the-art equipment, return it when you want to, and not have to worry about maintenance, depreciation, obsolescence, property taxes, etc.

◆ **Comparison shop.** If you need to make a major purchase or have major repairs done on your car, get more than one estimate. Often the prices will vary by several hundred dollars. The same holds true for your annual auto insurance and homeowner's insurance.

◆ **Pay cash.** This offers two advantages. First, you may be able to buy an item for less by offering cash instead of charging. Second, it forces you to "count the cost" of each purchase more carefully. You won't make as many impulse purchases.

◆ **Generic brands.** Major grocery stores offer generic or house brands. Don't be afraid of them! They are often made by the same manufacturer who makes the name brand but puts a different label on it. It doesn't hurt to try the product once; then if you don't like it you can go back to the name brand.

◆ **Stockpile or anticipate needs.** We have five children so we often buy in quantity when going to the grocery store or membership warehouse to take advantage of quantity discounts. If a store in our particular area is having a year-end clearance on items such as tennis shoes, shirts, or pants, we will buy half a dozen or a dozen of each. They may not fit our children now, but sooner or later one child will grow into them.

◆ **Baby sitting co-op.** Get together with other couples you know in your area to develop a baby sitting co-op or club, trading time on a child-per-child basis. This will provide quality care without the expense. I estimate that in one year we saved over $300 by using our baby sitting co-op, and we've developed stronger friendships as well.

◆ **Coupons.** Coupons can save you a great deal of money every week. It takes some work to clip them, but it's well worth the trouble. Why not make coupon clipping a family affair? Coupons can also benefit a family when eating out. Civic or nonprofit organizations often put together books containing coupons such as two-for-one restaurant offers or 10% off your purchase at various stores. We have one in each car plus one at home. If we are unexpectedly away from home at mealtime we are not forced to pay full price — we just pull the book out of the glove compartment and use a coupon.

◆ **Negotiate.** I am a great believer in negotiating price. Some time ago I was interested in buying a particular charcoal grill. After the salesman explained all the features to me, I asked him the simple question, "Is that price the best you can give?" I ended up saving 10%. I am not always a good negotiator when it comes to talking terms with salesmen. But I have found that the simple principle, "you have not because you ask not," really holds true. I do not negotiate hard; I simply ask if that is their best price.

◆ **Have a garage sale.** We usually have an annual garage sale to help us get rid of the stuff we normally would just keep accumulating. Frankly, it is unbelievable what people will buy in garage sales. We enjoy having them. Often we have free Christian tracts and books available. We have never had a bad experience with a garage sale. And we've never made less than $200. We typically join in with our neighbors, and it is a great time to get to know them better as well.

◆ **Dental schools.** If your county or state has a dental college or hygienist school, you may be able to get your teeth or your children's cleaned at a considerable savings. These hygienists in training are supervised by a dentist, and treat your children's teeth methodically. In the eleven years we have visited our community college clinic, we have never had a bad experience. For an average cost of $8 per child, they get their teeth cleaned, plus fluoride treatment, sealant, and X-rays if necessary. On top of that they also get a new toothbrush!

◆ **Medicine/generic drugs.** With a family of seven, we have many miscellaneous medical needs. Whether it is the local drugstore's house brand or buying our antihistamines via mail order, we rarely pay top dollar for a brand name drug. For the one antihistamine/decongestant we use for the kids' colds, we pay less than 10% of the price of a popular brand name, and the formula is exactly the same.

◆ **Matching price policy.** Most of the retailers in our geographical area have a policy of matching or beating any advertised price. In the course of a year we will take advantage of this policy several times. Recently, our local hardware store was more than happy to match prices of a discount store when I provided a copy of the store's ad. I've never had anyone "look down on me" for shopping price; in fact, most have been very appreciative of my patronage.

◆ **Avoid recreational shopping.** I have spent enough time in financial counseling sessions to know that people are not rational when they make purchasing decisions. Recreational shopping will cause you to buy items that you normally wouldn't buy. Shopping is like any other temptation. If you can't handle it, flee from it. Don't put yourself in circumstances that will cater to your potential weaknesses. If you're going shopping, know exactly what you're going for, make a list, and don't deviate from it.

◆ **Libraries.** Rather than buy books, our family is a faithful user of our neighborhood library. It's not unusual for us to have fifteen to twenty books from the library in our house at one time. Libraries today loan books, have story hours, provide meeting rooms, and are a great environment for your children to spend time in. Besides saving money, libraries are a great way to instill in your children the love of reading, which will benefit them throughout their lives.

◆ **Repair vs. replacement.** When we were preparing for the arrival of our fifth baby, as I looked at our crib my first thought was that it was rusty, beat up and just not suitable for our precious new baby. After a few hours of painting and the purchase of a new mattress cover, it almost looked better than when we bought it. The point is, don't be quick to think that you need a new item. Perhaps the old one can be repaired. Reupholstering furniture is another way to save. Often a reupholstered piece is better than new because the reupholsterer has repaired and reinforced structural components and probably used better materials than when it was originally purchased.

◆ **Haircuts.** People I know send their five-year-old to a stylist for a $15 haircut, and in our opinion, that money could be put to better use. So, every few weeks my wife has a haircutting night. If your family adopts this policy, my advice is to be one of the first to have Mom cut your hair. Usually, by the time the last one in line gets to the chair, Mom is tired and a little less careful, but hey, no system is perfect!

◆ **Budget Envelopes.** If you're one of those who can't stand a budget, try a "partial budget." For example, an expense that people have a hard time controlling is the money they spend eating out. Simply begin each month with the amount that you want to spend eating out in an envelope, and when the envelope is empty, stop spending. This time-tested method will save you money in the spending areas of most concern without causing you to come up with a formal budget.

◆ **Create your own money-saving tips.** Most people do not have an income problem but a spending problem. I trust these tips have been helpful and will spur you into some creative thinking on how you can save money in your own situation. What works for me may not work for you, but all of us can save money in certain areas, not sacrifice that much time, and perhaps even improve our quality of life.

◆ **The right perspective.** On a final note, don't try to squeeze every penny out of every dollar and make saving money into some kind of "second religion." Our family tries to be good stewards in order to provide us not with more money but with more freedom — the freedom to be flexible in our budget, the freedom to give more, the freedom to be spontaneous in our spending without being destructive to our overall financial plan. Balance is the key. We save on the spending side, but that gives us freedom in other areas. ◆

◆ 6

Cutting Credit Card Costs
By Marc Eisenson

A typical wallet holds eight to ten credit cards, groaning under 18% interest on some $2,000 in bills. But take heart. I offer this simple, step-by-step, debt-deflating makeover that will soon evaporate those money-siphoning, high interest rates and annual fees. First, I'll arm you for a quick shot at lowering the interest rate and excising the annual fees on the cards you already carry. Then, I'll teach you how to get an even better rate by transferring your revolving balance to the lowest-rate card you can get. Then you'll painlessly pay down your debt at a fast clip, ending up with a no-fee card that you'll use interest-free.

1. Look Homeward First. Begin your debt diet by putting your cards on the table — each with its most recent statement. See how much you currently pay in fees and interest. Then get a running start on becoming the new, credit-savvy you. I call it:

2. Dialing for Dollars. Each of your statements lists a customer service number. Call, and say the appropriate version of: "You're charging me a $20 annual fee, plus 19.8% interest. I'm seeing a lot of cards advertised with much lower rates and no annual fees. Will you waive my fee and lower my interest rate?" If you have at least a one year history of timely payments (even of only the minimum required), the answer will probably be "yes." You don't have anything to lose, and not asking is an automatic "No!"

3. Talk Tough, If Necessary. I've been calling my card companies and encouraging friends and family to do likewise. Most of our calls eventually result in savings, but we've learned not to expect an immediate "de- lighted to be of service." You'll be put on "hold" while your record is reviewed. If the verdict isn't to your liking, ask if they would pre- fer that you trade in their card for a better deal from one of their 6,000 hungry competitors. And always feel free to take it to a higher authority — ask for a su- pervisor. Getting an annual fee waived or an interest rate lowered from 19.8% to 15.9% should be relatively easy, but you may need to assert yourself. (When Nancy called her card company, she was passed off to three different op-

erators before she was eventually offered another card which has no annual fee and charges even less interest than the "preferred" rate she'd previously been given. Go figure it!)

Note: A variable rate card should pose little risk. Interest rates are at an historic low, and with careful management, you should be well out of debt before rates next go ballistic — at which point it won't matter to you. But if you're nervous about future rate hikes, hold on to one fixed rate card.

4. Stay on Top of Your Victories. To insure that they won't be fleeting or hollow, monitor your victories. You might get your annual fee waived, but only for the current year. You'll need to call again in twelve months. Another way I almost blew it: Since I don't charge more than I can pay off by the end of the grace period, the 19.8% interest rate on my no-fee Chase Visa Gold card didn't really cost me anything. But in the spirit of research, I proudly got Chase to lower my rate — only to find a $50 annual fee on my next bill. When I called to complain, I was told that I could have one or the other — no-fee or a low rate — but not both. Since I have a pocketful of other cards, I promptly cancelled this one.

5. Check Your Credit Report. Once you've shed an annual fee or two and lightened your interest rate by a few points, it's time to "refinance" any revolving credit card debts you may carry. How low an interest rate you can get will depend on your credit report. Get a free copy of yours from TRW — one of the "big three" credit bureaus. Call TRW at 800-392-1122. Have a pencil ready to jot down the information they'll need. Your report should arrive in a few weeks.

6. Shape Up. When your credit report arrives, take a hard look — 40% of the time there are errors that you should have cor- rected right away. Naturally, a record of late payments and other delinquencies will hurt your chances for low cost credit. Even if you're a model bill payer, there may be problems lurking. For example, if you're spending more than 28% of your gross income on credit card bills

TABLE #1

CREDIT CARD MATH
Based on Paying the Minimum Percent on a $2,000 Balance

Card	Interest Rate	Minimum Percent Payment	Total Interest Cost	Months to Pay Off
Chase	19.8%	2.00%	$7,636	502
Discover	19.8%	2.78%	$2,589	207
FCC/First	15.9%	2.08%	$2,944	265
Fidelity	15.9%	3.00%	$1,427	151
AFBA	12.5%	3.50%	$781	113
Amalgam	12.0%	2.50%	$1,103	131
Wachovia	8.9%	2.80%	$651	125

and installment loans, your application could be denied. Similarly, having more than four cards, carrying a balance close to your credit limits, or having too much open credit—even if you've never gone up to that limit—makes potential lenders nervous. Ask your current card companies to lower your credit limits to amounts more in line with your actual spending patterns—and cancel all of your gas and department store cards. With Visa and MasterCard so universally accepted, keep other credit cards only if they offer an extra special convenience or feature. For more on how issuers will rate you, get BHA's Credit Secrets Manual (800-553-8025) for just $3.

7. Lower Isn't Always Better. Seek out some lower rate cards. How low can you go? Eight percent, or less, is possible, but may not be right, or reachable, for you. Finding your best deal will require carefully attending to the rest of your makeover—and making a bunch of phone calls. Begin by getting a list of low rate and no annual fee cards. Ram Research's Cardtrak, a monthly newsletter, includes an easy to follow survey ($5 for a current issue, 800-344-7714). While helpful, it won't tell you a crucial fact—"The Minimum Percent." You'll have to call each card company to find it out.

Table #1 illustrates the effects of this hidden aspect of credit card math with some recent card offers. Look at the Chase and Discover cards, which both charge 19.8% interest. If you have a $2,000 balance, and pay only the minimum due, Chase's card would cost $5,047 more in interest than Discover's offering. That's because Chase requires a monthly minimum payment of only 2.00% ($40, the first month), whereas Discover's is 2.78% ($55.56).

Either deal is nuts, if you can get a lower rate. But if you can't, by regularly sending Chase 2.78% of your outstanding monthly balance, instead of the required 2.00%, your monthly payments as well as your total cost would equal that on the Discover card (e.g., $2,000 x 0.02778 = $55.56). You'd save over $5,000, and twenty-five years of payments! You'll notice the same discrepancy between the 15.9% cards. In fact, FCC/First's low minimum means it could be more costly for you than the Discover card, which charges almost four points more interest. Note: You can manage low minimum percent cards to your advantage. Send in as much as you can each month, to keep your costs down. But if times get tough—cut back to preserve your cash flow, without jeopardizing your credit.

8. Another Instant Money-Waste Reducer. As quickly as you can, transfer the balances from your high interest cards to lower interest ones. "Dialing for Dollars" may very well get you a reduced rate. While you seek out still lower rates, it's well worth the effort to transfer your balance from, say, a 19.8% card to one that charges 15.4%—assuming you make the higher minimum payment of the two. But first find out what the transfer process entails. Some banks provide free transfer checks, while others impose a cash advance fee in addition to interest (which may be 2%-3% higher for cash advances than for purchases).

9. And Now for the Nominees. If you've completed the plastic surgery on your current cards and your credit report, reach out for a still lower rate card. Salivate, if you must, over those with rock bottom rates—say 7.75%, like the Givens card (800-284-4082), or Arkansas Federal's 8.0% (800-477-3348)—but keep in mind that these dream boats carry high annual fees, grant low credit limits, demand a great credit history, and reject at least 70% of applicants. For most, a good next-step card might be the one issued by USAA (800-922-9092), by AFBA (800-776-2265), or by Amalgamated Trust Bank (800-365-6464). All offer no-fee cards with "convenience checks" to transfer your balances from other cards.

Tempted to apply to all these outfits? Don't. Applying for more than two cards in six months may get some lenders nervous about what they'll see as your sudden need for credit. Try for a card in the 12% range instead. If you get it, then go for an even lower rate.

10. Apply Carefully. If your credit report shows one thing, and your application something else, the bank's computer may get confused. List every credit account the report shows. Make sure addresses match, too, down to the zip code. Be honest, but not modest. Be sure to show extra sources of income, list your assets at present market values, and give the current balances on loans—not what you originally borrowed. Fill out the application completely and keep a copy. It'll be the model for your next application.

11. At All Cost, Avoid "MPS." Scott Burns, a columnist for the *Dallas Morning News*, coined a wonderful term "MPS—Minimum Payment Syndrome." Scott describes it as a "deadly" malady, which could afflict you for the rest of your life. Fortunately, the cure for MPS is simple and requires no doctor's visit. Always pay more than the required minimum. Table #2 shows the savings that a measly quarter a day—$7.50 a month—will earn you on each of our sample cards. For example, with Chase's 19.8% card, you could relocate $4,916 in otherwise wasted interest—from the bank's bottom line to your own—simply by investing two bits a day.

12. An Easy Way to Pay Off Credit Cards. Unlike mortgages, card contracts don't set a repayment term. The banks want you to send in just the minimum, on time, every month—and to keep on charging, happily ever after. To wipe your slate clean, just pick an amount that's larger than the minimum required this month—and send it in every month, until the loan's been repaid. The highest minimum among our sample cards is AFBA's 3.5%—which means $70 on a $2,000 balance. Table #3 shows what each card would cost if you made a flat $70 payment every month. While it certainly makes sense to go after low rate cards, I hope Tables #2 and #3 convince you that paying more than required—on a regular, but self-managed basis—is the real ticket to financial freedom.

TABLE #2

CREDIT CARD MATH
Adding 25¢ a Day to the Required Payment
Dramatically Reduces Your Total Interest Cost
Based on a $2,000 Balance

Card	Interest Rate	Cost without 25¢	Cost with 25¢	Interest Saving	Months Saved
Chase	19.8%	$7,636	$2,720	$4,916	334
Discover	19.8%	2,589	1,558	1,031	97
FCC/First	15.9%	2,944	1,553	1,391	137
Fidelity	15.9%	1,427	970	457	61
AFBA	12.5%	781	582	199	40
Amalgamated	12.0%	1,103	763	340	45
Wachovia	8.9%	651	469	182	45

TABLE #3

CREDIT CARD MATH
Regular Pre-Payments Are
Your Quick Ticket to Financial Freedom
Based on a $70 Monthly Payment on a $2,000 Balance

Card	Interest Rate	Cost with Minimum	Cost with $70	Interest Saving	Term (Mos)
Chase	19.8%	$7,636	$727	$6,909	39
Discover	19.8%	2,589	727	1,862	39
FCC/First	15.9%	2,944	529	2,415	37
Fidelity	15.9%	1,427	529	898	37
AFBA	12.5%	781	386	395	35
Amalgamated	12.0%	1,103	367	736	34
Wachovia	8.9%	651	255	396	33

13. Yet Another Way to Slice Debt Costs. Another quick way to cut your costs is to get a short term loan from a better-heeled friend, relative, or insurance policy—at a lower rate than your card charges. Then pay at least as much each month toward your new loan as you were sending to the card sharks. You'll save a bundle, and your benefactor will also profit. When your card balances are wiped out, start paying off your car, college loan, or mortgage. Soon you'll be totally debt-free, which is the best treatment I know for keeping those ugly worry-lines off your face.

14. When Interest Rates No Longer Matter, Grace Periods Do! While you're carrying a rollover balance, grace periods are of no benefit. But once you start paying your balance in full every month, grace periods generally offer you twenty-five days from the billing date, which could be a month from purchase date, to pay your bill. During this twenty-five to fifty-five day grace period your money can be earning you interest.

Therefore, when you're finally on a pay-as-you-go basis, get yourself a no-fee card with at least a twenty-five day grace period. While the interest rate will no longer matter—because you won't be paying it—be prudent. Stick with a no-fee, low interest card.

15. Deep-Six Dumb Deals. Be on the lookout for pseudo-personalized offers encouraging you to take advantage of yet another once-in-a-lifetime opportunity to charge your life away. For example, what say you to a "prestigious" Visa Gold Card with a $5,000 credit line, no annual fee, low monthly payments, and a 1% purchase rebate? Plus "at no cost," all purchases would be protected against fire and theft. You'd also get extended warranties, free checks, no transaction fees, $500,000 in travel insurance, and collision protection on car rentals. The catch? Accept an immediate cash advance of at least $2,000, at a mere 21.9% in interest. I say, "Thanks, but no," and hope you'll do the same. ◆

How to Save on Credit Card Interest and Fees
By Gerri Detweiler

As appeared in the Sound Mind Investing newsletter in 1995.
Excerpted from The Ultimate Credit Handbook, by Gerri Detweiler, former director of Bankcard Holders of America.
Copyright 1993. Published by Plume. Used by permission. All rights reserved. Available through Good Advice Press (800) 255-0899, $15.95.

It's inconceivable to think of taking out a mortgage or car loan and not being told the interest rate until after the papers are signed. Yet, for many years it was almost impossible to shop around for an inexpensive credit card, because few credit card issuers would tell consumers up front how much they charged. Congress put a halt to that practice, however, and in 1988 passed the Fair Credit and Charge Card Disclosure Act of 1988. Card issuers are now required by law to provide applicants with more information about the costs of credit cards up front.

Under this law, which is part of the Truth-In-Lending Act, the costs of credit cards must be displayed in an easy-to-read box format on most applications and solicitations. An example of a credit card disclosure table is shown below.

◆ **Finance charges.** You will see them listed on your credit card statement in two ways: as a "monthly periodic rate," and as an "APR." APR stands for annual percentage rate; for example, an APR of 19.8% is the interest rate the issuer claims you will pay over the course of a year on revolving balances. The stated charge may appear high, but the actual amount of interest you'll pay is often *even higher* because most issuers compound interest; that is, they charge interest on interest. That means that if you carry a balance from month to month, the effective interest rate you pay will be higher than the APR stated by the issuer. Suppose your card issuer compounds interest monthly, and charges a stated APR of 19.8%. Because of the interest compounding, you will actually pay an effective annual rate of 21.7%.

◆ **Annual fees.** Sometimes called memberships fees, they can run as high as $75 or more; the average is about $20. These fees can add up. Suppose you have three bankcards, each charging $20 apiece—that's $60 a year.

Some cards, however, carry no annual fees. Most consumers pay interest, so the card issuer makes money that way. In addition, every time you use your card the merchant pays a percentage of the purchase (called a merchant discount fee) to the card companies for the privilege of accepting the card. Some of the merchant discount fee, which ranges from 1.5% to 10% of the purchase amount, is passed on to the card issuer.

If your credit card carries an annual fee, your card issuer must notify you thirty days before the card is due to be renewed, so you will have an opportunity to cancel the card before you pay the fee. This notice will appear on your billing statement, and must disclose how much the annual fee will cost, and tell you how and when to close your account if you don't want to pay the annual fee.

◆ **Grace period.** As defined by the Federal Reserve Board, this free-ride period is "the date by which or the period within which any credit extended for purchases may be repaid without incurring a finance charge."

If your card has a grace period, the bill will usually read "Pay this amount to avoid further finance charges" next to the total balance. If your card does not have a grace period, even if you pay off your bill in full when it is due, the next month you will find that you nevertheless owe finance charges from the previous month's balance.

Many people are confused about the grace period. They often think that if their card has a twenty-five-day grace period, new purchases do not start accruing finance charges for twenty-five days, regardless of whether they pay them in full. In fact, if you carry over just one penny from the previous month, all purchases you make this month will start accruing finance charges immediately. In addition, you generally do not get the whole twenty-five days interest-free unless you meet two conditions: you've paid the "balance due" or "new balance" on your most recent billing statement in full by the due date, and you pay this month's new purchases in full when due. In that case, you will get at least twenty-five days interest-free on purchases made this month.

In short, *if you carry a balance from month to month, you don't get a grace period, even if your card issuer offers one. The exception is if your*

CREDIT CARD FEE INFORMATION FOUND IN THE FINE PRINT						
Annual Percentage Rate for Purchases	Grace Period for Purchases	Minimum Finance Charges	Balance Calculation Method for Purchases	Annual Fees	Transaction Fees for Cash Advances	Late Payment Fee
19.8%	Not less than 25 days	$.50 when a finance charge at a periodic rate is charged	Average daily balance method (including new purchases)	$25 per year	2% with a minimum fee of $2	$10

card issuer uses a balance calculation method that excludes new purchases, which ensures an interest-free period on all new purchases.

Late-fees, over-limit fees, and transaction fees on credit cards were uncommon, if not unknown, several years ago. But as soon as a few large banks realized that they could charge additional fees to cardholders who didn't pay their accounts as agreed, penalty fees became almost commonplace. Even worse, some banks will add the fee to your current balance, and charge you interest on the fee as well as the balance!

Cash advance fees are probably the biggest penalty fee rip-off. Card issuers already make a tidy sum off cash advances, because they charge interest from the day you take out the cash advance (regardless of whether you pay the balance in full at the end of the month), and sometimes they make even more by charging higher interest rates on cash advances than on purchases. On top of that, most issuers slap on a cash advance fee—often 2.5% of the amount of the cash advance—simply for the privilege of borrowing. Before taking out a cash advance, be sure to check with your bank to find out what fees they charge.

This can make cash advances an extremely expensive way to borrow money. For example, suppose you take out a $500 cash advance on the fifteenth of the month and you pay it back in twenty-five days when you get the bill. Your issuer charges you interest at 19% from the date of the advance, plus adds a cash advance fee of 2.5%. You'll end up paying about $6 in interest, plus $12.50 for the fee, which adds up to an APR of 44%!

How much your credit cards cost depends on the costs we've mentioned previously. It will also depend on the method the card issuer uses to calculate the finance charge. Because balances on credit cards are constantly changing, as new purchases are made and part or all of the balance is repaid, it is no simple matter to determine how to calculate interest. Card issuers have devised four main ways to determine the balance on which finance charges should be assessed, some more expensive than others. Most credit card issuers use the "Average Daily Balance, Including New Purchases" method.

FINANCE CHARGES FOR DIFFERENT CALCULATION METHODS

A consumer starts the first month with a zero balance and charges $1,000, of which he pays off only the minimum amount due (1/36th of balance due). The next month, he charges another $1,000. He then pays off the entire balance due. This same pattern is repeated three more times during the year. The interest rate is 19.8 percent.

1. Average Daily Balance (Excluding New Purchases)	$66.00
2. Two-Cycle Average Daily Balance (Excluding New Purchases)	$131.20
3. Average Daily Balance (Including New Purchases)	$132.00
4. Two-Cycle Average Daily Balance (Including New Purchases)	$196.20

Does the balance calculation method really make a difference in costs? Absolutely. Here's an example from a Bankcard Holders of America study, "Credit Cards: What You Don't Know Can Cost You." The calculation methods are listed in the example in order of "best" to "worst," although that will vary depending on how much you charge and pay off each month.

Fortunately, you don't have to find a card that has everything: a low fee, low rate, no extra fees, and a full grace period. Instead, the card you choose will depend on your personal credit habits. Which type of credit card user are you?

◆ **Credit User:** You often pay only the minimum payment each month, or you pay part—but not all—of the total bill at the end of the month. Credit Users should choose a card with the lowest interest rate they can find. If you're a Credit User, the annual fee is not as important as the interest rate. You do not need a grace period on your card, because you do not take advantage of it.

◆ **Convenience User:** You pay off your balance in full every month. Convenience Users should look for cards with no annual fees. If you are a Convenience User, the interest rate is not very important to you, because you don't revolve a balance. Make sure your cards carry interest-free grace periods. If there is no grace period, you are likely to wind up paying high monthly interest charges.

◆ **Combination User:** You do some of each. You pay off your balance in full at least half the time. If you're a Combination User, pull out your credit card statements from last year. For each card, compare how much interest you paid, and how much you paid for the annual fee. If there's not much difference between the two, it's likely you can cut your costs in half by choosing a card with a similar interest rate and no annual fee. If, however, you find there is a large difference between the amount you paid in interest and the annual fee, try to reduce the higher item first. If, for instance, your card carries a $25 annual fee but you paid $65 in interest, try to switch to a card with a lower interest rate. Make sure you avoid cards that use the two-cycle balance calculation method. ◆

◆ 8 ◆

Bankcard Holders of America
By Vicki Mosher

Gone are the days of closely guarded credit. Informed estimates indicate that the credit available on America's credit cards now tops $1 trillion. That's double what it was only five years ago. American consumers now have outstanding monthly balances to the tune of $415 billion (and growing), and that's $78 billion more than just one year ago! When I hear statistics such as these, it's obvious that the spendthrift ways of our federal government are being repeated at the family level month after month.

If your household is like mine, hardly a week goes by that you don't receive at least one solicitation for a new credit card. With offers of single digit interest rates, credit limits that topple an average income, and "free" checks, I'd be foolish to not accept such generous "invitations." Or would I?

Credit card solicitations are carefully crafted to primarily benefit the issuer, not you, the consumer. Consumers not paying attention to such things as when the special "introductory" interest rate period expires are sometimes startled to find they are now being charged double digit interest on their purchases. Or did you know that many card issuers, including CitiCorp and Chase, are hitting selected card holders who they consider higher risk with so-called "punitive rates" which can run as much as ten percentage points more than their standard annual rates? It's all in the fine print of that little brochure you get when you open your account.

And what about those cards offering points for free flights, merchandise or cash back? Most such cards carry higher interest rates than normal and tempt the consumer to spend more than usual in order to get that "free" rebate. Used wisely, some credit cards can save you hundreds of dollars. But which ones? What's a discerning consumer to do?

Take heart! Bankcard Holders of America (BHA) is a "watch-dog" organization that will help you sort through the flood of cards and their offers. Executive Director Ruth Susswein is committed to consumers. She and her staff offer excellent teaching tools on how to use credit cards to our advantage, along with up-to-date information on which cards are offering the lowest interest rate and best rebates. They are dedicated to helping bankcard holders become informed and responsible consumers, instead of debt-ridden victims.

Founded in 1980, BHA is the nation's only non-profit consumer group that deals exclusively with issues that are of importance to credit card holders. The information they impart is non-biased since they receive no government or foundational support and are independent of any bank, credit card company, or financial institution. I like that.

One glance through their resources caused my husband and me to question whether the $20,000 in credit available to us was really necessary. Since our goal is to pay our balance in full each month, and our budget calls for no more than $1,000 to be spent, why have all that credit? If an item were to dazzle our eyes, would we "justify" buying it since we had the available credit? If so, we would be playing right into our creditors' hands—being responders instead of initiators. We took BHA's advice and asked our bank to lower our credit availability to $1,000. It seems those requests are few and far between.

If you desire to change the course you're on and become (and remain) debt-free, you might consider BHA's "Debt Zapper Kit." After entering your information into a computer, a personalized payment plan will be sent to you to show you how to pay off all your credit cards as fast as possible and a savings summary will be provided. The cost is $15, which also includes BHA's list of low interest rate/no annual fee credit cards and the pamphlet, "10 Proven Strategies to Slash Your Debt."

A membership to BHA is $24 per year. The many benefits include: Bankcard Consumer News (BHA's very informative bi-monthly newsletter), credit card protection information, a listing of banks that offer no-annual-fee and low-interest-rate credit cards, a listing of banks that offer secured credit cards, and more than twenty educational BHA pamphlets. Priced individually, the pamphlets alone would total over $45.

For a free list of BHA's services, send a stamped, self-addressed envelope to: Bankcard Holders of America, 524 Branch Drive, Salem, VA 24153. ◆

BHA PAMPHLETS

The pamphlets below are only some of the special reports that are included in an annual BHA membership. The prices shown are the costs which apply when purchased separately.

Rebate/Frequent Flyer Card List	$5
Consumer Rights at the Cash Register	$3
What You Don't Know Can Cost You	$1
Credit Cards and Seniors	$1
Credit Card Fraud	$1
How To Re-establish Good Credit	$1
Your Next Car: Leasing vs. Buying	$1
Traveling With Credit Cards	$1
Credit Repair Clinics: Consumers Beware	$1

◆ 9 ◆

Housing Decisions: Should You Buy or Rent?

By Marc Eisenson

As appeared in the Sound Mind Investing newsletter in 1995. Adapted from The Pocket Change Investor. Copyright 1992 by Marc Eisenson & Nancy Castleman. Used with permission. All rights reserved. For a sample copy, send $1 to: Bulletin Sample, Box 78-A, Elizaville, New York 12523.

John and Mary Homeseeker need to move. After scanning ads and touring with local brokers, they're considering a $125,000 house in a nearby development. They're also intrigued by a thirty acre, secluded mountaintop home that they saw advertised for $950 a month. Putting aside the lifestyle questions, which alternative makes the most financial sense? To find out, I had to make some assumptions about the Homeseekers. Don't conclude that my numbers for the Homeseekers prove whether you should buy or rent. Decide based on *your own assumptions*, feelings, and willingness to take risks.

Here's what I assumed about the Homeseekers: They could negotiate the $125,000 asking price down to $112,500. They have enough cash on hand to put down 10%, and to cover an expected 5% worth of closing costs—totaling $16,313. (That up-front cash now earns them 5%, or $68 a month.)

John and Mary could borrow the difference at 8½% for thirty years. Because their down payment is only 10%, the bank will require mortgage insurance. They'd also have to pay property and school taxes, and their maintenance costs would be higher than if they rented. The Homeseekers have no other tax deductions, which means that if they buy, their tax breaks would be $118 a month—much less than they expected.

Their monthly housing costs would be $117 less if they rented than if they bought ($1,102-$985). This didn't convince them to rent the villa, because they expected that the early rental

advantage would be wiped out by equity gains and tax benefits over the seven years they expected to live in the house. Do I have a surprise for the Homeseekers! As buyers, they'd spend $26,141 *more* over the seven years than they would as tenants (difference shown at bottom of Table 1).

If John and Mary were to rent and systematically invest the $117 a month difference, say at 5%, it would grow to $11,738 by the time they get the seven year itch to move. If instead of going for the 5% return, the Homeseekers used that $117 a month to pay off consumer debt, they'd fare even better.

But how about all the money John and Mary would make as homeowners when they sell? Absent that crystal ball, let's look at a few scenarios:

◆ If home values drop, the Homeseekers clearly would come out ahead as tenants. That's no surprise.

◆ But maybe home prices will go up over the next seven years. If they do, we're looking at some real profits for John and Mary, right? Not if, as renters, they'd squirrel away that $117 every month! Even if they could get $150,000 for the house—a 33% jump—when you factor in the amount the Homeseekers could put aside as tenants, their real profit would be only $5,879—minus whatever capital gains taxes might be due.

Is it worth the risk? Renters can clearly end up wealthier than homeowners these days. And they can often find fabulous houses to rent—ones they could never afford to buy. ◆

TABLE #1: CASH SPENT AFTER 7 YEARS

Option →	Own	Rent
Negotiated Price	$112,500	$ 950
Down Payment/Security	11,250	1,900
Mortgage	101,250	None
Closing Costs	5,063	None
Monthly Payment	$ 779	$ 950
Taxes/Maint/Insurance	373	35
Sub-Total	$ 1,152	$ 985
+ Lost Investment Income	+ 68	None
– Tax Savings	– 118	None
Monthly Cost	$ 1,102	$ 985
Total Monthly for 7 Years	$ 92,568	$ 82,740
Plus Cash Up-Front	+ 16,313	+ 1,900
Cash Outgo	108,881	84,640
Less Security Refund	0	–1,900
Total Cash Outgo	$ 108,881	$ 82,740

TABLE #2: CASH FROM SALE AFTER 7 YEARS

Selling Price →	$100,000	$125,000	$150,000
Less 8% Commission	–8,000	–10,000	–12,000
Received At Closing	92,000	115,000	138,000
Less Remaining Mortgage	–94,242	–94,242	–94,242
Cash To Owner	–$2,242	$20,758	$43,758

TABLE #3: OWNERSHIP VERSUS RENTING

Selling Price →	$100,000	$125,000	$150,000
Owner's Cash Outgo	$108,881	$108,881	$108,881
Factor In Cash From Sale	+2,242	–20,758	–43,758
Homeowner's Net Cost	111,123	88,123	65,123
Less Renter's Cash Outgo	–82,740	–82,740	–82,740
Apparent Advantage of Renting	28,383	5,383	–17,617
Plus Renter's Earnings	+11,738	+11,738	+11,738
Actual Advantage of Renting	$40,121	$17,121	–$5,879

◆ 10 ◆

Big Savings Through Mortgage Pre-payments
By Marc Eisenson

As appeared in the Sound Mind Investing newsletter in 1994. Adapted from The Banker's Secret. Copyright 1991 by Marc Eisenson. Used with permission. All rights reserved. To order this book, which many consider to be "the bible" on saving money on your mortgage, send $17.95 to: Good Advice Press, Box 78-A, Elizaville, New York 12523.

When you take out a loan, you agree to pay back the amount borrowed plus interest. That's fair. But you've probably never realized just how much interest can be. For example, on a $75,000, 30-year mortgage, written at 10% interest, the total payback will be almost $237,000. That's nearly $162,000 in interest charges on a $75,000 loan. More than twice what was borrowed! Shocking, isn't it?

Well, take heart. Making small, frequent pre-payments with pocket change—that money most of us would never invest, or miss—will save a substantial portion of the nearly $162,000 in interest that this $75,000 loan would normally incur. *Pre-payments are not additional costs. They are simply small amounts paid sooner.*

Every month, or whenever you are expected to make a payment to your lender (for convenience we'll assume all borrowers are homeowners and all lenders are banks), the bank's computer calculates the amount of interest you owe for having used its money during the previous month, and subtracts that interest from the amount of the check you send in. What's left is credited toward the outstanding balance of your loan.

To make it easy to keep track of how much interest you are being charged and how much of each payment is being credited toward the principal of your loan, it is necessary to use an appropriate pre-payment schedule. These computer printed charts, often referred to as amortization schedules, separate out the interest and principal components of each monthly payment, along with the balance remaining after each payment has been made.

Shown above is a pre-payment schedule showing the payments during various time periods for our sample loan. When each payment is made, the balance of the loan gets reduced by the amount of the principal portion only, *not* by the amount of the total monthly payment. If the sample loan shown were your mortgage, you would be expected to pay $658.18 every month for thirty years. You could not pay less, or skip any payments without risking a foreclosure. But, you could pay more.

For illustrative purposes, let's assume that you are about to mail in mortgage payment #1. If you add $33.46 (principal payment #2) to the $658.18 which is due every month, and mail in a single check for $691.64, the bank will properly credit your pre-payment of $33.46 and you won't have to make interest payment #2. *You will never pay that $624.72!*

Next month, when you mail in your check for $658.18, it will be credited as if it were payment #3, since the principal portion of payment #2 will have already been credited, and the interest payment which the bank's computer will show as due, is the interest amount shown for payment #3. Now for the bonus: Not only will that $33.46 save you $624.72, but it will also reduce the term of your loan by one month. That's pre-paying in a nutshell. Where else but in your mortgage can you get such safe, high, guaranteed returns on such tiny investments?

You can begin pre-paying at any time; however, the sooner you begin, the greater your savings will be. That's because interest payments are higher and principal payments are lowest at the inception of the loan. Later on, the savings will still be substantial, although smaller. Let's look at a portion of the schedule of our sample mortgage ten years down the road. We'll assume that no pre-payments have been made.

Assume an additional principal payment of $90.57 is mailed in with payment #121 (for a total of $658.18 + $90.57 = $748.75). You will save $567.61 (interest payment #122) and retire the loan one month earlier. The following month's payment would be #123, not payment #122. Note that even after 120 monthly payments of $658.18 each have been made, totalling $78,981.60 (120 x $658.18), the balance on this loan has only been reduced by $6,796.76 ($75,000 less $68,203.24). The remaining $72,184.84 ($78,981.60 paid less the $6,796.76) all would have gone toward interest—almost as much as was borrowed in the first place!

If pre-paying seems like a good idea to you, get a pre-payment schedule for your loan and begin! No matter what type of loan you have, whether it's a fixed rate, adjustable, or bi-weekly, the more you pre-pay and the sooner you begin, the more you will save! ◆

MORTGAGE SCHEDULE

Amortization based on 30 year, $75,000 loan at 10% interest. Monthly payment of $658.18

Payment Number	Interest Portion	Principal Portion	Balance Remaining
1	625.00	33.18	74,966.82
2	624.72	33.46	74,933.36
3	624.44	33.74	74,899.62
120	569.10	89.08	68,203.24
121	568.36	89.82	68,113.42
122	567.61	90.57	68,022.85

◆ 11 ◆

Paying for College
By Scott Houser

As appeared in the <u>Sound Mind Investing</u> newsletter in 1995.
Copyright 1995 by Austin Pryor & Associates. Used with permission. All rights reserved.
Scott Houser is a partner in the financial planning firm of Ronald Blue & Co.

Paying for college is a lot harder for most people than selecting one. Since 1980, as measured by the consumer price index, college costs have grown two to two and one-half times faster than inflation. Estimates of $150,000-$200,000 are tossed out as the total cost package for getting one child through a good school. Some people may pay that amount, but I can't and you don't have to, either. What follows are some practical tips on tackling what can easily be the single largest expense item of your life.

1. Start early—saving, that is. Each of our children has a savings account that was funded primarily by the cash gifts received when they were born. You don't know whether your little bundle of joy is the next Albert Einstein or Cal Ripken, so you may as well hedge your bets by starting a savings account at birth. Over the years, each account has been added to with checks received for birthdays, earnings from yard work, babysitting, etc. Compounding is a wonderful tool. If one had invested $1,000 in an average growth mutual fund earning 10%, that sum would have grown to $5,560 in eighteen years—more than five times your money. Not bad. Not many of us can save the entire amount of our children's college education, but all of us can save more than we think we can if we start early and add periodically. Even having $5,560 in your pocket builds confidence when staring at the college-costs mountain.

2. Start early—distinguish your student. Last year, after applying to nine colleges and applying for at least two dozen scholarships, I know what makes a scholarship candidate look good. Above-average varsity athletes and applicants who graduated in the top ten percent of their class are a "dime a dozen" when competing for merit-based scholarships. Committees look for signs of achievement that are unique. Consistently winning high honors at the state science fair, extraordinary community volunteer service, or outstanding musical achievement can give the less academically-qualified applicant an edge when competing for merit scholarships. Get your children involved in an activity that may not only pay dividends in the future, but will make them feel good about themselves as they achieve. The number of hours spent playing Nintendo is not a strong scholarship qualifier.

3. Start early—get a job. My son was awarded several merit scholarships. Several students in his graduating class, all less academically gifted, were awarded better scholarships. How did they do it? They had worked during high school for some of our city's largest employers. Some of these kids were minorities, some were not, but all were good workers who had aligned themselves with companies who invest in their current and future employees. Finding out about these opportunities takes work. I am not aware of a published source, but most large companies have a person in their Human Resources Department who is aware of scholarship, student intern, and work-study types of opportunities. Call them.

4. Research, research, research. If you have a high school senior, you may have been solicited by a private search firm that claims millions of dollars of scholarship money goes unclaimed. For a fee, they will bring you scholarships "ripe for the picking." Don't believe it. The scholarship market is too efficient. The best facts come from do-it-yourself research. Recently, I went to a bookstore to see if I could find a book or two on financial aid. What I discovered was a whole section. Invest in two or three of these guides. Tip: Buy the most current book you can find by checking the copyright date on the inside, front cover. Many local and school libraries also have these books available.

5. Visit your high school counselor's office. Some parents leave this job solely to their children. I advise against it. Our high school has a computer program and a notebook that is kept current regarding local and national scholarships. Your child does not have time to read this information between classes, and after all, money grows on trees for Moms and Dads. We found that many scholarship opportunities were sometimes placed in the notebook that had a short application fuse, sometimes as little as two weeks. Use your high school to get oriented for your financial search. Home school? You may be able to hire a high school counselor who works after hours giving college advice.

6. Merit-based scholarships: College sponsored. One surprise for my wife and me was the level of competition in applying for the top merit-based scholarships offered by schools and other organizations. Your child may be a standout in his or her high school, but when applying for merit-based scholarships, he or she will be among equals. At every college that we applied to, we also applied for merit-based aid. All of these applications require your student to write one or more essays. Creative, non-traditional essays are what the evaluators are looking for. One tough decision Christian students will face is whether to include their testimony in some fashion into an essay question. Don't expect a pro-

Christian bias on selection committees.

7. Merit-based: National. Several companies and organizations offer scholarships aimed at target groups. Our son applied for the Schering Asthma Athlete scholarship. Tylenol awards several scholarships on a national basis. Research your high school's data base or the library to find out how to get an application and when the deadlines are. Some deadlines occur surprisingly early in the fall.

8. Merit-based: Local. This is a form of merit-based aid which offers promise for the industrious. In a small, local, throw away newspaper, we saw a one inch notice that a women's club in our area was offering a $2,000 scholarship. We applied and won. The local Kiwanis, Optimists Clubs, etc., often give scholarships on a local level. More often than not, these are not advertised at all, but an industrious parent with yellow pages in hand can search these out.

9. Need-based: College Source. Need-based aid generally depends on the parents' financial situation. When applying to a college, find out what percentage of their students receive need-based aid or grants. The figure may surprise you. It is not uncommon for over 50% of students attending private institutions to receive some type of need-based aid, but you have to apply and, again, hard work pays off. Tip: When visiting a college, always visit the financial aid office—it is usually separate from the admissions office.

10. Need-based: State. We were surprised to find out about the amount of financial aid available to a resident of Georgia. Georgia residents can automatically receive at least $1,000 in tuition equalization for all students who attend private schools in the State of Georgia. To find out about need-based aid, my advice is to not rely solely upon the literature that is available in the high school counselor's office, but call the Superintendent of Education's office in your state. Find someone who is knowledgeable to get information directly from the source.

Warning: It's not easy. You'll be put on hold forever.

11. Need-based: Federal. You may also be able to find out about federal grants and aids through the state Superintendent of Education's Office. Much of the federal aid is built around loans such as the Stafford, PLUS, and Perkins loans, etc. Tip: If you have to borrow money to send your child to college, I would recommend exploring a home equity loan as a source of college funds. The interest on home equity loans is deductible, and typically the interest on college loans is not. Even though you may pay a lower interest rate for a subsidized federal or state loan, on an after-tax basis it may cost you more.

12. ROTC scholarships. This is one of the greatest financial aid opportunities, especially for the academically average student. A friend of mine, who works for a Christian organization, sent his son to Vanderbilt University on an ROTC scholarship. In looking into this opportunity for our son, I was surprised at the small amount of payback time that was required to serve in the armed forces after graduation.

13. Hard work never hurt anyone. Statistics show that students who work part-time while in college have superior academic performance to those who don't work. The last time I looked, it wasn't in the U.S. Constitution that every parent owed their child a four-year college education. Even if financial resources are not a problem, I encourage my clients to have their children earn a bit of the privilege of going to college.

The purpose of this article was not to recite specifics as much as it was to increase your awareness of sources of possible financial aid. If you have a child of high school age, your sensitivity for the word "scholarships" and/or "financial aid" should be tuned like a Stradivarius. You should be able to open the newspaper, scan the entire page for two seconds, and have your eyes immediately come to rest on the word "scholarship." Cut it out, and start a file. You're going to need that information sooner than you think. ◆

12

How to Exchange Fund Shares Quickly by Mail
By Vicki Mosher

As appeared in the Sound Mind Investing newsletter in 1995.
Copyright 1995 by Austin Pryor & Associates. Used with permission. All rights reserved.
Vicki Mosher is a member of the SMI Reader Services Staff.

Often during periods of dramatic economic or market changes, investors are surprised (and frustrated!) when they find they can't get through on the telephone to their fund family in order to transact business. It may be that there has been a market selloff and you want to take advantage of the buying opportunity it presents by moving some of your assets from your money market fund to a stock fund. Or, perhaps you wish to reduce your risk and move in the other direction—from your stock fund to the safety of a money market fund. Either way, it's essential that you be able to communicate your instructions effectively even when the phone lines are busy. Come with me and I'll show you how to follow the example of the five wise virgins (Matt. 25:1-13) in preparing for an unexpected event.

❶ Locate the prospectus(es) of the fund(s) you currently hold. It should be a fairly recent one. If not, call and request a current prospectus to assure accurate information.

❷ Refer to the Table of Contents under "Exchanging and Redeeming Funds by Mail." You will find specific directions on the requirements from your fund family for exchanging shares by mail. They must be followed precisely. Any inaccuracies will cause a delay in processing. Familiarize yourself with the directions, and if you have any questions, call your fund's Shareholders Services for clarification.

❸ You'll now need to compose a letter of instruction which contains the necessary information required for the possible future transaction. The standard requirements for an exchange letter include: •For the funds involved in the exchange, give their specific name(s) and your account number(s). •The amount of the exchange you wish to make (leave this blank and handwrite in the amount at the time the letter is sent). •The signature(s) of the registered account owner(s) of the fund(s) is also required. •Most fund families require that the signature(s) be guaranteed since you'll be requesting that the funds be placed in a different account. Your fund will not accept a notary public seal. This is a procedure that can be obtained at almost all banks, savings and loan associations, and credit unions. Call your financial institution to see if they have the ability to guarantee a signature.

❹ To get your letter there quickly, you'll want to use one of the overnight delivery services (e.g., Federal Express). Pick up a mailing envelope from the service you wish to use. Fill out the delivery form completely (except for the date), paying special attention to the express mail address of your fund organization. Located in your prospectus should be a special address for receiving express mail (FedEx will not deliver to a post office box). Call your Shareholders Services if you're unable to find the address you need. Unlike fund organizations, Schwab has branch offices and requires that you send your instructions to the one that administers your account.

❺ Although you're going to prepare your overnight letter now, you may not have a need for it for many months. Find out how you should pay for the service when the time comes (Federal Express allows you to enclose a check or credit card number with the delivery form at the time you send your letter).

❻ Make a note of the location of the nearest drop box for your delivery service, and the time of their last pickup. If you really want to be thorough, you may also want to inquire where to take the envelope in case you miss the final pickup. Usually it's your local airport.

❼ Place your completed letter of instruction to your fund in your prepared overnight envelope, and store it within your (hopefully) organized file with your fund statements and other information.

❽ Relax, and know that if the time comes when you can't get through on the phone to communicate your instructions, you will have been an initiator instead of a responder. All you'll have to do is date your letter and the delivery form, and fill in the dollar amount of the transaction. Then affix your delivery form on the envelope, seal it up, and drop it in your local drop box. Don't forget to enclose your check or credit card number to pay the overnight service.

What happens after your fund family receives your redemption letter? They date stamp their express mail when received and give it top priority. When your request is processed, you receive the price for the close of the date received. Some of the fund families have arranged to bring in outside help in order to process the requests received each day and some even work around the clock until all orders are in. Call your particular organization and ask them for the procedures they follow during a volatile market.

Good job! You took the necessary precautions in order to get your plan in place for dealing with an unforeseen occurrence. Like the wise virgins, you took the initiative to be prepared! ◆

◇ 13 ◇

Load Funds and Classes of Shares

By Austin Pryor

As appeared in the <u>Sound Mind Investing</u> newsletter in 1995.

To keep track of the mountain of data generated by the mutual fund industry, I subscribe to a pretty neat service offered by Morningstar, the Chicago organization which monitors the investment performance of mutual fund and annuity products. For a mere $795 a year, I receive a computer CD each month that is packed with the equivalent of several thousand pages of data. The current one has information on 6,458 mutual funds. Three years ago, there were less than half that many.

Much of this dramatic growth is due to a feeding frenzy on the part of investors. The public's appetite for stock investing has been huge, and fund organizations have responded in fine capitalistic fashion by meeting the demands of the marketplace. A considerable number of the new funds, however, aren't really "new" at all. They're old load funds trying to look more like no-loads by creating new "classes" of shares. If you study the offerings of load fund organizations these days, you'll often find they offer three ways of investing in the same fund.

Class "A" shares. This is the traditional load fund arrangement where you pay a sales charge to the broker or financial planner who introduced you to the fund, and this charge is deducted from your investment at the time you make it. Whereas this used to run 8.50%, competitive pressures from the no-loads have taken their toll. The most common front-end load is now 5.75%, and some are as low as 3.00%. In addition to this one-time sales charge, you also pay the on-going annual operating expenses which are common to all mutual funds.

Class "B" shares. These shares move the load from the front-end to the back-end, where it gradually diminishes the longer you hold your shares. A typical arrangement might call for you to pay a 5% load if you sell your shares during the first year, a 4% load if you sell during the second year, and so on until you pay no load at all if you hold on for more than five years. Your broker still receives a sales commission, but it comes from the fund organization rather than immediately from your account.

How does the fund recoup this payment? By adding deferred sales charges to the fund's annual expenses, which makes them higher than they otherwise would be. So (surprise!) you're the one who ultimately pays; you just do it a little every day rather than all at once up front. After six or seven years, some fund organizations will automatically convert your Class "B" shares to Class "A" shares (which pay lower — that is, normal — annual expenses) on the basis that by then you'll have "paid your dues." Other organizations aren't so fair-minded and continue to gouge you indefinitely.

Class "C" shares. At first glance, these seem the most like no-load funds. They have no front-end loads, and the deferred load, a relatively small 1%, usually applies only to redemptions made during the first year you own your shares. The broker gets no up-front commissions for selling Class "C" shares. Instead, he receives a "level load" which is built into the annual expense charge and continues for as long as you own your shares.

The table below shows the effects of these various load arrangements over time on a $1,000 investment. The annual expenses column is an approximate average for each group. The initial advantage among the load funds goes to Class "C" shares, but if you hold them long enough, Class "A" shares win out due to their lower annual expenses. The ☑ symbol indicates the best deal for each holding period.

Two kinds of no-load funds are also included for comparison purposes. One group charges 12(b)-1 fees (marketing costs which the SEC allows funds to pass on to their shareholders as part of their annual expenses). The other group, for competitive reasons, elects not to charge 12(b)-1 fees. As the table makes clear, no-load fund investors enjoy the best of both worlds — no sales charges going in or coming out, and low annual expenses for as long as you stay. ◆

	Front Loads	Deferred Loads	Annual Expenses	Sell After Year 1	Sell After Year 2	Sell After Year 3	Sell After Year 4	Sell After Year 5	Sell After Year 6	Sell After Year 7	Sell After Year 8	Sell After Year 9	Sell After Year 10
HOW VARIOUS LOAD AND EXPENSE ARRANGEMENTS ERODE A 10% ANNUAL RETURN													
Pure No-Loads	None	None	1.10%	$1089	$1186	$1291	$1406	$1532	$1668	$1816	$1978	$2154	$2346
12b-1 No-Loads	None	None	1.65%	$1084	$1174	$1272	$1378	$1493	$1618	$1753	$1899	$2058	$2230
Class A Loads	5.75%	None	1.25%	$1025	$1115	$1212	$1318	$1434	$1559	$1695	☑$1845	☑$2005	☑$2181
Class B Loads	None	5.00%	2.05%	$1040	$1135	$1238	$1348	☑$1466	☑$1583	☑$1708	$1844	$1991	$2149
Class C Loads	None	1.00%	2.15%	☑$1079	☑$1163	☑$1254	☑$1353	$1459	$1574	$1697	$1830	$1974	$2129

How the Federal Reserve Affects Interest Rates and Bond Prices

By Austin Pryor

As appeared in the <u>Sound Mind Investing</u> newsletter in 1990.

The Federal Reserve is a kind of master bank. It serves as the bank for banks as well as for the U.S. government. In connection with its supervision of the nation's banks, it (1) performs periodic surprise audits on bank records to make sure the Fed's regulations are being followed; (2) serves as a clearinghouse for all the checks written on checking accounts nationwide; and (3) loans money to banks (at a special low rate called the discount rate) that might need it to meet regulatory requirements or simply wish to make more loans to their customers.

The U.S. government is also a customer of the banking services of the Federal Reserve Bank (or Fed). The Treasury and many governmental agencies have their accounts with the Fed, where they deposit and withdraw their money just like any other customer of a bank would do. The Fed also coordinates the money coming into the Treasury. When a worker or business pays payroll taxes, or when an investor buys Treasury securities, the money ends up at the Fed. Likewise, when it's time to send the monthly social security checks or the interest on Treasury bills, notes, and bonds, that money is released by the Fed.

But the activities of the Fed that get the most attention have to do with its role as the regulator of the supply of money we have in circulation. Have you looked at your money lately? Did you notice those words on the front at the top that say "Federal Reserve Note"? By increasing and decreasing the amount of those notes in circulation, the Fed has a powerful influence on the health of our economy. Here's how it works.

We face two constant threats to our economic well-being: recession and inflation. The problem is that it's impossible to combat both of these threats simultaneously. The antidote for one only aggravates the other. It's like finding that you are allergic to the only medicine known to effectively cure your illness. You have to decide: would you rather live with the illness or the allergic reaction? You can't avoid both.

Here's how this applies to the Federal Reserve. During the "illness" of a recession, the Fed tries to help the economy recover. The primary "medicine" it uses is lower interest rates (sometimes referred to as "easy money"). As the Fed floods the economy with money, interest rates fall and credit is readily available. This encourages more borrowing and spending by American consumers and businesses, which in turn creates additional demand for goods and services. Economic activity revives, and corporate profits rise.

The stock market looks down the road and anticipates this recovery, and stock prices rally. Everybody's happy. Well, almost.

The problem is that this additional demand also creates pressure for higher prices, which means (you guessed it) inflation may be coming back. Sooner or later, the economy is going to have an "allergic reaction" to all that money flying around—it's called inflation. In economist-talk, the money supply has exceeded our productivity. That means buyers with too much money are chasing after too few goods and services being made available by sellers. The heavy demand by consumers combined with the scarcity of supply from producers bids up the market prices.

This principle is regularly demonstrated on the sidewalks outside any major sports event. In that situation, it's easy to understand how scalpers can get such outlandish prices for their tickets: the greater the crowd of eager buyers wanting in, the higher the prices will go. How can ticket prices be kept down? Only by increasing the supply of seats inside or decreasing the size of the crowd outside.

In my analogy, the Fed can't do anything about the size of the sports arena. If it wants to fight the illness of inflation, it can only do this by reducing the number of buyers. It attempts to do this by using the medicine of "tight money." It wants interest rates to rise high enough to cool the economy down. As the cost of borrowing gets increasingly expensive, consumers and businesses cut back. This leads to less discretionary cash for purchases and effectively lowers the number of buyers all across the economy. If the Fed isn't careful, too much tight money medicine and the economy will have another allergic reaction: recession!

The goal is to maintain just the right amount of money so that the economy is growing moderately and the dollar will buy roughly the same amount of goods and services next year as it does this year. But it's tough! Usually it's feast or famine. When the Fed fights recession by lowering interest rates, the goal is greater consumer demand and a stronger economy. This, however, leads to rising prices and inflation. When the Fed switches strategies and begins fighting inflation with higher interest rates, we get weakening consumer demand and a weaker economy—which, if we're not careful, returns us to recession and the entire cycle begins all over again. Now you know why life at the Fed is one gigantic balancing act! ◆

The Risks of Index Funds
By Austin Pryor

As appeared in the <u>Sound Mind Investing</u> newsletter in 1996.
Copyright 1996 by Austin Pryor & Associates. Used with permission. All rights reserved.

Index funds offer several advantages. Among them are lower expenses, fewer taxable distributions, relative predictability, and easy accessibility. Our Just-the-Basics strategy relies on them almost exclusively. However, in my enthusiasm for index funds, I may have failed to sufficiently explain their drawbacks. They have a few disadvantages.

The most significant drawback is that index funds offer no protection during periods of market weakness. They are fully invested in a portfolio of stocks which reflects the index they are designed to mimic, and they *stay* fully invested at all times. Because they're on automatic pilot, they're often called "passively managed" funds.

The graphs at the bottom show the monthly results of Vanguard's S&P 500 stock fund during the past three bear markets. They show how far the fund dropped from its highest point preceding the bear market, and how long it took for an investor who bought at the top to break even. For example, a shareholder who bought the fund prior to the 1977-78 bear market would have needed twenty months to get back to where he started. During that time, he would have had losses as great as 14.9%.

A second drawback is that index funds are generally invested in a rather narrow fashion, that is, they invest only in securities that are part of the index they are imitating. An S&P 500 fund, for instance, invests only in the large companies found in that index. This means it owns no small growth companies or foreign stocks. When large company stocks do well, so will Vanguard's S&P 500 index fund. When stocks of small companies are in favor, as in 1992 and 1993, an S&P 500 index fund will be a relatively poor performer.

The fourth column in the table below shows how the S&P 500 index fund ranked among all stock funds over the past fifteen years. The percentage indicates the portion of stock funds which the index fund outperformed for the year, so a high number represents a high ranking.

For example, the fund returned 9.9% in 1993, not a particularly bad return in an absolute sense. But in a relative sense, it was a poor showing—the fund outperformed only 24% of U.S. diversified stock funds for the year. Indexing gains its advantage over the long-term, as you can see from the results for the entire fifteen year period.

Our Just-the-Basics strategy deals with these drawbacks by combining several index funds into one portfolio. By adding a bond fund, we hope to provide a cushion to bear market weakness. By adding Vanguard's Extended Market index fund and the International Growth fund, we increase our diversification by adding small company and foreign stocks to the mix. These additional funds will not enhance performance every year, but they do add safety and stability to the portfolio over the long-haul.

Indexing need not be an "all or nothing" proposition. Many investors use the Just-the-Basics funds as "core" holdings to anchor their portfolios. For example, you might invest two-thirds of your portfolio in a Just-the-Basics mix of funds, and then use the other one-third to be a little more flexible. With the remaining third, you could either be more adventurous (by investing in selected stock funds or individual stocks) or more conservative (by adding Treasuries, CDs, or other money market holdings). ◆

ANNUAL COMPARISONS

SOURCES: MORNINGSTAR, IBBOTSON

	Vanguard S&P 500 Fund	Small Company Index	Average All Stock Funds	Vanguard S&P 500 Fund Rank
1981	−5.2%	13.9%	−0.8%	31%
1982	21.0%	28.0%	26.5%	32%
1983	21.3%	39.7%	21.8%	48%
1984	6.2%	−6.7%	−0.7%	77%
1985	31.2%	24.7%	28.4%	68%
1986	18.1%	6.9%	14.9%	72%
1987	4.7%	−9.3%	1.5%	65%
1988	16.2%	22.9%	15.6%	52%
1989	31.4%	10.2%	25.3%	77%
1990	−3.3%	−21.6%	−5.8%	60%
1991	30.2%	44.6%	36.9%	39%
1992	7.4%	23.4%	9.5%	41%
1993	9.9%	21.0%	13.1%	24%
1994	1.2%	3.1%	−1.2%	73%
1995	37.4%	34.5%	30.9%	83%
Avg	14.4%	14.2%	13.6%	72%

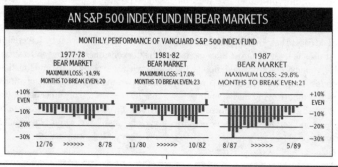

AN S&P 500 INDEX FUND IN BEAR MARKETS

MONTHLY PERFORMANCE OF VANGUARD S&P 500 INDEX FUND

1977-78 BEAR MARKET
MAXIMUM LOSS: -14.9%
MONTHS TO BREAK EVEN: 20
12/76 >>>>>> 8/78

1981-82 BEAR MARKET
MAXIMUM LOSS: -17.0%
MONTHS TO BREAK EVEN: 23
11/80 >>>>>> 10/82

1987 BEAR MARKET
MAXIMUM LOSS: -29.8%
MONTHS TO BREAK EVEN: 21
8/87 >>>>>> 5/89

16

How to CalculateYour Rate of Return

By Austin Pryor

As appeared in the <u>Sound Mind Investing</u> newsletter in 1996.
Copyright 1996 by Austin Pryor & Associates. Used with permission. All rights reserved.

Here's an easy way to calculate the approximate rate of return in any investment account. It won't be right on the money because we're giving up a little accuracy in return for simplicity—we're making the assumption that all deposit and withdrawal transactions take place at mid-year. This method will usually get you within one percent of the true return. That's close enough to provide a reality check.

Most financial institutions provide year-end account statements which include the data you'll need to perform the calculations. First, add up all the deposits you made during the year, and then subtract from that total all the withdrawals you made. Treat any dividends or interest checks you may have received as withdrawals. In Example 1 given below, deposits total $4,800 ($400 every month for twelve months). Subtract total withdrawals of $3,200 from the amount deposited, and the result is a net addition to the account of $1,600 over the course of the year.

You can track the rest of the calculation by following the examples. Steps two through four make adjustments to the opening and closing balances so as to take into account any deposits and withdrawals. In step five, the adjusted ending balance is divided by the adjusted beginning balance in order to measure how much the account has changed. Steps six and seven convert the result into more familiar percentage terms.

Example 2 shows a couple's retirement account which is being used to supplement monthly income. The ending balance is lower than the beginning balance; however, this doesn't necessarily mean the account lost money on its investments

during the year. After neutralizing the effects of the $600 monthly withdrawal, it can be seen that the account actually showed a positive return of about 8% for the year.

Similarly, just because an account climbs in value doesn't mean its investments were profitable. Example 3 shows an IRA which grew from $26,888 to $28,156. After taking into account the investor's $2,000 deposit, however, the calculation shows that the IRA account actually lost 2%-3% on its investments.

When comparing your investment returns to those of published benchmarks like the Dow Industrials or the S&P 500, remember that they assume the amount invested is unchanged throughout the year. If you're dollar-cost-averaging, it's unlikely your results will be similar. Because you weren't fully invested for the entire period, you'll tend to do better than the averages in a down year and worse than the averages in an up year.

If you want a more accurate measure of your results than the method shown here, your best bet is to purchase one of the many personal finance software packages available. Quicken and Managing Your Money are the two perennial leaders in sales. Included among the many useful reports they provide is a rate of return analysis on your investment portfolio. Be aware, however, that the process can be time consuming—you will need to enter every transaction that takes place in your account throughout the year. I suggest that you not purchase one of these programs unless you are ready to make full use of their many helpful budgeting and planning tools as well. ◆

EXAMPLE #1	EXAMPLE #2	EXAMPLE #3
What was the return in a college savings account which began the year at $18,692, ended at $22,919, and where $400 is added every month and $3,200 was withdrawn on August 20?	What was the return in a retirement savings account which began the year at $63,440, ended at $61,111, and where $600 was withdrawn at the beginning of every month for living expenses?	What was the return in an IRA which began the year at $26,888, ended at $28,156, and where a $2,000 deposit was made on April15?
1. Net additions/withdrawals for year + $1,600	1. Net additions/withdrawals for year − $7,200	1. Net additions/withdrawals for year + $2,000
2. Divide by two = + $800	2. Divide by two = − $3,600	2. Divide by two = + $1,000
Beginning balance from statement $ 18,692	Beginning balance from statement $63,440	Beginning balance from statement $26,888
3. Adjust beginning balance + 800	3. Adjust beginning balance − 3,600	3. Adjust beginning balance + 1,000
Adjusted beginning balance = 19,492	Adjusted beginning balance = 59,840	Adjusted beginning balance = 27,888
Ending balance from statement $ 22,919	Ending balance from statement $61,111	Ending balance from statement $28,156
4. Adjust ending balance − 800	4. Adjust ending balance + 3,600	4. Adjust ending balance − 1,000
Adjusted ending balance = 22,119	Adjusted ending balance = 64,711	Adjusted ending balance = 27,156
5. Divide ending by beginning = 1.135	5. Divide ending by beginning = 1.081	5. Divide ending by beginning = .974
6. Subtract 1 = .135	6. Subtract 1 = .081	6. Subtract 1 = − .026
7. Multiply times 100 = 13.5%	7. Multiply times 100 = 8.1%	7. Multiply times 100 = − 2.6%

Stock Market Seasonality

By Austin Pryor

As appeared in the <u>Sound Mind Investing</u> newsletter in 1990.
Copyright 1990 by Austin Pryor & Associates. Used with permission. All rights reserved.

The stock market is open an average of twenty-one days each month. For the past sixty-four years, let's assume that you and your family had a strategy of owning common stocks *only* during a certain seven-day stretch. Let's also say your neighbors thought you were crazy and, just to prove you wrong, insisted on owning stocks *only on the other fourteen days when you didn't*. Both families started with $1,000. Which family did the best?

Well, lucky you! Even though you were invested only one-third of the time, your family's nest egg has grown to a staggering *$4,400,000*! And your contrary neighbors, who were invested twice as many days each month as you were, watched with dismay as their original $1,000 shrank to a meager $433! (Commissions and taxes have been omitted to dramatize the point.) Curious? What seven days are we talking about here? *The last two trading days and first five trading days of each month.* From now on, I'll refer to this stretch as a "favorable period."

I first read of this tendency in the late 1970s in a book called *Stock Market Logic*, by Norman Fosback, who did the pioneering work in popularizing the seasonality concept. In 1990, the scholarly *Journal of Finance* published a paper by Joseph P. Ogden of State University of New York. He has offered an explanation of why there seems to be recurring buying activity at these times of the month that drives the market higher.

Professor Ogden's research discovered that 45% of all common stock dividends, 65% of all preferred stock dividends, 70% of interest and principal payments on corporate bonds, and 90% of the interest and payments on municipal bonds, is paid to investors on the first or last business day of each month. All this is in addition to the month-end contributions from salary checks that have been predesignated to go into various stock purchase plans. What do investors do with all this money? Dr. Ogden thinks they put a sizable portion into the stock market and believes this accounts for a significant part of the month-end phenomena.

Monday is historically the poorest performing of the five market days. Monday is the only day of the week to show a net loss. That means if you added up all the gains and losses of every Monday the stock market was open for the past sixty-four years, you'd end up with a negative number. So, when a Monday appears at the beginning or end of a favorable seven-day period, it is dropped. That's why some favorable periods only have six trading days rather than seven.

Here are a few ways you can use seasonality to improve your long-term performance.

◆ Let's say that your strategy calls for making regular monthly purchases (a dollar-cost-averaging strategy — see chapter 16), and that you are committed to investing $200 per month for the next fifteen years in a no-load growth stock fund. Why not do your buying before the other month-end investors start theirs? The favorable month-end period begins on the second to last trading day of each month; *the day to make your investment is the day before*. For example, assume the last five days in January fell as follows: 27th Thursday, 28th Friday, 29th Saturday, 30th Sunday, and 31st Monday. Since the financial markets are closed on the weekends, the second-to-last trading day in January is Friday, the 28th. You would then invest on Thursday, the 27th. A simpler approach (which I have tested and found to have roughly similar results) is to always mail your investment check on the Thursday before the last Monday of the month. Most of the time, it will arrive and be processed by your fund on the following Monday. This will be close enough to the day called for in the seasonality formula to still provide a benefit.

◆ Perhaps you're in retirement and part of your income derives from selling enough of your growth fund each month in order to withdraw $500. Wait until the favorable period has run its course; sell your shares on the fifth trading day of each month. A refinement of this takes into account that Friday has a tendency to be a strong market day; therefore, if the fifth trading day of a particular month falls on Thursday, wait one more day and sell on Friday instead. Over the long-term, you'll get a slightly better average price.

◆ Let's say that you're looking to move from one mutual fund organization to another. Sell your holdings in your present fund near the beginning of the month as a favorable period is concluded. Then, you've got time to receive your proceeds and get your account set up at the new organization. Initially, deposit your money into a money market fund. Then, near month's end just before the start of the next favorable period, make a phone call to switch into the stock fund you've selected.

◆ On a variation of the dollar-cost-averaging strategy, use favorable periods when investing a windfall (for example, an inheritance). If you haven't been investing regularly, it's a little scary to take a large sum and put it into the market "all at once." Divide it into several smaller amounts of equal size, depending on how long you want to stretch things out. For example, if you wanted to invest it over a period of six months, divide your total into six equal amounts. Then invest one-sixth each month just before the start of the favorable period.◆

18

Should You Use a Financial Planner?
By Dan Hardt, CLU, ChFC, CFP

As appeared in the <u>Sound Mind Investing</u> newsletter in 1996. Dan Hardt is a Certified Financial Planner with the Kentucky Financial Group in Louisville, Ky. Copyright 1996 by Austin Pryor & Associates. Used with permission. All rights reserved.

The need for "comprehensive" financial planning has emerged due to our changing society. Today, most of us have more disposable income, but the responsibility for financial success is falling increasingly on our own shoulders. We simply cannot count on working for the same employer, with big pension benefits and generous insurance plans, for the entire thirty-five to forty years of our working careers. According to the Social Security Administration, very few Americans are financially independent at retirement age. The reason for this bleak picture is primarily a failure to plan and an inability to spend less than what was earned over a long period of time.

According to the College for Financial Planning, "Financial planning is a process in which coordinated, comprehensive strategies are developed and implemented for the achievement of financial goals." In other words, developing a game plan in which all the interrelated aspects of your financial life—life insurance, investing, utilizing employee benefits and retirement plans, selling property, gifting strategies, and estate planning to name only a few—are given proper weight. Helping you through this process is the job of a financial planner.

Do not confuse a financial planner with a stock broker, money manager, insurance agent, or other professionals who have a limited focus. Although a financial planner may offer investment or insurance products, he/she does more than just look for the best investments for us or help us buy the right insurance policy. According to the International Association for Financial Planning, "Financial planners offer something you may not be able to get from the traditional stock broker, banker, accountant, or insurance agent—a way to consolidate *all* aspects of your financial life into one coordinated plan, so that every investment and activity can be viewed in the context of (your) specific financial goals."

A financial plan can be a valuable tool in helping you be a more effective steward. Many feel that only wealthy individuals need, or can afford, financial planners. The fact is most people have many facets of their financial affairs that could benefit from coordination. A planner helps you choose, from among almost unlimited alternatives, the appropriate financial strategy specifically suited for your situation. Also, a relationship with a financial planner can provide an ongoing, gentle accountability that many find vital in helping them keep focused and on track.

Finding a qualified financial planner is no easy task. Many individuals call themselves financial planners, financial consultants, financial advisors, personal planners, etc. Here are a few things you can look for that will increase your chances of finding qualified assistance:

☑ **Training.** Many planners have successfully completed formal courses of study to enhance their planning knowledge, and have further qualified for professional designations based on ethical and experience requirements. The most well known of these designations are those of Certified Financial Planner (CFP) and Chartered Financial Consultant (ChFC).

☑ **Experience.** You won't find many financial planners who have been around for thirty years, but you should be able to find plenty who have been in financial planning, or related fields, for ten years or more.

☑ **Team-backing.** I suggest that you work with a planner who is not a sole practitioner. Find one who has other competent planners in the office with them. You don't want the rug pulled out from under you if your planner retires, becomes incapacitated, etc.

☑ **Biblically-sound.** And of course, you want a planner who understands that your overall plan, and any specific planning strategies, should not be in opposition to God's word. Better yet, they should be *based on* God's word.

You also will want to know how your planner is compensated—fees, commissions, or both—and why they feel that is the most advantageous approach for you.

Should you plan? "A prudent man foresees the difficulties ahead and plans for them; the simpleton goes blindly on and suffers the consequences" (Proverbs 22:3 TLB). Combining a Godly attitude towards our finances, and adding the service of an experienced and knowledgeable financial planner, can help us be more faithful stewards of the money and possessions that God has placed in our care. ◆

19

Choosing Life Insurance That's Right for You
by Michael R. Cave, CLU, ChFC

As appeared in the <u>Sound Mind Investing</u> newsletter in 1994. Copyright 1994 by Austin Pryor & Associates. Used with permission. All rights reserved.
Michael Cave is a Chartered Life Underwriter (CLU) and Chartered Financial Consultant (ChFC) who lives in Augusta, GA.

The most common error in life insurance planning is forgetting God; this is our natural tendency. We must first recognize the necessity of faith in *all* decisions. With this firmly in mind, we can then proceed to the next step of choosing how much coverage to purchase (putting aside for the moment whether to buy term or whole life). Many people buy enough to feel secure; *to the degree God is our assurance, we'll feel less need for insurance.* I recommend you take rules of thumb lightly (for example, "you need six or ten times your annual income") because circumstances vary greatly. Rather, consider these reasonable guidelines which you can adjust to your comfort level.

♦ **Establish basic objectives.** I recommend leaving a paid-for home, no debts, an emergency fund, and income for basic living expenses. Admittedly I am frugal, but I think it's sound advice to not go overboard here. Just as we don't build mahogany staircases for fire escapes, it's best to insure basics — to do the job without undue expense. Reducing coverage by 30% reduces premiums by 30%. The savings here can be directed to other productive uses, like debt reduction, strengthening the family's contingency savings, or beginning an education fund.

♦ **Consider the probabilities.** Remember, insurance is a contingency plan which will likely never be used. Simply recognizing the odds is what I call "smart insuring." It's the same thing the insurance companies do that accounts for their massive wealth. For example, statistically the chances of a healthy non-smoking forty year old dying within the next ten years is less than 2%. (Conversely this means there's a 98% chance you won't get a penny for your premiums.) In contrast, what are the chances of a major economic disruption within the next ten years? The point is to not overly focus on the less-likely to the detriment of events that are more-likely. Our economic security dollars are limited, so be strategic with them (Prov. 19:2).

♦ **Distinguish between present life-style and insured life-style.** The large house (with its higher taxes, utilities, and upkeep) of a high-income family may not be prudent for a widow without that higher income. The issue here is are you willing to live more humbly if God ordains it? I Tim. 6:6 gives us God's perspective: "Godliness with contentment is great gain."

♦ **Don't automatically assume that a widow will remain unmarried.** A family, especially one headed by a young widow, may not remain exclusively dependent on resources left by the husband. Consider I Tim. 5:11 where Paul specifically commands the church to *not* support younger widows. Why not? After all wasn't the church's support their insurance program?

We read on to see his motive: "I counsel younger widows to marry." In fact, statistics confirm that younger widows usually do remarry. Although that may not seem likely in your case, God has a way of surprising us! Of four claims I've known, three have remarried after a few years (and the fourth got an unusually high-paying job). Remember the beautiful story of how God cared for the widows Naomi and Ruth through Boaz, without life insurance or Social Security? Death is not capricious. God is in control, and He has committed Himself to caring for His children, with special attention for widows.

♦ **Ask "How well am I insured already?"** Consider assets such as life insurance through your employer, Social Security, savings, retirement funds, family wealth, and the surviving spouse's income potential. Retirement accounts such as 401(k) or IRA are available to beneficiaries at death without the 10% early withdrawal penalty. However, they are subject to income tax; therefore, discount them by 20% (to reflect the family's lower tax bracket) when planning on their use.

Determine the adequacy of these assets to pay off a suitable house, funeral, and other debts, and to establish an emergency fund. I suggest a $25,000 emergency fund for a widow in lieu of the Level Two $10,000 objective. This could update an auto or large appliance. If assets are deficient for achieving your objectives, then you can supplement them through an insurance policy. View this as stabilizing the family.

Consider a young family with children ages ten, seven, and four that loses the father. The amount of cash needed immediately is easy to calculate: $90,000 to pay off the mortgage, $15,000 to pay off assorted debts, $25,000 for the emergency reserve, and $5,000 for funeral expenses. This need totals $135,000. To meet this, we'll assume the father has life insurance through his employer equal to his salary of $40,000, and that the family has $10,000 in savings. (There may also be a 401(k) or other retirement benefits, but we'll leave these for the mother's latter years.) So the cash available upon the father's death totals $50,000, which means the family will be $85,000 short. We need this much life insurance to stabilize the family — rounding up to a $100,000 policy is reasonable.

The next consideration is ongoing living expenses. Remember: the family without the hemorrhage of debt payments, and with one less mouth to feed, needs less income. A modest income will pay for groceries, clothing, and utilities. Here's where Social Security comes in. Survivor benefits, which can be substantial, make Americans among the best insured people in the world. For a family to qualify, the person who dies must (1) have paid into Social Security for six of the last thirteen quarters and (2) have surviving children under age eighteen. Here are *approximations* of the monthly income a family might expect:

Your Annual Earnings	Spouse & Two+ Children	Spouse & One Child	One Child Only
$20,000	$1,400	$1,140	$570
30,000	1,780	1,500	760
40,000	1,990	1,700	850
50,000	2,180	1,870	940

The monthly benefit is divided equally among the surviving spouse and each child. In our example, where the father earned $40,000 and left three children, the family would receive $1,990 per month. Although, as a practical matter the funds are pooled to support the entire family, the benefit would actually arrive in the form of four checks, one for the mother and one for each child. The spouse's check ends when the youngest child reaches age sixteen, and each child's check ends at age eighteen.

Thus, survivor benefits cover the most important child-rearing years. (If the system ever changes, you can buy replacement coverage at that time.) Depending on the age and earnings of the spouse who died and the number and ages of the children left behind, these benefits can total over $250,000 before they end. This amount, plus the $100,000 personal policy and $40,000 policy at work, effectively give our young family nearly $400,000 of coverage.

It may be best for widows to not work, or to work only part-time, since they would be filling the role of both parents; also, under certain conditions, their survivor benefits are reduced by 50¢ for each $1 of earnings over $8,040 per year. However, bear in mind Social Security provides nothing for a wife without children under age eighteen until she reaches age sixty. For more precise information, call your local Social Security office.

If you asked five life insurance agents for recommendations for this family, you'd get five different amounts. This is a subjective process that involves value judgments only you can answer. In summary, my suggestions for choosing an amount of life insurance:

☑ Don't forget God. See Deut 10:18, Ruth, and Psalms 146:9. Are you planning from fear or in faith?

☑ Establish basic objectives. Don't get carried away—a paid-for home, no debt, and an emergency fund.

☑ Take into account your current assets. You may already have group life insurance and savings.

☑ Consider Social Security survivors benefits as well as the wife's income ability after children are grown.

Term or Whole Life?

Only after choosing an amount of life insurance should you consider the type of policy—either term or whole life. ("Whole life" is commonly used to refer to insurance with cash value, as opposed to term life. Actually whole life is but one of many types of insurance with cash value, others being universal life, adjustable life, endowment contracts, etc. I am using the common, though somewhat imprecise, definition.)

This choice introduces a long-standing controversy between the industry and the consumer. Whole life sales are the bread-and-butter income of life insurance agents which are the distribution system (and therefore the very lifeblood) of the industry. For the industry to concede that whole life is a bad buy would be suicide. But that same factor—the large commissions which must be borne by the purchaser—makes whole life a poor performer among financial products. Once you understand how policies work, you can understand why.

First, let's take a quiz: What is the general difference between whole life insurance and all other insurance? (Think about it.) Answer: whole life, given time, *will* pay a claim (we all die); other insurance *may* pay a claim (the house may burn, the auto may crash, etc.). Thus, whole life must do something no other insurance does—accumulate a fund for the inevitable claim at death. This is called cash value.

Now, let's expand our definitions: Term insurance is pure insurance where the premium charged equals the probability insured against. Example: statistically, out of 1,000 healthy forty-year-old males, two will die before reaching age forty-one. Insuring them for $100,000 each requires a $200 annual premium from each. $200 X 1000 insureds gives the $200,000 needed to pay the two claims. (For simplicity we're ignoring expenses, time value of money, etc.)

Whole life is not just pure insurance. It combines pure insurance (term) with an accumulating fund whereby the risk is gradually self-insured as the fund, which is called cash value, grows. Therefore, within a whole life policy at age forty, initially we have $100,000 of pure insurance plus a zero cash value. Each year the cash value grows and the term reduces by like amount, so the two always total $100,000. By age 100 (for those who make it), the term is zero and the cash value $100,000. They'll pay it to you without your dying!

This combination of insurance and savings requires a higher premium, say $1,200 per year, to pay the pure insurance portion ($200 the first year) and have extra ($1,000) for the accumulating fund or cash value. The term cost per $1,000 increases each year as you get older but the amount of term reduces as you become self-insured through the cash value. Imagine that after ten years your cash value is $10,000. This means two things: [1] the amount of pure insurance has reduced (to $90,000) and, [2] the company's income from the policy has gone up—now it not only gets the $1,200 you pay but earnings from your $10,000 cash value as well.

Observation: With term, the company is insuring you; with whole life they are insuring you *and saving for you*. Most people do not realize that life insurance companies, to a large degree, do the same thing as banks—make a profit by lending money. Banks get theirs from savings accounts and CDs; insurers from policy cash values. Therefore, as one author pointed out, insurance companies really are "invisible bankers."

Next quiz question: Do insurers profit more by providing pure insurance (charging $250 for the term portion when it costs only $200 to pay claims), or by making a margin as do banks from the savings element of policies (crediting only 6% to your cash value earnings when they actually make 8%)? Answer: insurers make more on the savings element than the term insurance element! (Term insurance contains only one of the two profit sources, and it's the smaller one at that!) This explains why the industry promotes whole life. It also pays agents more (sometimes ten times more) to sell it. This makes for a material conflict of interest in getting advice on this subject from the industry, and explains why agents usually steer you to whole life.

We can summarize that "term = insurance" while "whole life = insurance + savings." Both have a term cost which increases yearly as one gets older and the chance of death increases. By cancelling this common denominator, we isolate the fundamental difference between term and whole life—the savings element called "cash value."

For a $100,000 policy where the annual premium is $1,200, only $200 is needed to pay for the actual insurance while the lion's share doesn't go to insurance at all. It goes to the investment element of the policy. It is because the cash value receives five times as much as pure insurance receives that I call whole life an "investment." Therefore we should evaluate it as such. The following are the three most important observations about cash value, the savings element within a whole life policy.

◆ **Transaction costs.** The expense load is by far the highest of any common financial product. It is many times that of other insurance company products (annuities), bank products (CDs and savings), or other mutual funds (even the highest loaded ones). It would be comparable to a mutual fund into which you put $1,000 per year, but the entire first year's contribution goes to commission and expenses.

Anyone considering whole life should compute the difference in its cost versus a comparable amount of term insurance. Then compare this difference to the *surrender* value of the whole life at the end of the first year. In the above example, the difference of $1,000 goes to cash value. Yet the cash surrender value at the end of the first year is zero. This violates a basic principle of investing—avoiding unnecessary transac-

tion costs. Over a ten year period, the high transaction costs always result in whole life giving a lower net worth compared to buying term and saving the difference (or using the difference to pay down debt).

◆ **Rate of return.** If you pay a high transaction cost to enter something, you hope the rate of return will make it up, right? Not here. In this investment you are a lender, not an owner. Insurers invest 80%+ of cash values in bonds, mortgages, policy loans, and cash. Although better long-term returns are available in stocks (over the past sixty-five years, stocks have returned around 10% compared to 5% for bonds), the buyer of whole life makes the longest possible commitment to a bond-type rate of return. The time horizon being death usually makes it even longer than retirement. Inflation may consume most of your earnings. Therefore this violates a second basic principal of long-term investing. Listed below are historic returns for 1978-1995 contrasting the returns of an S&P 500 fund to the approximate gross return credited to an exceptionally good cash value policy for the same year. These are gross returns before expenses and insurance costs.

◆ **Taxation.** This is a plus for whole life insurance. Cash value accrues on a tax-deferred basis. If held until death it becomes income-tax free as life insurance proceeds. Rarely, however, will this tax advantage overcome the economic handicaps of the first two points. Also, it may be unwise to presume on this advantage surviving forever, as the government has for many years had a covetous eye on cash-value earnings as a large possible revenue source. Finally, remember that term death benefits are also income tax-free, and annuities (even no-load, variable ones) accrue tax-deferred.

The decision boils down to this—do you want the insurance company to save for you in an extremely high-transaction cost long-term commitment to a debt-based return, or should you use them for pure insurance and rely on other vehicles to build your assets to the point where you no longer need life insurance. At that point, you are "self-insured." Whole life simply forces you to become self-insured through systematic savings.

Important qualification: This discussion primarily refers to the purchase of new insurance. Whether to continue old policies, where transaction costs have been paid, is a different consideration. However, despite the above limitations, cash-value insurance may be warranted in select situations, particularly after all debts are paid, and through using low-load products with a few outstanding companies. ◆

YEAR BY YEAR GROSS RETURNS

	1978	1979	1980	1981	1982	1983	1984	1985	1986	1987	1988	1989	1990	1991	1992	1993	1994	1995	AVG
S&P 500 RETURNS	7%	18%	32%	-5%	21%	22%	6%	31%	18%	5%	16%	31%	-3%	30%	7%	10%	1%	37%	15.5%
POLICY CASH VALUE	6%	7%	7%	7%	9%	10%	11%	11%	11%	11%	10%	10%	10%	10%	9%	9%	9%	8%	9.5%

How to Turn $10,000 into $20 Million
by Paul Merriman

Last March, my son Jeff became a proud father. I decided I wanted to do something really extraordinary for my new grandson, Aaron. I spent quite a bit of time thinking about what it might be.

I established five ambitious goals for my gift to Aaron. First, I wanted to make a one-time investment this year that would give Aaron a comfortable retirement when he reaches age sixty-five. Second, I wanted to make sure the money would be there at that time and not be used for anything else in the meantime. Third, I wanted my investment to grow without any tax liability on the income. Fourth, I wanted this investment to eventually provide at least $20 million to charity. And fifth, I wanted to do all this for only $10,000! That was ambitious enough for me, and with the help of Jeff and a couple of professional advisors, I found a way to accomplish all that.

Besides the $10,000, this turned out to require only three essential tools: time (lots of it), and a trust and a variable annuity. A trust is a legal entity that holds assets and is strictly governed, by the documents that establish it. A variable annuity is a product that combines the investment potential of mutual funds with the tax advantages of an insurance policy.

With the help of a Seattle financial planner and an attorney, Jeff and I have worked out the details. My wife, Doll, and I made a gift of $10,000 to an irrevocable trust for Aaron's benefit. This gift is not taxable to Aaron. Jeff and his wife, Barrie, will be the trustees of the trust. Since Jeff and Barrie are the trustees they cannot gift any money into his trust, without tax consequences, but anyone else can add to Aaron's account. (Any year that contributions are made the trustee must submit a simple tax return.)

Under the direction of the trustee, Aaron's trust invested the $10,000 in a variable annuity. Jeff will be the trustee as long as he is able, and the trust document tells how successor trustees may be appointed. Because the investment is in a variable annuity, it can compound on a tax-deferred basis. The trust is set up so that Aaron can't touch this money until he is sixty-five (in the year 2059). That will leave Jeff free to concentrate on very long-term investments, which we expect to provide a compound rate of return (CRR) of 10% to 12% over the decades ahead.

If these investments achieve a CRR of 11.2% until Aaron is sixty-five, the variable annuity will be worth $10 million. That's not bad for a $10,000 investment, but the best is still ahead. Under the terms of the trust, Aaron will receive 7% of the assets of the trust every year starting at age sixty-five and continuing as long as he lives. Hopefully, the first year that will be about $700,000. At an assumed inflation rate of 3%, that will be the equivalent of $102,500 in 1994 dollars. That won't make Aaron wealthy, but he'll have a comfortable retirement, especially if it is supplemented by his own savings and investments.

Meanwhile, if Aaron lives at least another twenty years after he starts receiving his annual distributions, if the investments achieve a CRR of 11.2%, and if he withdraws 7% a year, the variable annuity will be worth about $23 million.

At the end of Aaron's lifetime, the assets remaining will go to charitable organizations with a tax-exempt status. Those organizations are to be determined by the trustee or trustees, who could be Aaron's children or grandchildren. Jeff and I think there's a good chance that a Merriman Family Foundation will be formed by that time, and the remaining assets could go into it, with the earnings and proceeds directed to various charitable causes by our descendants. If a family foundation is established it will be possible to reasonably compensate the family members for running the foundation.

Jeff and I think this is an excellent plan, but some friends and other financial advisors have been critical. Friends say we should provide an "escape clause" by which Aaron could get the money before age sixty-five if, for instance, he is disabled or has huge medical expenses. Several of my colleagues have been critical of tying up money so irrevocably, for so long. "A lot of things can change in sixty-five years," they say. And of course they are right.

I realize that factors beyond my control, Jeff's control, or Aaron's control could potentially unravel these plans. The future is always uncertain. If you can't act until you know every fact, including those that can't be known, you will always be on the sidelines, never in the game. Now, in Aaron's first year, is the time to make this investment.

Are we doing Aaron a disservice by locking the money up tight until his sixty-fifth birthday? Possibly we are. For instance, if Aaron dies before age sixty-five, he won't receive a penny from the trust. If he lives only sixty-five years and six months, his long-awaited "pension" would be his for only the last half-year of his life. Some people think that is harsh and unfair. In addition, whatever family Aaron leaves behind at his death will get no benefit from this trust other than possibly the right to help give it away to charity.

Intentionally, we are setting up this trust so that it does not let Aaron off the hook. He will still need to provide for his family's security through life investments and insurance. He will need to earn a living and take care of whatever financial needs he has until age sixty-five without any help from this trust. And even when he is sixty-five, Aaron won't suddenly have great wealth at his disposal.

We think this trust will give Aaron something else important: a very real financial incentive to live a long and healthy life. He'll also have some peace of mind about retirement. We think that if he saves a "normal" amount of money through a working lifetime, he may be able to fund his own "early" retirement at the age of fifty or fifty-five, with the trust distributions kicking in after he's sixty-five.

Finally, the ultimate disposition of this trust's assets will be to charity, and Aaron may indirectly have much to say about that disposition. We hope this will prompt Aaron to think of himself as someone who plays an important role in society, encouraging him to pay close attention to charitable organizations he wants to support. We cannot know in advance how Aaron will respond to this gift. But we hope it will give him opportunities he wouldn't otherwise have in life. And it gives Doll and me great pleasure to be able to establish a legacy that will continue to benefit him and society long after we are gone.

I hope there are other people as excited about this concept as I am, and that some of them will want to use this example to establish some very long-term investments for their own children, grandchildren, nieces or nephews. I'm starting with $10,000, but a similar plan could be put in place for as little as $2,500. However, I think that is a practical minimum because of the legal costs of establishing a trust and the minimum investments required in most variable annuities.

For those who are interested, I have obtained permission to make copies of our trust document available. We are not offering this in order to give legal advice, and we don't recommend its use except as a starting point for discussion with your attorney and financial advisor. Nevertheless, we think anyone who wants to consider following in our footsteps could benefit from having a copy of the document we are using.

If you want a copy, send a check for $10 to Paul A. Merriman & Associates, 1200 Westlake Ave. N. Suite 700, Seattle, WA 98109. The $10 is only to cover our costs, and any excess we collect after meeting our costs will be donated to the trusts for our grandchildren. ◆

21

Are Living Trusts for You?
by Busby, Barber, and Temple

As appeared in the <u>Sound Mind Investing</u> newsletter in 1995. This article is excerpted from <u>The Christian's Guide to Worry-free Money Management</u>, Copyright 1995 by Daniel D. Busby, CPA, Kent E. Barber, CFP, and Robert L. Temple, CIC, CFP. The book is an up-to-date financial planning resource written by men who are professionals in their respective fields. Published by Zondervan Publishing House. Used by permission. All rights reserved.

What you own is called your estate. While you are living you are responsible as a steward/manager for everything you own and control. When you are gone, someone else has this responsibility. Preparing to pass the baton to the next person is called estate planning.

What is the most common problem with estate planning? Failure to make a plan that accomplishes one's objectives. Through a lack of information or having the wrong information, many people make provisions that do something totally different from what they really want.

Even if you have a will, some or all of your assets must go through a court procedure called "probate." In probate, the court determines if your will is valid. Your property is inventoried and appraised, and your creditors are paid. When all these conditions are met, your estate may be distributed to your heirs.

You may be attracted to alternatives to probate in a desire to handle the estate distribution process faster, cheaper, and more privately than through a probate court. It is possible to bypass probate, but it takes a great deal of planning and thorough comprehension of estate-planning rules. If you desire to sidestep much of the probate process, one of the techniques most frequently used is a revocable living trust.

A revocable living trust allows you to carry probate avoidance to the highest level. Simply stated, it is a strategy of giving your assets to a trust so the assets are out of your name. The trust allows you a change of heart later on if you so choose. But if you don't, it snaps shut at the instant of your death, and essentially you die owning little or no probate property.

This technique is called the revocable living trust—revocable because you are able to change your mind later if your circumstances or attitudes change, and living because you create the trust while you are alive. Some of the key aspects of a revocable living trust are:

◆ **Probate costs saved.** Most of the attorney fees associated with probate can be saved.

◆ **Title to assets.** The process of retitling all of your assets can be very time consuming up front. It may involve stock brokerage firms, transfer agents, mutual fund companies, and banks.

◆ **The trust must be funded.** This means that title to your assets must be transferred to the trust. If all of your assets (with

certain exceptions, for example, such as your car, personal effects, and furniture) are not transferred to the trust, your trust will not work as you intended.

◆ **Time saving.** Months or even years can be saved as compared to having all your assets go through the probate process.

◆ **Flexibility.** Revocable living trusts are very flexible. For example, the trust can be named as beneficiary of your insurance policies and other assets that provide you the opportunity to designate a beneficiary.

◆ **A will is still needed.** A revocable living trust is not a substitute for a will. Since assets often get inadvertently or intentionally left out of the trust, you still need a "pour-over" will that transfers all assets to the trust through probate.

◆ **No tax savings.** Contrary to popular belief, and to what some promoters would have you believe, a living trust does not avoid inheritance or federal estate taxes. It is simply not a tax-savings device. Nothing can be done through a revocable living trust to save taxes that can't be done with a properly drafted will.

◆ **Expense to set-up.** Up-front expenses typically start at $1,000 just to prepare the trust documents, and many trusts cost more. If you use an outside administrator, such as a bank, you'll pay a percentage of your trust assets each year for that service.

Not everyone should worry about probate. Depending on the size of your estate, the state laws where you reside, and other factors, probate may be the best alternative. If a competent family member is executor of your estate, working with a skilled and honest lawyer, the difficulties of the probate process can be kept to a minimum.

Who should consider using a revocable living trust? Anyone who has any substantial amount of assets should at least consider it. It may make the most sense for people who own property in several states (and don't want to pay probate costs in each of them), elderly single people whose children or heirs do not live nearby, and those whose children may disagree over the estate distribution.

If you are not certain whether you need a living trust, seek out an attorney to answer your questions. Probate avoidance is not lawyer avoidance. ◆

Charitable Remainder Trusts: A Win-Win Proposition
by Busby, Barber, and Temple

As appeared in the Sound Mind Investing newsletter in 1995. This article is excerpted from The Christian's Guide to Worry-free Money Management, Copyright 1995 by Daniel D. Busby, CPA, Kent E. Barber, CFP, and Robert L. Temple, CIC, CFP. The book is an up-to-date financial planning resource written by men who are professionals in their respective fields. Published by Zondervan Publishing House. Used by permission. All rights reserved.

A charitable-remainder trust may be used to make future gifts to charity and provide current or future income to you and to other beneficiaries.

Here's how it works: You place assets that will pass to a charity at a future date (or upon your death) in a trust. You retain an income flow from the assets. You get an income-tax deduction *now* for the value of the gift that will pass to the charity when you die. If you give appreciated property, you avoid paying capital-gains tax.

You must elect to take an annual percentage payout from the trust, such as 6%. The trust is tax-exempt, so investment earnings compound tax-free. You can be the trustee of the trust and control its investments.

The trust assets grow tax-deferred. Taxes are paid by the beneficiaries, based on the type of income earned by the trust.

Charitable-remainder trusts are irrevocable. While you may change the charitable beneficiary, *you cannot withdraw contributions to the trust.*

Contributions to a charitable trust are not subject to the dollar limits that apply to other retirement contributions — such as the $2,000 annual IRA limit or the annual limit for 401(k), 403(b), or 457 plans.

Here's an example: Joe and Mary are in their mid-60s. Their estate is valued at $1,500,000. Included in their estate is stock they bought for $50,000. It is now worth $600,000. If they sell the stock, the income taxes would be over $217,000. This would leave them only $383,000 to invest. If they earn 8% on the $383,000, their pre-tax income would be $30,640.

They would like to make a generous gift to their church. They decide to set up a charitable-remainder trust and make a gift of the stock to the trust. If the trust sells the stock, there is no income tax on the gain. If the trust earns 8% on the $600,000 and they chose an 8% payout rate, they would have pre-tax income of $48,000. This is $17,360 more than if they sold the stock themselves. They also have an income-tax deduction based on the value of the gift.

A charitable trust may also be the beneficiary of IRAs and other retirement funds. Life insurance is free from estate tax if it is placed in a charitable-remainder unitrust. You can use the current tax savings and increased income derived from the trust to buy life insurance that will pay your heirs an amount equal to what they would have received after taxes from your estate.

Property given to a charitable-remainder unitrust ultimately goes to the Lord's work instead of to your heirs. Assets transferred to a trust are removed from your estate, so the estate will pay less estate tax. The assets in the trust will also avoid probate. There are two types of charitable-remainder trusts:

♦ **Charitable-remainder unitrust.** You give the assets to the charity, which then pays you or you and your spouse a fixed percentage (5%-12%) of the fund until death or a specified date. At that time, the principal goes to the charity. If the money is invested properly, it will grow and you'll be getting a fixed percentage of a greater sum. This makes this type of trust a good hedge against inflation.

♦ **Charitable-remainder annuity trust.** Here, the donor receives a fixed dollar amount from the trust every year for life (or a fixed number of years), regardless of how well — or how poorly — the assets are managed by the trustee. This guarantees a fixed stream of monthly income that you may find comforting.

In summary, the benefits of setting up a charitable-remainder trust include:

☑ A current charitable-contribution deduction.
☑ No capital gains taxes on the sale of your property.
☑ No estate taxes on your trust's assets.
☑ Lifetime income from the assets.
☑ Future control over charitable gifts.

Check with your favorite charity or organization about their charitable trust arrangements. If you do not need lifetime income, consider a "gift trust" for an individual or charity through a mutual fund family: Twentieth Century Investors Gift Trust (800-345-2021; $250 minimum) and Fidelity Investors (800-544-0275; $10,000 minimum).

Charitable-remainder trusts require the assistance of a professional adviser who is familiar with estate planning and the tax law. Even though the tax savings may make giving very attractive, there should still be a basic motivation to give to the charity. Remember, in most charitable giving arrangements, you are giving up the right to get your principal back. ♦

23

Leave a Guide So They Don't Get Lost
by Robert E. Frank

As appeared in the Sound Mind Investing newsletter in 1996. Copyright 1996 by No-Debt Living Newsletter. Robert Frank is the editor of this monthly publication that provides financial, home management, and investment news with a Christian perspective. Subscription: $25.95 per year. To receive a sample issue, send $2 to: P.O. Box 282, Veradale, WA 99037-0282.

Jeff Camp, a graphic designer from Spokane, Washington, was stunned last year when his 69-year-old father, a robust wheat farmer, was diagnosed with liver cancer. The doctors were hopeful that the disease could be arrested through chemotherapy. The rigorous treatments began immediately, and Jeff's father moved in with him and his family. Despite all efforts, however, Ralph Camp died five weeks later.

From the beginning, Jeff found himself overwhelmed. Not only did he have a business to run and a family to take care of, he now was challenged with finding the necessary documents and information to manage his father's estate that included a large wheat ranch located 90 miles away, farming equipment, a house, a car, medical and life insurance and much more. In addition, he needed to work with family members to arrange his father's funeral. The weeks were stressful and emotionally charged as Camp also tried to deal with the fact that his father was gone.

Imagine for a moment that a close relative suddenly died and you were left in charge. Immediately the question arises: Is there a will or instructions telling you what should be done? Once that document is found, the thing you need most is a file or log telling you where you can find key papers and certificates, what creditors need to be paid, who that person's attorney and insurance agents are, and more.

Being named an executor is an honor; however, it is also a tremendous amount of work. Even after eight months, Camp is working to settle his father's estate. To help people avoid many of the difficulties he faced, Camp has designed a new product titled "LifeFile," which acts as a roadmap to a person's financial, health and personal records. True to his nature, he did a lot of homework, talking with attorneys, insurance agents, stock brokers, bankers and more. The result is a thoughtful, thorough, inexpensive product that should be a necessity for any adult.

"To some degree, I was fortunate," Camp said. "I had about a month to talk with my father, to pay bills and to begin to get a handle on his business and personal affairs. Not everyone has that. Even when you're in a circumstance like that, you don't want to spend that time asking your loved one about caskets, cemeteries, what should be done with clothes, what kind of service that person wants, or financial affairs. Up to the minute my father died, I never thought for a moment there wasn't a chance he couldn't recover. Plus he wasn't in the best of condition to answer a battery of questions."

The problem is, once a person dies, a variety of things begin happening. The executor and the attorney need information and documentation immediately to begin their jobs. The family needs information to handle funeral arrangements. And, numerous people need to be contacted.

"The world doesn't stop," said Camp, "your creditors still want to be paid."

That's where a list of information, like LifeFile, is useful. This simple form leads people to record the information relatives and friends might need in the event of an accident, serious illness or death. (It also provides a quick reference for people when they are alive and healthy.) For example, LifeFile prods a person to list information concerning his or her insurance policies (life, medical, auto, etc.), agents, mutual funds, credit cards, securities, loans, blood type, health history and more.

Camp said there are two major reasons for filling out the file. "First, it gives a person or a couple a sense of security that if something should happen to them, their wishes will probably be carried out. Second, it is a caring act on the part of the person completing the file. That person is making a genuine effort to help the people who are left to take care of their affairs."

Given his experience, Camp believes that anyone who is married or who has responsibilities to other people should at least make a hand-written list describing their personal and financial affairs. For survivors, the problem is compounded if the deceased person was disorganized or, worse yet, a packrat. In such cases, the executor and family members often find themselves staring at stacks of papers that are outdated, not knowing whether insurance policies or documents are current or expired.

One banker who works in the trust department of a large regional firm said, "If our clients would fill out forms like these, it would cut the cost and time involved in settling an estate by half."

Whether you're single or married, you may want to consider making such a list for yourself. And, maybe more importantly, you may want to encourage some of your relatives to do the same.

(Note: As a courtesy to readers of this book, *No-Debt Living Newsletter* is offering LifeFiles for $6 each, including sales tax and shipping. Group rates, involving orders of ten or more files, are available. To order, simply mail your check and a note designating how many files you want to the address shown above.) ◆

God's Plan for Systematic Giving
by Bill Bright

This article is excerpted from As You Sow: The Adventure of Giving by Faith by Bill Bright, founder and president of Campus Crusade for Christ. Copyright 1989. Published by Here's Life Publishers. Used by permission. All rights reserved.

The word tithe itself comes from an Old English term simply meaning a tenth. However, Christian leaders use tithe in two different senses. To some, tithe means the general giving of a tenth of one's income or resources to God. To others, tithe refers to the specific manner of funding God's work mandated by Mosaic Law. I use tithe in the first sense.

Denominational councils and parachurch organizations variously state their views on the subject. Among them, advocates of tithing substantiate their case with weighty premises.

Tithing is a practical guideline for systematic giving.

The apostle Paul emphasized this when he exhorted believers: "On the first day of every week let each one of you put aside and save, as he prospers." In 2 Corinthians, he again implores: "Let each one do just as he has purposed in his heart; not grudgingly or under compulsion; for God loves a cheerful giver."

Paul realized that systematic, purposeful giving ensures consistent stewardship. Without a functional plan, we fall prey to our whims. One day, we feel excited about giving, the next we may forget. Even worse, we may not feel like giving at all. A practical plan for giving, however, enables us to circumvent the emotions and circumstances that would hinder us from being faithful stewards.

What could better achieve this goal than the tithe? Originated by God, it has helped to build His kingdom and further the cause of Christ for centuries.

Tithing provides spiritual release.

Spiritual blessings are incomparably superior to material ones. When a steward gives the first portion of his income to God, he receives an abundance of joy and peace. R. T. Kendall writes:

"Tithing is one way to find great spiritual release. Sooner or later we come face to face with this matter and the failure to walk in the light results in a greater bondage than ever. But when one enters upon the life of faithful tithing there is a sweet release to be experienced that cannot be fully explained to another person. This release by itself is enough to convince one fully how serious God is about this matter of tithing. The peace and joy are so wonderful that a frequent reaction is a kind of sorrow that one had not been doing it sooner."

When we hang on to our possessions, they own us. Tithing releases us from the tyranny of materialism and clears the channel for God's abundant blessings.

Tithing acknowledges God as the Source and Owner of all that we possess.

Early biblical records date the origin of the tithe to Abraham. He gave a tenth of his spoils of war to Melchizedek, the King of Salem and the priest of the Most High God.

Returning victoriously from a battle, Abraham joined Melchizedek in giving God the glory. Melchizedek brought out wine and bread and blessed Abraham. In response, Abraham gave the priest the first portion of his spoils in public testimony of God's ownership over his possessions. As the spiritual father of every Christian believer, Abraham set an example for us to follow.

Tithing performs a role opposite that of mere giving, which suggests that we own all that we possess.

Through tithing we acknowledge that God created our increase. As stewards of what God entrusted to us, we set aside a proportion to use for the cause of Christ. We never consider any part of the amount to be our sole property but prayerfully tithe on the entire amount.

Tithing is a voluntary act of worship.

At Bethel Jacob affirmed his commitment to God by pledging his tithe. "If God will help and protect me on this journey and give me food and clothes, and will bring me back safely to my father, then I will choose Jehovah as my God! And this memorial pillar shall become a place for worship; and I will give you back a tenth of everything you give me!"

We, too, should tithe as an act of worship to the One Who blesses us. Through this act, we keep our focus on the heavenly Father and testify to His kindness and generosity toward us.

Jacob's family grew into a mighty nation and needed divine statutes to govern its new home in the Promised Land. What the children of Israel had given voluntarily, God now required to fund the new theocracy. Whenever Israel gave from a heart of gratitude and worship for God's provision, tithing brought blessing and prosperity.

Tithing teaches us to put God first.

Moses said, "The purpose of tithing is to teach you always to put God first in your lives."

As Israel established itself in the Promised Land, the people prospered. God blessed their obedience and subdued the godless tribes living in the land. Soon, however, the children of Israel lost their first love for the God of their fathers.

They began worshipping the idols of the pagans they defeated.

Their material prosperity or impoverishment directly reflected their spiritual attitudes. Whenever they put God and His commandments first, the children of Israel enjoyed peace and abundance. When their hearts turned away from Him, God chastised them. Israel followed this pattern throughout its history.

We can learn from this lesson. How often have we conceived grand strategies for giving, only to find that the money we intended to give vanished in day-to-day spending? Covetousness, greed, and frivolous buying all tempt even the most dedicated Christian. When budgets stretch unmanageably or a crisis depletes the paycheck, many Christians skimp on their tithe to cover a personal deficit.

God does not honor a gift that comes from the leftovers. As we have seen earlier, He requires the first and the best of our increase. Tithing ensures this.

Tithing in the New Testament

By Jesus' day, four hundred years after the close of the Old Testament, tithing had become merely a religious duty that served as a vehicle for self-commendation. The Old Testament age had marked the beginning and the end of the first of three cycles in tithing, each starting with the introduction of the practice and ending with its decline into legalism. The times of Jesus and the New Testament church would witness the genesis of the second cycle.

Our Lord mentioned the tithe twice during His ministry. In the first reference, He denounced the scribes and Pharisees for tithing meticulously without showing justice, mercy, and faithfulness to those around them.

In the second mention, Jesus related a parable of two men, one who tithed pompously for self-glorification, and another who humbled himself when he realized his sinfulness. Our Lord condemned the Pharisee for his pride and commended the sinner for his humility.

Although our Lord did not command His followers to tithe in these passages, He did not disapprove of the practice either. For our Lord, the issue of giving did not center on the method. Realizing that the religious leaders had distorted tithing into a tyrannical set of rules, He turned the issue from how much a disciple should give to his attitude toward giving. His challenge went beyond written ordinances to loving "the Lord your God with all your heart, and with all your soul, and with all your mind, and with all your strength." Love, gratitude and humility, not law, should motivate our giving. In this teaching we see the rebirth of the principles upon which the tithe rests.

Tithing, we have seen, did not originate with the Mosaic Law. The patriarchs tithed long before Israel became a nation. Since the principle precedes the Law, the fact that God compelled Israel to support the Levitical priesthood and fund the theocracy with their tithes has little bearing on the continued validity of the practice.

Under grace, everything we have is a gift of God. All we have belongs to Him. We tithe, therefore, not as a requirement of the Law, but as an act of loving obedience and worship. By applying the wisdom of Solomon to our giving, we testify to our dedication to godly stewardship.

Giving ten percent to the work of the Lord is a realistic starting point for a steward who wants to honor and glorify God with all his resources. As Dr. J. B. Gabrell declared, "It is unthinkable from the standpoint of the cross that anyone would give less under grace than the Jews gave under law."

We can be certain that if New Testament Christians tithed, they did so in the Spirit of Christ to help fulfill the Great Commission and not from a sense of obligation. What they put aside each week for the furtherance of the gospel signaled their return to the principles of giving which God established in the tithe: a humble attitude, an acknowledgement of God as the source and owner of all their possessions, a focus on worship, and a demonstration of His pre-eminence in their lives. ◆

TOPICAL INDEX

Sound Mind Investing

THE FINANCIAL JOURNAL FOR TODAY'S CHRISTIAN FAMILY

Dear Valued Reader:

I hope this book has been helpful to you. If so, I believe you'd be interested in knowing about my monthly Sound Mind Investing financial newsletter. Launched in 1990, it has rapidly grown to become one of the top 25 investment newsletters in the country in terms of circulation. Each month, it takes you out into the marketplace and helps you implement the investment philosophy and strategies explained in this book. It offers:

◆ Biblical goal-setting. Our Four Levels format, based on priorities taught in Scripture, helps you do "first things first." In every monthly issue, you get help in four areas.

> In Getting Debt-Free (the Level 1 column), you begin your journey toward financial peace of mind by receiving tips on budgeting and money-saving ideas on mortgages, credit cards, and how to cut your living expenses.

> In Saving for Future Needs (Level 2), you'll get information on the best ways and places to save, and primers on interest rates and the various kinds of interest-earning investments most useful to savers.

> In Investing Your Surplus (Level 3), you'll learn basic stock market investing principles and provides specific "getting started" portfolio recommendations.

> In Diversifying For Safety (Level 4), you'll learn how to reduce risk through diversifying among stock, bond, and international mutual funds.

◆ Earthquake Watch. Every issue includes a primer on basic economic principles you should understand in order to plan intelligently for the uncertain times that lie ahead. You also get graphs of various indicators that will warn you if an economic crisis seems to be approaching.

◆ Performance rankings. Each quarter you get a special mutual fund report that ranks more than 800 mutual funds—stock, bond, precious metals, and global—according to their performance and risk characteristics. Once a year, you get performance ratings on variable annuities.

◆ Easy to understand format. SMI makes very few assumptions about your level of understanding of economic and investing matters. That means using everyday, plain-English language (rather than industry jargon) to teach and inform.

If you'd like to learn more about the Sound Mind Investing newsletter, please write to: SMI, Post Office Box 22128-M, Louisville, KY 40252. For less than the cost of a daily cup of coffee, I'll lead you through the financial maze and show you how to make consistently sound investing decisions.

I hope to hear from you soon!

Cordially,

Austin